TOM HUGHES QC

TOM HUGHES QC

A Cab on the Rank

Ian Hancock

THE FEDERATION PRESS
2016

Published in Sydney by
The Federation Press
PO Box 45, Annandale, NSW, 2038.
71 John St, Leichhardt, NSW, 2040.
Ph (02) 9552 2200. Fax (02) 9552 1681.
E-mail: info@federationpress.com.au
Website: http://www.federationpress.com.au

National Library of Australia
Cataloguing-in-Publication entry

Hancock, Ian.
Tom Hughes QC: a cab on the rank / Ian Hancock.

Includes bibliographical references and index.
ISBN 978 176002 058 3 (hbk)

Hughes, Tom, 1923-.
Liberal Party of Australia - Biography.
Lawyers - Australia - Biography.
Attorneys general - Australia - Biography.
Politicians - Australia - Biography.

340.1092

Typeset by The Federation Press, Leichhardt, NSW.
Printed by OPUS Group in Australia.

Contents

Preface

Tom Hughes, a scion of a notable Sydney family, was one of Australia's top barristers for more than three decades, and has been a wartime pilot, politician, federal minister, a grazier and a racehorse owner. Throughout his life, he crossed paths with the great and the good, and with some who were neither. To mention his name to Australians who were aged around 20 in 1970, invariably evokes memories of the day when the Commonwealth Attorney-General, armed with a cricket bat, confronted anti-conscription and anti-Vietnam protesters outside his Sydney home. Anyone who saw him in the family gathering at Government House on 15 September 2015 would have learned or been reminded that he is the father-in-law of Australia's 29th Prime Minister, Malcolm Turnbull. Australians of a literary or artistic bent would be aware that he is the oldest brother of the late Robert Hughes, the internationally famous author and art critic. Those who have read articles and profiles about the law in magazines, colour supplements and media reports would have learned much about Tom Hughes QC. He was the expensive barrister who appeared in many significant cases and represented a multitude of high-profile individual clients and corporations. He had a dominating presence in court; a theatrical and intimidating style backed by a captivating use of language; and was so preoccupied and uptight that some lawyers and clients found him uncommunicative, even 'frosty'.

Many books and chapters have been written about Australian judges who were once barristers, but very few about barristers who never became judges. Although barristers influence decisions, they do not deliver the judgments that become the subject of analysis, criticism or approbation. The legal fraternity, however, frequently identifies them with great victories, and Tom Hughes has had several of those. After six decades at the Bar, Tom Hughes secured a better than the 60 per cent success rate he modestly claims and, more importantly, was considered a role model for a particular kind of advocacy and attained a legendary status as being perhaps the last of his kind. The case for a biography is substantial on these grounds alone, and reinforced because Tom Hughes' story comprises many other narratives.

There were three striking features about his various careers. First, family connections, friends of the family and friends he made along the way protected or promoted him or opened up opportunities that were not available to many others. Secondly, where Tom Hughes had a head start, he built on it with intelligence and concentrated hard work. He was not unlike the servant who, in the parable told in St Matthew's Gospel, was given five talents, invested them and earned five more. He learned the skills of advocacy by listening to mentors and watching other barristers at work, and by eagerly taking cases wherever he could find them. He spent long hours thoroughly preparing each case in all its dimensions, and demanded of those in his legal team that they exercise due diligence and punctuality. He was the complete professional, giving everything of himself for the client's sake and – win, lose or draw – moving swiftly to the next case. Because he was in such demand, there were normally at least two or more briefs awaiting immediate attention. Yet for a seemingly secure man he had an abiding insecurity, common to many barristers but surely misplaced in his case, namely, that he might not get work.

Thirdly, Tom Hughes kept his personal and professional life separate. He had to deal with many moments of sadness and times of difficulty. His beloved parents died at a relatively young age; he took a long time to find a relationship to replicate the happy marriage enjoyed by his parents; family relationships were sometimes fraught; Tom's long life has meant that he has attended the funerals of too many friends. Personal setbacks or troubles, however, never interfered with his work. He coped well with adversity. Sometimes it was hard, personally, to take a defeat in court. In common with all barristers, Tom did not like losing cases, especially when he felt that judges or juries had made a mistake, or where he felt a client deserved better or where his opponent happened to be disagreeable. But Tom never dwelt on what might have been or should have been. He simply immersed himself in the next brief.

There were bound to be many changes over a long life. He inherited an Irish and an English ancestry. Perhaps surprisingly, the former was barely influential. He has always been a Liberal, but not always the same kind of Liberal. Tom entered politics as a fervent anti-communist and supporter of national service and of the Vietnam War. By the 1970s he had become less of a 'conservative' and more of a 'liberal' within the Party's broad church, a change influenced by his non-partisan role as Attorney-General, an acceptance of changed circumstances, 'a cab on the rank' approach to taking briefs from all sides of politics and an intellectual gravitation to the centre. He never shifted from one core belief – a commitment to the free market – and never doubted his right to charge fees the market was prepared to pay (an approach tempered by lower charges sought from non-corporate clients, friends and deserving strugglers). Yet, even as Tom became a republican and took a more liberal stance on social and moral issues, he remained a stickler for the traditions of legal practice and remained the traditional advocate for whom the increasing reliance on out-of-court settlement and mediation had no attraction.

In researching this biography, I encountered an abundance of material, including Tom's official war papers, parliamentary debates, Cabinet Notebooks and other official records of his time in government, as well as law reports, case notes, academic articles, press reports and profiles and published biographies of politicians, judges and other barristers. The Hughes Family Papers and Thomas McKay's Papers held in the Mitchell Library, Sydney, proved invaluable for researching Tom's family history and his war years. The Hughes Papers in the National Library cover his time as Attorney-General.

The gold mine proved to be the trunks, boxes, files, press cuttings and loose papers of unsorted material kept at Tom's 'Bannister Station' near Goulburn. They contain school reports and letters written home during the War, Tom's RAAF Log Book and a war diary, voluminous personal correspondence files covering the post-war years to the present, intermittent, frank and intimate personal diaries, various short autobiographical writings and a number of briefing documents. Eventually, archivists or librarians will catalogue this material. In the meantime, all I can do is name the folders or areas where I found the evidence cited in support of my factual narrative, themes and analysis.

Tom's fee books, covering the period from 1949 to 2007, have been a priceless source. They provide a more accurate picture of his earnings than the myth-making profiles could ever do. They also offer solid evidence of a huge and varied workload, while recording Hughes' progress up to the time he took silk in New South Wales in 1962, the lull when he was in politics, the sharp revival of his career in the 1970s, its flowering in the 1980s and 1990s and the changing pattern of his practice in his final years at the Bar. The fee books also brought home the problem of selecting which cases among thousands to examine in trying to understand more about Tom's legal and life story. I began by asking him to choose those he thought were important to him and to his career, and then looked for others where transcripts were readily available, and were reported in the press and discussed in private correspondence and in Tom's diaries. I am very conscious of the fact that so many interesting and significant cases do not appear in this book, and of the probability that a lawyer or another historian would make different selections.

In addition to 21 separate taped interviews as well as many telephone conversations with Tom, I interviewed or communicated with Richard Ackland, Stephen Archer, Jenny Blackman, Mark Boileau, Don Cameron, Nicholas Carson, Carmen Champion, Deeta Colvin, the late Constance Crisp, Paul Daley, Sir William Deane, Robert Ellicott, Murray Gleeson, Ainsley Gotto, Dyson Heydon, John Howard, Chrissie Hughes, Geoffrey Hughes, Joanna Hughes, Michael Hughes, Tom Hughes Jnr, Michael Kirby, Lynette

MacDonald, Sir Anthony Mason, Michael McHugh, Jim Merralls, Maurice Neil, Philip Selth, Anne Sloan, Lucy and Malcolm Turnbull, Aleco Vrisakis and John Whittle. The Oral History section of the National Library has recorded interviews with many lawyers and politicians, including a lengthy one with Tom Hughes.

I am, as always, grateful to the staff of the National Archives of Australia, the Mitchell Library, and the National Library for their assistance.

Frank Bongiorno, Andrew Clark, Frank Crisp, Christine Fernon, Sebastian Hancock, Clare Hanley, Jenny Higgins, Stephen Holt, Rob and Sandie Little, John Nethercote, Wilfrid Prest, Phillip Price, Richard Reid and Sophie Torney advised me on particular subjects or provided editorial or technical assistance. Another historian, Philip Selth of the NSW Bar Association, helped me in countless ways. I particularly want to thank Douglas Craig, Ainsley Gotto, John Nethercote, Joan Ritchie, Paul Santamaria, Philip Selth and Susan Sharpe who read and commented on the whole manuscript.

Kathy Fitzhenry, Rebecca Fung, Jason Monaghan, Josephine Romeo and Trisha Valliappan of The Federation Press guided me through publication with patience, skills and professionalism; it was a great pleasure to work with them.

My special debts are to four people. Ainsley Gotto suggested the subject and, as always, pushed me to finish a book. The late Chris Holt of The Federation Press, one of the great encouragers, reacted immediately to my tentative email with an offer to publish and an assurance that a non-lawyer could write a book about a barrister. Chrissie Hughes always made me feel very welcome at Bannister, and offered many insights into her husband while indirectly helping me to understand why he has been so content the second time round.

My greatest debt is to Tom Hughes. He gave me full access to his records, opened up to all my questions, accepted intrusions into the deeply personal, looked at my drafts and gently corrected factual errors, grammatical blemishes and my misuse of legal discourse. He accepted my insistence on some interpretations; at times, we agreed to disagree. I also experienced a side of Tom Hughes I had observed in his relationships with his family, friends and acquaintances: a deep-seated concern for the health and happiness of others. He did wonder, occasionally, whether there was a story worth telling. I hope I have extinguished his doubts.

The errors, the focus and the interpretations are my responsibility.

Ian Hancock
April 2016

Abbreviations

AAP	Australian Associated Press
ABC	Australian Broadcasting Commission or Corporation
ACCC	Australian Competition and Consumer Commission
ACP	Australian Consolidated Press
ADB	*Australian Dictionary of Biography*
AFR	*Australian Financial Review*
AIF	Australian Imperial Force
ALJ	*Australian Law Journal*
ANU	Australian National University
ASIA	Australian Stevedoring Industry Authority
AWU	Australian Workers' Union
CLR	*Commonwealth Law Reports*
CO	Commanding Officer
CP	Country Party
CPD	Commonwealth Parliamentary Debates
CSM	Chief Stipendiary Magistrate
CT	*Canberra Times*
DLP	Democratic Labor Party
DRU	Draft Resistance Union
DT	*Daily Telegraph*
EFTS	Elementary Flying Training School
ENSA	Entertainment National Service Association
FEC	Federal Electorate Conference
ITS	Initial Training School
H/R	House of Representatives
KC	King's Counsel
LPA	Liberal Party of Australia
ML	Mitchell Library

NAA	National Archives of Australia
NCSC	National Companies and Securities Commission
NLA	National Library of Australia
OBL	Oil Basins Ltd
PIR	Pacific Islands Regiment
PKIU	Printing and Kindred Industries Union
PSB	Public Service Board
QC	Queen's Counsel
RAAF	Royal Australian Air Force
RAF	Royal Air Force
RFC	Royal Flying Corps
RPS	Reserve Price Scheme
SC	Senior Counsel
SDS	Students for a Democratic Society
SIFC	Stevedoring Industry Finance Committee
SFTS	Service Flying Training School
SJ	Society of Jesus
SMH	*Sydney Morning Herald*
Sqn L	Squadron Leader
SR (NSW)	*State Reports (New South Wales)*
TDT	*This Day Tonight*
UAP	United Australia Party
WLR	*Weekly Law Reports* (UK)

Hughes Family Tree

Thomas Hughes (1801-1863) *m* Maria Cogan (1805-1841)
had six children including:

John Hughes (1825-1885) *m* Susan Sharkey (1835-1907)
had eight children including:

(Sir) Thomas Hughes (1863-1930) *m* Louisa Gilhooley (1865-1948)

- Thomas Hughes (1888-1894)
- Roger Forrest Hughes (1990-1916)
- Geoffrey Forrest Hughes (1895-1951) *m* Margaret Eyre Sealy Vidal (1899-1963)

Children of Geoffrey Forrest Hughes and Margaret Eyre Sealy Vidal:

- **Thomas Eyre Forrest Hughes** (1923-) *m* Joanna FitzGerald (diss) *m* Christine Abel Smith
- Constance Margaret Patricia Hughes (Crisp) (1926-2015)
- Geoffrey Eyre Forrest Hughes (1928-)
- Robert Studley Forrest Hughes (1938-2012)

Children of Thomas Eyre Forrest Hughes and Joanna FitzGerald:

- Lucinda Mary Forrest Hughes (1958-) *m* Malcolm Turnbull
  - Alexander *m* Yvonne Wang
    - Isla
  - Daisy *m* James Brown
    - Jack
- Thomas Studley Forrest Hughes (1962-)
  m Marisa Fitzgerald (diss) issue Thomas
  m Samantha Magnusson (diss) issue Clemency
  m Georgina McMaster
- Michael Seamus Forrest Hughes (1965-) *m* Jane Madgwick
  - Harry
  - Benjamin

1

The inheritance

Thomas Eyre Forrest Hughes was born at 4.00 am at home, 26 Cranbrook Road, Rose Bay, Sydney, on 26 November 1923. He inherited an Irish and English ancestry. His father, Geoffrey Forrest Hughes, was the great grandson of Thomas and Maria Hughes of Ireland, who arrived in Sydney in January 1840. His mother, Margaret Eyre Sealy Vidal, was the younger daughter of a Church of England clergyman from the West Country of England and his Irish-born wife.[1] The Irish element of this inheritance was not immediately obvious in the 1920s. Three generations of Tom's paternal line regarded themselves as Australians, not as Irish expatriates. The Great War had confirmed for his grandfather and his father that they were Empire loyalists and not Irish republicans. Though strictly beholden to their Catholic faith, they turned against clergy who sermonised against conscription and for righting the 'wrongs' visited upon Mother Ireland. Their material advancement and a commitment to public service had placed the Hughes family near the upper end of Sydney society and made them acceptable to nearly all of its Anglo-Scottish and Protestant elite.

The Irish connection

Thomas Hughes, the eldest of the 10 children of Michael and Mary Hughes (O'Connor), was born in County Roscommon in 1801.[2] He married Maria Cogan in 1823 and, at some point, left Roscommon for the neighbouring County Leitrim, where he established a grocery business in Drumshanbo. By 1839, Thomas and Maria had six children and, on 20 September of that year, the family left the port of Kingstown just south of Dublin on the *Crusader* bound for the Colony of New South Wales.

There is no evidence presently available to explain why Thomas and Maria decided to emigrate. As Thomas probably continued to own and maintain a business, it is unlikely he was impoverished like so many of his countrymen who sought a future beyond Ireland. Thomas and Maria may have been seeking better opportunities. Their particular situation is intriguing because Thomas' occupation was given as 'farmer' in the *Crusader*'s passenger list. Maria's occupation was 'shopkeeping'. Perhaps the family had engaged in two different businesses or were supplying products to their own shop. Either way, assuming that the Hughes family were beneficiaries in full or in part of an assisted passage, the settlers in New South Wales would not have been impressed. They wanted labour, not potential competitors for labour.

The *Crusader* carried 286 passengers. The 'native place' of nearly half of them was the small town of Elphin in County Roscommon, and for another quarter it was somewhere in the adjacent County Cavan. Although the Hughes family had recently lived in Drumshanbo, their 'native place' was listed as County Roscommon. They emigrated with people from the same rural and semi-rural area of central-west Ireland. Some 90 per cent of the passengers were classified 'Roman Catholic'. Of the rest, 28 were 'Protestant' (probably Church of Ireland), six were 'Catholic' and one was 'Presbyterian'. A striking feature of the passenger complement is that whereas the largest single adult male occupation consisted of those described as 'labourer', and whereas the adult females who had an occupation were mostly dairymaids or servants, a number of the men had specific skills or training. There were four stonemasons, three farmers (including Thomas), three schoolmasters, three carpenters, three tailors and one apprentice tailor, two shopkeepers, two clerks, two land surveyors, one 'physician and apothecary', and one 'bird stuffer'. Clearly, a number of the emigrants, like Thomas and Maria Hughes, were not the 'ignorant and unskilful Irish Roman Catholics' which the *Sydney Herald* of 31 August 1840 claimed were flooding the Colony. Nevertheless, Thomas and Maria were Irish and Roman Catholic, and no doubt encountered people in Sydney who reminded them of that.

There is at least one surviving account of the *Crusader*'s voyage. James Gormly was aged four when he travelled on this ship with his family from Elphin. Seventy years after the event, and by then a member of the NSW Legislative Council and with his own colourful history, Gormly published an account of the journey in the *Wagga Wagga Express*.[3] Allowing for minor factual errors, and for the probability that Gormly was reporting his family's recollections, his account gives an idea of what the Hughes family experienced on their well-supervised migration to Sydney. According to Gormly, the immigrants were carefully selected; if one family member failed the health check, the whole family was rejected. (Just two passengers were among the 14 deaths at sea, as reported in the Sydney press, and three babies were delivered safely.) Gormly remembered the *Crusader* as a stout and fast ship with equipment and provisions 'of the best quality'. The captain and the officers were 'all good men' while the Surgeon Superintendent – James Birtwhistle, RN – was a 'strict disciplinarian' who insisted that the passengers remain on the deck for a good part of the day during fine weather.

Classified in subsequent histories as 'bounty immigrants', the Sydney press greeted the *Crusader*'s passengers on arrival on 15 January 1840 as 'Government emigrants'. The distinction soon ceased to matter because the bounty system of assisted passages replaced the Government scheme. In 1840, however, there remained a vigorous debate about which scheme was better. Under the original government scheme, surgeons or other agents sent from the Colony selected the emigrants. By 1839, British Government officials were overseeing the selection of emigrants and supervising shipping arrangements to prevent abuse and fraud and to ensure the health and safety of the passengers. Surgeons accompanied government ships on the journey to New South Wales; in the case of the *Crusader*, Birtwhistle superintended the voyage, aided by an assistant surgeon. The Colonial Government paid for the scheme with funds derived from land sales in New South Wales. Under the bounty scheme, the colonists chose the emigrants through their appointed agents in the United Kingdom. Provided an Inspection Board judged new arrivals as satisfactory, the Colonial Government would pay a bounty to the settlers responsible for their introduction. The bounty scheme was the one preferred by the colonists on the grounds, principally, that it was cheaper, and was more likely to produce the required labour force and keep out paupers and other undesirables.

The Catholic *Australasian Chronicle*, which favoured the Government system and denounced 'Bounty traffic', pointed out on 21 January 1840 that the captains and superintendents paid the greatest attention to the comfort of the emigrants. Those who arrived on the *Crusader* agreed, and with a 'unanimous voice'. Moreover, the Captain and the Surgeon assured the *Chronicle* they had exercised the 'strictest vigilance' and not detected any 'immoral action' among the emigrants. The *Chronicle* claimed that anyone who had seen all the children standing in line (presumably including the six Hughes children), and doing 'the most healthy exercises' under the direction of the Captain and the Surgeon, would have favourably compared the Government scheme to the bounty system. The *Chronicle* concluded that the 'bulk' of the adults on the *Crusader* were 'of a healthy working class', and went into jobs 'with rapidity'.[4]

The Hughes family initially settled into accommodation in Castlereagh Street and later moved to Campbell Street. There was an early and tragic setback. On 16 May 1841, 16 months after arriving in Sydney, Maria Hughes died, possibly just after giving birth.[5] Thomas never remarried. According to family legend, he once worked as a clerk at Darlinghurst Gaol, although there is no official record to support this claim.[6] At some stage, Thomas resumed his occupation as a grocer, opening a shop on the corner of George and Market Streets. Another family legend is that he brought the family material success by obtaining a franchise to sell Keen's mustard powder, used to counter the taste of unrefrigerated meat. Thomas lived until 1863 and died from gastro-enteritis while residing at the home of his eldest son, John, at 145 Elizabeth Street. Maria and Thomas were both interred at Devonshire Street Cemetery and later re-interred in the Hughes graves at Waverley Cemetery. Maria is commemorated in a stained glass window in the Lady Chapel of St Canice's Church, Elizabeth Bay, depicting the Girlhood of the Virgin Mary in the Temple.

John Hughes

John Hughes was born on 24 June 1825 at Drumshanbo, County Leitrim. He probably attended a national school that provided a non-denominational primary education.[7] On arrival in New South Wales, he appears to have spent just six months – from July to December 1840 – attending Sydney College before taking an apprenticeship with a grocer in George Street. He then worked in another grocery business in Market Street, before taking a position with Samuel Peek in George Street. Peek gave John advice, encouragement and material assistance when John set up his own business in about 1851 on the corner of George and Market Streets. John Hughes prospered, partly because he built on his father's business of selling Keen's mustard powder. After selling his retail grocery in 1862, he became a wholesale merchant and importer. He purchased an interest in Narromine Station, near Dubbo, and acquired and developed business sites in the city. An appreciation, published after he died, described his approach:

> Wholly free from the gambling instinct which impels many to hazard their money in risky speculations, and satisfied with the legitimate returns to safe investments, Mr Hughes could quietly calculate secure profits, and as quietly wait for their arrival.[8]

It was claimed in the same article that he was '[a]lways opposed to entering public life'; instead, he was 'devoted to the comparatively obscure path of business'.[9] Yet in 1866 and 1871, Hughes stood, unsuccessfully, for the Fitzroy Ward of the Sydney Municipal Council. In 1866, he was a last-minute entry to oppose 'Mr Kidman', a Protestant, who won by 629 votes to 614. It was an unusually high turnout, made more unusual by the inclusion of 40 ballot papers not issued by the Returning Officer. All 40 supported Kidman. Hughes declared his intention to challenge the result. Surprisingly, the Catholic *Freeman's Journal*, which referred to Hughes as 'our excellent citizen and fellow Catholic' and deplored the importation of the American practice of ballot stuffing, urged him to leave it to 'the good sense of the electors' on a later occasion. It appears that Hughes did let the matter rest, while saying at the poll declaration he had run the race 'fairly' and 'without any attempt to jostle the inside rider'. He thanked his 614 'independent voters'.[10]

In 1871, John Hughes was a member of what the *Freeman's Journal* called the 'liberal party'. An estimated crowd of between 400 and 500 gathered in front of Johnstone's Family Hotel, Darlinghurst, on the evening of Friday 24 November to hear Hughes 'recommend himself for municipal honours'.[11] Greeted with frequent cheers, he pointed out how he had a large business stake in Fitzroy Ward, and therefore an interest in its progress. He reflected the common view of the 'mercantile community' in attacking the wasteful expenditure approved by the Council, including the building of a town hall that was not needed on such a scale for another 50 years. He had found 'many prominent records of folly and extravagance to set off against works of utility and public convenience', and intended to work for improved public health and a better water supply. For good measure, he accused the sitting alderman, a glazier and painter, of being idle for three-quarters of his term and of 'going about in borrowed plumes' when claiming credit for setting up the fish market in Woolloomooloo.

James Green defeated Hughes by 703 votes to 627, and the 'liberal party' failed nearly everywhere else. The *Freeman's Journal* of 9 December had no doubt about why Hughes and his allies were defeated. While accepting that several factors were involved, '[i]t may be taken in the first place, as a sure and certain proof, that sectarianism and political ascendancy is still dominant'. In these circumstances a 'thoroughly incompetent candidate … need only ally himself with a disreputable faction and his election is a certainty'. John did not nominate again but his brother, William, later won Fitzroy Ward in 1888 and John's eldest son, John Francis, succeeded William in 1891. The Hughes family had an early commitment to public life.

John Hughes, though born an Irish Catholic, became an assimilated Empire man. He objected at a meeting on 11 March 1868 when someone nominated the young Richard O'Sullivan, the editor and part-proprietor of the *Freeman's Journal* and a fervent Irish nationalist, for the committee to select proposers of toasts at a luncheon during the St Patrick's Day Regatta. John recalled how O'Sullivan had remained seated the previous year during the toast to the Queen's health. O'Sullivan said he would rise and leave the table should it be proposed in 1868.[12] Following Hughes' intervention, O' Sullivan requested his name be withdrawn from the list of proposers. The incident became important because O'Sullivan's tirades in favour of Fenian causes coincided with, if not further inflamed, anti-Irish sentiment in New South

Wales, and because the day after the confrontation with Hughes, the Duke of Edinburgh was shot and wounded at Clontarf by an Irish-born Catholic. When, a year later, Hughes appeared before a Legislative Assembly select committee investigating an 'Alleged Conspiracy for Purposes of Treason and Assassination', he agreed with Henry Parkes that he 'never had much to do with Fenians'. While he did not think that O'Sullivan was one, or was involved in any conspiracy, 'I consider he did a very disrespectful act in refusing to drink the Queen's health'.[13]

On 2 July 1856, at St Mary's Cathedral, John Hughes married Susan Sharkey, a Limerick-born daughter of an architect who had been Clerk of Works at the Colonial Treasury and was later employed by the Colonial Architects Department at Hyde Park. John and Susan had eight children; four daughters and four sons. Two sons died early in childhood. The surviving boys – John (born 11 May 1857) and Thomas (born 19 April 1863) – became prominent citizens in Sydney, and (later Sir) Thomas would become Tom Hughes' grandfather. Family and church were very important to John and Susan Hughes. The 'comparatively obscure path of business' enabled Hughes to leave generous parcels of money and property to his children. In his lifetime, however, he gave much more to the Catholic Church. He was heavily involved as a benefactor, financial adviser and committee member in the rebuilding of his parish church – St Mary's Cathedral – following the fire of June 1865. John donated the site for St Canice's Church, Elizabeth Bay, marble altars for two other Sydney churches and a marble font for St Mary's Cathedral. He also helped to establish scholarships in honour of his good friend, Archbishop Vaughan, at St Ignatius' College. John's most remarkable action was to play the leading role in bringing the Sisters of the Society of the Sacred Heart of Jesus to Sydney. The French sisters had taught his two elder daughters and, approving of the results, John provided £500 towards their establishment in Sydney and, after their arrival in 1882, gave funds to establish a Sacré Coeur convent at Rose Bay.

In his will, John Hughes made other gifts to the Church. To the everlasting chagrin of his great grandson, Robert Hughes, he bequeathed to his oldest daughter, Maria, the family home, 'Kincoppal' (Erse for sea-horse), named after a rock formation on the harbour foreshore at Elizabeth Bay. This part of the will was to become operative on the death of John's wife. Maria had already committed herself to the Sisters of the Sacred Heart and another sister soon joined her. Maria, exercising her right to dispose of the property, handed it over to the Society.[14] John Hughes had indirectly ensured that the next two generations of the Hughes family would not inherit great riches.

The good Catholic, who was also a good citizen (he was a Justice of the Peace for many years, and sat as a magistrate in Sydney's police courts), was rightly appreciated by his Church. Taking the Grand Tour of Europe and the United States with his family in 1879, he had an audience with Pope Leo XIII. Appointed a Knight of the Order of St Gregory in 1882, he died on 29 June 1885 before receiving the brief promoting him to Knight Commander. In his generally quiet way, the good citizen had also demonstrated that loyalty to a church, which many Protestants in Australia associated with Ireland as much as with Rome, did not require obeisance to a nationalism forged in an ancient quarrel. He did not hide his Irish ancestry, but certainly did not flaunt it.

Sir Thomas Hughes

John and Thomas Hughes,[15] the surviving sons of John and Susan Hughes, attended Stonyhurst College in Lancashire, a school run on Jesuit principles, and matriculated to the University of London. John took articles in Sydney and began practice as a solicitor in 1884. His younger brother joined his family's Grand Tour at the end of his school days in England before taking articles with an Irish-born solicitor in Sydney. Admitted as a solicitor in 1887, Thomas joined his brother in the new family firm of Hughes & Hughes. The two brothers married two sisters, the daughters of James Gilhooley, a Sydney physician, who were also their second cousins. John married Mary Rose in July 1884 and Thomas married Louisa in October 1887. Both weddings took place at St Mary's Cathedral.

On their father's death in 1885, the brothers inherited Lyndhurst Chambers and a property at 26 Hunter Street. John Hughes acquired more property in Sydney, sat on company boards, and gave generously of time and money to Catholic institutions and charities, especially supporting the St Vincent de Paul Society and the Little Sisters of the Poor. In 1903, he was appointed Knight Commander of the Order of St Gregory and in 1906 John and Mary Rose had an audience with Pius X. After succeeding his uncle in Fitzroy Ward on the Sydney Municipal Council, John was appointed to the Legislative Council in 1895. Between 1894 and 1910, he served in the Reid, Carruthers and Wade ministries as Vice-President of the Executive Council; and, for just over two months in 1899, was George Reid's Minister of Justice. Widely regarded as a good man, who 'cut a commanding figure in Sydney's legal, business and religious circles', John Hughes died suddenly in 1912, survived by Mary Rose, two daughters and six sons. Four of his boys served in the Great War; one was killed in action.

Thomas Hughes had even more substantial business interests than his brother. He sat on the boards of many prominent Australian companies and chaired Washington H Soul Pattinson, S Bennett Ltd (publisher of the *Evening News*), Amalgamated Wireless and Tooheys. He also sat on the Sydney boards of two major insurance companies, and was a director of the Commercial Banking Company of Sydney and of the Australia Hotel. A gentleman of standing, he was elected to membership of the Australian Club and sat on the Council of Women's College at the University of Sydney.

Thomas made a significant mark in public affairs. In common with his brother, he formed a close association with the free-trader and anti-socialist George Reid and, supporting federation, accompanied Reid as his secretary to the third session of Australasian Federal Convention held in Melbourne in 1898. With the backing of the 'mercantile community', and representing the Citizens' Municipal Reform League, he won election by a large majority for Bourke Ward to the Sydney Municipal Council in September 1898.[16] Mayor of Sydney in 1902, he became, with the change in title in 1903, Sydney's first Lord Mayor and was again Lord Mayor in 1907-08. By 1906, he had managed to extend the franchise for the Municipal Council to joint and individual occupants of business premises, thereby ensuring for some time that reform continued within a conservative framework. From 1908 until his death in 1930, he sat in the Legislative Council and, declining many invitations to join ministries, became a respected figure in debates. Thomas was a member of several royal commissions including one on Sydney's water supply (1902-03) and another on the decline of the birth rate (1903-04). He worked with the Irish-born Alderman Sir Matthew Harris who, since 1899, had been campaigning for a unified 'Greater Sydney'. Thomas wanted Sydney to have a centralised municipal body owning and controlling key public services and undertaking a program of slum clearance and rehousing. In 1908-09, he presided over a wide-ranging royal commission whose final report, a planning document of lasting value, included recommendations on public health, transport, town planning, social welfare and beautification.

Thomas Hughes served as an honorary secretary of the first Australasian Catholic Congress of 1900. As a member of the 'gentlemen's executive committee' for the Third Congress in 1909, he successfully moved that the laity should present Cardinal Moran, Archbishop of Sydney for 25 years, with an address testifying to its 'loyalty and affection for the venerated leader of the Australian Church'.[17] Like his brother, though probably not to the same extent, he helped with financing St Mary's Cathedral and sat on its various committees. In 1915, in common with his father and older brother and after paying the requisite fee of £105, he was appointed Knight Commander of the Order of St Gregory. In the same year, Thomas was appointed Knight Bachelor in the King's Birthday Honours. The *Sydney Morning Herald* (*SMH*) of 4 June described Sir Thomas as 'a leading Roman Catholic churchman'. The Woman's Page of the *Freeman's Journal* declared that 'most people' expected this elevation to have occurred much earlier. 'Sydney's first Lord

Mayor and his handsome wife are eminently fitted to uphold the dignity of the position, so the honour conferred only adds a little to the lustre of lives unostentatiously lived with one objective – that of proving true and worthy citizens.'

Whereas church and state jointly honoured Sir Thomas in 1915, many prelates, clergy and members of the laity turned on him in 1916-17. A combination of events – the breakdown in the consensus of August 1914; the 'troubles' in Ireland in 1916 and the British Government's response to the 'Easter uprising'; the persistent industrial strife of 1916-17; the Bolshevik revolution in Russia – had exposed and widened fractures in Australian society. The Prime Minister, 'Billy' Hughes, intensified division by proposing to introduce conscription to increase the number of troops available for the Western Front. Dr Mannix, who became Archbishop of Melbourne in 1917, led the argument that Catholics had already done enough for the war effort. No man, he said, should be forced to take up arms. Sir Thomas and Lady Hughes, members of the Universal Service League, thought differently. They regarded the war against Germany as a just war against barbarism and believed every able man must do his duty for King and Country.

In November 1917, before the second conscription plebiscite, the Catholic Justice Heydon of the NSW Industrial Court whose son, George, was awarded a Military Cross, accused Mannix of disloyalty. Mannix in his reply accused Heydon of having an English father. On 23 November, the *SMH* published a response from Sir Thomas Hughes. He said the Mannix attack on Heydon, if delivered by 'a dignitary less highly placed, would be considered mere vulgar personal abuse'. Proud of his Irish descent, Hughes saw himself as 'above all … an Australian', and by that alone he should be judged. Mannix seemed to think that 'by setting race against race and class against class' he was serving the country 'which has so lately received him'. For Sir Thomas it was straightforward: 'Loyalty to the Empire is loyalty to Australia, and anything else is hateful to every true Australian.' Catholic parents who had boys at the Front (he once had two), or whose boys had given their lifeblood (he had lost one), 'resent to the innermost fibres of their being' the Mannix dismissal of the fight against 'the powers of darkness' as just a 'sordid trade war'.

Some Catholic Bishops fought the good fight in response. The Australian-born Patrick Dwyer, the Bishop of Maitland, had Sir Thomas in mind when referring to 'lick-plate Catholics who frequent Government House'. Presumably, the Bishop did not express his contempt earlier in November 1917 when he and Sir Thomas attended a welcome for the Papal Delegate at St Mary's and Sir Thomas stood behind him for the photograph to mark the occasion. Like Hughes, the other two laymen in the photograph were members of the Legislative Council, and one was a brother-in-law. All three were present as 'leading Catholics'. Speaking at a Catholic Federation breakfast at Casino, the Irish-born Bishop John Carroll of Lismore spoke disparagingly of 'some self-styled leading Catholics' who had the temerity to attack 'the great Archbishop of Melbourne'. Sir Thomas Hughes, he said, had more reason to feel proud of his Irish ancestry 'than Ireland had to be proud of him'. The Bishop could not recall Hughes making any act of sacrifice or uttering a strong or kindly word in support of 'the old Motherland in her chains'.[18] Speaking at St John's College at the University of Sydney, Mannix spoke damningly of well-off Catholics who 'are more Catholic than the Pope, and more loyal than the King' and who think 'they are able to instruct their bishops'.[19]

On his death from nephritis in 1930, the *Freeman's Journal* described Sir Thomas as 'a fine Catholic citizen'. It did not mention that he was also an Australian of Irish descent whose first allegiance was to Australia and the Empire, that he was not an expatriate looking over his shoulder to another loyalty. In two generations, the Hughes family had made a transition, assisted by their increasing prosperity and political prominence within an Anglo-Scottish world. The Great War, and the stark choices it posed, sealed the family's assimilation.

Geoffrey Forrest Hughes

Thomas and Louisa Hughes had three sons. The first-born, Thomas, arrived in November 1888 and died at Kincoppal in February 1894 of complications resulting from diphtheria. Roger Forrest Hughes, the second son, was born at Kincoppal in May 1890. He was a brilliant scholar at St Ignatius' College, Riverview, and at the University of Sydney where he graduated in Arts and Medicine. He was a versatile and noted sportsman in athletics, cricket, rugby and hockey. Roger married Eileen Maher at St Canice's Church on 2 March 1916 and, by the end of the year, was in France with the 1st Australian Field Ambulance based on the Somme. After five days at the Front, he died from wounds caused by a shell hitting the dressing station where he was working on a patient who was killed outright by the blast. His widow was then eight months pregnant.

Geoffrey Forrest Hughes, the third son, was born on 12 July 1895, ironically on the day Orangemen commemorate the Battle of the Boyne of 1690. There is a record of him attending 'Shirley, The New School and Kindergarten' in Edgecliff Road, Woollahra, in 1903. Shirley was essentially a school for girls, though a few boys up to about age 11 could enrol. The co-principals – Miss Harriet C Newcomb and Miss Margaret Hodge – had originally come to Sydney from England to assist with teacher training. Born in the 1850s, the two women became business partners, companions and feminists. They had travelled throughout Europe studying educational trends. Placing themselves at 'the cutting edge of progressive educational thought and practice', they took over an existing building in Woollahra with its large rooms and plenty of light, set in a substantial garden, and offered an education designed to 'develop individual powers and widen the range of sympathy in every direction'. The emphasis was on experiential rather than book learning, on open-air schooling, modern curriculum offerings, the cultivation of a family atmosphere and a concern for the 'whole child'.[20] On Geoffrey's First Term Report for Form I Newcomb wrote: 'Progress hindered by absence. Always a good boy.'[21]

The parents of young Geoffrey Hughes may have found the Jesuits more to their liking. In 1907, Geoffrey followed his brother Roger to Riverview where he became, in his final year of 1913, a House Prefect, a member and top scorer of the School's Rifle team, vice-captain of the First Fifteen, a member of the senior tennis team and a council member of the Senior Sodality. Academically, he did well in coming first in the senior class in English, Higher English, French and Greek. Earlier, in 1911, he had travelled with his parents and brother Roger to England where he attended the Coronation of George V and, having an interest in flying, visited the Hendon Aerodrome and the Paris Air Show.

Geoffrey entered Sydney University in 1914 to study Arts. Commissioned with the 26th Infantry Regiment in June of that year, he sought, at the outbreak of war, to join the Australian Flying Corps but encountered repeated rejections of his applications, bureaucratic hold-ups and diversions. In 1915, he served as an honorary aide-de-camp to the NSW Governor, Sir Gerald Strickland, thereby establishing a connection with the Catholic aristocracy which his son Tom utilised during the Second World War. Early in 1916, Geoffrey obtained an interview with the Army's Adjutant-General, who advised him to go to England and join the Royal Flying Corps (RFC). A few days after being best man at Roger's wedding, Geoffrey set sail for England bearing references from Michael Kelly, the Catholic Archbishop of Sydney, and Sir Ronald Munro Ferguson, the Governor-General of Australia.

He sailed via New York with a family party: John Hughes' widow, Mary Rose ('Aunt Mary'), her two unmarried daughters, her son Maurice and a nephew, Brendan Lane-Mullins. Aunt Mary already had two sons – Bryan and Gilbert – at the Front and Maurice and Brendan intended to join them. Bryan (wounded) and Gilbert (gassed) had been returned to England and, arriving there at the end of April, Geoffrey spent his first days visiting his cousins convalescing in Oxford.

Six weeks later, Geoffrey was commissioned 2nd Lieutenant in the RFC and started intensive training. He received his wings at the end of June and joined 10 Squadron RFC in France in August 1916. His principal duties consisted of observation, photography and night bombing. Geoffrey proved to have exceptional skills as a pilot. He understood that to beat the odds stacked against him, he needed to match courage with a sensible appreciation of the possible. He also believed that God was with him and moving, as ever, in mysterious ways, God had guided him to find, and to be with, the dying Roger early in December.

His grief over losing his much-loved brother and closest friend was compounded during 1917. He despised the 'shirkers' who refused to enlist in the great and just cause which claimed Roger's life, and the priests at home who opposed conscription and who had 'done more harm to the cause of Catholicity than the bitterest orangeman [sic] could ever do'. Geoffrey, 'as loyal a Catholic as I can be', considered it 'nothing short of criminal' for a priest to use his spiritual office to sway minds in a crisis affecting nations and to 'avenge his own wrongs or the wrong of his country by playing the traitor':

> If he is a priest, I will respect him for the holy office he bears, but there it ceases and I will have no more to do with him … some may forget such things – I won't.

As for the Irish element, Geoffrey was at one with his father, and grandfather, John Hughes: 'no one is prouder of Irish ancestors' but he had no time for the 'traitors' involved in the Dublin Easter Rising of 1916.[22]

Geoffrey was a training instructor in England for much of 1917. He was promoted to Captain, acquired a dog ('Girlie'), and used leave breaks to catch up with Aunt Mary and his second family, consoling them on the death of one cousin, cheering up another (Maurice) who was wounded just before the Third Battle of Ypres, and congratulating another on his engagement. He was not happy, however, when in September the RFC transferred him from Port Meadow near Oxford to a training station at Rendcomb in east Gloucestershire. Geoffrey was even less happy when he got there. He had to train pupils in a machine they 'cordially hated', he missed a squadron he really liked, and he found the closest main town, Cirencester, to be 'a dull spot'.

As much as he disliked his new posting, Geoffrey acknowledged that there were 'very nice people living around here and they are very kind to RFC officers'. On 4 October 1917, he told 'My own darling Mother & Father' that he and his Rendcomb CO had gone to Barnsley Park, near Cirencester, to have tea with Herbert 'Henry' Wykeham-Musgrave (the local squire) and his wife, and to pick walnuts. Two days later, Geoffrey and his CO dined with the Wykeham-Musgraves 'and tomorrow I am going to dinner with some people called Vidal who live at Barnsley'.[23]

The English connection

The Reverend George Studley Sealy Vidal was the Rector of St Mary's Church, Barnsley. He was born on 12 February 1862 in the village of Abbotsham in the county of Devon, the 13th child of Edward Urch (Sealy) Vidal and Emma Harriet Eyre who produced eight sons and seven daughters. Emma's ancestors included Humphrey Le Her of Wiltshire, a follower of King Richard I in the Holy Land. Over the following centuries, the Eyre family produced politicians, soldiers, lawyers, magistrates and a godson of Sir Robert Walpole. Edward Sealy (his original name) attended Christ Church, Oxford, and was called to the Bar by the Middle Temple, one of the four Inns of Court in London. He was living in Bridgewater, Somerset, where he owned several farms and properties, when a distant kinsman, Robert Studley Vidal, probably of French Huguenot descent, left Edward his property when he died in 1841. In order to claim his inheritance, Edward was required to adopt the surname and arms of Vidal and reside in the family seat – Cornborough House in Abbotsham. Meeting this condition, Edward also inherited several other landholdings in north Devon, two items of silver of historical significance and a name linking him in England to the Reverend Peter Vidal, MA (1702-41).

Edward's son, George, won scholarships to Winchester College in Hampshire and to New College, Oxford. William of Wykeham, the Bishop of Winchester, had founded both institutions in the late 14th century. Chancellor at one time to Edward III and to Richard II, the Bishop deployed his munificence in several directions. Winchester became the nursery for New College, providing it with 70 'poor scholars' trained in the classics, of whom the majority were to study theology and prepare themselves for the priesthood.

When George Vidal arrived at Winchester and New College, the two institutions were benefiting from reforms implemented from the mid-19th century. From 1854, a merit-based competitive examination replaced patronage as the means of awarding scholarships to Winchester, so Vidal must have established good academic credentials. George Ridding, headmaster from 1867 to 1884, expanded Winchester's focus on a classical training to embrace history, modern languages and science. Ridding also placed an emphasis on games, and Vidal was clearly an all-round sportsman. According to family legend, he might have played football (soccer) for England, a feat achieved by an older brother in 1873. Robert Walpole Sealy Vidal, the 'Prince of dribblers' according to football histories and folk lore, played in the first three FA Cup finals, in two of which he played for winning, albeit different, teams.[24] George Vidal was a member of the Winchester First Eleven (known as 'Lords' or 'Lord's'). The available records do not flatter him. In June 1881, batting at number seven in a one-day match against the Marylebone

Cricket Club, he made one run; and batting at number nine in a two-day match against Eton he scored just one and five in two innings. In those two games he neither bowled, nor kept wicket, nor took a catch.[25] His academic record appears to have been more impressive. He probably obtained his New College scholarship through a form of competitive examination and, late in 1881, at the beginning of Michaelmas Term, he went up to Oxford to take Honours in Classics.

Little is known of his Oxford years. Apparently, he played football for his college and university. He graduated with Honours, having obtained a Second in Classical Moderations at the end of his second year, and a Third in Classics in his final year of 1885. These results did not mark him out for an academic career. Perhaps he was already committed to seek holy orders. Perhaps, too, his results reflected a preoccupation with other activities. Treasurer of the Oxford Union for a term, he was President for the Hilary Term in 1885. Two histories of the Oxford Union mentioned the two Presidents who preceded him (including a future Archbishop of Canterbury) and one who succeeded him (Lord Robert Cecil, the third son of the Marquess of Salisbury who was three times Prime Minister), but there was no reference to the future Rector of Barnsley.[26]

Vidal formally graduated as a Bachelor of Arts in 1886 and took his Master of Arts two years later. On graduation, he tutored at New College and was ordained by the Bishop of Oxford in 1888. Curate of St Giles and Chaplain of St John's College, Oxford (1888-92), Vidal was also Chaplain of New College and Tutor at St Mary Hall at much the same time. For nine years from 1892, he was Rector of Stoke Abbott in west Dorset. In 1901, the father of Henry Wykeham-Musgrave, a student Vidal had met at New College during his chaplaincy, provided him with a living at Barnsley. By the time Geoffrey Hughes met Vidal in 1917, Henry had replaced his late father as the Patron.

In the year of his ordination, Vidal married Constance Isabella Homan of County Sligo, Ireland. Constance was born in 1866 and was one of the seven children of Samuel and Maria (Caxton) Homan. She was lucky to have been born at all. Nine years earlier, her father, a medical doctor with the East India Company, as well as her mother and elder siblings, had barely escaped death in the 'Indian Mutiny'. They survived because loyal servants had given false information to a band of rebels about their escape route.[27] Two of Constance's sisters – Clara and May – figure later in this story because Tom Hughes made a point of contacting them while on war service in England. A brother, Ernest, spent time in Africa where he either accompanied or later followed Dr Jameson's 'Pioneer Column' of 1890 that 'annexed' Southern Rhodesia. It is unclear how and when George Vidal met Constance, but he was probably smitten by her spirit and considerable beauty. She proved to be an invaluable asset in many respects, helping to supplement the family's resources by setting up a small business selling her homemade chocolates. In 1918, Vidal's living, supported by the Tithe Rent Charge, was valued at £300 a year, which he supplemented by tutoring Oxford students during the summer.[28]

Geoffrey told his parents on 8 October 1917 that his night with the Vidals was 'one of the cheeriest evenings I've had for ages'. There were about a dozen there 'and after Dinner we had a wild old rag'. There was a gramophone, dancing and a variation of a game of hide and seek where a dozen people ended up in a space big enough for one ('Sardines'), as well as 'Up Jenkins' and 'all the other mad old games'. The occasion was the 18th birthday of the Vidals' second daughter, Margaret, whom Geoffrey had probably first met at a Mess dance. 'We were just a wild crowd of irresponsible youngsters & all thoroughly enjoyed ourselves. <u>Of course</u> there were some awfully nice girls there – real cheery good sorts' (emphasis in the original). 'Mrs Vidal' made an impression: 'one of the very best. She simply loves to have lots of young people about the place and is full of fun.' Margaret, 'an excellent sport', was about to take a typist's job at the Special Medical Air Board in London. His initial view of the Reverend Vidal was more mixed: 'a funny old bird but quite a decent sort'. Evidently, Geoffrey himself made an impression. He was invited to tea the following day. Observing that the family was not well off – they had just one maid and Sunday was her day off – he lent a hand with clearing up.

For his parents' benefit, the pleasure of contact with the Vidals had to be placed in context.

> I cant [sic] tell you what a difference it makes to have nice places to go to and nice people to see. It really is just a little breath of home air and refinement that makes an enormous difference to life so far from home and everything that is dearest to me.

Although he liked the 'chaps' at Rendcomb – except for the 'rotters' – he was missing refinement and 'nice influences', and needed somewhere to go at the end of the day for distraction and relaxation. He had concluded that the colonials were the better types, and certainly better than the 'Pom' on the base who criticised the behaviour of the Australians in Egypt. It helped to receive many invitations to visit the Vidals and, on one occasion, he entertained the family at Rendcomb.

On 24 October, he asked his mother to write to Mrs Vidal ('a really good sort') to thank her for all she had done for him. Although 'old man Vidal is a funny old stick in the mud and a terrible old bore at times, I have had lots of very cheery evenings there when we danced sometimes till 2 AM!!'. He did not want his parents to get the wrong idea about Margaret: 'don't you start scenting a romance here because there ain't none! We are just excellent pals.'

Despite being 'only a kid', his experiences over the last two years 'have made me fairly level headed', and he did not want to make his parents unhappy so 'there isn't much likelihood that I would go and fall in love with a girl who is not a Catholic'.

Geoffrey was actually pursuing the vicar's younger daughter with enthusiasm and some inventiveness. Captain Hughes used flights in and out of Rendcomb to drop letters in a pouch at the Rectory. This means of contact lapsed when the supposed non-suitor transferred early in November to a training squadron in Hampshire and Margaret took her job in London. But short leave periods were spent in London for meetings with Margaret. Geoffrey stayed with Aunt Mary and his 'second family' now living in Maida Vale, and took Margaret to meet them. Even this level of contact could not last. In February 1918, Geoffrey returned to the Front as a Flight Commander of the Bristol Fighter No 62 Squadron.

End of the War, a conversion and a marriage

Geoffrey flew a series of engagements between February and May 1918 and registered 11 'kills'. On 13 March, after a successful morning escorting bombers and with enemy aircraft operating at a safe distance, he was leading his patrol home when a 'fool' in the formation dived on the 'Huns' below them. Unwilling to let one machine go down alone, Geoffrey led 11 planes against 40 to 50 enemy aircraft in a pitched battle he called 'simply indescribable'. The Hughes team had engaged Baron von Richthofen's 'Flying Circus' and Geoffrey was fired upon and outsmarted by the 'Red Baron' himself. At least, with his observer Hugh Claye, he could claim to have shot down the Red Baron's brother. Moreover, while nine of Geoffrey's 11 planes returned to their lines, at least eight of the enemy did not. Following this incident, Geoffrey was awarded the Military Cross. The citation, published in the *London Gazette* of 13 May 1918, referred to his record in three separate engagements and concluded that he 'always showed the greatest coolness and courage in action and as a flight commander led his formation with splendid courage and determination'.

By this time he was back in England. Sir Thomas and Louisa had prevailed upon Aunt Mary and she agitated in the right places to extract the surviving son from the Front. After Roger's death there was just too much anxiety in Sydney. Geoffrey was selected for a special flying course at Gosport in Hampshire. Just 20 per cent of the chosen ones actually passed, and Geoffrey emerged with the highest possible 1A grading. Assigned to a training post near Oxford, he learnt that his cousin Bryan, also a winner of the Military Cross, had been killed in Flanders. Like his father in Sydney, Geoffrey could not join the 'mad crowd' and its jubilation following the Armistice in November. Both men remembered what they had lost. For Geoffrey the fitting thing was 'just a prayer of thanksgiving' that the sacrifice had 'not been in vain'. Margaret Vidal had her own reasons for grief: 13 of her cousins had died in the Great War while her sister, Mary, lost the man she hoped to marry.

Geoffrey remained at the training school waiting for a discharge and preparing in his mind to study law. Now deeply in love with Margaret, he wrote to his father in October 1918 seeking permission to become engaged. Sir Thomas raised concerns about religious differences and hinted that his son should first secure his financial future. In the meantime, Geoffrey managed to get his extended family into the Throne Room at Buckingham Palace to witness his investiture for the Military Cross by King George V, an event memorable for the length of the queue for awards and by the brevity of his meeting with royalty. In April 1919, as he prepared for demobilisation, Geoffrey visited the graves of his brother and two cousins in France. He saw Margaret as often as he could before boarding a ship for New York to meet his parents at the end of May. The family arrived together in Sydney on 29 July, the month after Geoffrey received an Air Force Cross. Within the year he graduated with a Bachelor of Arts. He completed a Bachelor of Laws with Second Class Honours and, admitted as a solicitor in May 1923, joined the family firm of Hughes & Hughes.

His father persisted with objections to a formal engagement until Margaret agreed to become a Catholic.[29] Her parents made no recorded protestation. As the *Freeman's Journal* of 7 July 1921 explained: 'in order that there will be no division of faith between the young couple, Miss Sealy Vidal will enter the Catholic Church, as Captain Hughes belongs to one of the best known Catholic families in Sydney'. So, well into his 28th year, Geoffrey Hughes received parental approval to marry Margaret Vidal in St Canice's Catholic Church on 8 January 1923. The *SMH* called it a 'Society Wedding'. Sir Thomas gave the bride away. The Limerick-born Father O'Regan performed the service, assisted by two other priests, one of whom was Eris O'Brien, a future Archbishop and Australian historian. Mary Vidal sang an 'Ave Maria' during the signing of the register. The late Roger Hughes' son, Roger, was the bride's page. William Owen, later of the NSW Supreme Court and the High Court, was best man. Sir Thomas and Lady Hughes held a reception at the Hotel Australia and the couple honeymooned in New Norfolk, Tasmania.[30]

The Catholicity of the occasion was unmistakable, although the best man and the bridesmaid were Church of England. The Irish-ness was present without being significant. One branch of the descendants of assisted immigrants to New South Wales had been absorbed into another culture.

2

Childhood and education

'Thomas' was a natural choice for a Christian name of the first born son of Geoffrey and Margaret Hughes, at once honouring his Australian grandfather and linking him to the first of his family to arrive in New South Wales. Tom's second and third forenames did not commemorate two illustrious explorers of the Australian continent. 'Eyre', with its long history on his maternal side, was one of his mother's Christian names and had been the maiden name of Tom's maternal-great grandmother. 'Forrest' was a Catholic priest, the second Rector of St John's College at the University of Sydney, and a collateral relative of Sir Thomas Hughes.

A 'happy' childhood

Tom remembers growing up in a 'kind and loving' family and his childhood being 'happy and well-ordered'.[1]

An early memory is of his mother taking him to a children's party on board HMS *Renown*, which had brought the Duke and Duchess of York to Australia for the opening in 1927 of the new Federal Parliament in Canberra. Tom posted the gold-leaf invitation into the window casement of the family car just as it was reaching the wharf at Woolloomooloo. Fortunately, his father was present as an honorary aide-de-camp to the Duke and, despite what Tom called 'this breach of discipline', the party, without their invitation, was allowed on board. Tom has another memory of going to Circular Quay to farewell his first nanny, Betty Lindner, who was returning to England. He met her again in 1944 when, as Flying Officer Hughes of the RAAF, he stayed with her in Warwickshire.

Tom remembers clearly and not happily going to Turramurra to have his portrait drawn in crayon by the well-known artist Florence Rodway (she had previously drawn portraits of his father and of his late uncle Roger). Tom had to endure dressing for the event in the Hotel Australia where his grandmother, Lady Hughes, accidentally kept sticking pins into him for an outfit consisting of a smock and trousers. He then had to take the long journey from Rose Bay across the Harbour and on unsealed roads to the far North Shore. Nevertheless, Tom liked the portrait well enough to have it adorn invitations to attend his 90th birthday celebration.

Lady Hughes, known in the family as 'Ganny Gan', died in 1948. Tom recalls that she was 'always in decline' and 'plagued by religious scruples'. Towards the end, his 'saintly father' visited her twice a day at St Vincent's Private Hospital.[2] Tom hardly knew his paternal grandfather because Sir Thomas Hughes died in April 1930. His direct knowledge of him was limited to his grandfather's requirement that Margaret Vidal should convert to Catholicism before he would approve of his son's marriage to her.[3]

Tom's sister, Constance, was born on 17 March 1926. Her red hair and arrival on St Patrick's Day affirmed her Irish Catholic credentials and gave her bragging rights over a father born on the 205th anniversary of the Battle of the Boyne.[4] She confirmed Tom's point about growing up in a happy home, made even more so because their parents had 'a very lovely, happy marriage'. Early in 1928, Geoffrey Hughes described Tom and Constance to his own parents as 'splendid pals'.[5] They constructed their own world of make-believe, built a shop and a solicitor's office and, after making an aeroplane out of window boxes, Tom dressed up in his father's uniform and Constance wore the clothes of a nurse. They had their own language and wrote their own plays. For one, Tom dressed as Captain Cook, and for another he was Robin Hood, attended by Constance as Maid Marian. Tom liked to climb a gum tree in their backyard and he played with other children in the street. He had a primitive scooter and there were billy carts everywhere. His parents bought him the supposed prized possessions of any young boy – a Meccano set and a Hornby train set – but he was not interested in either of them. Tom preferred to read, and developed a great affection for the limericks and nonsense poems of Edward Lear. Other favourites included *Robinson Crusoe*, *Songs of a Sentimental Bloke*, *The Wind in the Willows* and *Winnie the Pooh*. Tom had his dreams. He wanted to own land, and importuned visitors to give him money so he could buy a station, and recalls one judge handing over a threepence.[6]

Constance remembered Tom as the more serious brother while Geoffrey, born on 9 May 1928, was the more mischievous and received more whacks. Tom was on hand after Geoffrey's arrival. His father reported to Sir Thomas and Lady Hughes that 'Tom is thrilled with his brother and sits outside the door patiently waiting to be admitted to the bathing ceremony each day'.[7] Much later, Tom used to help Constance with maths (it was his weakest subject at school), and was always very protective, and remained so. Yet he was also 'a bossy older brother'.[8]

The family had many holidays at Yaouk on the upper Murrumbidgee in the Snowy Mountains. The children would sail on the raft their father built, chop kindling, play tennis, fish and, when older, ride ponies. Their mother was a very accomplished equestrian, and arranged for the children to attend a riding school at Double Bay. Yet life at Yaouk was not always idyllic. During one scorching summer, Margaret remained there for a month with the three children and 'Nursie' (Anne Becker) after her husband returned to his law firm in Sydney. She wrote to him saying it was so unbearably hot she had remained in her bathing costume all day:

> The children were exasperating & Tom made an awful fuss when I went off for the ride. He kicked & squealed like a maniac after I'd left (Nursie said). They were all snarling & scratching at each other today till I got desperate & made them realise I really would pack them off to Sydney if they don't behave.
>
> Geoffrey is really adorable! I took them fishing this morn [sic] but they were all sick of it in half an hour. They are really too young for it up here. I hope it will be better when I can get the ponies for a decent ride for them.
>
> Constance has been quite off colour today, & we have put her on to a light diet & her mixture. I think she may have been upset by the heat & a whipping I had to administer yesterday.

Margaret was bored and miserable: 'I can only hope it really is doing the kids good.' Yet children do have restorative value. In the same letter, she wrote: 'They are rather priceless at the moment': they had a string of kerosene tins around their necks and 'are strolling about singing sweet songs very much out of tune'. She signed the letter, 'Your adoring wife Peg'.[9]

One trip to Yaouk might easily have ended in tragedy. Margaret, the children and Anne Becker stayed in Yaouk for some three months in the summer of 1931-32 because of a polio scare in Sydney. Together with a Great War veteran and a close family friend, HH McKay, they left for Sydney in the family car, a six-cylinder Hudson, with a trailer attached. McKay was driving when, at about 6.30 am and some eight miles from Goulburn, the car skidded on the gravel road, somersaulted, and landed on its roof and balanced on the ramp of a concrete culvert above a four foot drop. No one was actually hurt except 'Nursie', who suffered a bruised shoulder. But all were in shock. According to a newspaper report, the occupants escaped serious injury because the car was a sedan and had a steel body. The same report recorded that Margaret ran a mile to a farmhouse, borrowed a horse, and rode three miles to the nearest telephone. She contacted a Goulburn garage, which immediately sent assistance. A message went to Sydney and a Captain Leggatt flew Hughes to Goulburn, and the family boarded the afternoon train home.[10]

The children had another holiday venue. Their parents had bought a block of land on the crest of a hill at Whale Beach north of Sydney. Attracted to the site for its scenic view, Geoffrey and Margaret originally thought of building a shack for the summer holidays. Their plans changed following the death of the Reverend Vidal on 20 July 1928. The new plan was to build a place for the widowed Constance Vidal and her unmarried daughter, Mary ('Aunt Mim'), who could then make a reasonable income by selling afternoon teas. Geoffrey told his parents how he and Margaret were always hearing about the impossibility of getting a decent cup of tea while motoring around Sydney. Placed at the end of the loveliest drive, the enterprise, if well-managed, could not go wrong. He made another, not particularly subtle point: 'The spot is sufficiently near to be get-attable [sic] and yet not too near.'[11]

Gilbert Hughes, Geoffrey Hughes' cousin and an architect, designed the building and the enterprising Constance Vidal, assisted by her two daughters, established 'Jonah's' as a restaurant and roadhouse. The Hughes children spent many happy school holidays there.[12] The business gradually began to pay its way, and it survived the death of Constance Vidal in October 1937. 'Jonah's' was sold when the number of visitors declined during the Second World War.[13]

In 1938, Gilbert Hughes was retained to design substantial alterations to the Hughes home in Rose Bay now known as 'Marsland'. The cottage was already too small and now there was a need to accommodate Robert Studley Forrest Hughes, born on 28 July of that year. The new arrival was 14 years and 8 months younger than Tom. Although he expressed love and affection for his other two siblings, and especially for his sister, 'Bob' always felt closest to Tom, even in the late 1960s when they took opposite sides over the Vietnam War. The age difference mattered, however, when Robert was young. Whereas his siblings had shared a 'happy' childhood, he never really knew what it was like 'to grow up surrounded by playmates'. Aunt Mim, his adored 'second mother', became Robert's companion in his early years.[14]

A 'well-ordered' childhood

The Hughes family did not consider itself to be well off, even though a cottage in Rose Bay, a car, a nanny for the children and a maid for the housework, holidays spent at Yaouk or at Whale Beach were the outward signs of a comfortable, upper-middle class household. Geoffrey and Margaret Hughes felt they had to be careful with money, especially with the onset of the Great Depression when a solicitor's work became more unpredictable. Fortunately, Geoffrey held directorships with several public companies: the Commercial Banking Company of Sydney (worth £250 per annum), the United Insurance Company and the Australian Hotel Company Ltd. He became chairman of Tooheys Ltd and of Tooheys Standard Securities Ltd, and had good social and business networks through his membership of the Australian Club and of the Royal Sydney Golf Club. Geoffrey Hughes had status and connections, even if his grandfather's generosity to the Church had deprived him of commensurate riches.

The 'well-ordered' household of Tom's memory did not encourage physical displays of affection. The children grew up knowing they were loved but in an environment where good behaviour took precedence over the cultivation and release of feelings. The household mirrored the bearing, expectations and character of both parents. Constance recalled her mother being very enthusiastic about anything involving her husband. She adopted the military metaphor – 'follow the drum' – and looked upon Geoffrey as 'Number One', 'the centre of her life'. Not that he made all the rules. Margaret Hughes had no time for the cinema and the children had their first outing when their father took them to see Charlie Chaplin in *Modern Times* when their mother was ill in bed. More importantly, Tom grew up in a household regulated by women – his mother and 'Nursie' – and, while the former established and enforced codes of conduct, the latter helped organise the children's lives. Anne Becker presided over their regular hours, including evening tea in the nursery.

The whole family usually gathered for Sunday lunch, and occasionally the children would join the dinner table. If Robert Hughes is to be believed, and his memoir is demonstrably unreliable in places, 'Mum' produced food that 'usually tasted routine, and she had a way of overcooking anything and everything – the English kitchen vice of the day'.[15] Perhaps in reaction, Tom as an adult developed a liking for the best food derived from different cuisines.

Geoffrey Hughes led the family in daily morning and afternoon prayers and they all regularly attended Mass at the Church of St Mary Magdalene in Rose Bay. 'Mons' (Monsignor) Richard O'Regan, who had performed the Hughes' wedding ceremony in 1923, is best remembered by the children for being 'a long-winded preacher' and a regular guest for meals. Even their father's relationship with Monsignor O'Regan became strained because of his interminable sermons. For the Hughes family, 'the Retreat from Mons' had a special meaning.[16]

The children were not present when a new curate was a guest at the dinner table, but the occasion entered family folk lore. The curate made the 'mistake' of calling Countess Markievicz 'a wonderful woman'. The Countess, a daughter of the Anglo-Irish landlord and Arctic explorer, Sir Henry Gore-Booth, had shot dead a sentry at Government House in Dublin during the 1916 Easter Rising. She had defiantly told her trial she wanted to be shot and not imprisoned. After the Great War, Markievicz stood firmly by Éamon de Valera and the republican cause until her death in 1927. As in 1916-17, Geoffrey Hughes had no time for Irish rebels who rose up against the Crown when the Empire was fighting a war. The curate never received a second invitation.[17]

Geoffrey Hughes had a profound religious faith, high ideals, firm principles and a keen sense of what was right and wrong. Three of his commitments – to his Church, to King and Country and to public service – entered the public arena in the inter-war years. On 9 September 1928, Hughes led a formation of five Aero Club planes to escort the Blessed Sacrament as it crossed by ferry from Manly to Circular Quay as a part of the Eucharistic Congress held in Sydney. His reward for service to the church was appointment to the office of Privy Chamberlain of the Sword and Cape to Pope Pius XI.

Hughes frequently spoke out about future air force needs in Australia. Believing that hostilities in Europe would probably resume, and that aviation would play a greater part than it did in 1914-18, he wanted aero clubs to provide training grounds for instructors and flyers in preparation for the next conflict. A member of the NSW Aero Club since 1919 and President 1924-35, he vigorously lobbied government for the expansion of the RAAF and for improved civilian aviation facilities, all the time placing the greatest emphasis on ensuring safety for crew and passengers. Hughes had no time for 'glory boys' and risk-takers. He formed 'an unfavourable impression' of the two national heroes of the late 1920s – Charles Kingsford Smith ('Smithy') and Charles Ulm – before and during the time he served on a committee which investigated the forced landings of their *Southern Cross* and of its would-be finder, the *Kookaburra*, in central Australia in April 1929. He thought afterwards he had been harsh in his assessment of 'Smithy', but Geoffrey Hughes never retracted his view that daredevil flying had no place in war or peacetime.[18]

He briefly considered entering politics as one means of engaging in public service. His outlook was conservative, along conventional lines. Although Geoffrey and Margaret attended the first annual ball of the New Guard in October 1932, there is no evidence presently available linking Hughes to any further association with that paramilitary organisation.[19] In March 1928 SM Bruce, the Nationalist Prime Minister, asked him to nominate for the federal seat of South Sydney, which included Redfern, Randwick, Coogee, Maroubra and Botany. John Latham, the Attorney-General and future Chief Justice of the High Court, and Thomas Bavin, the State leader of the Nationalist Party, made similar requests. Caught in two minds – Hughes thought of becoming Minister for Air but the minuses included concerns for his practice, income and family life – he asked his father for advice, adding 'I suppose its [sic] in the family blood to do something in public life'. Sir Thomas, who was abroad, replied by cable saying the invitation had to be accepted. Nominations remained open beyond the official closing date, waiting for Hughes' decision. He agreed to stand, telling his parents that the selection 'will be all right, especially as the PM and the Ministry want it'. He was evidently unaware of having two liabilities rolled into one. He was neither a local nor a Protestant. Alderman George Baker, a former Mayor of Randwick and the losing Nationalist candidate in 1925, won the preselection. Geoffrey Hughes did not live to witness a delicious irony. In 1963, the Liberal Party chased after and chose his eldest son to stand for the federal seat of Parkes, precisely because he was a Catholic, and notwithstanding Tom Hughes' refusal to live in the electorate.[20]

The education of young Tom

On 7 August 1928, Geoffrey Hughes sent a letter to his parents to greet them on their arrival in Fremantle towards the end of their trip abroad. 'You will find the babes flourishing if they are still as fit as they are now. Constance has come on enormously and is full of mischief … Geoffrey is splendid and so good. Tom is a most important person going off each morning to school.'[21]

After attending a kindergarten in Bellevue Hill, Tom spent two years at a private primary school in the premises of the Royal Prince Edward Yacht Club in Point Piper. Miss Pile was in charge. She was 'formidable … very strict … [and] ran a tight ship'. Her response to acts of indiscipline or failure to meet her standards for learning was to hit pupils with the hard edge of a ruler. Miss Pile did, however, have a gift for imparting knowledge, and Tom was learning Latin at the age of seven, an experience not enhanced by dropping his text book into his grandmother's chamber pot.

In 1932, aged eight, he went to the Edgecliff Preparatory School for Boys, a school once attended by John Gorton, the Prime Minister with whom Hughes became closely allied. Miss Isabel Van Heuckelum ('Miss Van') founded the school in 1913. Tom remembers her as 'a strong personality … not plagued by doubts, firm but just'. Mr Butterly, originally the sole master, was 'a very impressive teacher' who taught the older groups. Tom travelled to school on a tram, and for a shilling could buy a hot lunch on the other side of New South Head Road. On Fridays, he briefly left the school to attend Catholic religious instruction classes at Kincoppal, where he encountered Anthony Mason, the future Chief Justice of the High Court.[22]

Speaking in 2009 at a function to celebrate Hughes' 60 years at the Bar, Mason recalled that his early impression of Tom 'was by no means favourable'. It was not his fault; Mason's mother held Tom out as 'a desirable role model':

> 'Why can't you be well-mannered, like Tom Hughes?' she would say. So the image I had of him was of a boy who handed around the scones and cakes at Eastern Suburbs' afternoon tea parties attended by Roman Catholic mothers in the early 1930s … Tom was a year, perhaps two years, ahead of me, this being a massive gap at that age in human experience and *savoir faire*. This meant that I did not fraternise with him to any extent. He seemed to be a distant, proper, upright boy and people spoke of him in terms of high praise. Had I then known that in later years he would earn the nickname 'Frosty', it would not have come as a surprise.

Hughes wrote to Mason saying 'I must have been a terrible prick'. Mason assured him he was merely expressing 'a mild resentment' about a comparison that, 'though justified, was unfavourable to me'.[23]

Tom's Edgecliff reports were not outstanding, though Miss Van was sure of his potential. In August 1932 he was placed ninth in a class of 15, and individual subjects were generally marked as 'Very Good'; Grammar and Writing were considered 'much improved' and Arithmetic was 'Better – but sometimes careless'. Conduct was 'Excellent'. Miss Van explained his low position in the class by frequent absences from school (he missed 14 half days because of winter chills), while noting that Tom had shown 'greater interest in his lessons and has improved'. The improvement took him to second in the class by December, with ratings of 'Excellent' or 'Very Good', and earning the comment 'Tom at last gets a fair report'. He slipped to 12th out of 18 in the report for May 1933, having missed 32 half days for the quarter. Miss Van evidently retained high expectations and liked his attitude: Tom had 'made a very good start in the year's work – he is anxious to excel & always does his best'. She saw a marked improvement in all subjects by the following August. 'He is ambitious to excel so is sure to succeed, for while in school gives his whole attention to his work.' The recurring problem was his absence through illness. His reports always improved with the warmer weather and a better attendance record. At the end of 1934, he came second in the class of 15 and, although he had slipped in Arithmetic where 'a little too much imagination [was] introduced', he came top in Latin and in the Dictation, Composition and Poetry sections of English and second in most of the other subjects. The two most consistent features of his Edgecliff reports were references to his keenness to do well and the word 'Excellent' in the Conduct column.[24]

In 1936, Tom went to his father's old school, St Ignatius' College, Riverview, as a boarder. Some country boys decided they did not like the English accent he had inherited from his mother. What they did not know, but soon discovered, was that Tom had taken boxing lessons at Edgecliff; three rounds in the ring sorted them out.[25] Tom also proved capable of matching the non-cerebral types in the fields they thought important. He played rugby at or close to the top in his age group throughout his school years, and in 1940 had three games as a breakaway in the Riverview First Fifteen. His principal successes were in athletics. In 1939 at Riverview, he won the 220, 440, 880 and mile races in the U-16 age group. At the Annual Schoolboys Championship on 7 October, he won the 880 yards in the U-16 age group after leading all the way. He came 'a good second' in the 880 yards in the U-16 age group in the Combined Public Schools meeting on 14 October, and broke an existing record in doing so. He was a member of the U-16 relay team that tied with St Joseph's College in the relay. Tom met stiffer competition in A-Grade in 1940 but still managed to come first in the 880, second in the mile and equal third in the 440.[26]

Tom's debating experience had long-term value. He considered that Greg Jones SJ, then a scholastic and in charge of debating for senior boys, was instrumental in his development as a public speaker.[27] In 1939, his second-last year, Tom was an active participant in the Second Division Debating Society. He narrowly lost in opposing the proposition that 'If we want peace then we must prepare for war'. According to the school magazine, *Our Alma Mater*, he was involved in some heavy 'crossfire' on the floor during a debate on whether, in the 20th century, the sword was mightier than the pen. He led for the defence in a 'mock trial' of one Peter Stevens, who was charged with disloyalty for expressing pacifist views and for deliberately allowing his physical condition to fall below the required standard for the defence of the nation. Tom entered a plea of 'Not Guilty' on the grounds of his client's insanity; he lost the case.

In 1940, Tom saw himself as 'a rather weak member' of the school team that won the Louat Shield for debating contested by the Great Public Schools. He 'tagged along as the middle speaker' between Thomas D'Arcy-Burke and D'Arcy Ryan. Both, he reckoned, were much more fluent. Burke, a brilliant classical scholar, was the outstanding debater at Riverview in 1939-40. Ryan and Hughes had regularly competed in the Second Division. Despite Tom's personal disclaimers, the senior team of three boys lost just one debate in 1940. As the school magazine saw it, the team demonstrated 'ingenuity, humour and wide reading'.

One of the debates – against three Riverview Old Boys – took place at the home of 'Mr and Mrs GF Hughes, Cranbrook Road'. Tom's cousin, Roger, was the adjudicator. He awarded the debate to the schoolboys by four points. In the competition debates, Riverview opposed the motion that 'The Arts have done more for civilisation than the Sciences' (according to *Our Alma Mater*, Tom 'urged the claims of philosophy, printing and engineering'); argued that European colonisation had benefited 'native peoples' (Tom spoke of the introduction of law and order in India); and that Sydney radio was inimical to culture (Tom stressed how radio distorted news stories). Riverview met Sydney Grammar School in the final and, as *Our Alma Mater* pointed out, had 'the unenviable task', given the school's tradition, of arguing that a scientific education was preferable to a literary one. Riverview won the debate, possibly because D'Arcy Ryan's 'intermingling of logic and humour was brilliant'.

Academically, Tom started well and continued to finish near to or at the top in most subjects throughout his Riverview years. A report in May 1936 covered his first term in Grammar A. Tom came third in a class of 36 boys with his best marks in Latin (99), French (96) and History (87). He got 85 for essay writing and 74 in English, but his marks slipped for Mathematics I and II and for Physics and Chemistry combined. Tom's Riverview reports echoed those of Edgecliff. His rating for Conduct read 'Excellent, nothing but praise for Tom', and for Application 'Very good'. He continued to do well in languages (he added Greek to the list in later years) and in English and History. He considered himself 'a keen student, but by no means a brilliant one'. Yet for the Leaving Certificate in 1940, he was awarded second class honours in English, Modern History and Latin, accounting for half the number of seconds awarded to Riverview boys. He scored A Passes in French and Greek and Passes in Mathematics I and II. Depending on how the results are calculated, he probably came second of the 27 Riverview boys who matriculated in 1940. D'Arcy-Burke, inevitably, was well out in front, securing the three Firsts awarded to Riverview and coming top in the State in Greek and third in Latin.[28]

Tom Hughes never doubted the value of his Riverview education:

> I owe a great deal to the Jesuits for the stamp with which they mark people by their educational system. Looking back on my years at Riverview, I can think of it best as a sort of junior university. If you were keen on your work, your scholastic work, and were prepared to work hard they left you to a considerable extent to your own devices to pursue your own scholastic interests.

One of the advantages of such an education was that 'its intellectual habits stick despite loss of belief'. The 'spirit of inquiry, or inquisitiveness, inculcated by Jesuit teachers, inevitably leads to a high loss rate, in terms of intellectual adherence to all the principles of Catholicism'.[29] His own questioning, and what he called 'deep and at times agonising self-communings', led him away from his faith for 25 years. He did not send his own sons to Riverview. Even at school, Tom was not completely at ease. He did not always take the sacraments, was never one for attending a daily Mass, did not regularly go to confession and experienced 'some emotional turmoil, partly in relation to sex'. Tom believes that Father Hehir SJ, the Rector at Riverview, may well have held this seeming uncertainty and irregular devotions against him.[30]

On not becoming School Captain

Geoffrey Hughes invested much of himself in Riverview and the school welcomed the material and emotional commitment. In 1939, he was a Life Member and a Vice-President of the Old Ignatians' Union and Vice-President of the Riverview Parents and Friends Association. The Association organised a special outing at 'Jonah's' and raised 'a substantial sum' for the Pavilion Fund. *Our Alma Mater* commented in the same year that Geoffrey Hughes was frequently at Riverview, where his two elder sons were making their mark in the classroom and on the football field. The magazine further noted how his third son, Robert, aged around 18 months, 'already looks as if you couldn't bluff him!'. The close relationship between the Hughes family and Riverview was disrupted, however, when the Rector selected Tony Liggins over Tom Hughes to be school captain for 1941. The resulting correspondence between Geoffrey Hughes and Father Hehir provides insights into Tom's character and outlook at the age of 17, as well as evidence of his father's influence on the choice of values and principles and of his directing hand in his son's education.

The context of the exchange was relevant in three particular ways. First, both Hughes and Hehir were concerned about the many breaches of school discipline during 1940 and about rebellious mutterings against authority, especially among the sporting types. Secondly, Geoffrey Hughes was back in uniform. Informed that at 45 he was 'too old' to enlist, Hughes had embarked on a round of recruiting speeches at the outbreak of the Second World War. Sir Charles Burnett, the distinguished British officer and Chief of the Air Staff of the RAAF, heard one of them and arranged for the First World War veteran to receive a citizen's commission. Assigned in July 1940 to the Administrative and Special Duties Branch, Flying Officer Geoffrey Hughes MC AFC was appointed to command No 8 Elementary Flying Training School (EFTS) at Narrandera in south-west New South Wales. Following two quick promotions, Squadron Leader Hughes was in command of 500 trainee pilots at the beginning of 1941, and held firm views about the need for discipline and for those in authority to act with authority.

Thirdly, Hughes had originally planned for his eldest son to leave Riverview at the end of 1940. He changed his mind after a conversation with Father Hehir late in 1939 and because of intimations from Father Meagher SJ, the previous Rector, and other members of staff. Believing that Tom would be appointed school captain for 1941, Hughes decided to keep him at Riverview for another year. In preparation, Tom spent part of the summer vacation taking an officers' course to fit him for a leadership role in the school cadet corps.

Against this background, the Rector wrote to Geoffrey Hughes on 12 February 1941, 'in case you may misunderstand or be surprised and hurt by my choice of the Captain of the School on Friday next'. He referred to the conversation in Hughes' office in 1939 where Hehir suggested Tom should have been pushed forward in 1939 so that he might be appointed a prefect in 1940 and captain in 1941. If Hughes recalled the conversation, he might be surprised by the choice of Liggins. Hehir assured him there had been long discussions on the issue. Prayers were said and Masses offered in the interests of making the right choice. With a group of young prefects, and the possibility of several prominent athletes not being 'on the Government side', 'it is important that we should have the best possible leader who will rally the most support to authority'. Everyone agreed that 'if the captaincy is looked at as an honour or reward to be won and deserved by past service to the School Tom was the obvious choice. His past record is far superior to Tonys [sic] … But we, and I especially, cannot regard the office mainly as an honour or reward.' It was primarily a post to be filled, and at 'a particularly important and difficult time'.

> We are convinced that Tony is more likely to rally sympathetic and willing cooperation of all sections and types. Tom, perhaps precisely on account of his clear view of duty and strict and rigid adherence to stern principles, might not gain the support that is necessary.

Tony was preferred over Tom because 'the latter's character is less likely to be understood by the average schoolboy of this superficial age'. The decision was 'purely and simply a practical one, the best solution of the actual problem'. He hoped that Tom's father would understand the reasoning and might 'say a little prayer that I may not prove to have been wrong'.[31]

Geoffrey Hughes replied on 15 February. 'Your letter has certainly surprised me, and it – not your choice – has hurt me very deeply.' He acknowledged there was 'no promise asked or offered' in their 1939 conversation, 'nor have I ever sought to influence your own or any other master's attitude to my boys – I would scorn any position or preferment secured by such a means'. Moreover, Hughes knew Liggins, and liked and admired him. Father and son, he wrote, could take the disappointment 'on the chin' and, if there had been no attempt to explain it, would probably have let it pass without comment. The 'hurt' and 'utter disillusion' lay in finding that the school 'yields so readily to the miserable policy of compromise that has bred the ruin that we face today'. Hughes believed that 'firm undaunted uncompromising leadership and example were the greatest need of Church and State'. It was, therefore, 'just tragic' that a school which ought to be producing such leaders should have the goal of finding one 'to rally the most support for authority' (Hughes liked to return Hehir's words to him).

Pointing out how he was presently commanding young trainee pilots, he asked a pertinent question: 'Does authority need such support from boys or does it command it?' Besides, he thought that a 'clear view of duty and rigid adherence to stern principles' (Hehir's words again) was 'the very ideal of a Jesuit education'. Yet the school was not prepared to stand behind those who upheld what should have been its principles.

Although Tom felt disappointed, he considered Liggins a good choice and was less upset than his father was about Hehir's explanation. His father withdrew him from Riverview and attention switched to Tom undertaking a year at university before enlisting in the air force. Although, ordinarily, he would have followed his father by first completing an Arts degree, 'we decided – my father and I – that the best thing to do was to go straight into law'.[32] Tom, therefore, enrolled at the University of Sydney in 1941 as a law student. He may have been involved in the decision-making, but Geoffrey Hughes was the key figure in determining Tom's educational direction, and his father's assumption was that his eldest son would eventually join the family firm. Tom almost certainly shared that assumption, and happily so.

While attending university in 1941, Tom also worked as an articled clerk in what had become Hughes, Hughes and Garvin. Geoffrey Hughes had taken on a junior partner in 1928 and James Garvin, who was unfit for military service, took over most of the senior partner's work during the Second World War. The firm remained seriously short-staffed and Tom's responsibilities in the office did not leave much time for a university life outside his studies, although he managed to attend some Union debates, and even maintained a connection with the Riverview cadet corps. He has a vivid memory of one part-time lecturer. Dr HV Evatt, the former High Court judge and future Minister for External Affairs, Leader of the Opposition and Chief Justice of New South Wales, had won the seat of Barton for Labor in the 1940 election. While an MP, Evatt taught constitutional law in 1941 and was the judge in a moot where Tom appeared in a case involving the *Colonial Laws Validity Act 1865* (UK). Tom remembers Evatt as not particularly fluent and, judging by the reminiscences of the Faculty Secretary, the part-time lecturer may not have been captivating.[33] Nevertheless, Tom did well in constitutional law. He heard later that he was awarded First Class Honours in Constitution I and II and achieved a mark of 65 (the Pass mark was 50) in Roman Law and 55.5 in Contracts (although the normal Pass mark was 60, the general standard of the year 'was a low one').[34]

At the end of 1941, what mattered to Tom was that he was ready and able to enlist.

3

'It's great flying all day, morning and afternoon'

After joining the RAAF Reserve in December 1941, Tom Hughes, Service No 422523, enlisted in the RAAF at No 2 Recruiting Centre, Woolloomooloo, on 22 May 1942. He was not particularly attracted to the idea of flying; it 'never had a fascination for me'. As a small boy, he flew once or twice with his father. When older, he flew over Sydney with one of his father's friends. The flying boats docked in nearby Rose Bay certainly attracted his attention. Yet Tom was more interested in the sea than the air and once thought of applying for the 13-year-old entry to the Naval College. In 1942, however, it 'seemed natural' to follow his father into the RAAF.[1]

Bradfield Park

Tom's enlistment papers recorded that he was aged 18 years and 5 months, five feet and nine-and-a-half inches tall, had a chest measurement of 34/37, was of fair complexion with brown eyes and brown hair, had moles on his right cheek and an appendix scar. He was 'RC' in religious denomination.[2]

After a medical examination, Tom was confirmed fit for 'full flying duties'. A bus took him from Woolloomooloo to No 2 Initial Training School (ITS), Bradfield Park, Lindfield, on Sydney's Upper North Shore. Bradfield Park was one of five Initial Training Schools established in Australia under the Empire Air Training Scheme, a program implemented during the Second World War to train aircrew from the Commonwealth or Empire for service with Britain's Royal Air Force (RAF).[3] If trainees passed that stage, they might proceed to one of 12 Elementary Flying Training Schools, and then join one of eight Service Flying Training Schools (SFTS). Alternatively, they might be assigned for further training in Canada or Southern Rhodesia. Recruits to the RAAF were also sent to other Schools to train as observers, navigators or gunners, and there was an infrastructure to support and supply all these Schools, including the means to train the trainers.

Bradfield Park had a long history, including a period as a racecourse.[4] At the end of 1938, some 10,000 boys met there for the Australasian Scout Jamboree. The RAAF occupied Bradfield Park in June 1940 and, by the time Tom arrived, the size and scope of the station had expanded to include, among other units, the Women's Auxiliary Australian Air Force and the No 2 Embarkation Depot, where aircrew assembled before moving to further postings.

Tom was one of 491 trainees who arrived at 2 ITS on 22 and 23 May 1942 which, a week later, recorded a complement of 43 officers, 104 ground staff and 1182 trainees.[5] Christened the 'Blue Orchids', on account of the shape of the white flash on their blue caps, the trainees were immediately subjected to hours of drilling and marching under the orders of corporals, many of the them ex-guardsmen, who 'were screaming at us to smarten up'. One Bradfield Park graduate said that meeting an Air Chief Marshal of the RAF did not instil in him the same fear 'as did the Lindfield corporal'.[6] Off the parade ground, successive intakes took subjects such as mathematics, navigation, aerodynamics and Morse code. Tom's academic background saved him from attending the preliminary classes devised to assist those with limited educational qualifications.

Tom settled in well at Bradfield Park. It helped having two longstanding friends join him. John Young, a future Qantas pilot, and Reg Bowman, a future obstetrician, had both attended The King's School, Parramatta. The three boys played golf together as junior members of the Royal Sydney Golf Club and spent holidays at a farm in Sutton Forest in the Southern Highlands.[7] Appointed under-corporal on his arrival – almost certainly singled out because of his family connection – Tom's leadership and disciplinary responsibilities further eased his passage through Bradfield Park. When it was his turn to face the aircrew categorisation board, where the Commanding Officer (CO) of 2 ITS and some instructors interviewed each trainee for about 10 minutes, his academic record, standing as an under-corporal and family background virtually guaranteed his 'mustering' as a pilot.

Apart from the drilling and marching, Bradfield Park was, for Tom, a pleasant existence. There was, however, one of those mind-numbing experiences which lead lower ranks to question the wisdom of those in authority. Aroused from their beds on the night of 31 May, the members of Tom's course were marched to adjacent bushland. Japanese midget submarines had attacked Sydney Harbour. 'It was difficult to understand how this compulsory nocturnal move contributed to our physical safety or served any remotely useful purpose.'[8] More seriously, Tom was in Rose Bay on leave on 8 June when one of the 10 shells fired from a Japanese submarine lobbed into a street a few blocks removed from the family home.

His mother had her own problems. She told her mother-in-law, Ganny Gan, how she missed Geoffrey (now with No 2 Training Group), 'most terribly at times, & feel we are missing the best years of being together with our darling family'. Margaret said 'he is so like his dear father in the way he wants to protect us from all care & anxiety. Not only has he got the ultimate responsibility but he has a really big job to do … & the added worry of his adored son going in to all the hurly burly & danger of the war'. Her youngest son, Robert, was 'badly in need of play fellows so I shall find a kindergarten for him'. Her other major concern was money, and she wondered about getting by. There was one very bright message for her mother-in-law: 'You will get such a thrill when you see [Tom] in uniform.'[9]

Tom heard in February 1943 that he came equal top with a new friend, Jock Wilson, in the ITS examinations. He told his parents by letter that they both scored 86.2 per cent; 'I never hoped to come first so its [sic] quite a surprise to me.' When he received this news, Tom was in the midst of pilot training at 8 SFTS, Bundaberg.

No 8 EFTS

As the CO of 8 EFTS, Narrandera, Geoffrey Hughes sought to apply the values he had been espousing throughout the inter-war years. He referred to them in a lecture he gave just before the graduation of the first course in December 1940. He hammered the point that lauding 'star turns' by supposed 'air aces' was anathema in the Service: 'the job must come before the individual', and teamwork at all levels in the air and on the ground 'is the very essence of efficiency and success'.[10] From November 1941, Geoffrey Hughes was second-in-command of No 2 Training Group but was ill with a chest infection for much of 1942. On medical grounds, acting Group Captain Hughes relinquished his commission in April 1943. Until then, he was clearly headed for 'senior executive duties'. A senior officer singled him out in a confidential report for his zeal and energy in performing his responsibilities, for his personality, force of character and leadership, and for his reliability, judgment, common sense and initiative.[11]

Geoffrey Hughes left the Service with an impressive reputation. He also left behind a number of contemporaries of similar and higher rank, and others he had trained or supervised, who were in positions to influence his son's progress in the RAAF. There were times when he could and did intervene on Tom's behalf; there were other occasions where his contacts acted without prompting. The downside of all this support was that Tom had to live with expectations he could not meet because he did not inherit his father's flying skills.

Early in September 1942, the newly-promoted Leading Aircraftman Tom Hughes and 18 other trainee pilots from 2 ITS arrived at 8 EFTS. Tom's move to Narrandera marked a new phase in his life. At Bradfield Park he could spend short leave breaks in Rose Bay. Narrandera meant a physical separation from the family, a separation that, apart from longer leave periods in 1942-43 and his mother's visits to Narrandera, lasted until December 1945. While training in Australia, he made occasional contacts by telephone, but principally kept in touch through regular letter writing, rarely going more than a week without writing to 'Mummy and Daddy', or separately to each of them when his father was in hospital. He also wrote to his two elder siblings, and to Aunt Mim and Ganny Gan, often sending two or three letters to Sydney a week. Thankfully, Tom's parents kept his mail – he did not keep theirs – and these letters provide a narrative of his life in the RAAF and an insight into the values, aspirations and anxieties of a young man preparing for, and living through, a war.[12]

JD Balfe, one of the instructors at Narrandera, who had served there under Geoffrey Hughes, described some of what Tom encountered.[13] 'Sunny skies and wide, rolling fields stretched out from the Riverina's flowing waterways around Narrandera making it safe flying country for trainer aircraft and aspiring young pilots and thus easy for their instructors.' Should an engine fail, a paddock was usually available for a forced landing. Flying accidents were rare, and caused mainly by delinquent flying or hot thermal currents. To avoid the latter, the beginners flew in the calmer mornings. During the war, some 4000 pilots were produced at Narrandera under these conditions, leading Balfe to claim that 8 EFTS 'characterised the bold concept of the Empire Air Training Scheme'. It was a thoroughly-organised operation which followed the program set by the Central Flying School's *Principles of Flying Instruction*. Each 12-week group of 120 pupils was divided into four 'Flights' and each Flight had 20 Tiger Moths and 20 instructors. Two courses ran at the same time: the junior one learnt the basics to the point of flying solo while the senior course undertook more sophisticated flying which included instrument procedure, aerobatics and cross-country flight. A Narrandera graduate, having logged 50 hours, half of which involved flying solo, was thought to have reached roughly the same standard as a civilian pilot who was applying for a commercial licence.

Arriving at Narrandera on Friday 11 September, Tom was disappointed to discover his assignment to 'A' Flight, consisting almost entirely of Queenslanders. Next day Wing Commander Ken Ranger,[14] the CO of 8 EFTS, called Tom to his office. He had already arranged for him to join the other Bradfield 'chaps' in 'D' Flight. They chatted for about 20 minutes, with Ranger seeking impressions of Bradfield Park and telling him that Flying Officer Clegg would be the instructor for the three friends. Tom left the meeting thinking Ranger was 'awfully decent'. Five days later Ranger wrote to Tom's father. After expressing regret about Geoffrey Hughes' 'bad luck' with illness, Ranger reported seeing Tom on the previous Saturday: 'He is looking exceptionally fit and is naturally very keen to start flying.' He told the Group Captain how he had placed Tom with Bowman and Young in 'D' Flight. Lindsay Rowell would be his Flight Commander and George Clegg his instructor. He expected Hughes to remember Clegg – 'tall', 'slight' and 'intelligent' – adding that Squadron Leader Plumridge, the Chief Flying Instructor at 8 EFTS, thought Clegg was the best instructor on the base:

> You can rest assured we will keep an eye on Tom, but he is a very fine lad and I feel confident it will not be necessary. Both Plum and I take it as a great compliment that you sent him here, and we will certainly be flat out to justify your choice of units.[15]

Ranger evidently knew that, whether or not Geoffrey Hughes had the authority to send his son to any post, his influence was considerable.

Tom found the early days very boring. Waiting impatiently for the opportunity to fly, he spent much of his time on general tarmac duties: washing the 'kites' or 'crates', starting engines, wheeling aircraft in and out of hangars, and guarding the installations. Some hours a day were devoted to aircraft recognition and signals, and one hour to physical training. Tom used his first day's leave to visit Narrandera. Expecting to find 'a pretty dead town', he 'never imagined it so deadly as it was today'. To be fair, it was a Sunday. His mood improved on later visits when he attended dances. One of these was 'quite a decent show' except that a woman – known to Tom's mother – 'bored every trainee in the room in quick succession' with stories about her 'own dear baby' who was attached to a brigade headquarters in the AIF.

He was soon learning to fly. Flying Officer Clegg, 'a cracker chap' who 'explains things awfully well and has a most reassuring manner', took him in the air on Monday 21 September. It was a 'simply wonderful' day. But he was having difficulties with his 'circuits and bumps', the training regime whereby pilots repeated a procedure of taking off, circling in a defined pattern, landing and then taking off without stopping. As Tom explained to his father, his wheels kept beating the tail to the ground. Increasingly frustrated, he told his mother on 1 October about having 'a very bad off day … I could not get anything right – I was landing the crate 6 feet up in the air with horrifying consistency. If only I could put her down alright [sic] I am ready for solo, but I must admit that I am finding it a bit difficult.' His two friends from Bradfield had now flown solo 'so that I am the only mug now. However it is no use letting myself worry about it as that will only make matters worse. I will get it taped somehow even though slower than the others.'

He was not very far behind. On 5 October, he sent a telegram to his father announcing he had just experienced his first solo flight. Next day he could put everything into perspective: of the 27 trainees in 'D' Flight, 19 were flying solo while a mere six or seven trainees in each of the other Flights had reached that stage. By 18 October, he had recorded 25 hours and 25 minutes of flying time, of which 8 hours and 50 minutes were solo. While he continued to face problems with the high winds later in the day, everyone else had trouble with them.

Tom was also doing well on other fronts. Appointed under-corporal for 'D' Flight, he joined the under-corporals from the other Flights at the end of September to meet Squadron Leader 'Bert' Beaumont, the RAAF's Chief Flying Instructor. Tom thought him 'a very fine chap', 'extremely decent', keen to hear suggestions and wanting to get things done. Tom reported how some non-commissioned officers of the guard grabbed trainees for long hours of night duty when they were due to fly the following morning. Beaumont assured him he would do a 'blitz' on this matter. The under-corporals were also singled out to meet the Governor-General, Lord Gowrie VC, who inspected the base on 1 October. Gowrie spoke to each of them in turn. Tom told his family how, when the CO mentioned that Tom's father had started the training unit, the Governor-General concluded by 'wishing me good luck'. Eleven days later, the CO called on the four under-corporals to give him a confidential report on the trainees in their flights who had been 'scrubbed'; that is, removed after failing as pilots. Ranger wanted guidance in determining their re-mustering. Tom applauded the approach because the under-corporals had a better idea of what the 'coves' were like as people.

Some days on the base were especially good. It was a pleasure to welcome Tony Liggins, Father Hehir's preference for school captain in 1941, who arrived at Narrandera from Bradfield Park with a new course in mid-October. Later in the month, Tom ran the 880 yards segment for the 'D' Flight relay team, which won the medley relay race at the RAAF's athletic carnival.[16] Tom had some good leave breaks in town, parcels from home were plentiful and the food especially welcome. Visits from his mother were always a delight. Yet the winds were often 'as cold as charity' and Tom had a mixed day taking a cross-country flight to the RAAF station at Wagga. Surrounded by Spitfires and Wirraways when making his circuit, he 'must have been suffering from an unconscious inferiority complex as the landing was not a very graceful one'. On the ground, he inspected the cockpits of a Spitfire and a Hudson and climbed into a Beaufighter – 'all intensely interesting'. Later, he did a solo test at night with Flight Lieutenant Rowell, 'a cracker chap … very encouraging & helpful & not at all harassing'.

Tom remained concerned about his father's continuing illness. His letters on this subject, his fears about his mother's workload (which included contact with Ganny Gan), and his interest in the progress of his siblings, reflected a continuing and deep attachment to family. The extended Hughes family took another blow when Tom's cousin, Pilot Officer Hughes, died after his reconnaissance plane crashed in northern Australia on 3 October 1942. Aware of the family history, Ken Ranger contacted Tom to break the news. Writing immediately to his father, Tom called his cousin's death 'very tragic', adding that it was 'very very hard for Aunt Eileen to have this tragedy after losing Uncle Roger in the last war. It makes you realise vividly how horribly cruel war is.' This branch of the Hughes family continued to endure more than its share of grief and misfortune. Eileen, who never remarried, was killed in an accident in Darwin when she went to visit her son's grave after the War.

Tom's record as a pilot was a persistent source of concern. Early in his training Plumridge noted in Tom's log book that he needed to 'develop smoothness'.[17] Geoffrey Hughes was aware that 'things were not going as well as they might have'. He contacted a friend, Thomas McKay of the General Duties Branch of the RAAF.[18] Telling him that Tom 'was on the borderline', he would greatly appreciate any assistance McKay could offer. McKay had 'no hesitation' in ringing Plumridge and 'asking him to use his best endeavours to ensure that the son of [Plumridge's] former CO attained the requisite standard'.

On 1 November, McKay reported the assessments of 'young Tom'. Ranger had talked to Clegg and Rowell. They both considered Tom's flying was 'a little below the average', though they also felt 'he is carrying a heavy burden, living up to his father's reputation and also being responsible for the discipline of his course'. The next test should show 'a marked improvement'. Tom's ground subjects were 'excellent' and so was 'his bearing and conduct'. McKay thought Tom should go to Bundaberg to train on the 'friendly Anson'[19] and, depending on his assessment there, go to the Central Flying School for an instructor's course direct or via another school, to build up his hours and 'put polish on his flying'. Ranger agreed with McKay, who felt sure Tom would not oppose the idea. McKay concluded: 'Unless I hear to the contrary from you I shall make the above arrangements.' In the meantime, he planned to find out where Tom's course would be going after finishing at Narrandera so that Ranger could ensure he completed his training in Australia.

Four days later, McKay wrote again to the father about 'your young man'. Bert Beaumont, the RAAF's Chief Flying Instructor, having returned to Narrandera and flown with Tom, had found 'his coordination was none too good but that his circuits and general flying were sound'. The trainee pilot had now flown 55 hours, and Beaumont gave instructions for him to be given as much flying as possible, and to undertake exercises such as rolling from turn to turn to improve his coordination. Beaumont agreed with McKay: Tom should go to Bundaberg rather than Point Cook in Victoria, the more composite and advanced training base. Beaumont would arrange for him to have a good instructor who would be told which faults to eliminate. Beaumont intended to re-visit the unit and fly with Tom again, and he imagined 'that Hendy will not dare to be difficult'.[20] McKay did not stop there. Tom was assigned to Bundaberg and, although McKay did not recall 'Geoffrey again asking for any direct assistance', he contacted the CO at 8 SFTS 'requesting him to see that Tom would get top instruction'.[21]

Bundaberg

No 8 SFTS at Bundaberg provided intermediate and advanced instruction for pilots as part of the Empire Air Training Scheme. Each course ran for about 16 weeks and involved intensive training in day and night flying, formation flying, dive-bombing and aerial gunnery.

Tom Hughes and John Young arrived together at Bundaberg on 23 November 1942 to join 28 Course. During a brief train stop in Brisbane on the way to Bundaberg, Tom observed that the city was 'jam full of Americans'.[22] This observation was the first of many comments he made over the next three years about a pervasive presence he did not always find agreeable. For no immediately apparent reason, Hughes and Young were listed separately from the other 17 arrivals from Narrandera.[23] Whereas at Narrandera Tom found that six of the staff had been there when his father was the CO, he was now in relatively new territory. Even so, on the day after his arrival, McKay talked to him at the base and the Chief Gunnery Instructor asked Tom to pass on regards to his father.

One of his first acts at Bundaberg was to send a telegram to his mother; he had left his pay book at home. Tom reported to his father how everyone was 'very disappointed' that 28 Course would probably have to wait more than six weeks before flying, filling in time with guard duty, range practice and lectures. For the following weeks his news home consisted mainly of reports about the weather, games of golf and tennis, guard duty, going to the pictures, swimming, visiting a sugar mill, an occasional drink in a pub in the town – and about his boredom. At least the station itself, and the food, were all good. On 29 November Tom reported that 'your aircrew guard is alive and well, but fed up with being an aircrew guard'.

When Tom did get to fly, his letters were enthusiastic about it. Not that he could say very much. The censor's signature began appearing on his mail home. He once evaded official notice by handing a letter to a friend for posting in Sydney: 'I shall be able to give you a bit of news in it.' He told the family that his instructor, Flying Officer Vaughan, 'is one of the very best'. Tom had now logged about 20 hours and the 'old crates are great to fly' although 'very bewildering and complicated at first'. He was finding them much easier to land than the Tiger Moths. He expected to be doing some cross-country flying and was looking forward to night flying. At the same time, Tom was enjoying his ground courses and especially navigation, for which he had a 'cracker' instructor who 'really knows how to teach'.

On one occasion what he could report would have been disturbing were it not comical. He told his parents in mid-January of 'a priceless bit of information' he had heard from someone who had just arrived from Narrandera. The story had been circulating there that Tom had been 'scrubbed' even before he started flying in Bundaberg. It was firmly believed, 'and the blokes who arrived from Narrandera were surprised to find me alive & kicking so to speak'. The rumour went even further. It was also believed that 'you [his father] had been making all sorts of enquir[i]es as to the reason I had been scrubbed'. Perhaps resentment provided the spur for the rumour. Other trainees and some instructors may have disliked what they saw as the workings of privileged connections, and believed what they wanted to hear. One particular instructor might have had a grievance. The committee of Geoffrey Hughes' Aero Club had grounded him for doing slow rolls over the Pymble golf course. Yet that instructor had given Tom a high 8/10 for a particular exercise.

Tom had obviously benefited from family connections when appointed an under-corporal at Bradfield Park and at Narrandera, although his performance at the former made him an obvious choice at the latter. It made sense, given his proven ability as a leader, to appoint him an under-sergeant at Bundaberg where he exercised similar duties. He may not have inherited his father's flying skills, and he may have lowered his colours to better pilots at Narrandera and Bundaberg, but no one could doubt his single-minded determination to succeed, or his willingness to take and exercise responsibility.

Tom's letters from Bundaberg were full of comments about wanting to do well, and there was no hiding the frustration when he did not. Early in January 1943 he said it was 'rather maddening' to learn how, while coming third in navigation in his written tests, he came just short by three marks of the top marks in the other subjects and lost six marks by not finishing a part of the paper. Happily, he got 96 per cent in Signals. Next month he reported having passed his wings test with a result of 'Average'. He knew he had not performed brilliantly and was worried until he received even that score. Tom also earned an 'Average' for the instrument flying test. After the exams he returned to flying: 'I flew badly, in fact worse than I have ever flown.' The recent break from flying had left him 'rusty'. Nevertheless, 'I'm not unduly worried about it – just very annoyed with myself'.

At other times he felt reasonably pleased with his efforts. Although he found it easier being a leader in formation flying, his instructor told him that his station-keeping was good. So, too, were his bombing results. In mid-March, he reported that his low-level bombing from 350 feet was satisfactory with an average error rate of 33 yards (50 were permissible), and it was all 'good fun'. His high-level bombing record was initially not so good. 'I'm very annoyed with myself about it. However, it's no use worrying now.' By late March, he could say that his average error rate for high-level bombing was 130 yards when an average of 210 yards was acceptable. Tom now knew he did not want to be an air gunner; sitting in a turret 'makes me quite squeamish'. Critically, he loved being in the air. On 19 March, he wrote: 'It's great flying all day, morning and afternoon.' The pilot also had the eye of a tourist. Cross-country flying at 10,000 feet enabled him to see much of Queensland, including a very good view of the Barrier Reef.

Family was always on his mind. He kept referring to his father's 'rotten luck' with a continuing illness, and felt for 'Nong' (Constance) sitting her exams early in December. Learning of his younger brother's escapades, he described 'Bob' as 'a young wag', and Tom could sense the 'relief' for both his parents when Ganny Gan was installed in the women-only Queen's Club in Elizabeth Street, Sydney. He received many letters and presents from home, as well as a cake, to mark the first Christmas he spent apart from the family. Christmas lunch at the station was 'a very good show' with the officers and sergeants waiting on them. Religious observance continued to matter. At the end of November, Tom told of serving at Mass at the station, the first time he had done so since leaving school, and in mid-January said he much appreciated both his parents saying a decade of the Rosary for him every night. Others thought about him too. On 7 December, Father Meagher replied to a letter where Geoffrey Hughes extolled his son's character and achievements: 'I am of course not one bit surprised at what you tell me of Tom, but I should have been greatly surprised if you had written anything else. There are very few boys like Tom – but I suppose he is a young man by this!'

For all his doubts and fears, Tom graduated with distinction from 8 SFTS. Along with 33 members of his course, he was awarded his Flying Badge on 5 April 1943. He was one of seven granted a commission as Pilot Officer, and he came fifth of the 34 graduates in the Order of Merit.[24] As for future assignments, he had expressed a first preference for flying boats and a second for heavy bombers. He knew his reactions were not quick enough to be a fighter pilot.[25] The immediate ambition was to join a Navigation and Reconnaissance Course, though he would be content, if not overjoyed, 'to be a Staff Pilot for a while and get valuable experience & more hours thus be as experienced and efficient as possible when I go on to ops'.

Posted abroad

Tom left Bundaberg on 7 April 1943 and spent two weeks with the family in Sydney, the first time they had been together for nearly five months. He was then posted to an RAAF station at Cressy in south-western Victoria to undertake a Navigation and Reconnaissance Course. In the meantime, he went to 1 Air Observers School, Cootamundra, to fly navigators mainly around northern Victoria and south-western New South Wales. Given that Jock Wilson and others from Bundaberg were posted to an earlier course at Cressy, it is probable that someone in authority thought he needed more flying hours. 'P/O WE HUGHES (422523) [sic]' reported to Cootamundra on 21 April and, after some initial test flights, he clocked 291 hours performing 'flying duties'. There were two more changes of course plan before Tom was posted to 2 Embarkation Depot at Bradfield Park.[26]

Squadron Leader McKay tried to keep him in Australia but explained to his father that he had been unable to obtain any satisfaction from the 'tight-lipped Postings people concerning your Tom'. He presented the case that Tom should remain in Australia, take the navigation course and then train on flying boats. Yet McKay had encountered a problem: 'The suggestion that he remain here created the impression that I was lobbying to cancel an overseas posting. As I feel I am now persona non grata, I have done nothing further for fear of prejudicing him in the eyes of the powers that be.'[27] McKay wrote this letter on 23 August, two days after the Curtin Labor Government won a landslide victory in the federal election. McKay was apparently unaware that Tom, after spending eight weeks at 2 Embarkation Depot, had sailed from Sydney on 12 August.

Pilot Officer Hughes had joined a 'draft' consisting of eight young officers and 150 other ranks of air crew on board an American troop ship. The United States Navy had acquired the luxury passenger liner SS *Washington*, re-named it USS *Mount Vernon*, and used the liner to ferry service personnel between San Francisco and a number of Pacific ports. Tom thought it a 'very nice ship'. His first dinner on board was 'an eye-opener – food being A1'. The voyage across the Pacific was in many ways a pleasant one. Despite the pitching and rolling in the first few days, Tom did not succumb to sea sickness. He had an upper bunk in a comfortable cabin with four others, spent much of his time reading, sleeping, walking the decks and playing deck quoits and volley ball and, importantly, 'one couldn't wish for better food'. Tom also met Raymond 'Bish' Russell, a Presbyterian minister and RAAF chaplain, who proved to be a stalwart friend both on board ship and in the United Kingdom.[28]

There was just one problem: Alexander MacKenzie Tyers, the CO of the draft. Born at Linton, Victoria, in 1895 and apprenticed as a civil engineer and surveyor, Tyers enlisted in the AIF in 1916, was appointed Second Lieutenant in the Australian Flying Corps and served in various administrative posts in the United Kingdom. Suffering minor epilepsy, he sailed home in January 1918 and his appointment was terminated in the following May. In the 1920s, he served with various Army Reserve units and later transferred to the Unattached List of Reserve Officers. Appointed Captain in a Reserve battalion in 1940, Tyers became a father in 1942, the same year as his promotion to Major. In August 1943, aged 48, Tyers was seconded to head the draft on its journey to the United Kingdom.[29]

The junior officers quickly concluded that he was not capable of managing a large body of young men. Within five days of boarding the *Mount Vernon*, they elected one of their number, the 19-year-old Tom Hughes, to be adjutant. Tom was, at first, pleased because 'I badly needed something in the way of a job to occupy me'. But the duties soon became 'moderately onerous' because the CO 'wasn't up to it'.

The *Mount Vernon* docked at San Francisco on the morning of 26 August 1943. A mist and low cloud spoilt the view. In any case, there was really no time to look around. The draft had to be quickly ferried to the north side of the bay to board an old train, previously retired for 14 years, for the journey across the United States. Tom had to organise much of the disembarkation and make arrangements with the train commander. Tyers was behaving 'like a very wet hen' and was almost totally ineffectual.

The journey to the East Coast took five nights and four days and left Tom 'feeling dustier and dirtier' than he had ever felt before: 'I've definitely had trains.' The heat did not help, and Tom became thoroughly exasperated with the CO, by now nicknamed 'Submarine Joe' (his head was always under water).[30] At one point, Tom pronounced himself sorry for 'the old joker because he was quite devoid of decision and drive'. More often, he felt angry about Tyers' stupidity and inefficiency, and wondered about the sense of those who selected 'Joe' for the job. Matters came to a head at station stops where there was always the possibility of leaving someone stranded, as 150 young men escaped confinement and wandered about regardless of the time. In Salt Lake City the train returned to the station to collect 10 men, including Bish Russell, who were left behind. 'Submarine Joe just about gave birth to twin foals.' Tom thought the mistake lay in trying to herd them 'like so much cattle'. The more sensible step, as he saw it, was to place the men on their honour to return to the station by a certain time. Self-imposed rather than imposed discipline seemed the better option.

There were ups as well as downs along the way. Tom liked what he saw of Salt Lake City, and the mountains and streams reminded him of the Snowy and trout fishing. He marvelled at the majestic Royal Gorge in Colorado, though he found Pueblo, Colorado, to be 'a most unattractive place', an impression not helped when the CO ordered a route march in hot weather with everyone wearing 'blues'. A black porter at the station in Dodge City amused them when he asked one of the sergeants what languages Australians spoke other than English. Tom saw nothing of Chicago because the train arrived after dark and pulled into the freight yards. If that was disappointing, the adjutant's mood was improving because 'the chaps' were behaving well and getting back to the train after the 30-minute station stops. Although Tom did not get a glimpse of Niagara Falls, he did see the rapids below them – 'a beautiful sight' – and liked the countryside of New York State as the train proceeded to its destination: an Army base 'somewhere in New England'.

Camp Myles Standish was located at Taunton, just south of Boston, Massachusetts. It served mainly as an embarkation depot for American and allied forces heading for the European theatre. On 1 September, one day after arriving at the base, the entire draft was quarantined because of a case of scarlet fever, forcing a ten-day postponement of leave in Boston or New York. Tom faced further tests in this 'rather grim' period because leadership issues 'very nearly came to a head on several occasions'. One bright moment reminded him of his good contacts in the RAAF. Air Marshal 'Dicky' Williams, the RAAF's representative to the Combined Chiefs of Staff in the United States, met Tom on a visit to the base, and passed on his good wishes to Geoffrey Hughes.

Tom eventually escaped to Boston with a four-day pass. The Anzac Club in the city had arranged a billet for Bish and himself with a warm-hearted family in the nearby affluent village of Chestnut Hill. Tom had 'a wonderful time'. He admired the Georgian architecture of the older parts of Boston, walked around Harvard University and its Widener Library and visited the Episcopalian church in Cambridge where George Washington and his family had worshipped. He saw a play and a Bing Crosby movie, went to a dance and a picnic and swam in the sea. Tom told his parents he liked America much better than he expected. He was 'left in a state of amazement and admiration', not least for discovering he could put a nickel in a machine and collect a bottle of Coca Cola. Americans were so hospitable and treated them 'like visiting royalty'. When Tom, Bish and Jock Wilson tried to pay for their meal at a restaurant in Taunton, a former mayor insisted on paying their bill. Above all, as Tom told his parents, it meant a lot to spend time in a home with a family, even though it was not his own. Americans, he concluded, were 'just tops', a view he later qualified after meeting or observing so many of them in London and Oxford.

As adjutant, Tom could pull strings and take a second leave: 'this rather lousy job has had its reward.' Due to go to New York on a Saturday morning, 'Submarine Joe' woke him at 0620 yelling, 'Tom, Tom, the system's buggered – the 45 KPs (the orderlies responsible for preparing and serving food) … aren't on the job.' Barely awake, Tom suggested that the Orderly Officer might be the one to arouse them. The CO went 'wild', returned to his room, sat on his bed, clasping his hands and telling Bish Russell that 'my bloody Adjutant's gone out of his mind – fancy – telling me to get the Orderly Officer'. Tyers then dashed from his room shouting that he would 'wake up every bloody officer'. Tom noted in his diary: 'Such is life and Joe.'

Tom and Bish went to New York together, where they ended up staying at the Columbia University Club. Tom packed a lot into two-and-a-half days. He ventured into four 'posh' pubs; attended Sunday Mass at St Patrick's Cathedral; visited the Metropolitan Museum, the Public Library, Radio City and the Empire State Building; shopped on Fifth Avenue where he bought shirts, underpants and nine squash balls; listened to Vincent Lopez's band while lunching at the Hotel Taft; and saw two plays on Broadway. Tom also linked up with Martha Eubank, a Texan girl he had met in Boston. They toured the famed night clubs – the Copacabana, the Stork Club and El Morocco – and ended up at a superior hamburger shop before Tom got to bed at 4.30 am. 'Nowhere else in the world', he told his parents, 'could be more cosmopolitan'. His appreciation was not absolute: 'there are far too many fat unattractive looking old Jews to be seen in the night clubs.' He noted that the taxi drivers were either 'wops or Huns with a Brooklyn accent'. Tom also observed, approvingly, that there was less public drunkenness than in Sydney, though bars were open well after midnight. He loved New York and wanted to go back.

Returning to Camp Myles Standish, Tom found that the CO had suffered a nervous breakdown. The other officers selected Tom to be Acting CO, an improvement on being an adjutant while offering 'great experience'. He took charge of the draft when it left New York on 9 October 1943 for the United Kingdom on board the *Queen Mary*. Tyers remained behind. It was no luxury cruise. There were some 16,000 on board and Tom joined 15 others in a cabin meant for two passengers. Fortunately, there were no dramas on the seven-day Atlantic crossing. Apparently, the fast-sailing *Queen Mary* did not need an escort though, as Tom observed, the other ranks had no chance should a torpedo strike the ship near their accommodation in the bowels.

When the *Queen Mary* docked in Greenock, Scotland, on 16 October, the acting CO of nearly 160 air crew from Australia, himself not yet 20 years of age, could reasonably claim to have justified his assisted passage through the system. Geoffrey Hughes' 'young man' had demonstrated a real capacity for leadership.

4

'A relatively lucky and safe war'

Disembarking from the *Queen Mary*, the draft immediately boarded a troop train for Brighton on the south coast of England. At Brighton they marched, carrying their baggage, for three-quarters of a mile in pouring rain to their station, 11 PDRC (Personnel Dispatch and Reception Centre), where they were to await a posting to an operational unit. Tom described Brighton as 'the most depressing station' of his experience, and doubted 'if it would be possible to find one more terrible'. He had little to do except fill in forms, collect equipment, and march up and down the parade ground on the orders of warrant officers. Officers, he found, 'were not treated as such'. There were compensations: he was billeted in a good hotel, 'we are fed very well', and the CO at Brighton knew Tom's father.

As officer commanding the draft, he had to deliver a report to the RAAF's Overseas Headquarters at Kodak House, London. He used the occasion to lunch at the Boomerang Club, located in the basement of Australia House and staffed by volunteers, which would serve Tom well in finding overnight accommodation in central London. After lunch, he took in the sights of a city he described as 'a wonderful place'. He visited St Paul's Cathedral, Westminster Abbey, and the Catholic Westminster Cathedral, pronouncing the latter to Constance as very ugly from the outside. Tom also went to the Law Courts, where the Lord Chief Justice, Viscount Caldecote, and Justices Hallam and Charles were hearing a case, and then walked along the Embankment before taking a taxi ride around Buckingham Palace.

Returning to Brighton, Tom had an interview on 21 October that proved to be a pivotal moment in his war. Squadron Leader Egbert 'Bert' Campbell Smith DFC, a car salesman from Horsham, Victoria, had enlisted in the RAAF in August 1940. After initial training at Bradfield Park, he joined the first course held at 8 EFTS, Narrandera, under Geoffrey Hughes' command. In April 1942, Smith joined the newly-formed 461 Squadron RAAF based at Pembroke Dock in Wales and flew and captained Sunderland flying boats.

After receiving his DFC in July 1943 – he had attacked a number of U-boats and sunk one of them – Smith completed his tour of operational duty and, in his new role with 11 PDRC, was seeking recruits for service on flying boats. Tom found him to be 'an awfully decent bloke and he yarned with me in his office for about half an hour'. Although Tom expected to be assigned to heavy bombers, Smith raised the possibility of his joining the flying boat 10 Squadron RAAF based at Mount Batten, Plymouth, on the English south-west coast.

In the meantime, Pilot Officer Hughes did some more travelling. On 24 October he returned to London for a half-day to meet a cousin, Gerald Biden, the son of his maternal grandmother's sister, 'Aunt May'. The pair cruised around the city on the top deck of a bus. Two days later, Tom used a week's leave to visit Aunt May, who lived in a cottage in Barnsley near the Rectory where the Vidal family had resided for nearly 30 years. Tom told his mother he had never met an old lady like her: 'so active and alert.' He had lunch with Mrs Wykeham-Musgrave at the Dower House, the widow of his maternal grandfather's friend from Oxford who had maintained the Reverend Vidal's living at Barnsley. Tom visited the rectory – 'a wonderful place' – and understood why the Vidals loved it. He met the current rector and his wife and many Barnsley residents who asked to be remembered to his mother. From Barnsley, Tom caught a train to Bude, a seaside town in northern Cornwall, to meet up again with Gerald. The two men then drove to Exeter where, as he so often did in England, Tom made a point of visiting its cathedral before returning to Brighton, 'the place of doom'.

The tourist admitted he was on 'rather a good wicket'. Late in November, he was appointed liaison officer at an RAF base at Whitley Bay on the mouth of the River Tyne near Newcastle. His duties included giving lectures to air crew trainees who were awaiting assignment. Confessing to his sister he was having an 'almost unbroken holiday', Tom was 'itching for some real work – as are countless others in the same position as myself'. He could tell his parents that England, despite its foul weather and the short days in winter, was a most pleasant place. It was also preferable being inactive in Whitley Bay than inactive in Brighton, and he liked sitting in the Mess by a fire and reading a book, attending a dance and seeing a few films. He conveyed a sense of guilt to Aunt Mim about the 'enormous' meat allowance in the Mess when rationing was affecting the civilian population. His immediate worries were feeling 'a bit homesick' in the absence of family news, and hearing nothing about his expected promotion to Flying Officer. When the promotion did come through, he was entitled to back pay of £9, and could now allot an extra 3/- a day to savings to help pay his university fees on returning to Australia.

One advantage of Whitley Bay was that officers were not subject to a roll call. Tom could catch a train to London, take in the passing view of the spectacular, Norman-built Durham Cathedral, spend the day at the law courts and visit the Boomerang Club, where he often met former fellow trainees. His experience of the Mess at Whitley Bay persuaded him he 'could get along just as well' in either an RAF or RAAF squadron. On the other hand, while he liked Whitley Bay and its immediate surrounds, Tom thought Newcastle 'a very drab place and the mean houses are very depressing to the eye and disturbing to the mind. This country will have to get cracking in double quick time to eliminate the slums and the unnecessary ugliness of its industrial towns as soon as this war is over.'

It surprised him to discover how many people feared that Australia 'has tendencies towards breaking away from the Empire'. It was sometimes difficult to convince them that 'we don't really want to cast ourselves adrift'. British servicemen intrigued him. Lecturing on subjects about which he knew little, Tom let one session develop into 'a general natter'. Several questions from the floor tested his knowledge of Australia and he found that many 'RAF chaps' wanted to know about their prospects should they emigrate. In another session, he led a discussion group with RAF aircrew sergeants who impressed him as being 'ardently pink'. Tom decided that a great many in the services favoured socialism in one form or another. More encounters of this kind convinced him that the United Kingdom would turn to Labour after the War.

In mid-December, Tom learnt the 'excellent news' that he was posted to flying boats. On security grounds, Tom could not be specific, yet told his parents more than enough. He would be flying the aircraft he wanted to fly, 'so nothing could be much better than that'. He would start out as the '2nd dickie' (second pilot), and his station was close to Bude so he could easily visit cousin Gerald on weekends. Arriving at his new post before Christmas, he offered a further hint: 'I cannot tell you what Squadron I'm in but the fact that it is a rather famous Australian one will convey something to you. It's just great to have the good luck to get the aircraft I've always wanted to fly.' He assured the family that 'there will be no cause for anxiety at any time'.[1]

Mount Batten

Flying Officer Hughes had been assigned to 10 Squadron RAAF.[2] Formed at Point Cook, Victoria, on 1 July 1939, the Squadron, with its motto 'Strike First', was originally equipped with assorted seaplanes. A small number of RAAF personnel went to Britain to train on the new Short Sunderland aircraft and to ferry six of them back to Australia. Following the outbreak of war in September 1939, however, the Australian Government decided that the Squadron should remain in the United Kingdom. In January 1940, the Squadron became part of No 15 Group (and, later, of No 19 Group), RAF Coastal Command, while retaining its separate Australian identity under Australian officers. The Squadron, first stationed at Pembroke Dock in Wales, moved to Mount Batten in mid-1941. It relocated to Pembroke Dock after Plymouth and Mount Batten were badly hit by German bombers late in 1941 and early in 1942. The Squadron returned to a refurbished Mount Batten in January 1943, by which time the intensity of German raids had eased considerably, the last of the major ones occurring in June and August 1943.

Allowing for the various modifications, the Sunderland flying boats weighed about 22 tons. Powered by four engines, they had a cruising speed of 110 knots at around 6000 feet, and could stay in the air for 12-13 hours. The Sunderlands have been described as 'board and lodging' for the 11-man crew as they included a rest room for those off duty, a wardroom, a workshop and, on the lower deck, a galley with a small stove and two crew compartments each containing two bunks.[3] Their armament consisted of six depth charges as well as twin Vickers .303 machine guns in the nose, four Vickers .303 machine guns in the tail and twin Browning machine guns in the mid-ship gun stations (hence the nickname of 'flying porcupine'). These machine guns were critical in defending the Sunderlands against formations of the faster JU-88s of the German Luftwaffe.

Initially, 10 Squadron's principal function was to escort convoys in the Atlantic, though it also hunted German U-boats and conducted air-sea rescue and transport missions. By the time Tom arrived at the end of 1943, the focus had shifted to hunting U-boats and enemy shipping in the Bay of Biscay. But the period of greatest intensity in the 'Battle for the Bay' had already passed. The Squadron's war continued to change shape and direction during 1944, partly because of the withdrawal of U-boats and fighter escorts from Biscay leading up to, and following, the allied landing in Normandy, and partly because the introduction of a new snorkel device made the submarines more difficult to detect. In 1945, up to the end of the European War in May, there were even fewer sightings and the Squadron concentrated more on escorting convoys. Tom's letters home between January 1944 and mid-1945 reflected some of the pervading sense of boredom and frustration over the lack of action.[4]

Tom arrived at Mount Batten at 9.30 pm on 21 December 1943. He got there in time for the Squadron's 'preliminary Christmas beer up', a 'riotous' affair with the gym 'knee deep in beer'. For 10 days, no one seemed interested in training six new pilots. He told his sister at the beginning of January that being a new boy 'is rather like beginning at a boarding school, and one feels small and insignificant'. At least, 'there are a few blokes I know quite well, which helps quite a bit'. One of them had been on the same course at Bradfield Park.

From the first week in January Tom attended lectures; he had 'bags and bags of stuff to learn', and found the work 'intensely interesting and I really am enjoying it – just as I always thought I would'. He also learnt from 'chaps' assigned to other stations how well-off he was. His single, well-furnished room had central heating and a view; he did not have to walk long distances for a bath or a meal; and the food, apart from the absence of 'real eggs', was very good. 'We really seem to fight our war in comfort down here and there's a lot to be said for this method of waging it.'

Tom's letters in the early months of 1944 reported on the weather, on dances in the Mess, his regular attendance at Mass, joining a poker school, taking up rugby again and playing a lot of squash. He also told his parents about going on a few operations, but could say no more. By February, he could tell of his expectation to be flying every second day and how one of the best features of an operation was having eggs for breakfast and steak on patrol. Tom was very happy that Flying Officer Jack Mabbett, 'a very nice bloke' from Victoria, would be his captain and that Squadron Leader Ron Gillies, 'a first class bloke', was the CO. From February to June, Tom flew and trained with Mabbett's crew as the second pilot. He formed close friendships with Mabbett, Stan Reeve, the first pilot who came from Campbelltown, NSW, and Tom 'Robbie' Robertson, a navigator from Cairns.[5]

Several things were always on his mind. He knew his job was 'in many ways a peculiar one', telling his parents on 13 February it was

> quite conceivable that a bloke will go through a whole tour and not see a sub. On the other hand there may be bags of fun. The tendency to ease up because nothing seems to be doing has to be combated all the time. We have to train constantly and keep in practice for an occasion which might crop up at any time – no one knows when. When the occasion arises – one has got to have everything taped and know precisely what to do – otherwise there's no chance of success.

He returned to the theme two months later. The main thing was to guard against false complacency, namely, 'the idea that because nothing has happened yet, nothing will happen in the future'. After the Allied landing at Normandy on 6 June – according to his log book, Tom was not on operations until 9 June – he returned to a much earlier theme. He assured his parents they had no cause whatsoever to feel worried about his safety. The job was getting 'tamer' and was likely to be less exciting as time went by. In fact, Tom saw less of a risk in the present circumstances than in flying would-be navigators round the wildernesses of south-west New South Wales.

He was always worried about his progress. In mid-May, he reported getting close to flying solo and, after doing circuits and bumps with Gillies sitting next to him, felt that he had them taped. Yet he had achieved nothing more than flying solo. At the end of June, Tom reflected on his situation. 'As time goes on, the chances of ever attaining my ambition & becoming a captain on one of these things seems to grow more & more remote.' It was, however, just a 'momentary annoyance'. 'I shall be perfectly cheerful again in the morning. It really pays to be philosophical these days. Cultivating worries does no one any good.'

Tom wrote this letter 11 days after an episode he described to his parents as 'rather eventful from my point of view'.

On the morning of 19 June 1944, Tom was watching a fitter working on an engine of the crew's aircraft when suddenly a fire broke out. Two other men jumped from the lower deck into the water, and the fitter soon followed. Tom went to investigate and found the upper deck alight, hot and smoky. He emptied a fire extinguisher at the centre of the blaze but the fire was out of control. To make his escape, Tom grabbed hold of the hand rails to lever himself up, but the metal was red hot. His hands burnt, he jumped into a dinghy waiting by the aircraft and on reaching land sprinted to the hospital. It was only after the event he realised that the bomb load or the petrol tanks could have exploded. He had 'acted on the spur of the moment and without much consideration of the situation'. If he had thought about it, 'my departure might have been as rapid as that of the other blokes'. As it happened, the petrol tanks blew up within a minute of his leaving the 'boat', which then sank. The aircraft, Tom had described to his parents as 'a jolly good one – quite new', was recovered but written off.[6]

Tom told his parents on 24 June that he was 'right as rain' by the following day. His left hand remained bandaged though it was not at all painful; the fitter had escaped uninjured; of the other two men who were worse off than himself, one remained in hospital. Relieved from duties, it was 'rotten dull' waiting to give evidence before the Court of Enquiry; once over, he 'felt glad to have it all behind me & finished with'. The enquiry failed to find the cause and precise location of the outbreak. If the investigation had been more thorough, it would have disclosed an important detail of which Tom became aware: the two men inside the aircraft had been using petrol as a cleaning fluid and one had lit a cigarette.

Clearly, Tom wanted to minimise the seriousness of the incident, both to reassure the family and because he was very conscious of what other airmen faced and suffered in combat. He could pass it off with the observation that he had 'no desire to participate in any further fires. One is enough in a lifetime.' The fact remains that he was fortunate to have survived a dangerous situation.

Excitement of the desired variety continued to elude him. Flying a replacement aircraft, what the crew thought was a U-boat proved to be a whale. Meanwhile, Tom continued to despair of ever becoming a captain. It used to take six months for a second pilot to reach that status; by September 1944, it might take 12-15 months. Fortunately, there had been no losses in 1944. Vacancies occurred only when a captain completed his tour of duty. Once again, Tom assured his parents he was not letting the situation bother him. Besides, there was some good news. He had received a score of 'Above Average' as a flying boat pilot, his first result ever above 'Average'.

The success of the Normandy invasion brought Tom an unexpected dividend. He and 'Robbie' Robertson had been given the two places available on a British warship which was sailing for Normandy. 'Rather a good show all round, I can't help feeling.' Even allowing for the limitations imposed by security, the account he gave his parents of the trip on 11-13 September suggests it was an interesting tourist experience rather than a thrilling adventure. Tom spent many hours on the bridge, had a great time with 'a fine crowd of blokes', ate better food and, though the sea was rough, never felt sick. Tom was hardly more forthcoming in his diary

On their way to join the frigate, HMS *Hapgood*, at Portland, Tom and Robbie had lunch at a horrible restaurant smelling of cooked cabbage: 'I dislike English seaside towns intensely.' Next day, the *Hapgood* joined a convoy of 21 Liberty ships and Landing Ship Tanks. From the bridge, Tom had a very good view of Cherbourg on the Normandy coast and of the U-boat pens and defensive forts. Boarding a launch, the tourists failed to persuade local French fishermen to sell some of their catch. The consolation for Tom was that they understood his French.

Two days after the tourists returned to Mount Batten, Mabbett's crew was involved in an incident that Tom passed off as 'nothing very momentous, but nevertheless quite interesting'.

From August 1944, Sunderland crews had been ordered to watch out for surface traffic in the Bay of Biscay. The withdrawal of all German fighters from western France meant that the Sunderlands could fly close to shore during daylight hours while looking for ships sailing between isolated German garrisons or escaping to Spanish ports.[7] On 16 September, Tom was first pilot on bay patrol when the crew encountered a vessel claiming to be a German hospital ship bound for a Spanish port. Mabbett was not convinced of its innocence. After radioing base, he followed MV *Rostock* for several hours until the arrival of two Royal Navy motor torpedo boats. While the aircraft circled the *Rostock*, Tom had a good view of the Brittany peninsular and thought it 'looks very pretty from the air'. As a Naval party prepared to board, Mabbett flew low over the deck to show off his armaments. The Navy escorted the German ship to Plymouth where it was found to be a converted minesweeper, which could be reconverted within days, and was carrying secret codes and engaging in weather reporting unrelated to hospital duties. Officially credited with the capture, Mabbett's crew subsequently made a claim for prize money. The British Government announced in December 1945 that it would pay prize money for captured merchant ships and cargo. In 1953, the Australian Government allocated £229,000 of all the prize money to an RAAF veterans' fund, claiming that an equitable distribution to individuals was impossible and would mean very small amounts being handed to participants. At least Tom could claim to have been a member of the one RAAF aircraft that captured an enemy vessel on the high seas in the Second World War.[8]

Within three weeks of the *Rostock* capture, Tom had what he called 'about my most interesting trip to date'. A Group Captain had joined the flight and was sitting alongside Mabbett during a 'coast-crawl' from the northern end of the Bay to Cape Ortegal in the south. After keeping out of flak range of the places known to be German-occupied, the crew sighted a small ship in the harbour of Le Verdon-sur-Mer on the south side of the mouth of the Gironde estuary. Mabbett decided to investigate, not knowing for certain whether the area was under German control.

> We soon found out! The Hun, in his wily fashion, held his fire till we were right in close – about 300 yards from crossing over the beach. Our height was only 800 [feet]. Then all of a sudden, I heard whoomph, whoomph, whoomph and saw streams of white smoke rising from a gun position on the beach.

The tail gunner thought some of the flak whizzed by just 15 yards from the tail of the aircraft. Tom saw 'stuff' bursting on the port and starboard bows. Mabbett took over the controls and engaged in 'violent evasive action' and 'we were out of range very smartly'. For the rest of the patrol Tom concentrated on the coastline scenery, especially between Biarritz, which he noted in his diary he would like to see in peacetime, and the mountainous country on the Spanish seaboard which 'certainly looks grand'.

There was little in the way of action to report for the remainder of the year. Personnel changes were noted in letters: Reeve seemed destined for another crew, Mabbett was finishing his tour of duty, one of the gunners was leaving and Gillies had completed his time as CO on 2 October. The new senior appointments – Wing Commander Harry Cooke DFC as CO and Squadron Leader Phil 'Happy' Adams DFC as Flight Commander – had made 'very good initial impressions'. Phil Oakley, Mabbett's successor, was 'a very good type' who 'will do a first-class job'. Tom replaced Reeve as first pilot and 'Red' Burt, a barrister and solicitor from Perth, arrived at Mount

Batten to become second pilot. Five years older than Tom, 'Red' – as he was called throughout most of his life – would also be known as Sir Francis Theodore Page Burt AC KCMG QC, Chief Justice (1977-88) and Governor (1990-93) of Western Australia. His great-grandfather, the son of a sugar planter in the West Indies, had been the State's first Chief Justice and his grandfather had served as the State's Attorney-General and Agent-General in London. Burt and Hughes formed a friendship at Mount Batten broken only by the former's death in 2004.

In mid-November, Tom learnt that he would start a captain's course within 11 days. Normally, as a new captain, he would take over a crew in December but 'Happy' Adams insisted on men taking their regular leave. After all his earlier foreboding, Tom could report that what he had been 'hoping and waiting for during the past 11 months is in sight. I feel as pleased as a cat sitting in front of a nice warm fire'. His confidence matched his greater contentment. There were hairy moments when taking off and landing in the deteriorating weather of October to November. On one occasion, cloud covered Plymouth Sound down to the 'deck', forcing him to land in 'a decent swell' outside the breakwater. The aircraft 'bounced in grand style three times before finally setting'. Tom managed to hold the wings level and avoided a 'prang', and Adams congratulated him on 'a good show'.

Life on the base in 1944

Life on the base in 1944 had its trying moments. Audiences were required for important visitors, and officers and other ranks often queried the value of such occasions. The Lord Mayor of London came in mid-January and, after lunch in the Officers' Mess, made a short speech saying 'how grateful people were to have us over here etc etc'. There was 'quite an array of gold chain' because the Lord Mayor was accompanied by the Lord Mayor of Plymouth, the second Viscount Astor.[9] The Duke of Gloucester, soon to become Governor-General of Australia, visited Mount Batten on 19 August. Tom labelled a story in the Sydney *Daily Mirror* as 'complete and utter balderdash and poppycock' for claiming that RAF officers accompanying the Duke had raised their eyebrows in surprise at some of the controversial comments made to him. Tom pointed out that there was no RAF officer with the Duke at the time.

There was a regular dance at the base on Saturday nights, a few of which were described as a 'jolly good show' but most were pretty 'dead' or 'dreary', enlivened only by the supper. After one dance in June, Tom commented favourably on the free beer and a good supper but, for his sins, 'I was introduced to a rather dim Naval nursing sister who was very difficult to talk to, and my valiant efforts to make conversation rather bored me after a while'.

Although he may not have met interesting female Naval personnel – he never formed a relationship during the War – he liked the 'cracker bunch of coves' he and Stan Reeve met on board the Tribal-class destroyer, HMS *Ashanti*, in July 1944. There were further references in his letters of visits to ships and of returned hospitality at Mount Batten.

Tom's recreational activity included games of bridge, seeing films in Plymouth and on the base, reading magazines and newspapers sent from home and books bought and borrowed. The Entertainment National Service Association (ENSA) offered another form of distraction, albeit of a dubious quality. ENSA put on concerts throughout Britain to entertain the armed services and regularly turned up at Mount Batten. Tom attended a few concerts and, like most of the Squadron, thought them pretty awful. The contrast was stark when a London West End company brought a play to the base. ENSA did employ some very talented performers like Joyce Grenfell, George Formby, Gracie Fields and Paul Scofield. Unfortunately, they never reached Plymouth. Tom liked the joke that ENSA actually stood for 'Every Night Something Awful', and the *Punch* story about ENSA teams being organised to follow the landing in Europe to give the invaders added impetus to drive forward.

Special occasions, like awards, were marked by beer-ups. Tom told his parents about a party in July after a Sunderland captain, Bill Tilley, was awarded a DFC, and his nose gunner, a Flight Sergeant, a DFM: 'gongs rarely come our way in view of the usually uneventful work we are engaged in. But when they do come, there is great celebration.' Sometimes any excuse would suffice. On 20 September, 'we had one of our rather infrequent mad parties in the Mess, with bicycle races round the ante-room and goodness knows what else. It's a good outlet for surplus energy, as people are apt to feel very browned off these days at the rather boring state of affairs.' Indeed, '[o]ur part in the war over here seems to be all over bar shouting'. Yet because of operational requirements, Tom's celebration of his 21st birthday had to be held three days before 26 November. Two friends organised a nine-gallon keg in the Mess to mark the occasion 'and it was open go till it ran out' and there was a 'certain amount of singing and general merriment'.

There were plenty of opportunities for sport. Tom played tennis and squash throughout the year, and rugby at the beginning and towards the end. Early in December, he flew the Squadron's rugby team to Pembroke Dock – there were 22 bodies on board – and they won a match 15-0 against 461 Squadron. Tom was full back 'and managed not to fumble the ball at all'. For him, the more testing time was the trip home in foul weather and 'my reputation was at stake with so many onlookers, and luckily [I] managed to grease the kite over the water rather smoothly'. In October, he saw his first game of Australian rules, a match between the officers and the non-commissioned officers at Mount Batten. It was an 'interesting' game but did not compare to 'rugger', though it was pleasing to see that Mabbett and four other members of his crew were the best players.

Tom maintained an active interest in politics, both in the United Kingdom and at home. The insights he gained at Whitley Bay about the voting intentions of British servicemen were augmented by the result of the West Derbyshire by-election in February 1944. An Independent Labour candidate overturned a Conservative majority of 5524 to take the seat by 4651 votes, defeating the Marquess of Hartington, the eldest son and heir apparent of the 10th Duke of Devonshire. Having followed what was a very lively campaign, Tom saw the result as 'rather a nasty slap in the eye for the Government' and 'a very clear indication of the way England will go politically after the war'.

Early in April, he surmised 'that Curtin & Co will be in power for years and years to come unless the opposition can extract the digit and present some sort of united front. The present dissensions and bickerings and defections seem to be suicidal.' At this stage, attempts to resurrect the United Australia Party or start a new organisation were either foundering or not progressing. The Labor Government's domestic policies continued to annoy him. Pleased that service personnel could vote in the 'Powers Referendum' of 1944, Tom said he intended to vote against surrendering more powers to the Commonwealth. He objected to 'being told exactly what to [do] and when and where and how, and in general being regulated like a lot of stupid sheep'. Late in September, Tom was pleased to learn that his former law lecturer Dr Evatt, the Attorney-General, was fighting with Eddie Ward, the Minister for Transport, over the latter's attempt to prosecute four Geelong Grammar boys for boarding a Sydney to Melbourne train without a permit. Tom enjoyed the very public spat; the earlier defeat of the Powers Referendum on 19 August was even more pleasing.

On another front, Tom expressed delight in learning early in July that his father was standing for election as President of the Returned Sailors' Soldiers' and Airmen's Imperial League of Australia. Told in September that the bid had failed, he decided it was just as well: the strain of office 'would not do your health any good'. In any case, the 'main thing' was that his father was successful in his campaign to widen the membership of the RSL to include ex-service personnel who had not left Australia.

The tourist

Throughout 1944, Tom used his 48-hour passes and more extended leave periods to visit London, his relatives in Barnsley and Bude and other contacts made through his family, as well as to explore south-western and western England. In addition to more visits to Aunt May and Gerald, he travelled to Gloucester where he met another relative on his mother's side – Clara – who 'is pretty old, and looks it' – as well as her daughter who was married to a nephew of Lord Derby. In the spa town of Cheltenham, he met another of his maternal grandmother's sisters, Aunt Clara, who 'is quite an old dear and amazingly well preserved for her 80 odd years'.

Towards the end of May, Tom travelled to Droitwich in Worcestershire to visit Betty Cobbold, his former English nanny who was staying with her parents. It was 16 years since Tom had seen Betty Lindner, as she then was. The pair then travelled to Bristol where Betty's husband, Lieutenant Colonel Reynold Cobbold, was in charge of the city's anti-aircraft installations. They had dinner together and went to a variety show. The Cobbolds and the Lindners were clearly impressed by the young man from Australia. Betty wrote to 'Mrs Hughes' on 27 May: 'we all agree that he is an absolutely grand person … I think I should have recognised him. He is certainly very good looking & most intelligent & quite charming. You have good reason to be proud of him. He is looking very fit.'[10]

Tom's letters provided detailed accounts of the villages, towns and countryside he observed and of the cathedrals and other buildings he scrutinised. He described the cathedral in Gloucester as 'a beautiful gem of architecture', and especially admired the cloisters for their 'intricate face-work' that he understood was the best preserved in Europe. Cheltenham had 'a sort of calm, ordered sedateness' of a kind he had not experienced elsewhere in England: 'If I were a retired Colonel, I would no doubt think it the nearest thing to paradise.' In Worcestershire he wrote of this 'very pleasant and peaceful part of rural England … I can't help wondering whether the inherent complacency of the British race is in some degree due to the face of the English countryside'. In April, he told his parents that he loved England and, in the main, admired it, though he cared little for the big cities outside London. Of the countryside, he definitely favoured the Cotswolds.

Owning a car was certainly an asset. In April, Tom bought a 1935 four-seater, dark blue Singer. It cost £35, and he serviced it himself. Ingenuity was occasionally necessary. Car tyres and tubes could not be replaced without a written application and negotiating with the bureaucracy. Motor cycle tubes could be more easily acquired, and adapted for the Singer. While he had to be careful with petrol coupons, Tom saw more of England west of Plymouth and north to the Cotswolds than would have been possible travelling by bus or train. The other advantage was that he could drive his mates – Mabbett, Reeve and Robertson – to a village pub for lunch, or to a seaside village in Devon where the beach did not have a grain of sand, or to a farm near Plymouth to collect strawberries.

Oxford

Of all Tom's trips around England, one could have had longer-term significance. Near the end of 1944, Tom and Red Burt organised their leave to spend a week in Oxford. They arrived on Monday 27 November and attended two lectures each morning as part of a course designed to show off the university to interested visitors from abroad. The course of about 80 consisted mainly of Americans and Canadians, though it did include 'a fair sprinkling of Englishmen', five Australians, two Poles and a Norwegian. Tom found the lectures to be stimulating and 'of a very high standard', delivered by 'dons' who really knew their subject.

Tom had a room in Balliol College. He quickly decided that the college architecture reflected 'an almost fiendish flair for discomfort', as he had to cross two quadrangles for a bath. Many of Balliol's *alumni* would have understood his irritation. Tom was more enthused when, on his second afternoon in Oxford, he joined a small group from the course which was taken around various colleges by 'a charming old lady', Miss Christine Burrows, who had succeeded her mother as Principal of St Hilda's College (1921-29). Tom was 'greatly impressed' by New College, his maternal grandfather's *alma mater*. He was especially attracted to its chapel and dining room, and was struck by the separate memorial for two New College Rhodes scholars who fought for Germany in the Great War. The tour finished at Magdalen College and, completing her two-and-a-half hour running commentary, Miss Burrows took the party to her house for an English tea.

Tom went to a dance at Rhodes House that night. He thought it 'about the best' he had attended in England. 'It was rather refreshing to see such an aggregation of intelligent people.' In all, he went to three dances at Rhodes House, each held in a 'very first-class ball-room' and given by 'Mr and Mrs CK Allen', the Warden and his wife.[11] Tom and Red agreed not to travel with the course to Stratford-on-Avon. They had no desire to watch Americans competing with each other to buy bits of Anne Hathaway's Cottage. Instead, they took a bus to the little village of Wytham, north-west of Oxford, had lunch at the local pub and afterwards called on some of Burt's friends who were living near the village. Returning to Balliol for dinner they went to a Chekhov play, *The Cherry Orchard*, which Tom did not rate well.

After lectures the following morning, he climbed the Carfax Tower in the centre of the city. He visited the University Church of St Mary the Virgin in the High Street where, following Queen Mary's restoration of Roman Catholicism, three Protestant divines – Cranmer, Latimer and Ridley – were tried for heresy in 1555 and later burnt at the stake just outside Balliol College. After a hurried look at the Bodleian Library, he visited the Christopher Wren-designed Sheldonian Theatre and thought it unimposing from the outside and musty indoors. In the evening, some members of the course attended the Union Debate. Tom found most of the speakers 'very youthful & very inexperienced' but considered the ritual was 'rather interesting' (35 years later he participated in the ritual, along with his future son-in-law, Malcolm Turnbull). The President of the Union, thinking the visitors were bored, sent a note 'making the useful and practical suggestion that we should find our way to the Bar'. They did. Tom clearly preferred the 'most interesting' Oxford-Cambridge rugby match he attended the following day. It ended in a three-all draw.

Tom managed both to immerse himself in Oxford and to stand back and observe. He explained that Oxford itself had become very crowded because of its large industrial population and the 'considerable hordes of Americans'. He divided the 1700 undergraduates into three main groups: the medically unfit, those waiting to join the forces, and the medical students. Tom noted how Oxford had its full quota of the varying shades of pink, 'the usual encumbrance of any University', even though the two MPs elected by Oxford University 'have been Tories from time immemorial'.[12] There seemed, he wrote, to be 'some brand of political thought or cult of philosophy' requiring its devotees to wear very long hair, which combined 'unwashed grubbiness with the coiffure of a Papuan native'. Oxford, he told his sister, differed from other universities as an institution, in part because it spawned 'hundreds of strange societies'. For him, the most amusing was the Jacobite Club. Each year it marked the anniversary of Bonnie Prince Charlie raising the standard of rebellion against the Crown in 1745. The club held a dinner where its members proclaimed Prince Albrecht of Bavaria as the legitimate king of the United Kingdom and of the British Dominions overseas. Tom saw good sense in tolerating rather than suppressing such idiocy among the young; they would soon grow out of it.

Tom was not the first, nor the last, 21-year-old Australian to be conscious of his age and of coming from a different world on encountering the university's predominantly English undergraduate population. Serving officers in wartime would be even more conscious of different outlooks and experiences. Had Tom gone up to Oxford immediately after the War, he might have considered himself years removed from the recent products of the English public schools and grammar schools. On the other hand, the Oxford he visited during the War had clearly appealed.

The final months of the European war

In his final letter for 1944 Tom referred to what he hoped would be his last Christmas away from home. Most of the Squadron had gone into town on Christmas Eve to see Australian newsreels especially prepared for the armed forces overseas. Everyone was 'disgusted' by the focus on horse racing, professional football, the latest in female bathing costumes and other 'extremely trivial topics'. To make matters worse, Viscount Astor and his wife were present. 'The impression of Australia at war … could not have been favourable.'

Following the show, Tom went to midnight Mass and, for the first time, had to queue to enter a church. Arthur Drakeford, the Labor Party Minister for Air and Civil Aviation, who was visiting the base, addressed the officers on Christmas morning. Drakeford told the officers to fire questions – 'which suited us down to the ground'. Tom asked two: what did the Government hope to achieve by nationalising interstate aviation?; and did the Government think it had a mandate to socialise the country? He did not report Drakeford's response. Tom heard later that the questioning by the non-commissioned officers and other ranks 'was not so polite'. The speechifying delayed the celebrations but Tom managed to fit in a beer with his old crew before serving 'buckets of beer' to 900 airmen assembled for their Christmas dinner. He then dressed up as a 'WAAF Sergeant Waitress' to serve dinner to the staff of the Officers' Mess before having his own Christmas dinner.

Tom started 1945 on a slow note. He now captained a Sunderland but had to wait until 8 April for his promotion to Flight Lieutenant. He was on leave for part of January, clocking just over 30 hours in that month, mainly on escort and patrol duties and on qualifying to fly Sunderlands solo at night. The patrol and escort work and training exercises increased from February, and he averaged 50 hours a month for the first four months of 1945 against 62 hours a month in the second half of 1944.

Incidents of any kind were rare, but there was a moderately serious one on 16 April. The day began with what Tom called in his war diary 'a minor taxying accident' just after slipping the buoy. Although the Sunderland had a damaged aerial, it was able to take off, albeit 30 minutes late. The mission involved a 'coast crawl' along the Bay of Biscay, flying past Belle Île, the largest of the islands off the coast of Brittany. Tom learnt at the prior briefing that the island 'was free of the Hun'. He came in low and close to the land. Just as the aircraft turned away from the island 'they let us have a mixed assortment of heavy, medium & light flak'. As another pilot occupied the captain's seat, and there was no time to change places, Tom flew the aircraft from the second pilot's seat. He took evasive action by undulating and turning at heights of between 200 and 500 feet. His aircraft was hit just once, a glancing blow on the perspex of the rear turret which knocked a piece into the turret and grazed a gunner's knuckle. Within five minutes the plane was out of range. Two-and-a-half hours later there was a further burst of fire from the west side of Belle Île. No damage was done. Tom recorded in his log book: 'Nothing else of interest.'[13]

There was a sequel. His log book contains an entry under the heading: 'ENDORSEMENTS REGARDING AVOIDABLE FLYING ACCIDENTS OR OTHER BREACHES OF FLYING DISCIPLINE.' Tom 'displayed carelessness' in slipping from the buoy and damaging two Sunderland aircraft. The Air Officer Commanding No 19 Group ordered that his log book 'shall be endorsed "Carelessness" in accordance with the provisions of AMOC A23/43'. Group Captain Caster RAF, the CO Mount Batten RAF Station, added his signature. It is unlikely that the Group Captain, or the CO or Flight Commander of 10 Squadron or anyone else, including the guilty party named as 'F/Lt TE Hughes', felt at all distressed.

Within a week of his 'minor taxying accident' and the incident in the Bay of Biscay, Tom arrived at Kendal in the Lake District to stay with the Hornyold-Stricklands. It will be recalled that Geoffrey Hughes had been an aide-de-camp to Sir Gerald Strickland, when he was Governor of New South Wales. Strickland had acquired Sizergh Castle from a cousin in the late 19th century, the castle having been in the Strickland family for 750 years. The estate was transferred to a daughter, Mary, in 1940 and she had married Henry Hornyold. Mary's sister and her family occupied the castle and Tom stayed with the Hornyold-Stricklands in the nearby Sizergh Lodge. He travelled around the Lake District – parts of the country reminded him of the Australian Alps – and visited the Wordsworth Museum, drove by a German POW camp and, in the Kendal cinema, saw the 'extremely funny picture', *Arsenic and Old Lace*, directed by Frank Capra and starring Cary Grant.

Tom was still on leave in Cambridge and London when the Germans surrendered. He caught a late night and very crowded train back to Mount Batten on 7 May. Next day – Tuesday 8 May, Victory in Europe Day – he did a taxi-test on his aircraft in anticipation of flying next morning. He listened to Churchill's speech at 3.00 pm, after which the ships in the Sound let off their sirens in unison and flags appeared everywhere. There was a party in the Mess that evening. Everyone paused from drinking to listen to the King's speech at 9.00 pm; Tom thought it 'a very good effort'. Although he could not join in the resumed festivities because of his early morning take-off, he considered that, altogether, 'it was a very memorable day'.

In the final reckoning, 10 Squadron had lost 151 men killed and 19 aircraft between 1940 and 1945. Six U-boats had been sunk, two of them while Tom was at the station. Several more were damaged and many enemy aircraft had been shot down. No lives in the Squadron had been lost in 1944-45 as a result of enemy action while in the air. The much-decorated, South African-born Air Marshal Sir Leonard Slatter, who headed Coastal Command at the end of the War, sent a signal to the Squadron when it was considered bound for the Pacific: 'You leave these shores with a record second to none.' The Squadron had received many decorations: 24 DFCs and one DFC and bar, while 55 officers and other ranks were mentioned in despatches.[14] Tom's own award was to come some 60 years later, when the French Government made him a Chevalier of the Légion d'Honneur for his role as a pilot during the Normandy landings. What mattered to him in 1945 was that he had survived. The burns received when fighting the fire had healed very quickly and left no scars. Tom had, as he put it, 'a relatively lucky and safe war'.[15]

5

'A mixture of frustration and hope ... followed by disappointment'

Tom's Squadron continued in May to escort convoys and undertake patrols. As U-boats were generally surrendering in northern waters, the work 'was very boring and everyone became fed up', especially with being 'sent out on footling useless night patrols which could not conceivably be of any earthly use'. The climax of 'clueless clottishness' was to order crews to provide escorts for convoys whose ships had been told to burn their navigation lights. One crew, sent out on anti-U-boat patrol, found a convoy before dawn fully lit up from miles away. This 'sort of idiocy' and the lack of information about the Squadron's future 'produced a somewhat gloomy and browned-off atmosphere'.

On 3 June 1945 in Melbourne, Thomas McKay told Geoffrey Hughes he was pleased that Tom had not witnessed the current political in-fighting of the RAAF High Command: 'He will leave the show I hope with a pleasant taste in his mouth.' Promising to get any information he could 'about the plans for 10 Sqdn – if they have any', McKay could imagine 'nothing more completely satisfying for you and for Tom than for him to come steaming up Rose Bay as captain of his own whacking great Sunderland. Let's hope it comes to pass.'[1]

Soon after McKay wrote this letter, Tom went on a course organised by the Joint Anti U-boat School near Londonderry in Northern Ireland. He pointed out that the course might have been instructive if held several months before the end of the War, though he valued inspecting a corvette and sailing in a British submarine. Within an hour of the final lecture, Tom and two friends from the Squadron were on a train to Belfast where, after beers and lunch, they tried to get train tickets for Dublin. Formally, they needed written permission from their CO to cross the border. Advised that an official in a happy frame of mind might not bother about the absence of requisite authority, the three men decided 'to have a go'. They reached Dublin in time for dinner. Tom recorded the details of his first meal in this 'amazing city': crab cocktail, soup, an enormous steak, Peach Melba and 'real whipped cream'. The tourist noticed that the shop windows of a neutral country were full of wares such as watches, pipes and silk stockings. He also heard the 'news' via an Australian in Dublin that 12 aircraft of 10 Squadron were to fly home. This information 'gave us much cause for speculation in the following week'.[2]

On 20 June, the Squadron formally ceased operations with RAF Coastal Command and more rumours circulated about it joining the Pacific War. Tom had visions of returning via one of the Gulf States, India and Ceylon and, as McKay had suggested, landing in Rose Bay close by the family home. Yet it was evident for at least a month before the Japanese surrender in August that 10 Squadron was not needed in the Pacific. Tom was asleep when the news of the surrender reached Mount Batten. Woken by the noise of ship's sirens and the glaring of searchlights, he joined his fellows in the Mess where free beer was served. The party lasted until 4.30 am but Tom Hughes was back in bed three hours earlier. He was appalled when he heard later of the Sydney celebrations and of the behaviour of the 'hooligan element', telling his parents there was not a single unpleasant incident in England.

Tom's letters home from July reflected increasing boredom and frustration.[3] In mid-July he thought he would be home in August; within a few days he spoke of September. By mid-August, when 'my store of philosophical calm will run out before long', he convinced himself that his best hope was to return for the beginning of the next university year. A few weeks later he wondered whether those who would decide his immediate future were actually capable of making a decision. Looking about him in mid-September he concluded: 'As a mob, I think we are all slightly insane as the result of four months futility & boredom – mad in a quite harmless way but mad nevertheless.' He felt 'full of impotent fury at this wretched delay … but there is nothing to be done about it'.

He was not exactly idle, and was certainly better off than airmen in other stations and soldiers pretty well anywhere. Apart from aircraft maintenance, there was golf, fishing, tennis and competitive sailing. Tom became 'a mild form of bridge enthusiast', read several books, listened to the BBC's live radio broadcasts of the 'Victory' cricket tests, and frequently visited London and travelled through the Lake District and the villages of the southern counties. On one visit to London he attended Mass at Westminster Cathedral and then walked to Buckingham Place where a guard stunned him with 'a shattering salute'. Next day Tom saw the film *I Live in Grosvenor Square*, starring Rex Harrison, Anna Neagle and Robert Morley. He thought it 'quite good'. Like the Londoners and a good many Australians, he felt bound to comment on the number of Americans he encountered. And he would not have been alone among young Allied servicemen from several countries in observing how 'the less pleasant products of the Chosen Race ... were very noticeable in the Restaurants and hotels. It has been a comfortable war for some people even in this country.'[4]

The intrepid letter writer kept up his flow of correspondence, with frequent reports on the weather (summer was 'a flop'), on dances he attended and dinners he enjoyed, including one 'magnificent meal' on board an Australian Navy ship consisting of cold turkey and salad and tinned pineapple pieces for desert, all washed down with ample supplies of Tooheys Pilsner. At another dinner, attended by thirty Australian officers at their Mount Batten Mess, 'the going was fast and furious' and included the firing of a salvo of red distress cartridges from the ante room. Tom recounted his efforts to buy presents for the family. He commented on issues ranging from Labour's landslide victory in the British election – there was general agreement that the Forces' vote 'was pretty solid for socialism' – to the rocketing prices for food and goods and the insipid quality of tea served on British trains made worse by unwashed and cracked cups.

He doubted whether 'the Australian masses' would show 'the same fortitude and common-sense' if faced with the same situation as the British people, who generally accepted the pain of continuing post-war shortages instead of living for the moment. At Paddington railway station in August, he encountered long train delays and huge queues but 'the whole spectacle increased my admiration for the good behaviour & common-sense of Englishmen en masse'. There was a continuing interest in Australian politics. On 12 July, he expressed his unhappiness about the Chifley Government's two Banking Bills, which expanded the powers and role of the Commonwealth Bank: 'I'm really serious in my intention to get stuck into politics when I get out of the Air Force – the more I read & hear about conditions at home, the more enraged I become.'

An assessment

Two months after the end of the European war, Wing Commander Cooke, as CO of 10 Squadron, completed a confidential report on Flt Lt Hughes. Dated 19 July 1945,[5] it was a standard document requiring the reporting officer to choose one of up to five options as best describing the subject in 14 different categories. In each case, the options usually ranged from the least desirable to the most favourable. Tom rated as follows:

1. **Appearance and Bearing:** creates a distinctly favourable impression, neat and smart
2. **Temperance** (observed on and off duty, in Mess; temperance was 'not to be confused with teetotalism): consistently temperate
3. **Mental Alertness:** catches on easily without too much explanation
4. **Power of Expression:** usually gets his ideas across
5. **Self-Confidence:** wholesomely self-confident and decisive
6. **Initiative:** satisfactory, displays minor constructive ability
7. **Emotional Stability:** fairly well balanced, cool headed
8. **Energy:** industrious and vigorous, shows willingness to do more than average amount of work
9. **Dependability:** completely dependable for the performance of all ordinary duties
10. **Cooperation:** keen to cooperate
11. **Leadership:** can lead in minor affairs
12. **Proficiency in Duties upon which Engaged:** superior – knows his work and does it well
13. **Administrative Ability:** moderately capable in routine manner
14. **Service Knowledge:** moderately well informed and steadily qualifying for greater responsibility

Tom received top ratings for temperance and self-confidence, and a second or third top rating in the other categories.

Not too much should be made of Cooke's assessment. Tom was a temporary employee with no intention of pursuing a career in the RAAF. In any case, these reports tended to hover around the average. Nevertheless, in view of Hughes' later appointment as Commonwealth Attorney-General, and of his standing as a leading QC, it is worth noting what Cooke did not say about him in three of the categories. On mental alertness, the Wing Commander decided against reporting that Tom was adaptable and quick in grasping the question and new ideas, or that he was exceptionally keen and quick on the uptake. On powers of expression, the CO rejected two higher categories, namely, of showing superior ability to express himself, and being most forceful and convincing. If this assessment was accurate in 1945, many opposing counsel of a few decades later would have wished it had remained so.[6] On leadership, Cooke thought Tom could lead in 'minor affairs' but not 'important' ones. Nor was he considered skilful in directing others, or capable of inspiring confidence and commanding respect. Cooke did not see him as 'a born leader'. If invited to comment, Bish Russell, who observed Tom on the trip to the United Kingdom in 1943, would have disagreed.

A Rhodes scholar?

Geoffrey Hughes rang his son on the morning of 4 October 1945, Sydney time. Prompted by Father Hehir, he raised the possibility of Tom applying for a Rhodes scholarship. Two scholarships were allocated to each State in 1946, open to service candidates only. Tom was eligible to apply: he had completed at least one year of 'war service', was a British subject aged between 19 and 25 years of age at some point between September 1939 and October 1945, and had lived for at least five years in Australia where he had completed the required minimum of one year at a university.[7] The Rhodes Will listed four groups of desired 'qualities', of which Rhodes considered the first two were the most important:

> (1) Literary and scholastic attainments;
> (2) Qualities of manhood, truth, courage, devotion to duty, sympathy for and protection of the weak, kindliness, unselfishness and fellowship;
> (3) Exhibition of moral force of character and of instincts to lead and to take an interest in his fellows;
> (4) Physical vigour, as shown by fondness for and success in manly outdoor sports.

Tom could fairly claim to have demonstrated possession of Rhodes' desired qualities.

To apply, he needed to submit an application by 31 October 1945 and attach a birth certificate, certified records of his university education and war service, a medical certificate, two photographs, a signed statement of 'general interests and activities', the names of six referees, the proposed course at Oxford, and 'the character of the work' aimed to be taken 'in after-life'.

Tom took his father's phone call on the evening of 3 October. He was very surprised to learn that Father Hehir of all people had suggested he should apply for a Rhodes. For Tom, however, the immediate importance of the call was that, after a break of two years, he heard his parents' voices again. In a letter home – written after he put the phone down – he explained his probable incoherence as the effect of 'elation and general amazement'; this day 'I shall not forget for a very long time.' He then considered the pros and cons of making an application, leaving his parents in no doubt that he wanted to go to Oxford.

He thought it 'well worthwhile' making the attempt. Tom realised that by going to Oxford he would deprive his father of a helping hand in the office. Yet 'I should love 3 years at Oxford' as it would be 'a great help in after life & perhaps fit me to play some part in the sphere of politics – as you know I have been harbouring vague aspirations of entering politics'. A Rhodes scholarship would help this cause and 'would also be a great thing for the family'. Oxford would give him a grandstand seat for observing 'the vital struggle for the rehabilitation of civilization as we understand it'. The next few years would mean recovery or collapse, and he would like to watch it all unfold. The opportunity should not be missed 'except for the gravest reason'. His father's wish to retire was a sufficient ground not to apply, but he could submit an application and defer a decision until called before the Rhodes Selection Committee. In the meantime, a family friend in England was already talking of pulling strings with the Headmaster of Winchester to secure Tom a place in New College, thus following the route taken by his maternal grandfather.

Geoffrey Hughes had no doubt that Tom should apply. Without waiting for a considered response, he became his son's campaign manager, organising his application and his return to Australia for an interview.

Within hours of telephoning Tom, Geoffrey Hughes spoke to Miss Hay, the long-serving Secretary of the Law School, and to JD Butchart, the Acting Secretary of the NSW Rhodes Selection Committee. He contacted Vincent John Flynn, a Sydney solicitor and the first Catholic in New South Wales to win a Rhodes (1927), who had sat on Rhodes Selection Committees. After collecting everything he could about the scholarship, Geoffrey Hughes composed a very long letter with many postscripts addressing what he saw as the immediate questions Tom had to tackle, namely, writing a good application, collecting all the necessary certificates, and meeting the deadline of 31 October.[8]

First, there was the matter of referees. Geoffrey Hughes compiled a list of names, headed by the two 'obvious' ones: Fathers Hehir and Meagher, the Rector and former Rector of Riverview. Miss Hay suggested Tom include Sir John Peden, the Challis Professor of Law at the University of Sydney, Dean of the Law Faculty (1910-42), and President of the NSW Legislative Council since 1928. She said Peden would remember Tom, he was an old friend of Sir Thomas Hughes, had a good regard for Geoffrey Hughes and could account for Tom's year at the university. Hughes added the names of Justice Owen of the NSW Supreme Court, the best man at his wedding, and Orwell Phillips, a leading Jewish businessman, who had a high opinion of Tom and was a prominent Sydney Grammar Old Boy. Finally, he included Bish Russell, while naming an Air Commodore and a retired Major as alternatives. Tom accepted all of his father's suggestions.

The campaign manager highlighted three tactical points in favour of Russell: he knew Tom well and regarded him highly; he 'is <u>not</u> an RC' (emphasis in the original); and he could speak with intimate knowledge of Tom's record as a young officer on the trip to England and of his relations with his fellows. While Geoffrey Hughes would contact the referees in Australia, and did not doubt their willingness to act, he wanted his son to arrange for Russell to forward a reference in advance of an invitation from the Committee. Time was critical. So was religious denomination. 'Get him to state that he is a Presbyterian Chaplain (this will tend to outweigh any sectarian bias on the part of the Selection Committee).' Bish should write 'a full but not over fulsome letter' (emphasis in the original), particularly mentioning Tom's interest in public policy and the present problems of the Empire. After all, only those associated with him in the War years 'can indicate the maturity of thought and interest of the Tom of today'.

The bulk of the father's letter focused on the writing of a good application. Flynn had told him that 'the most vital factor' was the statement about 'general interests and activities'. Hughes told Tom: 'you must set out your whole story and hopes and much depends on the framing of it.' He should outline his school career, sporting activities, the subjects in which he was interested such as Classics and History, and the reasons why they interested him. On sport at school, Tom should list football, rowing and the fact that he was stroke of a junior eight, boxing and athletics. He should also refer to his role in the cadets and his debating success 'and stress the age at which you passed Intermediate and Leaving' (emphases in the original).

Tom should expand upon his RAAF record: the appointments as under-corporal and under-sergeant during training, the commission awarded on completion of training, the highest marks achieved in written examinations during training courses, the appointments as adjutant and acting CO on the trip to the United Kingdom and the command of a crew of 11 in the Sunderlands. He should ask his CO to provide a certificate of service and, if possible, 'get him to include some personal opinion on your leadership [Geoffrey Hughes did not know that Cooke might not have been helpful here], fellowship and devotion to duty – these are important matters and give you a chance to put in something more than a bare certificate of time of service'. Appreciating that his son 'may think all this is shooting a line', Hughes urged him to 'remember you must indicate clearly that from school on you have had leadership and have carried responsibility'.

It was critical for Tom to expand upon his keen interest in public affairs and ambition to serve his country. He might mention a desire to follow the family tradition of public service exemplified by the activities of his paternal grandfather and his father. On the subject of tradition, his mother's side of the family should also be included. His maternal grandfather was a Scholar of Winchester and New College and President of the Oxford Union while his maternal grandmother's family, the Homans, had a record of involvement in the Empire. Great Uncle Ernest Homan, for example, was 'a Rhodesian pioneer'.[9] Hughes suggested that these points 'can be adroitly brought in as background to your interest in public & Empire affairs'.

The father was acutely aware of a gap that needed explanation. Tom had not undertaken activities in 1941 of the kind Cecil Rhodes preferred. He was a full-time university student who had not participated in university sport or university life. Tom should explain that, because his father had joined the RAAF and all the male clerks in the firm had joined up, the senior remaining partner – who was unfit for service – had to manage the practice single-handed. Tom felt, therefore, he had a duty to spend his first year at university undertaking full-time work as an articled clerk. Extra-curricular activities, in the circumstances, 'seemed of minor importance'. Just the same, Tom should not minimise what he had done at university, such as participating in moots, 'as debating indicates [a] desire to express ideas and [the] ability to do so'. He could also tell the Selection Committee that he was looking forward to being fully involved in university life after the War. Understandably, the father did not mention the particular circumstances that led to his son entering university in 1941.

There was also some preliminary advice on getting to Australia in time for the interviews. Tom should apply to Overseas Headquarters at Kodak House for all necessary assistance. Captain Lester Brain, the Flying Operations Manager of Qantas, had provided the names of two senior men in the British Overseas Airways Corporation who could ensure the application reached Sydney by the due date. Finally, the family firm could handle any necessary typing.

All of Geoffrey Hughes' 'suggestions' were subject to one qualification: 'you must necessarily tell your own story and not be afraid of line shooting as you will largely be judged on the general quality not only of your record but of your outlook as shown in your own statement.' At this point, the father remembered to tell his son to include his football record with 10 Squadron adding, almost by the way, 'your courses at Oxford … would be the Honours School of Jurisprudence and Bachelor of Civil Law'.

Hughes concluded: 'Well old man that is the story and I hope you will go to it in spite of any difficulties.' He thought it 'would be wonderful to get it and no disgrace to fail'. Tom should not be deterred because other applicants might be more advanced in rank and university study, and he would have at least two more chances under the normal requirement of being under 25 years of age in the relevant year of application.

> I will not enlarge upon the advantages of success to your career or how much I would love you to have Oxford – and so would Mummy. That is all very obvious. Don't worry about it interfering with the office. I am very fit and well able to carry on and what is a year or two with such an opportunity for you. You would not lack friends in England and certainly Mummy, Nong [Constance] & I would be likely visitors at some time in the next few years!

Conscious of probable mail delays, Hughes cabled Tom with the gist of his letter. Unfortunately, the cable arrived several days after Tom had completed and forwarded his application. The candidate was under the impression that modesty and reticence were assets when applying for a Rhodes scholarship. His seven paragraphs were at times self-deprecating and certainly did not 'shoot a line'.

Tom explained that, on completing his degree, he intended to practise as a solicitor in New South Wales and become a partner in his father's firm of Hughes, Hughes & Garvin. He also planned 'to take an active part in politics' by becoming an MP and trying 'to undertake, to the best of my ability, some part in national affairs'. Should he win a Rhodes scholarship and had not completed his law degree, he would read for the Jurisprudence Final Honours School. If he had completed his LLB by the time he went to Oxford he would take Philosophy, Politics and Economics, which he felt would assist him in a political career.[10] Tom briefly outlined his War service, acknowledging that, while his work with 10 Squadron was 'on the whole, extremely interesting', his 'actual contact with the enemy was an exceedingly rare occurrence'. The 'most persistent enemy was the feeling of boredom'. At St Ignatius he had rowed, played rugger and represented the school in athletics. His particular interest was running and he hoped to make 'a come-back' after returning home. He had played rugger and squash rackets at 10 Squadron, and was 'a very indifferent, but very keen player of golf'. While he could not pursue his interests in trout fishing and skiing in the United Kingdom, he had taken up competitive sailing. Tom concluded by apologising for his 'unpolished and sketchy' effort at self-description. 'For the first fault I must plead inexperience, and for the second, lack of time.' The idea of applying for a scholarship had been with him just one day earlier, and he had to send an application immediately to meet the deadline.

When Tom received his father's cable on 8 October he prepared an amended application. He admitted that his first effort 'was rather a hurried piece of work ... I shall take more time over the statement when forwarding the second application'. The final version took up one-and-a-half typed foolscap pages (but still shorter than his father's list of instructions). 'I gave quite a lot of time to composing it, and I think it more or less satisfactory.' Father Treacy of the Catholic chaplaincy and Bish had read it, and approved. As will be explained, this second version never reached the Selection Committee.

Meanwhile, Father Hehir in Sydney wrote to 'Mr Hughes' on 10 October, probably in response to receiving a copy of the application material which Geoffrey Hughes had sent to Tom. Hehir referred to the 'extremely interesting and useful document', and said he had taken notes in case he was asked for a testimonial. 'It has convinced me that we are doing the best thing in entering Tom, both from his point of view and from that of Mr Rhodes. I mean that I think he is the type that Rhodes wanted to get, and that he would benefit by the Scholarship very much.'

On the day Father Hehir wrote his letter, Hughes sent a memorandum to Squadron Leader Pat Crennan of the Overseas Headquarters at Kodak House. He wanted to ensure that Tom's application forms and annexures were sent through service channels or via British Overseas Airways Corporation to reach Sydney in time. For his son's sake, Hughes also wanted sea or other air passages arranged should 10 Squadron not be returning to Australia in December. Hughes pointed out to Crennan, as he had to the Director of Personnel and to Wing Commander Colin Gordon of the RAAF Rehabilitation Section in Melbourne, that those who set up the conditions and timetable for the Rhodes selection process had overlooked the problems facing eligible members of the RAAF in the United Kingdom. This was an important omission because the RAAF 'should contain, on the average, a higher proportion of eligible candidates than other services'. The Prime Minister, Ben Chifley, had promised that all candidates chosen for interview would reach Australia on time. Apparently, he assumed they would be returning from operational areas north of Australia. Hughes told Crennan he was doing all he could to bring the case of RAAF crew in England under consideration but was not very hopeful. At least Wing Commander Gordon had promised he would contact Dr Behan, the Warden of Trinity College, Melbourne, and the General Secretary for Rhodes scholarships, to inform him of the problem.

Tom's first application, and his cable of 12 October, reached his father on 16 October. Not surprisingly, the return cable to Tom, sent on the same day, expressed the hope that the second statement followed all the instructions. The first one was 'insufficient'. Tom answered with another cable assuring his father that the new version was 'ample'. He sent a further one on 19 October to say he was leaving by ship on 9 November and would reach Australia early in December. His father was 'simply delighted' to receive such good news.

The delight was short-lived. Tom had tried to get on a draft leaving by sea on 25 October but realised he had little chance of success. He did have another option. Air Commodore Charles Pearce of the RAF had met Geoffrey Hughes earlier in October before leaving Australia to take a staff position in the United Kingdom. Arriving in England, he put a call through to Tom and arranged to meet him in London on Friday 19 October. Tom found him to be 'a cracker bloke … I liked him immediately'. Pearce said he would try to get Tom a seat on a Transport Command aircraft: 'it is very decent of him to try to fix it up.' After their meeting, Tom had dinner with Pearce and his wife at 'quite a good night-club kind of joint'.

So, on Friday 19 October, there appeared to be many options. The members of 10 Squadron were scheduled to join a draft due to sail on 9 November, hence the good news cable to his father. Pearce was 'looking after my interests'. The 'posting people' would signal RAAF headquarters in Melbourne to keep in touch with the Rhodes Selection Committee so that Tom could be flown home 'in a hurry' if required for an interview. A confident Tom set off for a week's leave with the Hornyold-Stricklands at Sizergh Lodge. On this visit, he assisted the family's move from the Lodge to Sizergh Castle which, to make it habitable, was 'comparable with the cleaning of the Augean stables'. The cleaning process did have its rewards. Tom came across a mural which belonged to Henry, Duke of York of the Jacobite peerage, who would have been Henry IX of England had the Stuarts retained the throne, and who eventually entered the Church and became a Cardinal.

Tom shortened his stay in the Lake District to be in Mount Batten in case a flight became available. After making enquiries, Pearce advised him to take the sea route. The Squadron was now preparing for its departure, and Tom learnt he would be in the draft to sail on the Orient liner, the *Orion*, which had been a troop carrier during the War. It was 'a very minor disappointment' that he would not be flying his own aircraft home. He would be back before Christmas which, during 'the gloom of waiting', seemed only a remote possibility.

There was a pleasant diversion before the Squadron left Mount Batten. Tom attended the wedding of a fellow officer to a WAAF officer. Following the service, the party moved to the station commander's house where Group Captain Caster mixed 'a very potent cocktail' and Mrs Caster, a 'really cracker type' whose 'ability to entertain rather reminds me of you, Mummy', produced a wedding cake which was a pre-War masterpiece in style. After a formal parade and speeches on the following day, the draft boarded a train to Brighton where Tom looked for presents. He had to apologise to his mother for failing to buy her any underwear; his coupons did not extend to women's clothing. Moving then to Southampton to board the *Orion*, Tom joined a four-berth cabin with a wide porthole, had his meals in the first class dining room and the 'old bridge team' (which included Red Burt) had access to a large and comfortable officers' lounge. 'It is very pleasant to expect the worst and find one's expectations confounded.'

The *Orion* broke down in the Bay of Biscay and had to limp back to Southampton. While the other personnel of 10 Squadron remained billeted in Nissen huts before sailing home, Tom joined Air Commodore Pearce and his wife in Woking while Kodak House tried to find him a flight to Australia. His father, meanwhile, after learning that Tom's second application had not arrived in Australia, contacted Lester Brain of Qantas to trace the source of the delay. It transpired that the papers had arrived but the Rehabilitation Section could not locate them, and never did. Geoffrey Hughes reported the problem to the Acting Secretary of the Selection Committee while passing on Tom's original personal statement. Another Hughes contact now entered the story. Squadron Leader Lex Rentoul had returned to Australia after spending five years at the British Air Ministry. He took over from Gordon at the Rehabilitation Section, and sent a handwritten note to Hughes on 9 November confirming that the material Tom sent on 11 October was missing; the system for registering incoming mail was neither 'oversound [sic] nor accurate'. Rentoul did not know that Tom was 'your boy' when he 'had a hand' in getting him into 10 Squadron. He found him to be 'a very fine type of boy' who 'is very highly regarded and has done a fine job overseas'. Rentoul concluded: 'Let me know if you think I can do anything at all for the boy. I will be only too glad to help' (emphasis in the original).

Despite the absence of the improved application, the Rhodes Selection Committee in Sydney decided to include Tom among the candidates for interview on 7 December. No doubt Sir John Peden helped, and felt sure enough of his reference to send a copy to Geoffrey Hughes. Peden had retired from teaching by the time Tom reached the university, but he supervised the annual examinations in 1941, and described Tom's paper in Constitutional Law, a Peden speciality, as 'up to First Class Honours standard and had distinct merit'. Although he had no personal contact with Tom, Peden saw that 'his bearing throughout the year was admirable, and that his personality commended itself to fellow students and members of the staff'. Peden devoted the longest paragraph to Tom's father and his grandfather; he knew both of them well and both 'have exhibited qualities and set standards of achievement which should be an inspiration to the candidate'.[11]

Assuming that Tom would be arriving on the *Orion*, the Selection Committee asked Behan to arrange with the Department of Air for him to disembark at the *Orion*'s first Australian port of call and to fly to Sydney in time for the interview at Government House. When Rentoul heard what happened to the *Orion*, he contacted Behan – 'who I know very well' – and asked him to get in touch with Air Commodore Frank Bladin, the Deputy Chief of the Air Staff, to arrange for Tom to have a flight home. The Air Member for Personnel had already sent a signal to Overseas Headquarters requesting that every endeavour be made to fly Tom out by RAF Transport Command to arrive before 7 December. When Overseas Headquarters did not reply, Rentoul reported to Hughes on 24 November that he had requested the Air Member for Personnel 'to send a hastener'. A relieved Rentoul subsequently informed Hughes that his son had been appointed a crew member of an RAF Transport Command aircraft which should arrive in Sydney two days before the interview.

Tom had to cable his father to say that a revised departure date meant he would arrive in Sydney between 10 and 12 December. Hughes asked the Acting Secretary if it was possible to change the date of the interview. He then had to approach him a second time. The plane, an Avro-York, having reached Negombo airport in Ceylon (now Sri Lanka), needed spare parts that were not immediately available because of the cancellation of the US Lend Lease plan. Tom cabled his father, who immediately contacted Lester Brain, and Brain arranged for his airline's manager at Negombo to sign Tom on as supplementary crew on the first available aircraft. Hughes told the Acting Secretary that his son would arrive in Sydney by Friday afternoon, 14 December, adding that 'I feel I have exhausted my resources and can do no more, so I must await developments as patiently as possible.'[12] The campaign manager had overseen his application, organised his transportation, and prepared him for meeting the Selection Committee. Not many candidates received – or perhaps needed – the benefit of such good connections.

Tom landed at Mascot early on the morning of 14 December, and attended an interview at Government House that afternoon. Sir Frederick Jordan, Chief Justice of the NSW Supreme Court, sat in the chair as Lieutenant Governor of New South Wales. Jordan reputedly had a Rabelaisian sense of humour, though Tom saw only his cold, daunting and seemingly unsympathetic side. Although he failed to win a scholarship, Tom heard he had come third. He also learnt that the two older men were awarded scholarships knowing they would be ineligible to apply again.[13] Both had strong records and proved worthy winners. Lloyd Stuart Williams had attended Scots College, graduated in engineering from the University of Sydney, served in the Royal Australian Naval (Volunteer) Reserve (1942-44), went to Brasenose College, won a rowing Blue and subsequently spent many years with the Commonwealth Scientific and Industrial Research Organisation at Fisherman's Bend in Victoria. William Winslow Woodward had attended Shore, graduated in medicine from the University of Sydney, and served as a Lieutenant with the AIF in an Armoured Division (1942-45). He also went to Brasenose, won a rowing Blue, rowed for England in the men's coxed four in the 1948 Olympics, became a Fellow of the Royal Australian College of Surgeons and of the Royal College of Surgeons, and finished his career as a surgeon at the East Ham Memorial Hospital, London.[14]

Although eligible, Tom did not reapply for a Rhodes scholarship. If he had gone to Oxford in 1946, embraced the university life, participated in Union debates, made regular trips to the Old Bailey, become thoroughly familiar with the Inns of Court, he might well have revised the avowals made to please the Rhodes Selection Committee. There was a very real possibility that Tom Hughes would have settled for the life of a barrister in London where he would have been, and felt, substantially at home, fulfilled and financially very well rewarded. The NSW Rhodes Scholarship Selection Committee had indirectly made an important career choice for the young man it placed third.

In 1945, what mattered for Tom was that the period between the end of the European war and his arrival in Sydney had been 'a mixture of frustration and hope … followed by disappointment'.[15]

6

'With optimism as one's guiding star'

In February 1946, Tom Hughes returned to the University of Sydney to resume his law studies. His own assessment was that he 'plodded' through the degree, without setting his mind on any branch of the law. As a busy clerk in his father's law firm, Tom did not have time to experience the vibrant politics of university life in the immediate post-War years. In common with many of his ex-service cohort, he wanted to make up for the lost years of the War by graduating as soon as possible.[1] He completed his degree at the end of 1948, finishing with second class honours, and formally graduating at the beginning of 1949. His friend, Anthony Mason, graduated with first class honours in the same year. Denys Needham, a Vice-President when Hughes became President of the NSW Bar Association in 1973, also took a first. Other contemporaries included Lionel Murphy, a future Labor Senator, an Attorney-General of the Commonwealth and a High Court judge whom Hughes represented when Murphy's judicial career was in jeopardy.

Family connections continued to assist Tom's progress. In 1945, his father nominated him for election to the Australian Club, and Tom became the third generation Hughes to savour its benefits.[2] He spent part of his final year as an Associate to Justice Owen of the NSW Supreme Court whose links with the Hughes family have already been noted. Owen later chaired the Petrov Royal Commission and would probably have been Chief Justice of New South Wales had not the Labor Party decided to ease Dr Evatt out of federal politics. Owen ended his career sitting on the High Court. Tom Hughes appeared before him in appellate courts on several occasions. In the late 1940s, the connections were also social. Owen often joined Geoffrey Hughes and Hughes' two eldest sons on trout fishing trips to Yaouk. Everyone in the party, except Tom, was a skilled trout angler, his brother being 'very adept'.[3]

Geoffrey Hughes expected his eldest son to join Hughes, Hughes & Garvin after graduation. Tom had told the Rhodes scholarship committee of his intention to do so. But the young RAAF officer, who had little to do sitting in Brighton and Whitley Bay, had found 'the nucleus of an ambition' when visiting the courts in London. Though disappointed, his father did not stand in his son's way.[4] Tom was admitted to the Bar on 11 February 1949, and his brother took his place in the family firm, there being insufficient family funds to support Tom's brother Geoffrey's ambition to go on the land.[5]

Starting out

In 1863, Roger Therry, a former judge of the NSW Supreme Court, wrote that the Sydney Bar was 'modelled, as nearly as circumstances will admit, on the practices and observances of the English Bar'.[6] Crucial to the model was a separate, independent and self-governing Bar, which oversaw practice, conduct and etiquette, and which determined who could be admitted as a barrister. In some respects, it functioned like a medieval merchant guild. As Hughes pointed out much later, 'in the uninquisitive atmosphere of the times, the Bar [in 1949] was not subjected to the intense public scrutiny to which we have become accustomed as a constant factor in our institutional existence'. Importantly, too, the Bar was 'the product of a monocultural society', with a membership 'drawn from a fairly small human reservoir'. In 1949, all save one of the 335 practising barristers at the NSW Bar were male.[7] Moreover, it was a community assembled in one location. Apart from a handful of barristers located in the inner city suburbs and one each in the Blue Mountains and Newcastle, all were accommodated in and around Phillip Street. Fifteen years after Hughes' admission, by which time the numbers exceeded 400, John Kerr QC, the future Chief Justice of New South Wales and Governor-General, observed that it was 'impossible to be anonymous or lost as a barrister among barristers. What everyone did yesterday is known today to everyone else.'[8]

Finding accommodation was a problem in 1949. Connections assisted Hughes to secure a 'perch' on the first floor of Denman Chambers, a 19th century building with a rickety staircase and an even more rickety lift. Alan Bridge, a friend of his father and later a judge, let him have a corner of his room. Hughes remained there for three or four months when he had 'a stroke of luck'. Sir Henry Manning, the last UAP State Attorney-General before the Labor landslide of 1941, had a large room on the first floor of another 19th century building, the Old Selborne Chambers. It had a secure staircase, though no lift. Manning now led those members in the Legislative Council who supported the Liberal Party that had eventually replaced the UAP after its federal election debacle in 1943. Having no need for chambers, Manning let his accommodation to Harold Nicholas, who had retired as Chief Judge in

Equity. Nicholas and Hughes' parents were friends and next-door neighbours in Rose Bay. Nicholas was about to go abroad so he arranged with Manning for Tom Hughes to occupy a room which, despite its street frontage, was dark and uninviting because the windows were covered by the thick protective gauze applied during the War.

This stroke of luck provided the young barrister with a foothold on a floor once occupied by giants and which, in 1949, accommodated some contemporary titans and likely prospects. On the eve of his admission, Geoffrey Hughes took his son to meet one of the former grandees. Tom found Sir George Rich, a High Court judge since 1913, to be a 'lively old man with a mischievous twinkle in his eye' and a liking for gossip. FR Jordan, once a Rich pupil and whom Hughes encountered at the Rhodes interview, was another former denizen of the first floor. Sir Dudley Williams, a previous tenant, had gone to the High Court in 1940. Tom recalled watching him mow the lawns on the steep slope of his nearby house in Cranbrook Road. A very conservative man, Williams 'needed some such relaxation to temper the pervasive gloom in which the socialist excesses of the day (as he saw them) enveloped his whole personality'. Martin Hardie would soon leave the floor for the Supreme Court. John Evans, another tenant, did not take his 'rightful place' on the High Court because of his early death. 'Jack' Cassidy KC also occupied rooms on the first floor and, towards the end of 1949, Tom Hughes became a sub-tenant of 'Jack' Shand KC, on the same floor. It did not help the atmosphere on the floor that the once great Cassidy-Shand friendship sundered as they opposed each other through hearings and appeals in a long-running medical negligence case that went to the Privy Council in 1947. Hughes eventually secured his own room on the first floor, vacated by a barrister who had lost a leg in the Great War and happened to be an uncle of Gordon Jaques, Hughes' friend and contemporary at Law School.

The ground floor of Old Selborne Chambers housed William 'Bill' Dovey, Gough Whitlam's father-in-law, 'a very impressive silk but not an impressive judge'. Others on the floor included one who was 'quite mad' and another who lived in 'a paper cave'. Antony Larkins ('Lark' or 'Larko') had chambers on the ground floor, opening onto a small garden. Born in 1913 and educated at Riverview, Larkins was in many respects a conservative, yet maintained an aversion to authority that led to his departure from the Law School following a disagreement with the Dean, Professor Peden. Admitted to the Bar just before the War, and declared unfit for active duties, he served with the Army Legal Corps in New Guinea, where he stamped through enemy-infested areas 'armed with nothing more lethal than a monocle, a fearsome ginger moustache and a conspicuously large walking stick'. 'Larko' mentored the young Robert Hughes to whom he seemed 'in certain respects a character straight out of Wodehouse'. His influence over Tom, and over Anthony Mason, was more profound and enduring. 'Larko' set an example of disciplined work and attention to detail – an approach Tom had observed in his father – and the new arrival at Old Selborne observed the effect in court, and in conversation, of Larkins' command of language and theatrical manner. Mason also learnt a lot from him, not so much in terms of legal knowledge and practice but about a way of life: 'to the extent I am sophisticated … I would owe a good deal to Larkins.' Some of the mentoring was very practical. When Mason was due to speak as 'Mr Junior' at a Bar Dinner, Larkins gave the anxious young barrister some good advice: confine yourself to two whiskies beforehand, and don't drink any wine. Tom's father, who disapproved of 'show-offs' and 'glory boys' in the RFC and the RAAF, never warmed to 'Larko'; he probably thought him to be all about style.[9]

The young barrister benefited from having two very different pupil masters.[10] Bruce Macfarlan, who had moved his admission to the Bar, was the first: 'a very learned lawyer of a quiet demeanour' who was 'deliberate, slow, you might say ponderous, but very thorough and a master of detail'. Kenneth Asprey replaced Macfarlan towards the end of 1949. Hughes described him to his family as 'an extraordinarily able fellow and I feel I have done well for myself in making that arrangement'. Asprey was in demand as a pupil master. Kenneth Jacobs, a future High Court judge, was Hughes' immediate predecessor, and his successors were Gordon Samuels, who became a Judge of Appeal and State Governor in New South Wales, and Anthony Mason. Asprey had a well-founded high opinion of himself. He was a performer, 'at heart an actor' who 'loved the drama of advocacy'. He was quick, flamboyant and excellent in cross-examination, with ridicule as his weapon. Against expectations, Asprey became a very good judge in later years. 'It was almost as if being a consummate actor … he was acting the part of being a judge and acting it very successfully.' Hughes' father did not immediately appreciate Asprey's good qualities. When Hughes invited his pupil master home for dinner, Asprey talked incessantly about himself.

Asprey liked to test and reward his pupils. He took Hughes as his junior into a malicious prosecution case, which the junior regarded as a compliment. Hughes expected to learn a lot, and did, from his pupil master. Importantly, the teaching took place on the job. 'One of the best features of the Bar seems to be this system of paying juniors for giving them an opportunity to learn!'[11]

The first year

Tom's parents and his sister Constance went abroad for a large part of 1949, the highlight for his father being an audience with Pope Pius XII. The two older sons were left in charge of Marsland while Robert remained in the care of his beloved Aunt Mim.[12] Tom felt responsible for keeping the travelling family abreast of home affairs. He reported assiduously in May-October on subjects ranging from the unpleasant winter, exploits on the Royal Sydney golf course and domestic and personal matters, to his law cases, setbacks for the Chifley Government in the High Court and the crippling coal miners' strike that lasted from the end of June to mid-August.[13]

No game of golf escaped comment. While Tom had a very acceptable single figure handicap, Geoffrey was close to scratch and managed to win the club championship in 1949. Tom was very proud of him. He reported that the Marsland housekeeper was evasive; he could not abide 'her perpetual obsequiousness, which was quite obviously insincere'. The coal miners' strike was affecting ordinary work and living. Life in Sydney at the end of June 'is rather like a return to the dark ages', with strict rules applying to lighting. In addition, the drastic reductions in the suburban train timetable meant that the young barrister found it difficult getting to the suburban police courts. The brothers were concerned about the possibility of burglary because so many were out of work. To save coke, they only turned on the boiler in the middle of the week.

Tom was pleased in mid-July 1949 when the Arbitration Court gaoled two of the miners' leaders for contempt of court. He was also delighted when the police raided the Communist Party headquarters at Marx House in George Street, Sydney. He felt sure that, if the miners could freely express their views, a large majority of them would favour a return to work. On 7 October he told of the 'great news' that, against general expectations, the High Court had ruled 4-2 (Dixon and McTiernan JJ dissenting) that the Government's pharmaceutical scheme was unconstitutional. Tom also commended the decision of Justice Dwyer of the NSW Supreme Court to gaol the Communist 'Lance' Sharkey for three years for telling a journalist in March 1949 that if Soviet forces arrived in Australia in pursuit of aggressors, 'Australian workers would welcome them'. Sharkey served 13 months for sedition.

Tom's interest in politics extended to moderate activism. The Liberal Party had established a Speakers' Group in its NSW Division, mainly to train prospective politicians. Tom joined it and spoke at a public meeting at Kings Cross on Sunday 12 June. Although the meeting 'went off quite well' before an audience of about 70, 'I felt nervous and I'm afraid that my performance was not very good. I prefer the cosy and intimate atmosphere of the court room to that of a public platform!'. Tom was also a willing foot soldier. In mid-October, six weeks before the election that brought the Menzies Government to power, he walked along Bundarra Road, Bellevue

Hill, checking the electoral roll. 'It is a tedious and foot wearing job, but it helps one to realise the extent of foreign infiltration in this part of the world.'

Hughes wrote at length about his cases. Early in August, he spent two days in the High Court, called in because Garfield Barwick's junior took silk halfway through the case. Barwick, the outstanding advocate of his generation, was leading for the appellants in a tax case that eventually went to the Privy Council.[14] Hughes found it 'a most interesting and instructive experience ... Barwick is a wizard – he lacks charm and as a man attracts me not at all, but he is an amazing advocate'. Over time, Hughes' professional admiration for Barwick expanded, and his personal assessment of the man grew to one of warmth and affection.

One brief took Hughes to the Gosford District Court for a collision case. The local solicitor was shocked to discover the city representatives had chosen 'a callow youth' for a barrister. Hughes was a junior in another collision case, heard in the Supreme Court, where the jury awarded just £450 to a female victim who had a permanent incapacity. He saw the result as an example of 'the vagaries of the jury system', acknowledging that he undertook the jury selection because his leader was finishing another case. 'Needless to say, I did not feel very proud of my choice.' At the end of August, although he lost a collision case, the damages amounted to just £34 and the solicitors were pleased. Tom reported this story because, when he rose to address the court, Judge Holden said he had made up his mind and counsel was wasting his time. Hughes insisted on having his say. The court reporter later complimented him for standing up to a judge notorious for arrogance and rudeness.

Hughes heard in August of a tenancy available in Denman Chambers. There were 'two snags': it was in the basement with no natural light and was very cold; and he would have to retain a sitting lessee whose politics were 'very Left'. There was an even more serious objection: 'successful men don't live in basements.' Hughes thought it wiser to stay where he was; 'it's too good a place to give up lightly'.

Tom kept a close watch on his brother Robert, and was slightly bemused by what he saw. He told Constance in May about Bob's school report from Campion Hall, the Jesuit preparatory school. Their young sibling had come second in his class and remarks on his progress were 'very laudatory – more so than in any previous report'. The messages to Constance late in August were mixed:

> Young Bob starts his holidays soon and is at present sitting for his term examinations. As usual, he approaches such problems with an air of complete disdain – he didn't know, or wasn't quite sure, what today's exams are to be! I think he has grown up quite a lot in the last few months and is really a most delightful kid.

Tom and Geoffrey took him on a flight to Canberra early in October – Bob was 'thrilled' because it was his first time in the air – and the three of them went fishing on the Gudgenby River, where Tom despatched a 4'6" brown snake. 'Bob thoroughly enjoyed the day and did some fishing, to which he applied himself with great enthusiasm.' Tom had to leave early and, against his principles, flew with the Government-owned Trans Australia Airlines.

He did have something of a social life. In one week in mid-July, Tom had dinner with a visiting English couple, attended a cocktail party on HMAS *Sydney* and joined a dinner party at Romano's fashionable Italian restaurant in the city. He told his parents about a Bench and Bar cocktail party he attended with Bruce and Barbara Macfarlan, noting that Justice Owen was the sole Supreme Court judge present. The habits of wartime remained with him. He left parties early and alone. On 14 May, he attended a 'Come in Bad Taste' party at Bellevue Hill. Some 40 young guests dressed as commanded, and the *Sunday Herald* called the event the 'most amusing party of the season'. Tom was less than impressed. 'Altogether it was just a fair party and I beat a retreat as early as was decently possible.' In a letter to Constance he mentioned that the 'dreadful woman Robin Stanton was there – ogling as hard as she could go'. He took some pleasure in the photograph published on the following day where Stanton appeared in 'rather an unbecoming pose'. Presumably he kept his opinions to himself when Miss Stanton was one of the four bridesmaids who attended Tom's bride two years later.

Early days

He may not have appreciated it at the time but Hughes joined the Bar on the eve of it becoming 'more prosperous than at any time in its history', when there was plenty of work, 'most of it lucrative'. An expanding post-war economy, a rise in population and the greater use of the motor car led to an increase in accident litigation, in landlord and tenant work and in litigation over commercial matters.[15] Inevitably, however, the returns for a new barrister in 1949 were slow and small. His first fee yielded five guineas for a brief relating to a deceased estate. Sums of between three and five guineas were common. Between mid-February and 30 June, the relevant fee book recorded a gross income of just £145-5-0. The returns picked up in the second half of 1949. In September, Tom could tell his parents that he was so busy he had knocked back briefs; it was 'for the first time in my short career and probably for the last time for some considerable period to come'. His return from the first year totalled £769-12-6. In 1950, his return was £1172-14-0; in 1951 it was £2248-0-9. Over the same three years, average annual male earnings were, respectively and in round figures, £476, £567 and £699.[16]

It helped to have the support of Hughes, Hughes & Garvin. His father and Jim Garvin briefed him, and his brother Geoffrey kept up the supply of briefs during the 1950s. Other connections contributed. Hughes established a good relationship with another firm of solicitors – Allen Allen & Hemsley – because he had met one of the litigation partners, Fred 'Fearless Fred' Millar, at university. Millar, who told a young articled clerk around 1958 that Hughes was 'an outstandingly good pleader',[17] became a conduit to Frank Packer and Australian Consolidated Press (ACP) and a valuable source of briefs in the latter part of the 1950s.

Hughes had no difficulty in observing 'an essential principle which should guide a member of the Bar in practice', namely, that as 'a cab on the rank', the barrister must accept a brief in the barrister's field of practice from anyone prepared to pay the stipulated fee.[18] He wanted work, and counted himself fortunate because, while the volume was sometimes slim and he did not have a great many opportunities as a junior, the cases he fought in the 'rough and tumble' of the Court of Petty Sessions and in the District Court proved to be a great learning experience. Most of these cases involved negligent driving and minor crime. The experience proved 'very good for cutting one's teeth as an advocate'. The District Court was an especially 'harsh school' in which he appeared against senior juniors and had his ears 'boxed' a few times. Reflecting on the modern era, he noted how barristers of ability became perennial juniors and did a lot of paperwork but had little experience of standing on their feet in court. In his career, he learnt by trial and error and had to live with his mistakes. At the same time, 'it was all good fun' and, for all the 'agonising times when work was in short supply, it was stimulating. One was living in the real sense on one's wits, such as they were, and with optimism as one's guiding star.'[19]

There were some substantial cases in the early years. Hughes was briefed as a junior to RG Reynolds QC representing Tooheys Brewery at the Royal Commission into the Liquor Industry and Allied Subjects. Geoffrey Hughes was Chairman of Tooheys at the time of his death in September 1951, which occurred soon after the Royal Commission began its hearings. It is unlikely that the son acquired the brief without the solicitors and the company considering the family connection. Hughes received at least £1695 for appearances between September 1951 and June 1952 but decided to leave the case because he did not have enough to do.

Hughes appeared many times with Jack Cassidy. Cassidy had 'a jumpy sort of mind' and was difficult to work with. He did not keep his papers in order, and would say 'Son, get me that' without explaining just what he meant by 'that'. Nevertheless, Hughes regarded Cassidy as 'a warm, loveable character', even though 'unpredictable' and 'at times a little unscrupulous'.

Cassidy was at his best fighting cases where victory seemed impossible, and he had some remarkable successes. Hughes was his junior when ACP briefed Cassidy in a libel action brought by Dr Bialoguski, better remembered for his role in the Petrov spy case. 'Jack' Smyth KC – 'a formidable character who had a mind that made a steel trap look like an inviting refuge' – represented Bialoguski. The trial lasted 10 days. On the last morning Smyth, who knew that Cassidy liked to consume half a bottle of champagne before starting an address, took up a minor point of law to occupy enough time for the champagne to lose its effect. The judge said at the end of an hour that he would adjourn for morning tea, whereupon an anguished Cassidy said audibly: 'Oh, but your Honour, that means I have taken my champagne too early.' The ill-effects were not serious. Bialoguski was awarded what Cassidy and the client considered a relatively low verdict of £1000.[20]

Hughes' first reported case was in April 1952, when he appeared on behalf of Dudley Chalmers Clift, a member of a well-known grazing family in the north-west of New South Wales. Clift was charged with stealing 470 sheep from one Bruce Walker, who happened to be known to Hughes. Hughes had not met Clift before, but members of the Clift family had attended Riverview and one was at the school in Tom's time. A jury found Clift not guilty at his trial in Quarter Sessions at Narrandera. According to legend, no Narrandera jury had ever found anyone guilty of sheep stealing. Walker, the police and the prosecutors were livid. Clift was subsequently charged with the summary offence of having in his possession 470 sheep reasonably suspected of being stolen or unlawfully obtained and of failing to explain how he came by them. A magistrate found him guilty and Clift appealed. Hughes travelled by train to Hay on a very hot day in December 1951 to represent him. He appeared in Quarter Sessions before Judge Russell Brereton, a relative by marriage. The conviction upheld, Hughes advised Clift to take his case to the Court of Criminal Appeal. William Owen was one of the three judges who accepted Hughes' argument that, having been acquitted of larceny, it was not reasonable to suspect Clift had stolen or had unlawfully obtained the sheep. As Hughes put it, a Privy Council case was 'good enough to get me home'. The Court quashed the conviction in April 1952.[21]

There was almost a sequel. Some two or three years later Clift rang the Hughes home in the middle of the night. He had been arrested for stealing a ferry at Wiseman's Ferry on the Hawkesbury River. Woken by the call, Hughes pointed out there was little he could do at that hour. He never heard from Clift again.

Hughes had a 'bumpy' relationship with Frank Packer and ACP in the 1950s. Antony Larkins, who did a lot of work for ACP, led him in an adoption case in 1955 where a war between two newspaper barons – Frank Packer and Ezra Norton – added to its intrinsic interest. Miss Joan Murray, a bus conductor, gave birth to a boy in November 1952. She put him up for adoption, and Frederick and Gloria Mace of Erima, near Gosford, happily took him. Murray changed her mind and the issue was contested in several courts with Packer financing the Maces and Norton backing Murray. In March 1955, the full High Court ruled in favour of the Maces, after deciding that Joan Murray was not a woman of sufficiently good character to bring up a child.[22] Jack Shand represented Murray, who sought special leave to appeal to the Privy Council, which decided against granting leave. Tom attended a celebratory dinner at the Larkins' family home in Hunters Hill. Packer left the dinner before them. On his way home, Tom stopped in Kings Cross for the Sunday papers. He encountered Packer who saw him buying the rival *Sun-Herald* and did not see Tom carrying the *Sunday Telegraph* under his arm. Thinking Hughes had not bought his paper, Packer excluded him from legal work for ACP for some time. The adoption saga had its own sequel: Peter Mace later returned to live with his birth mother. For Larkins, who took silk in 1955, the case propelled him into the limelight, and he stayed there.[23]

Hughes appeared before the High Court on five occasions between 1949 and 1956. Two involved an introduction to 'the mysteries of s 92' of the Australian Constitution. Hughes took another step forward with a victory on his fifth visit to the Court. A general practitioner, convicted of a summary offence for not keeping a proper register of drugs, faced disciplinary action from the NSW Board of Health. Hughes was unable to persuade the Supreme Court that a conviction for a summary offence was not a conviction for a misdemeanour for the purposes of the *Medical Practitioners Act 1938* (NSW). The High Court granted special leave to appeal. Evans QC led Hughes and, building on his junior's argument, won the appeal.[24]

A marriage, two deaths, a near-death and two arrivals

While Hughes was making his way at the Bar in the 1950s, important events occurred within the family.

In October 1950, Tom met the spirited Joanna Paget FitzGerald at a cocktail party at the Royal Sydney Golf Club. Joanna's father had enlisted in the AIF and lost an eye when kicked by a horse in Cairo. He died a broken man in 1928, the year of Joanna's birth. Her mother came from a rich family, remarried more than once, and did not keep a watchful eye over her daughter. Joanna attended Ascham School, obtained her Leaving Certificate in 1945, worked in David Jones and in Elizabeth Arden shops and enrolled in Arts at the University of Sydney. She lasted just one year, although she liked Philosophy and English, was 'enthralled', as most were, by Arthur Dale Trendall's lectures – Trendall had replaced Enoch Powell as Professor of Greek – and generally had a good time escaping a very unhappy home. Joanna eventually went into journalism, and was working on the women's page of the *Daily Mirror* when she met the 'nice looking' Tom Hughes. He saw her as 'a very good looking woman' and liked her 'very quick mind'. Tom was then aged 26. For all that war does to a man, he was inexperienced in ways Joanna was not. Though non-religious, she agreed to become a Catholic after Tom, under pressure from his father, pressured her. Unlike Margaret Vidal, whom she found rather daunting, Joanna FitzGerald simply went through the motions. Her decision pleased Tom's father; she thought him 'gorgeous – the nicest man you could ever imagine'.[25]

On 5 July 1951, Tom and Joanna married at St Canice's Church, where Geoffrey and Margaret were united in 1923. The groom chose 'Larko' as his best man. Following a reception at the Royal Sydney Golf Club, Tom and Joanna travelled to Melbourne and then to Perth for their honeymoon. They rang home from Perth on Wednesday 25 July to learn that Geoffrey Hughes was in hospital with another case of 'rotten luck'. During their stay in Perth, where Tom managed to play some golf, Red Burt and his wife threw a party for them and they held one in return.[26]

Returning to Sydney, they found that Geoffrey Hughes' 'rotten luck' had extended to a life-threatening illness. Aged 56, he died of pneumonia in Lewisham Hospital on 13 September 1951. His eldest son blames his father's early death on the Macquarie Street specialist who treated him during the War by bombarding and weakening his lungs with radiation. As his youngest son pointed out, smoking 50 cigarettes a day for at least 35 years did not help.[27]

Our Alma Mater for 1951 described Geoffrey Hughes as 'a prominent Catholic layman' and, in acknowledgement of his standing, lawyers, judges, business associates and friends filled his parish church of St Mary Magdalene, Rose Bay. Father M Scott SJ, the Headmaster of Campion Hall, celebrated the Requiem Mass and 'Mons' (Monsignor O'Regan) performed the burial rites at the Catholic section of the Waverley Cemetery. Archbishop Eris O'Brien represented Cardinal Gilroy at the Mass. Hughes' estate was valued for probate at £29,492, a solid sum but hardly evidence of great wealth; his own father, Sir Thomas Hughes, had left an estate valued at £42,752. Evidently, Margaret was worried about income. Geoffrey had received a pension for a permanent disability resulting from service in the Second World War. His widow applied for a war widow's pension, claiming her husband's death was the result of a war-caused disability. The Repatriation Board on 18 December 1951 accepted her argument, and continued paying a pension of £1-4-5 per fortnight and an additional nine shillings and twopence a fortnight for one child (Robert).[28]

Tom lost someone very important in September 1951. Geoffrey Hughes MC AFC was the man he most admired and respected. His father had provided him with a firm moral outlook, the main features of which were the primacy of family, personal integrity, a work ethic, a commitment to public service and adherence to principles. The son sought to follow his father's example but for a long time had to do without two things that sustained Geoffrey Hughes in his adult life: a deep religious faith and a happy marriage.

Margaret Hughes was 'heartbroken' by the death of her husband. At 51 she was active and energetic, yet 'it was as if a light had gone out, leaving her emotionally adrift'. Friends from Tom's later years learnt in casual conversation that he had been very close to his mother. Yet Tom still felt guilty because he had not eased the burden of her grief. Newly married, and at first living in a house in Wahroonga on the far North Shore rail line, he had not been there for her. 'In sum, I fell short in filial duty.'[29] Margaret Hughes eventually picked herself up by opening a clothing shop at Thredbo. Constance, who had followed her own dream and become an architect, designed the building.[30] Margaret Hughes contracted hepatitis at Thredbo and died on 1 October 1963, just before her eldest son won Liberal Party preselection for the federal seat of Parkes.

Tom's brother, Geoffrey, had a near-death episode in September 1957. In addition to his golfing skills, he was also a very good skier, and had been instrumental in establishing the Crackenback Ski Club in the Snowy Mountains (Tom was also involved in the operation and enjoyed many skiing holidays). When Geoffrey smacked into a tree on the slopes, he sustained a severe head injury and was rushed to Cooma Hospital. Tom was involved in a case in Wollongong. He drove overnight to Cooma and met the attending South African-born doctor who proposed to perform a lobotomy. Tom said 'No'. He contacted Sir Douglas Miller, Australia's first neurosurgeon, who was based in St Vincent's Hospital. Miller flew to Cooma and arranged for Geoffrey's transfer to Sydney for a more conservative operation. After a few trying weeks, Geoffrey recovered to lead a normal life, grateful for the exertions of a determined brother and the skills of a top neurosurgeon.[31]

The 'arrival' of Robert Hughes at the University of Sydney in 1956 was an important event for what he called 'the Family'. His brothers, standing in for their late father, represented the 'authority' that experience at Riverview taught him to fear. Robert found it was 'Larko', the lapsed Catholic, and not his brothers, who helped him deal with a subsequent loss of faith.[32] University enabled Robert to break out and eventually to break away. Andrew Reimer, the Hungarian-born literary critic, academic and author, remembered this most talented young man always talking about becoming an expatriate. Robert, with two scholarships, had enrolled in Arts, but flunked the year because of a heavy extra-curricular workload. His brothers thought he should train for a profession; he wanted to draw and be creative; and the compromise was that he should follow his sister and take architecture. His brothers paid his education expenses, though Robert never quite completed the degree. It hardly mattered. According to Reimer, Robert 'came from a patrician family (of somewhat reduced circumstances) which gave him the social confidence to continue in his chosen role as an *enfant terrible* after he left youth and Australia behind'.[33] Nevertheless, Australia, and some members of 'the Family', remained constant factors in his life.

Lucinda Mary Forrest 'Lucy' Hughes was the second important 'arrival' of the late 1950s. She was born on 30 March 1958, nearly seven years after Tom and Joanna were married. A very excited father was at work on the day of her birth. On 6 July of the following year, he wrote to his mother, then travelling in the United Kingdom and Europe. Tom and Joanna had just celebrated their eighth wedding anniversary at a lunch hosted by 'Larko' in Double Bay. Lucy 'was in attendance, in magnificent form. She is a darling kid, and I shall miss her during the next three weeks [Tom was on holiday at Crackenback]. Not walking much yet but she does take a few steps when she decides to. She is talking, or doing what she regards as such, with increasing gusto and fluency!'. The one he liked to call 'darling daughter' would occupy a special place for him in the mid and late 1970s.

Two defamation cases

Hughes appeared in two defamation cases which 'really cemented' his position in that field in New South Wales.[34] In the first, he represented ACP, its editor-in-chief, David McNicoll, and the journalist Alan Reid. ACP's *Daily Telegraph* published an article by Reid in December 1959 alleging that 'Charlie' Oliver, the State Secretary of the Australian Workers' Union (AWU), had dismissed 10 members of the union after a 'Moscow trial', and that a former AWU organiser had claimed Oliver had sacrificed members' interests in negotiating with employers. Oliver sought damages for libel.

In November 1960 in the District Court, Hughes appeared alone before Judge Aaron Levine and a jury of four. Eric Miller QC, with Lionel Murphy, represented the plaintiff. Hughes knew that the article was 'pretty defamatory'. In court, however, the defence did not admit that either all or any part of the article was defamatory; and, if it was defamatory, claimed that publication was justified on grounds of qualified privilege. Provided the defendants acted in good faith, which they did, it was 'perfectly lawful' to publish defamatory material in the course of, or for the purpose of discussion of, a subject of public interest, and provided it was for the public benefit for this discussion to take place. Throughout his cross-examination and in his summation, Hughes made it clear that the defendants did not criticise Oliver or question his reputation. Hughes, in his words, 'scraped a win'. His strongest recollection of the case was of telling the jury how, although Oliver may have been an individual suing a company, it was not a case of *David against Goliath*. Rather, in view of Oliver's AWU connection, it was a case of *Goliath against Goliath*. Hughes saw the case as 'a great victory for me at that stage of my career', and it led to further work with ACP.[35]

The second case extended over a much longer period. On 27 February 1958, the *Manly-Warringah News* published a letter signed 'Ratepayer, North Manly'. The author claimed that, 'of all the appalling decisions made by the Warringah Shire Council, surely the one which takes the bun is that to allow Cr Jones [the Mayor] to convert his Harbord garage into servants' quarters'. The Council had consistently campaigned against allowing homeless people to live in garages. Gordon Jones, of known Labor Party affiliation, sought damages from Clement Skelton, who owned the *Manly-Warringah News*, alleging he was libelled by the published letter. Skelton may have been proprietor, but another man also had an interest in the outcome of the case. Robin Askin, soon to become the Leader of the NSW Liberal Party, obtained a financial and political stake in the newspaper because he represented the seat of Collaroy that was located within the Warringah area.

Allen Allen & Hemsley briefed Hughes on 3 March 1958 and the action commenced in the District Court, only to be transferred to the Supreme Court later in the same month. Jones based his case before a judge and a jury of four on the natural meaning of the words, namely, the claim that he had exercised undue and improper influence to secure Council's agreement to a scheme contrary to its declared policy. Denying that the allegations were defamatory, the defence argued they were true in fact and in substance, were made for the public benefit, and constituted fair comment. The trial judge ruled that the words used were capable of conveying the meaning that Jones had used his position to influence his colleagues. The jury, left to decide whether the words did have that meaning, found for Jones and awarded him £500. Skelton appealed, and Merlin Loxton QC, with two juniors, represented him before the Full Court of the Supreme Court in June 1961. Hughes appeared alone. He was unable to persuade the court (Owen, Brereton and Ferguson JJ) of his argument. They ruled that the words of the letter were directed at the Council and were not capable of bearing a meaning defamatory of Jones.[36]

Jones refused to give up, but where could he seek a remedy? Hughes and Larkins, whom he consulted, believed that an application for special leave to appeal to the High Court was unlikely to succeed, because no great principle was involved. Jones, however, could appeal to the Privy Council. Even though the threshold to an appeal as of right under a 1909 Order-in-Council was £500stg, the two barristers believed that the specified sum covered local currency despite its description in sterling. Hughes applied to the Full Court of the Supreme Court for leave to appeal as of right under the 1909 Order. The Court ruled in August 1961 by two (Evatt CJ and Wallace J) to one (Ferguson J) in Hughes' favour. Skelton then went to the High Court, which ruled that it was a matter for the Privy Council to decide whether an appeal qualified under the 1909 Order. Skelton unsuccessfully petitioned the Privy Council to set aside the appeal. Hughes represented Jones and, in April 1963, the Judicial Committee of the Privy Council allowed Jones to appeal. The case was heard over six days in the following July.

Hughes, who had taken silk by this time, appeared with David Hunt, a future Supreme Court judge and an authority on defamation law. Trevor Martin appeared for the respondent.

Hughes argued that, according to their 'natural and ordinary meaning', the words used in the published letter were defamatory, and that it was wrong in law to strain or force them beyond their literal or implied meaning. The Judicial Committee agreed.[37] 'So this indefatigable litigant, Mr Jones, who was pitted against another indefatigable litigant, Mr Skelton, recovered his verdict.' *Jones v Skelton* reinforced Hughes' standing as a defamation lawyer and became a landmark case in the defamation field.[38]

Jones v Skelton also had two interesting postscripts. During the summer vacation following the Privy Council hearing, Hughes passed Skelton in a street at Terrigal. Neither spoke a word but Skelton 'threw me a glance of utter hatred, for which I cannot blame him'. Some years later, Hughes heard that Evatt, who was 'away with pixies', had a message for his fellow judges hearing the application for leave to appeal to the Privy Council: 'I want to find against Askin.' Evatt was at least aware of Askin's relationship with Skelton's paper.[39]

On taking silk

By 1962, Tom Hughes was clearly winning the respect of the Bar and of the judiciary. Solicitors were seeking him out, his fee books were crowded and he could charge 50 guineas for a court appearance and more for a brief on hearing and a conference. He moved into the new Selborne Chambers, which alongside the recently constructed Wentworth Chambers – established on the initiative of Barwick and Manning – had expanded and improved working conditions in Phillip Street. Working in his chambers on a Saturday, Hughes frequently ate meals at the Australian Club where he met Chief Justice Sir

Owen Dixon of the High Court. It was gratifying to spend time in the company of Australia's pre-eminent jurist and common law lawyer. Hughes was flattered because Dixon treated him as an equal, and he enjoyed having 'occasional social discourse' with 'a most companionable man'. Dixon, who liked to gossip, was outspoken about people whose names came up in their conversation, and talked frankly about Evatt. Hughes felt that 'if he trusted you, he opened up'.[40]

It was possible to take some time out. Tom and Joanna had a holiday in England, Paris, Madrid and Rome in mid-1962. In the early stages of pregnancy, Joanna was not fit to do much but, as Tom explained in letters to his mother, at least she could rest.[41] The couple visited Barnsley and the Rectory in Gloucestershire, travelled to Cheltenham, dined well and saw plays in London, attended an opera at Glyndebourne, and Tom listened to a Common Market debate in the House of Commons. The tourists bought antique furniture to sell in Australia. They wanted to create a sideline for Joanna and justify further trips to the United Kingdom. Anticipating 'a handsome profit' – Sydney was 'so starved at the moment for genuine old furniture' – they could store their purchases at home if the market proved slow. Most of the furniture remains, at the time of writing, unsold. In Paris, Tom and Joanna lived for a week in 'quiet comfort' and in Madrid experienced 'opulence and luxury'. After spending a day at the Museo they spent part of the next one at a bullfight. Tom went into raptures comparing the final moments to a ballet. He was back in chambers early in July.

Hughes applied for silk on 22 October 1962. The Labor Attorney-General, Reg Downing MLC, informed him on 20 December that the Governor-in-Council had approved his appointment as one of Her Majesty's Counsel, 'with rank and precedence next after Edward Gough Whitlam Esquire QC'.[42] Thomas Desmond Forrest Hughes (Tom Jnr) was born four days later. Hughes received a bundle of congratulatory letters from leading silks, members of the outer Bar, solicitors, former clients and business houses. Some mentioned both events. Justice Asprey warned that, even with his ability and experience, he would need much assistance from the 'Goddess of Fortune'. Laurence Street, the future Chief Justice, said the sole surprise was that Hughes had not previously applied for silk 'which your stature in the profession has more than justified for some time past'.[43]

7

'Right out of national security central casting'

Tom Hughes had returned to Australia in 1945 determined to oppose the Chifley Government's socialist policies. The feelings he expressed in letters home in 1944-45 intensified in response to the Government's attempts in the late 1940s to extend controls over banking, aviation and medicine. The miners' strike of 1949, and the other disruptive actions orchestrated by the Communist-controlled unions, reinforced an already strong anti-communism. Nevertheless, the avowed aim in 1944-45 of undertaking a political career looked, by the 1950s, to be indefinitely on hold. The election of the Menzies Government in 1949, and its continued re-election, blunted the sense of urgency. The drive to succeed at the Bar became all-consuming. Joanna could even say she had 'no idea Tom was politically inclined when I married him', although it probably did not occur to him to talk seriously about politics with his new wife.[1]

For many years, Tom was happy to remain a foot soldier for the Liberal cause, handing out how-to-vote cards in federal elections. His brother, Geoffrey, was more involved at the higher levels in Party affairs, serving at one stage as a member of the finance committee of the NSW Division. Tom, however, did join the Liberal Party's City of Sydney Special Branch. Formed in 1953 and initially chaired by John Maddison, later Minister for Justice (1965-76), its membership consisted mainly of business and professional men in their 30s and 40s. The Branch discussed and developed policies on current political issues in the manner of a 'think tank'. Tom contributed as a member of the Special Branch committee that, in the early 1960s, recommended structural changes in the Party organisation. The committee's proposals met the usual fate of sensible reform ideas in the NSW Division; they came to nothing.[2] Hughes stood, unsuccessfully, for the Sydney City Council as the fourth member of the Civic Reform team for Gipps Ward in 1962, and he was a vice president of the Glenmore-Waverley branch of the Liberal Party at around the same time.

Yet if the ambitions of 1944-45 seemed to have faded, Tom claimed that his decision to go into politics 'had always been latent'. In 1963, having taken silk and experienced the predicted drop in the volume of work, and 'hating inactivity', the idea of entering politics 'seemed more appealing on the spur of the moment than it might have been in other circumstances'.[3]

John Atwill, an old friend, a barrister and a company director with strong Liberal Party connections, made the first approach.[4] Hughes, Atwill and John Holt, a future member of the Legislative Council and District Court Judge, regularly played tennis on Sunday mornings at the Royal Sydney Golf Club. Over a drink after a game in the mid-winter of 1963, Atwill raised the possibility of Hughes putting his name forward for Liberal preselection for the federal seat of Parkes in Sydney's inner west.[5] Les Haylen had taken Parkes from the UAP in the Labor landslide of 1943 and held it ever since. John Carrick, the General Secretary of the NSW Division since 1947, always believed the Liberals could reclaim Parkes, which included the suburbs of Earlwood, Campsie, Canterbury, Croydon Park, Ashbury and South Dulwich Hill. Haylen had persistently frustrated Carrick's hopes, albeit often by narrow margins, except in 1961 when, assisted by the swing that almost defeated the Menzies Government, he secured an absolute majority on primary votes over his Liberal and Democratic Labor Party (DLP) opponents. Haylen carried an 8.4 per cent margin on a two-party preferred vote into the next federal election.

Carrick sensed that the overall political climate had improved, and especially in New South Wales and Queensland where the Coalition had lost 13 seats in 1961. He welcomed the prospect of running an election campaign on defence and foreign policy, namely, the defence of Malaysia against Indonesian aggression, the developing conflict in South Vietnam, the proposed purchase of the F-111, the siting of an American communications base on the North-West Cape and Labor's commitment to a nuclear-free zone in the Pacific. In Carrick's mind, defence and foreign policy issues were ideal for re-establishing 'ideological' warfare between the Coalition and Labor, believing that a sharpening of differences usually benefited the Menzies Government.

In this more favourable environment, the General Secretary felt that the Liberal Party had an outside chance of taking Parkes. He just needed a good candidate, preferably a Catholic in a seat with a sizable Catholic population. The DLP candidate in 1961, standing on an anti-communist platform, polled 9.6 per cent of the primary vote, well above the DLP's average return in the NSW seats it contested. State Aid for non-government schools might entice some Catholics to vote Liberal for the first time. After all, they would be the principal beneficiaries of the Menzies Government's commitment to capital grants for independent schools to establish facilities for teaching science. Labor, on the other hand, remained firmly opposed to State Aid. Carrick could see that, with DLP preferences and the prospect of State Aid, there might be enough in an auspicious political climate to unseat Les Haylen.

He had to move quickly because there was a distinct possibility Menzies would call an election for sometime late in 1963, a year before it was due. Whether he asked Atwill to sound out Tom Hughes, or was responding to an Atwill suggestion, his intention in visiting Hughes in Selborne Chambers was unmistakable. As Hughes put it: 'Carrick did not hesitate to disclose the reason for his approach: he was looking for a Catholic to stand as the Liberal candidate.' The prospective candidate might not be a prominent member of the faith but he was a known Catholic and did go to Mass on Sundays. So, whereas the Nationalist Party had rejected his father in 1928 in part because he was a Catholic, the rebranded liberal-conservative party sought out his son precisely because he was one.

Carrick was persuasive, and Hughes was open to persuasion. He discussed the idea with Joanna, and she agreed 'it was worth giving it a go'. There were two conditions, and Hughes was open and uncompromising about both. First, he was not prepared to move from Bellevue Hill and live in the electorate. As he would not be standing for a safe seat and might, if elected, be defeated at the next poll, he could not risk further disruption for his young family. Besides, there was no settled convention about members living in their electorates. It was sufficient for him to open an office in Parkes should he win the seat. Secondly, he intended to continue working at the Bar. He had no private means, had a large mortgage and an expanding and dependent family.[6]

Preselection

Under the system then operating in the NSW Division, branches in an electorate chose 30 selectors and the State Council and the State Executive chose 10 each. John Carrick always denied picking out a particular candidate and organising his or her preselection. At most, he acknowledged making sure there was one candidate on the ballot paper who would be a good choice and, if chosen, would not embarrass the Party. Tom Hughes was, in that sense, Carrick's candidate. There was just one obstacle: a very experienced, dedicated and popular local man intended to nominate. Bill Dowd, a Second World War veteran, had served in the Army for 18 years. He had been President of the Campsie Branch of the Liberal Party, President of the Canterbury State

Electorate Conference and, for three years, President of the Parkes Federal Electorate Conference. Dowd had also been a delegate to State Council and to the State Convention and the endorsed Liberal candidate for Parkes in 1954 and 1961. He belonged to a host of community organisations, was an active Mason, and the co-owner and editor of a local newspaper, the *Weekly Flash*.

The Parkes Federal Electorate Conference had a new President in 1963. John Howard was a 24-year-old solicitor and the first President of the NSW Young Liberals. In Hughes' words, the two men 'got on well from the very beginning'. Howard had a key role. Guided by Carrick, his mentor and patron, he set about organising support among the local Liberals. He had 'mixed success', and was aware that some local Liberals were unhappy about the President of their Conference supporting an outsider. At the same time, Carrick and Atwill worked the numbers to ensure that the State Council and the State Executive delegates were open to the suggestion that Tom Hughes was a most suitable candidate for Liberal endorsement.[7]

Candidates for preselection usually provided a written statement.[8] Hughes highlighted his schooling, war service, university studies, and advancement in the law, mentioning his three appearances before the Judicial Committee of the Privy Council and his appointment as a QC in New South Wales in 1962 and in Victoria in 1963. Acknowledging he had not taken an active interest in politics, he pointed out how he had helped at polling booths in most elections since 1946 and referred to his role in the Glenmore-Waverley branch and his unsuccessful bid for election to the Sydney City Council. Unlike many contemporary and later candidates, he did not feel impelled to report every detail of his Liberal Party activities. There was no reference to his early connections with the Speaker's Group, or to speaking at public meetings in 'tiger country' such as Leichhardt during the 1949 election, or to his membership of the City of Sydney Special Branch. But Hughes wanted to make a point about service: he long 'had the ambition of entering some form of public service, of which there is a tradition in my family'. He named his grandfather, Sir Thomas Hughes, as an example of that tradition. There was another, perhaps more telling, argument likely to appeal to Liberals in Parkes who had endured Haylen for too long:

> One of the reasons why I have decided to offer myself for Parkes, and no other electorate, is that the sitting member is, perhaps more than others in his party, the exponent of views on questions affecting the safety and welfare of Australia which are thoroughly inimical to those interests. The opportunity – if it were given to me – of removing a left-winger of his ilk from the ranks of the Federal Parliamentary Labour Party would be an exciting challenge.[9]

Two well-placed referees spoke very warmly about him. RC 'Bob' Cotton, a former Liberal State President and future Senator and minister, had known Hughes for more than eight years. Cotton regarded him as a friend, had a 'particularly high opinion of his ability and personality' and had long thought he would be an excellent representative of the Liberal Party. Fred Osborne said he was glad to hear that Hughes had nominated. A decorated naval officer in the Second World War, Osborne had held the federal seat of Evans (1949-61) and served in the Menzies ministry and was soon to become State President. Osborne regarded Hughes as 'a very able and energetic man of the highest character and ideals'. Knowing what Liberals liked to see and to hear, Osborne told them that Hughes took silk at an early stage, was part of RAF Coastal Command during the War and had risen to the rank of Flight Lieutenant; the facts themselves constituted a reference. Osborne finished with a telling endorsement:

> Through his own inclination and his family background he has a deep interest in public affairs and a sense of personal responsibility to contribute to the country's welfare. It is encouraging to know that such a man is prepared to enter politics notwithstanding the cost both financially and in loss of independence. I strongly commend his candidature.

The preselection was conducted early in the evening of 16 October, the day after Menzies called an election for 30 November and a fortnight after Tom's mother died. The venue was the Liberal Party's State headquarters in Ash Street. There were four candidates: Hughes, Dowd, CS McPhee, the Treasurer of the Canterbury State Electorate Conference, and A Alexander, an Anzac with a Bachelor of Economics degree who had worked for a lifetime in the footwear and clothing trade, was a Methodist lay preacher and had stood for Maroubra in the 1962 State election. Each candidate spoke for eight minutes and answered questions for another seven. Hughes gave 'a very careful, thoughtful speech about national security'. (It is unlikely that anyone at the meeting, including himself, could have known enough to query his statement that the decision to buy what became the F-111 strike bomber was 'carefully planned'.) As Howard pointed out, 'Tom understood the sensitivities'. Hence, he stressed his intention of opening an office in the electorate. It was a shrewd move. Voters who wanted to see Haylen had to travel to the Commonwealth Bank building in the city where a number of MPs had offices.[10]

Tom later recalled how Alexander arrived late for the meeting and probably did not help his cause by saying he had come from another preselection meeting. Howard called Alexander 'a serial nominator'. Hughes saw him as 'subjectively overcoming all his improbabilities of success by a process of supreme optimism'. Whereas, in Hughes' words, McPhee was 'a dolt', Dowd was 'a fairly formidable opponent' because of his appeal to local sentiment. After all, 'why pass up dear old Bill Dowd in favour of some exotic outsider [,] some arrogant young lawyer [,] when you could have the editor of the local or one of the local weekly newspapers, a man who knew the electorate upside down and inside out as a true blue local representative'. When the two men met before the preselection Dowd made it clear he regarded Hughes as 'an irrelevant outsider' who had come 'to cruel my pitch'. Dowd said he was confident of winning Parkes in 1963, claiming untruly that he nearly won it in 1961. Dowd told Howard and probably many others that the Party had a chance in 1963 but not with an outsider.[11]

Tom won on the first ballot with 26 votes; Dowd received 18, McPhee 6 and Alexander none. The winner appreciated he had won on the back of nearly all the 20 State Council and State Executive delegates, though he needed at least half a dozen local votes, in addition to Howard's, to secure his absolute majority.

Bill Dowd took ill soon after the preselection. On his sick bed and waiting for an operation, he wrote a letter of complaint to Carrick.[12] Dowd did not want the preselection declared invalid; it was too late for that. Nevertheless, he set his sights on Howard. He wanted Carrick to understand that the selection of local delegates, the preselection itself and the Parkes Federal Electorate Conference had contravened the Party Constitution. Dowd wanted Carrick to make a statement explaining Howard's 'unconstitutional' actions. The Presidents of Federal Electorate Conferences, and especially the one for Parkes, should 'be instructed and directed to conduct Federal Electorate Conferences in accordance with the Constitution'. Carrick asked Howard for his comments but further action seemed unnecessary when Dowd died suddenly on 28 November. He was buried, with Masonic rites, on the day of the federal election.

The campaign

When Menzies called the election, he said it would be fought principally on the issues of foreign policy and defence. The Government also intended to exploit the damaging image of the '36 faceless men' (one of whom was a woman) who kept the Labor parliamentary leadership waiting outside the Federal Conference while it determined the Party's policy towards the American communications base. Although the Liberal Party went to the polls with a number of policies in relation to education and State Aid, housing, employment and northern development, the branding of Labor as dangerously 'left' on foreign policy and defence was central to its election strategy.

Les Haylen was an easy target. Whereas in 1943 he had entered Parliament as a right-winger, by 1963 he had travelled to his own version of the Left. Haylen had written a book extolling the virtues of Communist China. He was a leading opponent of the establishment of an American communications base on the North-West Cape, had demanded the withdrawal of Australian troops from Malaysia, described the Southeast Asia Treaty Organisation as 'useless' and had lobbied Labor's Federal Conference for a commitment to create a nuclear-free zone in the Southern Hemisphere.[13]

John Howard became Hughes' campaign director for the assault on 'Left-Wing Les'. Comparative youth was not a problem. Howard already knew more about running a grass roots election campaign than the raw candidate. Growing up in Earlwood, attending school at Earlwood Primary and Canterbury Boys' High and continuing to live at home, he was 'very familiar with the electorate'. His father's petrol station was located just outside it. So, while Howard was influenced by Carrick's strategic thinking and tactical planning, he was ideally placed to introduce Hughes to the Parkes electorate and to its communities and their leaders.[14]

The Liberal Party established its electorate headquarters in William Street, Earlwood. Howard and the temporary office workers arranged helpers to distribute literature, to organise what, for the Liberals, had always been the all-important postal votes and to staff the polling booths. Every election contest has its distinctive elements. In this case, Howard could write later of 'a memorable campaign blending together an army of Tom's legal mates and wide circle of friends with a band of enthusiastic locals'.[15] In addition to John Holt, the 'legal mates' included a future Chief Justice of the NSW Supreme Court and of the High Court of Australia in Murray Gleeson and a future judge of the NSW Supreme Court and Court of Appeal in Roddy Meagher.[16] Tom's family pitched in. Joanna filled envelopes and stuffed letter boxes, Constance and Geoffrey handed out leaflets and Robert lent his drawing skills for the one-off edition of the four-page *Parkes Examiner*. Volunteers hand-delivered the *Examiner* to letter boxes throughout the electorate after its publication by ACP on 27 November, three days before the poll.

Haylen had responded to the Packer involvement by dubbing Hughes 'Packer's pea for Parkes'. There is no hard evidence that Labor won any converts with this refrain. Haylen's other approach might have attracted some voters. He depicted Hughes as another of the 'visiting political seat-hunters', the sort who hurried home to their salubrious waterside houses after 'a distressing day in the dusty Western Suburbs'.[17] The Hughes campaign inadvertently assisted this line of attack. A cleverly devised handout introduced the Liberal candidate. It asked the question, 'WHO IS TOM HUGHES?', under a silhouette of the head and shoulders of the candidate taken from behind. Opened out, there was a head and shoulders front-on photograph of him, a family portrait, a biographical statement and a summary of his beliefs and commitment to national security, and his opposition to the neutralism of 'Left-Wing Les' and 'the 36 faceless men', along with a reminder that many of the latter were 'dangerous left-wingers'. Labor saw the silhouette too tempting a target: 'Little Tommy Hughes looking back wistfully at Bellevue Hill.'[18]

The 'outsider' tag may have lost some of its impact because Hughes kept pointing out that the State Labor member for Dulwich Hill had his home in Cronulla. He thought it wise not to mention Bill McMahon, the federal Liberal member for Lowe since 1949. McMahon never for a moment thought of moving into Drummoyne, Strathfield or Concord, remaining firmly ensconced in the Eastern Suburbs. For Hughes, the critical point was the one he made at the preselection: he intended to open an office in the Parkes electorate. It was also important to convince the local Liberals that he was fighting hard to win the seat. Within a short time, the 'outsider' won them all over, except for the Dowd diehards. As Howard explained, the local Liberal activists 'quite took to Tom'. He had charm, he worked extremely hard and he brought in so many others to help. Moreover, the local Liberals did not resent the Packer connection. Howard believes that many liked the notion of their candidate being close to the Packer family. They also enjoyed the increased outside attention given to Parkes, engendering the feeling of being involved in an event of some consequence.[19]

As the campaign gathered momentum, Hughes, armed with a loudspeaker and supported by Howard, Atwill and John Holt, arrived at railway stations early in the morning to deliver his message to commuters as they waited for their trains. At other times, accompanied by his campaign director and sometimes by Eric Willis, the State MP for Earlwood, he stood on the back of a truck at street corners and at the two large shopping centres in Campsie and Canterbury to harangue passers-by and knots of onlookers. Howard told the *Weekly Flash* how 'Tom starts his daily campaigning at 6.30 am and never finishes before 10 pm. I don't know how he keeps it up, but the fact is that he does'. Hughes' other major task was door knocking. Tom thought he must have knocked on 'literally hundreds of doors'. Forty-six years later Howard commented that Hughes 'spent every spare moment knocking on doors and must, in the space of a few weeks, have canvassed thousands of his future constituents'.[20]

Observing all this activity, a Packer journalist, almost certainly Alan Reid, described the Parkes election campaign in the *Sunday Telegraph* of 10 November as 'an "old fashioned" fight'. In one corner, Haylen: 'expensively dressed … age uncertain … with a flower always in his buttonhole … [and with] a gift for slick destructive phrases'. In the other corner, Hughes: about to turn 40, 'neat, good-looking, quick-tongued, a top libel lawyer, a member of a prominent Roman Catholic family … an infighter of some capacity'. It suited Haylen, the journalist claimed, for election contests to be conducted on television, fought between leaders and played out in living rooms. Haylen could hold his left-wing views and not be held to account; 'virtually unnoticed', he could ride back into Parliament on the 'TV shoulders' of the Labor leader, Arthur Calwell. Labor had one of the weaker machines in Sydney and, lacking the resources for a local campaign, depended on members of the Waterside Workers' Federation coming to Haylen's aid at election-time. Hughes highlighted Haylen's deficiencies as a local by hitting him with a 'whistle-stop type of campaign starting at train stations in the early morning and ending after sundown on street corners with amplifiers blaring'. The veteran of the Second World War also carried a very effective weapon: Haylen was a 'neutralist' whose every statement 'must be music to the ears of Australia's potential aggressors'. As a result, supporters of a politician who 'thrived on the rough and tumble of Sydney politics' were complaining that Hughes was not fighting fairly.

Hughes' assaults on the politics of 'Left-Wing Les' became more uncompromising and colourful as the campaign reached its final week. The context was critical. On Saturday morning, 23 November and a week before polling day, a number of Liberals met at the Parkes campaign headquarters. They had just heard the terrible news of President Kennedy's assassination. No one was quite sure what to expect, though Roddy Meagher was convinced the Russians would soon be on the move.[21] Yet they quickly grasped the point: with uncertainty came opportunity. Defence and foreign policy issues seemed even more pertinent.

On the Sunday afternoon, Hughes, along with his brother Robert and his campaign director, met with Clyde Packer, the older son of Sir Frank, in the offices of the *Bulletin*. Howard and Hughes had prepared some copy for a proposed handout of the *Parkes Examiner*. Their material was, in Howard's words, 'less colourful' than the published version. Clyde Packer edited and sub-edited their copy to produce what Hughes himself described 13 years later as a 'scurrilous piece of political adventurism in journalism'. Indeed, he almost cringed at the extreme views expressed. Nevertheless, it was 'war to the knife',[22] exemplified by Robert's cartoon depicting Mao and Haylen together dancing the 'Peking Two Step', with Mao's arm wrapped around Haylen's shoulder.

The lead story in the four-page *Parkes Examiner* was headed, 'LET'S GET ON WITH THE JOB!'. Hughes attacked 'Left-Wing Les' Haylen for his 'evasive behaviour'. Haylen had refused to repeat to the electors the views he had been expressing in the previous two years 'on certain vital questions touching Australia's safety'.[23] Hughes referred specifically to Haylen's opposition to the American communications base, to the stationing of troops in Malaysia and to his support for a nuclear free zone in the Pacific. Very simply, 'Left-Wing Les' held views which 'are dangerous to our national security'. Hughes' strategy was both legitimate and well-founded. The aim was to make Haylen's ideology visible to an electorate he had represented for 20 years. By publicising Haylen's professed views and standpoints, reproduced in the crudest possible form, the Hughes campaign sought to drive a wedge between Haylen's sympathies and those of middle-of-the-road Labor and uncommitted voters. It was an approach well suited to the Liberals' national campaign strategy.

Hughes attended two major public meetings during the campaign. On 15 November, Menzies addressed one at the Ashfield Town Hall, chosen because of its central location for Parkes and the Labor-held seats of Evans and St George. Tom Hughes and the Liberal candidates for Evans (Malcolm Mackay) and St George (Len Bosman) sat behind Menzies on the platform. They were not invited to speak but, in the course of commanding the attention of a crowded hall, Menzies did manage a wave of the hand in the direction of the three candidates and called them the future members for Parkes, Evans and St George. Nine days later Tom and Joanna joined him at a private dinner party in the home of Lady (Hannah) Lloyd Jones in Woollahra. Hughes remembered one particular conversation because Menzies manifested a 'friendly respect for Arthur Calwell'. More importantly, he found Menzies' mood 'much less confident, in truth pessimistic'.[24]

Sir Garfield Barwick, the Attorney-General and Minister for External Affairs, addressed the other public meeting, held at St Phillip's Presbyterian Hall, Campsie, on the Thursday evening before the poll. The *Parkes Examiner* advertised the occasion as a 'Haylen Farewell', and mentioned that 'Left-Wing Les' would not be attending because Arthur Calwell was addressing a meeting on the same night 'to speed his departure from Parkes'. Barwick, who arrived at the meeting driving his own car, a Jaguar, spoke warmly about his former junior to an audience of 250 people. He also made the now-familiar charge that Labor's foreign policy was controlled by '36 faceless men', and spent time explaining the emerging difficulties with Indonesia over Malaysia. Hughes did get to speak at this meeting.

'I've won the election'

The *Sunday Telegraph* article of 10 November, which had noted how Hughes was causing problems for Haylen, did not venture a prediction. It did report, however, that Labor was not seriously considering losing the seat while the Liberal Party had not listed Parkes as one it was likely to win. One week before the election, a writer for the Packer-owned *Bulletin* (again, probably Alan Reid) decided that the 'Member for Peking' might still be 'odds on' to hold Parkes 'but the price had shortened dramatically'.[25] The article listed three reasons for the change: the Liberal candidate was showing 'unexpected calibre', Haylen had exhausted his credit as a right-winger and there was a groundswell in Labor ranks against the 'once-loved Haylen'. Yet on the eve of the poll, when the *Daily Telegraph* identified seven 'key seats' in New South Wales, four of which were held by the Government, it did not mention Parkes. The pro-Labor *Daily Mirror* did. Excitedly quoting some alleged general and specific findings of the 'internationally famous public opinion poll' (Ashby Research Services), the *Mirror* predicted on 29 November that Haylen would clearly win Parkes and that Calwell would be Prime Minister of Australia. Calwell was confident for himself, and for Haylen. Speaking at the rally just before the election, he described Haylen 'a greater certainty than Gatum Gatum', a strange call given that the horse, which won the 1963 Melbourne Cup, had a starting on-course price of 25-1.

Six years after the election, John Carrick reminded Hughes of his suggestion that he 'should play a martyr roll [sic] in the Parkes seat'.[26] It is highly unlikely that, for all his customary caution, Carrick was totally pessimistic. The Liberal candidate for Parkes entered the campaign thinking he had 'an outside chance'. By the end, he thought his prospects were 'reasonable'.[27] Hughes' campaign director was sceptical at the outset but thought 'things had shifted' during the campaign and felt that Hughes had 'a real good chance'. In the event, he won, and with some ease. Leading Haylen by 537 votes on the primary count, Hughes finished with a majority of 1320, a margin of 1.7 per cent, after the distribution of DLP preferences. As Menzies originally predicted, the Liberals took all three Labor seats in Sydney's inner south and west. The swing of 5.9 per cent in Parkes may have been lower than in Evans (8.5 per cent) and St George (7.9 per cent), where DLP preferences were not required to win those two seats.[28] The Liberals who attended the victory party at campaign headquarters in Earlwood did not bother about comparisons. They knew they had achieved 'the stand-out victory' of the 1963 election campaign.[29] It proved to be a long night. Lucy Hughes went into her parents' bedroom at 7.00 am on Sunday to find both of them sound asleep, something very unusual at that hour in her father's case. He sat up, said 'I've won the election', and went straight back to sleep.[30]

Tom Hughes could expect a warm welcome in the Party Room in Canberra. He had defeated a Labor frontbencher whom long-serving Liberal parliamentarians heartily disliked (many on the Labor side felt the same way), and had regained a seat Labor had held since the middle of the Second World War. Hughes could also expect to find a general sense of relief among his new colleagues. In addition to winning Parkes and St George, the Liberals had reclaimed the three NSW seats lost in 1961 and the Country Party had regained its two seats, and the Liberals had won back three in Queensland. The Menzies Government now had a majority of 22 and was secure.

Many explanations were offered at the time, and much later, to account for what Menzies called 'a very remarkable victory, particularly remarkable in New South Wales'.[31] They usually included one or more of the following factors: the Kennedy assassination, 'the 36 faceless men', defence and foreign policy issues, State Aid and the Government's proposed housing assistance program. In a measured contemporary account, Colin Hughes argued that Menzies' support for State Aid was the single most important factor in New South Wales where the average swings of 3-4 per cent in country seats and 6-7 per cent in Sydney were not replicated elsewhere.[32] The Labor Party's Federal Executive had delivered a fatal blow by refusing to sanction a move by the NSW State Labor Government to introduce a very modest form of assistance to non-government schools.

Les Haylen, as ever, was not lost for words. On election night, at what became a wake in the Canterbury Municipal Chambers, Haylen said he was 'astounded' by the swing in New South Wales. He attributed his own defeat to Sir Frank Packer's *Daily Telegraph*, the DLP, and the campaign waged against him by 'Mr Hughes'. Asked what he thought of his opponent, he replied: 'I don't like him. He's a little Wentworth.'[33] There was also a reflective moment: 'I am a radical Labor man and there is just no place for a radical in a swing.' One week after the election, he ranged widely in a commissioned article for the *Sunday Mirror.* As he would often do, Haylen pointed out how the swing against him was one of the lowest in the State, despite the intervention of the *Daily Telegraph*, 'a virulent smear campaign', and the ignorance of youth 'bloated on soda-pop, exhausted by the stomp' and 'whose transistors never gave them a breath of Labor policy or ideals'. Tom Hughes and the Liberals had not beaten him; 'frightened Laborites' were 'caught up in the beer and bandit age'. Labor had become 'conformist' and 'respectable'. Haylen said it could start winning elections again by becoming 'the dissident voice … the raspberry on the outskirts of the cheering mob!'.[34]

Hughes sensibly left Haylen to his demons, invective and crude sociological analysis, though he did respond to accusations of being involved in a smear campaign. On the day after the election, he reminded journalists that 'Mr Haylen called me a silvertail from Bellevue Hill and a little Billy Wentworth'. He added: 'While we attacked Labor policies and not the man, they attacked me personally rather than my policies.' To underline the difference he went on to say that for all their disagreements over policy, he could not overlook the fact that Haylen had given his political life to a cause in which he believed.[35] On 10 December, Hughes expanded upon these points at the declaration of the poll at the Commonwealth Electoral Office in Campsie. He explained that to 'smear' an opponent meant to attack the personal qualities of a man standing for elected office with the intention of securing his defeat: 'I have not been guilty of that.' He admired Haylen as a man who had served Parkes ably and with devotion over 20 years. He just disagreed with his policies and attitudes, and feared Haylen's return to the lists in three years. The DLP candidate, not Hughes, was responsible for the acrimony at the declaration of the poll. He riled an already angry Haylen with his comment that while he and Hughes had 'provided the axe', the book on China 'provided the chopping block'. After congratulating 'the new member', Haylen called the DLP and not the Liberal Party 'the inveterate enemy'.[36]

In his 1969 autobiography, Haylen identified the Kennedy assassination as the major reason for Labor's and his own defeat in 1963. Shortly before his death in 1977, he claimed that the Liberals brought the best lawyer in Australia to beat him and maintained, wrongly, that the margin was just 114 votes.[37] Writing down his thoughts after leaving politics, Hughes emphasised the role of the Government's commitment to State Aid for independent schools, a view shared by John Howard.[38] Hughes could now be more open about the campaign waged against 'Left-Wing Les'. Haylen had 'concentrated on becoming a sort of national exemplar of the left wing of the Labor Party to the exclusion of the dull dreary round of performing electoral duties'. The Liberal campaign set out, 'quite mercilessly', to exploit this perceived weakness of Haylen being out of touch with the electorate and not ready to fight a hard campaign. The campaign went after him with 'unerring accuracy and political brutality' over his attachment to Mainland China: 'what a ball we had with him.' In the end, Haylen 'was overcome by crude, rude and thoroughly aggressive and I venture now to think obnoxious propaganda'. Whether this 'obnoxious propaganda' was critical in determining the result in Parkes, Hughes had, by fighting Haylen as he did, firmly aligned himself with the Cold War warriors in the Liberal Party. Or, as Howard later put it, in 1963 he was 'right out of national security central casting'.[39]

8

'I felt as if I was walking a tight-rope'

Tom Hughes attended his first meeting of the Liberal Party Room on Thursday 12 December. Peter Howson, the Deputy Whip, who had hoped for a ministry, cast his eye around the newcomers. He thought that Hughes and Wylie Gibbs, the brother of Harry Gibbs whom Tom, as Attorney-General, later recommended for the High Court, 'look the best at first impressions'. Promoted to Chief Whip, Howson interviewed Hughes just before the opening of the 25th Parliament in 1964. He decided that 'Tom seems ready to take advice'.[1] Hughes worked out that it was unwise to trespass upon what little kindness Howson could offer. The Chief Whip reminded him of a school prefect and he came to think of Howson as 'a jumped-up shop assistant'.[2] Seven years later, Howson was a prominent member of the 'cave' that brought Gorton down, an event which led to Hughes being sacked as Attorney-General.

On the morning of 25 February 1964, Tom Hughes made and subscribed the oath of allegiance and took his seat at the back of the more crowded Government benches in the House of Representatives. Later that day he sat in the Senate to hear Viscount De L'lsle, the Governor-General, dressed in the full plumage of his office – the last Governor-General to do so – deliver his speech. Nearly one-third of it was devoted to foreign affairs and defence, which had become Hughes' principal interest, and the rest outlined a legislative program covering communications, education, housing, industry, northern development and trade. An earlier event overshadowed a day of splendid ceremony. On 10 February, HMAS *Voyager* sank with the loss of 82 lives after a collision with the aircraft carrier, HMAS *Melbourne*. For Hughes, however, there was one highlight of the first day, with Menzies' brief remark: 'My boy, you have a future here.'[3] Not that Hughes had any illusions about his prospects. There were many in the Party Room who were queuing for promotion, and he had the disadvantage of holding a marginal seat, which a minister could not manage with the thoroughness of a backbencher.

The new member for Parkes delivered his maiden speech on 3 March at the prime time of 8.00 pm, immediately after the dinner break. The occasion was the debate on the Address-in-Reply. Arthur Calwell was due to speak next so that Hughes was doubly assured of a crowded House.

Unlike maiden speeches of the modern era, he did not begin by expressing gratitude to anyone and everyone who helped him win his seat. Nor did he deliver the now customary glowing commentary on his electorate or a statement of personal philosophy and world-view. Rather, he took up themes from his campaign, while moderating the rhetoric. He began: 'I propose to talk tonight about the threat to our freedom and to our survival as a free country.'[4] The threat was not immediate in the physical sense but present in the declared aim of 'militant revolutionary Chinese communism' which proclaimed 'that world revolution must be gained by military struggle'. The threat had 'two rows of teeth': China's development of nuclear weapons and an 'insidious form of warfare', as practised by internal guerrilla movements. Hitherto, Australians tended to ignore the Chinese threat because their upbringing had persuaded them not to bother about foreign policy. Before 1939, everything was in the safe hands of the Mother Country and, after the Second World War, the colonial powers had re-asserted their positions in South-East Asia. By then, militant communism had attached itself to emergent nationalism. Following the defeat of French colonialism at Dien Bien Phu in 1954, 'the dagger' in the form of North Vietnam was pointed directly 'at the heart of South-East Asia, and therefore at us'. Should South Vietnam fall, then Malaysia would be in danger from the north and 'we may stand next in line'.

Hughes argued that the current Australian Government was aware of the danger and had acted to meet it. The result of the recent election indicated a growing recognition among the Australian people of the importance of foreign policy. They had before them two broad alternatives: either to support the Government's commitment to the American alliance, or to adopt Labor's policies such as the nuclear-free zone which, if implemented, would weaken that alliance. The electorate chose to support policies that were 'clearly calculated and designed to keep the alliance strong and durable'. Labor should now accept the verdict and publicly embrace the policies acceptable to the electorate. 'As I see the position, no harm would be done to true Australian Labour Party principles if the Opposition could commit this act of statesmanship and join us on this side of the House in a unified approach to foreign affairs.' He cited the example of John Curtin embracing full cooperation with the United States during the Second World War. He referred to Dr Evatt who, as Minister for External Affairs, asserted that a principal aim of foreign policy was to create zones of security in this part of the world. Hughes concluded by quoting words spoken about 2000 years ago by a person 'much wiser than any of us': 'And if a house be divided against itself, that house cannot stand.'

From a later vantage point, Hughes' speech appears slightly naïve. Once the Menzies Government re-introduced national service at the end of 1964, and in May 1965 committed ground troops to the defence of South Vietnam, there was no possibility of Labor embracing a unified foreign and defence policy. In 1963, however, in the wake of the election result, of the limited commitment of a training unit in South Vietnam and of the existing defence arrangements with Malaysia, there were some grounds for thinking that a substantial degree of unity might just be possible.

The speech received little acknowledgement in the House. The English-born Robert Lindsay (Liberal, Flinders) coupled Hughes with Malcolm Mackay and spoke of 'two of the best maiden speeches that we have heard for some time'. He liked them because they were 'constructive and very much Australian in content'. Sir Wilfrid Kent Hughes frequently criticised the Government for failings or ignorance in defence and foreign policy and mostly walked alone as a malcontent on the backbenches. He said that Hughes was 'a great improvement on his predecessor', liked his comment that hope alone is not a sound basis for a foreign policy and disagreed only on insisting that the Chinese threat was imminent. Later that day, Labor's Fred Daly told Hughes he had forgotten to mention the Queen in his maiden speech, had committed 'a major error' in failing to praise his Prime Minister and did not even thank the people of Parkes 'who, temporarily at least, were silly enough to send him here'. Next day Daly quoted the late President Kennedy – 'We want neither the fanatic nor the faint-hearted' – and decided that Hughes exhibited both qualities. It is unlikely that Labor's court jester troubled the new member.[5]

The new member for Parkes had things to learn. Four Liberals voted against the motion to expel Wentworth from the Chamber after the Speaker named him for defying the Chair. Hughes was one of 10 other Liberals who abstained. Although he managed to avoid a wigging from the Chief Whip, John McEwen, the Leader of the Country Party (CP), later told Hughes and some of the others that it was very important to back the Government's choice of Speaker.[6] Tom Hughes never broke ranks again.

Attacks on Labor's Left

In September 1965, Brian Johns wrote an article about Tom Hughes for Sir Frank Packer's *Bulletin*. Hughes, he claimed, arrived in Canberra with a reputation that ensured he would face 'quick and bitter tests in Parliament'.

Comparatively young at 40, a QC, Les Haylen's nemesis, an Eastern Suburbs background and 'tall, pin-striped, groomed and full of social confidence': he was a perfect target for cutting down to size. Hughes knew it too. 'I felt as if I was walking a tight-rope.'[7]

Few seemed to notice that he entered debates on the law relating to compensation for Commonwealth employees, on State Aid for independent schools and trade practices legislation. In April 1964, he was quick to defend the appointment of Barwick as Chief Justice of the High Court, calling him 'a great Australian' who was 'admirably qualified'. He was equally quick to rebuke the Labor frontbencher, Allan Fraser, for his 'filthy remark' suggesting that the member for Parkes expected to do well in appearances before the High Court.[8]

In his first year in Parliament, Hughes' reputation in Canberra was of a hard-hitting anti-communist ever ready to bait and vilify Labor's Left and to claim it controlled or influenced Labor policies. In late March 1964, he defended the Government's refusal to recognise Communist China on the ground of Peking's refusal to accept the separate existence of Formosa as Nationalist China (Taiwan). Hughes noted the approach taken at Labor's Federal Conference in Perth in 1961 over a motion calling for the recognition of China. The resolution included a nebulous sentence suggesting there should be 'a sympathetic and informed attitude' towards Formosa. Hughes observed that the Conference rejected an amendment moved by a right-wing delegate from New South Wales affirming that Formosa was an independent state. He also recalled that when Calwell spoke during the election about recognising mainland China, he acknowledged the need for proper protection for the people of Formosa. Hughes queried whether Calwell was being genuinely independent of the Federal Conference or was engaging in a political hoax in order to win votes.[9]

In the latter part of 1964, Hughes attacked what he saw as the Left's refusal to give full support to Malaysia in the face of Indonesian aggression. On Vietnam, he was disgusted when Dr Jim Cairns, the notional leader of the Left, spoke of American aggression in the Gulf of Tonkin following an alleged incident involving two North Vietnamese patrol boats. He was especially critical of Labor's 'failure' to recognise that the Viet Cong in South Vietnam was dominated and supplied by North Vietnam, and that North Vietnam was supported and supplied by Communist China. Hughes identified Labor positions on foreign affairs as 'the emanation of the politically lunatic far left wing of a once great party'. He liked to single out Cairns as the centre of the 'little coterie of left wingers' who sought to drive a wedge between Australia and the United States. Labor speakers sometimes reacted angrily to Hughes speeches. An agitated Bill Hayden described one of them 'as characterised by conceit, arrogance and political dishonesty'. The more common refrain was to mock his growing status in the law. Cairns referred sarcastically to the presence in the House of a 'Queen's Counsel', and to his 'high standing' in the profession, saying it was no wonder the gaols were full when this advocate 'with forethought and consideration' had so distorted the arguments of his political opponents.[10]

Hughes' assaults backfired badly on 1 October 1964. Just after 11.00 pm, he set out in the adjournment debate to 'expose' Clyde Cameron, an Opposition frontbencher and former AWU warhorse from South Australia.[11]

On the previous day, Cameron referred to a recently published article by Tom Dougherty, the General Secretary of the AWU, with whom Cameron had been feuding for years. Dougherty had castigated Cameron for a letter written on 19 March 1963 to Jim Doyle, a known Communist, beginning with the words 'Dear Jim'. Dougherty, according to Cameron, wanted to create the impression that Cameron was being disloyal to the Labor Party and was therefore unfit to represent it in Parliament. Hughes took a copy of the letter into the House. He said he had never met or made contact with Dougherty, and the salutation 'Dear Jim' did not bother him. Instead, he stressed the importance of the date – 19 March – the day after the Federal Conference of the '36 faceless men' had begun to discuss the proposed American communications base on the North-West Cape. In the letter, Cameron said that Doyle had probably seen the decision of the State Council directing the six South Australian delegates to vote in favour of the base under certain conditions and, in doing so, had rejected Cameron's view. Hughes wanted to know why a Labor frontbencher, and someone of considerable power within South Australian Labor, should write to a Communist 'in terms of complaint and disapprobation' about a confidential decision by Labor's governing body in South Australia. Cameron had infringed 'a fundamental principle' of the Labor Party, namely, that any criticisms of the Party should be made within the Party's forums. Suggesting that disciplinary action might be the Party's response to this act of disloyalty, Hughes threw out a challenge: 'Let us hear from the honourable member for Hindmarsh.'

The member of Hindmarsh responded immediately, and with a mixture of glee and passion. He expected more from Sir Frank Packer's legal counsel, 'Packer's puppet from Parkes', who had so 'jumbled his brief'. The State Council's decision was not confidential. The relevant meeting was open to the press, which gave a full account of the decision to instruct the delegates to vote in a particular way. '[T]his wonderfully secret and confidential information that I allegedly gave to a Communist had been published in Australia some three or four weeks before the conference took place.' As for disloyalty, Cameron supported his State Council's decision at the Federal Conference, even though he disagreed with it: 'I have never voted against a decision of my party and … never will.'

Tom Hughes had been humiliated and there were murmurs of disapproval from his own side of politics.[12] He realised he needed to engage in the level of preparation that preceded his court appearances. As for Cameron, he had so enjoyed himself he felt no lasting enmity. The two men developed a respectful and civilised relationship, boosted by Hughes' helpful approach, when Attorney-General, over the public order legislation in which Cameron had an interest. In his later account, Cameron embellished the story or allowed his memory to play tricks. He claimed that in his reply to Hughes he spoke about his 20-year friendship with Doyle (he did not), and said that Hughes had sought to make something of Cameron beginning the letter with 'Dear Jim' (Hughes expressly did not do so). Yet Cameron was right on one score: 'Tom was thoroughly debunked, and knew it!' Cameron claimed that when Hughes was 'the leader of the Australian Bar' he frequently referred to my reply as 'the greatest bath' he had ever received.[13]

Unbowed, Hughes continued in 1965 to upbraid the Left. On 8 April, he joined an adjournment debate initiated by Gough Whitlam following a speech by President Johnson declaring that the United States remained ready for unconditional discussions for a peaceful settlement in Vietnam. Whitlam and Cairns joined forces to highlight what they claimed was a contrast between the American position and Menzies' outright opposition to any negotiations. Hughes focused, once again, on Cairns, accusing him of perverting ordinary language, of misrepresenting Johnson in order to make a cheap political point and of trying to drive a wedge between Australia and the United States. As Paul Hasluck, the Minister for External Affairs, had done, he explained that Johnson's reference to unconditional discussions was in fact a rejection of North Vietnam's pre-condition that the United States must withdraw from South Vietnam before talks could begin. He analysed Johnson's words in such a manner that Cairns felt bound to interject: 'Is your legal training helping you now?'[14]

Reserve Price Scheme

In 1965, Hughes became the most outspoken backbench critic of a scheme that had official government support and the very strong backing of the Country Party and of major figures in the Australian wool industry. In the process, he demonstrated that, for all the predictability of his attacks on the Left he was also, as Brian Johns had portrayed him, an 'unpredictable Liberal' or, more accurately, he was true to the strand of liberalism associated with the free market.

In July 1964, the Australian Wool Board sent a recommendation to the Government and to the Australian Wool Industry Conference, the 'parliament' of the industry, for the introduction of a reserve price scheme (RPS) within the prevailing auction system. In essence, the scheme involved fixing a minimum level below which prices at auction would not be allowed to fall. A statutory authority would purchase any wool where commercial bids failed to equal or better the reserve price. Thus acquired, wool would be stored and re-sold when prices recovered. Advocates of the RPS believed it would bring a measure of stability to the price of wool and to grower incomes and provide some protection to growers from short-term fluctuations in the market.

A large majority of Australian woolgrowers rejected a similar scheme in 1951 after the Menzies Government had negotiated a reserve price plan with the British, New Zealand and South African Governments. The 1964 proposal differed mainly by not involving any international arrangements, and by levying woolgrowers to raise £20 million (later raised to £30 million) of the funds needed to finance wool purchases. Reserve Bank loans of up to £50 million, guaranteed by the Commonwealth Government, would provide the rest.[15] Sir William Gunn, the formidable Chairman of the Wool Board, was the driving force behind the scheme, battering opponents with what he regarded as unanswerable arguments. In June 1965, the Wool Industry Conference voted 45-5 in favour of the RPS, thereby lessening fears about holding another referendum.

Officials in Treasury and in other departments noted that price stabilisation and orderly marketing schemes had fared badly in Australia and elsewhere. A reserve price set too high might lead to the accumulation of large stocks resulting in buyers holding back in anticipation of cheaper prices and in wool users switching to substitute fibres. The Graziers Associations of New South Wales and Victoria, and the NSW-based Committee for the Retention and Improvement of the Free Wool Market, rejected the entire scheme as unworkable and dangerously socialist. George Le Couteur, a wool broker, an economist and the General Manager of the Australian Mercantile Land & Finance Company, one of the three wool broking companies that opposed the RPS, emerged as one of its most effective opponents.

There was a link between Le Couteur and Tom Hughes, because their fathers had been friends, and Le Couteur sought to enlist the member for Parkes in his campaign. Hughes needed little persuasion. He may not have been a woolgrower in 1965, but he was instinctively opposed to the agrarian socialism practised by the CP. From April 1965, Hughes used Question Time to extract more information and to draw attention to some of the questionable actions and secretiveness of the Wool Board. He insisted there had been insufficient research and an insufficient supply of information. Hughes' persistent questioning clearly ruffled the CP's Charles Adermann, a peanut farmer from Queensland and the Minister for Primary Industry since 1958.

Menzies became aware of Hughes' interest in the subject. He knew that, with the encouragement of Sir Frank Packer, Hughes had approached the Attorney-General, Billy Snedden, to grant a woolgrower a fiat to allow him to test the validity of parts of the *Wool Industry Act 1962*. Snedden refused to act, Menzies asked him to change his mind, Snedden threatened to resign and the Prime Minister retreated. One night before the winter break, Menzies invited Hughes to his office for a friendly chat. Expressing some 'disquiet' about Snedden's performance as Attorney-General, he asked Hughes a number of questions about the law and about what he had been doing as a lawyer. Menzies also sought his views on whether woolgrowers should have the opportunity to express their views on the RPS. Hughes told Menzies that a referendum 'would be most appropriate'. The Prime Minister was already moving in that direction and Hughes believes that Menzies overrode any remaining opposition.[16]

On 18 August, Adermann introduced legislation authorising a compulsory referendum of woolgrowers, requiring a simple majority one way or the other and rejecting any weighted votes for the larger holdings. In the following week, Hughes pressed Adermann to release the original Wool Marketing Committee report, knowing that a minority on the committee did not agree with some of the recommendations. Gunn had said that the Wool Industry Conference could have a copy should it want one, and Hughes asked in an adjournment debate on 25 August if MPs might also have access. Malcolm Fraser, a woolgrower who supported the RPS, indirectly answered Hughes by saying there was already a lot of information available, sufficient for woolgrowers to make up their minds. Fraser also criticised opponents of the RPS for failing to offer alternative solutions to the industry's problems, conveniently ignoring the fact that the opponents, like Tom Hughes, regarded the auction system and the free market as the best approach.[17]

As two sides of the argument began forming into blocs, some 10 backbench Liberal MPs spoke out against the scheme. Gunn observed that all of them represented Sydney or Brisbane electorates and had no direct involvement in the wool industry. Sir William let fly at a press conference in Canberra on 8 September. He named them, in order, starting with Hughes, Gibbs and Wentworth. These 'backbench fools', he said, were using the wool industry 'as a political football for their own political gain'. Gunn did not specify the supposed 'political gain' but pressed on: these city types did not represent the interests of woolgrowers, and were causing confusion and bitterness.[18]

On 14 September, Hughes presented a petition praying that the Australian Wool Board be restrained from spending large portions of its funds putting its case for an RPS, and that Parliament did not pass legislation allowing a referendum until an independent and impartial committee of inquiry had investigated and reported.[19] Adermann, on the same day, announced that the Government had decided to invite organisations to make statements of not more than 2000 words supporting or opposing the scheme, which would be printed at government expense and sent to every grower who was entitled to vote. The 'Yes' case was to be prepared by the Executive of the Australian Wool Conference with the assistance of the Wool Board, while several grower bodies and three wool brokers would be invited to present the 'No' case.

Parliament debated the referendum legislation on the same day. Reg Pollard, Labor's shadow minister for Primary Industry, hoped that Australian woolgrowers would stand united against the purchasers of wool like Le Couteur who were spending millions to defeat the RPS. Fraser spoke immediately after Pollard. He felt that, as a grower, he had a duty beyond simply casting his vote; he should tell Parliament why he was going to vote 'Yes'. His central argument was that price fluctuations were hurting the industry because manufacturers were turning towards the more stable synthetics market. Fraser saw no inconsistency between supporting an intrusive RPS while arguing that industry needed to have a government in power that opposed interference in the 'domestic affairs of industry'. He made it clear where he stood as a democrat. A presumed minority had the right to be heard but not an equal right; the weight of argument in the literature should be given to the major bodies of the industry that rejected the minority view. Fraser also wanted the affiliations of the minority made known; for example, one of three broking firms had an all-English board.

Hughes welcomed the decision to allow the cases to go out with the ballot papers and to ensure that all the enfranchised woolgrowers would know of their entitlement to vote. He pressed again for the public release of the 12-month-old report of the Wool Marketing Committee. He wondered whether the report might disclose some disagreement. Gunn had said it was not convenient or proper to do so because of assurances of confidentiality given to the two non-Wool Board members of the committee. Hughes said, 'I do not admit the right of the Australian Wool Board to create self-imposed rules against the admission to the public view of documents that cannot but be of tremendous public interest'. Hughes wanted to know if the members of the Wool Marketing Committee had been asked if they wished to lift the veil of confidentiality. This comment led to the following exchange:

> Mr Malcolm Fraser: – They were asked.
>
> Mr Hughes: – Even if they have been asked –
>
> Mr Malcolm Fraser: – They were asked.
>
> Mr Hughes: – The honourable member for Wannon seems to be determined to interject. I listened to him in silence this afternoon and I thought he might have shown me the same consideration. He is … in point of fact out of his depth.

Unlike Fraser, Hughes chose to raise issues rather than express 'a concluded view'. He focused on the risk of setting a price too high or too low, and returned to a theme he had hammered since April: the absence of full and accurate information. Without it, growers might not reach 'the proper result'. Worse, he implied they might not be able to see through the inconsistencies, ambiguities and inaccuracies of the Wool Board's approach.[20]

Although there was palpable tension in the parliamentary debate, one observer felt that arguments within the wool industry were conducted 'with a ferocity not commonly … found in parliamentary proceedings'.[21] In the event, the 'No' case won by 7847 votes in a poll of 110,619 growers. The growers in just two States – New South Wales and South Australia – voted against the RPS but the majorities there were overwhelming. What Fraser had dismissed as a small minority of questionable affiliations actually had the numbers. Gunn did not take well to defeat and, far from going away, the advocates for a reserve price continued a campaign that eventually succeeded in 1971. Tom Hughes, committed as ever to the free market, became deeply involved in the demise of the scheme 20 years later.

The life of backbencher and a barrister

Tom Hughes assiduously observed his constituency duties. He sat in his electoral office in Campsie on Friday afternoons and Saturday mornings and attended meetings and social events in or near the electorate. He felt no difficulty about relating to the people of Parkes. Like all MPs, he encountered problems he could not solve. An early visitor complained about a noisy horse in her neighbour's backyard. When Hughes pointed out it would be more appropriate to take the matter to her local alderman, the woman explained she came to see him 'because you're a QC and that means qualified solicitor'.[22] Fortunately, Parkes was an easy electorate to manage. Hughes' Campsie office was the geographical centre of its seven square miles and the local member could easily cover the entire area in a day. John Howard, abroad for the first 18 months of Hughes' first term, knew him to be a 'very conscientious' local member. He never heard any complaints, and local mayors spoke well of what he had done. Howard also noted, however, that Joanna Hughes rarely appeared in the electorate. It may not have been simply a lack of interest in politics. In her view, 'if you want to find one of the most boring places on earth, try Earlwood'.[23]

The Hughes family moved briefly to Wickham Crescent, Red Hill, in the Australian Capital Territory, where Anthony Mason, the Commonwealth Solicitor-General, was a neighbour. More room was needed in Bellevue Hill – Michael Seamus Forrest Hughes was born on 23 February 1965 – and Constance was retained to design an extra storey. Hughes, meanwhile, continued to collect briefs. During parliamentary sittings, and after the House had risen on a Thursday, he would be at Yass station early on the Friday morning to pick up the Melbourne train for Sydney.[24] Winton Turnbull, the CP member for Mallee (1946-72), might have prided himself on never missing a day's sitting in over 26 years in the House, but his only other career was to tend the parish-pump. The *Australian* on 22 November 1966 recorded that Tom Hughes was just one of seven MPs who had attended all 196 sitting days of the 25th Parliament.

As expected, the volume of work at the Bar either began to fall away or did not rise sufficiently to his liking. In 1963, Hughes grossed just under $25,000 from his practice as a barrister. In the following year, he grossed $21,600 to add to a basic parliamentary salary of $5500, an electorate allowance of $1700 as well as sitting fees, an allowance to employ a secretary/typist, and a furnished electorate office. His income from the Bar fell away in 1965 to $7500 but jumped in 1966 to $14,000, while the basic parliamentary salary had risen to $7000 and his electorate allowance to $2200. Hughes felt sufficiently concerned to ask Carrick to approach Robin Askin, the NSW Liberal Premier since May 1965, to persuade the Government Insurance Office to include his name on its list of counsel.[25]

Hughes had one case that attracted the attention of the literary world. Hal Porter's *The Watcher from the Cast-Iron Balcony*, an autobiographical work covering his early life in the Melbourne suburb of Kensington and the East Gippsland town of Bairnsdale, was published in 1963.[26] A reviewer, Ronald Broinowski, in the Hobart *Mercury*, referred to an earlier Porter interview where the author spoke of the possibility of the book being banned. The reviewer took Porter's comment a step too far by referring to 'those "Anglo-Saxon words" on which Mr Porter based his hopes of being banned'. He also spoke of Porter's 'wailings of a lost soul'. On legal advice, Porter sued the *Mercury* for three imputations: he had inserted the Anglo-Saxon words, not out of literary necessity, but to promote publicity by attracting the attention of the censor; he had boasted that the book would be banned with the object of gaining notoriety and thereby improving sales; and 'he is a worthless character as a man'. Roger Jennings, a future Solicitor-General of Tasmania (1968-84), acted for Porter before Hughes was brought into the case on 19 November 1964. Senator Reg Wright, a Liberal Party colleague who had never taken silk and made a habit of crossing the floor, represented the *Mercury*.

The four-day hearing started on Monday 30 November. The two leading Tasmanian papers – the *Mercury* and the *Launceston Examiner* – gave the case considerable prominence. Whereas the former referred to Porter as 'a Victorian author' and provided more space for Wright, the latter called him 'an Australian author' and highlighted the Hughes cross-examination and final speech. Wright defended the *Mercury* by claiming that the published statements were either true or amounted to fair comment and were published in good faith. Hughes argued that newspapers that conducted smear campaigns against people with reputations should 'pay through their pockets'. He argued that the imputations made against Porter were as serious as those directed at Harry Hopman, the famous Australian tennis coach and known opponent of the professional game, who won £20,000 in damages from Mirror Newspapers Ltd for claiming he was paid to coach in South Africa (the case was settled on undisclosed terms after an appeal).[27] Hughes further claimed that the arrogant and careless conduct of the *Mercury* before the trial had aggravated the damages, and for good measure listed examples of dishonest reporting of the trial itself and of calculated misrepresentation of Porter's book in presenting its defence. The defence had presented Porter as a pornographer. Hughes responded: 'Even in staid Victorian England the book's beautiful prose would have been accepted.'[28]

Neasey J found the imputations made against Porter as a writer 'gravely defamatory' and awarded him £1000.[29] Not only had Hughes achieved a victory for his client, as much for the publicity as the immediate financial reward, and collected £435-15-0 plus expenses for himself; he had exposed a shoddy review and some even more shoddy newspaper reporting and editorial bias.

Hughes was continuing to make his mark at the Bar, and Johns' article in the *Bulletin* claimed he was successfully walking the 'tight-rope'. Johns also denied that Hughes had a limited repertoire characterised by 'repeated broadsides' against the Left. His course of 'self-education' had given him time 'to grow in the place'. He had stopped joining too many committees and had suffered no real loss of face after the Cameron debacle. In addition, he was prepared to criticise the Government in the Party Room and in the House over the state of the defence force, the approach to trade practices and the RPS. Johns concluded that Tom Hughes 'could easily take his place in the present Government Ministry'.

While walking the said tight-rope, Hughes had made some good friends, notably, Jim Killen from Queensland and Don Chipp from Victoria. Andrew Peacock joined them in April 1966 when he succeeded the retired Menzies in the seat of Kooyong. Hughes' relationship with Fraser was more ambivalent and rarely easy. At the end of 1964, Hughes was a member of the Government members defence committee of which Fraser was chairman. He felt obliged to turn Fraser's report into acceptable English. When Fraser said to him that either he or Hughes would one day become Prime Minister, Hughes assured the member for Wannon it would not be the member for Parkes.[30]

The 1966 federal election

When Harold Holt was elected unopposed to replace Menzies as Liberal Leader, he brought Fraser into his government as Minister for the Army. On 11 August 1966, the Prime Minister tentatively named 26 November – coincidentally, Tom Hughes' 43rd birthday – as the date for the federal election. Unofficially, the election campaign had been underway since the middle of the year when Calwell proclaimed his intention to live or die politically on the issues of Vietnam and conscription.

The campaign for Parkes took off on the evening of Friday 30 September at a public meeting held in the Masonic Hall, Campsie. Ostensibly, the Liberal Party had called the meeting to allow Hughes to report on a fact-finding mission to south-east Asia. Doug Sutherland, the Labor candidate, and a number of supporters entered the hall as the meeting was about to begin. Hughes was sitting on the stage with John Howard. He greeted Sutherland with a casual wave of the hand. Sutherland challenged him to participate in a public debate on election issues. Hughes cleverly deflected a similar challenge from a member of the Communist Party by pointing out that Liberals had one thing in common with the Labor Party: they did not share a platform with known communists. As for Sutherland's proposal, he would provide an answer in due course.

Alderman Doug Sutherland of Burwood Municipal Council, aged 33, was an accountant and a future Lord Mayor of Sydney. He presented himself in 1966 as 'Labor's dynamic candidate for Parkes'. Impressed by the Nixon-Kennedy televised debates in 1960, Sutherland hoped to replicate Kennedy's success. He pursued the idea in a letter to Hughes, suggesting that their respective campaign organisations could arrange the details. Hughes agreed to a debate, provided it was limited to the issues of Vietnam and conscription. Calwell, after all, had made them pivotal. Sutherland complained that Hughes was being 'unrealistically restrictive'. He wanted to debate issues ranging from housing, pensions and medical services to national development, foreign investment and economic growth. Hughes decided against providing Sutherland with a platform to shift attention to other matters. The idea of a public debate lapsed for want of two participants.[31]

Parkes was the fourth most vulnerable Coalition seat in Australia, the second most vulnerable Coalition seat in New South Wales and the most vulnerable Liberal seat in the State. Hughes would lose in a 1.71 per cent swing against him. There was also the unknown effect of Gordon Barton's Liberal Reform Group campaigning against Australia's participation in the Vietnam War and directing its preferences away from the Liberal Party. The DLP leaders in Parkes had already warned the Liberals of their own loss of support. The Parkes Liberals, however, were not worried. They believed that many DLP voters had finally crossed over to the Liberal Party, and drew comfort from Holt's general popularity, Calwell's low personal standing and from the euphoria which accompanied and followed President Johnson's visit to Australia between 20 and 23 October. The real problems in Parkes were the lack of financial resources to match Labor's spending spree. As Howard explained, Party members in Parkes had become 'complacent' because a Calwell victory seemed 'improbable'. On 16 November, a concerned campaign director had to issue a call for volunteers to distribute Hughes' personal letter to 42,000 homes and to ensure the staffing of 20 polling stations.[32]

Hughes could still count on the lawyers. John Holt organised booths at the Harcourt Public School and at other polling stations. He later handed Hughes a list of 24 helpers who did four-hour shifts. Clyde Packer was among them but most were members of the legal profession. Alec Shand was one: a son of 'Jack' Shand and a future QC, he later appeared against Hughes in some memorable contests. Robert Marsden Hope was another. Appointed QC in 1960, Hope became a Judge of Appeal of the Supreme Court and conducted important investigations into Australia's intelligence and security services.

Hughes campaigned much as he did in 1963, though without the same intensity. Doug Sutherland – 'a nice man'[33] – was not Les Haylen. Hughes kept to the script by focusing on defence and foreign policy while the advertisements published by Howard's organisation told electors: 'RETURN YOUR LIBERAL MEMBER TOM HUGHES QC FOR A SECOND TERM: You'll do well to choose HUGHES.' Fortuitously, the *Australian* piece on parliamentary attendance enabled the candidate to claim he was always conscientiously representing them in Canberra and deserved re-election. It is difficult to tell whether the publication of two photographs of Hughes in an early edition of the *Daily Mirror* on 17 November advanced or hindered his cause. In one, he wore a slight smile. In the other, he looked grim-faced and altogether unlikeable. Fortunately, the caption for the second one read 'Mr Crew', who happened to be the Liberal Reform Group candidate. Later editions corrected the mistake and 'Mr Crew' appeared as himself: well dressed, smiling and looking successful.

Sutherland campaigned with 'all stops out', adopting techniques passed on by the Democratic Party in New York. His followers wore straw boaters with bands of blue and white colours, smart-looking girls wore rosettes and blue and white sashes and Sutherland's team maintained communication by two-way radios. On the Saturday before the election, Gough Whitlam, 'Jack' Renshaw, the State Opposition Leader, and John Armstrong, the Lord Mayor of Sydney, joined Sutherland for street meetings where folk singers reportedly added some gaiety. The ABC's *Four Corners* program sent a crew to film some American-style barnstorming.[34]

On 15 November, Allen Fairhall, the Minister for Defence, addressed a rowdy meeting in the Earlwood Methodist Hall in support of Hughes' candidature. A section of the audience booed, heckled and stamped feet, providing a foretaste of what to expect when Harold Holt spoke in the Rockdale Town Hall on 23 November.[35] Hughes was a member of the official party at the Town Hall but could barely hear Holt because of the constant and organised chanting, booing and heckling. Demonstrators waiting outside the hall tried to stop Holt from reaching his car. Hughes, Bosman, Cotton and Howard formed part of a bodyguard to shield Holt, as police attempts to escort and protect him were not succeeding. One well-built man threw a punch at Hughes, who responded with one of his own for which a police officer, who had not seen the first blow, promptly arrested him. The officer released his grip once Hughes identified himself and explained he was merely trying to protect the Prime Minister.[36] Hughes later called it 'a pretty wild night'. Howard, who in his career experienced many hostile demonstrations, called it 'about the roughest election meeting I've ever been to'. The demonstrators acted with 'real venom', and Brigadier 'Jock' Pagan, the State President of the Liberal Party, who had seen a lot of action in the Second World War, looked 'visibly tense'.[37]

Hughes subsequently wrote to the Superintendent of Police in charge of the relevant district to praise those under his control on the way they behaved under such difficult circumstances. Contrary to various allegations, he never saw any officer behave with other than propriety, and pointed out that the police, trying to protect Holt, were heavily outnumbered by demonstrators who were 'bent on perpetrating real physical harm'.[38]

Results

The Government swept back to power with a majority of 39 in the House of Representatives. In Parkes, Hughes won 51.2 per cent of the primary vote and secured a 3.5 per cent swing on the 1963 figures. The Liberal Reform Group polled 6.3 per cent of the primary vote, more than doubling the DLP's return. Overall, Hughes finished with just under a 12 per cent two-party preferred margin over Labor. Seemingly, Parkes had become a safe Liberal seat.

The victor issued a press statement after the election expressing his gratitude to the electors, and said the overall result demonstrated that the Australian people had 'reached the full flower of political maturity' and wanted 'to stand by their friends and allies and … will not tolerate a retreat to isolationism'.

9

An 'insider' and an 'outsider'

The Holt Government experienced a few quiet months after its massive victory in December 1966, but a series of setbacks, some of them self-inflicted, left it struggling for much of 1967. Protests over conscription and the Vietnam War expanded, intensified and turned more violent as the vote-winning war threatened to become a political and financial liability. A revitalised Opposition, now led by Gough Whitlam, increased the pressure on a floundering Prime Minister who lost some of his customary equanimity. Something quite trivial – Holt's decision not to reveal the names of passengers who travelled on VIP aircraft – turned into a major embarrassment. With the connivance of Howson as Minister for Air and senior public servants, the Prime Minister – and Howson – lied to the Parliament about the existence of passenger manifests. John Gorton, the Leader of the Government in the Senate, extracted the Government from some of its mess late in October when he tabled the allegedly non-existent documents.[1] In the following month the Government's share of the primary vote, which was 50 per cent in 1966, fell to 42.8 per cent in a Senate-only election.

On the backbench in 1967

The member for Parkes had a quieter year in Parliament. He saw no point in debating issues on which the electors had already made a firm decision. Conscious that the real battle was taking place outside the House, Hughes spoke at teach-ins and public meetings and, like Malcolm Fraser, proved an altogether better performer for the Government than its principal spokesman, Paul Hasluck. Inside the House, Hughes seemed more interested in economics and finance. There was longer-term significance in his reply to a Labor MP who suggested he favoured price control. Hughes said he was 'advocating no such thing'. He believed that the best way of maintaining price stability was 'to allow a free market economy to run with proper supervision at the manufacturing end, [and] proper supervision of restrictive trade practices'.[2]

Hughes' fee books for 1967, and for the entire 26th Parliament, reflected an overall increase in workload and returns as a barrister, grossing $28,000 (1967), $27,000 (1968) and $26,000 (1969). Of all his cases in 1967, one stands out. It was almost certainly unwinnable; by taking it, Hughes sent a signal – the Vietnam 'hawk' was perfectly capable of working for clients from the other side of politics.

Clive Evatt Jnr was accused of misconduct as a barrister for assisting two solicitors to charge extortionate and grossly excessive fees between 1 February 1963 and 30 August 1965. One solicitor was struck off the roll and the other was suspended for two years. The cases related to 18 actions in the Supreme Court where clients had sought damages for injuries, mostly obtained in motor accidents. Evatt Jnr was either the sole counsel or junior counsel to his father, Clive Evatt QC, a younger brother of Dr Evatt, a former State Labor minister, a maverick and an unconventional barrister. Some colleagues regarded him as 'a likeable rogue' (Hughes' view); others, probably a majority, saw Evatt QC as 'beyond the pale'.[3]

The Ethics Committee of the NSW Bar Association reported in October 1966 that a special sub-committee had found sufficient evidence for the Bar Association to refer Evatt Jnr's conduct to the Court of Appeal. Evatt denied misconduct and sought an injunction in the Court of Equity to restrain the Bar Association from proceeding. Failing there, Hughes asked the Court of Appeal for a stay of proceedings until the Bar Association had properly examined Evatt and given him the opportunity to answer the allegations. He pointed out that the Association did not have the power under its own rules to prosecute the proceedings, and that it had transgressed those rules. The Court found against him.

On the substantive questions, Hughes argued it was not the function of a barrister to intervene between a solicitor and a client, and it was not open on the evidence to find that Evatt Jnr was either the architect or instigator of a conspiracy. Hughes added that in some cases Evatt QC had approved the proposed settlement and, in each instance, the client knew the gross figure. There was no evidence of Evatt Jnr knowing or appreciating that the amounts mentioned in the authorities were unlawful. The Court should take account of Evatt Jnr's state of mind at the time, that is, before the activities of the two solicitors had become public knowledge and the subject of Court proceedings. Finally, counsel was entitled to assume that a solicitor was acting properly.

In April 1967, the Court of Appeal found that Evatt Jnr 'knowingly was a party to, actively assisted in, and facilitated, a systematic course of action whereby two solicitors charged extortionate and grossly excessive sums as costs to lay clients'. He had also charged excessive fees as counsel that he knew would be paid in part from the amounts charged by the solicitors. The Court ordered Evatt's suspension as a barrister for two years. The Bar Association subsequently appealed to the High Court on the ground that the penalty was inadequate, and Evatt cross-appealed against the finding of professional misconduct. In May 1968, the full Court upheld the verdict of the Court of Appeal while finding it had erred in suspending instead of disbarring Evatt Jnr. Barwick told Hughes after the event that the case was 'in trouble' from the very beginning.[4]

Hughes believed the Evatts selected him to lead the defence precisely because he was a Liberal.[5] He explained the significance of the brief to Dudley Erwin, the Chief Whip, when seeking leave of absence to appear before the Court of Appeal. Although the facts of the case were 'very messy', he expected a quick finish and he was keen to do it for two reasons:

> 1. Whatever my personal feelings may be I am under a rather particular obligation to appear when requested for a professional colleague who is in trouble;
> 2. (to be brutally frank) there is considerable political mileage for me … in having a brief, as a well-known Liberal, to appear for the scion of a Labour family.[6]

The real 'mileage' was an opportunity to present the 'cab on the rank' as available for hire across partisan lines. Tom Hughes in his political afterlife represented such Labor notables as Whitlam, Murphy, Rex Connor and Neville Wran. Appearing for the Evatt clan probably advanced his legal career. It was also financially rewarding; his brief appearances netted over $7000.

A new Prime Minister

Tom Hughes was not directly involved in Harold Holt's troubles in 1967, though he did have one sad, brief encounter with the Prime Minister a month before his death. Peacock and Hughes were walking along the corridor behind the Speaker's Chair when they bumped into the Prime Minister. He greeted them saying it was 'nice to meet two real friends', and invited both to dinner at the Lodge. The dinner proved to be the last occasion when Hughes spoke to Holt.[7]

On 17 December, the Prime Minister disappeared in the turbulent waters off Portsea in Victoria. Hughes attended the memorial service at St Paul's Cathedral, Melbourne, where the lobbying for a successor was well under way. Gorton had put his name forward but neither he nor anyone else bothered to canvass Hughes. Everyone correctly assumed he wanted Gorton for the job. Hughes thought Paul Hasluck, the other major contender, represented the past. Elected Party Leader in January 1968, Gorton elevated Fraser to Cabinet as Minister for Education and Science, and Wentworth and Senator Wright to the ministry. Gorton overlooked Peacock in favour of another Victorian, Phillip Lynch, and dropped Howson and Chipp.

Hughes made a few interventions from the backbench during 1968, most notably in support of legislation to abolish appeals from the High Court to the Privy Council in federal and constitutional matters. While praising the Judicial Committee for its contributions to Australian constitutional development, particularly in relation to s 92, he said it was time to cut back the links because Australia had a High Court 'of which any nation could be and should be proud'.[8] Hughes spoke against an Opposition proposal to introduce equal pay for work of equal value for females in the Commonwealth Public Service and statutory authorities; while the principle was sound, overnight implementation would cause 'a serious dislocation of the economy'.[9] He opposed 'political conscientious objection' to the Vietnam War as a ground for non-compliance with the *National Service Act*. Subjects living in this parliamentary democracy had a duty to obey the law: 'Political objection is not a passport to infractions of the law.'[10] In August 1968, Hughes joined Gorton, Whitlam and Fraser on the losing side in voting for the lakeside rather than the hill site for the new and permanent Parliament House. Hughes said he belonged in 'the plain' and was not of the 'hill tribe'. He did not want the Parliament set apart as 'a lofty eminence'.[11] Hughes sided with Whitlam on another issue. The Leader of the Opposition wanted to lower the voting age to 18. Hughes would have surprised Whitlam who saw him as a conservative: 'I am not always so.'[12] The Whitlam proposal did not proceed to a vote.

Round One: Berowra

Tom Hughes had a more pressing issue on his mind in the latter part of 1968. The Electoral Commission scheduled five NSW electorates, including Parkes, for abolition, and proposed four new ones. There was immediate speculation that Hughes might try to move to the North Shore seeking either to replace the aging Sir John Cramer in Bennelong or to win the new seat of Hornsby (later, renamed Berowra). Situated in the outer north-western suburbs of Sydney, Hornsby was created by slicing solid Liberal territory from three existing Liberal seats and would become one of the safest Liberal seats in New South Wales. As Hughes did not intend to challenge a sitting Liberal, and as Gorton wanted him to contest Hornsby,[13] probably because he needed his talented supporter in the ministry, Hughes nominated for the new seat.

In July 1968, John Carrick alerted the Party's State President, Fred Osborne, to some difficulties. 'Bill' Bridges-Maxwell, the sitting member for Robertson, would lose 14,000 of his mostly-Liberal constituents to Hornsby and was in 'considerable anguish'. The Prime Minister wanted Bridges-Maxwell to recontest Robertson, because 'he is the one man who might hold it'. There was 'the problem of Tom Hughes' who would probably enter the Hornsby preselection.[14] Two other politicians were potential candidates. Nigel Bowen, Holt's distinguished appointment to replace Snedden as Attorney-General, might want a safer seat than Parramatta where he had succeeded Barwick. Jim Cameron, a State MP and outspoken moral conservative, had ambitions beyond Macquarie Street and the advantage of his own State seat lying within the proposed boundaries for Hornsby.

In mid-September, by which time Hughes and Cameron had signalled their intention to nominate, Osborne told Carrick that Cameron 'is unlikely to get any senior support from the organisation'.[15] The Liberal hierarchy had long considered him a pest. He would defeat Hughes but not Bowen, should the latter nominate. Bowen eventually decided to recontest Parramatta, leaving 12 candidates, including Hughes, Bridges-Maxwell and Cameron, to contest the preselection for the seat, now renamed Berowra. Ian Macphee also applied. A lawyer, he later won a Melbourne seat and became a minister in the Fraser Government and a prominent Liberal moderate.

Tom Hughes did not nominate any referees. Instead, he provided a statement highlighting his five years of experience in the Federal Parliament. He pointed to membership of the Joint Parliamentary Committee of Foreign Affairs and of several other committees of government members, including the Defence Committee and the Industrial Relations Committee (he chaired the latter). Hughes explained he would not stand against a sitting Liberal because all his colleagues were 'giving good service'. There was no point contesting a Labor-held seat in New South Wales because all had unassailable majorities. Guided by these considerations, he had nominated for Berowra in the hope of being able to give the same service to the electorate, the Government and the Party as he had done in Parkes.[16]

The preselectors met at the Party's headquarters in Ash Street on Monday 21 October. Hughes eventually won after six exhaustive ballots. Once again, he had to rely on votes from State Council and State Executive delegates, although he did have the support of the Chairman of the Berowra FEC, Trevor Thom. Bridges-Maxwell was typically generous, urging the presidents of the six branches of Robertson, now located within Berowra, to tell their members how fortunate they were to have Tom Hughes.[17] Others, however, were very unhappy about the preselection. John Maddison, the respected Minister for Justice and a long-time supporter of Bridges-Maxwell, unburdened privately to Osborne. For two days, he had been 'just a little short of seething with anger at the processes which have been employed in the selection of Executive & State Council delegates'. He had 'nothing against Hughes as a man, successful in his profession and successful in winning and holding a most difficult seat'. Maddison was upset because, having expected the fact and appearance of fairness, he found that members of the State Executive provided most of the outsiders on the panel.[18] He was now 'completely disillusioned' because of a deliberate campaign by the State Executive 'to ensure Hughes' preselection'.[19]

Other protests were more public. Four branches organised a function for 1 November at the Westfield Plaza in Hornsby. Joanna represented Tom who was attending a Commonwealth Parliamentary Conference in the Bahamas. Vi Lloyd, one of the prominent and progressive North Shore women in the Party's upper levels, reported later to Carrick that five committee members declared the preselection unfair.[20] She did not mention that Maddison made a speech praising Bridges-Maxwell and without ever mentioning Hughes. On 9 December at another Liberal Party meeting in Hornsby, and with Hughes present, Maddison spoke warmly about him. Aware 'that I was putting my head into the lion's mouth', Hughes spoke for 20 minutes justifying the Government's participation in mandatory sanctions against Ian Smith's 'illegal regime' in Rhodesia. Recently and unanimously, the Hornsby branch had called on the Government not to participate. Two of the disaffected Liberals peppered him with questions, after which there was another hour of grilling, though no one referred to Hughes' decision not to live in the electorate. Joanna and Tom decided after the meeting that he had answered the questions 'fairly expressively' and 'established a degree of ascendancy' which 'is needed if I am to ride out the storm winds being blown by the few dissidents'.

Three nights later and also in Hornsby, Hughes attended a meeting of the Berowra FEC. Chaired by Trevor Thom, whom he liked and respected, Hughes presented the case for increasing foreign aid, realising how difficult it was for politicians to sell the argument. Carrick then spoke for an hour, much longer than intended, about his trip to the United States, successfully forestalling discussion of a motion calling on the Government not to become involved in the imposition of mandatory sanctions on Rhodesia. Hughes left this meeting pleased that the dissidents now had to wait until next year to achieve anything damaging.[21]

Bahamas 1968

Hughes had joined a delegation of federal MPs to attend the Commonwealth Parliamentary Conference in the Bahamas. Sir John Cramer, a Catholic, an active member of the UAP in the 1930s, the Liberal member for Bennelong since 1949 and Army minister (1956-63), led the delegation. Fred Daly was his deputy and Hughes, Harry Webb (Labor) and Senators Dittmer (Labor) and Webster (CP) completed the numbers. Officials and some State MPs also attended the Conference in Nassau. Peter Howson was present by virtue of his position as Chairman of the Executive Committee of the General Council.

Conferences of this kind were regarded by MPs as one of the perks of the job. Judging by his letters home – it was considered too expensive for Joanna to accompany him – Hughes saw little pleasure. On 26 October, soon after reaching Nassau, he wrote to Joanna likening the Bahamas to 'institutionalised tourism'. After getting rid of 500 American dentists, the locals held out 'the rather tired hand of welcome' to more than 200 Commonwealth parliamentarians. Cramer, 'dear chap that he is', excelled himself at the dinner held upon arrival. He proposed a toast – 'Here's to the whites' – at a mixed race table. Red and white wines had been served, and he drank white wine. The only other white drinker happened to be black. Cramer asked the same black man, who was a local, 'And what is the name of your Prime Minister?' There followed 'a hush you could cut with a blunt knife'. Hughes feared that 14 days of Cramer and Webb 'dropping their little clangers' could be a major test. Indeed, if these conferences were designed to spread goodwill, 'more would be achieved by staying at home'.[22]

Hughes wrote again on 29 October telling 'darling wife' it was as well she did not come to Nassau. There were not many 'agreeably pleasant' people and it was impossible to choose those with whom you wanted to consort. Nassau was a 'clip joint', taking money for poor service and indifferent meals. The wives were best avoided, though he was interested in the double standards of one Australian spouse who clearly disapproved of the sexual imagery adopted by the African males but liked to watch 'a randy old Canadian [white] legislator' tickling the leg of 'a strange [white] girl from Atlanta with whom he spent the night'.[23]

Racial issues occupied several sessions as the Conference debated subjects such as Racial Harmony or Conflict, Britain's policy towards Rhodesia and Australia's immigration policy. Cramer later described the discussion on immigration as 'somewhat emotional' but praised Daly for his contribution in emphasising that anyone with the appropriate skills and qualifications could enter Australia and be granted citizenship. Hughes and Daly both pointed to what Hughes called the 'undoubted truth': all countries impose immigration restrictions. While the Conference was, as Hughes described it, 'never tranquil', he did at least draw comfort from Daly's non-partisan approach and from the delegation standing together in the face of criticism of Australia's policies.

Customarily, on returning to Australia after one of these excursions, delegates extol the value of the exercise and applaud the work and contribution of the Commonwealth Parliamentary Association. Whatever his private thoughts, Hughes could honestly say he had learnt something. As he told the House, he had never before 'seen or heard people at first hand expressing with great fervour controversial and bitter opinions'. Observing the 'explosive force and intensity' of the views expressed, he was not taken in by any of the fine words about solving these 'frightful problems'. Hughes concluded his remarks by observing another obligatory ritual; he paid 'a very sincere tribute to the leader of our delegation'.[24]

An election year

Sir Paul Hasluck's translation to Yarralumla in February 1969 created a ministerial vacancy. Gorton promoted Gordon Freeth to External Affairs with a seat in Cabinet and Dudley Erwin replaced Freeth as Minister for Air. Menzies told his daughter that 'Dudley has no possible qualifications for Ministerial rank', so that his elevation must have been a reward for helping Gorton win the leadership. Menzies could 'only guess what men like Tom Hughes QC, and Malcolm Mackay, and half a dozen others … are thinking about Dudley's promotion over their heads'.[25]

Hughes was untroubled. He supported Gorton in March 1969 when Bert James, the Labor member for Hunter, and Edward St John, the Liberal MP for Warringah since 1966, took rumours about the Prime Minister's private life into the House.[26] Hughes dissociated himself from St John by sitting in another part of the Chamber and publicly criticising him for his attacks on Gorton's personal behaviour.[27] By this time, a number of Liberal backbenchers – Howson was the most prominent – had morphed into anti-Gortonites, appalled by the Prime Minister's seemingly cavalier methods of government and by his assertive nationalism and centralist and 'socialist' tendencies. They did not share the Hughes view of Gorton as 'a breath of fresh air'. Nor did they approve of 13 avowed Gortonites affirming their loyalties through membership of the 'Mushroom Club'.[28] Max Walsh in the *Financial Review* of 29 August 1969 described Hughes as 'a foundation member'. Backbenchers who did not belong thought that the 'mushrooms' formed a bloc to support Gorton or, in Howson's eyes, were actually handpicked by Gorton. John Jess (La Trobe, Victoria) called them 'ruddy sycophants' who joined the Club 'by appointment'. He said the membership consisted of 'the Killens, the Hughes, the McLeay [sic], various nondescripts really. Not the great and powerful. But those who were seeking for further glory I would think. I could be wrong. I could be prejudiced.'

He was certainly wrong. The Mushroom Club was established after his own side gagged Andrew Peacock during a tariff debate in 1968. Gorton neither formed the Club nor determined who should belong. The membership was a self-selected and quite diverse group who liked to wine, dine and indulge in some ribaldry. They met once a week when the House was sitting and often invited a guest speaker to join them. Gorton, given the title of 'Chief Spore', attended just one dinner and eventually asked them to disband because some backbenchers thought they were dividing the Party Room. Appearances were everything. It was one thing for the anti-Gortonites to whisper, cabal and undermine in private – that was done for the good of the Party and of the Government – but it was damaging and divisive to engage in genuine and public displays of loyalty, even if those actions were secondary to enjoying good company.

Round Two: Berowra

On 4 February 1969, one Party member took opposition to the Berowra preselection a step further by announcing her intention to stand as an Independent. Councillor Edith Parrish MBE had helped found the Australian Women's Flying Club in 1939, was elected to the Hornsby Shire Council in 1959, and was a longstanding member of the Liberal Party and chaired its Hornsby Women's Committee. A tireless social worker, she had founded Meals on Wheels in Hornsby in 1965, was a patron of 30 local committees and active in the RSL, Legacy, the Red Cross, the Girl Guides, school and progress associations and the Old Age and Invalid Pensioners Association. She was also interested in animal welfare and owned 38 cats.[29]

Announcing her candidature, Parrish said she had been encouraged by numerous groups, including Liberal supporters, to stand. 'I do this only because it is right.' It was 'right' on three counts. First, there was no point in women seeking preselection. No woman, Parrish said, had any chance of being elected to the Lower House (Kay Brownbill was currently the Liberal member for Kingston, South Australia). Secondly, Hughes' endorsement was 'an organised attempt to make us prisoners of established politicians'. Parrish would be the non-politician to represent men and women who felt alienated by 'the professional politicians' who had 'foisted' Hughes upon them. Thirdly, Hughes was an 'outsider' who made it clear he had no intention of living in the electorate.[30]

Osborne as State President responded with a press statement on 7 February and distributed it to all branch and electorate conference presidents.[31] He said Parrish was not entitled to misrepresent the preselection system by saying Hughes was 'foisted upon us by the professional politicians'.

Of the 50 selectors just two were MPs. Thirty were elected by the Berowra FEC from 22 branches and the remaining 20 were drawn at random from the 350 members of the State Council across the metropolitan areas and from 15 State electorates. The system was 'the fairest that can be devised', the comments of political scientists were favourable and no one under this system could 'foist' a candidate. A 'clear majority' of the 50 selectors had chosen Hughes in a secret ballot. Osborne described him as 'still a relatively young man with a distinguished war record and an outstanding record as a Queen's Counsel in this State'. He had won a difficult seat facing great odds and earned widespread praise for his service to the Parkes electorate and to the Parliament.

Trevor Thom and Vi Lloyd added staunch local support, and so did a defeated candidate in the preselection – Jim Cameron – who later opposed Hughes' re-endorsement for the 1972 election. He assured Hughes that 'the local storm in a teacup' would be 'of a very short-term duration and of minor overall significance'.[32]

Despite Cameron's predictions, the 'storm' persisted right up to, and beyond, the federal election in October 1969. The *Hornsby Advocate* was bent on fomenting trouble. It claimed on 14 May 1969 that more than 800 Liberal Party members had not renewed their subscription. It reported how the Asquith-Mt Colah branch had voted unanimously to call upon the Berowra FEC to hold an extraordinary meeting of the Berowra preselectors 'to consider the wisdom of Mr T Hughes' continued preselection in the light of current developments'. The *Advocate* further claimed that Party officials acknowledged that support for the motion was 'snowballing throughout the electorate'.[33]

Head Office intervened to protect the 'outsider' who was the Party's 'insider'. Carrick issued Thom with riding instructions a few days before the extraordinary meeting.[34] The matter should be settled immediately and definitively. The Berowra FEC must understand the following: there were no issues relating to the mechanics of the preselection; a preselection ought not to be overturned 'except for the most imperative of reasons'; and the original preselectors elected by the 22 branches did not have a continued status. Thom might remind the FEC how Tom Hughes had won Parkes by defeating 'an outstanding Labor candidate' and had proved a strong vote winner. The Berowra selectors, like those in Parkes, knew his position on residency. Finally, the FEC should know of the State Executive's view that, in the absence of conclusive evidence of illegality, the Conference and the component branches had the responsibility 'to uphold the preselection and to execute a full campaign'.

Thom, assisted by Vi Lloyd, delivered the desired result. The FEC met on 3 June and rejected the Asquith-Mt Colah resolution by 54 votes to 11. The *Advocate* published a full account of the arguments expressed by the dissidents at a supposedly closed meeting. One KR Rowlings said Hughes was too much of an outsider, had refused to live in the electorate and made statements showing he did not understand the community's attitudes, circumstances or problems. The *Advocate* allowed Hughes, who spoke at the meeting, just one sentence, quoting him as saying he was 'quite prepared to visit it [the electorate] if required'. By contrast, the *SMH* reported him saying he would do his utmost for the electorate.[35] Undeterred by the FEC result, the *Advocate* backed the Parrish cause citing suspect and anonymous sources. At the end of July, it announced that 'a sampling of all sections of the electorate' showed Parrish collecting 'a whopping 55 per cent of the [primary] vote' in the federal election.[36] It quoted an unidentified North Shore State Liberal MP who praised her 'down-to-earth approach to politics', especially in relation to local government, and predicted she would win the seat.[37]

Meanwhile, Hughes was active on another front. Representing John Gorton, he joined Gough Whitlam and Wal Fife, the State Minister for Mines representing the Premier, at a capacity meeting in the Sydney Town Hall for a debate on State Aid.[38] The three other speakers opposed State assistance to non-government schools. Teachers formed a major portion of the audience and greeted Hughes with jeers, booing and stamping and, forsaking an exchange of views, tried to prevent him from being heard. Journalists reported Hughes saying that to abolish State Aid would now require the removal of the seven governments and five alternate governments prepared to stand up for 'a just and sound principle'. He also observed that sectarianism 'is pouring out tonight'. Whitlam received a better reception though he, too, met boos and hissing for suggesting that aid to Catholic schools was indispensable to any program for raising standards of Australian schools. The meeting overwhelmingly passed resolutions calling for an end to State Aid and for increased spending on government schools.[39]

The McLeod-Lindsay case

It may have been a rugged encounter but the Town Hall meeting was probably a welcome diversion from a major legal engagement where Hughes faced an unsympathetic judicial figure.

On the night of 14 September 1964, Pamela McLeod-Lindsay was attacked in her home in Sylvania Heights, south of Sydney. She received extensive head injuries and brain damage, and her four-year-old son was also injured. The police alleged that her husband, Alexander 'Sandy' McLeod-Lindsay, had driven home at around 9.30 pm from his work as a casual employee at a nearby hotel and battered his wife with a steel jackpick. McLeod-Lindsay insisted he arrived home after midnight to find that his wife and son had been attacked. Pamela barely survived the incident and remained unconscious for three weeks. Revived, she insisted her husband was not the attacker. Her one clear recollection before blacking out was of a man on the back veranda speaking to the family dog in an Australian accent. McLeod-Lindsay had a distinctive Scottish accent.

The Crown accepted its case was circumstantial, based mainly on four 'facts':

- the bloodstains on McLeod-Lindsay's clothing would have resulted from spattering at the time of the attack;
- his wind jacket, which bore the bloodstains, was never in contact with his wife after she received her injuries;
- a man seen at about 9.30 pm coming from the house carried a torch identical to the one owned by McLeod-Lindsay;
- a car answering a description of the one owned by McLeod-Lindsay was seen near his home at about 9.35 pm.

The Crown could not establish any motive for McLeod-Lindsay's alleged actions. Instead, it produced witnesses who more or less agreed that McLeod-Lindsay was near his home between about 9.30 and 10.00 pm. Experts testified that the bloodstains on his jacket were consistent with an attack on Pamela, whereas McLeod-Lindsay claimed he acquired them when moving and cradling his wife. Found guilty on 5 March 1965 of 'feloniously wounding and attempting to murder', McLeod-Lindsay was sentenced to 18 years in gaol. The Court of Criminal Appeal upheld the verdict in July 1965 while acknowledging that '(not) … every jury would have been satisfied beyond reasonable doubt'. A committee, whose members included Lady Herron, the wife of the NSW Chief Justice, and Robert Southern, a retired grazier who befriended Pamela, campaigned for an inquiry.[40]

Ken McCaw, the law-reforming and humanitarian Attorney-General, and his close ally John Maddison, had misgivings about the original verdict. In July 1969, the Government appointed Justice Lee 'to inquire into doubts or questions as to the guilt of Alexander McLeod-Lindsay'. The Deputy Public Solicitor, AG Knox, appointed Tom Hughes to represent 'the prisoner'. McCaw and Maddison knew that Hughes could be relied upon to probe the 'doubts or questions' and to provide the prisoner with his best chance of a favourable outcome. At the very least, those who had campaigned on McLeod-Lindsay's behalf could feel reassured by the appointment of a prominent silk.

Yet the prisoner felt uneasy about a Liberal MP representing him, because he was 'bucking the legal administration of a state liberal government'. Knox reassured him, and McLeod-Lindsay decided that, although on their first meeting Hughes was reserved and his conversation 'formal and business-like', he would be 'a strong and competent advocate'.[41] Robert Southern was suspicious on many counts. No one who cared about McLeod-Lindsay, a Presbyterian, 'chose the Roman Catholic Mr TEF Hughes' to represent him. The Government simply appointed him 'for its own reasons'. Southern believed that the 'real criminal' was a Roman Catholic who had 'bought' McLeod-Lindsay's conviction. Somehow, Hughes was part of a conspiracy to protect the real perpetrator. For a start, there was 'the fundamental (though of course concealed) antipathy which a Roman Catholic counsel might be expected to feel towards a Protestant client'. Southern added another factor to explain what he saw as Hughes' inadequate performance during the inquiry: he was preoccupied with the forthcoming federal election.[42]

Throughout the hearings, which began on 28 July and concluded on 5 September, Hughes sought to focus on the question of how another jury might react to fresh evidence placed alongside that produced at the trial. He believed it was not the judge's function to appraise all the evidence before him with a view to concluding whether it established McLeod-Lindsay's guilt or innocence. Nor should he be reaching conclusions on the reliability or significance of individual portions of evidence. It was sufficient, therefore, from Hughes' perspective, to show how new evidence or how a more forensic examination of old evidence might raise sufficient doubts to justify a retrial.

To this end, Hughes painstakingly took witnesses through their stories, drawing out re-interpretations and adding new evidence. He was able to show that the man seen walking near the McLeod-Lindsay home near the time of the murder was almost certainly not McLeod-Lindsay, and that the car parked near the home was very probably not his. Hughes also exposed several instances of inadequate crime detection, fiddling of records and dishonest testimony on the part of the police. Constable Jarvis was sitting in a car parked outside the McLeod-Lindsay house with a woman who was married to a gaol inmate and whose identity had to be protected. Jarvis told the trial that they left the area at around 8.50 pm, thereby creating a period of one hour for McLeod-Lindsay to commit the crime. Subjecting Jarvis to intense cross-examination, and taking other witnesses carefully through their statements and their memories of the night, Hughes clearly established that the constable and his companion were still outside the house at 9.30 pm and that McLeod-Lindsay was working in the hotel from around 10.00 pm until midnight. He was able to show that there was a very limited window of opportunity for McLeod-Lindsay to leave the hotel, commit the crime and return to work.

Justice Lee handed down his report on 3 October.[43] Rejecting the Hughes approach, Lee believed he had a duty to conclude whether McLeod-Lindsay was guilty or not. If the evidence given at the trial and put before him did not materially differ, then he felt bound to express an opinion whether, on the whole of the evidence, there was doubt about his guilt. He had none; the evidence 'confirms, in all its material aspects, the reliability and cogency of the case presented by the Crown at the Trial of the prisoner'. The Crown's four 'facts', apparently intact despite Hughes' careful reconstruction of events, together with other evidence, 'bear no other reasonable explanation but that the prisoner is guilty'. Lee did not accept the prisoner's denial on oath because there was no reliable corroborative evidence for accepting his testimony. Mrs McLeod-Lindsay's evidence 'cannot be regarded as cogent or of sufficient weight'. What Justice Lee called the 'unusual feature' of the crime – the apparent absence of a motive, the callous attitude towards his injured child, and his appearance of genuine grief after discovering his wife – did not 'alter the shape or size of a single tell-tale blood stain on his wind jacket and trousers'.[44]

Justice Lee dealt with contrary indications by dismissing them as immaterial or irrelevant. While he agreed that counsel had made some valid points about police actions and behaviour – a rare acknowledgement – he did not consider an amended time of the Jarvis departure made any difference. Presented with evidence of vaginal bruising and froth on the external surface of the labia, the details of which were not released at the trial, Lee brushed aside expert medical testimony that Pamela McLeod-Lindsay might have been sexually assaulted. He relied on the absence of semen, the assumption that McLeod-Lindsay removed his wife's pyjama pants to create an illusion, and the belief that in the overall picture, which included the bloodstains, the bruising could sensibly be explained without reference to sexual assault. Lee's line throughout was straightforward and consistent: 'In my view there is no rational basis for the proposition put by Mr Hughes that if the evidence, ie the whole of the evidence as has been given before me, had been given at the trial on this aspect, it might have resulted in an acquittal of the prisoner.'[45]

Notwithstanding Southern's sectarian ravings,[46] Hughes had worked very hard to demonstrate there was sufficient doubt about the original conviction. He found it difficult to believe that a jury, presented with the evidence placed before the Inquiry, would have found McLeod-Lindsay guilty beyond reasonable doubt. The bloodstains on the prisoner's jacket became the sticking point. Convinced they coincided with the attack, Justice Lee felt able to set aside anything inconvenient. McLeod-Lindsay, therefore, remained in jail until released on parole in 1973. Pamela divorced him in the same year, and he later married Valda Potts. Apparently, Potts contacted Hughes in 1978. He has no recollection of telling her that McLeod-Lindsay should enjoy the life he now had, and drop his obsession about clearing his name.[47] A second inquiry in 1991, based on new forensic evidence relating to the source of the bloodstains, cleared the prisoner just as they had originally convicted him. McLeod-Lindsay received a pardon and $700,000 in compensation.[48]

The 1969 election

On 22 September 1969, Robert wrote to his brother from London.[49] He was 'broke', trying to finish a book on Leonardo da Vinci, and going through a divorce and saw no point in 'delaying the revelation of this mess to the rest of the family'. As for his other brother, Geoffrey, 'if he starts coming out with some line about how this-is-the-inevitable-fate-of-irresponsible-Pinks-in-Degenerate-Europe … stick a cork in him. I am very fond of Geoff but I find his propensity to moralize a trial; and irrelevant in extreme situations like this.'[50] Robert was also responding to what was clearly a conciliatory letter from Tom about their political differences: 'whatever our divergences of opinion & explosions of temper we are a damn sight closer to one another than anyone else in the family.' He referred to a rumour in London that Tom was about to become Attorney-General. 'How nice to have such an exalted brother.' He expected to 'disagree furiously with every political pronouncement you make but THAT DOESN'T MATTER because we are too intelligent in our respective ways to ever agree about really important issues. (Pause for noise of RSFH and TEFH slapping each other on back: super sound effects, like copulating halibut).'

Gorton called an election for 25 October 1969. Whitlam presented a detailed and appealing social program and promised to end conscription and to withdraw all Australian troops from Vietnam by June 1970. Gorton wanted to focus on domestic policy. When, however, the opinion polls pointed to a probable Labor victory he revived Cold War rhetoric with claims that Labor was 'soft' on defence and foreign policy, and invoked images of the 'faceless men' and of 'communist-led trade unions' controlling a Labor government. As polling day approached, the Coalition cut Labor's lead to one percentage point.

Tom Hughes began his campaign for Berowra with an emphasis on domestic affairs. On 1 October, all five candidates addressed a public meeting organised by the Berowra Progress Association. Tom told the meeting that Australians had 'never had it so good'.[51] The standard of living was rising, there were more jobs available than applicants to fill them and the Gross

National Product had risen by 8.5 per cent. He defended the Government's policy on national service and, even more vigorously, State Aid to independent schools. The Hughes campaign literature focused on two objectives: to introduce him as the 'experienced' candidate who 'has emerged as a real political force' and had 'demonstrated strong potential for the future'; and to highlight the differences between the major parties over the 'live election issues' of defence and foreign policy. His Labor opponent, George Williams, was no 'Left-Wing Les' but, in keeping with the Gorton switch of emphasis, Hughes hammered Labor's 'isolationist outlook' and contrasted it with the Government's belief 'in helping Asian friends to resist externally-inspired subversion and aggression'. As for Parrish, the Hughes campaign had a quiet dig at her in the projection of Hughes as someone who could 'forcefully' represent the voters of Berowra 'on the wide stage of national politics where he is experienced in dealing with all types of national issues as they affect individual electors'. Hughes reminded voters that the election was determining who should govern the nation. It was not concerned with the powers or functions of a State government or a local council.

Parrish responded with her own swipe at Hughes, pointing out her dedication to serving Berowra 'on a full time basis – not just part time'. But she soon exposed herself as out of her depth on the national stage. With the possibility of a close result, Parrish imagined herself sitting in 'the ideal Parliament' where she had the casting vote in an equally divided House. Her plan was to vote for what the majority 'wanted on each individual thing'.[52] In combination, Berowra voters and the broader Australian electorate decided not to give her that power.

The Gorton Government won the election, while suffering a resounding rebuff. In a swing of nearly 7 per cent, the Coalition majority of 39 was cut to seven and the Government survived only because of DLP preferences in four seats. The Liberal Party alone lost 14 seats to Labor, including three in New South Wales. The 'Fashionable QC in a "hostile" electorate'[53] won 45.5 per cent of the primary vote, Labor came second with 30.6 per cent and Parrish finished third with 12.5 per cent. Hughes achieved an absolute majority after the distribution of DLP and Australia Party (as the Liberal Reform Group now styled itself) preferences. The 'outsider', and the Liberal vote in Berowra, had taken a serious knock.

10

'The Queen's Agent administering the law for her'

After the election, Hughes went to St Luke's Hospital to undergo a minor operation. The Prime Minister rang to inquire about his health and, without naming a post, said he wanted him in the ministry. Making a quick recovery, Hughes went to a post-election Party Room meeting. David Fairbairn, the Minister for National Development, had told Gorton he would not serve in his ministry and decided to contest the Party leadership. McEwen, who had threatened to withdraw the Country Party from a McMahon-led Government after Holt's death, retracted his threat following the 1969 election, and McMahon joined the leadership contest. On 30 October, Gorton won a narrow absolute majority on the first ballot, and reiterated his intention of promoting Hughes to the ministry.

Immediately after Gorton's re-election as Leader, Les Irwin, a Liberal backbencher, urged him not to promote Hughes and Killen. To do so, he wrote, 'would be an insult, and affront and an askance [sic] to the dedicated men serving under you. Both have been conspicuous by their absence and nonchalant in their parliamentary duties.' Irwin felt particularly bothered by rumours of Hughes' likely elevation. His animus towards Tom Hughes probably stemmed from Irwin's very different social, educational and employment background. No Eastern Suburbs silvertail, he was born in 1898 near Newcastle, attended State schools, became a bank clerk, served in the AIF, was wounded in France in 1917 and ended the war as a lieutenant with the Australian Flying Corps. For years he managed the Blacktown branch of the Bank of New South Wales with little prospect of advancement, but he surprisingly won the NSW federal seat of Mitchell in 1963. Irwin cared nothing for lawyers, blaming them for the 'procrastination and indecision over the years'. He told Gorton there were already too many of them in politics, and most were 'untrained in business practice, economics, feasability [sic] studies and the like'. As for Hughes, he 'gave little service to his Electorate – is laborious in debate – a slow thinker'.[1]

Within two days of receiving this gratuitous advice, Gorton informed Hughes he would be Attorney-General: 'This was a great moment in my life.' Hughes had never set his sights higher than this post because it was 'the summit of the legitimate hopes of a lawyer, turned politician'. He had not then realised that the position would give him an insight into all the operations of government and prepare him for other ministerial jobs. 'But this was not my current frame of mind; and as subsequent events proved, my mindlessness was entirely apposite.'[2]

Hughes was one of five new appointments to the ministry; Killen, Peacock, Chipp and Cotton were the other four. All, except Cotton, had been members of the Mushroom Club. Dudley Erwin, a casualty in the reshuffle, provided a stumbling much-quoted explanation for his sacking: 'It's shapely, it wiggles, and its name is Ainsley Gotto [Gorton's Principal Private Secretary].' Little attention was paid to another Erwin aside; unlike some of the new ministers, he was not a 'mushroom'. Howson, Erwin and the growing number of anti-Gortonites, believing that Gorton had surrounded himself with 'cronies', grumbled about the evils of 'cronyism'.

Hughes received many congratulatory messages from backbenchers, priests, diplomats, leaders of employer organisations, senior judges and barristers. Members of the NSW Bar were especially pleased that one of their own had been elevated to such a high office. Sir Garfield Barwick was appropriately circumspect. He offered congratulations and wished Hughes success, while adding that when the Attorney had settled into his position, 'there are various matters concerning the Court which I shall be pleased to discuss with you'. The mother of one of Hughes' Sunderland crew, who had died suddenly on returning to Australia after the War, wrote warmly about Tom's mother having invited the returned airman to dinner after hearing him talk on the radio about the problems of rehabilitation. There was also a reminder of a more recent past. The Chairman and the Secretary General of the Assembly of Captive Nations described Hughes' appointment as 'particularly gratifying' because 'we are well aware of your political ideological views'.[3]

John Carrick could not confine himself to a congratulatory letter. He told the new Attorney-General that he had 'a fascinating opportunity' because the portfolio had become much more significant during the past 20 years. Following Barwick and Bowen – Snedden, who figured between them, did not rate a mention – Hughes had inherited 'very high precedents', but the job 'offers enormous opportunities for solid homework and sound advice behind the scenes and I am sure that you can cope'. On another front, Carrick wanted Hughes to call a meeting of his Electorate Conference or of all the branches to 're-assure them that although you have moved to higher altitudes, you will still be keenly conscious of the needs of your electorate'. While this might irritate him, 'the fact is that electors even of blue-ribbon seats are not so keen on Ministers as they are on political servants. Perhaps we could talk about this aspect some time.'[4]

Whatever he did, Hughes remained an 'outsider' in a seat he described as 'a hotchpotch of disparate local interests'. The little towns between Hornsby and the Hawkesbury River reminded him of the Italian city-states. It was difficult to please them all. Hughes knew he was not very popular with the local branches, and did not foresee any change.[5]

The context

Tom Hughes took office as Attorney-General on 12 November 1969. He was 23rd of the 26 ministers in order of seniority. Unlike the other 12 members of the outer ministry, however, he frequently attended Cabinet meetings. Gorton needed him to be on hand to provide legal advice.

It is important, in looking at Hughes' tenure as Attorney-General, to be aware of three particular features of the political context in 1970. First, despite the Government's decision not to replace the battalion due to return from South Vietnam in November 1970, and despite it being obvious that Australia's involvement would continue to wind down, demonstrations against conscription and the Vietnam commitment became more popular, more disruptive and occasionally more violent during the year. An Attorney-General, who had administrative responsibility for prosecuting draft resisters and those who assisted draft resisters, and had the responsibility for preparing laws to deal with violence, inevitably became a butt for anti-government anger. At the same time, precisely because Hughes had these responsibilities, he was also a target for criticism by conservatives who wanted a crackdown on disorder.

Secondly, during 1970, John Gorton as Prime Minister faced growing hostility from his own side of politics. State Liberals and members of his Party Room continued to accuse him of being an aggressive centralist in a Party claiming to respect State rights. His 'socialist' tendencies became more obvious through his support for an Industry Development Corporation to raise overseas capital and regain Australian control over Australian resources. Identifying himself with Gorton, Tom Hughes attracted the attention of the mutterers and the plotters who formed the 'cave' of anti-Gortonites.

Thirdly, there was increasing agitation in the wider community for reforming the laws relating to abortion, homosexuality, divorce and capital punishment. Leaving aside the question of just what powers lay within the reach of a Federal Government, there was particular interest in how a known Catholic, occupying the position of Attorney-General, would respond to calls for change. At the same time, there were mounting fears within the Liberal Party, and among conservatives in the broader community, that moves to change the law in these fields would threaten the cohesion and undermine the values of Australian society.

In dealing with this myriad of issues, Hughes was obliged, and eager, to define his role as Attorney-General. At times deliberately, and sometimes unconsciously, he used his time in office to establish his persona as a non-political, principal Crown Law officer. He sought thus to defend himself from conservatives on his side of politics and persuade those on the other side that he was not the Cold War warrior who entered Parliament in 1963.

Setting out

In June 1969, the Attorney-General's Department had a permanent staff of 1482 and a total staff of 1741. The Department may have been a relatively small one but, on arrival, Harry Renfree, the Crown Solicitor and 'a charming and very wise man', could present the new Attorney-General with a 69-page paper detailing 'The Organisations and Functions of the Attorney-General's Department'.[6] In addition to those specified in the document, the Attorney's duties included administrative responsibility for the Office of the Commissioner of Trade Practices, the Commonwealth Industrial Court, ASIO[7] and the Commonwealth Police. He had to administer many Commonwealth statutes, such as the *Crimes Act 1914* (Cth), the *Marriage Act 1961* (Cth), the *Matrimonial Causes Act 1959* (Cth), the *Trade Practices Act 1965* (Cth), and the *Bankruptcy Act 1966* (Cth), and was responsible for administering Commonwealth laws relating to the extradition of criminals. As Hughes explained to a Liberal Party audience in March 1970, the Attorney recommended names for appointment to federal judicial office and undertook law reform. In the case of the latter, he was currently designing a uniform disciplinary code for the armed services. Like the British Home Secretary, the Attorney-General could recommend the prerogative of mercy. In Hughes' experience, that meant excusing people of fines for failing to make a tax return.[8]

Hughes had the highest regard for the staff of the Attorney-General's Department, though some of the grounds for his admiration might have seemed idiosyncratic to senior public servants in other areas. He recognised that the Department 'was well stocked with officers possessing a high degree of individuality, not to say eccentricity. This was a situation entirely to my liking. Lawyers, if they are any good at their task, must be expected to possess each of those qualities.'[9]

When Hughes arrived at the Department, Edwin 'Ted' Hook, the Secretary, was on extended leave for a stress-related illness. Hook never returned to work and, even before he formally retired in February 1970, Sir Frederick Wheeler, the Chairman of the Public Service Board (PSB), was working on a replacement. He initially proposed Sir Allen Brown, a former Secretary of the Prime Minister's Department who was retiring as Australian Ambassador to Japan. Wheeler was desperately trying to find any job for Brown whose better days – and they were very good – were well behind him. Hughes joined a number of ministers and senior public servants in rejecting Wheeler's approaches. The Chairman of the PSB next proposed John Ewens, Acting Secretary of the Attorney-General's Department and the Parliamentary Draftsman. AB 'Tich' McFarlane, another member of the Board and a Gorton favourite, also backed Ewens. JE Collings, the third member of the PSB, believed that Ewens was more suited to be First Parliamentary Counsel, and that Clarence 'Clarrie' Harders, Deputy Secretary of the Department since 1965, should be permanent head.[10]

Although Hughes said he would reflect on the Wheeler-McFarlane preference, he came down strongly for Harders. The new Attorney had a regard for Ewens, 'a man of imposing intellectual powers and lofty independence'. Like Collings, however, he saw Ewens as someone more suited as First Parliamentary Counsel. He regarded Harders, a graduate in law from Adelaide University, as a 'master of concise advice, legally impeccable and, most importantly, imbued with an innately sound instinct for the political realities of life'.[11] Hughes held out against Wheeler and won. In June 1970, Cabinet approved the appointment of Harders as Secretary and Ewens as First Parliamentary Counsel.

Hughes had a third victory over Wheeler. On his arrival at the Department, he encountered a log-jam in legislative drafting. He saw a clear need for more staff and, in order to attract quality people, there was a need for higher salaries matched by a lift in status. Wheeler informed Hughes that his proposals for upgrading, and for making three of the drafting staff statutory officers under their own Act of Parliament, would not work; they would distort the relativities of remuneration in the Public Service.[12]

Hughes took his recommendations to Cabinet on 21 January 1970. He explained that he wanted to make the drafting of legislation an attractive career with an appropriate salary and status. He encountered considerable opposition and many reservations. McEwen said he was not 'instantly favourable' to breaking up departments. Senator Wright – who opposed many submissions Hughes took to Cabinet – and Doug Anthony, Deputy Leader of the Country Party, saw no point in detaching the drafting staff from the Public Service. Sir Alan Hulme, the Postmaster-General, felt sure that Hughes would not mind his pointing out that the Attorney-General had been in office for just two months; there was a lot of history for him to learn, and other departments might see his proposals as a precedent and seek similar arrangements. Hughes had the perfect response to the opponents and the doubters; he kept reminding ministers of the 'dire situation' in relation to drafting. He also had a determined ally. A Prime Minister bent on change did not regard the maintenance of Public Service relativities as any sort of argument, let alone as a priority. Gorton had little time for Wheeler, noting somewhat scornfully that the PSB had found the sort of difficulties 'you would expect'. When McMahon added his concern about paying the First Parliamentary Counsel a salary equivalent to that of a Permanent Head, Gorton spoke quickly and decisively: the top man should be paid that amount. With the Prime Minister firm and determined in support, Cabinet agreed in principle with Hughes' recommendations.[13]

Hughes took the greatest pleasure in making one recommendation for judicial appointment. Sir Frank Kitto, a High Court judge since 1950 and approaching his 67th birthday, notified Hughes of his intention to resign. Hughes knew that a tense relationship with Barwick had contributed to Kitto's decision, but told Cabinet Kitto felt he needed relief after spending 20 years on the Bench and, recently, had found himself in the minority a few times. Hughes took one nomination to Cabinet on 21 July 1970: Harry Gibbs, 'the obvious candidate'. Barwick agreed. Ninian Stephen's name was mentioned during the Cabinet discussion. Hughes explained that age was an important consideration; Gibbs was 53 and Stephen 47. Hughes emphasised that Gibbs was a Queenslander and described him as someone having sufficient eminence. He also pointed out how Stephen had only recently been appointed to the Victorian Supreme Court. Snedden said he supported Gibbs, while observing that the Victorian Bar would object. Bowen and Anthony spoke in favour of Gibbs.[14] Cabinet agreed that Gibbs should be appointed.[15]

A liberal or a conservative?

There was early media curiosity about how the Attorney-General might approach issues of community concern. Interviewed by Allan Barnes of the *Age*,[16] Hughes said he opposed capital punishment; he was not 'a hanger'. Hughes did not expect to be a 'trend-setter' on abortion law and, while he had not made any detailed examination of the case for legalising homosexual relations between consenting males, 'I would tend to be a conservative'.

He respected the right of people to dissent and join demonstrations – of whatever persuasion – but that should be qualified where physical activity impinged on others. After reminding Barnes of his speech on the issue in Parliament, Hughes reiterated his support for lowering the voting age to 18. Explaining that he had never practised in the divorce jurisdiction, though he had acted in divorce cases, the Attorney said he had no views on divorce reform. He had not studied the new British law where the sole ground for divorce was the irretrievable breakdown of a marriage. Asked about courtroom procedures, he thought that the right to make an unsworn statement from the dock in criminal cases, which was not subject to cross-examination, might well be removed. He would not rush to dispense with wigs and gowns: 'I believe a degree of tradition is a good thing.' Inevitably, Barnes raised the question of whether Hughes' religious beliefs would inhibit him in his new post. In reply, the Attorney said he hoped to approach every issue without prejudice, but admitted that on the issue of abortion law reform 'it would be hard for me to go along with things being advocated in some quarters'.

Hughes was anxious to stress two things about his approach. First, experience of the law 'tends to make you pragmatic'. The law seeks practical solutions for situations that arise. He saw himself, therefore, as 'a practical fellow who goes down the middle of the road'. Secondly, he did not believe that law reformers should be leading public opinion. Barnes, rightly, marked this view as conservative. Yet the new Attorney-General, being both practical and open to ideas, said it would not only be a duty but a pleasure to listen to responsible persons who had views on law reform.

Some in the media highlighted Hughes' religious affiliations when considering how he might deal with the issues of abortion, divorce and homosexuality. Mungo MacCallum started with the proposition that Hughes was 'a devout Catholic', and that the Attorney told him, 'I haven't lost any of my essential Catholic beliefs'.[17] MacCallum was not to know that the private Hughes was already becoming another lapsed Catholic. It took Robert Hughes some years to appreciate the nature of Tom's beliefs. Whereas their brother, Geoffrey, 'was a pillar of piety and ancestor-worship whose faith never wavered for an instant … Tom's attachment to religion was more formal than emotional'.[18] The 'essential Catholic beliefs' on moral issues could, of course, survive a loss of faith and a detachment from the Church.

Capital punishment, a poignant issue since the execution of Ronald Joseph Ryan in Victoria in 1967, seized first place on Hughes' agenda. He took a submission to Cabinet in February 1970 proposing the removal of the death penalty for all offences against the Commonwealth except for the crime of treason. The politician, conscious of the middle of the road, noted that public opinion had hardened against capital punishment. Whereas 68 per cent supported the death penalty for murder in 1947, the approval rate had fallen to 43 per cent in 1967, with 46 per cent against. He reported that the Advisory Council of the Australian Capital Territory and the *Canberra Times* supported abolition. He proffered three arguments in support of change: the irreversible character of the punishment; the death penalty being inconsistent with the Christian ethic; and execution having a tendency 'to work a degrading and demoralising effect on all persons concerned'. He also claimed that the Australian Capital Territory did not have the facilities to apply the death penalty. Cabinet decided on 30 April to defer consideration until legislation to provide a uniform disciplinary code for the Services was ready for introduction.[19]

On 27 May 1970, five months after appearing to rule out homosexual law reform, the Attorney shocked many on all sides of politics. After careful thought, and working closely with Brian O'Donovan of the Attorney-General's Department, who was a devout Catholic, he addressed the sixth national conference of the Australian Council for Social Services at the Australian National University (ANU). Hughes questioned whether homosexual acts between consenting adults in private should remain a criminal offence. It was one thing to disapprove of homosexual activities on moral grounds; it was another to classify them as criminal.

> In a pluralist society it is no part of the function of the criminal law to uphold and preserve the Judeo-Christian ethic simply because that ethic exists. Any attempt to make the criminal law perform such a task would reflect a confusion between the respective places of law and morality in such a society.

But he thought it wise, in view of the longstanding application of criminal sanctions, to move cautiously before deciding to abandon them. He also said that exercising caution did not involve a slow pace of activity. Yet the law 'will do better to travel on a median course between the crest and trough of successive waves of public opinion rather than to conform itself to every prevailing mood'.

On 21 September, he told another ANU audience that the Federal Government was unlikely to give a lead on homosexual law reform. He described his May statement as 'kite-flying, designed to gauge public opinion'. The trend of the correspondence he had received since making that statement was against any change to the law. At the same time, he reiterated his central point: '[c]ertain categories of misconduct ought to be a matter between Man and his Maker, rather than a matter of criminal consequence between Man and his temporal lawmaker.'[20] Reflecting on these views years later, Hughes said they were 'a little ahead of their time', and did not find favour with the mainstream of the Liberal Party. Jim Cameron, who had previously supported him in Berowra, used Hughes' speech in May to justify opposing him for preselection in 1971.[21]

Hughes remained cautious on divorce law reform. In an address to the Family Life Movement in St James' Hall, Sydney, on 20 April 1970, he said he would study the British legislation on irretrievable breakdown as the sole ground for divorce. He was very conscious of the fact that there were currently 14 grounds for divorce in Australia, but was not disposed to make any decision until the British legislation had been in operation for some time. Speaking for himself, he thought that, because changes of the British kind would have such sociological significance, it was desirable and necessary to exercise caution. He stressed he had not reached any kind of conclusion.[22]

Whereas many Liberals regarded his approach to homosexual law reform as amounting to an attack on Christianity and Western Civilisation, others saw his reluctance to pursue divorce law reform as inhumane and illiberal. Soon after McMahon sacked Hughes as Attorney-General, Harold Harris, the President of the Divorce Law Association, told him that the Association was 'very happy that you got a taste of the treatment which you were giving to us people' (emphasis in the original). He accused Hughes of seeing it 'beneath your dignity' to work with the Association in finding ways to amend the iniquitous divorce laws, and said it would work against Hughes' re-election should the Party re-endorse him.[23] There is no record of the Harris reaction to Hughes' divorce of 1973 that was obtained under a law the former Attorney-General was not prepared to amend.

Early crises

Within days of his taking office, the *Daily Mirror* claimed that Hughes faced the possibility of gaoling Joanna's uncle, the poet RD FitzGerald. The new Attorney had inherited a policy of fining anyone who encouraged young men to defy the *National Service Act 1964* (Cth). Those who refused to pay the fine of $50 were liable for imprisonment for 25 days. FitzGerald, a member of an anti-Vietnam war group, was one of 39 people fined in mid-October for encouraging defiance. Nearly all decided not to pay the fine. Assuming that FitzGerald was also a defaulter, the *Mirror* approached Hughes for his reaction. He had not realised that 'Uncle Bob' was among those fined, adding that they got on well despite their political differences. FitzGerald would not cause any embarrassment. Unaware of the stand his associates had taken, FitzGerald, much to his later regret, paid the fine well before publication of the *Daily Mirror* story.[24]

A more significant issue arose out of a meeting held on 15 December 1969 called by the Trade Union Anti-Conscription Committee. Attended by some 200 unionists, the meeting passed a two-part resolution, urging already conscripted young men not to accept orders obliging them to act against their conscience, and calling on Australian forces in Vietnam 'to lay down their arms in mutiny against the heinous barbarism perpetrated in our name upon innocent aged men, women and children'. George Crawford, Federal Secretary of the Plumbers' Union and President of the Victorian Branch of the Labor Party, chaired the meeting. Gorton denounced the resolution as 'a stark incitement to mutiny'. The National President of the RSL said his organisation had asked the Attorney-General 'to use the full weight of the law in taking appropriate action'. Crawford declared he was not at all worried about any investigation, but stressed he was acting as a union official and not speaking for, or on behalf of, the Labor Party.

Hughes delivered a four-page memorandum to Gorton on 9 January 1970.[25] He and senior officers in the Department had carefully examined reports from the Commonwealth Police. The basic question, he argued, was whether the facts and circumstances warranted criminal proceedings for an offence under s 25 of the Commonwealth *Crimes Act*. This section provided, in part, that any person who knowingly attempted to incite any person serving in the Queen's Services to commit an act of mutiny would be guilty of an indictable offence with a conviction carrying a maximum penalty of life imprisonment. After deliberation, Hughes had reached the conclusion that the Crown should not proceed with a prosecution against anyone connected with the meeting on 15 December 1969 or, in a separate case, against a Law academic in Tasmania who had made a provocative speech. He noted that the Solicitor-General, RJ 'Bob' Ellicott, had independently arrived at the same position.

Before setting out his reasons, Tom identified two important considerations. First, 'it would be most unwise to prosecute for an indictable offence when the context is highly political, unless the Crown's case is clearly strong in law. An unsuccessful prosecution could do great harm to the Government's standing.' Secondly, because an attempted incitement had to be undertaken 'knowingly', a jury would not be entitled to convict unless satisfied beyond reasonable doubt that the accused intended the words to be understood by service personnel as an incitement to mutiny.

At this point, the Attorney listed the principal reasons for not taking action over the December resolutions. The movers of the motion had published a disclaimer in relation to the wording and an accused person could fairly argue that the disclaimer represented his intended meaning. It would be difficult to prove that handing a copy of the resolution to the press was intended to communicate the alleged incitement to servicemen in Vietnam. Although the meaning of the resolution accorded with Gorton's phrase – 'stark incitement' – the words contained 'a small germ of ambiguity' which the defence might develop in line with the disclaimer, and a trial judge could not simply dismiss this claim. Jurors would be well aware of the extreme gravity of any offence under the *Crimes Act*, and might be unwilling to convict if they had the slightest doubt.

Hughes concluded by proposing he should issue a longer press statement than normal. Ordinarily, he would not give a detailed statement of reasons for declining to prosecute. 'But the circumstances here are quite out of the ordinary.' There was a high level of public interest, a number of responsible citizens had written letters urging him to prosecute, the DLP had been agitating for action and the Government could be accused of pusillanimity unless it set out the reasons. Hughes, therefore, attached a two-page draft press statement to what became a Cabinet submission. In essence, he wanted to say that a prosecution for an indictable offence should not be instituted unless the case was strong in law. The prosecution would have to prove beyond reasonable doubt that the accused intended the words to be used as an incitement to mutiny. In light of these considerations, he had decided not to act. Reviewing the two cases, he bore in mind that public indignation was not itself a justification for instigating prosecutions. The criminal law should not be invoked unless all of the available evidence pointed to the fact of a crime having been committed.

John McEwen took issue with the Attorney before Cabinet met on 13 January 1971 to consider Hughes' submission. The Deputy Prime Minister insisted it was a matter for Cabinet to decide whether to proceed with a prosecution. Hughes took what he saw as the long-established view that it was up to the Attorney-General to make the decision. While he would take account of the views of senior ministers, he was not bound by the views of a minister or of Cabinet as a whole. McEwen and Cabinet eventually accepted the Hughes position.[26] Cabinet also endorsed the Attorney-General's conclusions that there should be no prosecutions but favoured a press statement 'on minimum lines'. That is, the Attorney-General had initiated inquiries and, after taking the advice of his senior officers, including the Solicitor-General, and considering the material himself, had 'formed the conclusion that no prosecution should be instituted in either of these cases'.[27] The last thing Cabinet wanted was a general debate about when to prosecute.

Despite the requirement to amend his press statement, the Attorney-General had achieved two important things at the beginning of what he hoped would be a long period in office. Cabinet had confirmed his authority as the principal law officer of the Crown to make the final decision on the issue of prosecution; and it had accepted that, in making his decision, he would consider what was both legally possible and politically acceptable.

The case of Wilfred Burchett

In March 1970, Hughes was asked for advice on another difficult political issue. Wilfred Burchett (1911-1983),[28] an Australian-born war correspondent and author, had reported the Korean War from the behind the North Korean and Chinese lines and was later accused of interrogating Allied prisoners and of working for the North Vietnamese in the Vietnam War. The British Foreign Office initially denied him entry to the United Kingdom after Burchett lost his British passport in 1955 and the Menzies Government refused to issue an Australian replacement. Subsequent applications for an Australian passport met the same result. Burchett's lawyers wrote to Prime Minister Gorton in 1969 to inform him that, to clear his name, their client had instituted libel proceedings against the Melbourne *Herald* and the journalist Denis Warner. They wanted Gorton to hold a judicial inquiry and to grant Burchett a passport.

Cabinet on 30 April 1969 had decided that, while the Government could not lawfully deny Burchett entry into Australia, the Government would not grant him any document and would not facilitate his return. Cabinet noted Nigel Bowen's advice as Attorney-General that it was doubtful whether a prosecution for Burchett's activities abroad could be sustained under the *Crimes Act*. If questioned, the accepted line was that Burchett would not be given a passport, having represented himself as a Cuban citizen, and there would be no judicial inquiry into the allegations. Burchett arrived in Australia in February 1970 by private plane from Noumea. There was no attempt to impede his entry. On 25 February, Ainsley Gotto sent the Prime Minister a memorandum relating to the handling of the Burchett issue in Parliament.[29] Convinced that Burchett was a traitor, Gorton explained in his marginal comments that he had no intention of dignifying 'the bastard' by saying there was not enough evidence to prosecute him for treason. Gotto asked whether he intended to make 'a reasoned, middle-of-the-road, unemotional statement … ?' (emphasis in the original). Gorton noted in the margin: 'unemotional but as vicious as possible'.

On 3 March, the Attorney-General delivered his written advice to the Prime Minister.[30] Hughes told Gorton he had concluded that, after studying the available material, the less said about the reasons for refusing to help Burchett to enter Australia the better it would be. If the Government made specific and detailed accusations about Burchett's alleged treachery, it may be forced to reveal to Parliament the source of those allegations and that there was no hard evidence to substantiate them. Apart from a statutory declaration made by an ex-POW, the available material consisted of signed statements by journalists and ex-servicemen who had been in Korea, cables from the US State Department purporting to summarise the views of unidentified US airmen, and magazine articles and transcripts of radio interviews between Burchett and those airmen (the tapes had been destroyed). Hughes did not want the Government relying on 'legally unverified or unverifiable material'. Should it be so placed, the Government would come under greater pressure to hold a formal inquiry. In these circumstances, Hughes advised that, in response to any question about its refusal to assist Burchett's re-entry, the Government should point out there was no legal obligation to help him and that, in light of his activities, it had no moral obligation to assist him.

On 4 March, the second parliamentary sitting day of 1970, both sides of the House of Representatives wanted the Government to explain its position. The Labor Party took up the issue of an inquiry. Gorton's response may be summarised thus: it was a matter of public record that Burchett had lived behind enemy lines in two wars where Australian forces were involved; he had engaged in propaganda helpful to the enemy; and he had visited POW camps where Australian troops were incarcerated. On this last point, Gorton said he believed there was evidence that Burchett sought to lower their morale and demean the cause for which they had been fighting. There was no need, in Gorton's view, to appoint a judicial inquiry to establish these facts, and the facts themselves justified the Government's decision not to provide Burchett with a passport or to ask Australian posts to assist him. Later in question time, Whitlam asked the Attorney-General whether he thought Burchett had broken any Commonwealth law or whether any investigation was underway to see if he had done so. Hughes declined to give an opinion on whether a Commonwealth law had been broken, while adding that he, as the Crown's principal law officer, did not intend to lay charges. David Fairbairn, from the Government's side, asked if there were plans to amend Australian law to cover future actions giving assistance to the enemy. Gorton said he would take up with the Attorney-General the question of whether changes were needed.

Tom Uren, from the Labor Left and a former POW in the Second World War, visited the Attorney-General early on the afternoon of 5 March to say he intended to raise the Burchett allegations during the adjournment debate. As Uren said in that debate, he had listened to many wild charges over the two days. For him, it was a matter of principle: if the allegations against 'this man' (he never mentioned Burchett by name) were true, then what he had done amounted to the crime of treason. On the other hand, no one should be convicted on the basis of 'a well-known fact'. The Government should take up Burchett's offer to face an inquiry and 'Put up or shut up'. While acknowledging that Uren had spoken with 'forbearance and restraint', Hughes followed Gorton's line in rejecting an inquiry. Addressing Fred Daly's question about why the Government had not charged Burchett with treason, the Attorney pointed out that the *Crimes Act*, which defined the offence of treason, had no extra-territorial operation at the time of the Korean War. Burchett could not be indicted for anything he did in Korea, 'however treacherous or traitorous or disloyal or indecent it may have been'.[31] Whitlam accepted the Hughes argument about the limitations of the *Crimes Act* as it then applied. Cleverly, however, he raised the possibility of charging Burchett with common law treason, an offence each State had inherited from English law. Hughes replied that the issue had not escaped his attention but there were other hurdles (he did not spell them out) which made that approach impracticable. Closing what had degenerated at times into a fiercely partisan debate, Clyde Cameron complimented the Attorney-General for approaching the whole question 'in the correct manner by discussing the law rather than the political implications and the political backwash'.[32]

The evening's proceedings were important for Hughes because he could present himself as a non-political Attorney-General, except for making the point that Labor opposed Garfield Barwick's attempt in 1960 to amend the legislation to provide for its extra-territorial operation. Hughes was no longer just another Vietnam hawk. As his Labor opponents came to terms with his translation to another role, they understood that the lawyer could more easily acknowledge and even accept different viewpoints and would look for workable solutions to intractable problems.

As Hughes found later in the year, radical opponents of conscription and the Vietnam War identified him as the unacceptable face of oppression, while conservative opponents of violent protest saw him as the unacceptable face of compromise. One could never accept he was non-political; the other did not want him to be so. Yet, even when it became harder to maintain his self-image, Tom Hughes had a clear view throughout 1970 of what he should be, and appear to be. As he explained to the Liberal Party branch meeting in March 1970, he had become two different people.[33] He remained 'a practising politician' who felt 'the political passions that usually course through the veins of all practising political animals'. He could and should make political speeches when the time was appropriate. As Attorney-General, he had to be dispassionate and non-political in administering the law. In that capacity, he was not a politician; he was 'the Queen's Agent administering the law for her'. If he decided to prosecute someone for committing 'a political offence', the decision itself had to be non-political. It should be based on considerations such as:

> Is there a prima facie case … ? If there is a prima facie case, what are the prospects ultimately of a conviction … ? If there are ultimate prospects of conviction, is the offence, looked at broadly and from a commonsense basis, only of a technical character … ? If there is an offence which is likely to be proved and if a conviction is likely,

> is it an offence where on balance a conviction would not serve the public interest because it perhaps tend[s] only to make the defendant or accused a martyr … ?

In deciding these questions, he had to isolate himself from party politics and political advantage. Only by doing so could an Attorney-General 'do his job as it ought to be done'. Not all his predecessors and not all his successors saw themselves in that way.

11

Public order: 'exercising caution, moderation and restraint'

When Hughes came into office as Attorney-General, he found that the Gorton Government had already been considering legislative action to maintain public order. Nigel Bowen, Hughes' predecessor, took a proposal to Cabinet in April 1969. He wanted comparable State and Commonwealth legislation to protect ministers and MPs from violence, to meet in full Australia's obligations under the Vienna Convention to protect representatives of other countries and their premises, and to give the Commonwealth power to take action against violence and lawlessness associated with demonstrations against Commonwealth policy and taking place on or near Commonwealth property. Cabinet addressed the Bowen submission in September without taking any action. Instead, Gorton spoke in the 1969 election campaign about introducing legislation to help preserve law and order. Whitlam kept reminding the Government of Gorton's statement during the first half of 1970. Even so, the matter remained in abeyance until July-August.

The first Moratorium

Contrary to government expectations, the Moratorium of 8 May 1970 did not provide the catalyst for a legislative response.

On 15 October 1969, the anti-war movement in the United States held a major demonstration – a 'Moratorium' – to indicate a refusal to accept 'business as usual' while the war in Vietnam continued. The anti-war and anti-conscription organisations in Australia took up the idea of one big demonstration to take place throughout the country. The stated aims of what became the Vietnam Moratorium Campaign were to secure the withdrawal of Australian and all foreign troops from Vietnam and the repeal of the *National Service Act*. Each part of the country would organise its own campaign. Although there was no formal leadership, Jim Cairns became the voice and conscience of the protest. The Government could do little as the Moratorium approached, except to demonise some of the sponsors and to warn of the probability of violence.[1] Faced with a restless backbench in Canberra, the Government decided to take an initiative. The Attorney-General made a ministerial statement late on the afternoon of 14 April 1970.

Hughes said he was hoping to persuade some of the Moratorium's sponsors and supporters to reconsider their association. He wanted to highlight the key role of the Congress for International Co-operation and Disarmament, a 'creature' of the communist-front organisation, the World Peace Council. He observed how supporters of the campaign included 'an assorted collection of Communists, Communist-sympathisers, Trotskyites and anarchists'. The Attorney raised questions about members of the Labor Party associating with communists and quoted Cairns' statement in 1964 that Labor was next to the communists on the spectrum and at times would be 'doing the same things for the same ends'. Yet Hughes stopped well short of accusing the Moratorium campaign of being communist-controlled, or even communist-influenced. It was more a case of inviting the Labor Party and the well-intentioned campaigners to take note of the company they were keeping. This approach was far too mild for the Liberal Party's hard-line anti-communists.

While accepting that many decent Australians supported the aims of the Moratorium, Hughes argued that the methods for achieving their objectives were not 'calculated to serve the public interest'. Attempts to change the law in a democratic society should be made within the framework of the law, and that principle applied especially to members of parliament. They should not be

> resorting to, or encouraging, activities based simply on the naked physical power of a mob, designed to force or embarrass a government into taking steps in conflict with the policies upon which that government secured a mandate to govern.

Hughes acknowledged that Whitlam, Lance Barnard, the Deputy Leader, and 'a very small minority' of Federal Labor parliamentarians did not sign statements sponsoring the Moratorium. Nonetheless, 75 Labor members of the Federal Parliament had done so, thereby calling into question their commitment to parliamentary democracy.

Hughes then focused on the issue of violence. He questioned whether the campaign could be conducted without violence, given that Cairns said he could not guarantee non-violence. Indeed, Cairns could not expect non-violence to prevail when, on 25 March, he called for workers and students and citizens to occupy the streets of Melbourne. Nor could Cairns expect the organisers to control all those who intended to participate. This point became pertinent after a public meeting in the Melbourne suburb of Richmond voted on 1 February to remove from the statement of aims of the Moratorium movement that 'all actions taken be of a peaceful, non-violent nature'. It was always good politics to highlight divisions between Whitlam and Cairns, to show that the former believed in the capacity of parliament to implement and manage change and that the latter did not share his Leader's faith. Hughes closed his speech, therefore, by calling on 'my honourable friend [Whitlam] … to get off the fence and denounce the methods to be used on 8 May'.

All those who followed Hughes on the Government side – no senior minister spoke – raised the temperature and lowered the rationality. A week later, McEwen chaired a meeting of the joint parties because Gorton had gone to Sydney to meet Queen Elizabeth II on the Royal Yacht *Britannia*. As a result, according to Howson, 'we had a united party, discussing objectively the issues of the proposed Moratorium, that is, the conservatives (almost all of them anti-Gortonites) took it in turns to 'expose' the Moratorium campaign as a communist conspiracy. They elected a committee, chaired by David Fairbairn, to organise publicity against the Moratorium.[2] In his new role, Fairbairn used a parliamentary question to invite the Attorney-General to name the hard-core communists who were among the sponsors of the Moratorium. Hughes said he had no intention of using and abusing parliamentary privilege for that purpose.[3] On the eve of the Moratorium, Fairbairn delivered a strong message about what was wrong with it, and Malcolm Fraser, as Minister for Defence, joined in with more of a rant than a speech that had the backbench cheering.[4]

There was just one problem. Apart from an incident involving some soldiers in Adelaide, the Moratorium was remarkably peaceful. Some 70,000 people joined Cairns for the march in Melbourne. They sat down and briefly occupied Bourke Street while marshals effectively controlled proceedings. Helen Williams, a young public servant in the Cabinet Office, correctly summed up the situation. 'Perhaps it [the Moratorium] may best be seen as an example of a self-destroying prophecy, the number and strength of the predictions that trouble would result increasing the determination of those involved to avoid it.'[5]

'The man students love to hate'[6]

Hughes later explained that the need for public order legislation arose from 'occasionally violent demonstrations'. He happened to be involved in two of them before a further cabinet discussion of public order legislation. Both incidents arose from opposition to the *National Service Act*.

At the end of July 1970, the Attorney-General was invited to address the University of Sydney Liberal Club at lunchtime on the subject of 'Problems Facing an Attorney-General'. His message might well have irritated radicals and conservatives alike. He said that launching prosecutions against those who invited charges for breaching the *National Service Act* would do more harm than good. They wanted to be martyrs and he did not intend to oblige them. Besides, he did not believe that all the 'posturing' and all the 'clap-trap' had any appreciable effect on the overwhelming number of young men who accepted the law as it was and did their duty.

As he was concluding his speech, about 150 members of the Students for a Democratic Society (SDS) walked into the lecture theatre in the Merewether Building. The President of the Liberal Club closed the meeting and, flanked by his private secretary and his press secretary, Hughes tried to leave. The SDS formed a barricade across the exit, but the Attorney's party managed to break through, assisted by some of the students who had listened to his address. Surrounded and jostled, Hughes eventually reached his Commonwealth car on City Road. One of its tyres had been let down and slogans – one read 'Fascist' – had been scrawled on the back of the car. Protected by friendly students, Hughes' party finally found refuge in the Anglican St Paul's College. The Attorney had a cup of coffee before escaping by a back door. A senior student drove him to his office. Meanwhile, more than 100 police and every available police car had arrived outside the University without attempting to enter the grounds.

Hughes described the SDS students as 'an atypical, unimpressive, motley mob'. He said they did not frighten him and, though they pushed and shoved, no one threw a punch – and that rather surprised him. 'Politicians and people in public life must be expected to run some sort of risks.' Hughes also made a point, sometimes overlooked by hotheads in his own Party: 'these yahoos' constituted a very small minority within the university student community. He hoped that the general public would recognise this fact.[7] Hughes said he would go to any university if invited, and without a police escort, because a police presence would ensure a riot. When, however, the Liberal Club invited him to speak at the University of Sydney on 8 September, he withdrew his acceptance after the President of the Students Representative Council requested him to cancel the proposed visit. The President referred to 'current feelings' on the campus, to 'the seriousness of the situation' and to the prospect of violent demonstrations. Hughes regretted that the 'very sound principle' of guests being allowed to express their view 'is being undermined by threatened violence on the part of an unrepresentative minority of the student body, fomented by at least one person who is not a student'.[8]

There was a particular reason for the concern about violence on 8 September. The second incident involving the Attorney, and the more personally disturbing one, guaranteed there would be violent protest.

On Sunday 16 August, following a meeting at the Boilermakers Hall in Castlereagh Street, an estimated 25 to 40 demonstrators went to the Hughes home in Bellevue Hill at around 2.00 pm. They brought a list of 182 names of young men from all States except Western Australia who had refused to register for national service. Hughes had claimed that only about 50 eligible males had failed to register. Arriving in a convoy of cars, the demonstrators walked to the front door and knocked. Hughes was inside the house with his two sons. Tom Jnr was then aged seven and Michael was five. Joanna and Lucy had left for the airport to holiday on the snowfields. Hughes, who had just arrived back from Western Australia and was expecting child-minding helpers, opened the door twice and slammed it shut each time. The protestors pinned their list of 182 names on the door and scrawled anti-war, anti-conscription and Moratorium messages on the windows. Hughes described how he locked his two crying and very upset boys in an upstairs bedroom, phoned the police and armed himself with Tom Jnr's cricket bat. Constable Pringle arrived, told the demonstrators to leave, and Hughes came out of the house carrying the bat. A dozen more police and two paddy wagons then turned up. Hughes walked up his driveway and had a brief scuffle with one of the protesters.

Joanna learnt of the incident when she rang home from the airport. She arranged for friends to look after Lucy and dashed back to Bellevue Hill. Joanna immediately phoned her uncle, RD FitzGerald, asking him to take whatever action he could to prevent innocent children from being terrorised. FitzGerald was 'terribly upset' and promised to speak at meetings against taking action of a similar kind. But he was probably right in saying he had little influence, though he was well aware that such incidents damaged the Moratorium cause for which he was a convener. Joanna also felt 'a sense of betrayal'; one of the very young female demonstrators had previously stayed with the Hughes family.[9]

The Commonwealth and NSW Police each suggested their continued presence, but Tom and Joanna settled for the offer of a police car making regular visits to their street. Some 20 uniformed and plain-clothes police were called to the house on the following night at around 10.30 pm, when about 30 demonstrators walked in single file up and down Bellevue Road just outside the Hughes home. They carried posters and some sang or whistled what had become John Lennon's anti-war anthem: 'All we are saying is give peace a chance.' Occasionally, some would chant so loudly the police had to warn them against disturbing the peace. Wearing a duffle coat, Tom stood at the driveway for a time to watch the parade. He spoke of 'a very nervous little boy' after what had happened the previous day and suggested that the demonstrators 'have done irreparable damage to the Moratorium'. The last of the demonstrators left the street at 12.40 am.

Understandably, someone who was both a parent and a politician wanted to underscore the threatening aspects of the 'invasion', and to make the point that on the Sunday he was protecting two small children as well as defending his house. But Michael Hughes, who claims a 'clear as crystal' memory of the event and of its immediate aftermath, does not remember feeling any fear. For him, it was 'quite an exciting time'. He was watching black and white television downstairs when his father asked him to go upstairs with him and his brother to look for a cricket bat in the cupboard. Michael recalled seeing a lot of 'hippies' outside the house, and later did a drawing of 'hippies in our garden'. It was 'fun' when detectives turned up and showed the boys the revolvers they carried in their holsters.[10]

In all, nine people were arrested at the scene that Sunday and were charged with being on 'enclosed land'. Released on bail, they appeared before a magistrate on 17 August. Several of them had earned the respect of the anti-Vietnam, anti-conscription community for draft dodging or participating in violent protest. Michael Hamel-Green and Ian Macdonald were students from Victoria and shared accommodation in Carlton. Macdonald had several convictions in his portfolio. He had helped form the La Trobe University Chapter of the SDS, and in September 1969 became the Business Manager for SDS at its National Office in Cremorne Point. When the National Office closed, he returned to La Trobe, where he became active in the SDS Chapter and the Labor Club and spent most of his time in 1970 organising radical activities and demonstrations. In June, he was suspended for three days from La Trobe University after leading more than 60 students on a forced entry into the Administration Building where two glass doors were smashed and a security guard was injured. By August 1970, he had become a credentialed and career demonstrator. His portfolio has since expanded and diversified. These days Macdonald is better known as the former NSW Labor minister found by the NSW Independent Commission Against Corruption in 2013 to have engaged in corrupt conduct to the benefit of the Obeid family.

The magistrate sentenced six of the protesters (including Macdonald) to 14 days hard labour for contempt of court. Each had raised his left arm with a clenched fist in what four of them described as 'an international gesture'.[11] On 20 August, Taylor J in the Supreme Court ordered the magistrate, the prosecutor and the Long Bay gaoler to show cause before the Court of Appeal why the six men should not be released. In the Court of Appeal Asprey, Holmes and Mason JJA refused all six applications for release.

Meanwhile, friends were quick to lend Hughes their support.[12] Sir James Plimsoll, Australia's Ambassador in Washington, wrote to the Attorney on 28 August enclosing a copy of a judgment by Justice Hugo Black of the US Supreme Court and comments by Justice Arthur Goldberg. Both men were regarded as 'liberals', and both concluded that a person was entitled to have the privacy of his home preserved without having it disturbed by picketing. Many commented on his 'fine innings'. Tom especially liked the note he received from Jack Fingleton, a journalist and cricket writer and a former Australian opening batsman of the 1930s: 'Footwork magnificent – cannot be faulted. Grip with bat just a little suspect. Perhaps hands should have been closer together although gap is permissible if stroke is improvised.' Strangers also contacted the Attorney-General. An English immigrant, a stonemason who had settled in Tasmania for 20 years, told the Attorney-General he was angry that university students, given a chance not available to him, were abusing their privileges; they should be expelled for participating in such demonstrations. Next time, Hughes should use the bat, and have a scatter gun handy. 'More power to your elbow.' The Attorney replied: 'I cannot tell you how much it means to someone with my problems to receive such kind words of encouragement.' Hughes expected to be in Launceston fairly soon and asked if he might get in touch.[13]

Tom Hughes and the cricket bat quickly entered folk lore. On the Sunday after the 'invasion' a number of protesters played a game of cricket on Bellevue Road opposite the Hughes house. After half an hour, the police moved them off the street, whereupon the demonstrators marched up and down the footpath displaying placards. The Hughes family were not at home. Labor MPs could not resist making oblique or direct references to the cricket bat. When Hughes arrived at the ANU at the end of September to address a Liberal Club meeting, students dressed in cricket gear greeted him. Batsmen wearing 'Tom Hughes' placards had been amusing onlookers outside the lecture theatre by missing the 'ball of dissent' aimed at the 'law and order' stumps. On Hughes' arrival, the cricketers formed a guard of honour and presented arms with cricket bats. The Attorney won some approval by inspecting the guard and signing bats.[14] Over 40 years later, the mere mention of writing a biography of Tom Hughes would provoke those who had a memory of that time to refer immediately to the incident with the cricket bat. Writing about Robert Hughes after his death in 2012, Catherine Lumby recalled that his older brother 'was an Australian federal attorney-general and famous for taking a cricket bat out to his front lawn to scare off anti-Vietnam war protestors'.[15]

Against this background, it is hardly surprising that journalists in the later months of 1970 were keen to write (mostly unfavourable) profiles of

Tom Hughes, the Attorney-General. They were prompted to draw parallels between the Hughes family and the Kennedys of the United States: the Irish ancestry, the second generation who prospered in the 'New World' (John Hughes), the achievements of the third (John and Thomas Hughes) and the fourth (Geoffrey Hughes) generations, the sense of feeling and being special. Gavin Souter quoted 'one of the Attorney-General's fellow silks' who said the Hugheses thought of themselves as an 'Australian aristocracy' and that Tom has 'a feeling of hauteur about him'. A 'fellow minister' saw nothing strange about this. 'What's he supposed to do – throw it away?' All the anonymous sources agreed that Hughes was a hard worker and was tense rather than cool like (some of) the Kennedys. A 'friend' said relatively few at the Bar liked him; many thought him 'reserved, slightly cold'. A QC, 'who is no longer a friend', said that removed from his context where he was an object of approval 'he is inclined to react in a haughty, arrogant way'. Claudia Wright supposed there were parallels that went beyond a similar story of 'the Irish who-made-good'. There was 'Tom the ambitious politician and aspiring PM [Wright failed to spot that he was neither]; Joanna the headstrong, attractive, wilful, intelligent mother who – like Jackie [Kennedy] was a journalist and comes from a family established in the arts.' Hughes himself pointed to the essential difference: 'We have no money', and the family owned just one house and one car.[16]

Legislating for public order

Three days after the 'invasion', Ray Whittorn, a Liberal backbencher from Victoria, asked the Attorney-General how long the Government intended to tolerate attacks on political leaders, the destruction of property, the shouting of obscenities and the involvement of innocent civilians 'before it enforces the law'. At first, Hughes replied with what the backbench wanted to hear. Nothing more concentrates the mind, he said, than having 'to defend one's home and one's children' from 'a wanton invasion by … idiotic vandals intent on defacing one's property'. While identifying himself with the victims of violent demonstrations, Hughes said he intended to continue exercising 'caution, moderation and restraint', which was the proper approach to matters requiring 'a semi-judicial discretion'. He drew attention to pending prosecutions, assured the House he would proceed where he thought prosecution was appropriate and said he was fully conscious of the need to preserve law and order 'by all proper means'.[17] Whittorn and others on the backbench wanted a more aggressive response.

Habitual Gorton critics – Jess, Mackay, Irwin and Kevin Cairns – used an acrimonious Liberal Party Room meeting on 26 August 1970 to demand action from the Government over violent demonstrations. They also wanted the Government to make a stand against the ACTU's decision to hold strikes and protests over the budget.[18] Gorton's response was to use a parliamentary question on the same day to lambast Bob Hawke, the ACTU President, as 'a would-be dictator', who incited people to break the law if their objects could not be achieved through proper political channels. He claimed that 'the vast majority of Australians' would back a government which, without interfering with the free expression of opposition, would take action against intimidation and interference with civil rights. In one brief sentence he added that the Government intended to ask parliament to take such action.[19] Sir Frank Packer's *Daily Telegraph* of 27 August said the action was coming 'not a day too soon'. While the *Age* on 28 August agreed that people and property had to be protected from the harmful effects of mass political action, it said society itself would suffer from 'an unnecessary stock-piling of powerful legal weapons'. Using the first Moratorium as an example, the paper argued that there was no clear and present danger to public order. The Government 'would be well advised to reconsider the wisdom of waving the big stick'. The Commonwealth Attorney-General, though thoroughly demonised by student protestors, was well aware of the risks involved.

On 2 September, Hughes asked Cabinet to authorise him to prepare a Public Order Bill with particular guidelines in mind. Everyone, he said, was familiar with deliberate breaches of the peace that harmed the rights of fellow citizens. He believed the great majority of Australians opposed this kind of behaviour and would welcome firm action by the Government. Three matters, however, should be kept in mind in preparing legislation:

> first, the Commonwealth's constitutional powers in this field are limited and the circumstances in which the provisions of the Bill creating offences will be applicable must be carefully defined;
>
> second, the Bill must carefully safeguard the peaceful expression of opposition against legislation and Government policy; and the use of legitimate means to pursue changes in law and in policy;
>
> third, while the Bill should include measures sufficient to meet existing and foreseeable circumstances, the Government must take care not to introduce legislation that goes beyond what is reasonably necessary; to do so would be undesirable, both in principle and politically.

Hughes sought approval to develop a Bill that took account of these guidelines while acting against a breach of the peace and the use of violence to prevent the implementation of Commonwealth laws. His other concern was that the States might be sensitive about new Commonwealth laws encroaching on their responsibilities. He proposed, with Cabinet's approval, to be in contact with State Attorneys once the Commonwealth's legislation had been prepared.[20]

Ministers wanted him to proceed except that, typically, McMahon did not want to act in haste and, typically, Gorton wanted to act quickly. McEwen stressed the necessity of legislating to deal with violence and breaches of the law and of not appearing to defend a political position. Doug Anthony spoke firmly in support of Hughes' three principles. While Gorton agreed with Anthony in accepting the three principles, he wanted to differentiate between what was being attempted now and what was involved in the *Communist Party Dissolution Act*.[21] Cabinet authorised the Attorney-General to produce a draft Bill along the lines suggested, with the rider that he should have it ready so that Cabinet could decide whether to introduce the Bill before the end of the year when a half-Senate election was due.

On the day Cabinet made this decision, the Commonwealth Police sent the Attorney-General a summary of demonstrations assembled by the Crime Intelligence Bureau and covering a 12-month period from 1 August 1969 to 31 July 1970. JM Davis, the Commissioner, did not believe that the situation was in any way desperate. He had sought reports, however, in the immediate aftermath of the incidents at the Hughes home, and on possible breaches of the *National Service Act* and of the *Crimes Act*.[22] The Draft Resistance Union (DRU) received special attention for urging eligible men not to register for national service and for calling on members of the public to submit registration forms containing false information. The 'evidence' gathered – patchy and inconclusive – simply magnified the difficulties in the way of achieving successful prosecutions.

Hughes returned to Cabinet on 2 October with the first draft of the legislation. He did so against the background of the second Moratorium held on Friday 18 September 1970. Smaller in numbers than the first, it led to violent clashes between demonstrators and police, especially in Sydney and Adelaide. The Attorney felt he had good grounds, therefore, for choosing 'Demonstrations Bill' as the title of his Bill. It was better than 'public order' when taking account of 'the viewpoint of presentation'. The Bill, after all, was mainly and essentially about conduct causing serious breaches of the peace arising from demonstrations. Its 'keynote' was to protect the innocent public and its property from threatened or actual violence.

The Attorney said he had three objects in mind when preparing this Bill: it should be capable of being explained as 'a desirable, and necessary, measure'; it should not be open to criticism as 'reactionary or retrogressive'; and it should avoid dealing with matters appropriate for attention by State parliaments. The emphasis, he said, was on moderation. For example, in common law a person who took part in an unlawful assembly was guilty of an offence even though the person's own conduct did not give rise to an apprehension of a violent breach of the peace. Under this Bill, a person may be guilty of an offence only if he or she gave rise to an apprehension of a violent breach of the peace. The Attorney felt sure that the Bill 'will let demonstrators know where they stand'; that is, the Government intends to protect citizens from violence. Yet there was no need to hurry. To press on with the Bill in this session would attract the criticism of acting with 'undue haste'. The Attorney recommended its introduction in 1971.[23]

Cabinet discussed the Bill again on 20 October.[24] It generally agreed with the Attorney's approach and authorised him to continue with the drafting, but asked him to consider alternative formulations for the title. After a lengthy debate, Cabinet decided to defer the legislation for a later parliamentary session. McMahon, as he often did, spoke firmly in favour of doing nothing. He liked the Bill, considered it moderate and said the Government had a responsibility to bring in legislation, but it should be 'ultra-cautious'. McEwen wanted Cabinet collectively to scrutinise Hughes' second reading speech. He was worried about talk of a 'police state'. Hughes saw the possibility of introducing the Bill and then letting it lie on the table until the following year; some ministers agreed with this proposal and others did not. Their overriding concern was the forthcoming Senate election. Was it better to reveal the details of the legislation and avoid speculation, or to avoid giving the Opposition the opportunity to portray the Government as bent on draconian measures? Gorton was characteristically blunt: there was no time left in the year to pass the legislation but he wanted to show that the Government was serious. It should have 'the guts' to go into the Senate election saying it will legislate to stop people sitting down in streets and invading offices. Cabinet eventually agreed with McEwen's view. He wanted the Prime Minister to make such public reference to the matter during the Senate campaign as may be necessary to confirm the Government's intention to proceed with the legislation and to talk about the principles, and the nature and extent of the legislative provisions. The matter rested at this point, except in the Attorney-General's Department where there were still many issues to traverse before the Attorney could deliver his second reading speech.

On 2 November, Hughes wrote to Gorton in response to a request for concrete examples of the unsatisfactory state of the law relating to demonstrations in the Commonwealth Territories and those involving Commonwealth property.[25] Hughes explained that one of the areas of obscurity related to the circumstances that justified forcible action to disperse a riotous assembly. The 'reading' of the *Riot Act* had fallen into disuse, and the language of the proclamation differed between the States and the proclamation was not available in the Australian Capital Territory or the Northern Territory. Hughes also drew attention to inconsistencies in State legislation over penalties for unlawful assembly, and the harshness of penalties in common law, where a person could be found guilty of an offence of unlawful assembly without actually committing a specific offence. The law relating to Commonwealth property was a problem because the *Crimes Act* provided that an offence is committed only where there is a notice that trespass is not permitted. In this situation, instead of devising new offences as part of a crackdown on dissent, the Attorney-General and his Department wanted to clarify and simplify existing federal laws and to strive for greater consistency with State legislation.

The Attorney-General had two pressing matters on his mind in December 1970. Accompanied by Tom Jnr, he attended Waverley Court on 9 December as a witness in a case brought against seven men charged with trespass on his property. Hughes told the court how he had informed Constable Pringle that these people were on his grounds without his permission and he wanted them arrested and charged with trespass. He had subsequently taken a position at the head of his driveway and held the cricket bat in a horizontal position to shepherd the demonstrators into the arms of police. He denied hitting anyone. It looked like an open and shut case until Jack Smyth QC, who represented one of the students, pointed out that the Hughes house did not meet the definition of 'enclosed land' as defined by the *Enclosed Lands Act*. Next day the magistrate inspected the property. He concluded that, in the absence of a gate at the head of the nine-foot wide driveway, it was not enclosed, and dismissed the charges against all seven men.[26]

The more pressing issue arose out of a signed statement published in the journal *Resist* on 7 October. In part, the statement read: 'In full knowledge and acceptance of the penalties involved, we, the undersigned, pledge sanctuary in the form of shelter, work and sustenance to all young men who courageously defy the National Service Act.' Five of the 28 who signed the statement were Victorian Labor MPs, of whom four were federal politicians: Cairns, Dr Moss Cass and Senators Hendrickson and Poyser. The fifth, David Bornstein, was a member of the Victorian Legislative Assembly. The Commonwealth Police conducted extensive investigations but, as was so often the case in 1970, it proved impossible to meet Hughes' requirement that, where the context was highly political, the Crown should have a strong case in law. Bornstein, alone among the MPs, co-operated with the police. Hendrickson said someone had added his name, and the others refused to answer relevant questions. Hughes announced that there was 'no evidence to justify the institution of proceedings'.[27] Arguably, both sides were happy to baulk at the first hurdle.

The Draft Resistance Union, the alleged publisher of *Resist*, attracted a lot of attention from the Commonwealth Police, ASIO and the Attorney-General's Department. Hughes had previously received advice from Peter Goldman, a Melbourne QC, on the question of whether the DRU could be declared an unlawful association under the *Crimes Act*. Goldman advised that there was probably sufficient proof that the DRU was an 'unlawful association'. While declaring it 'unlawful' might give some 'academic satisfaction', such an action could 'amount to nothing' because the individuals could scatter or reconstitute themselves under another name. Goldman uncovered all sorts of difficulties involved in charging four named individuals. Even though they could be prosecuted for conspiracy to commit an unlawful act, the evidence against them was not strong because their statements of intent took the form of affirmative answers to leading police questions.[28] Goldman and Neil McPhee, who later appeared opposite Hughes in some memorable cases, had met the Attorney-General in September to discuss ways and means of proceeding under the terms of the *Crimes Act*. Hughes' handwriting on the texts of their discussions suggests there were outstanding questions relating to distinctions between matters of fact and of law and to situations where the court's interpretation would be involved. Understandably, when facing the prospect in December of charging anyone connected with the DRU and *Resist*, the Attorney was inclined to be doubly circumspect.

Hughes informed Gorton on Christmas Eve 1970 that a further revised draft, with a revised title – Public Order (Protection of Persons and Property) Bill – was in preparation. He planned to bring it to Cabinet early in the New Year. Over the summer, the Attorney and his senior officials collected a mass of material relating to unlawful assembly and demonstrations, focusing on the key issue of how to preserve civil liberties while trying to maintain public order. Hughes and the officials also looked at the attitude of those in the community who regarded civil disobedience as an acceptable strategy. They gave much of their attention to the relevant laws and penalties relating to public order throughout Australia, and to the policies of British political parties on law and order issues. One paper examined British statutes covering unlawful assembly and riots from the time of Richard II, as well as looking at the relevant State and Territory legislation. It noted that some UK laws of 'considerable antiquity' applied in the Territories and in all States except New South Wales and Tasmania, and that common law offences were applicable in three States and the Territories. At the same time, the Attorney worked through many of his handwritten versions of a second reading speech, taking advice from officials along the way.[29]

Tom Hughes had at least one break from research and writing. He attended Waverley Court on 28 January 1971 where Ian Macdonald brought a charge of assault against him arising out of the 'invasion' at Bellevue Road. Tom Reynolds, later a Supreme Court judge, represented the Attorney-General. Macdonald claimed that when Hughes approached him with a cricket bat Macdonald told him to 'Calm it'. Hughes then held him in the area of the throat with his left hand, and used the bat to poke him just below the ribs. The blow winded him. Hughes said he grabbed Macdonald by his pullover and raised the bat because he feared an assault. Macdonald's counsel, reputedly a member of the Communist Party, asked Hughes at one point whether the people who came down his drive did so with hostile intent. Hughes replied: 'Well, I didn't think they were a friendly delegation of young Liberals come to admire me.'[30] The magistrate viewed ABC news film and some photographs and concluded they constituted the best evidence for the defence in showing that Hughes did not grab Macdonald by the throat and that he used no more force than was necessary. He dismissed the charge and ordered Macdonald to pay $105 costs.[31]

The Attorney-General took the revised public order legislation to Cabinet on 17 February 1971.[32] The objective remained the same: 'to make specific, simple, and effective provision for the protection of persons and property from violent action occurring in the course of a demonstration'. As promised, the Bill removed the provision that a person may be guilty of taking part in an unlawful assembly, a riot or a rout even without committing a breach of the peace, or behaving in such a manner as to give rise to the apprehension that a breach of the peace would occur. Penalties were reduced for a number of offences, and clearer and more limited definitions were applied. The Prime Minister's Department commented that the more objectionable features of the Bill had been removed, and Cabinet approved it on 23 February subject to some minor amendments.[33]

On 16 March 1971, six days after Gorton ceased to be Prime Minister and two days before McMahon told Hughes he planned to sack him, the Attorney-General delivered his second reading speech on the public order legislation.[34] The speech had become very much his own, and may have been too reasonable and balanced to excite some of those sitting behind him in the House.[35]

Hughes began by setting out the objects: 'to clarify, to simplify and, in important respects, to mitigate the severity of the law concerning assemblies of persons in areas of Commonwealth legislative responsibility'. Much of the existing law was archaic, hard to locate and difficult to apply. Laws dealing with 'potentially discordant situations' should be comprehensible both to those to whom they are directed and to those who are responsible for administering them and, therefore, should be accessible and 'expressed in clear and explicit language'. Hughes decried what he called the 'emotive slogans' about the need for 'law and order' and for preserving 'civil liberties'; such catchcries obscured the fundamental problem of formulating:

> just criteria for protecting social values of sufficient worth and durability to warrant the protection of the law. Calls for law and order must not be allowed to deteriorate into attacks upon the right to dissent. Calls in support of the right to dissent must be heeded, but they must not be allowed to deteriorate into attacks upon the rights and proper liberties of other people.

Overall, freedom of assembly and movement must be qualified by taking public interest into account, namely, that there should not be violence or the apprehension of violence, there should be no unreasonable obstruction, no intrusion upon the land or premises of lawful occupiers and no harassment or intimidation of foreign representatives.

The bulk of the speech dealt with definitions, the long and complicated history of laws relating to unlawful assembly and riots, the proposed penalties for breaches of the law and the structure of the Bill. In keeping with his overall approach, Hughes highlighted those parts of the legislation that substantially reduced the penalties applicable under existing law. He also pointed to the clauses laying down that only those persons who committed acts of violence or damage, or whose actions gave rise to a reasonable apprehension of violence or damage, would be guilty of an offence. Hughes finished by saying that 'law and order must be linked with moderation, liberty and justice' and the Bill provided 'such a link'.

As the Attorney prepared to resume his seat, Clyde Cameron asked if he might see the proposed amendments placed alongside the clauses of the existing laws. Hughes was very happy to oblige. He invited Cameron to come to his office where he would show him the relevant volume and he could take it away and read it 'and after doing so he will be as utterly confused as is anybody who has to administer the present law'. From the Attorney's point of view, it was a valuable exchange, both in reinforcing the reasonableness he wanted to convey and in keeping the focus on cleaning up the law. It also helped that Clyde Cameron and Tom Hughes had found a way to talk easily with each other.

The Labor Party did not oppose the legislation. Whitlam took pleasure in reminding the House that the Bill 'was conceived by a Prime Minister who has been discredited; it was delivered by an Attorney-General who has been discarded'. He argued that legislation was unnecessary and would never be used. Forty years later, one commentator described the 1971 Act as 'an over-blown legislative response to an over-estimated threat that seemed to dominate the concerns of a conservative government on its last legs'.[36] This judgment is at once harsh and inaccurate as it applies to its principal progenitor. The Tom Hughes who held the cricket bat was not the same Tom Hughes who spent most of his energy trying to clarify, modernise and moderate the law. He was a profound disappointment to the 'troglodytes' on the Liberal backbench.

12

Testing the extent of Commonwealth power

Tom Hughes angered the anti-Gortonites because of what they saw as his dilatory approach to prosecuting breaches of the *Crimes Act 1914* (Cth) and the *National Service Act 1964* (Cth). His more 'liberal' position on the issue of homosexuality raised doubts in their minds about his commitment to defend Christianity and Western Civilisation. What, however, sealed his fate in their eyes was joining Gorton's assault on one of the supposedly enduring principles of the Liberal Party, namely, 'the maintenance unimpaired of the federal system'.

The Menzies Government had impaired it with impunity but Menzies never made the mistake of advocating or acknowledging what he was doing. John Gorton believed that outmoded Liberal Party dogma had to conform to reality, and his reality involved the unequivocal assertion of Commonwealth control of the financial relationship and of the national estate. It has been pointed out that, throughout 1968-69, Gorton antagonised the 'States' rights' elements in the Liberal Party who saw him as a 'centralist' and a 'socialist'. Gorton compounded these felonies in 1969-70 by committing his government to control of the territorial sea as well as the continental shelf, thereby challenging the States' claim to sovereignty over 'their' territorial waters. The Attorney-General became his most important ministerial ally in the enterprise. Hughes, the lawyer, wanted to determine the extent and limits of Commonwealth power; Hughes, the nationalist, was not disposed to genuflect in the direction of 'States' rights'; and Hughes, the politician, appreciated and admired a Prime Minister who had vision and wanted to change things.

The Attorney-General had his own agenda, and Gorton keenly supported it. Hughes wanted Australia to have effective trade practices legislation. To achieve this objective, and in line with the broader aim of extending the boundaries of Commonwealth authority, he took a case to the High Court to test the scope of the corporations power of s 51(xx) of the Australian Constitution. Hughes, therefore, doubly offended the 'States' rights' faction in the Liberal Party.

Control of the seabed

The question of sovereignty over the continental shelf and the territorial sea had hovered in the background for most of the 1960s as Commonwealth and State governments wrestled with the question of how to give assurances to prospective operators in offshore oil and gas fields that they had a valid title. The States had been issuing permits for some years, covering both the territorial waters and the continental shelf. The relevant companies became nervous when the US Supreme Court ruled that the constituent States of the American Federation did not have authority over either the territorial waters or the continental shelf. In Australia, where the Commonwealth and the States had each claimed jurisdiction over both, the Commonwealth recognised that State co-operation was essential for administering licences issued for exploration and exploitation. After protracted discussions, the two sides agreed in 1964 on a joint arrangement in the case of petroleum. In 1967, all Australian parliaments converted a 'gentlemen's agreement' into legislation that came into operation on 1 April 1968.[1] By then, Gorton was Prime Minister. He later admitted having taken no interest in the matter, while believing that the Commonwealth had not given up any rights in enacting the 'minor' petroleum legislation.[2] He became involved when he refused to accept a proposal from David Fairbairn, as Minister for National Development, to extend the petroleum arrangements to other offshore minerals. Cabinet resolved on 27 February 1969 to assert Commonwealth rights from the three-mile limit to the outer continental shelf, while assuming that the States could establish their authority from the low-water mark to the three-mile limit. Cabinet also decided that, should an international agreement move the territorial sea limit to 12 miles, the Commonwealth would nonetheless regard the three-mile limit as the full extent of State authority.

On 3 March 1969, at a meeting of the Minerals Council, Fairbairn informed the State Ministers for Mines of the Cabinet decision, although he agreed to their request that the Commonwealth would not legislate unilaterally without further discussions with the States. At the end of July, Fairbairn sought Gorton's approval to tell the States that the Commonwealth would hold discussions with them before legislating. The Prime Minister told Fairbairn on 18 August he did not want any long and drawn-out discussion, and the Minister should not include in his letter to the States any suggestion that the

Commonwealth would not legislate unilaterally until after the completion of a full and frank discussion with them. Fairbairn decided not to write his proposed letter, and the States did not receive any more undertakings before another meeting of the Minerals Council on 26 September. Fairbairn left that meeting believing he had given the States a firm undertaking to consult them before the Commonwealth introduced its legislation, and had promised that the States' counter-proposal – to base any new legislation relating to offshore minerals on the petroleum model – would be referred to Cabinet.

Tom Hughes became closely involved with what did and did not happen at the September meeting. First, however, he submitted an opinion to Cabinet, signed by Ellicott as Solicitor-General and himself as Attorney-General, on the question of sovereignty over the territorial sea.[3] The advice was set against the background of two pronouncements in 1969. Sir Percy Spender, a former Australian politician, diplomat and President of the International Court of Justice at The Hague, had argued in a speech that, according to international law, the Commonwealth Government had total authority over the seas beyond the low-water mark. Secondly, two of the five High Court judges hearing the case of *Bonser v La Macchia*[4] – Barwick CJ and Windeyer J – expressed opinions appearing to support the Commonwealth's exclusive jurisdiction over all Australian territorial waters.

Notwithstanding these statements, Hughes and Ellicott said they could not confidently predict whether the High Court would uphold Commonwealth legislation controlling offshore mining other than for petroleum in this area. Two questions were central to any litigation: whether the sea within three miles of the low-water mark formed part of State territory, and on what basis the Commonwealth could legislate in those areas. The second question would not arise if the Court ruled that State territory extended to the three-mile limit. As to the first question, the Attorney-General's Department believed the Commonwealth had 'a strongly arguable case' before the High Court that the territorial sea did not form part of State territory. Therefore, the Commonwealth should not concede that State territory extended to the territorial sea. It was true that, until the late 1950s, both State and Commonwealth legal advisers viewed this area as State territory but this fact 'was not a sufficient reason for making any concession in derogation of Commonwealth power'. Should the High Court determine in favour of the Commonwealth, the Attorney-General's Department believed the Commonwealth would have the authority to legislate for offshore mining within the territorial sea. As for the continental shelf, the joint opinion pointed out that the Convention on the Territorial Sea and Contiguous Zone, approved in Vienna in 1958 and to which Australia acceded a year later, laid down that the 'coastal State' had sovereign rights over the exploration and exploitation of its natural resources. The Commonwealth was a party to the Convention and was the sole Australian 'coastal State'.

Reg Swartz, who succeeded Fairbairn as Minister for National Development after Fairbairn refused to serve under Gorton, had already prepared a submission for Cabinet. After reviewing the history, Swartz set out five possible courses of action the Government might take. They ranged from legislating unilaterally while seeking a co-operative arrangement with the States over administration, to taking 'the bit between our teeth' and legislating from the low-water mark outwards and facing protests from the States and litigation. Gorton's marginal comments on the submission left no one in doubt where he stood; taking 'the bit between our teeth' was part of his style of governance.[5] In Cabinet on 21 January 1970, he said the Government had sold the pass over petroleum. While accepting that nothing could be done about the petroleum agreement, he wanted the Commonwealth to assert control over everything else from the low-water mark, and there must be no going back on the earlier decision to assert authority from the three-mile limit. The States may choose to litigate, which would clear up the issue. McMahon wanted to be conciliatory. The Commonwealth should seek State co-operation; strong-arm action 'will harm us'; the Government should provoke a High Court case only as a last resort. Gorton, with Hughes' support, said that ascertaining the Commonwealth's proper legal rights within the federation was not an aggressive approach, and promised full co-operation once the legal limits of Commonwealth power were established. The Prime Minister acknowledged the States could cause trouble but did not regard that as a reason for not proceeding to act in the national interest.[6]

Cabinet adopted the course on 21 January 'of asserting Commonwealth jurisdiction over offshore waters from the low-water mark to the edge of the continental shelf'.[7] It also decided to implement this decision by legislating unilaterally in those areas in relation to the exploration and exploitation of offshore minerals other than petroleum. The aim was to precipitate a State challenge in the High Court 'to settle once and for all the doubts as to the constitutional position on jurisdiction over the areas in question'. If the Commonwealth should win the case then, while exercising its rights over issuing mining leases, it would be 'as conciliatory as possible towards the States', and this would mean working towards an agreement over royalties. Conciliation, however, stopped short of courtesy. The final sentence of the Cabinet decision read: 'It was agreed that the Commonwealth was under no obligation to inform the States in advance of the legislation of the course it proposed to take and that it should not do so.'

Sir John Bunting, the Cabinet Secretary, sent Gorton a draft of the decision that he and Hughes had formulated. He expressed his misgivings about providing a Cabinet minute with a greater degree of precision than the Cabinet discussion warranted. Bunting raised this question because Cabinet's discussion had focused on the broad joint opinion of the Attorney-General and the Solicitor-General, an opinion which formed the basis of what Hughes and Bunting had together drafted in such stark terms about the Commonwealth asserting its jurisdiction. Bunting was especially worried about the assertion that the Commonwealth was under no obligation to inform the States in advance of the legislation; he wanted to be sure he had 'understood the Cabinet correctly'. According to Bunting's account in the Cabinet Notebook, there was no discussion, let alone agreement on the matter of communication. Gorton assured Bunting that he had correctly reported Cabinet's decision.

The States received formal notice of the Commonwealth's intentions just before it made them public in the Governor-General's speech to Parliament on 3 March 1970. They were outraged. As they saw it, the Commonwealth had abandoned co-operative federalism in favour of rampant centralism. There were now two issues involved: the substantive one of whether the Commonwealth should have sole jurisdiction beyond the low-water mark to the end of the continental shelf; and the procedural one of whether the Commonwealth, in seeking to legislate unilaterally, had broken an undertaking to hold prior discussions with the States.

Swartz, accompanied by Hughes, presided over a meeting of State ministers and officials in Melbourne on 26 March 1970.[8] AF Griffiths, the WA Minister for Mines in David Brand's Liberal Government, accused the Gorton Government of 'discourtesy' and told the two federal ministers that feelings were running high within the States and within the Liberal Party organisation. It was not 'very heartening' for future Commonwealth-State relations. Other State ministers echoed Griffiths' protests and warnings. Hughes then outlined the legislative proposals. He explained there would be two Bills. A short one would assert Commonwealth sovereignty over waters extending to the three-mile limit but excluding what were State waters at the time of Federation. This Bill would throw up the question of sovereignty for the High Court to determine, and the Commonwealth would welcome a decision. It was especially keen when appearing before the United Nations – and the Commonwealth was the only government to which the UN related – to speak for Australia as a whole and not as a trustee for six different States holding six different views. The second Bill would implement legislatively the rights the Commonwealth acquired when it acceded to the Convention. This was also challengeable and the Commonwealth would welcome a challenge.

When Griffith drew his attention to the petroleum agreement, Hughes replied that the constitutional questions had simply been placed in 'cold storage' in 1964-68: 'This is not good enough. We must have a decision on where the rights lie.' Dr Peter Delamothe, Acting Minister for Mines in the Bjelke-Petersen Government of Queensland and Deputy Leader of the State Liberal Party, assured the Commonwealth Attorney-General that the States would fight and use all available weapons. Hughes chose to ignore Delamothe's repeated and pointed questions about whether, in exercising rights over the territorial sea, the States had adversely affected Commonwealth interests. The Queenslander wondered how long the petroleum agreement would survive after a complete Commonwealth takeover. Hughes insisted that the agreement was permanent and Swartz said the Prime Minister had given his assurance. Yet what if Labor won power? The Federal Opposition supported the extension of Commonwealth control. To calm tempers, Swartz suggested that the officials might take over and discuss details. When the State ministers refused to allow their officers to participate until they had seen a copy of the legislation, Swartz gave up peacemaking and announced that the decision to proceed was 'irrevocable'. He really had no choice; he knew that Gorton would not change his mind. At the end of the discussion, Delamothe neatly summed up the States' perspective: 'It is clearly a question of the States versus the Commonwealth.'

After the meeting, Swartz and Hughes issued a joint statement. They reiterated their view that a resolution of the issue of who had jurisdiction over the offshore areas had become a necessity in the national interest, and reaffirmed the Government's intention to proceed with the legislation. They held out two inducements to the States: those who co-operated with the Commonwealth would be eligible for royalties on the same basis as agreed in the case of offshore petroleum (that is, 60 per cent to the States and 40 per cent to the Commonwealth); and the States would be primarily responsible for government-industry contact over exploration and production.

Following the Melbourne meeting, Hughes went deep into 'enemy territory' to explain and justify the case for Commonwealth legislation. On 11 April, he addressed the Liberal Party's Bowman Federal Electorate Conference at Mt Gravatt, Brisbane. Clarrie Harders provided some of his material. The Attorney stressed one particular Harders point: the 1958 Convention required the Commonwealth to assure the right of passage of 'innocent shipping', and it needed legislative authority to do so. Hughes also insisted that the Commonwealth was not trying to grab power or money; it was merely taking steps to allow the High Court to decide the constitutional issue one way or another. His audience was unconvinced. 'I noticed very soon in the course of my speech that I was addressing a sea of faces frozen in disapproval.'[9]

Peter Howson was at once angered and delighted; angered, because Gorton was proceeding with 'another unnecessary piece of legislation which can only divide the party'; delighted, because the Bill would be sufficiently divisive to undermine Gorton's leadership. By 14 April, the day Tom Hughes delivered his ministerial statement on the Moratorium, Howson and Fairbairn, after discussion with the journalist, Alan Reid, were ready to turn the offshore legislation into 'a real crisis' and a confrontation between Gorton and Fairbairn. Next day, Gorton brought on the desired 'crisis' by refusing to delay the Bill to allow further discussion in the Party Room. On 16 April, after Swartz had introduced the legislation, Gorton agreed to table the papers dealing with the offshore minerals issue, including those relating to the meeting of the Minerals Council in the previous September. Attention now shifted from the legislation to the issue of credibility – who, of Fairbairn and Gorton, could be believed on the issue of prior consultation with the States. What, and on whose authority, had been set in stone at the September meeting?

Armed with the released papers, Fairbairn spoke in the House on 8 May, the day of the Moratorium.[10] His central point was that he, as Minister for National Development, had committed the Government to consider the States' counter-proposal and to hold a further meeting with them before bringing down any legislation. Unfortunately, as Wal Fife, the Minister for Mines in the Askin Government in New South Wales, acknowledged in a message to Gorton, not a single sentence in the transcript confirmed that Fairbairn had committed the Government.[11] Fairbairn nonetheless claimed a promise had been made and wondered about the state of public morality and the influence of the 'permissive society' when a government could override a legally unenforceable promise. Howson recorded in his diary on 8 May that Alan Reid believed Fairbairn had made 'a completely devastating speech'.

Fairbairn's speech brought Tom Hughes back into the picture because Gorton needed the Attorney's advice before giving his reply. Hughes in his memorandum acknowledged that the States had made a counter-proposal on 26 September 1969, having rejected the Commonwealth proposal of the previous March. Hughes wrote that Fairbairn, in a letter of 30 July, had sought the Prime Minister's approval to assure the States that the Commonwealth would not legislate unilaterally before a full and frank discussion of the views Fairbairn had expressed on 3 March. Gorton replied on 18 August saying he wanted to avoid drawn-out discussions with the States:

> For that reason I would prefer that you eliminate from your proposed letter the suggestion that the Commonwealth will not legislate unilaterally until after the completion of full and frank discussions with the States on this matter. I think we should preserve as much room for manoeuvre as possible in this matter.

According to Hughes, Gorton's reply could not, 'upon any reasonable interpretation', be regarded as conferring on Fairbairn the authority he had sought. By implication, if there had been a meeting of ministers before the introduction of legislation, Gorton did not want Fairbairn yielding to any proposal that would circumscribe the Commonwealth's freedom of legislative action, unless circumstances made a step back imperative.

There was, in other words, a clear limitation on Fairbairn's freedom of action. Hughes conceded, however, that if Fairbairn had made a commitment on 26 September, the fact he had exceeded his authority, and had not disclosed the limitation on his authority to other parties, did not detract from the binding quality of such a commitment. Yet, if Gorton had not in the meantime enlarged the terms of Fairbairn's authority, and if Fairbairn had not informed the Prime Minister of the commitment he believed he had made, it was unjust to accuse Gorton of breaking a promise of which he knew nothing. Hughes argued that Fairbairn's failure to tell the Prime Minister he had given an undertaking to the States must 'weigh heavily' against Fairbairn's accusations. Moreover, there was no reference to an undertaking in the press statement issued after the meeting on 26 September, the absence of which was 'a very eloquent and cogent piece of evidence' against Fairbairn's case. Looking at the September transcript, Hughes noted how Fairbairn began his remarks by saying he could not say what the Government would do, knowing it could be defeated at the next election and that he might not be the minister. Telling the State ministers, therefore, that there would be an opportunity for 'further discussion on this matter', could not be construed as an unequivocal undertaking to withhold legislation until such a discussion took place.[12]

If the Attorney was splitting some very fine hairs, his case on a literal reading of the transcript was strong. The transcript disclosed that Fairbairn acknowledged he could not make a binding commitment because of the coming election. There was no formal undertaking actually made on 26 September to withhold legislation until after consultation with State ministers. So Fairbairn had no authority to make a commitment, knew in any case he could not make a binding one, and never told Gorton that he had made what he claimed to have made and which was not recorded as having been made.

Hughes had given Gorton some of the material on which to base a legalistic response to the Fairbairn allegations. Yet, when Gorton applied his mind, he did not need a QC to guide him through a complex argument. Reading his speech it is evident that he had worked on it with diligence and intelligence. Listening to it, Howson thought the speech was 'weak' and failed to answer Fairbairn's main argument. Perhaps he should have paid attention to the way Gorton teased out material from the transcript to show there was an understanding about more discussions but no understanding linked to a commitment to forgo legislation until they had taken place. At another level, Gorton was generous in conceding Fairbairn's absolute sincerity in his beliefs, and astute in acknowledging that an impression may have been created around the table on 26 September about further discussions before the Government embarked on legislation. It was, nonetheless, just an impression; it never found a place in the transcript. Gorton could fairly claim that the records did not sustain a charge of bad faith.

After Gorton spoke, the Opposition moved an amendment. Labor supported the legislation but, presented with an irresistible opportunity, moved that the Prime Minister and his Cabinet lacked the confidence of the House for failing to honour Fairbairn's commitment, made on their behalf, to consult the States before the introduction of legislation. Gorton accepted the amendment as a censure motion and the House debated the question throughout the day.

Hughes entered the debate late in the afternoon. The barrister proceeded to pull apart the case against the Government just as he might have dealt with opposing argument in court. First, on the basis of the transcript of the meeting on 26 September 1969, 'one could not, I suggest, conclude that as a matter of reasonable probability, let alone certainty – and certainty would be needed on this issue if the government is to fall – an undertaking such as is asserted was ever given'. Secondly, central to an argument about bad faith was that the Prime Minister 'ignored or overrode or broke an undertaking', but Fairbairn accepted that Gorton did not believe an undertaking had been given to consult the States before introducing the legislation.

Thirdly, Hughes pointed out that, whereas in March 1969 Wal Fife had asked Fairbairn to give such an undertaking, no 'plain and unequivocal words' were used by State ministers at the September meeting. If experienced State ministers thought they had 'extracted' an undertaking, they would have said so in their press release issued after the meeting. After all, they did mention that ministers representing the Commonwealth had undertaken to present the States' views and counter-proposals to Federal Cabinet. Finally, and critically, Fairbairn had never claimed to have told Gorton before the Cabinet discussions that he had bound the Commonwealth to a certain course of action. The same was true for other ministers, in which case the Government 'should stand acquitted' of the allegation of bad faith.

The Attorney-General had made a good case for the defence, all the while stressing his respect for 'my friend', David Fairbairn. He never at any stage even hinted at what should have been obvious to anyone not distracted by the politics: the former minister, as Howson admitted, had 'gone out on a limb', and for a cause of little substance despite Fairbairn's histrionic invocations of civilised values. The anti-Gortonites, who were not prepared to cross the floor and bring down the Government, now had to find a way of rescuing their spear-thrower. Howson moved a convoluted amendment designed to appease both sides. The amendment passed, with Fairbairn absenting himself from the chamber. The Government, therefore, survived the crisis that the anti-Gortonites had sought to provoke while stopping short of a final rupture. They did win important concessions: Swartz would meet the relevant State ministers on 9 June, the Commonwealth would send them a draft copy of the Bill and a 'Heads of Agreement' as the basis for arrangements to control the exploitation of the seabed, and the Government would not proceed with legislation until the Budget session in August.

Tom Hughes continued to make the case for the legislation. On 10 June, he appeared on the ABC's television program, *This Day Tonight*. Philip Koch began the interview by suggesting centralism had reared its head because, if the Commonwealth insisted on controlling Australia's territorial waters, this surely meant the erosion of State power. Hughes said Koch was not looking at the question in the right way. The 'fundamental and crucial issue' was to determine where ultimate authority lay. The appropriate course was to determine that question by litigation in the proper constitutional tribunal. Until the matter was decided, it was beside the point to talk about the Commonwealth trying to filch from the States. Besides, if the States were not, in law, entitled to control those waters there was no infraction of State rights by the assertion of Commonwealth control. The Commonwealth's position had been misrepresented as an attempt to wrest from the States what belonged to them, the assumption being that, in law, the rights belonged to the States. The Attorney also made it clear that, should the High Court uphold the Commonwealth's view, the Commonwealth had no desire to keep the States out of revenue or royalties. If the States co-operated, the Commonwealth would make arrangements broadly along the lines of the petroleum legislation, and the States would receive, in the case of mineral exploration, including oil exploration, the same royalties they were getting under the petroleum legislation.

The Government eventually decided to hold over the legislation until 1971. In the meantime, it received important support. A Senate Select Committee, chaired by the Victorian Liberal Ivor Greenwood, handed down an interim report on 1 September 1970. It concluded that 'the larger national interest is not served by leaving unresolved and uncertain the extent of State and Commonwealth authority in the territorial seabed and Continental Shelf'.[13] The final report tabled on 8 December by Senator Harold Young, a South Australian Liberal who had succeeded Greenwood as chairman, called on the Commonwealth to control both the territorial sea and the continental shelf. At this point, Gorton and Hughes could reasonably expect to have the legislation passed in the coming year.

Sir Thomas Hughes: Tom's paternal grandfather.
(*Source: Hughes Papers*)

Constance Vidal: Tom's maternal grandmother.
(*Source: Hughes Papers*)

Wedding day, 8 January 1923: Geoffrey and Margaret Hughes.
(*Source: Hughes Papers*)

A make-believe world, c 1934: Constance, Geoffrey and Tom.
(*Source: Constance Crisp collection*)

Fishing at Yaouk, 1935: Tom, Geoffrey and Constance.
(*Source: Constance Crisp collection*)

The Hughes family, 1938. Clockwise from left: Constance, Geoffrey, Robert, Margaret, Tom, Geoffrey Jnr.
(Source: Constance Crisp collection)

Narrandera swimming baths, summer 1940-41: Robert and Tom.
(Source: Constance Crisp collection)

Group Captain Geoffrey Hughes and Pilot Officer Tom Hughes, 1943.
(*Source: Hughes Papers*)

Tom (fourth from the right) and his Sunderland crew, spring 1945.
(Source: Hughes Papers)

Wedding day, 5 July 1951: Tom, Joanna, Geraldyn Cowlishaw (Joanna's older sister), Janet Chapman, Robin Stanton and Constance.
(Source: Hughes Papers)

GREAT RECORD OF THE LIBERAL GOVERNMENT

THE LAST CARD IN THE PACK

In a last-ditch attempt to deflect the electors of Parkes from the real issues in this election, "Left-Wing Les" and his henchmen have been referring persistently to the fact that Liberal candidate Tom Hughes does not live in the electorate.

"The Liberal Party is committed, as it always has been, to a policy of 'Advance Australia Fairer'," said Liberal candidate Tom Hughes, Q.C., speaking in the electorate on Saturday morning.

Tom Hughes said:

"It is a matter of record that during the 14 years of the Menzies Government more social services and more vital social services, have been provided for Australian families than in the whole of the previous 47 years of Federation."

Parkes Examiner, 1963, featuring Robert Hughes' cartoon.
(Source: Hughes Papers)

Liberal Party campaign photo for the Parkes campaign, 1966:
Tom Jnr, Joanna, Lucy, Michael, Tom.
(*Source: Hughes Papers*)

The Mushroom Club, 1968. Standing from left: Don Jessop, Bill Arthur, Tony Street, John McLeay, Don Chipp, Bruce Graham, Bill Bridges-Maxwell, Fred Chaney, Jim Killen, Tom Pearsall, 'Duke' Bonnett.
Tom Hughes and Andrew Peacock (in front).
(Source: Hughes Papers)

Commonwealth Attorney-General, 1969.
(*Source: Attorney-General's Department*)

Tom 'cricket bat' Hughes, 16 August 1970.
(*Source: Bauer Media Limited*)

A '$1000-a-day QC', February 1978.
(*Source: Bauer Media Limited*)

Hon Justice Antony Larkins ('Larko') and Chrissie Hughes, c 1983.
(*Source: Hughes Papers*)

Tom Hughes QC and Clive Lloyd, 1984.
(*Source: Bauer Media Limited*)

Tom Hughes QC in Wardell Chambers, c 1987.
(Source: Hughes Papers)

Tom Hughes QC and Dyson Heydon, Phillip Street, 1988.
St James' Church is in the background.
(*Source: Hughes Papers*)

Robert, Geoffrey, Tom and Constance at Michael Hughes' wedding, February 1994.
(*Source: Constance Crisp collection*)

Tom Hughes at the NSW Bar Association celebration of his 90th birthday, November 2013.
(*Source: NSW Bar Association*)

Tom and Chrissie Hughes, February 2016.
(*Source: Hughes Papers*)

The corporations power

Tom Hughes involved himself in another constitutional question in the second half of 1970. He sought to confirm the validity of the *Trade Practices Act 1965* (Cth) and to test the extent and limits of Commonwealth power relating to corporations. In doing so, he became a central figure in the High Court case, *Strickland v Rocla Concrete Pipes Ltd*,[14] better known as the *Concrete Pipes case.*

Early in the 1960s, Sir Garfield Barwick as Attorney-General sought to protect free enterprise from the development of injurious monopolies and restrictive trade practices. He wanted to legislate for the compulsory registration of a very wide range of restrictive arrangements, their examination by a tribunal, and de-registration if the arrangements materially reduced competition or were deemed not to be in the public interest. It was to be unlawful to continue trading after de-registration while the failure to register a registrable practice would attract heavy penalties. In 1965, Snedden, having succeeded Barwick as Attorney-General, introduced what Hughes later described as a '[r]uthlessly emasculated piece of legislation'.[15] Although the Snedden Bill required the registration of collective restrictive agreements, it did not extend to bilateral arrangements, vertical resale price maintenance and exclusive dealerships. Snedden abandoned Barwick's plans for controlling mergers and reduced his list of inexcusable practices to collusive bidding and tendering.[16] Even in this truncated form, Ray Whittorn on the Liberal Party's backbench described the Snedden Bill as an 'unjustifiable intrusion into normal business affairs and an intrusion by public servants into the activities of free enterprise about which they knew very little'. Tom Hughes, who wanted comprehensive and enforceable trade practices legislation, tried to sound enthusiastic: this 'truly liberal measure … is to preserve fair competition, reasonable competition, where this is consistent with the public interest'.[17]

As Attorney-General, Hughes sought to revive the original Barwick proposals. He told the Awards Dinner of the National Packaging Association, held at the Wentworth Hotel, Sydney, on 11 May 1970, that, as a Liberal, and allowing for some exceptions, 'efficiency and public satisfaction in the production and selling of goods and services are more likely to be attained in a competitive environment'. To oppose legislation to fix prices, one must equally oppose price fixing by private prescription. If the public saw that the *Trade Practices Act* was not working there would be pressures on the States to introduce price fixing, and on the Commonwealth to get the powers to introduce it.[18]

It was important, therefore, to ensure that the 1965 legislation was effective and had the widest possible application. There was, however, a known obstacle. The *Australian Industries Preservation Act 1906* (Cth) had made it an offence to form combinations in restraint of trade in foreign and interstate commerce, and among foreign corporations or trading or financial corporations formed in Australia. It was assumed that Parliament had the authority under s 51(xx) of the Australian Constitution which gave the Federal Government power to make laws 'with respect to … [f]oreign corporations, and trading or financial corporations formed within the limits of the Commonwealth'. In 1909, the High Court held in *Huddart, Parker & Co Pty Ltd v Moorehead*[19] (*Huddart, Parker*) (Isaacs J dissenting) that the Act did not cover intrastate trade because the Commonwealth's legislative ambit was limited by the reserved powers of the States. In 1920, a differently constituted High Court overturned the doctrine of reserved powers in the *Engineers' case*.[20] This landmark decision was a critical factor in enhancing the power of the Commonwealth. Yet *Huddart, Parker* stood unchallenged. In 1970, Tom Hughes, working closely with Clarrie Harders, wanted to ensure that the *Trade Practices Act* validly covered intrastate trade. To achieve this objective, they needed to take a case to the High Court to overrule *Huddart, Parker* and, in the process, to test the extent or limits of the corporations power.

Three companies presented Hughes with an opportunity. Rocla Concrete Pipes Ltd and Humes Ltd (both Victorian-based) and Concrete Industries (Monier) Ltd (located in New South Wales) agreed in April 1969 on price and credit arrangements for manufacturing and supplying concrete pipes and associated products solely within the State of Queensland. In October 1970, Keith Strickland of the Commonwealth Police laid information that the three companies had failed to furnish particulars of their agreements within 30 days after the date on which their agreement became liable for registration under s 43 of the *Trade Practices Act*. The companies, relying on *Huddart, Parker*, believed it was beyond the power of the Commonwealth to apply sections of the trade practices legislation to an intrastate agreement.

In July 1970, the Commissioner of Trade Practices recommended prosecution. He thought it important to deal with the case immediately and openly. 'Prosecution would bring the matter to public notice, and I think it would be defended by challenging the corporations power.' Ellicott, the Solicitor-General, took the same view. He was a centralist who wanted to expand the role of the Commonwealth. When the Victorian Government challenged the Commonwealth's attempt to impose a payroll tax on State governments, as it did on all other employers, Ellicott advised Hughes, who received different messages from his Department, that the legislation was defensible in the High Court. Between 26 November and 3 December 1970, the Solicitor-General led for the Commonwealth in the so-called (and ultimately successful) *Payroll Tax case*.[21] Ellicott's central argument was that the *Engineers' case* in effect confirmed the Commonwealth's power to pass laws 'with respect to' corporations within the limits of the Commonwealth, the phrase 'with respect to' having a very wide application.

According to Michael Pelly, Murray Gleeson's biographer, 'Ellicott also decided to test the reach of [the] corporations power' by taking up the case involving the *Trade Practices Act*.[22] In pursuing the matter, Ellicott said there was 'no question in my mind that the two juniors are going to be [Bill] Deane and [Murray] Gleeson'. Deane and Gleeson provided an important joint advice on 15 October 1970.[23] Their instructions from the Crown Solicitor stated that, in deciding whether prosecutions should proceed, the constitutional question should be put to one side. The Deane-Gleeson advice indeed assumed 'the complete validity from the constitutional point of view' of the provisions of the Act. The reasoning and the decision of the High Court judges in *Huddart, Parker* were, 'in the light of accepted constitutional thinking since the *Engineers' case*, irrelevant'. They advised that a prosecution would succeed, but suggested more evidence be obtained by issuing further notices. Both Deane and Gleeson were, as Ellicott firmly believed, in 'the Commonwealth-power camp'.

Pelly's account gives the impression that Ellicott was the prime mover behind the *Concrete Pipes case*. Ellicott was certainly on the lookout for opportunities to extend Commonwealth power. It is also true that some of the arguments employed in the *Concrete Pipes case* paralleled those utilised in the *Payroll Tax case*.[24] Yet Hughes' own papers, the records of the Attorney-General's Department, and the testimony of interested parties at the time make it clear that Tom Hughes was central to the initiation and conduct of the case. A key point is that, whereas the Solicitor-General was prepared to use any case to test the scope of Commonwealth power, the Attorney had a particular commitment to this one because of a longstanding objection to restrictive trade practices. Hence, 'Harders and I organised the litigation' to establish the validity of the *Trade Practices Act* of 1965; getting movement on trade practices was 'my major achievement [as Attorney-General]'.[25]

Hughes, Harders and senior staff in the Attorney-General's Department provided energy and drive, working through the Convention debates and Imperial legislation, the relevant case law, Quick and Garran's *The Annotated Constitution of the Australian Commonwealth*[26] and a multitude of commentaries. They wanted to challenge *Huddart, Parker* and to promote a broader interpretation of the corporations power, aiming to ensure the validity of existing trade practices legislation and to open up opportunities for greater Commonwealth involvement in managing commercial affairs. To this end, Hughes decided he should lead the case for the Commonwealth in what was to be his second and last appearance in the High Court as Attorney-General.[27]

Rumours began circulating that the Attorney-General's Department was considering a prosecution. Hughes, in an address to the Annual Convention of the Tasmanian Bar Association on 10 October 1970, signalled that action was imminent and that its implications were enormous: 'The consequences of any judicial re-consideration of the extent of the [corporations] power would have great political and legal significance.'[28] Hughes let it be known on 14 October 1970, on a non-attributable basis, that advice was being sought from counsel.[29] On that same day, Richard Ackland broke the story in *Jobson's Investment Digest*: manufacturers of concrete pipes were about to be prosecuted under the *Trade Practices Act*. Proceedings against the three companies were instituted in the Commonwealth Industrial Court on 23 October. The Trade Practices Commissioner was firmly with the Attorney- General, telling him in mid-November that the case was critical, not only for establishing the extent of the corporations power but also 'in showing the resolution and credibility of the administration in one of the few cases that the public knows about'.[30]

A hearing began in the Industrial Court on 2 December 1970 before Spicer CJ, Joske and Smithers JJ. The defendants argued that four sections of the Act were invalid and void because they were not referable to any head of power conferred on the Parliament by the Constitution. Hughes said the Court was bound to disregard the reasoning in *Huddart, Parker* because the doctrine of 'implied prohibition' or reserved powers had been 'exploded' by the Privy Council in *Webb v Outtrim*[31] and by the High Court in the *Engineers' case*. The Court reserved its decision after a two-and-a-half-day hearing. On 18 December, it unanimously dismissed the charges against the three companies because, insofar as the Act required the registration of restrictive trading agreements confined to trade within a State (in this instance, Queensland), it was invalid. While acknowledging the force of Hughes' arguments, the three judges held they were bound by the decision in *Huddart, Parker* because the High Court had not formally overruled it. Hughes announced that officers of his Department would begin work immediately on preparing an application for leave to appeal to the High Court.[32]

Proceedings before the Full Court – Barwick CJ, McTiernan, Menzies, Windeyer, Owen, Walsh and Gibbs JJ – began in Melbourne on Monday 1 March 1971. Hughes had what he called 'a galaxy of talent' to help him:[33] Ellicott, Deane and Gleeson. Richard Fullagar QC, a son of the late High Court judge Sir Wilfred Fullagar, led a team representing Rocla and Humes, Jack Smyth led one for Monier and Harold Snelling QC, the NSW Solicitor-General, appeared for his State.[34] Hughes' 'galaxy of talent' became a real team, as evidenced, Hughes claimed, by Ellicott leading the reply to opposing arguments (and enduring something of a frontal attack from Barwick). Ellicott might well have taken this role anyway. He gave his reply on 9 March, the day Hughes was in Canberra as the political crisis over Gorton's leadership finally came to a head.

Hughes began his argument for leave to appeal by pointing out that the sole basis of the Industrial Court's decision was that the High Court had never expressly overruled *Huddart, Parker*.[35] When Hughes rose to respond to Fullagar's several lines of argument for rejecting the application, Barwick intervened to say that the Court did not wish to trouble the Attorney further; it granted leave.

Hughes opened his substantive argument with an examination of the relevant sections of the *Trade Practices Act* and engaged in an extensive discussion with several judges over meanings of words and phrases, and over definitions of corporations and the relationship between particular sections of the Act. Hughes was not at all fazed by the discursive nature of the exchanges, nor by Barwick's testing interventions. In the afternoon of the first day, and for much of the second, the Attorney focused on the reasoning in *Huddart, Parker*. Hughes argued that the doctrine of reserved State powers obviously and materially influenced the findings of Griffith CJ, Barton and O'Connor JJ, and to an extent of Higgins J, although the latter was more driven by a view, no longer accepted, that a law can be made only with respect to one subject matter of power. Hughes wanted the Court to follow what he saw as the correct reasoning of Isaacs J in his dissenting judgment; that is, the Commonwealth had legislative power to control the trading activities of trading corporations and the financial activities of financial corporations. If anything, the Attorney considered that Isaacs J's view was too narrow in interpreting the extent of the corporations power but was wide enough for the current case. Hughes acknowledged that a favourable decision from the Court could lead to a major expansion of Commonwealth power over commercial activity at all levels: national, interstate and intrastate. For the moment, however, he wanted the Court to accept that the relevant provisions of the *Trade Practices Act* came within the ambit of s 51(xx) in that they were confined to the trading activities of trading corporations, and trading and financial corporations were expressly singled out by sections of the Act. By overruling *Huddart, Parker*, the Court could conclude that the Act was valid in all its aspects.

Fullagar argued that the Act sought to preserve healthy competition in Australian trade and commerce, and the power to make laws with respect to trade and commerce was the sole head of power to which it could be referred. The Act exceeded that power by not confining its operation to interstate and foreign trade. At the time, Snelling's intervention did not greatly bother the Commonwealth Attorney-General. The NSW Solicitor-General urged the High Court to postpone a decision on the scope and limitation of the corporations power because its ultimate determination was vitally important to the States. Reference to that issue, he argued, was not necessary in determining the current case. Many years later, Hughes came to believe that the NSW involvement, reflecting as it did a concern about the expansion of Commonwealth power, explained some of the hostility that led to his dumping as Attorney-General.[36] Hughes' identification with anything smacking of 'centralism' assured him of opposition from Askin's State Liberals wanting to protect 'States' rights'.

After they concluded the first part of their case, the Commonwealth team repaired to the Australian Club in William Street for a celebratory drink. Ellicott, a Methodist who was virtually teetotal, asked for something soft. Hughes took a decanter filled with what he thought was water and poured the Solicitor-General a glass of neat gin. Ellicott survived the ordeal. The legal team got on well at the Club, even though they were not entirely of the same mind politically on the Vietnam War. But a sharper exchange occurred when Senator Magnus Cormack arrived at the Club. Once described as 'the stormy petrel' of post-war Victorian Liberal politics, Cormack correctly saw the implications of a Commonwealth victory in the *Concrete Pipes case* as a setback for 'States' rights'. His friendship with Hughes did not deter him from starting a row.[37]

The Attorney-General left Melbourne confident of a good result. Harders felt the same. Soon afterwards, Barwick spoke to him over morning tea at the Reserve Bank: 'My word, your Attorney-General presented a very powerful argument in that case the other day.'[38] Returning to Canberra, Hughes looked forward to making his second reading speech on the Public Order Bill, resuming the challenge to pass the Continental Shelf and Territorial Sea legislation and perhaps introducing more far-reaching trade practices legislation.

13

'You change the course with no regrets for the past'

Shortly after 3.00 pm on Monday 8 March 1971, and without warning of his intentions, Malcolm Fraser delivered a letter to John Gorton's office announcing his resignation as Minister for Defence. He explained his action in a single sentence: 'I regard your conduct as Prime Minister as one which indicates significant disloyalty to a senior Minister.'[1] Fraser's resignation precipitated Gorton's downfall and Hughes' sacking as Attorney-General.

For some days, Fraser and the Army had been briefing journalists over conflicting interpretations of the Army's commitment to the 'civic action' policy in South Vietnam. Fired by his habitual loyalty to the armed services, and wanting to hear the Army's version of events, Gorton met the Army's Chief of the General Staff, Lieutenant General Sir Thomas Daly, for 15 minutes on 1 March. Denials notwithstanding, a story circulated after this meeting that Daly had accused Fraser of being disloyal to the Army and to its minister, Andrew Peacock. In his resignation speech of 9 March,[2] Fraser indicted Gorton's actions on two counts. First, he had violated the chain of command by directly consulting the Army without reference to the Minister for Defence. Secondly, he had failed to 'kill' a journalist's story about Fraser's alleged disloyalty to the Army and to Peacock and, by not doing so, placed silence above loyalty to a senior colleague. He concluded by saying that Gorton was unfit to be Prime Minister. He offered three examples to support his general denunciation. Two involved the meeting with Daly. The third was of particular interest to Tom Hughes.

According to Fraser, Gorton had 'a dangerous reluctance to consult Cabinet, and an obstinate determination to get his own way'. He ridiculed public service advice unless it supported his view. Fraser cited as evidence Gorton's attempt to prevent a Cabinet discussion of the proposed call-out of the Pacific Islands Regiment (PIR) in July 1970. Fraser told the House that the Prime Minister wanted the call-out to assist the civil power in dealing with unrest on the Gazelle Peninsula in New Britain. Fraser was asked as Minister for Defence to arrange the call-out in preparation for an order-in-council to be signed by the Governor-General Sir Paul Hasluck. Advised by his Department and by officials on the Defence Committee that the necessary legal conditions had not been met, Fraser refused to act until Cabinet had been consulted. But Gorton 'resisted Cabinet discussion from the outset'. The Attorney-General subsequently flew to Port Moresby 'and I received his advice'. Cabinet met on Sunday 19 July and, with its authority, Fraser co-signed the call-out order.

Hughes knew that Fraser, by omission, had misrepresented the story.[3] Clarrie Harders and Hughes had been visiting departmental offices in the Northern Territory when, in Alice Springs on Friday 17 July, the Attorney received an urgent message from his Department requesting an immediate return to Canberra. Arriving at Fairbairn, he took a phone call from the Minister for Defence, who was attending a function in Tasmania. Fraser told Hughes that the Prime Minister wanted the Governor-General to issue a proclamation calling out the PIR to assist the civil authorities in dealing with a threatened uprising by the Mataungan Association on the Gazelle Peninsula. Fraser spoke of his concern that Gorton intended to act without prior Cabinet approval. Hughes agreed that Cabinet should first endorse an approach to the Governor-General, and said he would consult the law books to prepare advice on when a call-out in aid of the civil power was justifiable.

After examining the legal position, and reading the telexes from Port Moresby, Hughes concluded that, on the evidence available, a call-out could not be justified. He prepared a handwritten opinion, adding his own view that it would be inappropriate to seek a call-out without Cabinet approval. After delivering his findings to the Treasury building, where the Prime Minister was working on the budget papers, Hughes caught a late afternoon plane to Sydney to spend the weekend with his family. He was not at all surprised when 'a very displeased' Gorton rang him while he was having dinner, and asked Hughes to be at the Lodge the next morning. Fraser telephoned soon after Gorton had done so, and asked if the 'Boss' had called. Fraser and Hughes – who held the same views about due process – agreed to meet in Canberra over breakfast before proceeding to the Lodge.

Tamie Fraser prepared a meal while her husband, Hughes and a senior Defence official paced up and down the frost-covered lawn outside to plan their encounter with Gorton. Hughes made a suggestion: he and Harders should fly to Port Moresby to gather more information in order to advise Cabinet on the legally appropriate course. Fraser and Hughes took this idea to the Lodge where they met the Prime Minister, flanked by Charles Barnes, the CP Minister for External Territories, and Doug Anthony, the Deputy Leader of the CP. Within the hour, Hughes and Harders were on an RAAF flight to Port Moresby. They went straight to the Army barracks, had radio conversations with the authorities in Rabaul, and learnt that the Peninsula was on 'the cusp of civil insurrection'. Following intensive discussions with the Administrator, David Hay, and members of the Territory's Executive Council, Hughes and Harders concluded that the legal requirements for a call-out had been satisfied: there was a real danger the police would not be able to contain the expected level of violence.

After limited sleep, the two men flew back to Canberra on Sunday morning. Hughes then attended a hastily convened Cabinet at the Lodge. He advised that it would be proper to authorise a call-out. Cabinet approved, and Hughes accompanied Fraser and Gorton to Yarralumla for the signing of an Executive Council order. Fraser suggested that Gorton should join Hasluck in signing it, but Gorton wanted Fraser alone to do it, and Fraser did so.

For Hughes the matter rested there, until Fraser's resignation speech on 9 March 1971. To his astonishment, Fraser had made Gorton's conduct over the events of mid-1970 a centre-point of his attack on the Prime Minister (Fraser had called it 'one example' of Gorton's 'obstinate determination to get his own way'). For Hughes, what happened between 17 and 19 July amounted to 'a strong-willed Prime Minister submitting to the advice of strongly minded ministers, namely, Fraser and myself, who had acted in unison'. After Fraser had delivered his speech and Gorton had replied, Hughes fell in step with Fraser and Peacock in the government lobby and asked both men to come to his office. There he recounted his recollection of the events. Concluding, he asked Fraser if he had got anything wrong. 'No', said Fraser. In that case, Hughes said he could not understand why Fraser had made the events relating to the call-out a point of his attack on the Prime Minister. Fraser said nothing in response and the conversation ended. Evidently, Fraser had either forgotten the full circumstances or preferred the simplicity of a tale about Gorton wanting to get his own way. A resignation speech would lose some of its punch if, in truth, Gorton did not get his own way because two ministers obliged him to observe due process – which he did.

Hughes was not alone in his surprise. Gorton was puzzled. Fraser had never mentioned any lasting dissatisfaction over the matter. Moreover, at no stage during the Cabinet meeting on Sunday 19 July did Fraser voice any concern about Gorton's handling of the issue. Fraser did insist, however, that he had sent a message to the Secretary of the Prime Minister's Department saying he had accepted advice not to sign the order and believed the call-out should be a subject for Cabinet discussion. Perhaps what Gorton did remember was that after Hughes delivered his report, and McMahon made his habitual plea for inaction, Fraser joined the CP ministers in supporting an immediate request for an Order-in-Council, saying, '(w)e would be more culpable in that failure [to obtain an order-in-council] than in going to call-out'.[4]

Sacked

Fraser's resignation became the catalyst for a Party Room showdown on 10 March. Two Gorton supporters on the backbench moved a motion of confidence in the Prime Minister. Several backbench 'troglodytes' and 'termites' (Hughes' description) proceeded to denounce Gorton and all his works. Malcolm Mackay said the Prime Minister had finished a game of darts with a number of drinkers in the Western Suburbs Leagues Club in Ashfield where, upstairs, those attending an Evans electorate dinner organised by John Howard were waiting for him to arrive.[5] It is just possible Gorton had an idea about where to find swinging voters in a marginal seat. Howson invoked the Almighty and the spirit of Dunkirk, and quoted Leopold Amery's charge to Neville Chamberlain – 'Depart, I say, and let us have done with you. In the name of God go!' – apparently unaware that Cromwell had first used those words when dismissing the Rump Parliament. McMahon placed a hand over his forehead trying to look inscrutable. Hughes sat at the table alongside Gorton, ready to reply to questions on the call-out. As tension mounted, Killen twice begged Gorton to let him speak, but the Prime Minister thought an emotional Killen might damage the cause.

The ballot papers were counted in front of the meeting, and the Gortonites despaired as the piles looked roughly even. When the result was announced – 33-all – Gorton exercised a casting vote, to which under Party Room rules he was not entitled, and voted himself out of office. Hughes asked Gorton whether he should leave the room to alert the Governor-General. Gorton told him to stay: he was going to stand for the deputy leadership. McMahon was subsequently elected Leader and Gorton replaced him as Deputy Leader, an arrangement which could not, and did not, last very long.[6]

The new Prime Minister needed to reward his backers and meet his many promises. McMahon wanted to know the legal position in relation to the appointment of assistant ministers, ministers without portfolio and parliamentary under-secretaries, and sought the advice of the Attorney-General. Hughes sent him a memorandum on 18 March pointing out that an MP, who was not a minister in charge of a department, could do and be many things but could not be paid emoluments except for travelling expenses. The acceptance of emoluments 'would give rise to the real risk of disqualification'.[7]

On the day Hughes delivered this memorandum, McMahon told him he wanted Nigel Bowen to be Attorney-General. As Hughes remembered the conversation, he responded by saying 'you want me on the backbench'. McMahon: 'Yes, I have been under great pressure in the Party to get rid of you.' Atwill and Carrick had tried to persuade McMahon to retain Hughes. Ellicott urged Bowen to act. But the new Prime Minister was bent on what John Howard called 'an act of malicious spite'.[8] McMahon did not tell Hughes who was applying pressure for his dismissal. He told Killen, the first to be sacked, that he could not ask why he was being removed. As Killen found, the moistened hands, the clearing of the throat and an uncomfortable demeanour were signs that McMahon wanted job-ending interviews to be brief. In any case, Hughes and Killen realised that the two most outspoken Gortonites had to go. Hughes knew the 'troglodytes' had him in their sights over the territorial sea legislation, and sensed later that 'States' rights' Liberals in New South Wales objected to him using the *Concrete Pipes case* to expand Commonwealth power. Malcolm Mackay, promoted to the ministry and in effect filling the gap in NSW representation caused by Hughes' removal, was an opponent on both issues. The 'unctuous' Mackay greeted Hughes in the corridor after the sacking to say how sorry he was. As Hughes recalled, 'I did not attribute to this statement the quality of veracity'.[9]

Hughes continued to attend Cabinet meetings for almost two weeks before his sacking was formalised. On 19 March, the day after McMahon revealed that he was under pressure to remove him, Hughes clashed with the new Prime Minister in Cabinet over resale price maintenance. The Attorney had prepared a paper proposing to open up even wider issues. McMahon was reluctant to do anything, let alone be expansive.[10] Hughes could already feel his isolation.

The sacked Attorney received a pile of genuine messages of sympathy, and kept them in a folder marked 'Condolence Letters'.[11] Judges and barristers from Sydney, Melbourne and elsewhere, while welcoming him back to the Bar, expressed commiserations. Justice Laurence Street wrote:

> If I could presume to offer advice it would be to keep all your options open – no apparent disenchantment with Canberra (I realise this may not be easy) but at the same time a willingness to pick up your practice again and run it much along the same lines as you did immediately before your appointment as A-G. One way or another you have a rosy future to look ahead to.

A number of past and present politicians sent letters. Senator Magnus Cormack spoke of the 'villains' who had drawn their daggers 'and accepted the proffered salatium [sic]'. Robert Southey, the Federal President of the Liberal Party, felt bound by his office to be restrained, and had to suppress his dislike of McMahon. Peter Barbour, the Director-General of ASIO, thanked Hughes for his assistance both personally and to the organisation. JM Davis, the Commissioner of the Commonwealth Police Force, thanked him for his 'enthusiastic support' for the Force on a number of counts, including his attendance with Mrs Hughes at the Police Ball. Davis and Barbour both pointed out they could not comment on the reshuffle because it was a political matter, but were obviously very unhappy about the outcome.

One official dared to be more open and less than subtle. Lieutenant General Daly sent a hand written note to 'Dear Tom' on 28 March:

> I was very sorry to learn this morning that you are leaving the Ministry. I have a very high regard for your ability and an even higher regard for your integrity, a quality in Ministers of the Crown which I have come to value very highly in the past few years.
>
> You must sooner or later be recalled. I hope sooner, but in the meantime I will be barracking for you from the sideline.
>
> Yours sincerely
>
> Tom Daly

Malcolm Fraser sent Hughes a telegram: 'VERY MUCH REGRET TO SEE YOUR EXCLUSION FROM THE MINISTRY STOP SORRY TO SEE YOU WERE CAUGHT IN THE BYWASH.' It was a handsome, perhaps guilt-ridden, gesture. Sir Frank Packer also sent a telegram, addressed to 'Mr Ted Hughes': 'BAD LUCK BUT YOU WILL LIVE TO FIGHT ANOTHER DAY KINDEST REGARDS.' McMahon's media backer may have helped to end Hughes' political career but would soon assist his progress at the Bar.

One interested observer later recalled that Hughes was 'bitterly' and 'visibly' disappointed at being sacked. Clarrie Harders had a special affection for the man who organised his appointment as Secretary of the Attorney-General's Department. He saw Tom as 'a vibrant personality', 'full of good humour', who would do the unexpected such as suggesting that, while they were in Melbourne, they should go to a test match. Unfortunately, it rained all day; it was the test where not a ball was bowled for the scheduled five days. Tom took him to the Australian dressing room where the Attorney seemed to know all the players. Harders as Secretary worked under eight Attorneys, and regarded Hughes as 'not only my favourite but as the best Attorney-General under whom I served'.[12]

Returning to the Bar

Hughes took a week to clear out his Attorney's offices in Canberra and Sydney. He then began looking for accommodation to resume practice as a barrister, and needed to move quickly to meet 'the necessity of making some money after the arid years in politics'.

Chambers were not readily available in the city. Fortunately, Jim Staunton QC created a vacancy on the 11th Floor of Selborne Chambers by accepting appointment as Chief Judge of the District Court. Hughes applied to join the floor and there was immediate controversy. Under the existing practice, the Board of Directors of Eleventh Floor Pty Ltd chose the candidate who could purchase chambers. In April 1971, the purchase price for occupying a single room was $8500. All members of the floor met to consider the claims of two candidates: Hughes and Jenny Blackman. Blackman had first joined the floor as a stenographer in 1958. In 1965, she became an associate of Judge Rae Else-Mitchell while taking the Barristers Admission Course, which she completed in 1968. Douglas Staff QC, a powerful figure on the floor, supported Blackman. So did AB Kerrigan, the most senior QC on the floor, and Frank McAlary QC, the famed 'dancing man' in Sydney on Victory in the Pacific Day 1945, who owned several properties in the Kimberley region and in Glen Innes and often represented sporting figures in court. Tom Hughes received strong backing from Bill Deane, 'a man of great brilliance and compassion', with whom he had been associated in the *Concrete Pipes case*. Deane wanted to help Hughes secure a place and, at the same time, to boost the standing of the floor. Hughes narrowly won the vote, and Staff did not speak to him for at least a year. McAlary, who disagreed with Hughes politically, probably maintained his rage for longer.[13]

Hughes joined 'this holy band', 'this curious collection of people', in April 1971. He found that the floor, which could once boast being home to Rae Else-Mitchell and Robert Marsden Hope, among others, was 'now living on its past glories', and the quality was continuing to run down.[14] At first, Hughes occupied a tiny room, barely enough to accommodate his books and his secretary. He soon began to get briefs to appear in various jurisdictions, though it was 'not great work'. From April until the end of June 1971 he collected fees of $11,802; in the second half of the same year his return was $28,100. In the following year, his earnings at the Bar totalled $72,720 (on its own, roughly 14 times the average male earnings), dwarfing his salary as a backbencher. Whereas in April 1971 he was charging $300 a day for court appearances; by the end of 1972 he could command $500. By that time, Hughes had improved his earning capacity by appearing for Sir Frank Packer's ACP in defamation suits.

He had also made an important appointment. Soon after joining 11 Selborne, Hughes interviewed a young woman for the secretarial position to which he was entitled as a backbench member of Parliament. Anne Sloan brought with her an impressive reference, plenty of experience, a calmness and an obvious capacity. The meeting lasted for just 10-15 minutes. The sole interviewee, she began working with Hughes on 26 July 1971. Apart from one short break, taken for personal reasons, Anne remained with him until her employer retired from the Bar in 2012. In all that time, and ever since, she always addressed him and referred to him as 'Mr Hughes'.

Anne had attended Catholic schools in Sydney, considered nursing and, instead, enrolled in the 12-month course at Miss Hale's Secretarial College in Margaret Street, Sydney. Her first job was with an insurance company, and her second with a firm of solicitors, Sly and Russell, which occupied the same building as Hughes' brother, Geoffrey. She always wanted to travel and, vowing never to work for lawyers again, left Australia with a friend in August 1966. She travelled around Europe and the United Kingdom, worked for various employers in London – including the BBC for one day, and New Scotland Yard as a cleaner for three months – and spent a very happy three months working in West Berlin. Returning to Australia in December 1969, Anne enlisted the support of a job-searching company and they directed her to 11 Selborne.

Initially, she spent three-quarters of her time in Hughes' electoral office at Hornsby dealing with constituents. She became a full-time legal secretary after he left politics in 1972, and discovered that working for a barrister was infinitely more interesting than sitting in a solicitor's office. Perhaps it helped that this particular barrister was also taking on such a variety of work. In a very short time, she was the secretary who also made sure that robes were in order, clients and solicitors and conferences were managed, the Hughes children were supervised, shopping trips and appropriate presents were organised and, above all, that the office reflected more of her serenity than his intensity. She proved to be an exceptional appointment.[15]

The backbencher

At the beginning of August 1971, McMahon removed Les Bury from the ministry and replaced him in Foreign Affairs with Nigel Bowen. One week later, Gorton began publishing a series of articles in the *Australian* headed 'I Did It My Way'. In the first, he breached Cabinet solidarity by implying that McMahon and Fairbairn had themselves breached Cabinet solidarity. McMahon finally screwed up the courage to sack a very relieved and amused Gorton as Minister for Defence. On 20 August, Fraser returned to Cabinet as Minister for Education and Science. There were now four former ministers – Gorton, Bury, Hughes and Killen – sitting on the backbench and identified in the eyes of the media, and of the Prime Minister, as malcontents and rebels.

Tom Hughes was not disposed to cause problems for the Government, except over the issue of offshore minerals legislation. The striking feature of his renewed career on the backbench was how far he had moved from conservative positions he held when first arriving as the member for Parkes. His combative days were well behind him, pushed there by the reduced level of Australia's involvement in the Vietnam conflict and by his required and preferred non-partisan approach as Attorney-General. His parliamentary interventions became those of the detached observer prepared to criticise his own side of politics, and of someone eager to lift the standard of argument from all sides.

Hughes signalled his movement on several fronts during the latter months of 1971. In a wide-ranging and measured speech on 23 August, he acknowledged that participation in the Vietnam War – which he had strongly supported – had generated a deep-seated and long-lasting aversion within Australia to military involvement in Asia. It was 'a fact of life', which had to be recognised in formulating defence policy; 'no strategic design can be maintained except upon a firm base of domestic support'. He argued for a greater focus on the security and welfare of the South Pacific. Like it or not, he said, Australians should understand that, because of Britain's decision to enter the European Economic Community, 'we are fast coming to the end of any meaningful special relationship with the United Kingdom'. Hughes wanted to maintain the link with the Crown but wished to abolish the distinction between 'ambassador' and 'high commissioner'. Australia should accept that the Commonwealth was 'a greatly diminished utility' because its members had few interests in common except to meet in supposedly 'family gatherings' which were used 'for vituperative recrimination against other members' (the memories of the Bahamas remained vivid). He hoped that meetings of Commonwealth heads of government 'will diminish consistent with their virtual inutility'. Above all, Hughes wanted public discussion of foreign affairs to focus on policies not personalities, and for the major parties to develop a bipartisan approach because it would be 'a wasteful and expensive luxury to indulge in avoidable divisions'.

This speech was important for its context. The prospect of the People's Republic of China joining the United Nations had become foremost among the shifts underway in outlook and alignments in international affairs. Against this background, Gough Whitlam had made a controversial visit to China early in July 1971. McMahon condemned and ridiculed the venture. He said on 12 July that 'Mr Chou [Zhou En-Lai, the Chinese Premier] had Mr Whitlam on a hook and played him as a fisherman plays a trout'. Embarrassingly for the Government, President Nixon announced on 16 July that he planned to visit China in the following year. Nonetheless, McMahon and other Liberal and

Country Party ministers and backbenchers kept up their attack on Whitlam's visit as 'dangerous', 'irresponsible' and 'conceived in sin', not least for allegedly abandoning Australia's south-east Asian allies. Fraser, then still on the backbench, accused Whitlam of making secret promises to the Chinese Premier, declared he had 'clearly become a Chinese candidate for the next Australian elections' and called him 'a disgrace to Australia'. Hughes in his speech of 23 August agreed that the Whitlam visit was 'in some respects … not such as to serve Australia's best interests'. Pointedly, however, he saw no ground for denigrating Whitlam as 'a disgrace to Australia' or as 'the Chinese candidate in our next general election'. Nor could he detect any evidence of Whitlam making a secret pact with the Chinese Government. 'Verbal ballistics in the end serve no great purpose.'[16]

Hughes had another crack at Fraser after the newly elevated Minister for Education defended the increased concessional deductions for educational expenses announced in the Budget. Fraser considered that the concessional allowance was the sole means whereby people in remote rural areas, and especially woolgrowers, could afford to send their children to boarding school. Hughes argued that the deductions themselves had a regressive and inequitable element because they provided a greater benefit to higher income earners. He was further out-of-step with his own Party after saying in the budget debate that it was important to consider the imposition of a capital gains tax. While not yet firmly in favour of such a tax, he saw it as a possible means of dealing with the expanding tax avoidance industry. Tax avoidance, he argued, was certainly legal but also 'essentially inequitable' because the better-off were its principal beneficiaries.[17]

Hughes' finest moment of recognition occurred on 3 September 1971. The High Court, sitting in Sydney, handed down its decision in the *Concrete Pipes case*.[18] Although five of the seven judges held that, because of technical drafting deficiencies, sections of the *Trade Practices Act 1965* were invalid, the Court unanimously disapproved *Huddart, Parker & Co Pty Ltd v Moorehead*.[19] As Hughes put it: 'We lost the battle and won the war.'[20] Yet the precise reach of the corporations power remained unclear. Barwick had refused to set its 'outer limits'. He saw constitutional interpretation following the same method as the common law. 'The law develops case by case, the Court in each case deciding so much as is necessary to dispose of the case before it.' Professor Geoffrey Sawer warned against 'grossly exaggerated and over-optimistic assessments' of the decision in the *Concrete Pipes case*. The decision 'is certainly an invitation to the Commonwealth to have a lash, but it is no guarantee of success'.[21]

Whitlam launched a short debate when the House first met after the High Court announcement.[22] The Leader of the Opposition called the decision 'historic', and he knew who deserved much of the credit:

> The Australian people and Parliament should acknowledge the drive and skill of the honourable, learned and gallant member for Berowra who, on their behalf, secured this decision after litigation in the Commonwealth Industrial Court and the High Court.

Whitlam proceeded to list what he saw as the opportunities created by the High Court decision. They included the restoration of the original Barwick proposals for trade practices legislation and new laws for consumer protection and consumer credit, for creating a securities and exchange commission, and for dealing with overseas control of Australian companies.

The former Attorney-General described the decision as 'having momentous consequences for our future as a country and as a nation'. In effect, it had unlocked the doors for a 'very important ideological disputation' over how the country's economic life should be managed. Hughes imagined that the other side of politics would want to use the corporations power differently, and he expected to be fighting them all the way. His own priority was for the introduction of effective trade practices legislation to ensure that 'private enterprise' was actually 'free enterprise'. Above all, Hughes wanted to see the full operation of a basic common law principle, namely, that the onus was on a person who wanted to restrain competition to show that such restraint was in the public interest. He hoped that the Government would seize the initiative and, unlike the Asquith Liberals in Britain during the early 20th century, would not advance reform with 'noisy mouths and mouse-like feet'.[23] But Hughes was under no illusion that the McMahon Government would engage in root and branch reform. In the case of trade practices, he had to wait until the election of the Whitlam Government to get his wish.

A preselection and a retirement

During the short debate on the High Court decision, Hughes said he hoped to be in the Parliament 'in the years to come', but 'that is perhaps a matter of doubt'. Few in the chamber would have been unaware of what lay behind his qualification. The *Australian* on 3 September had reported rumours about two sitting Liberals facing preselection difficulties. One was the anti-Gorton Jeff Bate, aged 65 and married to Harold Holt's widow. Bate had represented Macarthur since 1949. Tom Hughes was the other potential casualty. Jim Cameron, the crusader against the iniquities of the permissive society, wanted to despatch someone he believed had not stood firm. Mrs Dorothy Simons of Greenwich told the *Review* on 25 September 1971 that Cameron's ideal society was Cromwell's England. Yet Cameron had created sufficient unrest among some Liberal branches for the *Australian* to suggest that, while Hughes could count on the State Executive and State Council delegates, he faced a problem with the local branches.

Whereas the Macarthur preselectors soundly rejected Bate, Hughes won his preselection on 8 October with an absolute majority over four other candidates on the first ballot, securing most of the local votes.[24] Hughes, it transpired, had the great advantage of not being Jim Cameron. And he won despite being greeted on arrival for the preselection at Party headquarters by a line of homosexuals standing outside the building holding balloons aloft and chanting, 'We want Tom'. The object of their support wondered '(w)ho needs enemies if one has friends like these'.[25]

Six weeks after winning the preselection, Hughes informed McMahon of his intention to leave federal politics at the next election. In a letter to the Prime Minister, Hughes denied belonging to any 'rebel group' in the Liberal Party, and said he had never considered himself a rebel. Nevertheless, McMahon told his associates that Gorton and Killen were now isolated. The Prime Minister did not feel obliged to express public regret about Hughes' foreshadowed departure, having previously tried to achieve it by covertly organising Hughes' appointment to the NSW Supreme Court (Hughes declined the invitation).[26]

The former Attorney-General made his decision after receiving a very good proposition. Antony Larkins was elevated to the Bench on 18 October 1971 and Sir Frank Packer, who had retained Larkins as chief legal counsel for ACP, offered the position to Hughes. Following this announcement, Vi Lloyd, who had succeeded Thom as the President of the Berowra FEC, appeared on the ABC TV program, *This Day Tonight* (*TDT*). It was put to her that 'they' (unidentified) were suggesting Hughes had been 'bought off' by Packer to stop him from embarrassing the Prime Minister. Lloyd replied: 'I don't think Mr Hughes could be bought off on anything.' Packer pointed out he had already given Hughes a retainer after he left the ministry and resumed general practice, and Hughes was presently engaged in a case on the company's behalf. Hughes described the *TDT* question as 'grossly offensive and baseless' and its very form 'convicts the questioner of reckless disregard for ordinary decency'.[27]

Hughes formally announced his decision at a meeting of the Berowra FEC on Monday 29 November.[28] He told the FEC that his decision to retire should end persistent and 'false and unfounded' allegations that he belonged to a rebellious group of ex-ministers who were trying to bring down the Government. He would remain loyal to the Party and its leader during his remaining time in Parliament, adding 'I have always had an agreeable personal relationship' with the Prime Minister. He admitted feeling 'wronged' by his dismissal as Attorney-General but had come to see 'I had no just cause for complaint' (his second remark was plainly untrue, and wasted if it got back to McMahon). Hughes said his decision to retire followed significant opposition he faced when seeking re-endorsement for Berowra. He would always encounter opposition inside and outside the Party: 'I am hardly an uncontroversial person.' Besides, he would now receive more legal work, and attract the sort of publicity where people might find an incompatibility with his other duties. He had found himself at the 'crossroads'.

> Would I go back to my first love – and it must always be so – the law, or would I chance my arm on the manifest uncertainties of politics? Events have proved that I am, politically speaking, accident prone. I have had better luck in my primary profession. I thought upon reflection that I would be pushing luck a little far if circumstances like those of March ever required that I should attempt a second resurrection at the Bar.

Understandably, Hughes left some matters unsaid. After all, the ACP offer merely precipitated a decision that was in the making from the time McMahon sacked him. Hughes knew months before the preselection he had no future in politics. There was no place for him in a McMahon Government should it survive beyond 1972; there was no guarantee of a front bench appointment should it lose; and there was no appeal about remaining in a parliamentary party possibly led by Malcolm Fraser. Given these circumstances, and his awareness of remaining an outsider in Berowra and his preference for a career at the Bar, Hughes should never have nominated for re-endorsement. Now the Liberal Party faced the expense of a second preselection.[29]

The final year

Hughes saw out his final parliamentary year by continuing to stand apart from or above party politics.

On 29 February 1972, Hughes intervened in a debate on the current and prospective state of the economy.[30] He pointed out that in an election year such a debate was unlikely to be objective. He described his own views as not entirely orthodox, while hoping they 'will not be too entirely heterodox for my Party to stomach'. He did not want to be accused of 'rocking my Party's boat', yet could not 'lie inertly in the scuppers while the ship of state ploughs through rather heavy seas'. Hughes proceeded to blame employers for contributing to rising inflation and escalating industrial disruption, and saw no sense in criticising Labor for standing up for a strong trade union movement. Hughes' main point, however, was that the Government would find it hard to persuade the electorate it was doing all it could to curb cost-push inflation until it moved effectively against restrictive trade practices and ceased its opposition to a prices justification tribunal.

Nearly two months later, Hughes became embroiled in an issue where, along with Gorton and Killen, he seemed ready to rock the Government. In April 1972, Whitlam had moved a motion to require the Government to proceed with the original Territorial Sea and Continental Shelf Bill before moving ahead to the Marine Science Institute Bill. 'Duke' Bonnett, a loyal Gortonite, wanted the latter because the Institute would be located in Townsville, the heart of his marginal seat. Hughes wrote to McMahon on 19 April saying he was 'irrevocably committed to the opinion that the question of sovereignty and control over the territorial sea and continental shelf ought, in the national interest, be resolved … with the least possible delay'. McMahon and Bowen had told him that the Government was moving towards high-level discussions with the States with a view to reaching an agreement. The former Attorney knew that, even in the unlikely event of a unanimous agreement with the States, there would remain outstanding areas of difference requiring litigation for their resolution. His 'deep conviction' was that the current Parliament must pass the Bill, unless an agreement with the States obviated the necessity. He wanted an assurance that, if the projected discussions with the States failed, the Government would secure passage of the Bill. If this assurance was not forthcoming, 'I would have to use my voice and my vote to bring the Territorial Sea Bill on (assuming the Government still wanted it shelved) during the last few weeks before a general election'. For the moment, he could offer no more than to vote for an amendment to the Whitlam motion to postpone discussion on the Territorial Sea Bill until immediately after passing of the Marine Science Bill.[31]

On 17 May, the Party Room voted unanimously to proceed first with the Marine Science Bill. Bonnett was happy, and Gorton decided that it was more important for the Government to stay in power. On the same day, Tom Hughes spoke on the Whitlam motion.[32] He said the Opposition was entitled to use the forms of the House 'to promote the idea that there is a basic disunity in the Government ranks'. But it knew 'that at times members of a Party have to submerge their quite profound convictions on matters of personal conscience in order to support the Party to which they belong'. He was not going to be used as a 'plaything' by the Opposition to create an impression of such disunity in the Liberal Party that he could not submerge his strong views 'in the general party interest'.

Next day, and more than two years after the original debate was adjourned, the Government brought on the second reading of the offshore legislation. With the support of Gorton, Hughes and Killen, the Government adjourned the debate without resolution. Hughes spoke for 20 minutes affirming his support for the Bill, describing opposition to it as based on 'obduracy, obscurantism or prejudice'.[33] He added another argument to those he used in 1970: it was the prime duty of a federal government in a federal system to explore the boundaries of federal power. As Attorney-General, he had done so in relation to the corporations power. Hughes was not prepared, however, to vote against the Government. On 18 October, a little more than six weeks before the 1972 election, Gorton and Killen voted against a motion that effectively postponed further consideration of the Bill until the next Parliament. Tom Hughes abstained, and the Government had a majority of one on the floor of the House.

On the last day of the 27th Parliament, 26 October 1972, McMahon spoke briefly about two retiring ministers (Sir Alan Hulme and Sir Reginald Swartz), acknowledged the retirement of three former ministers (Adermann, Barnes and Hughes) and spent more time talking about Arthur Calwell. Whitlam, as always, had more sense of occasion and more grace. He noted that of the 10 members who were leaving of their own free will, 'one is retiring from public life at a much earlier age than honourable members ordinarily choose. No party can lightly suffer a loss such as the departure of the honourable member for Berowra. I am sure that his service in this Parliament has in no way diminished his forensic future or disqualified him from judicial office.' Snedden also spoke warmly about Hughes, and thanked Whitlam for doing so. Lance Barnard said Hughes had made 'a very significant contribution' as Attorney-General and that the House would be the poorer for his leaving. Labor's Jim Cope, the former glassworker who became Speaker after the election, spoke of another side: 'Tom Hughes is a genial fellow who always had a nice "good morning" to say and a little chat outside in the lobby.'[34]

Hughes had a valuable 'self-imposed rule': if you have a good reason to change course, 'you change the course with no regrets for the past'. Friendships should not be discarded but it was important not to 'live the past or live in the past'. He never joined ex-service associations after leaving the Air Force and never involved himself in the Association of the Former Members of the Parliament of Australia. Hughes rarely went back to the Parliament, though he did attend the memorial service in the former Senate chamber for Magnus Cormack, 'my dear friend, for whom I had enormous admiration'.[35]

Hughes did leave many good friends behind in Canberra. He had shared a flat for a time with Andrew Peacock and found him to be 'a most agreeable companion, a loyal friend'. Like so many Liberals, Hughes never saw Peacock as 'true leadership material … he lacked a capacity to articulate in clear terms a political creed on serious subjects. He lived for the moment.' The paths of the two men diverged after Hughes left Parliament, but Peacock sought his advice when having difficulties with Fraser. Hughes also had 'a close and very cordial association and friendship' with Don Chipp. Again, in common with his contemporaries, Hughes found Chipp 'very intense', 'given to expressing himself in strong language with frequent use of superlatives', and 'too emotional … ever to lead the parliamentary Liberal Party'. As will be seen, Chipp and Hughes did have a falling out though they re-established contact at John Gorton's wedding to Nancy Home in 1993. Jim Killen was the one closest in 'political friendship'. The two men developed 'a great bond of affection' and it survived their post-politics separation. Hughes saw him as 'a mercurial character, gifted with great fluency of language' and with 'an orotund style'. Killen, above all, was 'a conspicuously honourable man'.[36]

John Gorton remained a good friend. Hughes saw Gorton as someone who wanted to make a new beginning for the Liberal Party and 'had some very good ideas, which he did not always articulate with great precision'. Unlike Fraser, he never saw Gorton as determined to get his own way. Attending Cabinet, he observed Gorton to be a good chairman, 'not given to the unilateral assertion of inflexible positions'. He had strong views but 'was always prepared … to listen to argument and to modify a position in response to what he regarded as sensible, persuasive argument'.[37]

Hughes' assessment of McMahon was scathing.[38] He could not understand why Fraser made the short-sighted move against Gorton because McMahon 'carried all the baggage of potential disastrous failure'. Given that Fraser was heard to remark after McMahon's election as Leader – 'At last, a real Prime Minister'[39] – perhaps he had discerned qualities few others of any standing had noticed. According to Hughes, McMahon 'was devious, scheming and consumed by ambition … his devouring ambition was not matched by leadership ability … a shocking little person'. Menzies, he knew, had no time for him and it was a measure of 'the intellectual bankruptcy' of the NSW Liberal Party that McMahon climbed to the position he attained. Hughes agreed with Sir Paul Hasluck's oft-quoted assessment where, after applying a broad selection of derogatory adjectives and adverbs, Hasluck settled for McMahon being 'a contemptible creature'.[40]

Hughes sat on the sidelines during the 1972 election campaign. He was not surprised by the defeat of the McMahon Government on 2 December. The surprising element was that, despite the Whitlam bandwagon, the backing of the media and McMahon's failings as a campaigner, the anti-government swing was just over 2 per cent. Gortonites who believed that their man might have held onto office needed to remember that the adverse swing in 1969 was nearly 7 per cent. At least Berowra moved more firmly into the Liberal corner. Harry Edwards, a university economist, retained the seat with 53.5 per cent of the primary vote, an 8 per cent improvement on Hughes' vote in 1969. Edwards, however, did not have to contend with a Liberal spoiler. Hughes wrote to Whitlam after the election offering his congratulations and best wishes. The new Prime Minister replied on 28 December saying he was 'very touched' by a 'most generous letter'. Whitlam added that, while the 28th Parliament 'would be a great improvement on its predecessor, it will be very much poorer for your absence'. He felt sure 'there will be greater opportunities for your qualities to be used in the service of Australia in the years to come'.[41]

There was no possibility of Hughes looking over his shoulder. He was back at the Bar, where he wanted to be.

14

President of the NSW Bar Association

Within three years of returning to the Bar in 1971, Tom Hughes took office as Chairman of the Board which managed 11th Floor Selborne Chambers, and was elected to the Council of the NSW Bar Association and became its President. Hughes considers that one of his major achievements in Selborne Chambers was to persuade the senior clerk to take early retirement. Jack Caffrey, a former first grade rugby league player, had passed his prime and Hughes had no doubt that the junior clerk, Paul Daley, who had joined Wentworth Chambers in 1961, was a better option. The Chairman had to sway Caffrey to accept it was time to go, and to convince reluctant barristers to pay for his early retirement. Daley recalls that, in relation to Caffrey, it was an 'awkward situation' which the Chairman handled 'beautifully'. Hughes' efforts had a longer-term significance. Daley remained in office until he took retirement in 2015, someone universally liked and respected. He was on first-name terms with luminaries such as Sir William Deane, and with everyone else he encountered on the 11th Floor. Yet, like Anne Sloan, he always addressed Hughes as 'Mr Hughes', and did so even when the two men met occasionally at Randwick racecourse.[1]

After Hughes' election to the Bar Council he was elected to be one of the two Vice Presidents. On 17 September 1973, he replaced Harold Glass QC as President when Glass was appointed to the Bench of the NSW Supreme Court. Completing his predecessor's two-year term, Hughes occupied the position for 26 months. Two of his Vice Presidents were Denys Needham QC and Douglas McGregor QC, and the members of Council during his term included Mary Gaudron, elected as a barrister of under five years' standing and a future Solicitor-General of New South Wales and High Court judge.

Incorporated in 1936, the Bar Association 'was very much a professional association created solely to represent and advance the interests of its members'.[2] Membership was voluntary, though about 90 per cent of practising barristers paid their annual fee in 1973, compared with some 75 per cent in 1949. Fees were levied on a graduated scale. Tom Hughes as a QC (in 1973 he was listed at no 21 in seniority at the NSW Bar) paid the top annual subscription of $120; a barrister of under two years' standing paid $15. The Association itself had no statutory powers but exercised a number of functions designed to uphold 'the honour and dignity of the bar' and to promote its interests. While the Supreme Court or a higher tribunal alone could disbar a barrister, the Council of the Association could expel, suspend or reprimand its members, and the Supreme Court regarded the Council as the appropriate body to commence disciplinary hearings against barristers, regardless of whether they were members of the Association. The Council was, therefore, both a general regulatory body of the profession and the governing body of the Bar Association. In the former capacity, it was in a position to protect the public interest; in the latter, its task was to advance and defend the interests of members of the Association.

In 1973 there were 562 practising barristers in New South Wales. Almost three-quarters of them had chambers in Phillip Street. The various law officers, including the NSW Attorney-General and the Solicitor-General, the Commonwealth Solicitor-General and the Crown Prosecutors, who were domiciled elsewhere, and many barristers – often recently admitted – had chambers at 225 or 233 Macquarie Street or at 60 Martin Place. A number of barristers were based in the inner or outer suburbs, while 13 were located in the Australian Capital Territory, five in Newcastle, four in Wollongong and one in the Blue Mountains.

Despite the increase in numbers by nearly 68 per cent since Hughes' admission in 1949, and a greater dispersal in their location, the outlook and assumptions within the NSW Bar had not undergone any fundamental changes. Writing of the Bar in 1969, its principal historian thought it:

> seemed comfortably settled in traditional ways. Its members, except for a few stragglers, had become housed under the common roof of Bar Association premises at Selborne and Wentworth Chambers. Reproductions of the arms of the Inns of Court graced the entrance: the English connexion was immutable. The institutional perceptions of the Bar were those of men, brought up in a regime of 'fraternity' that set great store on dining together and maintaining quaint rules of etiquette, many of which seem absurd to later observers.[3]

An article in the *Australian Bar Gazette* in 1964 identified 10 'problems' when addressing the question 'Whither the Bar?'.[4] The anonymous author argued that the NSW Bar had to determine the appropriate forms for its organisation, the Bar's future participation in legal education, law reform and community affairs and issues relating to discipline, the independence of the Bar and of individual barristers and relations between the Bench and the Bar. There was an exchange in the same year between EA Lusher (later a judge of the Supreme Court) and Kerr QC over the question of whether the expansion of the Bar Association's corporate activity, and the need for corporate solutions to problems, would emasculate the hitherto 'fiercely independent, vigorous and colourful' NSW Bar.[5] All sides recognised that the traditional Bar had to be ready to meet challenges but there was a limited appreciation of where they might originate or of what they might entail. In any case, the underlying and sometimes stated assumptions were that the 'traditional ways' could and should survive scrutiny.

There were some areas requiring immediate attention. The Askin Government established the Law Reform Commission in New South Wales soon after replacing Labor in 1965, and law reform issues were regularly discussed at Bar Council meetings during Hughes' presidency. So were matters arising out of the introduction of Legal Aid. More immediately, in 1965 Ken McCaw, the Attorney-General in the Askin Government, asked the Council of the NSW Bar Association to investigate possible changes to two rules. Rule 64 laid down that a QC 'may not appear for a party without a junior barrister' except in criminal cases; and Rule 62 stated that a junior counsel 'is entitled to mark a fee equal to two-thirds of the fee payable to his leader'.[6]

The Bar Council responded to McCaw's invitation by appointing two sub-committees. A draft report went to the Council and, during the next six years, the Council discussed and approved minor amendments. It appears from the Minutes that the issue provoking the most debate was the rider to Rule 64 allowing a QC to appear without a junior in criminal cases. A majority on the Council feared it diminished the 'dignity' of a QC to appear without a junior. Council revisited the two-counsel rule in October 1972 and, by a narrow majority, agreed to allow some leeway in criminal cases. The revised wording of Rule 62 made it clear that a junior counsel was not *required* to mark two-thirds of the leader's fee. Clearly, the Council felt it had to respond to external criticism of the increasing costs of litigation. Nevertheless, the hallowed principles underpinning the two-counsel and two-thirds rules were considered inviolate.

Defending the status quo

External criticism of these principles gathered during Hughes' presidency. It did not help that the English Bar appeared to respond to a more concerted attack in the United Kingdom by abrogating the 'two-thirds' rule in 1971, though it remained in practice for most of the 1970s. In Sydney, the Council returned several times to the subject of the two rules, increasingly condemned by critics as involving restrictive trade practices. It felt especially obliged to react when James Ramsden published three articles on the legal profession in the *AFR* on 12, 13 and 14 March 1975. In the first, Ramsden argued that the profession 'is rife with restrictive trade practices' which had been carefully nurtured, rationalised and preserved 'to foster their well-developed sectional self-interests'. Ramsden highlighted what he called 'the famous or infamous "silk" rule'. As he represented it, if a solicitor employed a QC, which could be for anything between $320 and $1000 a day, and even up to $1500 a day, he must engage a junior barrister at two-thirds of the QC's fee.

Hughes responded on behalf of the Bar Association in the *AFR* on 8 April. He accepted that the Bar ought to be open to 'thorough scrutiny' and should not shrink from exposure to informed comment. Misinformation was another matter. He quoted the two relevant rules. Under Rule 62, where two counsel are briefed and junior counsel's brief is unmarked, junior counsel is not required by etiquette to mark two-thirds of the leader's fee but should not exceed two-thirds of that fee except in special circumstances. He also quoted Rule 59, whereby a barrister should not, except in special circumstances, accept a lower fee on a brief than what was commonly allowed on taxation to the successful party recovering the largest amount that might reasonably be obtained in the action. On this basis, Hughes argued that the Bar did not engage in an unjustifiable trade practice of an inflexible application of the two-thirds rule. A junior would normally mark two-thirds of a normal leader's fee. If the leader marked a special fee, the junior would normally make a special arrangement for the fee to be marked on his brief. Fees of $1000 or $1500 a day would be special fees and no junior would be entitled to mark two-thirds of them except by special arrangement.

Hughes concluded his response by saying that, if Ramsden wished to exercise his 'undoubted right' to criticise the Bar, he hoped the journalist would seek any relevant information from the Bar Council. Had he done so, 'his article would have contained fewer errors'. Perhaps Ramsden should have sought, not more information, but a cogent argument in favour of rules whose costs had to be borne by clients. After all, Hughes had not addressed what many solicitors and some commentators considered the critical issue: why should there be *any* requirement for a QC to appear with a junior?

Ramsden returned to this issue and several others in the *AFR* on 13 June 1975 when claiming that the law in Australia 'is riddled fore and aft by restricted [sic] trade practices'. He contacted the President of the Bar Association to suggest that s 45(2) of the *Trade Practices Act 1974* (Cth) appeared to make it unlawful for competitors to fix or maintain prices charged for services unless previously authorised by the Trade Practices Commission. He asked Hughes whether the Association had applied for authorisation and, if not, why not.

The President, whose opposition to restrictive trade practices was unmatched except by Sir Garfield Barwick, had a ready response. The *Trade Practices Act* did not apply to professional services rendered by members of the NSW Bar Association. Asked whether the Bar should determine whether its restrictive trade practices were in the public interest, Hughes responded that barristers were not engaged in 'trade'. Moreover, the Bar had not purported to determine whether Rule 59 was in the public interest. The object of that rule was to prevent a barrister from offering services lower than the economy scale fee allowed on a 'party and party' taxation of costs.

Ramsden quoted Michael Zander, a persistent critic of the restrictive practices of the English Bar, who replied to the lawyers-are-not-in-trade argument. Zander himself quoted Professor Lees' comment: 'to an economist schooled in the theory of competitive markets, it seems at first blush suspiciously like mumbo jumbo. Of course, the professions sell their services, just as do dry cleaners and British Railways. It seems to be sheer verbal obfuscation to insist that the services are not "sold".'[7]

Hughes advised the Bar Council on 26 June that he had discussed the two-counsel rule with the AH Loxton, President of the NSW Law Society, who had told him that several firms of Sydney solicitors were seeking the abolition of the rule. They wanted to make it optional for QCs to appear alone. After discussion, the Council formed an *ad hoc* committee with Hughes in the chair. The committee drafted a report, and Council resolved on 16 October that it would repeal Rule 59. Hughes signed a letter informing Loxton of the decision. But neither the Council nor the Bar Association was prepared to undertake root and branch reform.

Protecting a livelihood

The advent of the Whitlam Government in 1972 threatened areas of the legal profession's livelihood, notably, in relation to family law and accident litigation. One of Hughes' early tasks as President of the NSW Bar Association was to supervise the Association's case to place before the Government's National Committee of Inquiry on Rehabilitation and Compensation, which was established in March 1973.[8]

Gough Whitlam had a longstanding interest in what he called 'the most prevalent and the least appropriate form of litigation in Australia', namely, motor accident cases.[9] He committed his government to establishing a national scheme for rehabilitation and compensation to cover all cases of personal injury. He arranged for Justice Owen Woodhouse, who chaired the Royal Commission that led to the implementation of such a scheme in New Zealand, to inquire and report on the scope, form and manner of implementing one in Australia. In the expectation that Woodhouse would recommend a national system to override existing remedies, the legal profession, the insurance industry, the trade union movement and State governments acted quickly to press alternative views. The lawyers were defending livelihoods. A government estimate for the 1974-75 financial year reckoned the legal costs arising from accidents would amount to $25 million for workers' compensation and $32 million for compulsory third party injuries.[10]

Hughes had experience of what 'running down cases' and workplace accidents meant for a young barrister trying to make a mark. On the other hand, as Bar Association President, he believed that the profession could not afford, either in practical or moral terms, to oppose reform. As he said in his 1973 address, 'the Bar should not oppose change just because it might be thought to affect the financial interests of many of its members'. In this vein, the Council supported the Australian Government's broad objective of rehabilitating and compensating every person who had suffered an injury. As Hughes explained, however, there was a rider: 'the Council expressed its strong view that such a scheme should not sweep aside and replace all existing remedies because … there would be a risk of grave injustice to those victims of serious injuries who are presently entitled to a full measure of damages on proof of negligence.'[11] Neville Wran QC put this view on behalf of the Bar Council at a hearing on 29 September 1973. The Law Council of Australia, representing solicitors, followed suit.

Woodhouse was unmoved. His Report of June 1974 recommended 'the replacement of negligence action for personal injury claims by a general system of social insurance'. While appreciating that the legal profession would experience a substantial reduction in earnings by imposing a 'no-fault scheme', Woodhouse felt there was plenty of other work available and plenty of opportunities to exercise initiative and ingenuity. The Bar Association appeared to lose on another count. Under the Whitlam Government's proposed legislation, the final arbiter in cases of dispute would be the Secretary of the Department of Repatriation and Compensation. As Hughes argued, a non-judicial administrative tribunal was not the appropriate body to determine the complex issues likely to arise under the proposed scheme.

The lawyers could relax. After the Bill passed through the House of Representatives, the Senate in October 1974 handed it to the Standing Committee on Constitutional and Legal Affairs. That Committee broadly favoured a no-fault compensation scheme but wanted the Bill reconsidered because of doubts about its constitutional validity and about the removal of common law remedies for negligence in the case of work and road injuries. A redrafted Bill was ready for introduction when the Whitlam Government was dismissed, and the Fraser Government did not allow Whitlam's private member's Bill to go to a vote in 1977.

Collegiality

Tom Hughes worked hard to maintain a number of the Bar's social customs. The Common Room continued to provide for a corporate social life through the traditional Friday night 'fifteen bobbers' and held functions to mark new judicial appointments. In 1973, it held one for Lionel Murphy, the new Commonwealth Attorney-General. The Council and members of its various committees – there were 36 in all in 1974, one covering sport – entertained judges of the High Court and the Supreme Court as well as members of the Industrial Commission and judges of the District Court. Hughes was in office when Lords Denning and Hailsham arrived in Sydney in 1974 to celebrate the 150th anniversary of the opening of the Supreme Court. Hughes noted in a Presidential address how the Bar Association welcomed the appointments in 1974 of Sir John Kerr as Governor-General and of Laurence Street, who replaced Kerr as Chief Justice of the Supreme Court, observing that the latter appointment met with 'warm approval' from the Bar.

In the same year, Hughes welcomed Michael Kirby's appointment to the Arbitration Commission and, in later years, Kirby liked to remind him of one sentence from his speech: 'Your Honour is well known for Your Honour's vanity.' Hughes always claimed that he used the word 'urbanity'. Kirby referred to the subject in 1983 in a speech he made on becoming a judge of the Federal Court, claiming that 'the court reporter' remained 'unconvinced and immovable': the word was 'vanity'. At his judicial farewell on retiring from the High Court on 2 February 2009, Kirby, in thanking Hughes for his presence, said: 'Lawyers love ceremonies. It is not just the "vanity" in us. Ceremonies like this help to cement our corporate life and to remind us that we are all but temporary travellers in these parts.'[12]

Hughes' best intentions for promoting a corporate life had to contend with three considerable obstacles: the growing size and expanding locations of the NSW Bar; barristers belong to a profession that is not inherently nor necessarily collegial; and the costs of developing and maintaining existing levels of social contact had to contend with galloping inflation in 1973-75. On the latter point, the profit from bar sales in the second half of 1974 was just $34, while the dining room lost $2986 in the same period, mainly because of two large retrospective increases in wages for employees under the NSW Club Employees [State] award. One of the props of 'fraternity' faced possible liquidation.

Perennial issues and duties

Much of the President's and Council's time in 1973-75 was taken up by two hardy perennials: ethical issues and non-payment of barristers' fees.

The Council often delegated Hughes to follow the time-tested and approved method of having a quiet chat, possibly over a drink, with a barrister allegedly engaging in non-ethical behaviour. On investigation, many complaints were judged to be groundless or requiring no further action. There was a difficult situation in December 1973 when a barrister accused a solicitor before a Stipendiary Magistrate of aiding and abetting an escaped prisoner and of consorting with a known criminal. After Hughes spoke to the barrister on several occasions, the miscreant was persuaded to make what the Council required – an open and unconditional apology in open court – and no disciplinary action was taken. Maintaining proper etiquette was critical. The Council was asked on 20 March 1975 whether a member of the Bar Association who had moved to Canberra to join a firm of solicitors could remain a member of the Association and could still appear as a barrister in New South Wales, and, if so, be instructed by a solicitor from his Canberra firm. Led by Hughes, Council resolved that he was no longer entitled to be a member of the Association, and it would be unethical to exercise within New South Wales his right of audience as a barrister no matter who instructed him.[13]

Claims of non-payment meant chasing up solicitors after the Council had sent a letter and a follow-up letter and had placed the offending solicitor on a list. Hughes had many discussions with the Law Society in attempting to formulate guidelines for the payment of fees. He also had to deal with public misconceptions. For example, James Ramsden claimed that the NSW Bar Association maintained a 'black list' of solicitors who had not paid fees, thereby in practice denying defaulting solicitors and their clients access to counsel until the fees had been paid. Hughes pointed out that Ramsden had made two errors of fact in relation to the so-called 'black list'. No solicitor was placed on a list while there remained a dispute about counsel's entitlement, and no listed solicitor was denied access to counsel. The sole restriction relating to access was that counsel must not accept a brief unless a fee accompanied the delivery of the brief.[14]

One of the President's regular duties was to recommend appointments to the rank of Queen's Counsel. Hughes met McCaw, the Attorney-General, on 2 September 1974 for what he described as 'a long and detailed discussion'. Next day he forwarded a memorandum containing the names and respective dates of admission of those whom McCaw had agreed should be appointed. Hughes had already advised the successful applicants to arrange a time to call on the minister. It had been a difficult selection process. There were 46 applicants at a time when 42 silks were in active practice (Hughes had not counted four of them, including Neville Wran and Bob Ellicott, who were absorbed with their political careers). There had been a significant diminution of silks in private practice following elevations to the Bench and appointments and retirements, of which there were eleven in 1973 and another eight thus far in 1974. With some juggling, Hughes fixed the wastage rate at 23, reduced by 10 to take account of the silks appointed in 1973.[15]

In the event, 16 barristers took silk in 1973, 24 in 1974 and 8 in 1975, the three years when Hughes delivered recommendations to the Attorney-General. They included Alec Shand and Michael McHugh. Hughes would have some memorable contests with both of them. In the case of McHugh, a future High Court judge, the contests did not intrude upon what became Hughes' closest personal friendship at the Bar. Murray Gleeson, who appeared several times with Hughes as a junior after the *Concrete Pipes case*,[16] was also appointed in this period, as were Roddy Meagher, Chester Porter and Barry O'Keefe who, among others, were destined for greater prominence. There were bound to be instances of hurt and anger but in 1973-75, when the Attorney-General formally made the decision and when there seemed to be no formal selection procedures, let alone formal selection criteria, those who failed to gain silk had really nowhere to turn and probably 'copped it sweet'.

Unless there is further paperwork in the Bar Association's files, it appears from the limited documentation available in the Hughes Papers that a handful of senior silks made lists and ranked those on their lists, and Hughes and perhaps one or two others collated everything and made the recommendations which went to the Attorney-General. One conclusion is probably unavoidable: the selectors just *knew* who were the 'best' candidates, based on what they had read in the application, and on what they had observed and had heard. In 1975, something similar to this process had a long history but a short future.

Two difficult issues

Following a riot at Bathurst Gaol on Sunday 3 February 1974, when a section of the prison was burnt down, 47 prisoners were subsequently charged with assembling to disturb the peace and unlawfully causing damage.[17] The authorities ignored the alleged criminal activity of prison officers. The Bar Council became involved after a deputation of barristers expressed concern about the lack of legal representation for prisoners awaiting committal proceedings, and about the right of a prisoner to consult legal advisers in privacy. Hughes met McCaw to discuss these issues and to offer assistance in the assignment of counsel should legal aid be approved. There were further meetings throughout 1974, where Hughes represented the Council's concern to ensure adequate representation and a prisoner's right to private consultations with legal representatives.

In the latter half of 1974, Hughes became involved in a delicate matter arising from the Bathurst affray. During a hearing on 29 August, the Crown Prosecutor objected to particular questions being asked of a medical officer who gave a statement to police about the nature and causes of injuries to prisoners. When Harry Berman SM upheld the objection, the radical and maverick Jim Staples, counsel for the defence, stalked out declaring that the court was not interested in the law or in the truth or in fairness to the prisoner. Staples then published an article in the 30 September-5 October issue of the *National Times* claiming that a number of recent cases demonstrated how justice in New South Wales meant that not everyone was equal under the law.[18] In particular, he accused John Maddison, the Minister of Justice, of engaging in a cover-up over possible assault charges against prison officers equivalent to that used by President Nixon over Watergate. Maddison called the Staples article 'shameful' and said it was based on 'completely false premises'.[19]

Hughes reported to Council on 31 October that Berman had brought Staples' conduct to the attention of the Bar Association. The Ethics Committee had asked Staples for his comment and Staples, in replying to the President, handed over his press statement. The Council also noted a letter of 31 October 1974 from Walter Lewer, Deputy Stipendiary Magistrate, forwarding a tape from the master tape of the proceedings. The Registrar was requested to get copies of the parliamentary debates together with press cuttings for the Ethics Committee. The Council subsequently called a special meeting for 21 November to consider Berman's complaint against Staples. Hughes tabled the recommendation of the Ethics Committee meeting he had chaired, advising Council to find that Staples had on three counts exceeded the proper limits of professional conduct as a barrister. The Bar Council accepted the recommendation, while acknowledging that the evidence Staples had sought to adduce was 'arguably admissible'. Hughes invited Staples to a special meeting called for 4 December, where an explanation of his behaviour convinced the Council to take no further action. No vote was formally recorded but Staples believed he was acquitted by 19-0, and that Hughes, after addressing Council on the seriousness of the charge, declared: 'Gentlemen, I want to tell you we'll convict Staples over my dead body.'[20] There was an intriguing sequel. Clyde Cameron, as Minister for Labor and Immigration, asked Hughes for advice in February 1975 on whether to appoint Staples as a Deputy President of the Arbitration Commission. Staples was duly appointed and the Hawke Government had to abolish the Commission in 1989 in order to get rid of him.

Of all the difficult issues that arose while Hughes was President, one was potentially explosive. Conservative lawyers, especially in Melbourne, where there was already hostility towards Murphy generated by some of his actions as Attorney-General, objected angrily to Murphy's appointment in February 1975 to fill the vacancy on the High Court created by the death of Sir Douglas Menzies. Much as Barwick disliked the appointment – he told Whitlam that Murphy was 'neither competent nor suitable'[21] – the Chief Justice contacted Hughes to say that any action would be inappropriate. Hughes also believed the appointment should be accepted, and felt sure the Bar Council was of a similar mind. He assured Barwick he would make a speech of welcome.[22] Speaking, as President of the NSW Bar Association, at the swearing-in ceremony at Darlinghurst on 14 February 1975, Hughes delivered what a critic from the past described approvingly as an 'eloquent reaffirmation of the Bar's impartial tradition'. Murphy grinned when Hughes deployed his favourite quotation from Dangerfield's *The Strange Death of Liberal England*: 'it could not be said of Your Honour that, like Asquith's Liberals, you advanced upon reform with noisy mouths and mouse-like feet'.[23]

That evening, Barwick contacted the Chairman of the Victorian Bar Association, RE McGarvie QC, who reportedly read out Hughes' speech to a meeting of the Victorian Bar Association and recounted the warmth of the Sydney welcome. The Association proceeded to debate a motion stating 'it is essential that positions on [the High Court] should be offered only to persons who are pre-eminent within the legal profession and whose fitness for office is not a matter of public controversy'.[24] The motion was rejected by 188 votes to 64. Hughes subsequently played a central role in the NSW Bar Council's decision not to make a submission to a Select Committee of the NSW Legislative Assembly set up to recommend changes to the Constitution to ensure that judicial appointments 'were made in a more equitable and acceptable manner'.[25]

Standing firm

On his appointment as Attorney-General in 1969, Hughes said that he did not believe law reform should lead public opinion. As President of the Bar Association, he had to defend legal practices against a small but growing body of (mainly external) opinion. Hughes was acutely aware of the new situation in which the Association now found itself. In his 1973 Presidential Address he said that 'if we are to survive successfully in times of challenge and of more intensive public scrutiny, we must recognise the need to subject our corporate habits and performance to critical self-examination'.[26] Yet Hughes was equally aware that a reformer could not successfully lead the membership to accept anything other than minor changes.

In 1976, Frank Walker, the Attorney-General in the newly-elected Wran Labor Government, asked the Law Reform Commission to review a number of matters relating to the organisation, regulation, obligations and privileges of the legal profession and its practitioners. Every Bar Council submission in 1977 made the case for retaining the *status quo*. It was one thing to accept the principle of public scrutiny; it was another to commit to substantive change. As for 'accountability', it was two steps removed. The 'guild' wanted it understood 'that the present system whereby the Bar itself primarily administers the ethical requirements of the profession is eminently satisfactory'.[27]

Tom Hughes' timing was perfect. His successors, particularly those in the 1980s and 1990s, had to deal with invasive changes that, in the time of his presidency, were barely on the horizon.

15

'The best of times' and 'the worst of times'

Between 1972 and 1977, Tom Hughes experienced a roller-coaster ride of many successes in his professional career and some lows in his personal life. In these years, while establishing a second life on the land, he became widely recognised as a leader of the NSW Bar. Despite his customary doubts about getting enough work, his fee books confirm that he was always busy and that, by 1977, could command fees of up to $1500 a day. Hughes was also developing the distinctive court manner that captivated public galleries and members of the fourth estate, panicked witnesses and some opposing counsel, while causing a few trial judges to wonder who controlled the courtroom. Standing erect, immaculately turned out in wig, gown, collar and jabot, with one hand resting on the lectern, his head and body turned side-on to the witness, his stare fixed towards a high point at the rear of the courtroom: his very presence foretold dominance. Sandra Hall later described his style as 'declamatory and theatrical, full of hectoring flourishes, airy swoops and lethal pounces'. Andrew Clark wrote of his 'rich vocal pitch, penchant for the pregnant pause, flashing eyes, imperious mien, razor sharp mind, brutal cross-examination, pomposity, wit, apposite quotes from the Bard'.[1]

Alongside Hughes' progress to the pinnacle, he had separated from his faith and from a marriage that had petered out. He tried several relationships – including a very happy liaison that became an enduring friendship – but failed to persuade the woman he most loved to accept the permanent relationship he needed to emulate his parents' ideal marriage. His support for her career fractured his connection with 11 Selborne where he had re-established his legal career after ceasing to be Attorney-General.

It is enlightening to place Hughes' personal life alongside the professional one to show how the barrister could separate the two lives and prosper at one while enduring disappointment and frustration in the other.

The personal

During his final two years in Parliament, Tom Hughes turned his mind to buying a rural property. Later, he wondered whether it was an atavistic urge, inherited from his Irish forebears. Whatever the explanation, he paid $46,000 for 900 acres a few miles west of Goulburn. The place was 'moribund' and the house 'run down', if weatherproof. Tom named his new possession 'Marsland', linking it to the home where he was born.[2]

It was not in his nature to become an occasional weekend visitor, leaving the management and work to others. He took on a new career as a part-time grazier, albeit a calling secondary to the law, in which he invested considerable capital and thousands of hours. Over the years, he added another two blocks of 1000 acres each to Marsland and, by the end of the 1970s, the best of his herds and flocks were winning prizes at shows around New South Wales and his diaries are replete with rainfall figures and seasonal information. From the early days, Marsland had another function, neatly captured in 1974 by a visitor. Judge Raine, appointed to the Supreme Court of Papua New Guinea through the good offices of Tom Hughes, Attorney-General, observed how his school friend had benefited from his rural acquisition:

> I can't tell you how impressed I was by Marsland. Its [sic] certainly done you no harm, you look as tough as old rope, and it very obviously gives you rest (not physical, I really mean mental repose) and enjoyment. Also its [sic] wonderful to be able to have the boys there – like you & I spent most hols at school in the bush ...[3]

'Mental repose' was critical. The rejuvenated lawyer and would-be grazier of 1972 had to deal with another disruption. While the Hughes marriage maintained the requisite public appearance of togetherness, the couple had drifted apart and both had, as Tom put it, already 'strayed' from the vows made in 1951. A chance meeting provided the spur to formalise the breach.

When Joanna took the children to Bowral for the school holidays in mid-1972, she met Catharine ('Kate'/'Katie') Weigall and her son and daughter. Kate's father, a grazier, an ex-serviceman and a member of a prominent Victorian legal family, had married a Catholic of Scottish descent. The family had moved from a property at Yarrawonga to Wagga Wagga during the Second World War and then to another property near Dubbo. Following Kate's father's death in 1951 – he died the day before Tom's father – the family moved to Bellevue Hill and Kate attended Rose Bay Convent in Sydney's Eastern Suburbs. Although clever, she never bothered with a tertiary education beyond spending a year at the University of Sydney. In 1963, she married Graham Ducker at St Peter's Church, Watson's Bay, an occasion which attracted the attention of Ita Buttrose's column 'Social Round

About' in the *Women's Weekly*. After an unhappy marriage, that probably influenced her never to marry again, she became something of a free spirit and a Bohemian, and was living in Vaucluse at the time she met Joanna Hughes. The two women got on well at Bowral, and Kate invited Joanna and her husband to a dinner party at her house. Within a few months, she was a co-respondent in the Hughes divorce case.

The formal dissolution of the marriage was a civilised affair. The couple separated in September 1972 and divorced in March 1973. Tom agreed that Joanna should be the one to sue, leaving her to make a confidential discretionary statement. Neither attended the brief court hearing, and it all ended with 'polite, dispassionate affidavits revealing the essential parts' and, 'as we each believed, not before time'.[4]

Custody and maintenance arrangements proceeded fairly smoothly as both parents were determined to do what seemed best for their children. Tom, through the family company, bought a house in Paddington for $70,000, and Joanna has lived there ever since. The company also took care of her rates, service charges and maintenance. She was not especially well-off, though she did have an income derived from BHP shares inherited from her aunt, Kitty FitzGerald. As Tom saw it, Joanna had been 'a large part of my life', and he did not want to seem 'stingy'. The children went different ways. Lucy mostly stayed with her father when home from school (she boarded at Frensham School in Mittagong), and the boys moved into Joanna's Paddington home, an arrangement which bothered Michael, the younger one, who missed his friends in Bellevue Hill. After selling the Bellevue Hill home, Tom lived in different places in the Eastern Suburbs before buying a house in Darlinghurst, which overlooked the city.[5]

Tom reflected on his earlier relationship many years after the divorce, and when happily married for the second time.[6] He turned his attention to the Christian ideal of indissoluble marriage, the best aspects of which he had witnessed in his parents' very special and enduring relationship.

> But what is to happen if, for any number of diverse reasons, the ideal is incapable of practical effectuation? And what about the children of warring parents, neither of whom is partially or at all responsible for the breakdown of their relationship, are they to remain locked within a continuum of marriage? The answer is: potentially disastrous in terms of the impact on the developing personalities of the children; and quite destructive of the peace and happiness of the parents.
>
> But according to Catholic principles, such a situation should not lead to divorce. What nonsense! I am a divorced man; and I know that my children, each of whom I deeply love, would have been destroyed in important aspects of their personality if there had not been a decision to sever the matrimonial tie.

> So, the decision was taken, and very sensible it was. My wife, a woman of remarkable personality and great quality, realised that 21 years of marriage could not sensibly be the subject of continuation.

The 'enforced permanence' had at least produced 'three beautiful children, each of whom gives each parent great joy and is the source of great interest and pride'. This was a marriage, Tom wrote, 'in which the fruit from the tree of sexuality was of better quality than the enjoyment that produced the fruit'. No one was to blame for sexual disappointment or for the incompatibility of mind, except those who decreed, and whom he obeyed, that couples should not sleep together before marriage. 'What utter crap! But if we had slept together, we would perhaps have discovered such incompatibility as would have prevented us from going on with marriage. Hence what irony – the children would not have been produced.'

Hughes had a few relationships in the 1970s in his quest for the preferred form of permanence. He encountered some very interesting women. One of them, the actor Kate Fitzpatrick, wrote about her 'little love affair' with Tom and about his proposal of marriage.[7] Observing that she described him as 'sweet', Michael McHugh wondered whether Fitzpatrick was a good guide in such matters. After all, she called Murray Gleeson the sexiest man she had ever met: 'Poor Kate. She must have led a sheltered life.'[8]

Deeta Colvin became an important person in Tom's life, and has remained a good friend. The daughter of an eye surgeon based in Orange, she had graduated with an Arts degree from Sydney University, travelled abroad and, back in Australia, taken a marketing position. Introduced to Hughes in 1975 at a party, Deeta found him to be good-looking, charismatic and a very young 52-year-old. She might have been 'a bit of a wild child', and he might have seemed at first buttoned-up and conservative, but they had 'a brilliant couple of years together' living in Sydney, riding horses at Marsland, and attending and giving parties. Deeta liked to watch Hughes perform in court – 'it was like being at a play'. The 24-year age difference seemed immaterial when she was 28, though her father did warn that it might count for more after she turned 60. Lucy Hughes, who had become Tom's closest confidante, clearly approved of the relationship. There might have been problems, however, because the two boys, each in their early teens, were not comfortable. Tom Jnr thought that his father's mistake was to ask for their opinion. Deeta, wisely, thought it best not to risk family difficulties and moved on, pleased later that the boys apologised for their opposition.[9]

Throughout the 1970s, Kate Weigall retained a presence in Tom's life even when she was not present. On meeting her, Tom had fallen deeply in love. She was a 'great beauty', 'singularly beautiful', 'off-beat' and his 'first great love'. He encouraged and supported her career in the law, wooed her with passion and persistence, and tried to persuade her to settle with him. Kate did not, or could not, respond as he wished, which was probably just as well. Judging by Lucy's letters to her father, Tom's daughter understood something that he took time to accept: Kate and Tom did not 'belong'.[10] But their association continued to have consequences, one of them leading to Hughes moving from 11 Selborne to 16 Wardell Chambers in Martin Place.

Moving chambers

Edward St John had previously tried to lure Hughes to new chambers. Following his defeat in the 1969 federal election, St John had begun looking for other forms of employment. Eventually, he returned to the Bar and, regarding Phillip Street as a very expensive closed shop, sought to establish new chambers elsewhere in the city. Despite their clashes over his attack on Gorton in 1969, St John contacted Tom Hughes in September 1975 in the hope of persuading him to join the enterprise. A barrister with what St John called 'a very big and fashionable practice' would add to the stature and allure of new chambers. After 'much agonizing consideration', Hughes decided to stay at Selborne. He told St John of his experience in 1971 after losing office as Attorney-General and trying to pick up the threads of private practice. 'It was very much line-ball whether I would be allowed to make the 11th floor and I owe my position here to the goodwill and effort of people, nearly all of whom are still on the floor, who wore down some entrenched opposition to my presence.' Although these events had occurred four-and-a-half years ago, and although confident he had discharged his debt of gratitude, 'I think my conscience would properly chide me if I were to leave the floor which has been the base of the position I am now lucky enough to occupy'.[11]

He had a clear conscience in mid-1977 because of what he regarded as the callous treatment of Kate Weigall by colleagues at 11 Selborne.[12] After taking the requisite examinations, Weigall was admitted to the Bar on 28 May 1976. In the following year, Hughes, as Chairman of the Board of Directors, moved for her appointment to the next vacancy on the 11th Floor. The Board approved this arrangement at a meeting in May 1977. In addition to Hughes, the other Board members at the time were Douglas Staff, Richard Conti, Simon Sheller, Vince Bruce and Jenny Blackman.[13] The Board had the authority to take this course, and Hughes assumed the matter was settled once Weigall paid the requisite fee. Conti, who was in London, confirmed in a letter to Hughes on 1 June that the Board had taken the necessary steps to admit Weigall to membership and that she was entitled to attend and vote at floor meetings and to all the privileges of floor membership. In the meantime, while Conti was overseas, she worked in his room.

Hughes was absent from Sydney when members of the floor held a meeting to test feelings about Weigall's placement. Blackman voted for her acceptance but the overwhelming majority voted against it, and she felt bound to support the majority decision. Conti and Staff believed that, as a matter of courtesy, the complainants should have waited until Hughes had returned to Sydney. Learning of the vote after he returned to Sydney, Hughes wrote to Conti on 24 June to bring him 'up to date regarding the acutely unhappy position on the floor'. Weigall's cheque had not been banked. Hughes contacted Sheller, who agreed she was entitled to membership of the floor having fulfilled the sole condition to which the invitation was subject, that of tendering her membership subscription. Sheller said he was 'shocked by the spate of intrigue', and told Hughes 'to expect a visit from McAlary'.[14]

After speaking to Sheller, Hughes contacted Jenny Blackman (it will be recalled that Hughes had pipped her for admission to the 11th Floor in 1971 for which McAlary and Staff had supported her). Blackman said the cheque was not banked because she believed membership did not become effective until formal ratification by the Board meeting held after the cheque was tendered. Hughes demurred, pointing to the 'simple contractual situation'. Blackman asked, in deference to her views, for a Board meeting to pass a resolution, 'as a mere formality', accepting Weigall's application. Hughes agreed to this proposal, with the reservation that it was 'quite an unnecessary step'.

In the meantime, McAlary visited Hughes, telling him 'this will be painful'. He told Hughes that 20 members of the floor objected to Weigall's membership and asked whether the Chairman would consent to a rescission of the resolution inviting her to join. Hughes replied that 'such a course would be a distinct breach of contract and quite dishonourable'. McAlary said he was not interested in the legal position, whereupon Hughes 'was constrained to retort that an evaluation of the legal situation seemed to be the essential starting point of any discussion'. Hughes told Conti that McAlary offered no specific or even general ground of complaint. 'It was a painful interview – but perhaps more for him than for me.'

The Board met in Hughes' chambers at lunchtime on Tuesday 14 June. Just as it was due to begin, McAlary entered the room and placed a petition on the desk (Hughes attached a copy to Conti). There were 18 signatories to a document dated 10 June 1977; and two names were typed but not signed.[15] Addressed to the Board of Directors, the petition read:

> 1. We take the view that it is contrary to the best interests of the Floor to allocate the next available room to anyone in advance, thereby denying the Floor the opportunity to select the best available applicant when the occasion arises.

2. We take the same view about admitting any person to membership of the Company before a room has actually become available.
3. For these reasons and without reflecting personally on the member of the Bar concerned, we request the Board to rescind its recent resolution to invite a member of the Bar to apply for membership of the Company.
4. Irrespective of whether recission [sic] of that resolution is possible and for the same reasons, we request the Board to rescind its recent resolution allocating the next available room to the member of the Bar concerned so as to give effect to the views contained in paragraph 1.

The Board, consisting of Hughes, Sheller, Bruce and Blackman, considered the petition and decided by two votes (Sheller and Hughes) to one (Bruce), with Blackman abstaining, to admit Weigall to membership. Hughes reiterated his earlier position: there was no need for such a resolution. He also realised, however, that a majority vote on the Board was not sufficient. Within a week, Hughes decided to leave 11 Selborne. He expressed his feelings in his letter to Conti of 24 June:

> Katie is close to broken: but I think that her inner strength will just pull her through and keep her at the Bar. There is, of course, no way of her staying on the floor and she is looking in other directions.
>
> It goes without saying that I am appalled and disgusted by the cruelty and injustice of it all. I have had it from one member …, that the petition is founded on a belief that I have been instrumental in bull-dozing the Board to accept Katie. If ever I can bulldoze you or Douglas [Staff] or Sheller, I shall throw a large garden party for no less than 1000 people and provide French champagne and caviar from the Caspian sea [sic].
>
> What puzzles me is why some of the signatories – old friends I thought – would not see me before they signed to ask what was the rationale of the Board's decision.
>
> I was naïve enough once to think that escape from politics would bring me back to a gentlemanly environment. Now I know better.

At least six of the signatories wrote to Hughes after hearing of his intended departure. Most regretted any misunderstanding, assured Hughes of no intentional discourtesy, spoke of their respect and admiration for his ability and leadership, and urged him to change his mind. Blackman spoke to Hughes after the event; he was 'bitter and accusatory'; she resented being called a 'liar'. She subsequently wrote to him, concerned he might hold to his reported statement that 'I will never forgive and never forget'. Blackman referred to her own 'traumatic' experience in 1971 and recalled how 'the storm blew over'. She was sorry he had experienced 'such deep unhappiness' and hoped he would 'at least forget the hurt'. For her part, Jenny Blackman 'continued to be friendly with and, so far as possible, supportive of Katie Weigall'.

Hughes did not forget. He had a chance encounter in a Sydney street in November 1979 with one of those who had signed the petition and who, in June 1977, had expressed the earnest hope that Hughes would reconsider his decision to leave the floor. Referring in his diary to their casual meeting, Hughes described the barrister as 'in his strange way a good person ... But I can never entirely eradicate from my mind that he was one of those who behaved so badly on the 11th floor 2½ years ago – causing my departure to Martin Place.'[16]

Was it really such bad behaviour to hold a meeting in Hughes' absence when the critics did have legitimate objections and strong arguments, and when they knew that the Chairman of the Board was not enamoured of participatory democracy? Notwithstanding his denial that he could bulldoze Staff and Sheller, Hughes did acquire a reputation at Selborne Chambers, and later in Wardell and Blackstone Chambers, of expecting to get his own way. Now separated further in time from the events of 1977, and well over his obsession with Kate Weigall, Hughes accepts he made unwise decisions and choices, while remaining disappointed that no one on the floor ever confronted him over Katie. He suspects that, in addition to not liking the idea of her being on the floor, some feared there could be problems if his relationship with her 'went off the boil'. He had to leave 11 Selborne because there was a schism, and 'I bore responsibility for its creation'. Hughes never regretted, however, continuing to support Weigall, who appeared several times as his junior. Characteristically, he maintains concern for her well-being.[17]

Joining Wardell Chambers did not interrupt the upward trajectory of Hughes' legal career. As Head of Chambers and Chairman of the Board, he acquired the best accommodation in 16 Wardell, with sufficient space for a conference room, in addition to his own work area, and a separate room for his secretary. Anne Sloan remembers the floor as by far the best work environment she experienced in all her time with 'Mr Hughes'.[18]

Some early high profile cases

In June 1973, Hughes represented Mrs Pamela Warrender, who was pursuing a 15-year-old claim for a greater share of the estate of her father, the late Sir Norman Myer. Heard in the Victorian Supreme Court, the case exposed deep rifts within the Myer family and between Pamela and the trustees, as well as the financial troubles and other misfortunes of the Hon Simon Warrender, Pamela's English-born husband. Hughes failed to persuade Pape J to rule in favour of his client after hearings that titillated the Victorian public and left the Warrenders feeling humiliated.[19]

In the same month, Hughes appeared with Murray Gleeson for his friend and former boss, John Gorton, in a defamation suit in the ACT Supreme Court. Gorton claimed $200,000 from each of the ABC and the *AFR* journalist, Maximilian Walsh. On 4 March 1971, Richard Carleton had interviewed Walsh on the ABC's *TDT* in relation to the developing crisis for the Gorton Government. Hughes said that Walsh, in response to questions, effectively accused Gorton of dishonesty and falsehood, and claimed it would be difficult to envisage graver libels of a man holding high office. Hughes highlighted two defamatory imputations: Gorton was guilty of complicity in Fraser's publication of a false denial of a true Peter Samuel story in the *Bulletin*; and Gorton had sought to discredit Fraser by giving Alan Ramsey approval to publish a false story about Fraser knowing that, without such approval, the story would not be published. The defence – Jack Smyth QC appeared for Walsh and JT Hiatt QC represented the ABC – denied any defamatory imputation on the first count and, while admitting that the second was defamatory, relied on the defence of fair comment. Hiatt reminded the Court of Gorton's admission that he could not remember actually seeing the interview on the night it was aired. Summing up his case, Hughes argued for very heavy damages, both compensatory and aggravated compensatory, the latter because the interview was pre-recorded which meant the ABC and Walsh knew of its defamatory nature beforehand.

Justice Russell Fox reserved his decision after a six-day hearing, and handed down his findings on 24 July. In what Hughes acknowledged was 'a disappointing result', Fox awarded Gorton just $7500 and required Walsh and the ABC to pay half Gorton's costs. Fox found 'some slur' on Gorton's reputation on the first count, and so the plaintiff should succeed in the case of publication in Victoria and the Australian Capital Territory. Nevertheless, Fox considered the first imputation to be 'the less significant and less serious'. In reaching this conclusion, he specifically rejected Hughes' attempts in cross-examination and in his final submission to show that Walsh had acted with malice. Fox found for the defendants on the second imputation. He agreed it was defamatory but Gorton was well aware that his failure to deny the story would lead to its publication and that publication would damage Fraser.[20]

Hughes' costs amounted to $2150. Gorton was at once embarrassed and puzzled. He had received a letter from his solicitors pointing out that Hughes had charged full fees, although they were under the impression that Gorton may have had some private arrangement regarding fees. The solicitors now wanted Gorton's confirmation before they paid the account. 'It is probable

I gave them some such impression because, in fact, I thought we had some such imprecise understanding at the beginning of the business but, of course, I could have been mistaken.' Hughes should let him know at once if Gorton had made a mistake and he would inform his solicitors. It transpired that the 'imprecise understanding' was that Hughes would charge a special daily appearance fee of $250 compared to the $300 he charged Pamela Warrender and the more common figure of $500 a day he commanded in the latter half of 1973. Gorton had another concern: 'Is it illegal, or unethical, or something, for us to pay you half the cost of your full fees, recover the other half from the defendants, and make some arrangement about distribution of the amount recovered?'[21]

Hughes appeared briefly for 'Lennie' McPherson (the alleged 'Mr Big' of the underworld) in September 1973 at the Moffitt Royal Commission into organised crime. Hughes challenged a Commission subpoena requiring McPherson to produce certain documents, namely, his passport, tax returns, bank statements, correspondence with the Taxation Commissioner and documents relating to the ownership of property. Moffitt rejected the Hughes argument that these documents were not relevant to the inquiry, whereupon McPherson's 'expensive lawyer' (Hughes charged $500) retired from the Commission.[22]

In 1974, Hughes successfully defended Sir Robert Askin when Jack Mundey, the President of the Australian Communist Party, sued him for defamation. Mundey, when Secretary of the NSW Builders Labourers' Federation, claimed that the Premier had described him and other trade union officials as 'vermin' at a Liberal Party federal election rally in the Sydney Town Hall on 15 November 1972. The plaintiff also objected to suggestions he favoured violence as a method of political action.

The two-week hearing attracted considerable publicity, partly because Mundey kept abusing the trial judge, Justice Taylor. Mundey also accused Hughes of employing McCarthyist-type questioning methods. Clive Evatt Snr – Mundey called him 'a revered legal figure' – periodically contributed to the tension by objecting to Hughes' questions, including one to a journalist which referred to the 'faceless men' and which Evatt saw as 'a political speech'. Mundey's exchanges with Askin's counsel were not without humour. Hughes sought to probe the extent of Mundey's avowed abhorrence of violence:

> Mr Hughes: 'When you say you abhor violence with guns and pick handles …'
>
> Mr Mundey: 'Including cricket bats. (Laughter)'

At one point, Mundey raised the subject of Vietnam, telling Hughes it was the place 'where you sent conscripts to die'. The judge asked counsel if he was willing to continue taking this sort of treatment. Hughes replied: 'I am quite prepared to. It takes longer this way, but one is not unused to taking it.' The long route also involved Hughes getting Askin to explain how his attacks were political not personal, and general rather than specific, a tactic that probably affected the outcome.

After deliberating for two-and-a-half-hours, the 12-member jury found for Askin and, overriding Evatt's complaint that the verdict was 'unreasonable', Taylor J entered the judgment Hughes requested and awarded costs to Askin. Mundey took his case to the Court of Appeal (Moffitt P, Reynolds and Samuels JJA), where Evatt once again appeared for Mundey and Hughes, with David Hunt, appeared for Askin. The Court dismissed the appeal and awarded costs to Askin. Mundey found consolation in claiming to have uncovered further evidence of contradictions between the treatment of those high up in the establishment and those who questioned the class nature of society.[23]

The Ratten case

In March 1974, Hughes returned to the High Court in a case which, although in many ways dissimilar and conducted in a different setting, was bound to remind him of an earlier and unhappy experience at the McLeod-Lindsay inquiry of 1969.

On 7 May 1970, Beverley Ratten, eight months pregnant with her fourth child, was killed by a single blast from a shotgun held by her husband. Leith and Beverley Ratten were alone at the time in their kitchen in Echuca, Victoria. Ratten claimed that the gun accidentally discharged while he held it under one arm and was cleaning the outside rust on both barrels. He also claimed to have been unaware that the weapon was loaded. The Crown argued at Ratten's trial at the Supreme Court sitting at Shepparton in August 1970 that the circumstantial evidence clearly indicated a deliberate act of murder. There also appeared to be a strong motive. For more than a year, Ratten and Mrs Jennifer Kemp, a family friend, had been conducting what in court was described as 'an adulterous relationship'. Kemp was pressuring Ratten to leave his marriage in the days just before the shooting, and Ratten sensed that his wife was unlikely to give him a divorce. In summing up, the trial judge, Winneke CJ, told the jury that the Crown's case depended on circumstantial evidence and warned it against being swayed by moral issues. After deliberating for 10 hours, the jury returned a verdict of guilty. Ratten was sentenced to death, but the sentence was later commuted to 25 years in gaol with the requirement that he serve at least 20.

There followed two appeals, first to the Full Court of the Supreme Court (dismissed in September 1970), and then to the Privy Council (dismissed in July

1971). After Professor Brett, who had been involved in the McLeod-Lindsay case, investigated the trajectory of the bullet, he successfully moved for the exhumation of the body. More experts on ballistics and firearms became involved, with many questioning the original medical findings. Several lawyers and members of the public agitated for a re-assessment of the evidence. The Victorian Attorney-General invoked s 584 of the *Crimes Act 1958* (Vic), and referred the whole case again to the Full Court of the Supreme Court to determine whether the conviction of the Petitioner [Ratten] constituted 'a miscarriage of justice … in the light of evidence now available'. The Court concluded that the additional evidence presented did not point to a miscarriage of justice at the original trial, nor did it warrant a fresh trial.

Don Chipp, Hughes' good friend from his parliamentary days, wrote to Brett on 24 December 1973 referring to an application for leave to appeal to the High Court. Chipp had prevailed upon George Madden, the Public Solicitor, to brief Tom Hughes. Chipp told Brett that Hughes had been interested in the case since 1971, 'and is delighted to have your thoughts'. Brett proceeded to correspond with Hughes, claiming that the Victorian judges 'went sadly astray in their evaluation of the evidence'. The two men spent some time discussing the angle of entry of the bullet. Hughes soon became fully involved, except to the point of rejecting Chipp's plea to visit Ratten in gaol. He was about to engage in a complex legal and evidential argument and regarded a gaol visit as a distraction. This decision cost him a lengthy break in his friendship with Chipp.

Hughes began preparing his case late in February 1974 and addressed Barwick CJ, McTiernan, Menzies, Stephen and Jacobs JJ in the High Court on 7 and 8 March.[24] He wanted the Court to consider the impact of the additional evidence on the whole case as it emerged at the coroner's inquest, the trial and the full bench of the Victorian Supreme Court. As in McLeod-Lindsay's case, Hughes sought to cast sufficient doubt about the guilty verdict to warrant a re-trial. He stressed that the Crown's case depended on three things: the angle of the bullet; the distance between the gun and the body; and the evidence of the telephonist who received what she interpreted as a call for help from Beverley Ratten. Hughes sought to show how in all three instances experts had raised doubts about the Crown's case. Moreover, the key Crown witness at the trial, Dr Charlton, had since given additional and contradictory evidence in relation to the bullet wound. Finally, Hughes broached the question of how the jury might have dealt with additional evidence that was available at the time, Ratten's legal advisers having wrongly persuaded him not to present it at the trial.

Hughes opened up a number of legal angles and evidentiary arguments, but Barwick had a direct and simple answer for each of them: Ratten had a gun, it was loaded, he fired it, and the Court should not be 'too diverted by the frills'. When Hughes pointed out that the trial judge did not treat matters such as pre-meditation or the angle of the weapon as 'frills', Barwick came back quickly: the Court should not be too worried about what someone else did. He was particularly dismissive of the experts who had offered opinions on the medical evidence, given that not one of them had been present at the autopsy and only one of whom had examined the exhumed body. Barwick also dismissed Hughes' argument that the Full Court had failed to distinguish between challenges to credibility and the acceptability of a case. The former, Hughes argued, were sufficient to cast doubt on the original finding. He failed, however, to convince any of the five judges who turned down the appeal. The most he achieved was that four of the five agreed that the appeal should be heard, Menzies J having dissented even on that issue.

Brett wrote to Hughes on 21 October 1974 giving his review of the High Court judgment.[25] He accepted that the Court had applied sound legal rules but queried some of its assumptions and conclusions. In particular, he was bothered by Barwick's view that fresh evidence must produce the likelihood of a different verdict. After all, if there was such a likelihood, then that could only mean a finding of not guilty, and there would be no need for a trial. How could the Court leave a conviction standing if a new trial would produce a verdict of not guilty? Despite all the problems he had with the Court's decision, Brett thought it would be 'extremely difficult' to persuade the Privy Council to interfere, though 'a good advocate' might persuade them to listen by showing how the High Court 'virtually poured scorn on [the Privy Council's] own doubts about the reliability of the telephone call evidence'. There is no evidence of Hughes responding to this letter, or of his being further involved when others pursued Ratten's cause.[26] Ratten remained in gaol until 1983, and kept protesting his innocence until his death in January 2012.

Constitutional cases

The High Court heard a number of important constitutional cases between February and May 1975. Tom Hughes appeared for the Commonwealth in two of them as part of legal teams led by Maurice Byers QC, who had replaced Ellicott as Solicitor-General.

At Whitlam's request, he joined the Commonwealth's defence when all six States challenged the validity of the *Seas and Submerged Lands Act 1973* (Cth). It will be recalled how, in government and on the backbench, Gorton and Hughes wanted to assert Commonwealth sovereignty over the territorial sea and the continental shelf. They expressly sought a High Court challenge to determine the extent of Commonwealth power. The McMahon Government had pandered to the States' sensibilities and shelved the original Bill. The Whitlam Government had seized the day, and Hughes was delighted to join the defence of legislation for which he had previously advocated. Each State briefed a formidable legal team, a number of whom would one day sit on the High Court: Deane and Gleeson (NSW), Keith Aickin and Daryl Dawson (Vic) and Ronald Wilson (WA). Although Byers, a lawyer and man he admired and respected, presented the case for the Commonwealth, the crux of it consisted of arguments Hughes had used in 1970. Hughes himself had a limited public role during the 14 days of hearings in Sydney in March and April 1975. He did, however, derive considerable satisfaction when, on 17 December, the Court handed down a unanimous decision in favour of Commonwealth sovereignty over the continental shelf and, by a 5-2 majority (Gibbs and Stephen JJ dissenting), acknowledged Commonwealth sovereignty over the territorial sea.[27]

Hughes was on the losing side when he assisted Byers in the so-called *PMA case*. The Victorian Government had challenged the validity of Rex Connor's *Petroleum and Minerals Authority Act 1974* (Cth) passed by the joint sitting of the Parliament after the 1974 election. The authority was to explore and exploit Australia's petroleum and mineral resources and to promote Australian ownership and control of resources through cooperative ventures with private enterprise.[28] The Liberal and Country Parties had originally opposed the Bill as tainted with socialism, and delayed its passage in the Senate. The issue before the High Court was whether the Senate had failed to pass the original Bill within the meaning of s 57 of the Constitution, thereby validating its reference to a joint sitting. A majority of the High Court (McTiernan and Jacobs JJ dissenting) declared the Act invalid because the mandatory requirements of s 57 had not been met. Therefore, the Bill had not become a 'proposed law' within the scope of s 57. The High Court ruled, in effect, that while the legitimacy of the Parliament elected following a double dissolution granted under s 57 could not be challenged, a law enacted by a joint sitting of that Parliament may be considered invalid, because of events preceding the double dissolution.[29]

Hughes led for the Commonwealth in his third case before the High Court in 1975.[30] A central question was whether s 24 of the Constitution, which provided that 'the House of Representatives shall be composed of members directly chosen by the people of the Commonwealth', required that the electoral divisions within each State should contain, so far as practicable, the same number of people or, alternatively, the same number of voters. Hughes' argument was a straightforward one. There was nothing in the wording of s 24 or any other sections mentioning, let alone requiring, equality between the numbers in electoral divisions. A 6-1 majority (Murphy J dissenting) agreed with this argument.

'Political' cases

Hughes appeared in several 'political' cases in the mid-1970s. In November 1975, he successfully represented the former DLP Senator, Jack Kane. Wilfred Burchett had previously failed to win a million-dollar libel suit launched against Kane who, in 1971, had used his newsletter, *Focus*, to report the testimony of the Soviet defector, Yuri Krotkov, that Burchett was a paid agent of the KGB. Although the jury found that Burchett had been defamed, it determined that Kane's article fairly reported a speech in the Senate by Vince Gair, the DLP leader. Burchett took his case to the Court of Appeal. Michael McHugh, on his behalf, argued that the jury should not have been asked whether the article was a fair record of Senate proceedings when, in fact, it was not. Hughes argued that Burchett was precluded from raising that issue on appeal because all parties had consented to leaving the issue of fairness to the jury, and the jury had made its decision. The Court decided that, while Kane's article was not a fair report of Gair's Senate speech, Burchett's barrister at the original hearing had failed to argue his case before the jury. The trial judge was not in error.

In March 1976, Hughes represented Victor Garland, the federal Liberal MP for Curtin since 1969, at a hearing before Charles Kilduff, the Chief Stipendiary Magistrate (CSM) in the ACT Court of Petty Sessions. Garland and a fellow West Australian George Branson, a former Liberal senator, stood accused of offering $500 to Michael Cavanough, an Independent candidate, to offset his campaign costs in return for directing his preferences to the Liberal Senate candidate, John Knight, in the 1975 federal election. Their object was to thwart John Gorton's attempt to enter the Senate by taking one of the two seats available in the Australian Capital Territory, the other being certain to go to Labor. The charge itself had already cost Garland his appointment as a minister in the Fraser Government and now threatened his political career.

Hughes approached the case with many arguments on many levels. Cavanough had publicly committed his support to Knight *before* the bribe was proposed. The *Electoral Act* distinguished between a promise of support and support itself, and the former might not be unlawful. A bribe had to go beyond a contribution to expenses and leave the receiver better off. If an offence had been committed, Cavanough could be charged as an accomplice, and a trial judge would have to warn a jury about accepting uncorroborated evidence. Hughes, in effect, offered Kilduff a way out. He might accept there was a *prima facie* case against Garland yet rule it was not strong enough to go to trial. Kilduff concluded that, properly directed, a trial jury would be unlikely to convict either of the accused.[31]

Hughes appeared in another 'political' case in February 1976. Bernard Clark, an offset production manager for Kerry Packer's ACP (Sir Frank Packer died in May 1974) was expelled in November 1974 from the Printing and Kindred Industries Union (PKIU) for working during two strikes in June and July 1974. The Industrial Court ruled the expulsion invalid and adjourned its hearing on Clark's application that certain PKIU rules were themselves invalid. It emerged that Packer was financing the Clark appeal against his expulsion. The PKIU State News of September 1976, in referring to 'the legal team assembled by Consolidated Press', noted that it was 'headed by ex-Liberal Attorney-General "Cricket Bat" Hughes'. The same former Attorney-General managed some hits of his own. In court, he claimed that to describe the union hearings of the Clark case as akin to those of a 'kangaroo court' would be both an understatement and 'an insult to a great Australian marsupial'. The Assistant Secretary of the union's NSW Branch admitted during Hughes' fierce cross-examination that he had referred to Clark as 'a lying bastard', that while acting as the 'prosecutor' he had seconded a motion recommending Clark's expulsion, and that he had presented supposed details of Clark's work during the disputes without knowing whether they were true or not. The Assistant Secretary also agreed he had treated Clark unfairly during the hearings, and was proud of it. The State President of the PKIU acknowledged under persistent pressure that the proceedings at the expulsion meeting, over which he presided, were 'manifestly unjust' and amounted to 'disgraceful conduct'. From this point, Hughes took no further part in the case.[32]

A leader of the Bar

Tom Hughes never allowed personal complications and setbacks to disturb the progress of his career. In the traumatic year of 1977, he grossed, not including retainers, just over $290,000 in fees. He was at the top of the top bracket of the NSW Bar, both in terms of income and stature, and there was never a shortage of briefs. The 'best of times' more than compensated for the 'worst' of them.

16

The Robinson Royal Commission

In May 1978, Tom Hughes accepted a brief to represent Eric Robinson, the (suspended) Minister for Finance in the Fraser Government, before a Royal Commission appointed to investigate allegations that Robinson had interfered with a federal electoral redistribution in Queensland and revealed confidential information related to uranium mining. Hughes' achievement – the total exoneration of his client – seemed insignificant placed alongside the unintended and mildly absurd outcome. Malcolm Fraser sacked Senator Withers, the Minister for Administrative Services, Leader of the Government in the Senate and Fraser's crucial ally in the events leading up to the dismissal of the Whitlam Government. Yet Hughes' cross-examination of Robinson's principal accuser, and of the accuser's supporting witnesses, is worth exploring for observing the 'cab on the rank' in action.

Background

Don Cameron at age 26 won the Brisbane seat of Griffith for the Liberals at the 1966 federal election. Against expectations, he retained Griffith in subsequent contests but decided against re-contesting the seat at the federal election of 1977. An electoral redistribution had made it virtually unwinnable for a Liberal. Instead, he stood for the new seat of Fadden in south-east Queensland, which he won after the distribution of preferences. On 21 December 1977, Cameron delivered a prepared statement at the declaration of the Fadden poll. He claimed that a 'fiddler' had interfered in the Queensland redistribution.[1]

Eric Robinson was unaware on 21 December that he was the alleged 'fiddler'. A wealthy businessman who owned a chain of sporting goods stores, Robinson, as State President of the Liberal Party in Queensland, had publicly called for Gorton's removal as Prime Minister in March 1971. Elected to the Gold Coast seat of McPherson in the 1974 federal election, he was one of the kingmakers who supported Fraser for the Liberal leadership in 1975. He was Minister for Posts and Telecommunications at the time of the 1977 redistribution and became Minister of Finance with a seat in Cabinet after the 1977 election.[2]

Although Robinson had no formal ministerial responsibility for the redistribution, Cameron believed he had engineered the appointment of one of the three distribution commissioners, thus enabling him to influence the Commission's deliberations. Cameron also believed Robinson had promoted John Teulan, a young local businessman who opposed Cameron in the Fadden preselection. According to Cameron, Teulan had, at Robinson's request, drawn up a map of the proposed new seat carved out of McPherson, and this map closely resembled the Commission's final version. Furthermore, Cameron claimed Robinson had prior knowledge of the Commission's proposals and had persuaded the commissioners to retain the name 'McPherson' for what was left of the existing electorate. A seat with the same name was not a 'new' one, thereby preventing the Country Party under Coalition arrangements from entering the contest.

Within a week of his poll declaration speech, Cameron told journalists that there was 'direct proof' that a senior Liberal 'has fiddled the boundaries'.[3] Two other Queensland MPs shared his suspicions. One was David Jull, who held the marginal Brisbane seat of Bowman. Cameron believed that Robinson had tried to 'get' him through the redistribution. The other was Kevin Cairns, one of the 'termites' who had undermined Gorton and who had regained his Brisbane seat in 1975.

After Cameron wrote to the Prime Minister setting out his general concerns, Fraser called a meeting for 18 January 1978, bringing together Cameron, Jull, Cairns, Reg Withers (responsible for election matters), and Robinson. Unnerved and unhappy about Robinson's presence, Cameron refused to divulge any of his evidence. Robinson firmly denied any wrongdoing, and left the meeting when Cameron repeatedly declined to lay out his case. Cameron remained unprepared to disclose all his evidence and kept insisting on a judicial inquiry, while rejecting Fraser's and Withers' preference for a police investigation. Cameron wanted to force Robinson to give evidence under oath, and was not convinced of the competence or the trustworthiness of the Queensland Police to conduct a proper inquiry. The Prime Minister sought to end the stalemate by calling on the Attorney-General, Senator Durack, and the Solicitor-General, Maurice Byers, for advice. The two principal law officers concluded that the matter neither required nor warranted investigation by the Government. They conceded only that those claiming impropriety did so 'in good faith and for reasons that seemed weighty to them', but their suggestions were 'unfounded'.[4]

After Cameron rebuffed Fraser's request to drop the matter, the Prime Minister sacked him in mid-March as Deputy Government Whip, thereby removing a significant constraint on his actions. In the meantime, Cameron had learnt of a Liberal Party lunch held on 26 July 1977 at the Logan and Albert Hotel in the town of Beaudesert, south of Brisbane. Prompted by Cameron, four of the 11 persons present at the lunch signed statutory declarations. They swore that Robinson had revealed details of the redistribution before they were published, that he was promoting Teulan and had advised everyone present to buy uranium shares because the Government was about to bring down a decision favourable to uranium mining. On 7 April, Cameron delivered a long personal explanation to the House and publicly named the 'fiddler' for the first time, albeit in his final sentence. Three days later Robinson said he 'utterly and completely' rejected Cameron's allegations.[5]

Following a Cabinet meeting and several informal meetings of ministers, the Government agreed to establish a Royal Commission to investigate the allegations about Robinson's involvement in the redistribution, to see if there had been any illegality or impropriety. Douglas McGregor was appointed Commissioner. He had succeeded Hughes as President of the NSW Bar Association and was recently elevated to the Federal Court. On the same day, 27 April, Fraser suspended Robinson from Cabinet. The terms of reference were widened on 10 May to include the claim that Robinson had disclosed the Government's intentions in relation to uranium mining. The terms were further expanded on 30 May after it was revealed that Senator Withers had contacted Keith Pearson, the Chief Electoral Officer, to suggest changing the proposed name of the electorate from 'Gold Coast' to 'McPherson' which included substantial portions of Robinson's existing seat. The Commission was now required to investigate the actions of any person in relation to the redistribution.

Hughes v Cameron

The Royal Commission opened with a formal session in Brisbane just after 9.00 am on 8 May 1978. Hearings began on 15 May and were held over 21 weekdays and concluded on Tuesday 13 June.

The Attorney-General appointed Murray Gleeson QC as counsel assisting the inquiry. Ian Callinan QC, a future High Court judge, appeared for the three Queensland Distribution Commissioners. Des Sturgess, a future Queensland State Director of Public Prosecutions, was later authorised to represent Cameron. Unwisely, as it turned out, Withers, who had practised as a solicitor and later as a barrister, did not seek representation.

Tom Hughes was surprised to receive the Robinson brief. Indeed, the irony was not lost on those who knew recent history. Don Cameron and Hughes supported Gorton in 1971 and no Gortonite could forget how Robinson backed McMahon and worked on Fraser's behalf to help him replace Billy Snedden as Liberal leader. Nonetheless, the 'cab on the rank' had no qualms about taking the brief, and quickly forged a good relationship with Robinson. The divorced barrister was especially struck by the very close relationship between Robinson and his wife, Narelle.[6]

Gleeson spent part of the first day of hearings outlining the way ahead, presenting exhibits and identifying a number of key issues. Pearson was the first witness, followed by a cartographer who had assisted the 1977 Redistribution and who had seen no evidence of Robinson communicating with the Commissioners. Cameron was next and, when Sturgess applied for authorisation to appear, Hughes intervened during a prolonged discussion to support approval. He said:

> [I]t may be thought proper that [Cameron] should have the skills of counsel available to him because it would be my melancholy duty, but nevertheless my duty, to conduct a cross-examination of Mr Cameron, which consistently with my instructions will involve reflections upon his public conduct in this matter, his fitness for public office arising out of his public conduct and his credibility.[7]

The Commissioner agreed, given the 'specifically forecast' attack on Cameron's 'credit and character'.[8] Hughes also foreshadowed another line of approach. Whereas Callinan had warned against casting the net far and wide – for example, to include material relating to Jull's seat of Bowman – Robinson's counsel wanted everything included. He intended to demonstrate the full extent of 'the total insubstantiality of the material upon which these grave imputations were raised'.[9]

For nearly three days, Hughes conducted a cross-examination which was at times brutal and always relentless and unsettling. The technique derived from his early days as a barrister. Hughes observed how Asprey, Shand and Dovey would induce witnesses to accept general principles and then undermine their 'credit' by exposing a failure to implement them. Adopting this approach, Hughes led Cameron into acknowledging what should constitute correct behaviour. For example, Cameron agreed he had a 15-year political and personal friendship with Robinson, and regarded his political colleague as a confidante and someone he respected. Cameron felt bound to agree when Hughes pointed out that 'common decency' required him to confront Robinson with any suspicions, be they minor or major. Cameron might deny it would be 'reprehensible' not to do so, and take refuge in what became his mantra that the issue was too grave for ordinary standards to apply. But

Hughes could portray him as a man who forsook 'common decency' to make damaging accusations at the declaration of the Fadden poll, to make them without having any hard evidence or direct proof and without being prepared to confront or even consult his friend.

Another aspect of the Hughes technique was not to allow the accuser to develop his own narrative. Cameron wanted to tell a story by linking seemingly unconnected actions or words and tracing the development of his suspicions to the point where he was convinced Robinson had interfered with the redistribution. Hughes blitzed Cameron with questions on events or topics that he deliberately kept separate and extracted from their chronological sequence. Most questions required 'Yes' or 'No' answers, thereby enabling Hughes to control the pace and direction of the cross-examination, to cut short Cameron's many attempts to evade, elaborate or explain and to deprive him of a comfort zone. Hughes could further diminish Cameron's 'credit' by pinpointing the many instances of contradictory and evasive replies, and it helped when the Commissioner felt obliged to intervene several times to remind the witness of his responsibility to provide direct answers and to abstain from 'non-responsive' replies.

Early on, Hughes pressed Cameron over his conversation with Teulan on 30 October, held six days after Cameron had nominated for Fadden. The two men were sitting in a car outside a house where a function was taking place. Cameron said the conversation consisted of his talking about the possibility of nominating for the Liberal-held seat of Brisbane and of Teulan trying to dissuade Cameron from proceeding with the Fadden nomination. Teulan also let Cameron know that 'a minister' had asked him to prepare a map of the proposed new seat. In the space of an hour, Hughes had Cameron agreeing to the following:

- he was suspicious about Robinson's conduct at the time he spoke to Teulan;
- his suspicions fell short of proof of misconduct;
- he was not anxious to explore any avenue to confirm or allay his suspicions;
- he did not have a 'set attitude' about Robinson;
- as a result of his conversation with Teulan, he started for the first time to think that Robinson 'may have had more to do with the redistribution than events which had gone beforehand may have suggested';
- he had a 'set attitude' about the propriety of the redistribution before talking to Teulan;
- at no stage did Cameron ask for the name of the minister or any questions about the map;
- before he talked to Teulan he knew 'something was wrong' but his suspicion was not directed at Robinson;

- Robinson 'was involved in the suspicion';
- his suspicions before talking to Teulan were not directed at Robinson;
- it would not be true to say that, before talking to Teulan, Robinson was not a subject of suspicion;
- prior to talking to Teulan, Robinson was a subject of suspicion 'to a minor degree'.[10]

Amidst the confusion, Robinson's counsel had successfully elicited important admissions: although Cameron became more suspicious of Robinson on 30 October, he did not have any actual evidence of malpractice or of impropriety, and he had not taken the obvious steps to see if there was any. At least his responses on the latter point were succinct:

Mr Hughes: I want to have it quite clear in my mind, you say this conversation in the car took 20 minutes? – I said it took 15, maybe 20.

And the length of the conversation would not have been in any sense prolonged would it, if you had asked three simple questions? – No

Mr Hughes: Who is the minister? – That is correct.

Have you got a copy of the map? – Correct.

Can I see it? – Correct.

That would have taken less than ten seconds would it not? – Correct

Those questions would have been of enormous relevance would they not in resolving one way or another a suspicion in your mind, what was a matter of considerable concern to you? – Yes it would have had that effect.

Hughes also raised the possibility that Teulan was 'having [Cameron] on' in order to shift him out of the Fadden contest. Cameron agreed it was a possibility and said he had considered it. He also agreed with Hughes that the map 'might have been a load of rubbish', and that it was incumbent on him to inquire whether such a map was ever drawn. Hughes then elicited something even more damning: Cameron never at any stage saw any map, and never asked to see one.

Hughes turned later to a second – and this time taped – conversation with Teulan held in Cameron's home on 9 November and after Cameron had won the Fadden preselection. This exchange lasted 40 minutes. Cameron arranged it so that he could pursue inquiries about malpractice or improprieties in the course of the redistribution. Hughes had him admitting, however, that he did not ask about, or see, the map, or ask what happened to it, or ask for a reproduction. Nor did he ask for the name of the minister. Cameron agreed that the latter question was an important one though, apparently, not critical: after all, he happened to be aware of a 'firm link' between Robinson and Teulan, a link – as Hughes kept pointing out – resting on supposition and hearsay.

Hughes then targeted Cameron's character. Having exposed Cameron's failure to live up to his own standards of 'common decency', Hughes now submitted he was 'a back-stabber' and 'a coward', and someone who had 'a scant regard for the truth'. Cameron acknowledged that not giving advance warning to a political colleague and a friend amounted to back-stabbing. As the questions kept coming, Cameron managed to say within a few sentences of each other that:

- he was neither proud nor ashamed of being a back-stabber;
- he did not regard himself as a back-stabber but as someone who had very strong convictions about the redistribution in Queensland;
- because he acted outside the norm on one occasion did not make him a back-stabber for all time [Hughes had not suggested he was];
- what he did amounted to back-stabbing.

As for telling the truth, Hughes reminded Cameron of the article published in the Brisbane *Telegraph* of 29 December. The journalist quoted Cameron saying he had 'direct proof' to support his claim that a Queensland Liberal parliamentarian brought pressure to bear on the Distribution Commissioners. Recalling that, under questioning, Cameron had admitted not having 'direct proof' of wrongdoing, Hughes suggested he had 'a rather scant regard for accuracy'. Was this kind of approach 'in accord with your standards of public conduct'? Cameron agreed it was a departure from 'ordinary standards'. Hughes sought to add the word 'lamentable' to describe his departure from these standards, especially given the seriousness of the charge Cameron was making against Robinson. Cameron said he did not agree with 'lamentable' until, under more pressure, he accepted Hughes' phrase 'a lamentable disregard for accuracy' for using the term 'direct proof'. When Cameron repeated this response, he began to laugh, possibly out of relief or as an act of bravado. His reaction invited a chilling riposte:

> Mr Hughes: It is a matter of mirth is it that you showed lamentable disregard for accuracy and fairness in pressing your attack against Mr Robinson, unheard – that is a matter of mirth, is it? – No.

Another of Hughes' strategies was to show how Cameron had drawn conclusions about possible impropriety from actions and statements that, to anyone else, would seem innocuous or otherwise explicable. Of the many examples Hughes pursued, perhaps the most telling was Cameron's interpretation of a Robinson comment in March 1977 about a National Party approach concerning the appointment of the third Distribution Commissioner. Robinson allegedly said: 'I am not going to have a bar of them having their fingers in it.' Leaving aside Robinson's denial of using those exact words, there was a perfectly straightforward and acceptable explanation for the comment. Hughes had no trouble securing Cameron's acknowledgement that Queensland Liberals believed the Country Party carried out Queensland State redistributions 'without much regard to objective standards of electoral justice'. He put a proposition to Cameron as a 'hypothesis', first making sure that Cameron knew the meaning of the word. It would be in the Liberal Party's interest and in the interest of electoral justice to exclude a distribution commissioner who had been involved in State redistributions. Cameron agreed that Hughes' interpretation of Robinson's attitude was a 'reasonable one'. In this case and in all the others, the unexceptional interpretation was the obvious and appropriate one. An inference of wrongdoing, drawn from gossip and casual remarks, simply fell away under cross-examination as either inconsequential or groundless.

Hughes' cross-examination had done more than expose the 'insubstantiality' of Cameron's case. It also revealed an obsession, bordering on irrationality. Hughes wanted his Honour to notice how Cameron remained upset about the loss of the electorate he had loved and nurtured and how his 'sense of bereavement' had distorted his judgment. Fortuitously, Reg Withers provided supporting evidence. Cross-examined about the change of the name from 'Gold Coast' to 'McPherson', Withers effectively cleared Robinson of any involvement. 'Why', Justice McGregor asked Withers, 'could you have not gone to Mr Cameron and told him what had happened?' Withers said the aim was to get the maps approved in October 1977, 'not start new hares running', to get on with the early election and to avoid 'squabbles'. Pointing out that 'one hare was still running strongly', Justice McGregor again asked why no one told Cameron. Withers replied that ministers believed 'no explanation would satisfy him and he would go off on another tack … and he would only have made it worse … Mr Cameron's sort of rage of indignation over what had happened to the seat of Griffith was such that talking to him would not achieve anything'.[11]

Cameron exited the witness box with 'back-stabber' and 'a scant regard for truth' hanging over him, and having seen his charges exposed as untested inferences and imaginings. At least the law officers had let him down gently with references to acting in 'good faith'. Hughes left him with nothing.

The evidence from Beaudesert

The Robinson team knew from the start that the four Beaudesert witnesses who swore statutory declarations on 28 March 1978 represented a significant obstacle to a successful outcome. The declarations appeared to provide hard evidence to sustain three charges: that Robinson demonstrated prior knowledge of the findings of the Distribution Commissioners by talking about a seat named the 'Gold Coast' before the publication of the report; that he promoted John Teulan at the lunch; and that he advised those attending the lunch to buy uranium shares. Tom Hughes took on the twin tasks of challenging the reliability of the statutory declarations assembled during consultations between the signatories, and of undermining the 'credit' of two particular signatories – Mrs Mavis Rostedt and Mrs Jane Blunck.

Rostedt lived in Beaudesert, and had worked for both Robinson and Cameron in previous election campaigns. She described herself as 'a wife, mother, part-time teacher and student'.[12] Cameron had approached her upon learning of the lunch at Beaudesert. After an initial reaction of 'polite non-co-operation', she changed her mind when Fraser sacked Cameron as Deputy Government Whip. Rostedt arranged for Blunck and two of the men (Messrs Joyce and Trier) who had attended the lunch to meet at Blunck's house. There, they assembled their recollections into a common account of what they claimed to have remembered.

Try as she might to downplay her role, Rostedt acted with zeal in preparing a case against Robinson and in making sure that everyone was in step. Hughes portrayed her as the shop steward in the industry for creating statutory declarations. She certainly achieved solidarity on 28 March 1978, when they all signed the declaration. The unanimity fell apart, however, under cross-examination in May. It appears that Rostedt arrived at Blunck's house with a prepared draft, read it out, and said that was what she remembered. She told Hughes that the others agreed with her. Yet Joyce told him that the draft was changed considerably. Three of the four signatories agreed that the procedure was not calculated to ensure independent recollections of what happened at the luncheon. One of them said he would not have participated if he had realised that the purpose of the meeting was to support a campaign for a judicial inquiry into grave allegations against Robinson. Another had no vivid recollection of anything said during the lunch.

Rostedt agreed with Hughes she had 'some intelligence' but also admitted she was not 'an attentive listener'. Hughes seized upon her listening inadequacies to cast doubt on her capacity for accurate recollection. He also decided that her frequent requests to have questions repeated or explained reflected another deficiency. When asked yet again whether the meeting in Mrs Blunck's house was held to compare recollections, Rostedt seemed hesitant about the meaning of Hughes' question. He felt bound to ask: 'Is there anything difficult about it, except possibly the task of providing the answer …?' Gleeson intervened on this occasion, and on others, to protect her. Later, when Rostedt was giving an answer that threatened to become interminable, Hughes intervened: 'You find it a little difficult to stop talking?' Justice McGregor, assuming the protective role, told counsel 'it is not easy for the lady, she is at a disadvantage, and it would be better if that sort of comment were not made'. Yet his Honour was not forever patient and tolerant. He agreed Hughes had a problem when the witness gave 'exactly the opposite' answers to a previous answer: 'I do not know what else you can do about it.'[13] What Hughes could do was all but state the obvious: Rostedt was having trouble getting a twisted story straight.

Jane Blunck had her own problems. She, too, lived in Beaudesert and described herself as a housewife and a part-time teacher. Like Rostedt, she was unhappy when Fraser sacked Cameron. Questioned by Hughes, she agreed that it would be 'wrong' to have talked to Rostedt on this or any other matter in preparing a statement. She felt obliged to agree, therefore, that she had not followed her own precept when making her declaration on 28 March. What she had done then was 'very wrong'. At this point, Hughes drew the Commissioner's attention to the fact that 'the lady is distressed' – Justice McGregor had not noticed it – and Hughes suggested it would be 'quite unfair' to proceed. Blunck was given leave to compose herself. While sensitive at one level, Robinson's counsel quite properly used Blunck's confession to make a telling point: 'she was prepared to stoop to what she regarded as wrongdoing to help Mr Cameron's baggage train to roll along the road.' Hughes added this instance to others he uncovered in cross-examining her 'to show how thoroughly discreditable this operation of assembling evidence against Mr Robinson was and how improperly it was conducted'.[14]

Almost half the witnesses present at the Beaudesert lunch disagreed with a large part or all of the evidence provided by those who believed that Robinson had acted improperly. Ted James, the local Liberal Party chairman, became Hughes' 'star turn'. He was firm, clear and consistent: nothing untoward had happened. Sitting at the table next to Robinson, he felt best placed to deny that the minister made any reference to buying uranium shares. James, Teulan and others gave Hughes what he needed. He could complement his exposure of error, inconsistency and confusion among the ranks of the adverse witnesses with evidence of disagreement across all ranks sufficient to make it very difficult for Justice McGregor to reach any definite conclusions about what happened that day in the Logan and Albert Hotel.

One more witness had to be discredited. Mrs Beryl Hodgson, a journalist and editor with the *Logan and Albert Times*, had arrived late for the lunch to take photographs for her newspaper. She appeared self-assured: yes, she had made notes on a coaster during Robinson's short speech after the lunch and boasted to Rostedt about obtaining a 'scoop' because of the minister's alleged remarks about uranium shares. But Hodgson failed to keep the coaster and did not deliver the story to the newspaper. Hughes seized on her failure to publish the 'scoop'. He elicited a dubious explanation: the *Logan and Albert Times* was a conservative country newspaper that did not carry national news stories; there was a difference between a city and a country reporter; and Robinson said, looking directly at her, that anything said in the room should not leave the room. Hodgson started to flounder as Hughes pounced on her excuses, and in his summing up argued that she invented Robinson's remark. No one else in the room actually heard it; in this respect, 'her evidence is false and deliberately so'.[15]

Hughes' summing up

Hughes presented the Commission with an oral and a written summing up. The striking feature of both is that he did not bother with a detailed rebuttal of Cameron's allegations. It was sufficient to assert in 'blunt, broad terms' that his 'grave imputations' against Robinson and the Distribution Commissioners should be dismissed because they were not supported by 'a scintilla of substantiation … a scintilla of evidence'. He gave more time to explaining how Cameron's 'wild allegations' could be traced to 'morbid suspicions' which developed in his 'febrile mind and imagination' as a result of being deprived of his seat of Griffith. Cameron 'suffered from a misplaced sense of bereavement'. Hughes highlighted an 'exquisite' irony. Cameron had sent a letter of exhortation to the Distribution Commissioners after reading their first report telling them, '[i]n the name of the Electoral Act, decency and justice', they were obliged to re-think the redistribution of Griffith. The man who appealed to the Commissioners for 'decency', allowed his bereavement over losing Griffith to abandon decency to betray a long-standing friend 'and to do so with the cloak and dagger of the would-be political assassin, a back-stabbing political assassin, on his own admission'.

Hughes devoted the bulk of his submission to two matters arising out of the Beaudesert lunch. First, he sought to show how Cameron manipulated the evidence of the Beaudesert witnesses. Cameron had 'a well-deserved reputation as being a grass roots politician' whose 'movements through the political grass possessed a rather reptilian quality'. He used information from the Beaudesert lunch to overcome the unpalatable conclusions of the law officers, and did this through a 'mind conditioning' exercise with the Beaudesert witnesses 'which was hardly calculated to bring into bloom the fragile plant of truth'. Unable to provide his own admissible proof, Cameron enlisted the aid of Mrs Rostedt, who became his deputy organiser in the enterprise to bring Robinson down. Hughes said that Cameron told Rostedt how Robinson had asked Teulan to prepare a map of the boundaries which proved to be 76 per cent accurate in relation to the final boundaries. Yet, if Teulan were to be believed, he never told Cameron there was such a map; if Cameron were to be believed, Teulan never mentioned Robinson's name.

Hughes' second task was to dent any impact of the supposed 'hard' evidence emanating from the Beaudesert lunch. Hence, he devoted a special section to Mrs Hodgson's failings and another to the procedure adopted in preparing the statutory declarations. He showed how the declaration contained a palpable falsehood. The signatories said Robinson actively promoted Teulan. Confronting them with evidence given from many sides during the hearings that Robinson did not promote Teulan, the four signatories acknowledged their error, allowing Robinson's counsel to use their false assertion as a measure of their prejudice and unreliability. Moreover, their remorse 'cannot restore them, as it were, to a state of testimonial grace'. The Commissioner: 'You did not leave out the word "testimonial", I am glad to see, Mr Hughes.'[16]

Murray Gleeson also made short work of the Cameron allegations, recommending in a polite and careful manner they be totally dismissed. Following Hughes, he reminded the Commissioner of the problems in trying to determine just what Robinson said at the lunch in Beaudesert. To highlight the difficulty of trusting recollections, Gleeson reported how his team conducted some research of their own. The witnesses were asked whether Robinson addressed them while standing or sitting. Seven said he stood and four thought he sat. Gleeson noted that Robinson showed himself to be the 'consummate politician', saying he started his remarks while standing and continued them when sitting down.

Counsel assisting felt he should comment on the approach of 'my learned friend Mr Hughes' towards the witnesses at the Beaudesert lunch. It was 'both his right and … his duty' to make 'a trenchant attack' upon their credit. The lawyers present understood that challenging the reliability of evidence did not necessarily reflect on the honesty of witnesses. Gleeson thought the distinction particularly important where witnesses, without the benefit of representation, faced powerful challenges. Both counsel assisting and the Commissioner thought that Hughes had on 'one or two occasions' questioned their subjective honesty, though Gleeson had to agree with Hughes that putting people in the same room and working out their recollections together was not the way to get at the truth.

The Report

Justice McGregor submitted his 275-page Report at the beginning of August.[17] While he completely exonerated Robinson, the Commissioner did not comment directly on Cameron's evidence, or lack of it. Nor did he refer to the cross-examination that shattered his 'credit'. But the outright and almost summary rejection of every Cameron allegation and inference was telling. Just as Hughes and Gleeson had done in summing up, McGregor devoted much more than twice the space to the Beaudesert lunch than he assigned to all of Cameron's allegations. McGregor did have one kind word for Robinson's accuser: if he had been informed of 'certain significant facts' about the name change of the electorate, he and others would not have been 'left to speculate about something that did bear curious and unexplained features'.[18]

The 'certain significant facts' led the Commissioner to find that Senator Withers had used his position 'to further a political purpose by an approach (not open to members of the public) to the Distribution Commissioners'. McGregor found that Withers sought to influence and did influence the three men who were unaware of the significance of changing the name of an electorate from 'Gold Coast' to 'McPherson', and what he did constituted 'impropriety'.[19] Fraser sacked Withers when he refused to resign; a Prime Minister publicly committed to propriety could not blink when faced with a finding of 'impropriety'. On reading the Report, Tom Hughes remembered Withers' remark to him just before taking the witness stand: 'it'll be a breeze.'[20]

Not surprisingly, the press virtually ignored Cameron and Robinson in the days following the release of the Report. The news stories and the editorials focused on the sacking of Withers. Nearly all agreed it was the right thing to do. Some did notice that under oath Robinson said Fraser learnt of Withers' intervention on three occasions.[21] The Prime Minister tried to deflect difficult questions by asking Robinson to write a letter admitting to a lapse of memory. Advised by Ellicott to consult Tom Hughes before he took this step, Robinson demurred, obliging the Prime Minister to admit his own failure of recall. Judging by the omission of this confession in his book, Fraser continued to have no recollection of having had no recollection. Perhaps he just thought it best to ignore the embarrassing fact that he failed on three occasions to recognise 'impropriety'.[22]

Eric Robinson survived the Cameron allegations, but they hurt. His relations with Cameron never recovered, though it mattered more to him that Fraser had not provided the expected support. In one mad week in February 1979, Robinson resigned from Cabinet for undisclosed reasons and then re-joined it. Offered a demotion to the outer ministry after the 1980 election, he chose the backbench. Aged 51, Robinson died suddenly of a heart attack in January 1981. Cameron fared better. The preselectors of Fadden re-endorsed him for the 1980 election, and the preselectors of Moreton chose him to replace the retired Jim Killen after Cameron lost Fadden in 1983. Cameron 'bears no malice' towards his tormentor at the Commission: Hughes was 'just doing his job'. At least, having endured that ordeal, no future courtroom held any fears. Moreover, he was later reconciled with Robinson's widow.[23]

Tom Hughes left Brisbane in good spirits. He had conducted one of his 'best-ever cross-examinations', collected appearance fees of $1000 a day, received a total of $24,700, 'won' his client's case and earned his gratitude and respect. Hughes genuinely 'felt' for Robinson, whose experience provided 'a stark example of the vicissitudes that have to be endured by men who choose to give public service to their country in the hazardous field of politics'.[24] For Hughes, the one discordant note was the finding in relation to Withers. It was a 'poor' judgment delivered by a stranger to politics.[25]

17

'From silk to riches'

A 23-year-old journalist arrived at 16 Wardell Chambers early in the summer of 1977-78 to interview Tom Hughes QC. Educated at Sydney Grammar, Malcolm Turnbull had completed his arts and law degrees at the University of Sydney and won a Rhodes scholarship. During his final year at university, he wrote for Kerry Packer's *Bulletin* magazine about law and politics. As ACP had every reason to promote its leading counsel, Turnbull's article became the *Bulletin*'s cover story for 21 February 1978 with the arresting headline 'FROM SILK TO RICHES: Portrait of a $1,000-a-day QC'.

There had been earlier profiles of Tom Hughes. Brian Johns' piece of 1965 on the rising backbencher was the first; several brief articles in 1970 offered insights into a different and intriguing Attorney-General; *Vogue Australia* for September 1970 carried photographs of Hughes, Peacock, Harry M Miller and other 'splendid men of Australia … who get things done … and manage to look pretty smashing'. Turnbull's portrayal highlighted several crucial features of Hughes' career. Quoting unnamed sources, Turnbull cited his versatility and long hours of disciplined hard work. There was a reference to Riverview – 'Hughes owes a lot to the Jesuits' – and a stress on the value of family contacts in advancing the young barrister's career. Turnbull drew attention to Hughes' inheritance: a father who was 'an eminent Sydney solicitor and businessman', a grandfather who was Lord Mayor and a member of the Legislative Council, and a great grandfather who was 'a wealthy 19th-century property developer'. Referring to the great, great grandfather who arrived from Ireland in 1840, Turnbull made use of the (unproven) family legend: '[a]ppropriately enough for a man who spawned a line of lawyers, the first Tom Hughes worked as a clerk in Darlinghurst jail.'

Unnamed friends and colleagues provided insights into Hughes' personality. For example, the barrister's life is 'very lonely', which suited someone who 'is a very solitary fellow'. The same source regarded himself as 'a close friend' yet 'couldn't say I knew him'. Aware of Hughes' sobriquet – 'Frosty' or 'Frosty Tom' – implying that he was cold, distant and even dismissive, Turnbull believed that 'Frosty' was less commonly used in 1978. Besides, 'Hughes is a gregarious man'. Those who knew Tom over a longer period regarded 'reserved' as more apposite than 'frosty'. They also observed, however, and here Turnbull may have held his peace, degrees of frostiness and of impatience bordering on anger in Hughes' relations with non-performing juniors, slow-paying solicitors and anyone who failed to meet his standards of punctuality.

Turnbull touched on the changes that occurred in Hughes' life from around the time he resumed full-time practice at the Bar. By 1978, he had long abandoned an 'old Catholic view of the world', exemplified in part by sending his two sons to the non-denominational Sydney Grammar instead of Riverview. Tom also had adopted a different political outlook; he had been 'too fervent, too unquestioning' in opposing communism and was 'wrong on Vietnam'. On the subject of divorce, Turnbull quoted an 'old friend' (probably 'Larko'): 'There are all sorts of divorces, but Tom Hughes' is the most civilised of them all. He gets on well with his ex-wife and this is reflected in his three confident and talented children.' Perhaps the most striking confirmation of this civilised divorce was that Tom liked to have family lunches on Sundays at Joanna's house or at a nearby restaurant. But the conventional and convenient wisdom, as expressed in the *Bulletin* article, was not entirely accurate. The 'civilised' relationship had strained moments, often provoked by Joanna's bouts of instability and turbulence and intensified by her former husband's reaction to them. In February 1978, while the two boys were living with their mother, and Lucy was staying in Darlinghurst with her father, it was apparent that Michael, the youngest of the children, needed another arrangement.

Turnbull's interview with Hughes had an unintended consequence. The younger man met Lucy who was working in her father's chambers for the summer vacation after completing first year law at Sydney University. 'I fell in love with Lucy the moment I met her.'[1] He sent her flowers after their first meeting. There are different versions of the immediate outcome. The popular media version is that the father thought the flowers were for him. The other is that he took them home to present them to his daughter.[2]

A brief self-portrait

Tom Hughes kept a handwritten diary between July 1979 and June 1980.[3] At the beginning of this period he wrote an entry every day. Towards its end, he often caught up a week or more after the events he described, and collapsed several days into one. There was just one, brief, occasion where the diarist discussed his motives for engaging in the exercise. On 15 August 1979 he did wonder if it would be of any interest to posterity; 'but it is at least something to which I can look back to catch moods of the moment that would otherwise be lost and forgotten'. Tom Hughes did not have, or need, Manning Clark's 'eye for eternity'.[4] His diary is not the work of an egotist. Its revelations of self are neither self-conscious, nor studiously contrived, nor deeply probing. He described what he felt, saw and thought at the time. Next day, in a different mood or frame of mind, he might tell a different story.

The diary began at a time when the author was appearing before the Copyright Tribunal and concluded soon after his 'darling daughter' had married Malcolm Turnbull. It records frank assessments of judges, barristers and solicitors, and of the downside of representing John Fairfax and Sons. The diary tells of contacts with Joanna and the boys, and with girlfriends, and of the enduring presence of Kate Weigall. There are fears expressed about not getting enough work and about not meeting debts. The defamation lawyer worried about a sudden increase in the size of awards for damages. The grazier kept a record of trophies and blue ribbons won at shows, of rainfall figures at Marsland and of stock purchases organised with his manager, Don Stanton. The racehorse owner noted the unsatisfactory performances of his horses 'Make Mine Candy' and 'Singing', and kept a record of his bets, and those of his sons, at the track. The 'gregarious man' was always meeting someone of note, and was often out lunching and dining.

Although the diarist may not have engaged in sustained self-analysis, he did occasionally reflect upon some of his character traits. On 26 July 1979, he described himself as 'being uptight and thoroughly tense' before addressing the Copyright Tribunal, where he was representing the Australian Recording Industry Association. He found 'everything coming together' when he got to his feet:

> This idiosyncrasy must be difficult for those around me at the time; but that is the way I am made; and I fear that nothing will alter me. On the other hand, I was relaxed & calm & polite in the late afternoon when I had to spend 2 hours dealing with the odious Mr [a client]. This means, I think, that the feeling that one has done a task well in Court engenders a relaxed attitude towards the next succeeding problem.

The professional Hughes saw the importance of ordering priorities: 'I am pleased that I am totally unattached at the moment. I suppose that I would not be displeased if it were otherwise. But at least I am able to concentrate entirely on my work, which I must needs do if obligations are to be met between now & year's end.' Yet his inherited and developed work ethic was not alone responsible for this focus on meeting obligations. In the previous week, he had taken a woman out to dinner: 'A pleasant enough evening, but nothing further will happen. We are not really on the same wave-length.'

Tom's 12-month diary has much to offer a biographer. It records a life whose many strands, professional and personal, were lived simultaneously. It reveals Hughes' intense emotional and time-consuming commitment to clients and to cases, even as he concurrently attended to other clients and cases and planned two or three briefs ahead. The diary, read alongside the relevant fee book, indicates that this very expensive barrister was never short of work. It also offers insights into the kinds of problems and tensions that were masked by strong theatrical performances in court.

This chapter explores these themes by examining Hughes' role in, and accounts of, a defamation case in the Federal Court, a criminal case before a naval Court Martial and an appeal case before the Privy Council.

Punch v Fairfax

In August 1979, Tom Hughes represented Leon Punch, the NSW State Leader of the National Country Party (NCP), in a defamation suit against John Fairfax & Sons and Australian Associated Press (AAP). Alec Shand QC, the son of the late Jack Shand and a former Hughes pupil, led for the defence. Once again, but this time in Canberra and in very different circumstances, Hughes found himself appearing on a 'political' matter before Justice Douglas McGregor.

On 30 April 1976, the day before the Labor Party's victory in the NSW State election, the *SMH* reported that on 29 April about 250 dairy farmers and members of the NSW Country Party (as it was then named) resigned from the State Party at a meeting in Bega over a dispute concerning the milk quota. Under the statutory system, only some 2700 dairy farmers in designated areas could sell fresh milk in the lucrative Sydney, Newcastle and Wollongong markets. Some 1200 farmers, excluded from the quota, had joined the Dairy Action Group to oppose the system, and they figured prominently at the Bega meeting. According to the *SMH* report, those who resigned from the State Party at Bega also called for the resignations of Leon Punch, then Deputy Premier and State Parliamentary Leader of the CP, and Bruce Cowan, the CP Minister for Agriculture, both of whom were direct beneficiaries of the quota system. Three other newspapers – the *Canberra Times*, the *Newcastle Herald* and the *Northern Star*, Lismore – published similar accounts, all based on the story originally filed by a *Herald* journalist, Gordon Hunter, and distributed by AAP. All four newspapers claimed that those who resigned from the State Party took steps to maintain their membership of the Federal Country Party.

It transpired that a staff member in the office of the then Leader of the Opposition, Neville Wran, had contacted Hunter and told him of the coming meeting in Bega and of what was expected to happen. He also provided Hunter with names of people to contact for amplifying the story. Based on what he had learnt from these sources, Hunter wrote a piece in advance of the meeting. Although senior Fairfax editors ordered the article to be 'held' pending verification, the journalist did not inform the copytaker, who passed on the story for publication. Hunter had transgressed several 'house rules'. Worse, as the defendants later acknowledged in court, the published story was an almost total fabrication; only about 50 people had attended the Bega meeting, no one resigned and no motion was passed demanding that Punch resign as leader. Fairfax duly sacked Hunter, and later editions of the *SMH* on 30 April did not carry the original story. At no stage, however, did the *SMH* issue an apology, although AAP did offer a form of one.

A Sydney firm of solicitors briefed Tom Hughes at the end of July 1979, and *Punch v Fairfax* began in the Federal Court in Canberra on Monday 6 August.[5] Hughes recorded that he 'opened the case high, wide and handsome, which pleased the client & those with me. As political libels go, it is a bad one, considering the electoral context in which it was published.' Moreover, some internal Fairfax memoranda showed just how reckless the journalist had been in beating up a story 'based', as it was, 'on inspired & poisonous rumour from Neville Wran's office', though Hughes said that he did not want to say anything 'pejorative' about Wran himself. A Nimmitabel grazier and a senior CP official in the region ended a good first day with his emphatic denial that any formal motion calling for Punch's resignation had been proposed at the Bega meeting. Hughes accentuated this point, and the defence never cross-examined the witness on the subject. The Punch team was embarrassed when Shand later produced witnesses who had either proposed or voted on a resignation motion.

Leon Punch, Hughes' second witness, told the court he was 'most upset' by the report. It implied a loss of confidence in his leadership, and questioned his integrity and reputation. He was also 'outraged' because the report was 'so untruthful'. Shand spent most of the second day cross-examining Punch – 'not very well', in Hughes' view, though Shand was aided by McGregor J's 'obfuscated views about relevance'. 'Really, Doug is a nice, well-intentioned but blinkered and inept lawyer. As a judge he is as disappointing as he was at the Bar. But so well-intentioned.'

Hughes and Shand were soon in each other's sights. David Levine, later a judge of the NSW Supreme Court, could have been referring to *Punch v Fairfax* when he described a Hughes-Shand contest as 'gladiatorial advocacy at its best: you know, blood on the wall and one would be down and fight his way up, and the other one would go down and fight his way back.'[6] Hughes won a crucial victory on the question of 'contextual justification'. In order to extend the scope of 'contextual justification' for the *Herald* article, Shand intended to show that large numbers of dairymen who were not CP members had lost confidence in Punch. McGregor J ruled in favour of Hughes' argument that the words of the article criticising Punch should be taken as referring only to those dairymen who were also members of the CP. Having criticised McGregor J's performance on the second day of the trial, Hughes decided on the third that McGregor J 'seems to be much more in command of the case'. Hughes also managed to stall Shand's argument for three days by questioning the admissibility of the CP's computer records of membership. He initially persuaded McGregor J to reject these records because, under the ACT Evidence Ordinance, someone who could reasonably be said to have personal knowledge of the matters on the records was obliged to supply the information in the records to the person compiling them.

The plaintiff's case began to wobble when Shand produced a minute book of the Bega meeting of April 1976 showing that a motion calling for Punch and Cowan to resign was defeated by 30 votes to 20; that is, a motion had been moved calling for Punch's resignation. A dairy farmer, who was a member of the CP, said that beef producers opposed the motion while dairy farmers supported it. Hughes restored equilibrium when he pointed out that the minutes referred to a meeting of the 'Bega branch of the National Country Party'; the CP in New South Wales did not insert the word 'National' into its title until June 1977. Hughes told a hostile witness – 'very bluntly' – that the minutes presented in Court were not the correct minutes of the night. Witnesses, who swore there was a vote, restored Shand's advantage.

By the second week, Hughes was convinced that the defence, by calling a succession of non-credentialed witnesses, was 'fighting a war of attrition, hoping to wear us down by the mounting expense of the fight'. Shand claimed that Hughes clearly implied he was deliberately prolonging the case, and denied doing anything improper. Hughes replied that 'my learned friend must be very sensitive'. Shand argued that Hughes himself was delaying proceedings by objecting to defence attempts to introduce computer membership records, but Shand seemed untroubled about introducing more witnesses whose CP credentials remained in question. At this stage Hughes thought the case was on 'an even keel', and that the defence was at '6's and 7's' after he had persuaded McGregor J to reject a defence proposal to tender CP membership cards. Hughes also 'winkled some quite valuable admissions' from the *Herald*'s news editor. By the middle of the third week, however, the case again looked to be in trouble. McGregor J finally rejected Hughes' argument opposing the admissibility of 'the bloody computer print-out lists', an argument that Hughes considered, 'even by my stern standards', to be 'really good'. On the other hand, McGregor J did allow Hughes to reopen the plaintiff's case, and to call Bruce Duncan, the State NCP member for Casino. Duncan swore, 'quite convincingly', that no motion calling for Punch's resignation was moved at the Bega meeting. But the advantage was lost when Shand's 'skilful' and 'pertinacious' cross-examination led Duncan into making simple mistakes. Hughes' star witness did not have the sense to answer questions simply and directly.

Nevertheless, after the trial concluded on 30 August, and McGregor J reserved his decision, Hughes thought 'we shall win in Punch. Disaster for him if we do not.' Hughes' confidence rose as he reflected upon the core arguments of the two sides. Shand in his final address said that politicians, by their very occupation, were involved in controversial issues and could expect to be criticised by those who were on the opposite side. Any reasonable person would see that discontented dairymen were protesting over a scheme that affected their industry and their livelihood. The articles did no more than express an opposite point of view from Punch on the divisive milk quota issue. They did not reflect on his competence or fitness for office, and were not capable of being, or in fact were, defamatory. And AAP was entitled to the defence of qualified privilege, having published reports in the ordinary course of accepting news material from Fairfax.

In his closing address, Hughes argued that the articles in question carried the imputation that, through his support of the milk quota system, Punch had lost the confidence of a significant body of the party membership, who judged him incapable of providing leadership. Hughes described the Shand approach as an 'ocker' and 'knocker' attempt to apply different rules where the plaintiff was a politician operating in a world of controversy. The law, he said, was clear: the same rules of defamation applied. The highest courts had rejected the 'legal heresy', the 'obnoxious legal fallacy', which had permeated the whole defence approach. In full theatrical mode, Hughes said Fairfax and AAP had adopted 'the mask of the cynic … the cynic with the sneering smile … an ocker attitude that politicians were there to be knocked … it does not matter what you say about them'. In effect, he assigned to McGregor J the responsibility for ensuring that public affairs commentary remained on the highest level.

Hughes' confidence at the end of the hearings disguised his continued frustration with the way his side had managed the case. Right at the start, he concluded that everything was 'a balls up'; there were 'too many mistakes made by other people on the way through'. He had no time for one of the instructing solicitors, was very critical of his junior's inconsistent performance and counted himself fortunate to have Peter Hohnen, a solicitor with the Canberra firm of Macphillamy Cummins and Gibson, as a part of the team: 'a beacon of good sense & a tower of strength.' The defence did not escape criticism. It inveigled the former General Secretary of the NSW CP to come from the Gold Coast – he wanted to help Punch – without disclosing to him that it was the defence who would call him. 'Stupidity and deviousness are a dangerous mixture.' Hughes' diary comments on some of the hostile witnesses were typically hard-hitting. He referred to the current General Secretary of the NSW NCP as 'that arch-oaf', and to a prominent member of the Dairy Action Group as 'an arch shit from the far North'.

One advantage of appearing in a case in Canberra was that Hughes could drive to Marsland at the end of most days. He may have taken dark thoughts with him but at least he avoided the legal teams of both sides who were staying at the Lakeside Hotel. Besides, pleasant dinners with Don Stanton and his wife Betty awaited him, and he was 're-invigorated by agreeable talks about sheep and so on'. He could also worry about other problems, such as the 'unavoidable' costs of acquiring water tanks and oats for an empty silo, and finding an alternative source of finance after the Head Office of Dalgety/Winchombe turned down a loan request to buy some ewes.

Tom did have one happy encounter at the Lakeside. On the second night of the trial, he had dinner with Carol Thatcher, the daughter of the newly-elected British Prime Minister. Jonathan Aitken, a British Tory MP, whom Tom first met in Sydney in 1968, had asked Tom to meet Aitken's then girlfriend when she came to Australia to pursue a career in journalism. Tom had first entertained Carol for lunch and dinner at Marsland on the Saturday before the Punch trial. He found her to be 'a remarkably intelligent girl. I like her.' He was unaware of her inner hurt; Aitken dumped Carol just after the May 1979 British election and announced his engagement to another woman a month later.[7] Another evening at the Lakeside was not so pleasant. Hughes had arrived back at the hotel after 'a lovely dinner with lots of good conversation' in the mountains outside Canberra. Peter Hohnen and Alec Shand were two of the other guests. One of the plaintiff's solicitors confronted Hughes on his return, upbraiding him for his approach to the case. Hughes responded, 'sparing him not at all'.

Weekends in Sydney were a blessed relief, although driving to the city was a slow trip because Tom had lost points for two speeding convictions since 1977. On Friday 17 August, pleased to be home at the end of the second week of the trial, Tom took time off for reflection. He had just spoken to Tom Jnr on the telephone: 'I believe that we are getting closer to each other.' He decided to set down 'how I feel at this moment, within and about myself'.

> I have not been together with a woman for nearly 4 months. And I do not greatly feel any desire. Katie is at last out of my system.[8] For

> which I am thankful. It has taken a long time – too long. But I am sure, at the moment, that I shall never fall in love again and am quite resigned to that prospect. I am really resigned to a solitary life. It isn't all that bad. I have so many other demands on my time and attention, not the least of which are my two great sons.

Next day, he drove to Sydney and went to lunch at the 'May Sun' Chinese restaurant in Dixon Street, Haymarket. He was a guest of the journalist and broadcaster 'Red' Harrison and his wife Pamela, a horticulture writer and a sixth generation descendant of John and Elizabeth Macarthur of Camden. Pamela's sister was also present. Tom referred to her in his diary as 'the legendary Phoebe McA-O (Atkinson) now separated'. Within two weeks, he could write about 'a delightful evening with Phoebe. What a great girl. I almost think we might make it. But who knows? I am by now the ultimate cynic about these things.' Their relationship lasted another seven months.

Tom Hughes might have worried about not getting enough work, but there were limits to what the 'cab on the rank' would accept. A wheat-stealing case in Gunnedah and Parkes had no appeal. On 15 August, Hughes quoted a fee of $3000 on brief and $2000 a day in court: 'Should frighten them off!' He learnt, two days later, he had been successful: 'Very pleasing to me!' He could afford rejection. Hughes' fees for the Punch trial were those of a '$1,000 a day QC'. His total fees for the case amounted to $18,700. Within the same period, he also received $3200 for conferences and opinions. Of that sum, he 'managed' on Friday 24 August 1979, 'a very rushed day', to put $1200 into the fee book. 'I need it all, because … the bite of inflation into my earnings is unpleasantly noticeable.'

That same day, while lunching in the Australian Club, he met Barwick 'who was his usual ebullient self & very chatty'. The Chief Justice offered his opinion on defamation issues; any statement concerning a person, and injurious in the sense that it is likely to cause loss, should be actionable even though it did not reflect on the person's reputation. At the time, Hughes had more than Leon Punch on his mind. He was due to represent Fairfax in a defamation suit brought by Tom Uren, with whom he had occasionally sparred in Parliament. A *SMH* editorial, published on 3 April 1975, just before the fall of Saigon, had accused Uren of being a racist and a traitor. His barrister, Michael McHugh, had phoned Hughes to discuss an adjournment of the case because his client wanted to attend the Mountbatten funeral.[9] Fortunately, McHugh wanted no more than a week's suspension because Hughes could foresee clashes ahead with the Copyright Tribunal hearing.

Hughes' Punch commitment had already caused his withdrawal from another Fairfax case, which would also have pitted him against McHugh. John Andrews, an Australian architect with an international reputation, sued Fairfax over claims that the government buildings in the ACT he had designed, and whose construction he supervised, leaked like sieves and were a property manager's nightmare. At the end of August, Hughes learnt that Andrews was awarded $480,000. Excluding the United States, Hughes thought it must be the largest verdict in the common law world: 'I wonder if it would have been different if I had been there.' McHugh had already contacted him in confidence expressing his own fears about the size of the award. Fairfax wanted Hughes back for the appeal. It was all very worrying because the Uren case was due to begin in September, work was piling up and the copyright matter was also imminent: 'I shall have to finesse as best I can.'

In the week following the Punch trial, Hughes had to deal with the Uren matter. He had received instructions to make an offer: $25,000 inclusive of costs to settle two actions, plus a deed of release, and an acknowledgement in the deed that Fairfax had never published anything maliciously:

> I do not think it will appeal to the other side; but I could be wrong. I do not enjoy working for Fairfax [emphasis in the original]. What a difference between the close rapport I have with Packer, when I am working for him, and the distanced relationship with the Fairfax people – they are, as I described them in my *Punch* address last week, a stiff-necked mob.

On the following Sunday, 9 September, and after 'a delightful lunch' at Paddington with Joanna, Lucy, Michael and Larko, Hughes spent the afternoon working on Uren: 'Unless we can settle, disaster looms.'

David Levine, Hughes' junior in the Uren case, recalled that when the plaintiff walked into the courtroom on the Monday morning, 'the whole of the jury panel-in-waiting waved and smiled'. The defence team knew then they had to settle. Agreement was reached at a morning conference.[10] Hughes noted: 'Disaster was averted.' The settlement consisted of $40,500, inclusive of costs, together with a release of all claims for defamation to date, and an undertaking on Uren's part not to use the article complained of as evidence of malice or to defeat a defence of comment in any subsequent proceedings. Hughes read out an agreed apology in open court. He said the *SMH* unreservedly withdrew the allegation that Uren was racist, withdrew any other imputation Uren found damaging and apologised to him for any hurt he may have suffered through the editorial. Justice Nagle congratulated the parties on reaching an agreement and told the potential jurors the case might have lasted up to two months. Hughes, in his diary, called the apology 'quite a mild one' in the circumstances and was greatly relieved. 'Fairfax was well out of it. It was a defenceless position … Had the case gone on, in the climate created by Andrews and by his [Uren's] recent trip to London for Mountbatten's funeral, there would have been another enormous verdict.' Hughes and Uren shook hands at the end of the proceedings and talked briefly. According to Uren, Hughes told him much later that the libel was impossible to defend.[11]

Hughes was immersed in other cases when McGregor J returned on 5 October with a 61-page judgment awarding Punch a total sum of $27,250 in damages ($18,860 against Fairfax and $8660 against AAP) as well as costs. He found that the articles did reflect on Punch and, by implication, accepted Hughes' contention that politicians were entitled to equal treatment under defamation law. At the same time, McGregor J rejected a number of Hughes' arguments, most notably that no motion was moved at the Bega meeting.[12] Shand and Hughes faced each other again when Fairfax and AAP appealed to the Full Federal Court. Blackburn, Northrop and Brennan JJ unanimously dismissed the appeal with costs, arguing it was capable in law of being defamatory to say that a leader of a political party had lost the confidence of a significant number in his party, their loss of confidence demonstrated by the calls for his resignation.[13]

A Court Martial

Tom Hughes, appearing again with David Levine, was briefed to appear for Lieutenant John David Napier of the Royal Australian Navy, who was charged with 36 offences allegedly committed while in command of the patrol boat, HMAS *Adroit*. Eight of the charges related to conduct unbecoming an officer. The others concerned theft, receiving stolen goods, assault and making demands with menaces. Most of the charges arose out of the boarding of foreign fishing vessels in the Gulf of Carpentaria in June 1978 and of a Taiwanese fishing vessel off the coast of Darwin in the following November. Hughes and Levine decided to 'object to the jurisdiction; then plead not guilty; then, after the inevitable result, go to the High Court on certiorari' (a writ or order by which a superior court will review the decision of an inferior court and quash the decision if it has exceeded its jurisdiction). Hughes spoke to Napier about this approach and thought he appeared 'to have come to the dawn of understanding what deep trouble he is in'.

Hughes considered it 'a tragic case'. Napier was now 27 and 'must have had the ball at his feet'. Yet, as CO, he had turned HMAS *Adroit* into 'a pirate ship'. Hughes concluded that Napier had 'a defective personality' and considered his appointment did not reflect well on the Navy. There were aspects he knew to be 'desperately worrying' but could not spell them out, confiding to his diary that 'I feel the burden of it'. Legally, he decided, Napier was in 'an impossible position': he 'sang like a canary' in his record of interview, tried to cover up by lying to the Board of Inquiry and to his own Captain, and concealed the two sextants he took from the Taiwanese vessels. It did not help that Napier's Executive Officer had already been dismissed from the Navy after being found guilty of nine charges, including the stealing of a sextant. Hughes thought the most he could achieve was to keep Napier out of gaol.

The Court Martial began on the morning of Tuesday 18 September 1979 on the ninth floor of Westfield Towers in Sydney. Captain John McDermott was President of the five-member panel and Lieutenant Commander Murray Tobias QC was Judge Advocate. Tobias immediately impressed Hughes with his 'quiet and incisive methods'. Hughes tried every legal angle. He started with the proposition that the Court had no jurisdiction because it purported to exercise the judicial power of the Commonwealth. When this approach failed, he argued that the *Theft Act 1968* (UK) and the *Criminal Damage Act 1971* (UK) were both inapplicable in this case. Tobias overruled him, a result Hughes found 'somewhat doubtful and very disappointing'. On the other hand, he thought Tobias 'was probably sensible to rule as he did', while any error could be cured on appeal. Hughes' other submissions on matters of law were more successful; Tobias ruled that five of the charges should be withdrawn, though Hughes had hoped 'for a somewhat better result'. He also had success on matters of fact, exposing inconsistencies in the evidence of the Master of the Taiwanese fishing vessel. It helped that the prosecution became tied in knots over the charge of stealing money. Several members of the ship's company contributed by displaying 'their esprit de corps' and 'letting their Captain down lightly', thereby not providing proof of malfeasance.

Just before and throughout the six-day hearing, Hughes and Levine spent several hours together in chambers, and Hughes spent even more hours alone, working on the case. Hughes spent still more time on other professional and personal matters. He drafted an opinion for the Corporate Affairs Commission relating to the Barton case,[14] and accepted a brief and began preparations for appearing in a case before the Family Court. He had conferences with the oil companies immersed in a crisis at the Kurnell Refinery. The ABC wanted to brief him in its copyright dispute with ATN-7 that had used the former's film of the Rugby League Grand Final. Believing that his Fairfax retainer included ATN-7, Hughes contacted the Fairfax solicitor, Graham Bates, who promptly claimed him.

During this period, Tom attended several lunches and dinners, often with Joanna and the two boys. At the end of one day at the Court Martial, and after talking to the oil company representatives, he drove to Leura in the Blue Mountains to dine with Phoebe 'at a very ordinary place' with its 'slight air of misplaced pretentiousness'. On Friday 21 September, and accompanied by Michael, Tom went to Shore School where he was an adjudicator for the prestigious Lawrence Campbell Oratory Competition. Established in 1935, the competition was open to representatives of the Greater Public Schools and Associated Grammar Schools. A boy from Trinity Grammar won; Tom thought him 'brilliant in the style of a low key orator'. He disagreed with Alastair Mackerras, Headmaster of Sydney Grammar, that the Riverview boy was better; in Tom's view, he 'was totally lacking a sense of humour'. The personal meeting at Shore was valuable. Mackerras warned Tom Jnr's father that his son would get a bad report. At least the Head believed the boy had the capacity to do well. Tom received better news on another night when, at a large birthday party, he found 'Mrs SS still wants me'.[15] Although he considered an affair would be too difficult, 'it is nice to know someone still finds me attractive!'. An early morning run at Bondi on a Sunday made him feel fit, and wishing he could do more.

On the second last afternoon of the Court Martial hearing, Monday 24 September, Napier made a statement in which he admitted several of the charges. Two 'impressive witnesses', one of them Commodore Peter Sinclair, a future Governor of New South Wales, gave character evidence in his defence. Next day, the prosecution and the defence made their final addresses. Hughes spoke for 90 minutes: 'I thought it was alright. But this case has all the inevitability of Greek Tragedy.' He considered that Tobias gave an excellent summation, and thought he would be a worthy addition to the Supreme Court (Tobias retired as a judge of the Court of Appeal in 2011). The Court was out for nearly five hours before returning to convict Napier on 13 charges, including seven for conduct unbecoming an officer. It acquitted him of several serious criminal charges. There was a 'great hassle' while the Court was considering its verdict. 'A shit-headed Commodore' (later, a Rear Admiral) wanted Napier placed in close or open arrest at HMAS *Penguin*, a shore establishment. Tobias intervened – 'what a fine man he is' – and spoke to the President of the Court, who agreed Napier could spend the night at home. On the following morning, Hughes spoke for 20 minutes arguing for mitigation, and thought that the Court 'was very lenient' in sentencing Napier for discharge from the service: 'It could have been worse.'

There was, throughout Hughes' account of the Court Martial, a sense of frustration and despair. He was engaged in 'a hopeless case', without any possibility of acquittal. His task was limited to minimising guilt and pleading mitigation. Yet he maintained an intense personal engagement. Hughes' diary entry of 24 September is especially revealing. 'I am sad at heart for him, and sense that, in a curious way, I am more emotionally involved in his inevitable downfall than he is.' In the following sentences, Hughes could stand back and assess himself: 'I find the task of being a criminal advocate exquisitely difficult. But I feel I am tolerably good at it.' He later described how, on the night after Napier was sentenced, he joined a family dinner that Lucy had prepared: 'Very pleasant, but too much to drink … it was perhaps a much needed let down from the strain of the Court Martial.' Next day, Hughes worked on two cases in chambers. Just as he was capable of a strong emotional commitment, he was equally adept at moving on.[16]

Mukta Ben v Suva City Council

On Sunday 7 October 1979, Tom Hughes flew first class to London. Malcolm Turnbull, now at Oxford, met him at Heathrow – 'it was so good to see him again' – and the pair lunched at a wine bar at Aldgate Circus, full of people from the nearby Old Bailey. Characteristically, Tom recorded the fare: a roast beef sandwich, two smoked salmon sandwiches and a bottle of French ordinaire cost £6. Geoffrey Robertson, who was making his name at the English Bar, joined them in the city for dinner. Hughes' junior, Kate Weigall, arrived in London nearly a week later. Early in the previous month, when the pair met in Hughes' chambers to prepare for the case, Tom noted that 'she is as thin as a rake: thinner … than I have ever seen her'. Before that meeting, he had not seen her for six weeks.

Hughes had gone to London to represent the Suva City Council in a case that originated in 1968. The Council had compulsorily acquired 20 acres of private land to build an auxiliary power station. Over the years, Mukta Ben and Shanta Ben, the landowners, proceeded through the Fijian courts to challenge the validity of the acquisition. Tom Hughes represented the Council at the hearing in the Fiji Court of Appeal in 1977 that found for his client. KH Gifford QC of the Victorian Bar represented the appellants, and the two barristers squared off again at the Privy Council. The appellants had identified 10 separate grounds where they claimed that the Suva Council had acted beyond its power and that the requirements of natural justice had not been observed. The Council admitted to making errors along the way, but the majority on the Fijian Court of Appeal did not consider that in sum these actions invalidated the acquisition. The same issues were canvassed again in London.

The hearing before the Judicial Committee began on Monday 15 October before Lords Wilberforce, Davies, Russell of Killowen, Keith of Kinkel and Lane. Hughes wrote little about the case itself. He preferred to focus on Gifford's demeanour and performance. After noting that Wilberforce and Davies 'gave a friendly smile as we entered the room', he embarked on a savage summation of his opponent:

> Gifford is incredibly gauche: he is rude; he interrupts; he asks rhetorical questions; he gesticulates; he is thoroughly frightful and he sets my teeth on edge as if he were a piece of coarse sandpaper. He is unfair and untruthful. Whatever may be the result of this appeal, his advocacy can only be described as counter-productive so far as his case is concerned.

Hughes was pleased to observe the responses of the Law Lords. Davies to Gifford: 'Please do not be so supercilious.' Russell of Killowen, with 'a look of sardonic contempt' and in 'a drily sarcastic tone of voice', observed: 'Mr Gifford, you have said that before – many times.' Wilberforce just 'wore his look of saintly boredom'. The diary entries for the following two days added more examples of Gifford being 'remarkably inept and ill-mannered'. Hughes believed their lordships could not abide Gifford. By contrast, they responded well to his own submissions. When he apologised for not finishing sooner, Wilberforce said he should not worry 'as your argument has been very compact'.

John Winneke, the son of the former Victorian Chief Justice and current Governor of Victoria, and himself a future President of the Victorian Court of Appeal, met Hughes and Weigall by chance at the Royal Automobile Club on Friday 19 October. 'He confirmed how greatly disliked Gifford is and was amused by our account of his gaffes.' Hughes acknowledged that, on the following Monday, the final day of the hearings, Gifford 'hit his best form and was heard attentively'. The appellants' solicitor told Hughes that Russell of Killowen had been deputed to write the judgment. 'The inference is that we must win … Russell was throughout the hearings thoroughly unimpressed by Gifford's arguments.'

If Gifford occupied more space, there was always room in the diary for Kate. One morning she arrived at the Privy Council a few minutes after Tom:

> She professed to be put out because once again she had not beaten me to work. How lovely she looks when away from the hassles of Sydney. Despite all her neuroses she is the most enchanting woman I shall ever meet or have met. What went wrong? I shall never know; except that she is frightened of strength and permanency. But I must have the question discussed again.

Three nights later they had a long telephone conversation in which Katie 'gave expression to her conviction that she is not worthy of me – an idea that I tried to dispel, but probably never will'. Phoebe rang from Australia two days later, 'full of love and affection'.

Hughes' London trip included important extra-curricular activities. He bought silver spoons and forks in New Bond Street as well as a new suit in Jermyn Street. Lunch with Jonathan Aitken at an Italian restaurant provided an opportunity to talk about politics in Australia and the United

Kingdom. Hughes was understandably curious about Aitken's failure to secure a ministry under Margaret Thatcher. Aitken offered two explanations: in November 1978, he had opposed the continuation of economic sanctions against Rhodesia; and Thatcher disapproved of his affair with her daughter, Carol. Hughes correctly surmised that it was the 'termination' rather than the 'subsistence' of the relationship that influenced Carol's mother. (Aitken remained on the backbench for Thatcher's entire prime ministership.)

Towards the end of the hearings, Tom headed to Oxford with Malcolm Turnbull, who had returned from a quick trip to Sydney, where they were due to appear in a Union debate supporting the proposition 'That the private lives of public figures should be solely their own concern'. Kate Weigall and Beryl Whiteley (a patron of the arts and mother of Brett Whiteley) joined them in Oxford, Malcolm having arranged for the two women to stay in Brasenose College. Clement Freud, a grandson of Sigmund Freud and himself a British Liberal MP and a noted wit, broadcaster and writer, spoke against the motion. The debate was memorable for clashes between Turnbull and Freud. While sympathetic to Malcolm's anger and believing Freud to be 'a queer customer' (many in his own party considered Freud unlikeable), Tom thought that Malcolm 'will have to learn the art of taking it on the chin'. Deciding that the humour of the occasion was wearing a bit thin, Tom decided to make a reasoned contribution to the debate, and thereby impressed a speaker on the other side, the recently resigned editor of the *New Statesman*, Anthony Howard.

After the Privy Council hearing concluded, Hughes and Aitken attended a party in Kensington hosted by Sir Humphry Wakefield, Bt. They met Ian Smith, the former Prime Minister of Rhodesia, who was attending the Lancaster House Conference that prepared the way for the independence of Zimbabwe. Smith 'railed against the perfidy of the British Government'. He complained especially about the decision to appoint a Governor to run the country during the proposed election campaign. He said it would erode the credibility of the predominantly black and pliant Muzorewa Government – which Smith had simultaneously helped into power in April 1979 and effectively sabotaged – and would give the Mugabe-Nkomo Patriotic Front an easy victory. Hughes thought that Smith's judgment 'may be clouded by fanaticism and his intense dislike of the Brits'. Aitken and Hughes decided that Smith's pessimism had 'a somewhat bogus ring', a view they found corroborated when the Justice Minister, Chris Andersen, a liberal-minded Afrikaner, 'was not nearly so gloomy'. As it turned out, Smith's prediction was largely vindicated.

Lord Russell of Killowen, in delivering the judgment on 12 December 1979, rejected all 10 grounds of the appeal and proposed to advise Her

Majesty to dismiss the appeal with costs.[17] Hughes could feel well satisfied. He received a fee of $40,000, as well as $200 a day for living expenses, a considerably 'better deal' than the one proffered by the instructing solicitor in London who was unaware that Hughes had arrived with a pre-arranged agreement. In all, it was a good year. According to his records, Hughes received nearly $320,000 in fees in 1979 (worth close to $1.5 million in 2014), which is not taking into account what was left over from retainers with Packer, Fairfax and others. On 11 January 1980, he noted that 'the weight of the last year is being lifted from my shoulders'.

18

Two 'happy & auspicious' events

Two events – one in March 1980 and another in June 1981 – gave Tom Hughes the personal and emotional satisfaction missing from his thriving career at the Bar. In the first, his 'darling daughter' married Malcolm Turnbull, an occasion spoilt only by the fact he was not present. In the second, he married Chrissie Abel Smith, the woman with whom he achieved something approximating to the marriage of his parents.

'What a happy & auspicious event'

On 11 January, Fred Lind of Allen Allen & Hemsley asked Hughes if he would take a Packer case in Perth. 'Of course I said yes.' Apart from anything else, it was a good opportunity to see Red Burt – by now Chief Justice – and his wife Margaret.

Packer's Publishing and Broadcasting Ltd (PBL), which controlled the very popular midday television program, 'The Mike Walsh Show', had sold the rights to STW-9 in Western Australia. A rival television station, TVW-7, had exercised these rights for four years until the end of 1979. Early in February, TVW-7 sought to obtain an order preventing Channel Nine from screening the program until the court decided which station was entitled to show it. Hughes flew to Perth with Lind for a case that began in the Supreme Court on Tuesday 5 February. Next day, Hughes reported a win; the judge refused to grant an interlocutory injunction.

He then referred in his diary to 'the most important event of the day'. Tony Larkins rang him from Sydney with the news that Lucy and Malcolm had telephoned to say they were getting married. 'How delighted I am! I'm sure that this marriage must have a great chance of success.' He talked the next day to 'darling daughter' and his future son-in-law, and learnt there was a problem. Joanna announced she was flying to England to attend the wedding. Lucy, who was not getting on with her mother, promptly had a rare asthma attack. She could not face the inevitable dramas on her wedding day, fears probably aggravated if both her parents were present.[1] Upon reflection, Tom believed that the 'strong and hard decision' to exclude her mother 'cannot be described as unfair'. Two telephone conversations with Joanna, a few hours apart, convinced him that Lucy and Malcolm were wise to have a quiet wedding in England. He accepted he could not go himself if Joanna did not attend, and instead suggested holding a reception after the newly-weds returned to Sydney. This proposal met approval on all sides, and so Lucy and Malcolm could have their small private wedding in Oxford where almost all the guests would be in their age group

They were married on 22 March 1980 at St Michael's Church, Cumnor, just outside Oxford. The Vicar, an Oxford graduate, was a former member of the British Colonial Service in East Africa who had taken Holy Orders late in life. Lucy had told her father that he was not 'at all Dickensian … but is more in the starving missionary mould', probably the result of spending so many years in Uganda. Malcolm had to use some ingenuity to persuade the Vicar to marry a Catholic (Lucy) and a Presbyterian (Malcolm) in an Anglican Church. Apparently, he convinced the Vicar that, as part of the Established Church, he had a duty to prevent fornication in his parish, and Lucy and Malcolm were a young couple and, admitting nothing, were 'sorely tempted'. The Vicar was so amused he agreed to marry them.[2]

On the day itself, Hughes arrived back from Perth where he had again been appearing for Packer in the Walsh case. The case had been stood over until 25 May, but he was very confident of winning, and he did. Having fallen asleep at Perth airport, he missed his overnight flight, and did not reach chambers until early on Saturday afternoon, when he worked on the Andrews case. He noted in the diary: 'We did well at [the] Goulburn Show.' He added the following to the Saturday entry, probably two or three days later: 'Lucy's wedding. Spoke to her with Mike and Joanna on the phone. What a happy & auspicious event.'

There were three older guests at the wedding. Bruce Turnbull, the much-loved father of the bridegroom, arrived about two days before the ceremony, determined not to miss the marriage of his only son.[3] The two other older guests wrote letters to the father of the bride telling him 'what a joy it was'. Betty Fairfax, once married to Sir Warwick Fairfax, reported that the groom, the best man (John Glover) and the 'giver awayer' (Geoffrey Robertson) were all Rhodes Scholars. She sat next to Malcolm at the wedding lunch in the nearby pub, and assured Tom he was 'a very remarkable young man – very like you in lots of ways … you need not have any worries about Luce's future with Malcolm'. Francis James[4] told Tom he had attended many weddings but 'Lucy's, yesterday, was about the most joyous of them all'. He noted how the small congregation consisted almost entirely of 'The Young from Oxford, heavily laced with future LCJs [Lord Chief Justices] if one judged by their conversation'. James spoke of Lucy in glowing terms: 'a beaut young woman', bright with a quality of humility acquired earlier than most manage to achieve but with a 'streak of toughness' to balance 'a quality of quietness, repose, which is quite natural' allied to 'good straight judgement'. As for Malcolm, James, for the first time, 'detected the slightest indication of self-consciousness in that young man'.[5]

Much work and some pleasure

Hughes own life was taking a familiar course: cases upon cases, all of them bringing good returns for the long, disciplined hours given to them; and a growing sense that his personal happiness would remain, outside of his family, very much work-related.

Early in 1980, he was spending time with Tom Jnr and Michael, often lunching or dining with at least one of them, attending race meetings with them and sharing with Michael the disappointment when 'Make Mine Candy' finished third last in a field of 11 in the final event at Randwick on 9 February. The rains were good over the summer, the Marsland sheep took many prizes in the Gunning Show, 134 ewes were with lamb and the prize ram, 'Lord Louis', had joined 31 of them, 'a very satisfactory tally', and had been given another 35 'to look after'. Triumphs at the Royal Easter Show for some of the Marsland flock offered some more cheer.

A problem with Michael had been resolved. He had not been getting ahead at Sydney Grammar. His father had written to Alastair Mackerras, the Headmaster, on 31 August 1979, the final day of the Punch case, giving notice that Michael would be leaving the school at the end of third term to complete his last three years at Cranbrook as a weekly boarder. Tom greatly regretted making the move. He had come to admire the school but, for Michael to improve his performance, he needed to improve his organisation and output. Michael himself thought he would be better able to achieve these objectives if tied to a regular boarding school routine. His father agreed, adding in his letter to Mackerras, 'I trust you will understand my feelings: you may also read between the lines'.[6] Mackerras agreed that a boarding school 'is probably the best solution of the problem'. Tom noted in his diary that the Headmaster's reaction to Michael's departure showed him to be 'a good and understanding man'. Although there were some initial difficulties, eliminated by moving to another study room, Michael had fitted into Cranbrook in 1980 and made some 'impressive' friends, much to his father's delight.

Tom was very happy with Phoebe for several months, not least because she fitted in well with his schedule of preparations and court appearances and, during January 1980, with his time at Marsland working on house improvements and buying stock. Tom often commented on her excellent cooking and she helped him host some very pleasant lunch parties at the farm. As he saw it, however, they had incompatible lifestyles. On Good Friday 1980, he decided '(t)his is ending. Much as I like her … (p)rivilege unaccompanied by hard work is not my scene'. Not long after breaking with Phoebe in April 1980, Tom wrote of another woman who later achieved prominence in the law: 'What a great girl she is; but there is still only one for me, and I suppose that I shall never have her. I mean my beloved Katie. What a balls up life can be; but I have learned how to live with loss. And the hurt has gone.' Some weeks later, in what was the final entry for this particular diary, he wrote of driving Susan Smith and her young son to Marsland. He made no further reference to the event, except to note that, on arrival, the rain gauge had collected 75 points in his three-week absence from the farm, the oats 'look quite good' and a dam was full.

'The legal profession's highest flyer is Tom Hughes QC'[7]

Journalists, observing the Australian Bar in the 1980s, liked to assert or speculate on two matters: how much barristers charged, and who was the leader, or were the leaders, of the Bar. After reporting that Hughes was 'the legal profession's highest flyer', James Murray claimed he could be charging $3000 a day. Hughes declined to disclose his preferred fee because 'solicitors will think that is what I always get'. Murray found that, while some 'sources' agreed that Hughes could charge $3000 a day, others said he could not possibly charge more than $1500. Hughes' fee book for 1980 recorded the highest charge for a refresher as $2700 but, for most of the year, he sought $1600 for a day in court. By November-December, he occasionally received fees in the region of $1800-$2000. Even so, Hughes continued in 1980 to worry about getting enough work and about the kind of work he was getting. He noted at one point that he did not have a case in court in the week following the Easter break, a gap 'which always fills me with neurotic thoughts about what is happening to my practice'. On the other hand, he was able in that week to enter $6950 as payments for seven conferences and two opinions. His fee book entries for 1980 were just shy of $400,000.

The *AFR* surveyed solicitors in Sydney and Melbourne in November 1980. The 16 solicitors contacted in Sydney were mostly located in the big corporate firms, though some were suburban solicitors. Invited to name the 'best' in six fields, namely, tax, criminal law, workers' compensation, defamation, industrial law and companies/equity, a number also volunteered nominations in other areas. Valerie Lawson reported in the *AFR* for 21 November 1980 that Murray Gleeson was considered the 'number one glamour boy among Sydney solicitors'. Gleeson's 'glamour' was no doubt enhanced by his stunningly successful defence of Ian Sinclair, the Deputy Leader of the National Party and a senior Fraser Government minister, who had faced charges of forgery, of intending to defraud and of making false statements.[8] A telephone survey found that Gleeson scored 20 'mentions' as the 'best' barrister across the chosen fields and other nominated categories. McHugh received 16 and Hughes 14. McHugh rated first as a defamation lawyer, followed – and this might have been galling – by Shand, ahead of Hughes. Hughes received six mentions in the companies/equity field and headed the solicitor-nominated constitutional field. Some solicitors referred to him as 'Mr Constitution'. There was no clear winner in Victoria, except that Neil McPhee QC absolutely dominated the defamation field. Hughes would encounter him in this field in two notable cases in 1985.

Hughes did not have a case in 1980 to attract the sort of headlines that followed the Sinclair story through committal proceedings and the NSW District Court. He was, however, involved in several matters which were of public interest or had significant legal implications. He appeared, successfully, for Kerry Packer's companies in defending Channel Nine's exclusive rights to televise test and one-day international cricket. Hughes worked hard in March on the Andrews case, finding it 'very difficult to run an appeal that arises out of a completely fucked-up trial'. He succeeded to the point where the Court of Appeal agreed that the damages awarded to Andrews personally, in contrast to those for his company, were excessive. It ordered a re-trial on this particular issue.

Early in April, Hughes appeared as counsel assisting the Australian Broadcasting Tribunal, chaired by his friend, Bruce Gyngell. On Hughes' advice, the Tribunal rejected an inquiry into Labor Party allegations that Rupert Murdoch's joint takeover of television Channel 10 in Melbourne breached Commonwealth legislation and the criminal law. Hughes represented the Tribunal when, in mid-May, the Labor Party took the case to the High Court. The Full Court brusquely dismissed the Hughes-Gyngell argument that the Tribunal had acted lawfully over the Murdoch licence for Channel 10, despite the Tribunal receiving an all-clear from the Attorney-General's Department. By the time the Tribunal returned to the question of Murdoch's application, as required by the Court, it had acquired a new member. Hughes noted in his diary that Kate Weigall's appointment to the Tribunal took effect from 17 April: 'I hope that the job will lead to greater happiness for her.'[9]

In July 1980, Hughes represented Professor Harry Messel, then head of the School of Physics at the University of Sydney and founder of the International Science School in 1962, who faced charges at the Darwin Magistrates Court. Messel stood accused of taking barramundi from closed waters, discharging a shotgun in a protected area, killing a protected animal and keeping part of its flesh. These alleged offences occurred in mid-October 1979 at Andranangoo Creek on Melville Island, where Messel was heading a study of sub-adult crocodiles. Hughes argued in his defence that taking 150 fish was incidental to the professor's research licence, that Melville Island was not a protected area, and that the 40 magpie geese were not protected animals at the time of the alleged offences. After a five-day hearing, G Galvin, Chief Stipendiary Magistrate, found Messel guilty on four counts and fined him $5527.60. In addition, he had to meet Hughes' fees of $7050 that included daily appearances of $1200 and preparation of grounds for appeal. Hughes was not further involved in the case that went to the Supreme Court of the Northern Territory, to the Federal Court and the High Court, and came back again to the Supreme Court where Gallop J allowed each of the four appeals and quashed the convictions and the orders of the Court of Summary Jurisdiction, Darwin.[10]

Tom Hughes was one of several silks from Sydney and Melbourne who represented the major players in the frenetic days of credit expansion, and takeover bids of the 1980s. The election of the Hawke Government in 1983 had provided much of the impetus for the so-called 'heady days' by floating the Australian dollar, deregulating the banking system and dismantling the tariff system. Corporate entrepreneurs – including Rupert Murdoch, Robert Holmes à Court, John Elliott, Alan Bond, John Spalvins and Christopher Skase – took advantage of readily available credit (16 foreign banks had entered the market) and launched takeovers, restructured and expanded companies and, in some instances, created lavish and very public lifestyles. Hughes' connection began in May 1980 when he appeared on behalf of the Bond companies in their takeover bid for White Industries and its coal operations in New South Wales. It was a frustrating exercise because he encountered Justice Robert Franki in the Federal Court who, he considered, 'knows nothing about evidence and really nothing about the law except for the little corner in which he used to practise … [and] is unused to the forensic techniques involved in fighting a war of "goodies & baddies"'. Hughes did not have personal contact with Bond, for which he is now grateful. The financial return was considerable. In late May to early July, he collected $20,225; for eight days at the beginning of August he received $11,900 for representing Endeavour Resources and collected another $30,970 later in that month when representing an associate company of the Bond Corporation. In the latter instance, White Industries fought hard to prevent a Bond takeover by enlisting the support of the Mitsubishi Corporation and, significantly in view of Hughes' retainer with Packer, ACP. Hughes' brief involved an assault on the illegal issue of 450,000 shares to the staff share scheme. It was all to no avail. Bond failed in his bid.

During his appearances for Bond, Hughes spent time in mid-June to work with Sir Lenox Hewitt, who was seeking a renewal of his five-year contract as Chairman of Qantas. The Whitlam Government had appointed him to the position in 1975 and, finding itself unable to sack Hewitt in 1976 – Hughes claimed to have 'cemented' the Hewitt appointment – the Fraser Government refused in 1980 to go beyond a 12-month extension. It was a time for old wounds to re-open. The former Secretary of the Prime Minister's Department under John Gorton had many enemies, and Hughes wrote in the diary that Fraser 'hates' Hewitt.[11] Hughes also believed that Phillip Lynch, the Deputy Leader of the Liberal Party, was tired of the political game and had 'cast covetous eyes' on the Qantas job: 'What a plastic person he is!' Hughes believed that Fraser, in 'inimitable fashion', leaked the 12-month offer to the media, causing speculation to grow. Together, Hughes and Hewitt prepared a letter stating Hewitt's reasons for rejecting the 12-month extension, offering instead to stay on for three months to ensure a smooth transition. Hewitt then made the mistake of going on television where, without mentioning the 12-month offer, he made the case for renewing his appointment for another five years. As Hughes put it, 'unhappily he did not consult me' before speaking out. 'His sworn enemy' (Fraser) could construe Hewitt's action as an attempt to appeal to public opinion over the Government's head. Next day the Government withdrew the 12-month offer. Hughes said that Hewitt should have refused the 12-month offer, stated his reasons for doing so as set out in the letter prepared with Hughes and made the offer to go on temporarily. By ignoring his legal adviser, 'Len was really left flat-footed' and 'the rug was pulled out from under him'.

In November 1980, the Commonwealth took a case to the High Court relating to the private publication of the book *Documents on Australian Defence and Foreign Policy 1968-1975*.[12] The book reproduced some leaked classified official documents, and the Departments of Foreign Affairs and Defence considered that their publication might damage Australian-Indonesian relations over the Indonesian invasion of East Timor in December 1975. Aware that the *SMH* and the *Age* intended to publish excerpts on Saturday 8 November, the Commonwealth persuaded Justice Anthony Mason in the early hours of Saturday morning to grant an *ex parte* injunction against publication. On the following Monday, Mason granted a further injunction forbidding the publication and distribution of the book. This second injunction arrived too late to halt the distribution of 662 copies to bookshops. Apparently, the Indonesian Embassy in Canberra bought a number of them. On 11 November, the Commonwealth subsequently sought an interlocutory injunction on the publication of the book and of excerpts from it.

Fairfax briefed Tom Hughes to appear before Justice Mason when the Commonwealth sought to continue the injunctions, and David Syme & Co Ltd briefed JL Sher QC to represent the *Age*. LJ Priestley QC, for the Commonwealth, told the Court that publication would breach confidentiality, copyright and the *Crimes Act*. On 11 November, 'the familiar, now rather gnarled figure'[13] of Hughes QC responded to each of these claims. In relation to confidentiality, he referred the judge to the High Court decision in the Sankey prosecution of Gough Whitlam, and its ruling that merely because a document was in a certain class, it was not conclusive on the question of privilege. In the case of copyright, the appropriate approach was to seek damages after a breach had been established. On the *Crimes Act*, an injunction in respect of an apprehended breach had to be at the suit of the Attorney-General, as guardian of the public interest; this part of the Commonwealth's case, therefore, was not properly constituted.

Justice Mason rejected the Commonwealth's claims of breaches of confidentiality and of the *Crimes Act*. He said it was 'unacceptable in our democratic society' to restrain the publication of information 'when the only vice of that information is that it enables the public to discuss, review and criticise Government action'. Mason, however, did uphold that publication of the material would contravene copyright. He remained unmoved by the Hughes and Sher arguments that the defences of 'fair dealing' and 'news reporting' would stand up in a hearing for breach of copyright. Yet, as Jack Waterford, Hughes' sparring partner in 1970 over possession of a Viet Cong flag, pointed out in the *Canberra Times*, the Commonwealth won on the weakest of its three legs in trying to protect itself from damages flowing for giving access to information. No one may directly quote the documents but could pass on the message in another form of words, for example, that a named senior public servant had advised the Government to lie about what was happening in East Timor.[14]

Hughes continued to reflect on the quality of judges and barristers he encountered in court appearances. He admired Howard Smith of the Supreme Court of Western Australia who was the presiding judge in the dispute over rights to 'The Mike Walsh Show'. He thought him 'urbane and pleasant … enjoying himself testing me out to the utmost, while being extremely polite in the process'. He was less than complimentary about Hutley and Glass JJA, two of the three members of the NSW Court of Appeal hearing the *Andrews case*. 'Hutley cannot stop talking' and Glass 'joins with him in cross-interruptions'. Worse, they 'try to ape the High Court by resorting to the Socratic dialogue; unfortunately they are an intellectually inferior breed of judicial monkey'.

Hughes formed a high opinion of Justice 'Bill' Fisher and, on the same occasion, one of Edward St John QC that simply reinforced the contempt he felt when St John attacked Gorton in 1969. Fisher presided over a drawn-out trial in 1980 arising out of the use of Deep Sleep Therapy at Chelmsford Private Hospital in Pennant Hills. Barry Hart, a former gymnasium proprietor, actor and male model, sued the hospital and a psychiatrist, Dr Herron, claiming he had been detained at the hospital in 1973 against his will, kept unconscious against his will and treated negligently and improperly. St John appeared for Hart, and Hughes represented Herron and the hospital. Hughes immediately applied for the jury to be discharged following what he called St John's 'mad opening', delivered 'with all the perverted zeal of which St John, with his total lack of judgment, is capable'. St John then proceeded to fight 'a desperate rearguard action' to ward off a discharge. 'He is a strange mixture of dishonesty, stupidity and sanctimoniousness; and demonstrates his complete lack of knowledge of the mechanics and techniques of a jury trial.' Next day, Fisher agreed to discharge the jury. Yet Hughes' mood did not improve. It was clear the re-trial was going to be drawn-out affair. The defence was ready to settle by paying $40,000 plus costs but the plaintiff was not interested, and had 'a zealot/fool/knave as his leading counsel and a senile oaf, SSW Davis, as junior counsel'.

Hughes also had complaints to make about his own side. At least Fisher kept the case 'on an even keel'. Importantly, in Hughes' mind, Fisher had a grasp of the rules of evidence and of basic trial practice. 'He is a man to be reckoned with but is becoming far too fat for his own safety.' Fortunately, Hughes had work commitments that enabled him to withdraw from a case that continued until mid-July and, in different forms, for another three decades.[15]

The 'extremely attractive Chrissie Abel Smith'[16]

Tom Hughes began a new relationship towards the end of 1980 that would become central and permanent.

Christine 'Chrissie' Hilda Taylor was born on 2 November 1941. Her father was an Adelaide stockbroker of English and Scottish extraction who, with his brother, had served in the Second AIF. Her mother was of part German background while her mother's father, in a profligate life, managed to avoid any form of employment. He did, however, fight in the Boer War with a South Australian contingent and, at one stage, served as ADC to the Governor of that State. The Taylor family – Chrissie had two much younger brothers – lived in a very large house on expansive grounds in the well-off suburb of Netherby. Christine had a pony, attended Unley High School and completed Leaving Honours despite the disruption of her final year, when she contracted encephalitis and her boyfriend died in a car accident. She travelled abroad twice and for extended periods, partly financed by casual jobs. Returning to Adelaide to be a bridesmaid, she met a divorced Englishman, John William 'Billy' Abel Smith, eight years older than Chrissie, a glamourous stockbroker, a former officer in the 10th Hussars and a cousin of Sir Henry Abel Smith, Governor of Queensland (1958-66). They married within three weeks. Chrissie saw Billy as 'wonderfully original' in the surrounds of Adelaide of the mid-1960s. In England, where they first resided, she realised that there were 'hundreds like him'. They had two daughters – Victoria and Georgina – but the marriage petered out, and they divorced in 1974.[17]

Chrissie had met Tom and Joanna Hughes at various parties in Sydney from 1968, and she met Tom again in 1980 when she was living at Darling Point. At that stage, after he had broken up with Phoebe, Tom was also seeing Susan Smith. Around Christmas of that year, Chrissie needed a partner for a fund-raising Ball she was helping to organise. Her current partner, who did not intend marriage, was overseas at the time. She rang Anne Sloan to ask if her employer was available. The return call was in the affirmative, a bunch of flowers arriving at Chrissie's house. A relationship developed very quickly; in Tom's case because he appreciated that Chrissie offered him more contentment and companionship, and more chances of permanence, than he had so far experienced. The couple married on Saturday 25 July 1981 at the home of Tim and Pru Allen. The Rev Ted Noffs of the Wayside Chapel performed the ceremony after first securing Tom's agreement to provide some advice to the notorious criminal Darcy Dugan, whom Noffs was always trying to help.

Instead of a reception, the Hughes gave a cocktail party at the Royal Sydney Golf Club on 29 July, the same day as the wedding of the Prince of Wales and Lady Diana Spencer. A number of the more than 200 guests drifted into an upstairs room to watch the televised Royal wedding. Chrissie did not know, or know well, most of the guests, mainly because they inhabited Tom's world: judges, barristers, solicitors, as well as notables such as Kerry Packer, John Howard, Bill Wentworth, Charles Curran, Harry M Miller, 'Jock' Pagan, James Fairfax and Bruce Gyngell; nearly all accompanied by wives. The Barwicks, Deanes, Killens and Gortons sent their apologies and so did Andrew Peacock. Kate Weigall was unable to attend, but Joanna was there and so was Deeta Colvin and her husband Rod McGeoch.

There were entries in the Hughes fee books for 27-31 July and for all of a busy August. Tom's second honeymoon had to wait for the end of the legal year when the couple went holidaying and skiing in Europe.[18] They lived briefly in Tom's house in Thomson Street, Darlinghurst – but with Michael and two daughters it was a bit crowded – and they jointly bought a house in Bathurst Street, Woollahra. The age difference of 18 years seemed unimportant. Besides, Tom continued to look younger than his chronological age. He had given up a long-term smoking habit at Chrissie's behest, kept fit with farm work and occasional running and swimming and a doctor had told him in March 1980 that his blood pressure reading would rate him A1 for life assurance purposes.

19

An 'exquisitely difficult case' and a 'difficult' client

At the end of 1984, a High Court judge (Lionel Murphy), a District Court judge (John Foord), a former State Labor minister (Rex Jackson), a former Chief Stipendiary Magistrate (Murray Farquhar) and a high-ranking police officer (Roger Rogerson) were all facing trial.[1] Although their guilt or innocence had yet to be determined, they had been subjected to intense media and public scrutiny and their cases had become highly politicised as questions were raised about judicial propriety and corruption in high places. Interviewed in November 1984, Tom Hughes expressed concern about a public perception of widespread corruption within the political and legal systems.[2] While he could not talk about the Farquhar and Murphy cases – he was representing both men – he did speak about the 'ill-founded campaign' conducted by the media against Neville Wran, the Premier of New South Wales (whom he later represented). Hughes pointed to 'obsessive suspicions' clouding public perceptions, and to the lack of evidence to back up the rumours and innuendos circulating about Wran. Believing that Australia was verging on a period of McCarthyism, he blamed the *Age* newspaper and the conservative Federal Opposition, and some of the happenings at the Costigan Royal Commission, where the legal rights of individuals, notably those of Kerry Packer, were not being protected.[3] Hughes found himself defending public figures who were also being tried by public opinion, and in circumstances where he had to insist that a public figure was entitled to the same rights as other individuals.

Hughes resumed his diary for part of this period and, along with letters and other personal papers, it provides further insights into his actions and attitudes while representing Farquhar and Murphy.[4]

Farquhar

On Saturday 30 April 1983, the ABC program *Four Corners* aired 'The Big League', an investigation into the administration of rugby league. *Four Corners* alleged that in 1977 Wran had influenced the then Chief Stipendiary Magistrate, Murray Farquhar, to drop a case against Kevin Humphreys, the secretary-manager of the Balmain Leagues club. Humphreys had been charged with misappropriating $52,519 from the club. In August 1977, Kevin Jones, the magistrate appointed by Farquhar to hear the case, cleared Humphreys of all alleged offences. Wran said he would sue the ABC for defamation, claiming the allegations concerning him were 'absolutely false'. The NSW Government appointed a Royal Commission, and Wran stepped aside for its duration. The Commissioner, Sir Laurence Street, the Chief Justice of New South Wales, cleared Wran of any involvement in the Humphreys case. He recommended, however, that Farquhar, who had stepped down as CSM in May 1979, be charged with perverting the course of justice and that Jones be granted immunity so that he could testify against him.

Murray Farquhar was born in Broken Hill in 1918 and, before the Second World War, worked in the Petty Sessions branch of the NSW Department of Justice. During the War, he served in 2/48th Infantry Battalion of the Second AIF, rose in rank from private to captain, and saw action at Tobruk and El Alamein, and in New Guinea and at Tarakan. After the War, he reached the rank of Lieutenant Colonel in the Citizen Military Forces. He studied law, and was appointed a Stipendiary Magistrate in 1962 and CSM in 1971. Professor Gordon Hawkins of the Institute of Criminology described him as 'one of the more enlightened and intelligent of the magistrates'.[5] In retirement, Farquhar published a biography of his friend in the 2/48th Battalion, 'Diver' Derrick VC.

During his final years as CSM, Farquhar found reasons for not committing some highly suspect individuals for trial. He also liked to punt on the races and his contacts included several 'colourful racing identities'. In June 1981, Farquhar sued Mirror Newspapers over articles published in March and July 1978 imputing he had a close association with George Freeman, a prominent Sydney criminal. Tom Hughes appeared for Farquhar in this case that ended abruptly on the third day in an out-of-court settlement on undisclosed terms.

Hughes became further involved in Farquhar's tribulations immediately after Farquhar and his barrister, Maurice Neil, the former federal Liberal member for St George and Hughes' colleague in 16 Wardell Chambers, learnt of Street's findings. Neil suggested that Farquhar needed a fresh mind on the case. After a quick visit to Hughes' chambers, Neil returned to say, 'Tom's … deeply concerned'. They went to see him. According to Farquhar's account,

Hughes said this was not the time for a briefing; instead, they demolished a bottle of scotch and arranged to meet again. Farquhar received a summons in August 1983 and Neil managed to secure delays by citing Farquhar's obvious stress and ill-health, and his need to get away from media harassment. Summonsed again in November 1983 for a preliminary hearing, Farquhar attended lengthy conferences with Hughes, later describing his leading counsel as 'certainly the epitome of the successful "silk" – debonair, trim, patrician'.[6]

Hughes appeared for Farquhar in December 1983 before Slattery J in the Common Law Division of the Supreme Court in a failed attempt to stop committal hearings due to be heard by Greville Reidy SM. Reidy, in common with all other magistrates, was currently under assessment for inclusion on the bench of the new Local Courts destined to replace the Courts of Petty Sessions. Hughes argued that Reidy would be considering charges related to the same matters upon which Street had adjudicated, and Street chaired the committee responsible for deciding the magistrate's future. Slattery J did not accept the argument nor, subsequently, did the Court of Appeal.[7]

On 9 February 1984, Reidy rejected Hughes' application to dismiss the charges and declared himself satisfied, on the evidence of five prosecution witnesses, that a *prima facie* case had been made out. The two key witnesses were Walter Lewer and Kevin Jones. Lewer, Farquhar's deputy, swore that Farquhar said to him on the morning of 11 August 1977 that the Premier had phoned to say he did not want Humphreys committed for trial. Farquhar asked Lewer to change the magistrate listed for the Humphreys case. He said Jones 'will do'. Jones said he was 'stunned' when Farquhar called him into his chambers on the same morning and told him, '[t]he Premier has contacted me, he wants Humphreys discharged'. Farquhar said he was not guilty and reserved his defence.

The case did not move immediately to trial and there was a further complication when Jones died of a heart attack in November 1984. His evidence, not contested at the committal hearing, was available at the trial in the form of a deposition. Hughes accepted the Farquhar brief, negotiating fees of $1600 a day with $12,000 in hand. After reviewing the evidence, he noted in his diary for 1 March: 'What a difficult case. The prospects are gloomy indeed.' The 'tragic aspect' was that Farquhar's written statement to the Street Royal Commission half-admitted the accuracy of Lewer's account of their conversation of 11 August 1977.

The trial began on Monday 4 March 1985 before Judge Muir of the District Court and with WH Gregory QC as Crown Prosecutor. Hughes thought the jury was 'a mixed sort': 'I don't know what to make of them.' There was an opening argument about whether the Jones deposition was admissible as evidence. Hughes considered admission inevitable, and it was indeed accepted. Lewer was the Crown's key living witness. Hughes thought him 'bitter and twisted'. Farquhar had beaten Lewer for the position of CSM in 1971, and Hughes sought to expose Lewer as bent on revenge. Lewer's evidence, he said in summing up, was 'unreliable and tainted', and the jury should 'evaluate the spleen and rancour in his sneer and his snarl'.[8] Hughes felt sure that Lewer's prejudice shone through during cross-examination, and he endured Lewer's occasional insolence because it matched the impression of the witness he wanted to convey. Hughes caught him out over inconsistencies between his evidence given at the committal hearing and now presented at the trial, and noted how Lewer 'recalled' conversations he failed to mention during the Street hearings. He hoped the jury would accept that Lewer had manufactured two conversations – 'each damaging to the accused' – that bore too close an affinity with Jones' deposition to be above suspicion.

Nevertheless, Hughes' problems were mounting. Lewer testified that Farquhar was once highly regarded but his reputation declined as his health deteriorated, as his interest in horse racing became 'very visible' and as his association with George Freeman became known. A number of retired or sitting magistrates backed Lewer on the subject of Farquhar's declining reputation. Hughes now noted in his diary: 'This is an exquisitely difficult case.' His own witness might have been more helpful. Lewer claimed that Farquhar's clerk, Cam Abood, had been present when Farquhar told Lewer about the Premier's alleged phone call and asked Lewer to change the listed magistrate. Abood denied he was in the room where the Farquhar-Lewer conversation supposedly occurred, thereby casting doubt on the reliability of Lewer's recollection, Yet Hughes felt that Abood was even more 'wishy-washy' than his performance at the committal because he 'is a wishy-washy person who wants to be all things to all men'.[9]

Friday marked the final day of the trial. Hughes thought he had never put so much effort into a final address, except for the Clive Lloyd case (see the next chapter). 'As I spoke, I sensed that my words were having an effect on 3 or 4 of the jurors, but others were very po-faced.' After the judge completed his summing-up, Hughes left for the Australian Club to have lunch with Roddy Meagher and Henric Nicholas 'to whom I revealed my fear about the result'.[10] At around 2.40 pm, back in his chambers, he wrote a note for Neil to pass onto Farquhar. Hughes wanted to explain why he could not be present at the verdict.[11]

> If you do not mind, I do not propose to take the verdict in this case. I hope you will understand why. Perhaps it is cowardly: but I do not think I could maintain my composure if the jury downs you. Mind you, I do not think they should; but life is a lottery.

> Wherever you go, you carry my best wishes. I appreciate the generous compliment you paid me this morning. I doubt whether it was deserved.[12]

Maurice Neil does not recall receiving the note. Hughes may have changed his mind, and left the message in his personal files. He was certainly distracted, telling his diary he could not work in the afternoon as the hours ticked by. He thought the chances of a disagreement grew until he turned on the 6.00 pm news and heard that Farquhar had been found guilty. 'I felt a bit let down, but then the case had all the inevitability of a Greek tragedy.' Later he heard the rumour that a majority in the jury room opposed conviction until persuaded otherwise by a very forceful juror.[13]

Tom went to a dinner that night hosted by Charles and Eva Curran. Curran, another Old Ignatian, 'immortalised' by the contrived tax avoidance scheme that bore his name, chaired the Greiner Government's Commission of Audit in 1988. The other dinner guests included some Labor identities – Graham Richardson, the McHughs and the Breretons – as well as Rowena Danziger, the long-serving Headmistress of Ascham School in Edgecliff, and Victor Chang, the cardiac surgeon who was later murdered. Hughes called it 'an interesting miscellany'.[14] It was a good way to wind down and move on.

On Friday 15 March 1985, Hughes made 'an unavailing plea for a deferred sentence'. He described Farquhar as 'very sick', a point brought home by the young doctor Hughes called in for support. Hughes also produced two QCs as character witnesses, one of whom said Farquhar had 'an impeccable character'. Yet, 'I was aware very soon after I started my plea that nothing could keep him out of gaol'. The *Australian* said Hughes made 'an impassioned plea'. He did not see it that way; he 'tried to keep it all in low key'.[15] Judge Muir sentenced Farquhar to gaol for four years with a non-parole period of 18 months and, because he had other cases, Hughes bowed out of any further involvement. The NSW Criminal Court of Appeal unanimously dismissed an appeal against the conviction and the High Court, by a 4-1 majority, rejected an application for special leave to appeal that decision. Released in 1986, Farquhar was acquitted in 1991 on a charge of receiving stolen paintings. In 1993, facing a charge of conspiracy to obtain false passports, he died of a heart attack.

Murphy: 'not an easy client'

In November 1983, when proceedings against Farquhar were under way, the *National Times* published an article sub-headed 'Big shots bugged'. It referred to alleged telephone conversations between a judge, an organised crime figure, a solicitor and police. On 2 February 1984, the Melbourne

Age published transcripts of telephone conversations allegedly and illegally recorded by the NSW police between 1978 and 1981. The two central figures in the '*Age* tapes' were Lionel Murphy and Murphy's friend Morgan Ryan, a solicitor who was facing forgery and conspiracy charges. On 28 March, the Senate appointed a select committee to inquire and report on whether this material was authentic and genuine and, if so, whether the conduct of the judge met the condition laid down by s 72(ii) of the Constitution. That is, judges of the High Court and of the other federal courts:

> Shall not be removed except by the Governor-General in Council, on an address from both Houses of the Parliament in the same session, praying for such removal on the ground of proved misbehaviour or incapacity.

The select committee consisted of three Labor senators – Michael Tate in the chair, Nick Bolkus and Rosemary Crowley – along with two Liberals – Peter Durack and Austin Lewis – and Don Chipp, Tom Hughes' Liberal colleague in his parliamentary life and now leader of the Australian Democrats.

The committee examined documents purporting to be transcripts and summaries of conversations and three cassette tape recordings purportedly of conversations, and decided it could not authenticate them. It unanimously cleared Murphy of all allegations arising from the '*Age* tapes'. The matter might have rested there, at least in the short term, but for the intervention of Clarrie Briese, Farquhar's successor as CSM. Briese believed that Murphy tried on two occasions in January 1982 to influence him into intervening with the examining magistrate in the Ryan case, culminating in Murphy's alleged question: 'And now what about my little mate?'

Briese tendered a written statement to the committee and gave sworn oral evidence. Justice Murphy received a copy of the Briese statement though not, initially, of his oral testimony. On advice from counsel, Murphy declined to appear before the committee. Instead, he forwarded a 28-page statement to the committee responding to Briese's written submission. Murphy's advisers used their client's statement to identify 24 'relevant' conflicts between the Briese and Murphy statements.[16] The aim was to raise questions about the accuracy or honesty of the Briese recollections, principally as they related to a dinner party he attended at Morgan Ryan's house in May 1979, and one held at the Briese home in January 1982. The question relating to 'my little mate' – variously regarded as innocent or infamous, as mis-reported or a question never even asked – was listed as no 23. Nearly all of the 24 'conflicts' went beyond slightly different recollections or slightly different interpretations; most of the differences were irreconcilable.

Tom Hughes first became involved in the Murphy case on 12 August, when he attended a conference of Murphy's legal team. It included David

Bennett QC, a future Commonwealth Solicitor-General, and his wife, Annabelle Bennett, a future judge of the Federal Court. The Bennetts had prepared a paper based on research into English and Australian sources arguing that the entire investigation was flawed.[17] A critical dilemma confronted the committee:

> If what is being investigated is the possible commission of a criminal offence, that is not a matter for a committee of the legislature. If what is being investigated is something less than a criminal offence, it is outside the scope of Section 72.

'In short', the Bennetts claimed, the Senate investigation:

> is quite inappropriate, an intrusion upon the independence of the Judiciary, a misconception of Section 72 of the Constitution and a denial of natural justice to attempt to interrogate a Judge whose conduct is being inquired into for the purposes of Section 72 as if he were an ordinary witness in a routine legislative inquiry.

Hughes, accompanied by the Bennetts, his juniors, as well as two instructing solicitors from Canberra, met the Senate committee *in camera* on 14 August.[18] After a short discussion of the tapes, Hughes moved briefly to the Briese evidence, providing the committee with a foretaste of his assessment of Farquhar's successor. He noted that the original version of the Briese statement given to Murphy excluded the last four lines where, drawing on his experience and coupled with material on the tapes, Briese said there was an 'inescapable' inference that Morgan Ryan and Murphy had advised or assisted Murray Farquhar in pursing illegal or improper activities. Hughes observed that the committee had not invited counsel to comment on an allegation amounting to Murphy being guilty of a criminal conspiracy. 'Mr Briese did not condescend to tell us exactly what it was', but Hughes guessed that the committee felt that this 'appalling allegation' was not 'worthy of any answer'.

Almost all of the remaining morning session focused on what Hughes described as 'a constitutional question of enormous significance'. The Parliament, he argued, had neither the power nor the jurisdiction to determine whether a federal judge was guilty of misbehaviour or to determine incapacity within the meaning of s 72(ii) of the Constitution. In addition, Hughes argued that the question of whether a federal judge was guilty of 'proved' misbehaviour or incapacity 'lay within the ambit of the judicial power of the Commonwealth and nowhere else'. 'Parliament's function begins when proved misbehaviour or proved incapacity – one or the other – is established by curial judicial process outside the Parliament … then the Parliament takes over, weighs the conduct and decides whether to address.'

Hughes dealt with the Briese evidence for much of the afternoon session. His core argument was that, in hindsight, Briese had constructed a conspiracy theory to replace what he had originally viewed as inconsequential or innocent occurrences or comments. This theory defied ordinary rules of evidence and was 'entirely conditional on the authenticity of the transcript of the tapes that he saw'. Just as in 1978, when he deconstructed Don Cameron's conspiracy theory aimed at Eric Robinson, Hughes showed how the Briese case was composed of connected assumptions and interpretations of otherwise innocent events and statements. Briese, Hughes argued, had resorted to the discredited technique of establishing guilt through proof of association; that is, Ryan was convicted of an offence and Murphy was associated with Ryan. But what if Ryan's appeal against conviction succeeded? Briese said he might then change his mind. Recounting this story, Hughes embraced both outrage and contempt: someone who engaged in such 'a shocking pollution of legal principle' was 'a fool', 'an utter fool'.

Hughes drew attention to a Briese remark that appeared to undermine the CSM's case. Senator Chipp had asked Briese whether he interpreted the alleged Murphy question about 'my little mate' to mean 'Okay Clarrie, I have done something for you, one for you, what about one for me, what about my little mate?'. Briese responded: 'I do not think you could necessarily interpret it that way …'. Hughes made the simple, effective point that, unless it *was* interpreted that way, the question did not involve any impropriety. When Chipp pointed out that Briese had been 'quite unequivocal' on another occasion, Hughes had the perfect riposte: can the committee make a finding on the basis of a 'bewildering array' of interpretations? As Hughes put it, the true value of the many Briese interpretations of the same event or statements lay in measuring the reliability of his evidence, not to mention the degree of his 'stupidity'.

Hughes concluded his argument with an attack on the entire procedure. He said that 'the elementary requirements of natural justice had not been extended to the judge'. Justice Murphy was entitled to the same rights as an ordinary person charged with an offence, and that included an entitlement not to speak until he had heard and tested the full range of evidence adduced against him. His counsel did not know who had been called as witnesses, nor how the '*Age* tapes' were regarded, and was not allowed to cross-examine Briese. When reminded by Senator Durack that he had not been given the opportunity of questioning Briese, Hughes replied, 'I feel that would be to his advantage'.

The Senate committee tabled its findings on 24 August 1984. The three Labor senators decided that the evidence was not of sufficient weight to warrant a *prima facie* charge of misbehaviour against Murphy; the two Liberal Senators concluded that a *prima facie* case had been established; and Chipp said that nothing could be decided until Murphy was questioned.

In September, the Senate appointed a second committee of four senators – Tate, Bolkus, Lewis and Janine Haines (Australian Democrats) – along with two retired judges to advise the committee on matters of fact and law. Theo Simos QC was appointed to assist the committee on matters of law, evidence and procedure. There was a significant rule change that allowed the examination and cross-examination of witnesses by counsel assisting the committee and by counsel for other witnesses. On the first day of public hearings, 24 September, Hughes sought the removal of the three senators who had sat on the first committee and hinted at a High Court challenge if they did not step down. He warned of his intention to petition the Senate for a change in the terms of reference if counsel for Briese, Murray Gleeson, was allowed to cross-examine Murphy, should he appear. He would also petition the Senate if Murphy's written statement and Hughes' submission given to the earlier inquiry were made available to Briese's counsel.

On Monday 1 October, Hughes told the committee he would not be pressing for the resignation of the three senators. Rather, he wanted to focus on procedural issues. He argued that, because his client was effectively on trial, safeguards should be introduced of the kind enjoyed by all individuals on trial. The committee should not roam far and wide, especially now that new evidence had come to light. Judge Flannery of the NSW District Court claimed that Murphy had referred him to a recent High Court ruling on conspiracy two days before the judge was due to preside over the Ryan trial. Ryan's counsel subsequently mentioned the case in his opening statement. Chief Judge Staunton of the District Court said Murphy had approached him to arrange an early trial date for Ryan. Given the increasing number of allegations, Murphy should immediately receive particulars of what exactly he had to answer.

Hughes insisted that counsel for other witnesses should not have the right to cross-examine Murphy, just as the chief prosecution witness did not have the right to examine other Crown witnesses or the accused. The committee must observe this principle; if it did not, the inquiry would degenerate, and be seen to degenerate, 'into an exercise in injustice'. Hughes would seek a hearing before the Bar of the Senate should it consider the issue of cross-examination or the question of giving counsel for Briese access to Hughes' submission to the first committee. The committee and the Senate must take a strong stand now: 'Otherwise we will be going down a path that is full of danger, and I'm [not] only thinking of my client. I'm thinking of the institution of justice in this country.' Despite these pleas, the Senate voted on 2 October to allow the cross-examination of Murphy. The Democrats voted with the Opposition to defeat a motion put by Tate, and effectively agreed to give witnesses Murphy's statement to the previous committee.

At least Hughes now had the opportunity of grilling Clarrie Briese. He began cross-examining him on 4 October. Janet Hawley in the *Age* on the following day called it 'vintage Hughes'. He 'poured on withering righteous indignation with long sweeping stares around the room, as Mr Briese, looked [sic] uncomfortable or downright annoyed, answered the unremitting attack of questions'. Characteristically, Hughes led him back and forth on particular issues – one of them being whether he had prepared his statement to the first committee carefully or in a rush – and Briese managed to give different answers at different times. In the main, however, the object was the same one Hughes took to the first committee. He wanted to show how Briese had allowed suspicion, conceived in hindsight, to place constructions on conversations that either did not have the support of hard evidence or were open to other interpretations.

On 12 October, Hughes explained why his client would not be appearing as a witness. He pointed out that the House of Representatives had adjourned indefinitely the previous evening and would be dissolved on 26 October. Even if the Senate committee found misbehaviour, the procedures envisaged in s 72 – removal by both Houses in the same session – could not be followed before the election, and so the Governor-General could not act on any recommendation. The Senate would be acting inappropriately, therefore, if it contemplated a removal before the expiry of this Parliament. To do so 'could be seen as a futile step taken solely for political reasons' and could also be seen as an attempt to pre-empt the role of the new Parliament. It was also clear that the committee's proceedings were being conducted 'in a highly politicised political environment and are being treated as a factor in the opening stages of a political campaign'. If Justice Murphy gave evidence, he could become a 'political football' and that would be 'intolerable'.

In these circumstances, Murphy thought it would be inappropriate to appear as a witness. Hughes continued: 'Few things could be more detrimental to the constitutional position of the Court than that one of its justices, not charged with any alleged offence and not the subject of any charge formulated by the Senate, should give evidence in the present circumstances.' Another, though less important, factor behind the decision not to appear was that the Senate, voting on party lines, had deprived Murphy of a fundamental protection available to any sole defendant in a criminal trial, namely, protection from multiple cross-examination. Finally, Murphy's participation would, or could, create a precedent that should never be tolerated in the relations between the judiciary and the Parliament. Hughes said his client refused to lend his aid to such a procedure and had instructed his counsel to say that 'Mr Justice Murphy categorically denies any misbehaviour and will, if necessary, insist on exercising his constitutional rights under s 72 of the Australian Constitution in the next Parliament'.

It was a strongly worded and forthright statement. Hughes delivered it without any hint of his disagreement with Murphy's stand. He believed Murphy made a mistake by not appearing before the second Senate committee, and giving up the opportunity to confront and quash the Briese allegations.[19]

Summing up on Monday 15 October, Murray Gleeson described Briese as 'decent, honourable and dignified' and said he had 'heaped coals of fire on his detractors'. Gleeson stressed how Murphy's non-appearance left many of the Briese allegations 'uncontradicted'. Briese 'had nothing to gain by coming forward with these allegations. He had a great deal to lose – he may have lost it.' Perhaps mischievously, Gleeson also suggested the committee might come to the view 'that five minutes of evidence from Mr Justice Murphy would have been of more assistance than a day of argument from Mr Hughes'.

Hughes claimed that Briese was 'gripped by suspicion' and suspicion, coupled with hindsight, had acted 'to corrode judgment and corrupt recollection' and render his evidence 'unreliable'. He did not want to accuse Briese of lying. 'But to say that a person is not a liar is not to concede that his evidence is reliable.' At the same time, Hughes was notably circumspect in his personal references to Briese, content to argue that, on the weight of probabilities, the Briese evidence could not be substantiated. Hughes reserved his strongest statements for the '*Age* tapes'. Briese, he said, had relied on unauthenticated material that was 'garbage emanating from the NSW Liberal Party to its great discredit'. The tapes constituted a 'farrago of fact, falsity and fiction'.[20]

Three members of the second select committee – Tate, Haines and Lewis – reported on 31 October that, on the balance of probabilities, Murphy did attempt to influence the committal hearings against Morgan Ryan. Lewis went further, arguing that the case against Murphy was proved beyond reasonable doubt. Bolkus concluded there was no case for Murphy to answer. On 13 December, Ian Temby QC, the Commonwealth Director of Public Prosecutions, announced that Murphy would be charged on two counts of attempting to pervert the course of justice in line with the Briese and Flannery allegations. Murphy said he had not committed any offence and welcomed the fact that the allegations would be tried by a judge and jury and not by the media.[21]

Murphy decided against using Hughes for the trial, and probably compounded Hughes' disappointment by preferring Alec Shand. On Friday 8 February 1985, Tom and Chrissie attended a dinner given by 'Australia's most fashionable couple',[22] the boulevardier Snow Swift and his publicist wife, Georgie. The Whitlams were also present. Hughes' diary reads as follows:

> Everyone was sparkling, the conversation rolled at breakneck speed. The food & wine perfect. Pink Bollinger before dinner. Gough agreed with me that Murphy is a graceless person.

A few days later, Hughes appeared in a case before the High Court, and earned a 'smiling' compliment from Gibbs CJ when Hughes apologised for taking an extra 10 minutes: 'we didn't stop you because your argument was entrancing us.' Hughes lunched that day with Anthony Mason, one of five judges hearing the case. Mason 'opened a very good bottle of 1978 Langhorne Creek'. Hughes learnt that Murphy had ceased to speak to Mason and 'Tony thinks it is because he is ashamed of his treatment of me'. Thirty years later, Mason had a slightly different recollection. He believes that Murphy refused to speak to him simply because he was Hughes' friend.[23]

Murphy's case was heard before Cantor J in the Central Criminal Court, Sydney, over five weeks in June and July 1985. On 5 July, a jury of eight women and four men threw out the charges relating to Flannery but found Murphy guilty of attempting to pervert the course of justice in his approaches to Briese. Murphy's lawyers immediately began planning an appeal, supporters rallied to his side and Bill Hayden, the Minister of Foreign Affairs, announced that Murphy was innocent. Academics and unionists, almost none of whom had attended any day of the trial, joined the chorus. The foreman of the jury went on John Laws' radio program to defend his fellow jurors and left listeners with the impression that the jurors were unclear about what they were doing and about what they had done. Murray Gleeson, speaking as President of the NSW Bar Association, was surprised that public figures felt free to comment on a case that was still before the court. Justice Yeldham of the NSW Supreme Court defended the jury system. He attacked Hayden, though not by name. He also referred to 'the spectacle' of 'a journalist', Malcolm Turnbull, asserting in a *Bulletin* article that there had been a miscarriage of justice, and included Turnbull in his general condemnation of 'lamentable and grossly improper comments'.

Murphy contacted Hughes on the afternoon of 8 July asking him to return to the case. He explained that his decision not to engage him after the Senate committee findings 'was made when he was "mad" as a result of the pressures on him'. Murphy may or may not have mentioned that Shand was actually unavailable because of previous commitments. The legal issues were mounting in number, and were further complicated when two other jurors wrote letters explaining their problems in reaching a decision. There were now so many angles to take that the Murphy camp had to hire more lawyers.

After negotiating a path through TV cameras and photographers, Tom Hughes walked into the Old Banco Court on Thursday 18 July. It was to be a 'strange' experience for him – cast, for the first time in 10 years, as junior counsel. Once again, his leader was Maurice Byers. Observing and admiring him, Hughes wrote in his diary:

> [Byers] is, in the best sense, an extraordinary character. His rotund ungainliness is the exact physical opposite to his acute mental ability, albeit it finds expression at times elliptically.

Observing them in court, the journalist Evan Whitton found it 'unclear who was leading whom'. The several changes in Murphy's legal representation did make for some confusion. At one point, Byers advised Cantor J that Shand had written the note Hughes had slipped to him. According to Whitton, Hughes murmured, 'Gone but not forgotten'. The journalist reported the next day that Hughes gave him a 'birching'. Hughes insisted he had said 'The misnomer is no dishonour'. It was 'unthinkable' that he would have used the reported words. The report, he said, was offensive as well as inaccurate, and he had apologised to Shand, describing him as a friend and former pupil.[24]

When Cantor 'bristled with hostility' after Byers raised the subject of a juror's letter, Byers 'was equal to the occasion and calmed him down'. Byers jousted well with Ian Callinan, who had prosecuted Murphy, as they argued over whether jury members could or should be recalled, and whether Cantor should declare a mistrial. For the rest of the day and the following one, discussion concentrated on the form of the legal questions to be reserved. Hughes, through Byers, believed he had put paid to any idea of sentencing Murphy before the reserved questions were determined. Two separate matters were to go to the High Court. One involved 21 reserved questions of law. The other raised questions about whether a magistrate in a State Court could hear committal proceedings for a federal offence, as a magistrate had done in the Ryan case, and whether legislation vesting federal jurisdiction in State courts was valid.

On Saturday 10 August, Hughes described in his diary how he spent the morning in chambers 'supplementing the tedious work during the week of putting together written submissions on the reserved questions of law'. He described Dermot Ryan, his fellow junior in the case, as 'a <u>very</u> hard worker' with 'a good, orderly mind' (emphasis in the original), an assessment which said much about the values of the assessor. Tom and Chrissie drove to Marsland on Sunday. The country looked 'good' after plentiful rain and the merinos were starting to lamb. Arriving at the High Court in Canberra on Monday, Hughes worked all morning on the case with a large team of barristers and solicitors, the latter including Clarrie Harders who, on retirement from the Public Service, had joined Freehill, Hollingdale & Page. Their case, on the constitutional issue, was that Murphy had been charged under a Commonwealth law that attempted to create an offence with respect to committal hearings. Committal hearings were not judicial in nature and therefore any law attempting to create a criminal offence with respect to them would be beyond the Commonwealth's legislative power to make laws with respect to the exercise of the judicial functions of the Commonwealth.

The case opened after lunch before six judges. The *Canberra Times* reported on 13 August that there were 13 barristers at the table, and almost as many instructing solicitors. Once again, Byers led the Murphy team, and Callinan led for the Crown. Dr Gavan Griffith QC, the Commonwealth Solicitor-General, intervened to support the validity of the Commonwealth legislation and Mary Gaudron QC, the Solicitor-General for New South Wales and a strong Murphy supporter, had also intervened. Looking about him, Hughes was surprised that the public gallery was not as full as he expected but decided that the 'dry atmosphere in this Court tends to drive people away, except the journos, the tourists and the true aficionados'. It bothered him more that 'Maurice was <u>not</u> at his best' (emphasis in the original) because of a painful leg injury he had received at the weekend. Perhaps Hughes' concern partly explains why Clarrie Harders 'could see Tom twitching at times, being almost ready to jump to his feet to either support or supplement what Byers was saying – not that Byers did a bad job. He did a magnificent job.'[25]

Hughes soon detected that 'Gibbs and Mason are clearly against us, the former because of "what he says" and the latter because of "how he looks"'. Even though Byers was in 'better shape' on the second day, and Mary Gaudron's 'presentation of argument has greatly improved', Hughes could see that the constitutional point 'is <u>very</u> unattractive to the Court [emphasis in the original]. Mason has the appearance of someone underneath whose nose there is a rotten and noisome smell. In terms of the purity of constitutional principle, how wrong they are.' The High Court rejected the constitutional challenge. It held that committal hearings relating to Commonwealth offences had a relationship with the exercise of the judicial power of the Commonwealth. The Commonwealth law that made it an offence to pervert the course of justice in relation to those hearings was a valid law. The Court returned the 21 reserved questions to the NSW Court of Appeal.[26]

The immediate question was whether it was appropriate to sentence Murphy while waiting for the Court of Appeal to make its decision. Callinan argued before Cantor J that it was in the interests of the community and of the administration of justice to complete the trial proceedings as quickly as possible. Hughes, now leading counsel, countered that sentencing Murphy now would do untold harm to his position. Publicity had harmed him over one-and-a-half years and a sentence might make a new trial 'a more difficult vehicle for ultimate justice'. After listening to two hours of legal argument, Cantor accepted the Callinan submission. Invited to speak, Murphy protested his innocence and said a properly directed jury would have acquitted him.[27]

On 3 September, Cantor sentenced Murphy to 18 months' gaol, with a non-parole period of 10 months, saying that this crime 'has done a terrible injury to the administration of justice' and for many 'has adversely affected and raised doubts as to the integrity and standing of every judge in this country'. Cantor compared Murphy and Farquhar, saying that 'here the prisoner was using and abusing a much more exalted office'. In passing judgment, Cantor observed that Hughes refrained from making any submission on behalf of the prisoner in relation to sentencing. 'This deliberate negative course adopted by senior counsel makes my task no easier.' Hughes also declined an invitation to respond to the Crown's and Cantor's interpretation of the jury's verdict, namely, that the jury agreed Murphy made certain statements to Briese, that it rejected Murphy's own evidence, agreed the prisoner had the guilty intention of attempting to pervert the course of justice and disbelieved the prisoner's contrary claim. Cantor J took one further step. He said this 'construction' of the jury's verdict 'is to some extent fortified by the attitude adopted by Mr Hughes of Queen's Counsel'. It was Hughes' duty to refute or attempt to refute this interpretation if the prisoner did not accept it as valid.[28] Cantor J's lecture and his admonitions did not trouble defence counsel: why make representations about a sentence he believed should have been postponed, or about a verdict he expected to be overturned?

The Court of Criminal Appeal began its hearing on 5 November 1985 before Street CJ, and Hope, Glass, Samuels and Priestley JJA. Hughes presented arguments on each of the 21 reserved questions of law and 19 grounds of appeal against conviction. One caused some merriment. Hughes referred to Cantor's rejection of the evidence of three witnesses who would have testified that Murphy had an aversion to the use of the word 'mate' in conversation. If, Hughes argued, Murphy had asked the alleged question in French, it ought to have been legitimate to show that Murphy did not speak French. When Hughes said he would not inflict his French on the Court, the Chief Justice insisted he do so. After hesitation, Murphy's counsel obliged: 'Eh bien, Clarrie, et maintenant comment va mon petit copain'. Hughes did not win this point. The Court decided that Cantor J correctly rejected evidence that Murphy did not use the word 'mate', because the evidence was too generalised or related to circumstances too dissimilar to have any probative value.

The Court delivered its unanimous verdict on Thursday morning, 28 November.[29] It quashed Murphy's conviction and, finding there had been significant misdirections of law, ordered a retrial. The Court ruled that Cantor J had erred by saying Murphy's character could be used to determine his guilt but not his credibility, by excluding the evidence of Murphy's wife and his secretary concerning Murphy's conversations with Briese and by giving 'confusing, misleading and erroneous' directions concerning motive and intention.

At the same time, the Court rejected seven of Hughes' arguments on the reserved questions, decided that a further eight did not need consideration, and disagreed with Hughes' severe assessment about the conduct of the trial and with his claim that 'justice demanded … this chapter of history be closed' by acquitting Murphy without a further trial.

While his supporters greeted Murphy outside the court as some kind of conquering hero, the journalist Errol Simper pointed out that in 'legal circles' Tom Hughes was being hailed as Lionel Murphy's 'judicial saviour'. Simper referred to Hughes' 'apparently flawless advocacy' and quoted another barrister who had followed the case: 'It's a throwback to 19th century English advocacy; it's an incredible education just to sit and listen to him.'[30] Clarrie Harders, who had worked closely with Hughes on the appeal, thought he put in 'one of the best performances as a barrister that I ever heard'. Hughes:

> worked hard on the case, he had all the case law at his fingertips, was able to joust with the judges on the earlier decisions and he far outshone his opponent … Callinan was a robust prosecutor, a robust lawyer, and I'm sure a good one, but he was not in the class of Hughes as an appellate counsel.[31]

Murphy sat behind Hughes during the hearings. He was either less than ecstatic or more than demanding. Once again, he dumped his counsel.

On 23 February 1986, Hughes wrote to an English friend, Hugh Griffiths (Baron Griffiths of Govilon PC QC MC). Griffiths had congratulated Hughes on his Murphy 'triumph', while noting that it was undoubtedly 'a considerable strain presenting his appeal'. Griffiths assumed that Hughes 'must be [Murphy's] first choice' for the retrial. Hughes explained that Murphy had chosen Ian Barker QC, 'whose principal claim to fame is his successful (at the time) prosecution of Lindy Chamberlain'.[32] Murphy, he wrote:

> is a curious person. After the result of the appeal was published, he went into a fugue of Hamlet-like indecision – a condition into which the poor fellow has not infrequently fallen. He couldn't make up his mind as to choice of counsel.

Hughes provided a range of dates for Murphy's solicitors, other dates being difficult because of the prepayment of 'availability' fees. In the event, the trial was fixed for 14 April 1986 and, though this date was affected by prepayment, Hughes could have made changes if Murphy had made up his mind sooner.

> Maybe he didn't want me anyway, because there is a school of thought according to which I am more inapt as a jury advocate than as an appellate one. Anyway, Chris is very relieved that I shall not have the

> strain of looking after him. He is not an easy client and would have wanted me to spend much more time on preparation than necessary.

Murphy was acquitted on 28 April 1986. More allegations surfaced and, in mid-May, the Commonwealth Government appointed a Parliamentary Commission of Inquiry. Three retired judges were to determine whether any of Murphy's conduct might amount to 'proved misbehaviour'. The Commission began proceedings in June with the intention of inquiring into 14 matters. The Government decided to abandon the inquiry, following the announcement that Murphy had inoperable cancer. After briefly returning to the High Court – his relations with Chief Justice Harry Gibbs were probably irreparably damaged – Lionel Murphy died on 21 October 1986, little more than a month after the death of Justice Cantor. Tom Hughes was one of the 'notables', as the *Sydney Morning Herald* put it, who attended the packed memorial service in the Sydney Town Hall on 27 October.

Four days later, Tom Hughes wrote to Murphy's widow, Ingrid. He was always solicitous when people he knew personally – whether they were close to him or not – experienced tragedy, sadness or any other misfortune. Like his closing arguments, he chose the words carefully.[33]

> For all of you the unjust ordeal of the past three years has been a journey through the darker extremities of human experience. Yet you and Lionel bore it with consummate dignity, a quality equalled only by the courage and endurance which marked all of you during a period of stress which no one should have undergone.
>
> I shall always have fond memories of Lionel. Although we spent the major part of our respective careers on opposite sides of one fence or another, there was never any rancour, indeed there was nothing but essential comradeship, between us.
>
> I counted it as a very considerable honour to be asked to appear as his counsel at several stages of his trial by ordeal.

This was not the time to speak the whole truth.

20

Four defamation cases

Tom Hughes' fee book for the mid-1980s indicates that he was always in work and always well-rewarded. In 1984, he could charge $2500 a day for court appearances, and two years later was charging $3000-$3250 on a regular basis, along with fees of up to $5000 for preparation and advice.[1] He was briefed to represent major companies – for example, Bell Resources, FAI Insurance and Ansett Industries – as well as briefs with television and newspaper interests and the racing industry. Settled and happily married, he could look upon his family with some contentment. Lucy and Malcolm had presented him with two grandchildren. Tom had advised and helped Malcolm early in 1980s, and took his son-in-law as his junior in some cases. On top of representing Kerry Packer at the Costigan Royal Commission, Malcolm had attracted further public notice because of the 'Spy Catcher' case, and was becoming seriously wealthy. Tom Jnr had married and decided to become a lawyer. Michael was progressing through university and making his name in student politics as President of the Sydney University Liberals. Anne Sloan had willingly answered Tom's pleas to return to the office after her departure in 1981 to deal with personal matters. A new manager took over at Marsland in February 1983 and proved such a 'find' that, at the time of writing, he is still managing Hughes' country estate.

In the mid-1980s, Hughes appeared in four high-profile defamation cases, and all figure prominently in his diary and other personal papers. He won three of them, one against Fairfax following the company's decision to brief another barrister. Two cases involved the reinstated Clive Evatt Jnr (it will be recalled that Hughes represented him when he faced disbarment in 1967), and in two of them Hughes was pitted against Neil McPhee, a leader of the Victorian Bar.[2] Two cases went to the Privy Council in October 1985. Both appeals had their origins in sport, both were important cases hinging on interpretations of the *Defamation Act 1974* (NSW), and both marked Hughes' final appearance before the Privy Council. Within a few months of this visit to London, Commonwealth, State and UK statutes came into operation abolishing all appeals from Australia to that court.[3]

Elizabeth Evatt

On 14 June 1985, Hughes was offered a brief to appear for Elizabeth Evatt in a defamation suit against John Fairfax and Sons. Evatt, a daughter of Clive Evatt Snr, and a niece of Dr Evatt, was the Chief Judge of the Family Court. She claimed to have been defamed in an article published by the *Sun-Herald* on 8 July 1984. Graham Gambie had undertaken a special investigation of the Family Court in the wake of the bomb explosion in the previous week that had killed Pearl Watson and injured her husband, John Watson, a Family Court judge. This outrage followed the earlier shooting assassination of Family Court judge, David Opas, as well as two other bomb attacks, and a number of death threats made against other Family Court judges. In the article, headed 'Shutting the door after the terror has bolted', Gambie reproduced some virulent writings attacking the Court. In one piece, Elizabeth Evatt was said to control the destruction of fathers' and children's lives 'with the same cold-blooded efficiency that Ilsa Kuhn and her like used in disposing of Jews in Auschwitz and Belsen'. Evatt contended that the article had exposed her to hatred and physical danger and that she had been shocked and hurt to be 'singled out as someone who had done infamous and inhuman things'. The specific imputations were that she was unfit to be Chief Judge of the Family Court of Australia; she had participated in destroying the lives of thousands of fathers and children; had behaved with the same cold-blooded efficiency as Ilsa Kuhn and her ilk; and had committed judicial frauds and was inhumane. The defence argued that the article was not defamatory, was a matter of public interest and was not likely to harm Evatt's reputation.

When approached, Hughes laid down one condition: Clive Evatt Jnr must withdraw from the case because 'it would be quite unseemly for him to be appearing for his sister'. Although Elizabeth Evatt was reluctant, 'Clive took it very calmly'. Alec Shand, originally briefed to lead Clive Jnr, acted 'with characteristic ruthlessness' by hanging onto the brief until 14 June, when he knew some days beforehand that the Murphy trial would preclude him from appearing.

From Hughes' perspective, his Fairfax retainer was the more serious matter. In July 1984, he had spoken to Graham Bates, a senior partner in a firm of Sydney solicitors and who did much defamation work for Fairfax. He told Bates he reserved his position about taking opposing briefs should Fairfax persist in hiring barristers other than himself. Fairfax had briefed Neil McPhee to lead its defence against Evatt. Hughes believed that Max Suich, then editor-in-chief of Fairfax's Sydney and national papers, was 'enchanted' by McPhee, whom Hughes regarded as 'an exceptionally able advocate' with 'a great power of persuasion'. Learning that Fairfax had briefed McPhee, Hughes rang Bates to remind him of their conversation a year earlier. He told Bates 'it has happened'. Bates responded with, 'Oh God'. Hughes told him he felt free to take the Evatt brief and 'Graham was, as usual, perfectly equable and understanding'.

The trial began on 17 June 1984 before Justice David Hunt and a jury of seven men and five women. Hughes made a short opening speech, concentrating on the tendency of the article to incite hatred and contempt. Evatt's evidence in chief was brief but McPhee's cross-examination, 'rugged and full of sneers', extended for six hours and 50 minutes. He wanted Evatt to admit that her hurt was 'contrived'. In response, she spoke 'calmly and with considerable dignity'. At one point McPhee suggested she had 'over-reacted' to the article. 'This was the breaking point: she wept, not for long; but her break-down, perfectly genuine I am sure, served to emphasise the cruelty of the cross-examination.' Hughes was an interested observer of McPhee's manner of conducting the case, seeing it as 'completely attuned to the taste of the wild men of Jones St [Fairfax]. I could never conduct a defence to this kind of case in the same way.' He also noted that McPhee's final address, lasting just over two-and-a quarter hours, 'was not lacking in misrepresentation, particularly inasmuch as he stated that I had sought to protect the Plaintiff from hard cross-examination on the ground that she is Chief Judge of the Family Court!'

Hughes spoke for 75 minutes and decided he had no way of 'reading' the jury. Hunt's summing up was 'quite favourable', though Hughes was concerned that the judge omitted one of his principal arguments. Hughes requested the jury's return and, when they finally retired in the late morning of 21 June, he attended a High Court hearing of special leave applications. He had two to oppose, and won them both. In one, he represented Fairfax in an application brought by Jim Cairns and Junie Morosi, Cairns' one-time chief of staff and lover. They were seeking damages over accusations and implications about what they had done together, about what they denied they had done, and about what in fact they actually had done. In the Evatt case, the jury returned with a verdict at 6.55 pm finding two imputations and awarded damages of $85,000.

Tom and Chrissie dined with the Currans and, after dinner, they went to a film through which Hughes 'slept in utter exhaustion'. But he had 'got a good result' for Elizabeth Evatt and also won something for himself, having bested McPhee in a head-to-head exchange, repaid Fairfax for dumping him, and collected a fee of $16,000.[4]

Lloyd v David Syme & Co Ltd

The first of Hughes' Privy Council cases, in order of hearing in London, involved Clive Lloyd, the West Indian cricket captain. Lloyd and many of his players had participated in the breakaway professional competition, World Series Cricket (WSC), organised and financed by Kerry Packer in the late 1970s. Although there was a rapprochement between WSC and the Australian Cricket Board in 1979-80, the former continued to influence cricket in Australia with the adoption of its marketing techniques, along with higher player earnings and links with sponsorship and Channel Nine. A WSC innovation – a three-team international series of one-day cricket matches – evolved into the Benson & Hedges World Series Cup as part of the Australian summer of cricket. Three international teams competed in a round robin series of one-day games (some of them day-night), and the top two sides played each other in a final series. Australia, the West Indies and Pakistan competed for the Cup in the summer of 1981-82. The West Indies under Lloyd easily qualified for the play-offs and Pakistan would have joined them if Australia failed to beat the West Indies in the last game of the round robin series. Lloyd had influenza and did not play in the match at the Sydney Cricket Ground on 19 January 1982. The Australians, led by Greg Chappell, chased 190 runs to win and had scored 7/168 with 41 balls left when the game was washed out. Australia was awarded the match because of a better run rate per over bowled.

On 21 January, David Thorpe, an English-born journalist, published an article in the *Age* under the heading, 'Come on dollar, come on', a clever take on 'C'mon Aussie, C'mon', the jingle first associated with Packer's WSC. Thorpe began with a quotation from F Scott Fitzgerald's *The Great Gatsby*, referring to the fixing of baseball's World Series in 1919: 'It never occurred to me that one man could start to play with the faith of fifty million people – with the single-mindedness of a burglar blowing a safe.' Thorpe pointed out that if the West Indies had won on 19 January and played Pakistan in the finals, crowd numbers, television ratings, gate revenues and returns from sponsorship would have been well down. The West Indies knew it did not matter if they lost. 'This thought edges perilously close to taking a dive.' Moreover, both sides and Packer's Channel Nine, with its exclusive television rights, might want the finals to stretch for the full five games. 'Somebody is playing with the faith of the people – with the single mindedness of a burglar blowing a safe.'

Incensed by what he saw as an attack on his integrity, Clive Lloyd sued the proprietor of the *Age*, David Syme & Co Ltd, for defamation. Kerry Packer provided the financial backing for his legal challenge. Tom Hughes, his retainer now amounting to $50,000 a year, appeared for Lloyd.[5]

The defendant applied for a separate trial pursuant to Part 31 of the Rules of the Supreme Court to determine whether, in its natural and ordinary meaning, the article as a matter of law was capable of conveying the imputations pleaded on Lloyd's behalf. There were four imputations: Lloyd had committed a fraud on the public by being a party to prearranging the result of a game for financial gain; he could be suspected of doing so; he would do so again in the future; or he could be suspected of being prepared to do so. On 21 June 1982, Maxwell J decided that the article was capable of bearing the four imputations pleaded.

The trial before Begg J, the Chief Judge at Common Law, and a jury of three women and one man, was held on 16-18 April 1984. Hughes' words and phrases were customarily robust. The allegations in the article were 'filthy' and 'atrocious', the article itself was 'a disgraceful piece of journalism', Lloyd had been defamed 'in a horrible and horribly serious fashion', and it would be difficult 'to imagine a more serious libel upon an international cricketer'. For the defence, Michael McHugh argued that the article did not refer to Lloyd by name, did not defame him, would not cause him harm, and expressed an honest opinion. Hughes and McHugh occasionally sparred, especially when the latter – over Hughes' objections – asked Greg Chappell whether he and members of both teams had also sued for libel. Hughes claimed that the question sought to influence the jury to reduce the damages awarded in this case because there may be other verdicts delivered against the newspaper. He pointed out there was no principle of law which laid down that if 'a large and powerful newspaper commits a bulk libel it is entitled to a discount on the damages payable'.[6] The jury awarded damages to Lloyd of $100,000 on the final day of the trial. A Victorian QC wrote to Hughes congratulating him on his win: 'That will set the smartypants [sic] of Spencer Street back on their heels for a while.'[7]

David Syme & Co Ltd took the case to the NSW Court of Appeal, citing 13 grounds for the appeal on account of the trial judge's judicial errors, and one claiming that the jury's verdict was 'excessive to the point of perversity'. Hughes and McHugh faced each other again over three days early in September 1984, and this time McHugh emerged successful. On 21 December, the majority, Glass and Samuels JJA, found that Begg J 'fell into a number of errors of law' when instructing the jury, and set aside the original decision and awarded costs against Lloyd.[8] The majority ruled that the article was not capable of conveying a defamatory message, that the statements in the article were expressions of opinion relating to a matter of public interest and that the statements were based on materials 'shown to be substantially true'. Critically, as Glass JA put it, allowing for the loose thinking of a lay reader, the words used in the article could not support the first and third imputations, since they involved 'an adverse reflection on the players' which the author disclaimed and which he achieved by using words that could not be applied to them. Priestley JA dissented, arguing that the article would convey to a reasonable reader that the West Indian team had joined a match fixing operation and would do so again.

In January 1985, the Court of Appeal gave leave for Lloyd to appeal its decision to the Privy Council. In June, however, the Court held that Lloyd could not appeal as of right because his solicitors had failed to comply with conditions laid down by the appeal court. The conditions included depositing $50 within 14 days as security for the cost of preparing appeal papers and a further $1000 within three months. Tom Hughes was unimpressed. He noted in his diary on 11 June 1985 that Kirby P, Mahoney and Priestley JJA 'would like to help but it is a hopeless situation'. He saw it as 'a paradigm case of solicitors who, getting too big for their boots, fail to do the work that makes big litigation go … Everyone wants to be a chief & disdains the necessary work of the Indian.' The problem was that a senior partner in Allens had left the matter in the hands of a young woman who was not up to the task.[9] Lloyd now had to petition the Privy Council for special leave to appeal.

Robert 'Bob' Alexander QC,[10] another of Hughes' good friends at the English Bar, handled the matter in London. After receiving two telephone calls from Hughes, Alexander wrote to him on 15 July to say the Board reacted very well when he told them that 'we' had a very good *prima facie* case on merits. 'For your private encouragement, Hugh Griffiths (who is now a Law Lord and was sitting) later told me privately that he thought that the Court of Appeal's decision was all wrong. Please do not tell anyone this – he may, after all, be sitting and also could change his mind.' Leave was granted and the hearing was set down for the beginning of October. Alexander wrote again, enclosing invitations for Hughes to attend a buffet supper at Gray's Inn on 30 September and for Tom and Chrissie to attend a function in the House of Lords on 1 October to mark the opening of the legal year.[11]

Austin v Mirror

The second action related to Rugby League. Ron Casey, a sports writer of strong opinions, had a regular column in the *Daily Mirror* featured as 'Casey's Corner'. On 27 April 1981, he claimed that Sydney's top rugby league players were 'being trained into the ground by over-zealous conditioners'. They had been hoodwinked by coaches into believing that three nights of 'tortuous conditioning' were needed in addition to an 80-minute match. Casey referred to Reg Austin as Manly's 'fitness fanatic'; under his conditioning, Manly had 'gone from being a great side to being a tattered band of former champions'.

Austin was not totally to blame but Casey advised Manly to sack him, while acknowledging Austin's personal achievements as a sprinter in world competitions for older athletes (in 2010 Austin was inducted into the Australian Athletics Masters Hall of Fame).

Austin complained that the article contained two defamatory imputations: he had conducted the conditioning and preparation of the Manly Rugby League team in a wrong and incompetent manner and was not fit to hold the position of trainer; and he was an incompetent conditioner of the Manly Rugby League team. Mirror Newspapers employed several defences in denying that the imputations were defamatory, relying in part on the defences of fair comment and qualified privilege. At the end of the five-day trial held in the Supreme Court in March 1983 the jury rejected all the defences except for qualified privilege, a defence reserved under the *Defamation Act 1974* (NSW) for determination by the judge. The jury awarded Austin damages of $60,000. But Lusher J held that the defence of qualified privilege had been made out and he overrode the jury's verdict. He held that the article consisted mainly of comment based on facts that were substantially true, placing himself in conflict with the jury's finding that they were substantially false. Lusher J also ruled that newspaper readers had an interest in the results of rugby league matches, on the performance of teams, players, coaches and trainers and related matters. That information could include comment and opinion as well as facts. He also found that Casey honestly believed that what he had written was true. After delivering his finding, Lusher J recalled the jury and directed it to bring in a verdict for the newspaper company.[12]

Austin said he would lodge an appeal. A superannuation tax consultant, he was having a break from training teams but had received offers from five clubs for 1984 and hoped to resume his relationship with the game. He felt the jury's finding had vindicated his training methods, and thanked the Manly club and others for their support. Maurice Neil, who had represented Farquhar and Austin, arranged a conference with Tom Hughes for 29 March, a week after Lusher J handed down his decision. Austin did appeal and the Court of Appeal heard the case on 7 and 8 June 1984. Hughes led Maurice Neil, and Henric Nicholas QC and John Sackar appeared for the respondent. Glass, Samuels and Mahoney JJA ruled on 23 August that the trial judge was bound by the factual findings of the jury and, because he had contradicted them, the Court was bound to find his reasoning erroneous and set his judgment aside. As the two parties did not want the expense of a further trial, they asked the Court to decide whether the defence had been established, paying regard to the jury's findings while itself deciding the primary facts as a prelude to determining the questions of qualified privilege. Glass JA decided that 'the conduct of the defendant in publishing the matter defamatory of the plaintiff was in all the circumstances reasonable and that the defence is made out'. The Court dismissed the appeal with costs.[13]

Austin did not intend to give up. Advised that the High Court would not grant him leave to appeal to its jurisdiction, he appealed to the Privy Council.

Two victories and a packed vacation

Tom and Chrissie decided to combine Hughes' appearances in London with an extended holiday. They left Australia on Friday 20 September 1985. Travelling first class on Qantas, they flew to Hong Kong where they did some sight-seeing and dined with several friends. Sir Patrick Neill, the Warden of All Souls, Oxford, was one of them. He had appeared against Hughes in a commercial case in 1976 that was settled on the doorstep of the Privy Council. Kerry Packer laid on a limousine to meet his leading counsel at Heathrow on 25 September, and Tom and Chrissie went to the Savoy Hotel, Hughes' base during the appeals. He kept a full diary for this period overseas. Along with accounts of the appeals, the diarist recorded outings and travels with Chrissie, meetings with new and old friends and visits to restaurants and meals taken and costs incurred (an 'excellent meal' at Boulestin on 27 September, where they took Bob and Marie Alexander, was 'quite expensive – £135-70, incl service').

John Sackar, Hughes' junior for the Lloyd case, arrived in London on 26 September and the pair immediately settled down to work. On Tuesday 1 October, Tom and Chrissie attended the special service at Westminster Abbey to mark the beginning of the English legal year, a ceremony dating from medieval times. Afterwards they joined some 140 other guests at the Lord Chancellor's Breakfast. Next morning, Hughes went to 9 Downing Street, the home of the Judicial Committee of the Privy Council, for the first day of the Lloyd appeal. He appeared before a Board comprising Lords Keith of Kinkel, Elwyn-Jones, Diplock (obviously ailing), Roskill and Griffiths. The team representing the *Age* was substantial. Neil McPhee QC led an English junior from Robert Gatehouse's chambers and Ruth McColl from the Sydney Bar, backed up by a number of English and Australian solicitors and 'at least two acolytes'. Hughes led one junior, Sackar, and, '(by) contrast [with the numbers on the other side], we were instructed by a very agreeable para-legal from Linklater's [sic], who organised an excellent lunch'.

Hughes felt they got off to 'a good start'. He had the impression that 'they are with me on the imputations'. On the question of comment, however, 'the going was a little sticky'. But they all seemed attracted to the idea that a new trial would be inappropriate in view of the interrogatory answer in which the defence said it did not intend to convey the imputations. Hughes finished at

3.45 pm and McPhee made an inauspicious start by attempting to tender two copies of the original newspaper. 'All in all a good day. They did not want to hear me in chief on a number of points.' Tom and Chrissie had dinner that night in an Italian restaurant with John Sackar and Henric Nicholas. Hugh Griffiths delivered a note saying how delightful it was to see Tom and Chrissie at the appeal, 'and to listen to you'. He was about to go to Cyprus but suggested they go to the Garrick Club for dinner after he returned.

On Thursday it soon became clear that 'we are alright on imputations'. On comment, the board warmed to the idea Hughes had implanted on the previous day: the interrogatory denying intention to convey the imputations was decisive against a new trial. Everything was 'looking very good' by lunchtime. 'When poor Neil McPhee got to the question of identification' – claiming that the article could not and did not refer to Lloyd – 'they began to get quite short with him. Diplock said he was wasting time; and even the urbane Hugh Griffiths said that the argument was an affront to common sense.' McPhee came to a halt at 3.15 pm and all counsel and solicitors were invited to leave the room. Called back after 10 minutes, the Board asked Hughes to reply on just one point: did the denial that the article intended to convey the imputations amount to evidence that David Thorpe (the servant) who wrote the article did not hold the opinions represented by the comment? Diplock especially wanted to hear Hughes on this point, and Hughes took just five minutes to deal with it. McPhee jumped to his feet and tried to 're-agitate' the point by citing a case not previously mentioned; at this stage 'he had really lost the place & lapsed into confusion'. Hughes was asked if he wanted to say anything more. Before he could speak, Diplock intervened: 'Do I win my bet – is that case irrelevant?' Hughes said it was and sat down.

'The people on the other side spoke to us outside and congratulated us on winning.'[14] Ian Robinson, the in-house lawyer with David Syme & Co Ltd, 'was particularly gracious'. Graeme Brister, a partner at Linklaters, took the winners to Leith's in Kensington, 'a very good restaurant – and very expensive'. Next day, Friday 4 October, Hughes noted that Maurice Neil had not arrived for the Austin appeal – or, if he had, did not show up. Hughes worked all morning and most of the day on Austin. He and Chrissie then entertained guests who arrived for a celebratory drink: they included Clive Lloyd, Bob and Marie Alexander and John Sackar. Between them, they drank the three bottles of the Moet et Chandon Chrissie had bought at £14.50 each. The party broke up when Tom and Chrissie went to see the Tom Stoppard play *Jumpers* with Felicity Kendal in the lead role. The plot was 'incomprehensible' with a 'sort of stream of consciousness dialogue', but the gymnasts were 'very good'. After dining late at a small brasserie near Aldwych, Hughes learnt that Neil had rung to say he had arrived early in the morning. He had been with the instructing solicitor and thought everything 'seemed to be in good shape'. Tom had one word for his diary: 'Phew!'

Over the weekend and on Monday, and in addition to working with Neil at the Privy Council, Hughes lunched and dined with friends and new acquaintances. Among the latter, he met Piers Dixon of Eton, Cambridge and the Harvard Business School, a former Conservative MP and a one-time member of the right-wing Monday Club.

The Austin case began at 10.15 on Tuesday 8 October. Lord Hailsham, the Lord Chancellor, sat with Lords Diplock, Keith, Roskill and Griffiths (back from Cyprus). Hughes knew it would be 'closer to the line' than in *Lloyd's case* but Neil was 'reasonably confident'. The diarist was struck by Hailsham's 'mental agility', and noted he was troubled by the question of whether the defendant intended to convey the imputations, and 'described it as a catch-22 question'. Even so, Tom thought the argument went well. Their lordships agreed it raised as a significant question the proposition that 'it cannot be reasonable to publish defamatory comment which cannot be defended as such'. Diplock, 'more frail than last week' (he died six days later), tended to regard the question as devoid of content. 'But he is disposed to listen to me. He and I obviously have a degree of rapport. Even when he is not disposed to agree with me, he is unfailingly polite. More than can be said of his performance with McPhee last week.'

Hughes thought that, at the end of the day, Keith ('certainly'), Roskill and Griffiths ('probably') were running with his argument. Hailsham was in 'a state of equipoise' and Diplock was 'probably contra'. At one stage in the afternoon, the Board sent the legal teams out of the room, and then called them back, but made no announcement. 'The ball is still therefore in play.' Henric Nicholas began his submission the following morning and spoke for just under two hours; he 'did it very well but left a number of points untouched, as perhaps he had to'. Hughes replied for two hours and felt he made 'some good points' and, like the rest of 'our camp', thought 'we are just in front'. Hailsham appeared impressed when Hughes cited authorities that indicated a dividing line between giving information and making charges of misconduct. Another of his points seemed to appeal, particularly to Griffiths: in determining whether people have an 'interest', you must have regard to the nature and quality of the 'information'. In the evening Griffiths told Hughes over 'a most agreeable dinner' that he was writing the judgment. Maurice Neil has nothing but praise for his leader. Hughes, he recalled, was 'outstanding', handling so many complex points relating to qualified privilege 'very, very well'.[15]

The result was a clear win for Reg Austin, who recovered the original award of $60,000. Their Lordships decided that 'the critical issue' was whether, in all the circumstances, it was reasonable for Casey to write, and his employers to publish, an article 'which contained a wholly untrue description of the appellant's training methods and on this basis to comment in such hostile terms'.[16] They concluded that 'slipshod journalism' – which included misquoting and misrepresenting another journalist as well as reporting untrue facts – did not entitle the defence to 'the shield of qualified privilege'. Reflecting later on the two appeals, Hughes observed that:

> In one case the plaintiff was supported by the financial might of the Consolidated Press organisation. In the other Austin was a litigant with no financial backing, who decided as a matter of principle to fight the case out to the ultimate tribunal and his courage was properly rewarded.[17]

On the day after the Austin appeal concluded, Tom and Chrissie travelled to West Sussex to stay with friends, and then flew to Jersey, the largest of the Channel Islands, to visit David and Margita Wheeler. The Wheelers had lived in Sydney for three years and David, a pioneer of the offshore hedge fund industry, had moved his operations to Jersey. The Wheelers' home had served as the residency of the German Commandant during the Nazi occupation in the Second World War. Tom's visit to the museum at Jersey 'did nothing to allay my sentiments about Germans'. Chrissie and Tom then spent a week driving through the Brittany, Normandy and Picardy regions of north-western France followed by a few days in Paris.

Hughes was back at work in Sydney on Monday 28 October. He joined Jim Spigelman, Dyson Heydon and others to prepare an application for Rupert Murdoch to go before the Australian Broadcasting Tribunal. Next morning he worked on both the Murdoch and Murphy matters. Setting out for lunch in the company of Heydon and Murray Gleeson, he encountered Barwick in the street and talked briefly about Diplock's death, Barwick describing him as someone who had no interests outside the law and hunting. The former Chief Justice then launched into a criticism of his successor, Harry Gibbs, for lacking firmness in coming to a conclusion. Hughes noted in his diary: 'The old leopard has not changed his spots and never will.'[18]

Seidler case

In the course of his letter to Hugh Griffiths of 23 February 1986, telling him that Murphy had once again dispensed with his services, Hughes raised two other matters. One concerned Lindy Chamberlain, who had been released from serving the balance of her life sentence. He told Griffiths there was now to be a full judicial inquiry. At a dinner party before Christmas, Hughes had fallen into a discussion with two fervent Chamberlain supporters – Barwick and Bill Wentworth – and the latter, 'a brilliant (but erratic) crusader in many causes', was then organising a movement to back Chamberlain at a political level. On the day of her release, Hughes telephoned a member of the Opposition Shadow Cabinet urging him to stir his colleagues into action. In his opinion, one of the features of the trial 'was that it became a sort of stadium for the unleashing of that nasty animal – Northern Territorian prejudice against people from the Southern and Eastern parts of Australia'. Chamberlain was well defended by a 'competent man', John Phillips QC from Melbourne and a future Chief Justice of Victoria, and the trial 'became at one level a personal contest with overtones of localism'.[19]

The second matter was the defamation suit brought against Fairfax by the famed architect, Harry Seidler.[20] The libel itself had arisen out of a cartoon by Patrick Cook published in the Fairfax-owned *National Times* on 15 August 1982. As Hughes explained to Griffiths, the cartoon depicted roof-less box-like structures dotted around an arid landscape. Each box had an aperture at the front and food was delivered on a tray; at the back was another aperture through which excrement was being shovelled. Inside the box, like a prisoner, was a hopeless-looking individual. The caption read, 'Harry Seidler Retirement Park'. The defence had argued that the cartoon and the caption were comments on the plaintiff's architecture, and the jury found in favour of the defendant. Hughes added in his letter that it was accepted as common ground that Seidler had never designed a retirement park.

The trial, held before Justice Miles and a jury of four, lasted seven days, concluding on 26 June 1984. The original claim was that the cartoon conveyed three imputations, each of them defamatory to the plaintiff: he had been brutal and anti-social; he lacked aesthetic sensibilities; and he was incompetent as an architect. The jury agreed that the cartoon conveyed the imputation that the architect lacked aesthetic sensibilities and was defamatory of him. At the same time, it found that ordinary readers of the *National Times* would have seen Cook's cartoon as an expression of opinion. The expression of opinion was one an honest man might have made on material upon which the cartoon was based. The defendant had established that Cook's comment expressed in the cartoon was based on proper material for comment. In accordance with this verdict, the judge directed a finding for the defendant.[21]

Twenty-one years after this trial, Hughes pointed out in a talk at the NSW Art Gallery how, in a sworn answer to an interrogatory, Cook said he did not hold the opinion represented by the comment.[22] In Hughes' view, this answer should have destroyed the defence. At the trial, however, the matter was put to Cook again, thus giving him the opportunity of saying he did hold the relevant opinion. The jury, therefore, had the choice of accepting Cook's written statement or his oral evidence as representing his true state of mind. The jury accepted his oral testimony.

Hughes had represented Seidler and Harry Seidler & Associates at the Court of Appeal in March 1986. The main issue was whether the trial judge had erred in submitting the defence of comment to the jury. Hughes put forward three arguments on behalf of his clients. First, the jury's verdict affirming that the cartoon said the plaintiff 'lacked aesthetic sensibilities' could not be held as comment. Secondly, if it were held as comment, the jury did not sufficiently state the facts on which the comment was made. Thirdly, if it did state the facts, one of them – that the plaintiff had built or designed a retirement village of the relevant kind – was false.

The Court, comprising Hope, Glass and Mahoney JJA, unanimously rejected these arguments. Glass JA focused on the third of Hughes' submissions. He found it was open to the jury to determine that the reference to a retirement park was fictitious and not a factual assertion about Seidler's architecture. A cartoon of this sort was bound to range through caricature and fiction and ordinary readers would not regard it as literally true. The jury must have decided that the cartoon made its comment on Seidler's architecture by representing the retirement village in allegorical form and of the kind an architect lacking 'aesthetic sensibilities' would design. Consequently, the judge was not in error 'in ruling that the jury was not bound in law to find that the cartoonist was misrepresenting the facts by alleging as a fact that the plaintiff had ventured into that particular field'.[23] The appeal was dismissed with costs. After three significant defamation victories in the previous year, it was a disappointing result, and Hughes remains convinced that the Court was wrong.[24]

21

'The venerable lion of the Sydney bar'

The takeover frenzy of the 1980s and the stockmarket crash of 20 October 1987 provided Hughes with many financially rewarding briefs from banks, major media organisations and insurance, construction, finance and industrial companies. He represented or opposed most of the prominent corporate raiders in these years in cases requiring weeks of preparation and court appearances, sometimes ending in stalemates and out-of-court settlements. In the 'heady' days before the crash, he appeared for Rupert Murdoch who had set his sights on the Herald and Weekly Times of Melbourne, and for Robert Holmes à Court, who wanted to take over BHP and much else besides. The crash opened up a different source of employment instigated by bankruptcies, investigations, negligence actions and a myriad of company restructuring schemes. As one commentator pointed out, the realities of corporate life meant that when 'the economy goes bust, the demand for lawyers goes up'. He predicted that, far from experiencing the after-shocks of the crash in the form of recession, QCs were 'about to enjoy a bonanza'.[1] Tom Hughes certainly benefited, and his immediate post-crash briefs brought him into contact with 'Young Warwick' Fairfax and 'Laurie' Connell, whose business activities occupied newspaper columns, television news and commentary for months on end in 1988-90.

Meanwhile, Hughes the all-rounder continued to appear in many jurisdictions and in a variety of cases. His name was constantly in the press because he represented individuals who were always in public view or had brief moments of fame or notoriety. In 1990, Hughes won $100,000 for a dentist in the WA Supreme Court for being defamed by Channel Seven and Derryn Hinch, with Hughes at his persistent and vigorous best in portraying Hinch as arrogant and reckless.[2] Between June and August 1990, he represented Darren Brennan at a NSW Police Tribunal inquiry. Brennan, naked and unarmed, was shot in the face during a pre-dawn police raid on his home in Glebe. The NSW police did not emerge well from this and other very-public inquiries in 1989-90 and, in Brennan's case, Hughes highlighted the falsification of a search warrant that amounted to 'a most grave irregularity'.[3]

In November 1990, Hughes appeared for Jane Makim, the older sister of Sarah Ferguson, Duchess of York, in a defamation suit against Nationwide News. He invited the jury to join him in outrage: a false and 'scandalously defamatory' article in the *Sunday Telegraph* imputed that Makim had conducted an adulterous relationship with an Argentinian polo player and implied she was 'a promiscuous adulteress … a slut, a multiple adulteress … Can you imagine anything more shocking than to say that falsely about a decent woman?'. Makim was awarded $300,000.[4] In 1991, Hughes successfully defended Coopers and Lybrand in an action brought by Bart Cummings, the legendary horse trainer. Wilcox J in the Federal Court found against Cummings, whose rambling, if amusing, replies in his cross-examination had Hughes insisting he observe the 'Golden Rule', namely to give 'Yes' or 'No' answers to 'Yes 'or No' questions.[5] On a different level, Hughes appeared in two high-profile defamation cases in 1989 and in 1992-94 that raised questions about the appropriate compensation for damaged reputations, about the correlation between damages awarded for defamation and those awarded for personal injury and about the wisdom of allowing juries to assess damages.

In the period between the mid-1980s and the mid-1990s, the media often referred to Tom Hughes as 'a top silk', sometimes as 'the top silk'. Two journalists in the *Australian* in 1989 said he was 'generally accepted as leader of the Australian Bar'. In 1990, Mike Carlton called him 'the venerable lion of the Sydney bar'.[6] When a newspaper won a defamation action in the Australian Capital Territory for the first time in 28 years, its Deputy Editor, Jack Waterford, described the paper's counsel as an 'ageing war-horse'. The newspaper hastened to publish a 'clarification'; to call Hughes an 'ageing war-horse' meant no more than saying he was 'a very senior and experienced counsel'. He was also probably Australia's most expensive senior counsel. By the end of 1986, Hughes was regularly charging $3000-$3500 a day; 10 years later, he could ask for $6000. In 1996, the year he turned 73, Hughes' fee books recorded total charges of $1,582,015. The books also indicate that, except for brief holiday breaks, he was never without work.

As head of 16 Wardell Chambers in Martin Place, Hughes presided over a distinguished floor to which Bob Ellicott, the former Solicitor-General, added further prestige when he returned to the Bar after leaving the Federal Court in 1983. Malcolm Craig QC, who was appointed to the Land and Environment Court, saw them as 'two great exemplars of the barrister's craft'.[7] They may have come from different socio-economic and cultural backgrounds but they worked well together in the Gorton years, when

Hughes and Ellicott jointly tested the limits of Commonwealth power. They were together again in 1991, circulating a letter to all members of the NSW Bar Association deploring the emergence of voting 'tickets' for the coming Council elections.[8] Unity was essential when facing 'the current hostility in some quarters towards [the Bar] as an institution'. The two men, however, may not have had the same approach to leadership. Hughes cast many pearls of wisdom in Craig's direction but one proved 'particularly pertinent' for a future head of chambers. After Hughes had quickly terminated a hearing of a barrister's grievance he said: 'You know, Malcolm, there's only one way to govern a floor of barristers and that is by doing so as a benevolent dictator.'

Robert Holmes à Court

Although the 'top silk' took well-remunerated cases on both sides of the Australian continent during the 'heady' 1980s, he had mixed feelings about the adventurers from Western Australia. His contact with Robert Holmes à Court did not have a pleasant conclusion.

Holmes à Court, born in South Africa and a law graduate from the University of Western Australia, proved to be the sharpest and the shrewdest of the corporate raiders of the 1970s and 1980s.[9] Hughes first appeared for him in 1981, when Holmes à Court pulled out of a takeover bid while collecting a profit of $16 million. Hughes represented Bell Resources, part of Holmes à Court's Bell Group, when Holmes à Court launched his second takeover bid for BHP in 1985-86. He again represented him at the Australian Broadcasting Tribunal in May 1986, when the Tribunal had to decide whether the entrepreneur was 'a fit and proper person' to have his radio licences in Western Australia renewed. Hughes' most significant association, however, began in October 1986.

Holmes à Court had acquired an interest in Oil Basins Ltd (OBL), after taking over its operator, Weeks Petroleum Ltd. In 1960, BHP had agreed to pay OBL's predecessor, Oil Basins Inc, an overriding royalty of 2.5 per cent of the gross value of all hydrocarbons produced and recovered by BHP within what became the Bass Strait oil field. The dispute between OBL and BHP (and its partner in a joint venture, Esso) centred on whether BHP could deduct its payments of excise duty when calculating gross value. At the time, Holmes à Court was a member of the BHP board. Initially, the case was heard in the United States because OBL was a Bermuda-registered company. It was subsequently moved to Melbourne because OBL's sole active business was located there.

Hughes did preparatory work on the case in the United States in the last two weeks of April 1987. In Melbourne, he spent virtually the whole of

May and much of June with his formidable team of QCs and a very talented junior, Neil Young, opposing Murray Gleeson who led Esso-BHP's team of four QCs. Although the three arbitrators – Lord Roskill, Bob Ellicott QC and an American judge – ruled in favour of Esso/BHP in August 1987, Hughes assumed he would be briefed for any further litigation. On 30 September, Alan Newman of Weeks Petroleum Ltd thanked him for his efforts. He noted Hughes' advice that an appeal to the Victorian Supreme Court over the excise tax issue could place the arbitrators offside. Nevertheless, Weeks Petroleum and OBL felt they could not forgo a last opportunity to prevail. The solicitors had advised that the appeal could be a relatively simple matter being limited to law rather than facts and, this being the case, Weeks Petroleum wanted the matter handled by a smaller Melbourne-based team of barristers. Newman added, 'I am sure you can see the wisdom of the decision'. Hughes took comfort in learning that his removal had nothing to do with 'inadequate performance', but his 'disappointment' was 'real' because 'the development of the excise argument, both in writing and orally, was very much the brainchild of Neil Young and myself'.

Young wrote to Hughes on 2 October, calling his removal 'a miserable decision' and 'wholly contrary to OBL's best interests' to retain only himself and another barrister. Young told Hughes how much he liked working with him. 'I learned a tremendous amount about the advocate's art' and did not believe that OBL's case could have been put 'more lucidly or more powerfully'. Hughes replied with a handwritten note four days later:

> I was greatly touched by your kind and generous letter which has done much to restore my spirits. As you rightly imply, the decision to sack me has been taken by a client who knows nothing of the way the argument was presented and regards all lawyers as expendable scapegoats to be thrown overboard to gratify petulant disappointment. Your approbation means much, much more to me than any that he [Holmes à Court] might have chosen to bestow.

Hughes said he really enjoyed working with Young, who had been 'unstinting' in giving time to the case, and who 'made me realise how much a good junior of your industry and enormous intellectual capacity can mean to a leader'. Hughes hoped the two barristers would do more cases together, but 'a sense of realism' compelled him to accept that 'you will not remain much longer in the ranks of the juniors'. He urged Young to stay with the case because, in that way, 'the client will get such residual benefit as it deserves from our joint labours'.[10]

Hughes might have been surprised to learn from the *AFR* of 3 July 1986 that he was 'a close friend' of the corporate raider. He saw Holmes à Court as 'a cold fish' who treated those he employed as his private property.

Hughes believes he was dumped from the OBL case because he led Rupert Murdoch's legal team when Murdoch out-manoeuvred Holmes à Court in the takeover of the Herald and Weekly Times.[11] If, indeed, Hughes' removal was payback, then Holmes à Court clearly observed the truism that revenge is a dish best served cold. After all, the Murdoch takeover was completed in February 1987, and OBL paid Hughes just over $200,000 in fees and expenses between February and the following August before sacking him. Perhaps Hughes was 'thrown overboard to gratify [a more recent] petulant disappointment'.

'Young Warwick' and 'Last Resort Laurie'

Hughes represented the interests of another Perth entrepreneur, Lawrence Robert 'Laurie' Connell, in a case involving the 26-year-old Warwick Fairfax, Sir Warwick's son by his third marriage. On 30 August 1987, 'Young Warwick' launched a bid to take over and privatise John Fairfax & Sons Ltd. His principal qualifications for the task were the family name, the support of his mother (Lady (Mary) Fairfax), his devout Christian faith, an education at Oxford and Harvard and some work experience at the Chase Manhattan Bank and the *Los Angeles Times*.[12]

To acquire the company, 'Young Warwick' first needed to buy out the family's shares at a time when prices were rising and other predators, including Robert Holmes à Court, were reportedly circling. After the stock market crash of October 1987, he had to pay for shares at pre-crash prices. But the ANZ Bank was a willing lender, and Warwick had enlisted three men – Martin Dougherty, a public relations consultant, Bert Reuter, formerly Holmes à Court's right-hand man, and Connell – to 'advise and assist' his company, Tryart, in raising what became the $2.5 billion required to win total control of the Fairfax empire. Connell was the key figure. Aged 41, a self-made millionaire merchant banker and an associate of Alan Bond and of Brian Burke, Premier of Western Australia (1983-88), Connell was renowned for his extravagant lifestyle, speculative adventurism and string of racehorses, and for being a lender whom borrowers could engage as 'a last resort'. Under the so-called 'Tryart Agreement' of 28 August 1987, Connell's merchant bank, Rothwells, was to receive $100 million 'in consideration of and conditional upon Rothwells properly performing its services' in relation to the takeover. Dougherty, Reuter and Connell were to share the fee.

Hughes appeared for Connell on several occasions in 1988-89. According to Stephen Archer, the Sydney barrister then operating in Perth and frequently Hughes' junior, 'Tom and Laurie hit it off immediately'. Hughes saw Connell as 'an engaging fellow'; that is, likeable, but with suspect tendencies.[13] Warwick Fairfax appeared not to have any doubts. When he finally won control of Fairfax in December 1987, Warwick especially thanked and praised Connell during a celebratory dinner at 'Fairwater', Lady (Mary) Fairfax's home in Double Bay. The old board and senior executives departed and new managers – including Dougherty as editorial director and Connell as a director – replaced them. A falling-out between the bid allies, occurring in the midst of staff upheavals early in 1988, escalated when Warwick sent Connell a letter on 4 March requesting his resignation. Rothwells had reached the point of collapse. Owing $1.6 billion, Warwick described Connell's position on the Fairfax board as 'a serious embarrassment' for a company seeking 'suitable financial accommodation'. The Fairfax board was currently receiving advice from a new merchant bank, Whitlam Turnbull, founded by Gough Whitlam's son, Nicholas, previously head of the State Bank of NSW, and Malcolm Turnbull. The latter's criticisms of Rothwells' actions during the takeover helped to persuade the Fairfax board not to pay the $100 million fee. Bond Media, which had acquired this $100 million debt in raising cash for a Rothwells rescue package, sued Fairfax for the fee. Fairfax cross-claimed for $160 million alleging, among other things, that Rothwells had not performed the required service.

The trial began on 17 October 1988 against a background of 'Byzantine perplexity and complexity',[14] and with the prospect of Rothwells going into liquidation and of an investigation into its activities by the National Companies and Securities Commission (NCSC). Justice Roger Giles, a recent appointment to the NSW Supreme Court, presided. Eight QCs, several juniors and numerous solicitors assembled in Court 11A in Queens Square, Sydney. Hughes led Dyson Heydon QC, Francis Douglas QC and Stephen Archer for Rothwells and Bond Media, with Julie Bishop[15] as one of the solicitors. Neil McPhee, who had replaced Murray Gleeson after the latter's appointment as Chief Justice of the NSW Supreme Court, led an impressive team for Tryart, by now renamed John Fairfax Group Pty Ltd.[16]

Gavin Souter described Hughes' opening address as beginning 'like the prologue for a play within a play', and its author as 'one of the most redoubtable silks of his day, and the most theatrically accomplished'. Hughes presented Warwick as 'a young man in a hurry' who wanted 'to gain control of the company whatever the risk and virtually whatever the cost'; that is, he was prepared to sell off the jewels in the crown so long as he secured the principal gem, the *SMH*. Hughes challenged Warwick to enter the witness box and tell why he did not meet Connell personally to explain the demand for his resignation. If he did not enter the box, 'the view is open that he is a coward'. McPhee pointed out that the defence intended to call Fairfax to give evidence.

Hughes focused on the Tryart Agreement, stressing that Rothwells was appointed to 'advise and assist', and that 'advise and assist' actually meant providing 'advisory assistance' with the takeover offer but not with the implementation of the Agreement. The Agreement expressly barred Rothwells from entering dealings on Tryart's behalf, and did not require Rothwells to perform adequately in relation to refinancing the Fairfax debt. McPhee joined the debate about definitions, translating 'advisory assistance' into 'advise and advise'. Warwick, he said, was inexperienced in the takeover field, and needed more than just advice from Connell and Reuter – hence the words used in the Tryart Agreement. Moreover, the $100 million fee was not merely substantial; it was 'outrageous'. Proficient merchant bankers would normally charge $10 million for a comparable operation. Yet, as Hughes pointed out, Fairfax had voluntarily entered the arrangement.

Warwick was in the witness box for 24 days. Hughes' cross-examination occupied 14 of them. Whereas in his prime, according to Dyson Heydon, Hughes engaged in trenchant cross-examinations, using short sentences and not wasting time, he drifted away from this practice in the Fairfax case. He went on for too long and lost sympathy.[17] If, indeed, Heydon was right, Hughes was unable in this case to control the pace of the cross-examination. Warwick kept asking for questions to be repeated, and often took up to a minute to begin answering them. He had a stock response to questions about whether he had made a particular statement – versions of, 'I don't recall saying that but I won't specifically deny it' – making it difficult for Hughes to establish anything concrete about Warwick's conduct of the takeover bid. Despite, or because of, his education, Warwick needed to have words such as 'remonstrate', 'peremptory' and 'furtive' defined for him.

Or did he? Souter wondered whether Warwick was prevaricating in order to 'disconcert' Hughes, and 'it seemed to have that effect'.[18] He certainly had a disconcerting way of using non-answers and equivocation to defuse a line of questioning. For example, Hughes wanted to use notes Malcolm Turnbull had taken of a meeting at Whitlam Turnbull in April 1988 to show that Fairfax did not see himself as a novice and, therefore, could not claim Rothwells had failed to reveal the risks involved in his takeover bid. Turnbull had warned Warwick of the risks he was taking in refinancing the Fairfax debt. Warwick apparently replied:

> When I decided to do this takeover, I knew all the risks and I assumed them. It was entirely my decision. I am not financially illiterate. I understand the situation and I will deal with it in my own way.[19]

Warwick told Hughes he could not remember speaking in this manner at Whitlam Turnbull. Hughes asked whether, if he had said something like that, it would have been the truth.

Fairfax:	No. I don't think it would have been.
Hughes:	So you would have been lying to Mr Turnbull and Mr Whitlam, if you said that?
Fairfax:	If I said that I don't think I would have been describing the situation accurately.
Hughes:	Would you have been lying?
Fairfax:	I find it hard to answer the question.[20]

At another point, Hughes tried to unsettle Warwick by firing a simple question: 'Is the company now viable?' To answer 'Yes' undermined an attack on Rothwells. To answer 'No' undermined the standing of the company when it was desperately trying to deal with debt. After more equivocation, Warwick evaded the trap by saying there was no simple answer.

Laurie Connell had not even entered the witness box when Justice Giles decided that, after 12 weeks, the case had seriously interfered with court timetables. Tom Hughes invited his team home for drinks, and extended the invitation to McPhee, who lived up to his reputation for enjoying a party and mixed company. As all sides needed resolution, they worked out a settlement at the end of January 1989. It pleased no one, least of all Fairfax. Warwick's ailing company had paid out $3.2 million in legal costs and probably lost on the public relations front.[21] The lawyers, however, came out well ahead. Tom Hughes collected fees of nearly $300,000.

Meanwhile, Connell was facing his own problems. He appeared before the NCSC late in December. In the following January, O'Bryan J of the Victorian Supreme Court rejected his application to stop the NCSC from proceeding with its wide-ranging inquiry into the collapse of Rothwells. On Friday 3 March 1989, Federal Police, armed with an interim Supreme Court injunction, escorted Connell off a British Airways flight as it prepared to leave Perth for Singapore and London. Henry Bosch, the Chairman of the NCSC, said the Commission feared that Connell was trying to avoid charges relating to Rothwells' collapse. Connell denied he was running away and, on Tuesday 7 March, Hughes accused the NCSC of failing to peruse Connell's business diary detailing his travel plans, including his proposed return to Perth. The NCSC had received the diary on 26 February. Hughes said Connell's trip reflected a genuine need to conduct commercial transactions, including the sale of Rothwells' corporate structure. Rowland J of the WA Supreme Court rejected Hughes' request to allow Connell to travel because he remained unconvinced of the urgency of Connell's proposed trip

On 9 March, appearing before Pidgeon J in the Supreme Court in Perth, Hughes set upon James Gaffey, the Melbourne-based NCSC lawyer and ANU law graduate, with a 'ferocity' matched only by his later treatment of Derryn Hinch.[22] Gaffey had prepared the affidavit presented with the application for an injunction the previous Friday. He had not revealed knowing that Connell had a return ticket for his London trip, or that Connell had travelled overseas twice in January and February and returned to Perth as scheduled on both occasions.

Hughes:	Wouldn't you agree that even a lawyer of moderate competence or intelligence making an application for an ex-parte order should make a full disclosure of information to the court?
Gaffey:	Yes.
Hughes:	That non-disclosure of information was nothing short of deplorable, wasn't it?
Gaffey:	In hindsight, yes.
Hughes (later):	Wouldn't you agree that it was professionally reckless that that information wasn't put before the court?
Gaffey:	In hindsight, yes.[23]

Hughes extracted two other pieces of information: Gaffey at one stage believed there was no difference between a one-way and a return ticket, and he had told the WA Corporate Affairs Division that possession of a return ticket was 'irrelevant'.

Armed with these admissions, Hughes in his summation accused Gaffey of 'trying to hide the truth' from the Court, and of seeking 'in a slimy and slippery way' to create an image of Connell as a fugitive who did not intend to return to Australia. In doing so, Hughes argued, Gaffey stood convicted of 'nothing short of conscious deliberate concealment' of what he knew to be relevant facts. Nor did Hughes spare Henry Bosch, claiming he was 'careless with the truth, to put it mildly'. He also attacked the NCSC's methods and raised questions about the 'bona fides' of the corporate watchdog. In all, it was a savage assault, accompanied by references to the Stuart kings of England and individual rights and liberties, and by quotations from a British law lord and Alice in Wonderland.[24] Counsel for the NCSC did not oppose Hughes' request that Connell be allowed to leave Australia. Pidgeon J made the order; Connell did leave and he did return.

Hughes continued to appear for him before the NCSC inquiry but Connell's world was falling apart. In 1994, he was jailed for five years for conspiring to pervert the course of justice by paying a jockey to leave the country. By then, Alec Shand was representing him. Typically, Hughes sent a solicitous note to Connell who was in the maximum security Casuarina Prison, south of Perth. Connell replied to 'Dear Tom' on 2 July 1994, writing that the letter had given him 'a great lift'.[25] He described his experience as 'a bit of a culture shock but I have adapted. I get on well with all the blokes & most of the screws.' Connell was exercising every day and attempting to read James Joyce, and was heartened by news of an appeal date in August. He hoped for 'a half decent panel who may be able to overcome the "CONNELL" factor'. He also hoped to see his former barrister 'before too long'. Paroled, Connell, aged 49 and officially bankrupt, died of a heart attack at his Peppermint Grove home on 27 February 1996.

The Packer connection

Tom Hughes had enjoyed a long professional association with the Packers, preferring to work with them rather than Fairfax. Nor was the relationship purely professional. Kerry and Ros Packer attended Hughes' wedding reception in 1981. When, in October 1990, Packer had his near-fatal heart attack while playing polo, Tom wrote to Ros Packer expressing 'heartfelt sympathy in this very anxious time'.[26]

Everything changed when the American 'Chainsaw Al' Dunlap arrived in Sydney as managing director of the Packer organisation, Consolidated Press Holdings (CPH). Hughes' retainer, held since 1972, was due for renewal in 1991. Packer told Hughes on 11 December 1990 that there would no problem, but Hughes should talk to Dunlap. On the same day, Hughes received what he called a 'curt letter' from David Barnett, the organisation's in-house lawyer, telling him that CPH would not henceforth be putting anyone on a retainer. 'I am sure that you have done excellent work for the CPH group ... and would very much like to thank you for it.' Hughes faxed Packer on 12 December to ask whether Barnett's letter represented his decision; if so, 'I accept it without question or complaint'. On the same day, he wrote to Barnett, telling him of the conversation with Packer on 11 December, while saying he would accept the decision if Barnett's letter was written on Packer's instructions.

Barnett replied that he had written the letter on Dunlap's instructions. He expected there would be opportunities in the coming year for Hughes to advise and appear on behalf of CPH, and he would value the opportunity of working with him. Hughes responded on 20 December, in terms similar to those he put to Fairfax in 1984. He assumed that Dunlap understood the ramifications: in the absence of a general retainer, Hughes had a professional obligation to accept briefs against Packer companies. 'I have lost count of the number of times I have been able to refuse, on the basis of my retainer, to appear against the companies in the CPH group. If I cannot refuse in future, so be it.' There is no record in the Hughes Papers of a formal response to this letter.

Hughes also wrote to Kerry Packer's son, James. Being 'most anxious' to avoid appearing against CPH, Hughes suggested an alternative. That is, CPH might give him a retainer, so he could avoid accepting briefs from the other side, and he would discontinue charging fees for work exceeding the prepaid retainer. James Packer explained that, while CPH still wanted to give him some of its work, Dunlap's attitude meant a retainer was out of the question. At the beginning of 1992, when Hughes took a brief to appear against a company for which Kerry Packer was a director, James asked him not to take the case. Hughes said he could not return the brief. He never spoke again with James Packer, and never again worked for CPH or its 'emanations'. He did have 'a very strained conversation' with Kerry Packer, which became 'somewhat explosive' on Packer's part.[27]

Damages out of control: Carson

Tom Hughes had a long professional and personal association with the 'victim' in the first of the prominent defamation cases mentioned earlier. Nicholas 'Nick' Carson, a senior partner with Blake Dawson Waldron, sued Fairfax and John Slee, a senior journalist, over two articles published in the *SMH* on 21 April 1987 and 6 May 1988. Carson's case was one of many offshoots of what became a long running legal battle starting in 1981 between Tectran Corp Pty Ltd and Dr Leszek Rajski over the delivery of a computer software system.[28] In the course of claims and cross-claims, Rajski turned his attention to Carson, whose firm had acted for Tectran, and who in 1985 was representing Allen Allen and Hemsley, against whom Rajski had filed abuse-of-process proceedings. Rajski made a number of allegations, some of which appeared in Slee's two articles. Carson pleaded two imputations in the case of the first article:

> the plaintiff wrongly attempted to intimidate Dr Metcalf [a psychiatrist who had examined Rajski] by threatening to sue him for defamation in respect of his medical report [Metcalf had reflected unfavourably on Carson]; and
>
> the plaintiff wrongly brought defamation proceedings in his own name against Mr Arthur Carney, solicitor, for the sole purpose of causing Mr Carney to forthwith cease to act for his client Mr Rajski.

The imputations pleaded in the second article were:

> the plaintiff was wrongfully party to a conspiracy with Mr Moshe Yerushalmy and Mr David Bruce Cowper [of Tectran] to obstruct the course of justice by evading service of criminal process; and

> the plaintiff so conducted himself as to give rise to a suspicion that he was wrongfully part of a conspiracy to obstruct the course of justice by evading service of criminal process.

Carson also claimed aggravated damages for, among other things, the failure to offer a proper apology and to contact Carson before publication, and for Slee publishing the first article while knowing the two imputations were false.

The hearings began on 5 June 1989 before Loveday J of the NSW Supreme Court and a jury of four. Hughes, with Guy Reynolds, appeared for Carson and Neil McPhee represented Fairfax. Hughes needed Carson to explain his approach to launching the defamation suit, partly because Carson's initial response to the first article was simply to 'wear it'. He changed his mind after Antony Larkins, who by this time had retired from the Supreme Court Bench, told him the article was 'disgraceful' and, in the absence of an appropriate apology, he 'must sue'. The *Herald's* response to Carson's request for an apology was to admit there were two factual errors and, much later, to make a gesture of contrition that Hughes said stopped well short of meeting Carson's requirements. Carson had no hesitation about responding to the second article, and Hughes made sure that three past Presidents of the Law Society, including Rod McGeoch, the chief executive of the Sydney 2000 Olympic Bid Committee and husband of Deeta Colvin, who told the Court what this imputation of criminal conspiracy meant for Carson's high reputation.

Hughes described one of the Slee articles as 'a piece of greasy insinuation', and Slee as a 'pedlar of deliberate falsity'. He made much of the defence decision not to put Slee in the box. When McPhee countered that it would require a deliberately perverse interpretation for Slee's words to become adverse inferences, Hughes insisted there were members of the legal profession whose streak of malice would lead them to listen with composure to allegations about a colleague. He countered McPhee's argument, that Carson had made no claim about loss of income, by saying Carson would never know how many potential clients he had lost. In a key moment of his summing up, Hughes seized on McPhee's suggestion in cross-examination that Carson had acted improperly in relation to the Rajski litigation and had instigated defamation proceedings to silence Slee. Hughes pressed for aggravated damages: 'It is about time this defendant [Fairfax] was brought down to the ground.' The *Defamation Act 1974* (NSW) might have removed a jury's option of awarding punitive damages but a jury could award aggravated damages for the manner in which Fairfax had defended the Slee articles. Hughes' reference to bringing Fairfax 'down to the ground', however, rebounded on him in the appellate courts, where the view prevailed that the damages awarded were of a punitive character.

The jury verdict – $200,000 for the first article and $400,000 for the second – reached after just 47 minutes of deliberation was the highest for libel in Australia at that time. Fairfax and Slee appealed. The Court of Appeal, by majority (Kirby P and Priestley JA, Mahoney JA dissenting) set aside the verdicts as excessive. In Kirby's words, they 'smacked of the punitive.' The Court ordered a retrial on each of them, limited to the question of damages.[29]

Carson appealed to the High Court, where Hughes again led Reynolds with Tom Jnr at a two-day hearing in August 1992. DF Jackson QC of the Queensland Bar appeared for Fairfax. Hughes argued that Justice Kirby was in 'error' by treating the two verdicts as one aggregate verdict, and by comparing the damages awarded to Carson with those given in a personal injury case. Referring to Hughes' 'powerful address' to the trial jury, Jackson said the atmosphere created was hardly that of 'a vicar's tea party'; Hughes had invited the jury to punish Fairfax. Hughes replied: 'Even today, the namby-pamby school of advocacy ought not to be encouraged. There is still room for red-blooded advocacy in trials. If not, we may as well abolish juries altogether.' Besides, he had stressed three times in opening the case that the damages sought would be compensatory; 'punishment is no part of this remedy'.[30] The High Court in June 1993 endorsed the Court of Appeal decision by a 4-3 majority (Mason CJ, Deane, Dawson and Gaudron JJ, with Brennan, Toohey and McHugh JJ dissenting).[31]

The retrial began in Sydney on 29 April 1994 before Levine J and a jury of one man (a waiter) and three women (a librarian, a shop assistant and a courier driver).[32] Maurice Neil from 16 Wardell Chambers represented Fairfax. Carson's wife, Ainsley Gotto, sat with her husband at the trial and Sir John Gorton periodically joined them. Rajski also took a seat in the gallery. Levine J had to order him to be silent as he kept talking at Hughes while counsel was on his feet. Slee entered the witness box for the first time, and Hughes could now cross-examine him. He led Slee to agree that a journalist had a responsibility to tell the truth, and to accept that the imputations in the first article were false. Slee's 'credit' noticeably slipped as he managed to say over a period of persistent inquisition that the imputation relating to Dr Metcalf was at once 'close to the truth', 'substantially true' and 'false'.

A combination of two factors – Hughes' advocacy, and Levine J's decision not to direct the jury against making excessive awards – probably explains the jury's decision to award Carson $1.3 million. Advised by Hughes and others that the verdict was 'vulnerable', Carson accepted a lower figure of $810,000, comprising $500,000 for damages and $310,000 for costs, as well as a full retraction and an appropriate apology.

Damages out of control: Ettingshausen

The second defamation case aroused intense public interest in Sydney, partly because the 'victim' – Andrew 'ET' Ettingshausen – was a well-known and highly-regarded rugby league player. He was a member of the Australian team, the Kangaroos, which toured overseas at the end of 1990. In April 1991, *HQ* magazine, part of the Packer stable, published a black and white photograph of three naked team members standing under a shower, identifying them as 'Benny Elias, Laurie Daley and Andrew Ettinghausen [sic]'. The accompanying article was headed 'hunks' in large red letters and the opening paragraphs in yellow print appeared over part of Daley's body and nearly all of Ettingshausen's lower half. The photo is grainy and not well lit but, if not at first glance, at least with a studied look, the shape between Ettingshausen's legs was, in the words of Justice Hunt of the NSW Supreme Court, 'certainly capable of being interpreted as his penis'.[33]

Ettingshausen felt 'anger and deep hurt' when he saw the photo, and was especially embarrassed when female fans asked him to sign autographs across the photograph. At a preliminary hearing, Hunt J held that two revised imputations should go before a jury:

> the plaintiff deliberately permitted a photograph be taken of him with his genitals exposed for the purposes of reproduction in a publication with a widespread readership; and
>
> the plaintiff is a person whose genitals have been exposed to the readers of the defendant's magazine 'HQ', a publication with a widespread readership.

ACP subsequently published an apology in *HQ*, which, though it appeared to withdraw the first imputation, had diminished sincerity because of its placement on a page advertising condoms. Solicitors from both sides attempted to negotiate a settlement but the gap between Ettingshausen's willingness to accept $85,000 and ACP's final offer of $60,000 proved too substantial.

Tom Hughes represented Ettingshausen at the trial that began on 1 February 1993 before David Hunt, by then Chief Judge at Common Law, and a jury of two men and two women. Guy Reynolds appeared as Hughes' junior, and Ian Callinan represented ACP. Sir Michael Davies, a visiting former judge of the High Court in England and noted for supporting large defamation damages, subsequently described Callinan as a 'heavyweight silk … brought in to try and knock ET over. This he failed to do – don't blame him, he had neither powder nor shot.'[34]

Tom Hughes had what Davies called 'an ideal plaintiff' for a client: an outstanding sportsman, married with a child, university educated, articulate and with 'no skeletons in the cupboard'.[35] Hughes led Ettingshausen carefully through his evidence to build the picture of a man unfairly wronged. Yes, it was his penis in the photograph and, no, he had not given his consent for the photograph to be taken or published, being 'against all my beliefs and morals to pose naked for any magazine'. Yes, the photo had caused him harm because of sleepless nights, stress for himself and his family and taunts from teammates. Hughes used these answers to assure the jury they could 'readily see' how the meaning projected by the magazine – of someone deliberately exposing his genitals for publication – 'strikes at the heart of a decent man's sense of decency and his proper sense of modesty'.

Counsel for the plaintiff could call on excellent support players. Ettingshausen's wife, Monique, his teenage sweetheart, described her husband as 'very distressed, very angry, very upset and very astonished' on seeing a full-frontal nude photograph of himself in the magazine. Wayne 'Junior' Pearce, a former Australian test player and NSW and Balmain captain, was the decent face of rugby league throughout the 1980s and had been awarded an OAM in 1988 for services to the code and to the community. Pearce said Ettingshausen 'is regarded as being of outstanding morals … [and] sets a great example for kids'. John Quayle, the NSW Rugby League general manager, described Ettingshausen as 'certainly a family person'.

Callinan sought to undermine the plaintiff's professed 'modesty' by getting him to admit he promoted himself as a sex symbol, and to accept he had profited financially after the photograph was published. Callinan also claimed that Ettingshausen's penis was not actually in view. Rather, there was 'that tracery of deep shadow and greyness and darkness'. ACP's sole witness – Shona Martyn, the 27-year-old, New Zealand-born editor of *HQ* – told Callinan that the picture did not show 'Mr Ettingshausen's penis'. All she could make out was a 'grey shape'. While 'some people may have possibly construed the shaded area [as a penis]', she did not think the 'shadow' could 'reasonably' be construed as one. Martyn's refusal to acknowledge the obvious, inspired what has been described as 'one of the most famous pieces of cross-examination in Australian legal history':

Hughes: It is a penis is it not … ?

Martyn: Well, I assume if it's in that part of the body, maybe it could be and maybe it might not be.

Hughes: What else could it be?

Martyn: I guess it could be a shadow …

Hughes: (appropriating Martyn's pronounced New Zealand accent): Is it a duck?

Martyn: I don't think it would be a duck.[36]

Callinan followed three lines of approach in his summing up: the tasteful photograph showed nothing more of 'the groin area' than 'a very, very indistinct collection of shadows', which were 'in no way defamatory'; there had been 'a great deal of fuss over nothing much at all'; and Ettingshausen's modelling career as a sex symbol had 'flourished' since the photograph was published. Hughes said that Ettingshausen never claimed to have suffered financial loss because of the photograph. He did claim damage to his reputation among *HQ*'s estimated 154,000 readers who did not know him personally. There was a major difference between Ettingshausen posing for photographs 'decently' and emphasising his 'sexual attributes and good looks', and publishing 'an indecent photograph' without his permission and making it available to a wide audience.

On Wednesday 10 February 1993, after Hunt J had warned the jury that 'absolutely staggering sums' did not survive the appeal process, it awarded Ettingshausen $350,000. Adding the agreed interest, the final amount was assessed at $363,416.66. One press report described Ettingshausen as 'dazed', though he was 'very relieved' to be vindicated. Tom Hughes emphatically denied having said: 'That's one in the eye for Mr Packer.'

> You do take personally the end of an association that is of 35 years' standing. Those events don't fail to touch you. It was a long and agreeable association and I'm sorry it's over. But that was not my expressed reaction.[37]

ACP's solicitors said they would appeal against the verdict and the size of the damages. A representative of the Law Society said the award to Ettingshausen highlighted the difference between compensation for personal injury and damage to reputation, adding that a maximum payment for a severed penis and severed testicles would be just $45,000.[38] Sections of the electronic media attacked the findings on damages as outrageously excessive, prompting Hunt J to issue a statement explaining that aggravated damages were relevant because of the 'flagrantly unjustifiable conduct by the defendant … in a manner most hurtful to the plaintiff'. He thought, wrongly as it turned out, that the damages were not such as to make the Court of Appeal feel it must interfere.[39] After a successful appeal on the extent of damages (Hughes was not involved), Ettingshausen received a reduced sum of $100,000.

The personal and the political

Always busy, Hughes had many other grounds for contentment between the mid-1980s and the mid-1990s. In 1988, the Bicentennial year, he was appointed Officer of the Order of Australia 'for service to the legal profession.' In the same year, Tom and Chrissie acquired another, and larger, farm,

'Bannister Station', some 19 kilometres by road from Marsland.[40] They proceeded to extend the existing weatherboard homestead, which became their principal home from January 1993. After participating in the successful campaign in 1965 to defeat the proposed reserve price scheme for wool, Tom, as an active grazier, campaigned again in 1990-91 against the reserve price scheme imposed in 1974, and which effectively collapsed in 1991.[41] Lucy and Malcolm continued to prosper and Malcolm, after breaking with Nicholas Whitlam, had established his own merchant bank, Turnbull & Partners. For a time, Tom Jnr did not prosper as expected, having developed a range of personal and financial problems that greatly troubled his father who bore much of the monetary cost.[42] Admitted to the Bar in 1989, he joined 15 Wardell Chambers, and often appeared as his father's junior.

After taking his Arts degree at the University of Sydney, and experiencing uncertainty about career choices, Michael joined Turnbull & Partners in October 1990, where he stayed for four years. In February 1994, he married Jane Madgwick, who had worked as a research assistant for Ian Macdonald MLC, the former serial demonstrator who had clashed with Tom Hughes at Bellevue Hill in August 1970. Macdonald, a wedding guest, along with several Labor luminaries and John Howard and Sir John Atwill, apologised to Michael's father for his earlier actions. Politics, for Michael, remained an option. He contemplated standing as a Liberal against Clover Moore, the sitting independent in the State seat of Bligh, but nominated instead for preselection for the State seat of Vaucluse in 1994. Supported by some of the right-wing faction, he came third behind John Brogden, a future State leader, and Peter Debnam, the future State leader who won the preselection. From this point, Michael chose not to pursue a career in politics.[43]

There was one moment of great sadness. On 27 November 1989, Tom Hughes lost 'the best friend anyone could ever have', and a link with the Bar he joined in 1949. Antony Larkins died after a long period of poor health, probably the result of partaking too liberally of the banquet of life. Sitting with 'Larko' in his last days, Tom asked the lapsed Catholic if he would like a priest to be present. His friend replied that he did not intend to come in 'by the back door'.[44] In the obituary, published in the Autumn 1990 issue of *Bar News*, Tom commented on Larkins' aversion to authority, the ever-present monocle, his 'reputation for sound law, good advocacy and prodigiously hard work, all garnished with his own very individual style' and his remarkable capacity to inspire the loyalty and admiration of the young. Tom described Larkins in words that in some measure could be applied to himself: his 'solicitude, and his selfless generosity were of legendary proportions. In his eyes, his friends could do no wrong (quite often contrary to the fact). He would defend them to the utmost with an obstinacy of undoubtedly Irish origin.' Tom's words – 'our world has lost some of its colour' – reflected his sadness about the passing of a time when those who might be called 'originals' stood out from the rest.

Whereas 'Larko' rejected his inherited faith, Tom Hughes regained his after meeting Father Emmet Costello SJ in June 1993. Born of Australian parents in Fiji and educated by Jesuits in Melbourne, Costello was ordained in 1955, served on the teaching staff at St Aloysius College, Milsons Point, and at Riverview, and spent the last years of his priesthood at St Mary's, North Sydney. Costello befriended and counselled the rich and influential – a colleague dubbed him 'apostle to the silvertails' – and mentored many leaders in business and politics, including Tony Abbott. Father Brennan SJ, delivering the homily at Costello's funeral on 21 October 2013, said he was a 'great communicator' of the message that 'Christ was divine as Son of God and human as our brother'.

Costello contacted 'Mr Hughes' after reading Sandra Hall's article in the *Australian Magazine* of July 1993 where Tom explained that the Pope's Encyclical on birth control 'accelerated' his departure from the Church. Costello sought to reassure him. Paul VI had not designated contraception a mortal sin and had 'made it clear that the document was NOT infallible'. Besides, about 90 per cent of Catholics ignored it and 'many top theologians' thought the Encyclical had 'gravely undermined papal authority'. Costello plied Hughes with books and articles, including some of his own writings. At the end of 1994, Tom launched Costello's book, *Saints: Popular and Relevant*, referring to the author as 'my dear friend'. He later told a Jesuit gathering that Costello's 'wise advocacy led me back to a path I should never have left'. Yet, while forever grateful to Costello, Hughes later felt uncomfortable with his persistent criticisms of Pope Benedict XVI and of the Australian hierarchy.[45]

Tom Hughes remained a firm if not overly active supporter of the Liberal Party. He donated funds to election campaigns, handed out how-to-vote cards at elections, and proffered advice to, and wrote references for, candidates seeking preselection. Hughes had become even more firmly a 'liberal', most notably in aligning himself with the Australian Republican Movement of which Malcolm Turnbull became Chairman in 1993. Neither immediate family connections nor his Irish ancestry explain his support for a republic. For him, it was a common sense acknowledgement of Australia's independence and separate identity. He had been heading in that direction for 25 years, as his earlier comments on the legal links to the Privy Council and on Britain's entry into the Common Market clearly attested.

Hughes was sympathetic to the 'moderate and progressive' values represented by Kevin McCann, a Liberal Party office-holder of distinction and a prominent company director. He wrote a reference for McCann who was the 'hot favourite' to win preselection for the federal seat of Warringah in 1994. Tony Abbott, a comparative outsider, defeated him by 10 votes in the final ballot. McCann later told Hughes that he 'could not match Abbott's public speaking excellence', nor his support from 'certain sections' (the Right) of the Party.[46]

For all his 'liberal' instincts, Hughes had no reservations about supporting the Party's most notable conservative, John Howard, whose triumph in the 1996 federal election gave the former Liberal member for Parkes one of his happiest moments since leaving parliament. He wrote to 'Dear John' on the day after the election. 'What a stunning victory! You have made it to the top by dedicated hard work in the face of setbacks that would have deterred anyone else.' Remembering what happened to the Liberals after Holt achieved a massive majority in 1966, Hughes hoped that Howard's stamp of authority 'will be firmly imprinted on the parliamentary party'. Of Parkes in 1963, he wrote: 'What fun we had in those days developing and honing our campaign skills – skills that you developed to the level of an art form.' He was sure that Howard's 'elixir for success' would mean he could solve 'some' of the nation's problems. In reply, Howard also recalled those 'heady' days of 1963, adding that, after a difficult 13 years, 'the new team has a splendid opportunity to make its mark and effect necessary change and reform'.[47]

22

'I am still enjoying practice'

On Friday 9 April 1999, the NSW Bar Association held a special dinner to mark the 50th anniversaries of the admission of Chester Porter, Frank McAlary and Tom Hughes to the Bar.[1] Ian Harrison SC, later a President of the Bar Association and a judge of the Supreme Court, proposed the toast for Tom Hughes. Interspersed with his generous tribute, Harrison delivered a witty and creative 'roast'. He observed that Hughes' technique of cross-examining witnesses by standing side-on, and staring towards the back of the courtroom, 'has unintended consequences. Members of the public gallery often break down and answer his questions.' One of Harrison's fictional flights had perhaps the intended consequence of demonstrating that his subject appeared to stand apart from, as well as above, the modern Bar.

> I thought I'd check … to see if he was keeping abreast of state-of-the-art contemporary forensic concepts. I asked Tom 'What do you understand by the term case management?' He looked at me with a very straight back (Tom has a very straight back) and said 'My boy, that's what the porter at the Dorchester does with your luggage when you arrive'.
>
> I thought I'd take a chance. I said 'Well, what about differential case management?' He said 'That's just an instruction to the porter not to get my bags mixed up with those of my wife'.

The NSW Bar, and the context in which it operated, had changed markedly from the time of Hughes' admission in 1949, but most notably during the final two decades of the 20th century. The immediately obvious changes included an expansion of the numbers in practice, a modification of the gender composition and a proliferation of both chambers and courts. In 1999, 1825 practising barristers – 13 per cent of them women – were members of the NSW Bar Association. While Wentworth and Selborne Chambers accommodated 430 barristers, 902 other barristers occupied 32 other chambers in the city, and the remainder were mostly located in suburban, regional and interstate chambers or official offices. Given that dispersal, it is not surprising that 'collegiality', something Hughes tried to advance when President of the Bar Association, was confined to individual floors or, in some cases, to the smaller chambers.

By 1999, barristers were required by law to hold a practising certificate, renewable annually upon payment of a fee. They also had to hold a policy of indemnity insurance. There had been a formalisation of independent disciplinary procedures for barristers designed, among other things, to promote accountability and transparency. The Bar had abandoned the two-thirds rule and determined that silks (Senior Counsel, or SC, if appointed after 1993) could appear alone. Tom Hughes adjusted to these changes, and even to those introduced or further advanced in the 10 years between the 50th and 60th anniversaries of his admission to the Bar. In fact, he may have surprised some by his readiness to adapt. A number of barristers objected to the introduction of the 'Continuing Professional Development' program. Hughes wrote to Ruth McColl, the President of the NSW Bar Association, supporting the program, stating that the time was past when the Bar as a professional body could rely on 'on the job training'; it had to be seen as 'determined to upgrade our efficiency'. He also offered to help with the program. The letter was published in *Bar Brief*, August 2001, which had the immediate effect of sending some of the hostile muttering underground.[2]

For Hughes, the important adjustment was not to ever-growing formal requirements, or to the new technologies that mostly passed him by. Rather, he faced a shift in the amount and kind of work available. Most of the solicitors who supported him with work had retired. 'As I have grown older practising solicitors as a tribe have grown younger.'[3] At the same time, media companies were shying away from costly defamation cases and they, and the journalists, were more careful. The 'Big Six' firms of solicitors – Freehills, Allens, Mallesons, Blake Dawson, Minter Ellison and Clayton Utz – wanted to avoid long days and weeks in court. Although Hughes continued to get briefs, increasingly cases proceeded to settlement. He liked a contest, so the growing enthusiasm for mediation had no appeal. Hughes realised he needed to move further into the field of commercial litigation and, in 2001, left 16 Wardell to join Blackstone Chambers at level 62, 29 Martin Place, which specialised in this area. He also explained his decision as a desire for change and having received an invitation.[4]

Significantly, his fee books for the Blackstone years record many more entries for 'Preparation' than 'Refresher', and very few charges above the $6000 he regularly sought at 16 Wardell Chambers. Hughes' briefs were beginning to dry up after he turned 85. On 1 February 2010 he referred in his diary to a 'very bleak start to the year'.[5] He had practically no work save for preparing a mediation due a fortnight later. Whispers around the Bar suggested that he was no longer at his very best in court, was losing his train of thought and had to rely more on his juniors.

Some high profile cases

Until 2009-10, Hughes continued to appear in cases that attracted media and popular attention. One of the more spectacular began in Perth in March 1999. Gina Rinehart, the daughter of the mining magnate Lang Hancock, who died in 1992, began an action in the Supreme Court of Western Australia to reclaim cash and property from Hancock's widow, Rose Porteous. Rinehart claimed that the $20 million in cash and properties her father lavished on Porteous rightfully belonged to Hancock Prospecting Pty Ltd and the Hancock Family Memorial Foundation. Hughes, with Stephen Archer, took the brief to represent Rinehart. A Melbourne QC, Julian Burnside, led the legal team for Porteous.

Hughes did not hold back. Lang Hancock faced something as 'old as human nature – the struggle between duty and avarice'. The scales weighed against duty because 'an old man' yielded to a clever and much younger woman and succumbed 'to her very large demands for property and monies'. Porteous formed a relationship with Hancock and, her eyes 'firmly fixed on the main chance', she 'went at it with her ears back'. Hancock had 'plundered' the assets of the two companies to provide her with cash to buy the properties she wanted: the Perth mansion, 'Prix D'Amour' (a kitsch replica of 'Tara' from *Gone with the Wind*, and bulldozed in 2006), another mansion in Florida, office buildings in Sydney and Perth and a Bentley.

Gina Rinehart, brought into court by the Porteous legal team, expanded upon Hughes' picture of Rose as the scheming woman she called 'a Filipino prostitute'. Rinehart said her father could not escape an unhappy marriage because Porteous threatened to ruin his reputation. Burnside took a risk and put Porteous on the stand, the main effects of which were to entertain the packed gallery and to exasperate Rinehart's leading counsel. By design or because she was naturally talkative, Porteous never gave a direct answer to a question when a long explanation was available. On one occasion, Hughes called a halt: 'Do you mind if I interrupt you to ask a question?' At times, Porteous was disarming – her only crime 'was to marry a rich man'. At others, she was opaque – on business matters, 'Hancock was the cake, I was only the icing'. She pleaded language difficulties in understanding Hughes: her English was 'American-English' and his was 'English-English'. When Hughes asked whether she had poor relations with Rinehart, Porteous replied: 'Yes, or we wouldn't be here and you wouldn't be earning so much money.' On another occasion, she told Hughes to calm down and to get on with his job: 'you are being paid for it.'[6] Ian Harrison claimed in his 'roast' that 'Tom is writing a book at the moment, tentatively entitled *Filipinos Behaving Badly*'.

Hughes was well paid. He started charging $7500 a day and soon lifted the daily figure to $8500 (his highest-ever charge for a refresher) and, overall, collected $312,750. Yet it was not a successful visit to Perth. On 10 June 1999, on what would have been Hancock's 90th birthday, Anderson J ruled in favour of Porteous. He found no evidence that Hancock had breached his fiduciary duties or that Porteous was implicated in a breach of fiduciary duty. Rinehart's subsequent appeal to the Full Court in Perth failed and, on 8 September 2000, the High Court refused to grant special leave to appeal. By this time, Rinehart had dispensed with Hughes' services, as she often did with 'the top minds' she engaged in her campaign to crush Rose Porteous.[7] In 2003, the two women declared a truce, ended their legal actions and refused to disclose the agreed terms.

At the end of 1999, Hughes appeared, unsuccessfully, for Radio 2UE in the Australian Broadcasting Tribunal's investigation of two of the station's stars – Alan Jones and John Laws – accused of taking cash for favourable editorial comment in their radio programs. In March 2000, he represented the 30-year-old Sydney-based Shari-lea Hitchcock, with whom the 65-year-old packaging billionaire from Melbourne, Richard Pratt, was conducting a long affair, and with whom he fathered a daughter. In this case, Hughes succeeded in extending an injunction to restrain a former nanny from revealing secrets on a Channel Nine television program. A few months later, Hughes appeared without success before Finn J of the Federal Court representing South Sydney in the early stages of its battle for readmission to what is now the National Rugby League competition. In the first half of 2003, he appeared for Channel Seven in its continuing argument with the well-known solicitor John Marsden over the damages to be awarded after an earlier, long-running defamation case where Marsden, a gay man, had been accused of being a paedophile. An embittered Marsden noted that Seven had 'instructed a new barrister, Tom Hughes QC, who used to be a top barrister but is now fairly old'.[8]

Hughes had a long professional association with someone who was 'not an easy client'.[9] Rene Rivkin was always in the news. Born in Shanghai of Russian-Jewish parents who fled after the 1917 revolution, Rivkin was a flamboyant entrepreneur, investor and 'celebrity' stockbroker, noted for an ostentatious lifestyle and his worry beads. His client list during the 1980s included Kerry Packer, Alan Bond and Laurie Connell. In 1998, he sued Channel Seven for depictions of him on its *Witness* program, and Fairfax for three newspaper articles, two published in the *Sydney Morning Herald*

(25 February and 5 March) and one in the *Australian Financial Review* (21-22 February). Both the television program and the articles arose from a coroner's decision to return an open verdict at the inquest into the death of Sydney model Caroline Byrne, the 24-year-old girl friend of Rivkin's chauffeur, Gordon Wood. The Coroner could not decide whether she 'jumped, slipped or was pushed' to her death in June 1995 at The Gap, a cliff at South Head in Sydney's eastern suburbs, infamous for suicides.

The action over the newspaper articles began on 17 April 2001 before Justice Carolyn Simpson of the Supreme Court and a jury of four women. Hughes led Tom Jnr for Rivkin, while Henric Nicholas QC appeared for John Fairfax Publications Ltd. Hughes argued that the newspaper articles contained 17 imputations. One *Herald* report was 'overladen with venomous insinuations', implying that Rivkin had engaged in homosexual sex with Gordon Wood, and was a close associate of criminals. There was a clear imputation Rivkin had 'counselled and procured' Byrne's murder because of her knowledge of the 'homosexual connection' and of the alleged involvement of Wood and Rivkin in 'unsavoury business dealings'. One report implied he had engaged in 'unlawful conduct' with the public company Offset Alpine,[10] thus diminishing the reputation of 'a sagacious and astute stockbroker'. Above all, Hughes said the reports did nothing to dispel the suggestion that this married man with five children was involved in Byrne's death. In response, Nicholas said readers would need to engage in 'flights of fantasy' to conclude from the reports that Rivkin was connected with Byrne's fate.

The jury faced a two-part question. Did the articles convey certain imputations? If so, were they defamatory? The four women took just 50 minutes on 23 April to decide that the articles did not convey any of the 17 alleged imputations. Rivkin said he was 'flabbergasted'. His leading counsel did not comment. Hughes had to contend with other matters on the same day. Robert Hughes had arrived in Sydney following the death of his 33-year-old son, Danton, found on 19 April in the home in the Blue Mountains he shared with the fashion designer Jenny Kee. Only after nearly three months did Hughes comment privately on the jury's decision to his friend, Hugh Griffiths. He described the result as 'a severe blow'. Nevertheless, 'our client is rich and has decided to appeal the verdict as unreasonable/perverse'. Hughes had heard that the trial judge was 'affronted' by the verdict. 'The general reaction of the profession was that the jury strayed from their task.' Hughes appreciated how hard it was to set aside a jury finding in a libel case but thought in this instance there was 'a reasonably good chance'. He felt encouraged by a recent decision of the Court of Appeal in England to reject a jury verdict as perverse.[11]

Rivkin did appeal, and Hughes, with Tom Jnr, continued to represent him. They had initial success. On 26 May 2002, the Court of Appeal unanimously decided that the jury verdict was, as Hughes had proposed, perverse and unreasonable. The jury had acted too quickly in dismissing the defamation action. The Court ordered a new trial on all 17 imputations. Granted special leave to appeal, Fairfax asked the High Court to set aside the order for a new trial and for restoration of the original trial verdict. Hughes, with Tom Jnr, appeared for Rivkin, and Bret Walker SC for the appellant. By a 4-1 majority, on 10 September 2003 the High Court held that just five of the 17 imputations were unreasonable and ordered a retrial in respect of these alone.[12] McHugh J was the dissenting voice. In his view, provided that a jury's view 'cannot be described as irrational, it must stand'. Hughes could not shift him. Nor could he persuade the other judges that the trial judge's refusal to grant a right of reply was both wrong in procedure and significant in the outcome. Nor did they accept that the speed of the jury's deliberation provided a basis for rejecting its findings. The matter went no further. Rivkin ceased to use Hughes, and eventually decided to withdraw from legal action when his own world started imploding before and after his conviction for insider trading in April 2003.[13]

Hughes carried a jury with him in February 2004 when he represented Greg Hodge, a former Olympic swimming coach. Hodge sued Channel Nine for airing the allegations made against him by a former student, Emma Fuller, who lived with the Hodges when aged around 12 in the mid-1990s. Hughes said the program depicted Hodge as an 'obsessive, mentally sick, sexual predator, as a pervert and a creep who subjected Emma Fuller to sexual harassment'.[14] It took the jury just 30 minutes to decide that three imputations had defamed Hodge. The judge awarded him $320,000 in damages.

Hughes did not get the desired result, however, in a case brought by Mercedes Corby, sister of Schapelle Corby who was jailed in Bali in 2004 for smuggling drugs. In April-May 2008, Mercedes sued Channel Seven for interviews broadcast in its *Today Tonight* program. Her legal team identified 31, mostly drug-related, imputations drawing upon allegations made by a former close friend, Jodie Powell. The case was the first held under amended defamation laws: in addition to determining if the imputations were conveyed, juries should decide if they were defamatory and whether the defence of truth had been established. Hughes, along with Kieran Smark SC and Tom Jnr, represented Channel Seven, the Seven Media Group having agreed in December 2007 to pay Hughes a general retainer of $50,000 for the following year and Tom Jnr one for $25,000. GST was added to both fees.[15] Stuart Littlemore QC appeared for Corby.

During the trial, accusations and denials about drug taking were tossed about and between one-time friends, tears seemed to be mandatory, the public gallery was always full and Justice Carolyn Simpson appeared irked by what one commentator called 'the antics of a somewhat truculent bar table'. Hughes complained about Littlemore's 'minatory tone', his 'bullying' and 'theatrical posing' in his cross-examination of Powell. After deliberating for six hours, the jury decided that 29 of the imputations were defamatory and that Seven's defence of truth succeeded on just one count: Mercedes Corby had been guilty of possessing marijuana. Corby was exultant and Littlemore, who had lost to Hughes on other occasions, looked very pleased.[16] There followed an out-of-court settlement for undisclosed damages. When Hughes later sought to renew the two retainers for 2009, Bruce McWilliam, Seven's Commercial Director, who had a longstanding association with Malcolm Turnbull and who had worked with Hughes over many years, warned that times were tough and queried the necessity of retainers.[17] Like the journalists responsible for the *Today Tonight* program, the Seven Media Group may have been unhappy about the conduct of the defence.

Final years in the High Court

Hughes relished appearing before the High Court. In June 1980, he appeared in the first case held in the new building in Canberra, successfully representing a solicitor convicted of contempt in a custody dispute before the Family Court.[18] In a long diary note for 3-6 June 1980, he noted that the 'ugliness of the building on the outside is more than compensated by its magnificent inside. It is all very impressive and something for the country to be proud of. The finished job makes Barwick's detractors look mean and unimaginative.'

Appearing before the High Court, Hughes had to adjust to changes in judicial approach and style. Whereas there was little judicial intervention in counsels' arguments in the Latham and Dixon Courts, counsel in the Barwick Court received what Sir Anthony Mason called a 'gruelling interrogation, dignified by the description, "Socratic dialogue"'. Hughes appreciated rather than begrudged the Barwick approach. He adjusted to the curtailing of lengthy oral argument and the extensive use of prior written submissions that accompanied the greater equanimity of later courts.[19] As he took account of changes sought or imposed by the Bench, Hughes also had to adjust his manner and style. Perhaps he was not always successful. At one point in the Crimmins case (discussed below), Hayne J asked whether an example Hughes had chosen to advance his argument was 'for the better inflaming of our passions'. Counsel replied: 'I am sorry Your Honour. I am not trying to address Your Honours as if Your Honours were a jury. Sometimes I am accused of doing that.' Michael Kirby noticed that Hughes took some of his habits into the appellate courts; he never looked at judges sitting on the Bench but turned sideways and gazed into the distance 'as if to a higher court'.[20]

Between 1999 and 2009, Hughes appeared in a number of significant though not widely noticed cases in the High Court. In 1999, he represented Mrs Maureen Crimmins, the widow of Brian Crimmins who had died the previous year. Crimmins, a waterside worker, had contracted mesothelioma after inhaling asbestos fibres in the course of his employment at the Port of Melbourne between 1961 and 1965. Although the Australian Stevedoring Industry Authority (ASIA) did not directly employ him, it did assign Crimmins to jobs and it had disciplinary powers over all the workers on the wharves. The Stevedoring Industry Finance Committee (SIFC) had replaced the ASIA in 1956. The first question in 2009 was whether the SIFC had inherited the original authority's liabilities. The second was whether those liabilities included a duty of care to workers on the wharves.

Hughes had failed to win the case in the Victorian Court of Appeal, which upheld the appeal from the SIFC that there was no transmission of liability (3-0) and no duty of care (2-1). Hughes came to the High Court with two other QCs and a junior. Jackson QC appeared for the respondent. Aware that the Court looked favourably on the issue of transmitted liability, Hughes concentrated on making his case for the SIFC having a duty of care. He was at pains to point out that, although the direct employers had the greater responsibility, the SIFC had regulatory functions and, 'in the ordinary course of things', it was in a position to tell employers they could not have men working in holds 'with dust enveloping them'. It was not just a case of the SIFC merely omitting to exercise its statutory powers; it omitted to use them in circumstances that called for decisive intervention. The SIFC knew from 1960 about the hazards of asbestos yet took no part in stevedoring operations, except to act as the operator of the employment bureaux.

The High Court decided by 6-0 that there was a transmission of liability and by 5-2 (Gummow and Hayne JJ dissenting) that the SIFC had a common law duty of care. The case established a precedent based on the six questions McHugh J had identified as essential to ask when a plaintiff alleged that a statutory authority owed a common law duty of care and had breached that duty by failing to exercise a statutory power.[21]

Hughes had a severe rebuff in the High Court in 2005. The Court in November upheld by 6-0 the right of BP Australia Pty Ltd to buy back three service station sites on their terms, because the relevant companies had breached contracts to supply only BP fuel from the stations. The companies had already failed before a single judge and the Full Court of the Federal Court. Hughes appeared with Tom Jnr, and against Bret Walker, over two days in May 2005. He argued that BP had failed to take account of goodwill in determining the price paid for the buy-back; that BP had obtained a double penalty for the same breach; and that the penalty was 'indiscriminate' and 'oppressive', considering the breaches were minor. The High Court found that the service stations had not demonstrated the monetary value of goodwill; that there had to be a good reason for judicial intervention in a freely-agreed contract; and, on the law relating to penalties, it must be 'extravagant and unconscionable in amount' and, not just lacking in proportion', it must be 'out of all proportion'.[22]

In May 2006, Hughes appeared for Dragan Vasiljković (aka 'Captain Dragan' or 'Daniel Snedden'), a naturalised Australian citizen, in what proved to be the early stages of a drawn-out and losing battle to prevent his extradition to Croatia. The Croatian Government wanted to try him for offences allegedly committed early in the 1990s while Vasiljković was a captain of Serbian paramilitary unit troops then at war with the Croatian armed forces. Hughes challenged the constitutional validity of the combined operation of the *Extradition Act 1988* (Cth) and the *Extradition (Croatia) Regulations 2004* (Cth) that gave Croatia the opportunity to secure his client's involuntary detention and removal from Australia based on untested and untestable allegations of criminal conduct against Croatian law. Hughes argued that the Act and the Regulations denied his right to have a judicial examination of the evidentiary basis of the charges alleged against him, and breached the constitutional principle that an Australian citizen cannot be involuntarily detained except through the exercise of the judicial power of the Commonwealth. In August, the Court (Gleeson CJ, Gummow, Hayne and Heydon JJ, Kirby J dissenting) ruled that the 'no evidence' model of extradition detention was constitutionally valid, and was not inconsistent with the separation of powers requirements embodied in the text and structure of Australia's Constitution.

In 2008-09, Hughes was in the High Court opposing an appeal by the Australian Competition and Consumer Commission (ACCC) against a decision of the Full Court of the Federal Court. It was commonly agreed that Channel Seven Brisbane had broadcast episodes of *Today Tonight* containing false statements about the 'Wildly Wealthy Women' program that offered training for women who wished to invest in real estate. The misrepresentations contravened s 52 of the *Trade Practices Act 1974* (Cth), the legislation Hughes had once wanted to introduce. The question was whether s 65A of the legislation which exempted 'prescribed information providers' – the so-called 'media safe harbour' – applied in this case. Arguing that it should,

Hughes embarked upon some ingenious redefining and repositioning of words, but to no avail. The High Court by a 4-1 majority (Heydon J dissenting) held that the exemption conferred by s 65A did not apply to situations in which a media outlet published matter in relation to goods or services where the publication is pursuant to an arrangement with a supplier of goods or services.[23]

In a letter to his brother, Robert, of 17 December 2009, Tom wrote that at 'age 86 I am still enjoying practice. It is a great antidote to senility.' He had a very good reason to feel pleased. In what he called a 'landmark constitutional case', he had just won a 4-3 majority in the High Court. Soon after, he appeared before the seven justices of the High Court 'in another significant case'.[24]

In May 2008, the NSW Crime Commission made an *ex parte* application to the NSW Supreme Court under s 10 of the *Criminal Assets Recovery Act 1990* (NSW) to obtain restraining orders against dealings in property suspected of being derived from serious crime. The Supreme Court was required to make an order where an authorised officer in an affidavit had deposed to a suspicion that the relevant property was derived from serious crime, and where the Court considered there were reasonable grounds for suspicion. If affected parties wanted to overturn an order they had to prove it 'more probable than not' that the property was not acquired fraudulently or illegally. The target on this occasion were the bank and share-trading accounts of two companies owned and operated by a firm of accountants in Vanuatu. The Crime Commission believed that Robert Agius, the senior partner of the firm and an Australian citizen, was engaged in tax fraud. A judge of the Supreme Court made the necessary order but, by a 2-1 majority, the Court of Appeal found there was no admissible evidence providing reasonable grounds to support the authorised officer's suspicions. At the same time, the Court of Appeal unanimously rejected the argument that s 10 was constitutionally invalid, thereby depriving the Supreme Court of any discretionary judgment as to the manner of hearing an *ex parte* application under s 10 of the Act.

Tom Hughes successfully applied on behalf of the two companies for special leave to appeal on the constitutional issue. The Full Court of the High Court heard the case on 26-7 May 2009. Ian Temby QC, a former Commonwealth Director of Public Prosecutions and NSW Independent Commission Against Corruption Commissioner, represented the respondent, and the Commonwealth Solicitor-General and the Solicitors-General of the five mainland States intervened in support of the first respondent. Hughes argued that the legislation substantially impaired the Court's 'institutional integrity'. Section 10 vested in an external administrative agency the right to determine how a court exercised its statutory function while depriving it of the opportunity to hear the other side. In the course of his argument, he invoked the *Kable* principle. In 1990, Gregory Kable stabbed his wife to death during a custody dispute and was sentenced to gaol for five years for manslaughter. In gaol, he wrote several threatening letters to various people about the custody of his children. The NSW Government legislated for his continued detention in anticipation of his release in 1995. Declaring the Act unconstitutional, the High Court ruled that it vested powers in the Supreme Court that were incompatible with the Court's role in the federal judiciary.[25]

A majority of the High Court (French CJ, Gummow, Heydon and Bell JJ, Hayne, Crennan and Kiefel JJ dissenting) held that s 10 was invalid 'because it engaged the Supreme Court in an activity repugnant to the judicial process in a fundamental degree as understood and conducted throughout Australia'.[26] Murray Gleeson's biographer assessed the decision as a return to 'judicial activism', where the High Court grabbed for power at the expense of parliament. 'This would never have happened on Murray Gleeson's watch.' Perhaps not, but it cannot have been wholly remiss to render invalid what Hughes rightly called 'a bad law', and to affirm a fundamental legal principle that both sides of a case ought to be heard.[27]

The other 'significant case', to which Hughes referred in his letter to Robert, originated in a Crown prosecution of two men – referred to as 'LK' and 'RK' – who were charged with conspiring to deal with money to the value of $1 million and 'were reckless to the fact that the money was the proceeds of crime'. In July 2008, the trial judge directed the jury to acquit the two accused on the ground that the indictment did not disclose an offence known to law. The NSW Court of Criminal Appeal dismissed the Crown's appeal, and the High Court in June 2009 granted special leave to appeal and heard the case on 1 December 2009. John Stratton SC represented LK and Hughes appeared for RK. Both barristers argued that the prosecution had to prove the accused believed, at the time of their agreement to lodge the funds in Switzerland, that the money was proceeds of crime. Although the Court rejected a number of Hughes' ancillary arguments, all seven judges agreed that intention was the fault element of the offence of conspiracy, and that proof of intention required the accused to believe that their proposed conduct was an offence. The Crown had not alleged that the accused knew or believed that the money was the proceeds of crime. In May 2010, the High Court handed down a 7-0 decision in Hughes' favour; it 'was not open to find that either accused had intentionally entered an agreement to commit an offence'.[28] Hughes had won a decisive victory in what proved to be his final appearance in the High Court.

Two other activities

In 1998, Tom Hughes joined the Appeals Panel of the Thoroughbred Racing Board of NSW as Principal Member (this position had to be a legal practitioner of seven years standing). The Panel constituted the first level of an independent two-tier system of appeal from decisions imposed by a racing authority. In 1999-2000, Hughes chaired all 17 sittings of the Panel – five members usually sat at any one time – and heard 21 appeals, most against conviction and penalty. He enjoyed working with the other 19 members of the Panel, who included Wayne Haylen QC, later a judge of the NSW Industrial Court, who was the son of 'Left-Wing Les' Haylen, whom Tom had defeated in Parkes in 1963. Hughes met several 'colourful racing identities' and 'a very interesting group of people' from a world removed from the boardrooms and chambers of his other life. His pleasure soured, however, when early in 2003 Racing NSW decided not to renew his appointment. In August of the previous year, the Panel had voted 3-2 to dismiss two of the charges laid against Robbie Waterhouse arising out of a betting scam at the Canterbury Racecourse. Racing NSW wanted to deal severely with Waterhouse. Hughes pointed out that the industry would link his removal to the Panel's decision and offered, instead, to retire when he turned 80 in November 2003. Racing NSW accepted his proposal.[29]

In June 2005, Edmund Capon, the Director of the Art Gallery of New South Wales, invited Tom to give a lecture exploring the relationship between art and the law.[30] Explaining that 'Art is not an Alsatia where the Queen's writ does not run', Hughes said that courts did sometimes have to make judgments on artistic works, but usually when artists sued for defamation. Although Australian courts avoided making judgments about quality, they should and did interpret formal prize requirements in a manner that allowed and encouraged artists to follow their creative instincts. He cited the Archibald Prize, and notably Roper J's decision in the NSW Supreme Court to accept Dobell's 1943 prize-winning painting of Joshua Smith as a portrait and not a caricature. By rejecting the traditionalist's invitation 'to confine portraiture in a cage', Roper J had circumvented 'any suppressive effect on innovative artistic enterprise'. Without that decision, the Archibald 'would not have developed its magnetic drawing power, reaching out to many thousands of people to inspire in them an interest in art'. It did not matter that the defeat of the traditionalists 'generated a lot of rubbish masquerading as portraiture' because the long-term effect was 'to put Art on the town'. Hughes' approach to art, consistent with the one he adopted in the seemingly unrelated areas of trade practices legislation and a reserve wool price, was to liberate rather than inhibit.

Losing friends

Sir Garfield Barwick, aged 94, died on 13 July 1997. One of Hughes' last professional contacts with him occurred three years earlier, when Barwick sought his advice about responding to the paperback edition of David Marr's biography.[31] Barwick did not want his descendants and others accepting Marr's version that he had 'instigated Kerr's action'; to do so 'would have been a gross breach of the duties of my office'. Barwick feared that such an assertion, 'even though made by a person perhaps of little worth', would receive a wide circulation. He was 'very touched' by Hughes' offer to represent him without fee: 'it warmed my heart to know that the brotherhood of the Bar still exists.' Hughes nonetheless advised against legal action, and Barwick decided that ch 24 of his 1995 autobiography, *A Radical Tory*,[32] should constitute his response to David Marr.

Two months after Barwick died, Tom Hughes spoke at a memorial service held at St James' Church, King Street. Hughes considered it a 'sad thing' that Barwick's death had 'evoked in some quarters a repetition of the cacophonous chorus of criticism to which he had been subjected'. Hughes talked about a distinguished Australian citizen who had driven himself from humble beginnings to become an outstanding barrister and minister of the Crown and to hold the office of Chief Justice for 17 years. He acknowledged that Barwick's time on the High Court was controversial but focused on his approach in court rather than on the dismissal of the Whitlam Government. Hughes defended Barwick's 'pronounced habit of intervening in argument', though he understated the general reaction by saying it was not a 'universally popular approach to the judicial task'. Admitting that facing the Chief Justice was 'not always a comfortable experience', it was 'seldom dull' because Barwick 'was given to testing propositions in the fire of a debate which he would originate'. Hughes concluded: of 'this true disciple of the law … let us say, in the words attributed to Christ in St Matthew's gospel: Well done thou good and faithful servant … enter thou into the joy of thy lord.'[33]

Fifteen years later, in 2012, Hughes delivered the annual Garfield Barwick Address, an event organised by Liberal lawyers.[34] He worked long hours on several drafts, wanting to leave behind a considered account of a man he greatly admired: 'By any acceptable standard, [Barwick] was a truly great Australian.' Hughes revisited the subject of Barwick's judicial methods. Working in Barwick's Court 'was not a task for the faint-hearted'. Yet, for anyone holding themselves qualified for appellate work, 'an ability to face fast judicial bowling, including short-pitched bumpers, should be part of one's forensic equipment'. The analogy was a good one in highlighting the force of Barwick's many interventions. It does not, however, apply to those occasions where sarcasm, dismissiveness and incivility were his weapons of choice.

Hughes also referred to two subjects that had long been on his mind. First, Tom's father was the solicitor for Atlantic Union Oil when it issued a bankruptcy petition against the newly married Garfield Barwick. Barwick had assumed the primary responsibility for his younger brother, a minor, who conducted a service station business hit by the Great Depression. The matter appeared settled when, ill advisedly, Barwick sued Atlantic for defamation based on words published about him during the dispute. Hughes likened this action to that of someone who, having escaped the lion's den, returned to recover his hat. Atlantic sought a rehearing of the original petition and Tom's father briefed a fearsome silk who went after Barwick. The court made a sequestration order and the Barwicks endured a period of 'crushing penury'. Barwick knew that Hughes, who had arrived at the Bar in 1949, was the son of the solicitor who had procured his bankruptcy. Yet he never allowed the past to intrude on their relationship.

Hughes – perhaps sensibly – never raised the second subject with Barwick. He had long believed that the Chief Justice had 'erred in principle' in advising Kerr on 10 November 1975 that, in the then existing circumstances, the dismissal of the Whitlam Government would be a proper exercise of the Governor-General's executive powers. This advice, though 'legally unimpeachable', had placed Barwick in a role adjunctive to the exercise of executive power. 'No judge in whom the judicial power of the Commonwealth is vested should participate in any way in the exercise of its executive power.' When Barwick was Attorney-General, he decided that he, not a judge, should authorise telephone interceptions on behalf of ASIO. Barwick would have avoided the later criticism if he had adhered to the principle that no judge should exercise an executive function unrelated to the exercise of judicial power. Fortunately, Hughes noted, there was no legal challenge to Kerr's withdrawal of Whitlam's commission, as Barwick would have been obliged to disqualify himself from any adjudication.

In his 1980 diary, Hughes wrote of Barwick: 'I do revere him.'[35] He might not have revered John Gorton but he admired and loved him. Tom saw Gorton in hospital just before he died on Sunday 19 May 2002. Gorton recognised his friend and, for a brief moment, they held hands. Gorton was privately cremated and a State memorial service was arranged for Friday 31 May at St Andrew's Anglican Cathedral, Sydney. Hughes had earlier attended the condolence debate in the House of Representatives, after which he joined John Howard, members of Gorton's family and Ainsley Gotto in the Prime Minister's suite. Over lunch, they discussed the question of whether Malcolm Fraser would, or even should, attend the memorial service. Wisely, the prevailing view was to let matters take their course.

Gorton had asked Hughes to deliver the eulogy. Tom undertook 'a very considerable preparation'; everything was 'very carefully thought out'.[36] The text went through several drafts, each one a little more strongly worded. Hughes believed that Fraser's action in 1971 was founded on misrepresentation and poor judgment, and should not be ignored or smothered by anodyne prose. Fraser knew what to expect, once he learnt that Hughes would deliver the eulogy. He, too, 'was prepared'.[37] Others thought Hughes might have an additional or a different target. Bill Haffenden, a Sydney barrister, wrote to him three days before the service: 'We Anglicans would not regard any "accidental" derogatory remark about Sir William McMahon in our Cathedral as a major sin!'[38]

Some 400 people attended the service. Whitlam and Fraser sat with their wives in a fourth row pew. The proceedings were notable for the hymns loved by Anglicans of all traditions: 'And Did Those Feet in Ancient Time', 'My God, How Great Thou Art' and 'Praise my Soul the King of Heaven'. There was a thunderous fly-past by FA-18 aircraft from Gorton's wartime unit, No 77 Squadron, in 'missing man' formation. Yet, unquestionably, Tom Hughes' eulogy was the memorable event.

Hughes spoke of Gorton the private man, of his unconventional upbringing, of the fighter pilot and his ministerial career. He captured the unique mixture of 'the larrikin and the gentleman' in Gorton, his candour and magnetism, and his considerable intellectual capacity. He referred to Gorton's determination to be an agent of change in the machinery of government. There was a reminder of his eye for the talented misfit in the promotion of Bill Wentworth, whose 'absolute disbelief in the virtues of tact' was one of many factors that had kept him on the outer in the Menzies and Holt years. Hughes also highlighted Gorton's individual stamp on Australia's defence and foreign policy and his firm belief that Australia was a single national entity for the purposes of economic management.

No one in the Cathedral could reasonably judge any of the above as inappropriate. Everything changed when Hughes turned to the 'political assassination' of March 1971.

> No treatment of the life of Sir John Gorton would be complete without some reference to the events surrounding his political demise as Prime Minister, and I realise that what I am about to say is said in the distinguished presence, amongst many others, of a former Parliamentary colleague [Fraser]. But I have to speak the truth, and I will.

Internal opposition came to a head when Fraser resigned, 'quite unnecessarily', because of Gorton's supposed disloyalty over dealings with a journalist and his alleged refusal to listen to ministers in making decisions. Hughes provided a shorthand version of the story, discussed earlier, of the call-out of the Pacific Islands Regiment, and referred to his own successful association with Fraser to dissuade Gorton from taking unilateral action. He recalled Fraser's agreement, in Andrew Peacock's presence, with Hughes' recollection of events. Hughes added that Gorton had intended no disloyalty, and in the House had complimented Fraser, who had just described him as unworthy to hold the high office of Prime Minister. As for the internal opposition, which seized upon Fraser's resignation to oust Gorton, their actions 'resembled the downhill stampede as described in St Matthews Gospel of the proverbial Gadarene swine'. There was a final thrust: 'History's judgment will be kinder [to Gorton] than it will be upon those who conspired to bring him down.'

Outside the Cathedral, and during the next few days, the chatter revolved around Hughes' eulogy. Whereas long-time Gorton supporters were mostly delighted, the journalist Alan Ramsey thought that funeral rites were 'supposedly about resolution'. He contrasted Hughes' 'charmless, graceless eloquence', with Whitlam's compassion. Whitlam had touched Fraser on the shoulder and whispered words from St John's Gospel quoted in the service: 'Let not your heart be troubled.' Responding to Ramsey, Hughes explained that a eulogy 'to have enduring value should include a truthful account of the main events in the life of the subject'. He had to set the record straight or be 'unfaithful to history'.[39] Hughes also said he had spoken only about Fraser's lack of judgment and his selective recollection; he had not attacked his character.

Ramsey had written that, by 'dumping' on Fraser, Hughes had 'squared the ledger' for his own 'political assassination' in 1971. Yet Hughes had long come to terms with his sacking. He regretted only the *manner* of his departure from politics, and of being deprived of the opportunity to promote effective trade practices legislation and Commonwealth sovereignty over Australia's territorial sea. Otherwise, as he told a judge of the WA Supreme Court in 2009, his sacking by McMahon 'was a turning point for the better. I would never have been happy in, or supporting, a government led by Fraser.' Besides, 'it is really a badge of honour to have been dismissed by Australia's worst Prime Minister to date. Perhaps, however, the present incumbent [Kevin Rudd] will run him close.'[40]

Two other deaths reminded Hughes of a more distant past. Red Burt, aged 86, died on 4 September 2004. Hughes was overseas and missed the State funeral. Tom wrote to Burt's daughter describing her father as 'one of my oldest and dearest friends'. He explained that Burt's oft-quoted remark – the Sunderland, piloted by the pair of them, was 'the most dangerous in the Bay (of Biscay)' – referred to the safety of the rest of their crew. He spoke of Burt's 'enviably powerful armoury for a judge', and listed qualities Hughes himself liked to see on the Bench: 'a limpid mind, a great grasp of principle, a capacity for clear and simple expression and a tolerant understanding of the foibles of human nature.' The letter included a significant revelation. Early in 1970, Hughes as Attorney-General asked Burt to consider appointment to the High Court. Red replied that he had a young family, the travelling would have been onerous and he was already enjoying judicial office in his own State.[41]

Stan Reeve, the first pilot in Mabbett's Sunderland crew of 1944, died on 22 June 2011 aged 93, survived by his wife of 64 years, five of his children, 21 grandchildren and seven great grandchildren. Reeve had enlisted in 1942 while working as a factory foreman in Brisbane, trained first at Bradfield Park and then at Point Cook, and joined 10 Squadron two months before Tom arrived at the end of 1943. After the War, Reeve took over the family dairy farm at Campbelltown, NSW, where he spent the rest of his working life. A devout Christian, Reeve's funeral was held at St David's Presbyterian Church, Campbelltown, and Tom Hughes was among the mourners.

Disasters and triumphs

Tom had a great affection for Robert, and kept press cuttings of all his Australian visits. There was bound to be tension, however, when the much older brother assumed his role of authority, such as the occasion when he instructed the world-renowned art critic on the correct method of extracting toothpaste from the tube.[42] Robert's almost-fatal car accident near Broome on 30 May 1999 traumatised the entire family. Tom and Chrissie went to Perth for a few days to visit him in hospital but Robert did not regain consciousness while they were there. Malcolm told Tom in October 2000 that Robert felt his brother lacked interest in what was happening to him. Tom assured Robert 'this is not so and never has been'. He pointed out that Robert either eluded or ignored Tom's efforts to contact him, leaving Tom to assume that 'your lack of communication was a matter of choice on your part'. He had done his best to keep in touch with developments through the Turnbulls.[43] In fact, Lucy and Malcolm were in the best position to take charge, and their efforts over the months and years after the accident explain why Robert dedicated *Things I Didn't Know* to them and to their children.

Lucy Turnbull published her book, *Biography of a City*, in 1999. In the same year, Malcolm led the failed campaign for a republic and Lucy was elected to the Sydney City Council on Frank Sartor's 'Living Sydney' ticket, and became Deputy Lord Mayor. Sartor entered State Parliament in March

2003 and a proud father sat in the Gallery when the Council unanimously elected Lucy as Sydney's first female Lord Mayor. Given the approaching merger with the South Sydney Council, she decided not to stand for any position in the April 2004 elections, her position being made all the more difficult because Malcolm, who had been the Federal Treasurer of the Liberal Party, was seeking Liberal preselection for Wentworth. He defeated the sitting Liberal, Peter King, for whom Tom Hughes had once written a warm reference.

Lucy and Malcolm had commissioned Jiawei Shen, who was born in Shanghai and emigrated to Australia in 1989, to paint Tom's portrait. The completed portrait was presented to the National Portrait Gallery in February 2004. Lucy made the presentation and spoke of her father's insight, focus and formidable ability to hold people's attention.[44] The painting made the short list for the 2004 Archibald Prize, won by Craig Rudd's portrait of the Aboriginal actor David Gulpilil. Edmund Capon ensured that Tom was hung next to the magistrate Pat O'Shane with 'the crusty old silk in his robes … pointing menacingly at the controversial magistrate'.[45] Shen painted another portrait of Hughes, which a number of senior members of the Bar presented to the Bar Association at a ceremony on 18 March 2005. In the same year, the French Government made him a Chevalier of the Légion d'Honneur for his role as a pilot during the Normandy landings.

Malcolm Turnbull won the seat of Wentworth at the federal election of 9 October 2004. His father-in-law joined a convoy of Wentworth Liberals to hear his maiden speech in the House of Representatives. Howard brought Turnbull into the ministry early in 2007. Defeated by Dr Brendan Nelson in the ballot for the leadership after the 2007 election defeat, Turnbull successfully challenged Nelson in 2008 only to lose the leadership to Tony Abbott by one vote in December 2009. Although he was no longer in such close and frequent contact with his son-in-law, Tom's strong sense of family loyalty, and his preference for centrist policy positions, fired up his anger at Turnbull's defeat. He sent a handwritten note to Malcolm on 16 December urging him to remain in politics and promising the support he had given at the 2004 and 2007 elections. 'There is room only for improvement and the Party's present folly will pass.' Next day, Tom wrote to Robert about the Party Room vote:

> This is a potentially catastrophic decision. But Malcolm, to his great credit, stood up for his principles and paid the price. To elect Abbott in his place is the equivalent of putting the bull in charge of the china shop or the principal lunatic in charge of the asylum. Abbott's behaviour in relation to the risks of global warming may be compared to the oscillations of the weather vane.[46]

Looking ahead, the decision, in terms of immediate electoral success, did not prove to be 'catastrophic'. Nevertheless, Hughes' assessment in 2009, stripped of the strong metaphors, reflected legitimate fears within the 'liberal' sect of the broad church, and were partially borne out after the Party won government in 2013.

23

'The profession has every reason to be grateful to you'

Tom Hughes wrote to the President of the NSW Bar Association on 28 June 2012 regarding his decision not to renew his practice certificate.

> This was not an easy step to take; but one cannot go on for ever and I have finished up where I want to be: a semi-skilled grazier with a very good manager and a wife who loves the country, as I do. It was my good fortune to be at the Bar in its salad days.[1]

Although he told a colleague in Blackstone Chambers that he did not want to give it all away, he was not getting enough work and realised that his time 'had come'. Just as in 1972, when he left politics, he was 'not consumed by regrets', even though he had more reason to grieve leaving his first love, the law. His philosophy was unchanged. As he said of his departure from politics, 'you change the course with no regrets for the past'. He claims not to miss the Bar, but retains one connection, having accepted an appointment as an honorary member of Blackstone Chambers.[2]

Life on the estate

Tom always wanted to retire to the country and not to the city, and Bannister Station admirably suits his purpose. The refurbished and extended home provides a comfortable setting for reading newspapers, biographies and histories. Much as he likes to read, the former barrister, who had been accustomed to long hours of activity, needs to do more. Although his greater age restricts him physically, he has not lost any of the determination to remain involved. Tom spends many days driving around Bannister, inspecting and working on the property, and regularly recording rainfall figures. He visits Goulburn and Canberra, takes trips to Sydney, where Chrissie owns a large flat in Bellevue Hill, drives with his manager to stock sales and is constantly in personal or telephone contact with family and friends. The fact that email and the internet have always been foreign territory has never inhibited him.

The country estate now consists of three parts: Marsland, Bannister Station and 'Burragurrundah'. Marsland comprises nearly 3000 acres, slightly reduced because Tom sold poorer quality land as seven residential blocks. Initially, Marsland produced fine wool; these days, the primary function of the whole estate is to produce beef cattle and prime lambs for the domestic and export markets. Bannister originally consisted of 2500 acres to which another 2700 were added when Tom and Malcolm Turnbull bought a neighbouring farm, 'Pomeroy', which was later sold. Chrissie recently bought another 903 acres adjoining Bannister. Burragurrundah, neighbouring Marsland, comprises 2500 acres of land leased from Roden and Gabrielle King. Overall, his land aggregation is substantial, placing him in the top 10 per cent in the region and, in terms of its operation, perhaps in the top 20 per cent in New South Wales.[3] Tom owns a profitable enterprise – a very profitable one in good seasons – and continues to draw income from a variety of sources.

Mark Boileau has managed the Hughes properties since his appointment in March 1983. Born in 1959, the son of a soldier settler of French Huguenot extraction, Boileau took a two-year course at Orange Agricultural College. Chrissie Hughes had wanted to change managers and she and Tom met Boileau who, at the time, was working on his family's farm, managing another property and doing casual work for Elders. A real estate agent was present at the meeting, because selling Marsland was also under consideration. Mark was appointed, but it was not an auspicious moment to start a new job. The region was in the midst of drought. Not that he worked exclusively for the Hughes; that came much later. When Marsland was the sole property in operation, Boileau ran a contracting business where he employed up to 13 workers as well as managing seven or eight other properties. He now works exclusively for Tom and Chrissie at an hourly rate and receives bonuses. There is no contract, just a 'handshake agreement'. Mark can trust his employer; he knows that 'integrity is a very big thing with Tom'. The main paperwork consists of the manager's weekly report, summarising the work done and outlining the next week's schedule.

Tom has an impressive record for retaining those he employs. Anne Sloan worked as a secretary for 'Mr Hughes' for four decades and Mark Boileau is about to start his 33rd year as manager. Tom is a generous man who pays well and on time. When Tom and Chrissie moved house to Bannister, they arranged for Mark to live in their house at Marsland. For a manager, keen to implement the advice of an agronomist and the local Elders branch manager, it helps that his employer is ready and able to hire or buy whatever is deemed necessary. It helps, too, that the employer takes the advice of his manager. Prudently, Boileau learnt to accommodate Tom's moods and idiosyncrasies, and his desire to get things done quickly. Occasionally, the 'semi-skilled grazier' needs guidance as well as advice, and Tom always accepts it without taking offence. He likes stock auctions, likes to bid, and likes to win, and there were times when Mark felt bound to counsel restraint.[4]

Tom retains his interest in the racing industry. On his own admission, he has not been an overly successful racehorse owner. There have been occasions, however, when a horse gave cause for optimism. The most recent example was 'Party Dress', jointly owned by Chrissie and Tom and trained by the late Guy Walter. Her most significant victory was at Royal Randwick on 18 January 2014 where, starting at 25/1, she won the Benchmark 80 Handicap and collected $48,750 in prize money. She then finished fourth at Randwick on 8 February and a disappointing ninth at Rosehill on 5 July. The horse subsequently raced at Canberra for three near-last finishes before passing to a new owner. Tom Hughes explained his motivation and reasoning behind racing horses in an address to the Australian Club on 21 March 2001.[5] He and Chrissie avoided expensive purchases at yearling sales and chose instead to breed animals that they hoped, 'with supreme optimism', would eventually win races. What they both enjoyed was watching 'the interaction between horses', experiencing 'the interaction between horses and humans', and observing 'the interaction between humans and horses' on a racecourse. 'Altogether the mixture of perceptions is utterly absorbing.'

Family and friends

Tom has always been generous in supporting charitable causes, and has been extraordinarily caring for, and loyal to, his family and friends. With his brother Geoffrey, he was on hand when Constance went through a divorce. Tom helped her financially thereafter and, with Robert, enabled Constance to take a trip to Italy, England and New York in 1990.[6] He continued in different ways to support Tom Jnr, to the extent that some juniors in Wardell Chambers felt aggrieved because of what they saw as a commensurate lack of support for their careers.[7] Always inclusive, Tom looks upon Chrissie's daughters as his own, just as he takes delight in the company of his granddaughter by Tom Jnr's second marriage. Joanna continues to be part of his life, and she was a guest, along with Deeta Colvin, at the grand 90th birthday party for Tom at the Turnbull's' home in Point Piper in November 2013.

There have been times of sadness. Robert Hughes died at Calvary Hospital in the Bronx, New York, on 6 August 2012. His third wife, Doris Downes, an American botanical artist, was at his bedside. They had married in 2001 and, of his three marriages, this one proved the happiest. Robert's death deeply affected his oldest sibling. After a period of ill health, Constance died on 10 July 2015. She had taken sole ownership of a house in Cremorne following a legal battle with her former husband and, after selling the property, moved into the Emanuel Retirement Village in Woollahra. Both Constance and Tom had assisted Robert in research for his memoir *Things I Didn't Know*, and felt disappointed by the number of factual errors and particularly by what they saw as misrepresentation or misunderstanding of their parents.

Friends, colleagues and clients who were ill or in some sort of trouble could expect to hear from Tom. He stood by those, like Laurie Connell and Robbie Waterhouse, whom he thought had been through enough. In 1983, he supported Harry M Miller for continued membership of the Australian Jockey Club (AJC), after Miller had served 10 months in prison for fraud, and a member of the AJC had queried his future association with the club.[8] Hughes was one of many who backed Neil Forsyth QC when the Australian Taxation Office in 1985 charged him with conspiracy to defraud the Commonwealth of $30 million. Forsyth, a foremost tax lawyer, had provided legal advice to five others who were engaged in a tax avoidance scheme. Hughes assisted Forsyth in June-July 1989, mostly at $3250 a day and at a time when he regularly sought between $4000 and $6000. Appalled by what he saw as an unjust and relentless pursuit of a lawyer legitimately advising his clients, he was delighted when a judge in 1990 ordered the jury to acquit Forsyth because the Crown had presented insufficient evidence against him. Hughes and Forsyth maintained a congenial friendship[9] until the latter's death at the age of 58 in 1997, an event possibly hastened by what Hughes and others regarded as persecution by the Australian Taxation Office. In 2000, in a letter to Ruth McColl SC, the President of the NSW Bar Association, Hughes and Dyson Heydon supported Stephen Archer's unsuccessful application for what they called 'long overdue' appointment as Senior Counsel. After downplaying several factors mitigating against success – including Archer's former bankruptcy and failure to file tax returns – they emphasised, among other things, Archer's busy practice, his conduct of major and lengthy litigation, his capabilities as a trial lawyer, 'deep knowledge of the law' and willingness and ability 'to advance the interests of his client with all proper vigour'.[10] During the summer vacation of January 2004, Hughes rang Lynette MacDonald, the Clerk of Blackstone Chambers, as soon as he heard the news that her mother had been savagely murdered by a white man in Johannesburg. He told her that the chambers would pay her fares to attend the funeral. For a long time thereafter, 'Mr Hughes' was on hand with 'masses of compassion' as MacDonald struggled to come to terms with this horrific event.[11]

In one instance, Hughes' readiness to stand by friends and colleagues reflected a degree of unworldliness. Dyson Heydon recalled attending an early morning meeting with Hughes in November 1995 when the papers were reporting the suicide of former Justice David Yeldham. Hughes had written to Yeldham the night before expressing sympathy over the rumours being spread about him, apparently unaware that they had been around for some time, and that they were accurate in so far as they referred to homosexual trysts in the toilets at a railway station.[12]

Hughes is perfectly aware that he had a good start in life. He was born into a comfortable world, had a happy childhood, attended excellent schools and enjoyed varied and exciting holidays. His father's name and connections protected and promoted him at critical stages in the RAAF and, later, helped him find chambers and to get work in the 1950s. Atwill, Carrick and Howard eased him into preselection for Parkes; Carrick and Osborne were on hand to help with Berowra. Gorton gave him a ministerial position and Deane assisted his return to Selborne Chambers. Perhaps he was conscious of these advantages, and of how he added value to them, when a guest at a dinner party in July 1979 contended that Lucy would do better in life than a woman 'struggling along' without the assistance of a well-placed father. Tom wrote the following in his diary: 'What bullshit all this is! Lucy may get her chance partly because of me. But in fact, if she does not capitalize on this opportunity she will be buried much faster than Lucy Nurks would have been.'[13] Lucy did more than make the most of opportunities created by her father. She became the most successful of Tom's children both in material terms and in being able to make a difference to the world in which she moves.

Tom never hesitates to speak highly of his children. Lucy is very much the 'darling daughter'. Malcolm Turnbull once described her as 'the family glue'; if there is to be a family gathering she is likely to be the one to organise it.[14] Importantly, Lucy has recently taken over the financial responsibility for Joanna. Observing that Tom Jnr is building a criminal law practice at Ada Evans Chambers in Pitt Street, is happily married to his third wife and has good relationships with the two children of his previous marriages, Tom is confident about his elder son's future. Michael is not widely known outside family and business circles. Securely married to Jane, he has two sons, is well liked and never enters troubled waters. After leaving Turnbull & Partners in 1994, he continued to work in banking and investment companies before becoming Head of Corporate Finance at Ord Minnett. In September 2014, he took a position as Commercial Director in the senior management team of SeaLink Travel Group, where he has the task of identifying and securing new business opportunities. Lucy became a director of SeaLink in August 2013, just before its listing on the Australian Securities Exchange, and was appointed Deputy Chairman in July 2015 but resigned after her husband became Prime Minister. Proud of his children, Tom delights in his son-in-law's elevation to high office. Tom looked very much the proud patriarch of the four generations of his family who attended Malcolm Turnbull's swearing-in-ceremony at Government House on 15 September 2015.

The patriarch is also proudly Australian. His ancestry did not leave him with an allegiance elsewhere. It says a great deal that Tom's sole visit to the land of his Irish forbears occurred in 1945 when, after attending a naval course in Northern Ireland, he and two friends crossed the border to visit Dublin and to eat a good dinner before returning to their base on the English south coast. Tom has never been to County Roscommon where his paternal great-great-grandfather was born, nor has he seen Drumshanbo in County Leitrim where Thomas and Maria Hughes lived before migrating to New South Wales with their six children in 1839. In time, London became a workplace abroad, and England, France and the European snowfields became his holiday destinations. Although Tom later recovered the Catholicity of his inheritance, he has not chosen to explore or advertise its Irish component. In retrospect, the Great War of 1914-18, the 'Easter Uprising' in Dublin and the conscription crisis in Australia, all occurring before Tom was born, marked a dividing line in the history of his branch of the Hughes family. His professional and cultural attachment to his English inheritance has been more enduring, but not to the extent of forging or sustaining another loyalty.

Tributes, reflections and habits

As the law has been Tom Hughes' principal occupation since 1949, it is appropriate to end this book by reflecting on his time as 'a cab on the rank'.

There were many occasions, leading up to and following Hughes' retirement from the Bar, when former and current judges, and barristers and solicitors, commented publicly or privately on his career as an advocate. Predictably, nearly all came to praise him. Tom Hughes was, and still is, highly regarded in the profession, and the Bar, whether welcoming or farewelling colleagues, indulges in magniloquence on public occasions. When journalists hunted for critics of Hughes, they either returned to their desks empty-handed, or reported the comments of those who took refuge in anonymity. After Richard Coleman published a profile of him in the *SMH* in 1985, and Hughes said Coleman had treated him more kindly than he deserved, Coleman replied that he had 'presented a number of people with a golden opportunity to have a free kick at your expense, but nobody did'.[15]

By temperament intense, demanding and impatient, Hughes could become cold ('frosty') or explosive in responding to pressure. These moments soon passed. His seniority and stature guaranteed him respect and deference as Chairman of the Board but an authoritarian tendency did irritate some barristers. Even a good friend and admirer acknowledged that his time in charge at Blackstone Chambers was 'not a huge success'.[16] Given that up to 80 per cent of barristers struggled to make a good living, inevitably some never bothered to hide their envy of a colleague who attracted so many rich clients. What perhaps was less well known was the Tom Hughes who could tell a colleague '(t)here is nothing as satisfying as winning a case for the little man'.[17] Some younger barristers, admitted during the final third of Hughes' time at the Bar, dismissed his declamatory and theatrical advocacy as a relic of a disappearing era. Nevertheless, as Philip Selth, Executive Director of the NSW Bar Association since 1997, pointed out, Hughes remained the respected elder statesman and 'an icon of the Bar'.[18]

On 24 July 2012, Terry Tobin QC, the Chancellor of the University of Notre Dame Australia, conferred the degree of Doctor of Laws *honoris causa* on the Honourable Thomas Eyre Forrest Hughes AO QC. Members of his family and of the NSW Bar Association as well as several judges and MPs attended the ceremony. The Chancellor described Hughes as 'the greatest advocate of his era'. Whether he was actually 'the greatest' is a question for which there is no agreed answer. Much, obviously, depends on the definitions of 'era' and of 'greatest'. Besides, Tom Hughes does not stand out in the way that Barwick clearly did in the 1940s and 1950s. Perhaps it would be better to settle for 'great', or to leave the debate to that stage of the night when sporting buffs argue the relative merits of halfbacks, batsmen, or netballers. The more useful exercise is to examine just what it was that made and distinguished Tom Hughes as a leading barrister for more than three decades. Here, at least, there is a remarkable consensus.

Michael McHugh reflected this agreement when speaking at the lavish and well-attended party organised by the NSW Bar Association to mark Tom Hughes' 90th birthday. McHugh said Hughes

> embodied the public's perception of the great advocate – dashing, dominating, charismatic, patrician and handsome – equally at home cross examining a cowering witness or addressing a jury or the High Court or the Privy Council. As an advocate, he was an elemental force of nature. In court, he was a sight to behold with his sculptured jaw, his icy stare at a dissembling witness and his habit of wheeling around to face the back of a court after he asked a question, a habit which a journalist once described as "a menacing pirouette". When addressing the court, he would stand like a 19th century actor, extending one arm in front of him with the other arm behind his robe at his back. He dominated judges and juries and was, I can tell you, as formidable an opponent as any barrister has had to face. By some means or

> other, he always knew the point that judges and juries would find most persuasive.

Other former judges drew similar pictures. Murray Gleeson described Hughes as 'a charismatic advocate'. Dyson Heydon considered that Hughes and Gleeson stood out for their capacity to dominate a courtroom. Sir Anthony Mason explained some of the means at Hughes' disposal: the 'arresting, even archaic, language'; the 'imposing presence and voice, evocative of the image of an aristocratic Guards officer', and the habit of looking at the judge or jury but not the witness in the course of cross-examination. Jim Merralls, the Victorian QC who appeared with him and against him, said Hughes 'could capture a court'. Journalists took up many of the same themes. Coleman, for example, also used the word 'patrician' and wrote of Hughes' 'theatricality' and of his being a 'dominating figure' in the courtroom. Not all, however, depicted Tom Hughes as 'dashing' and 'handsome'. During the Rivkin trial, DD McNicoll claimed that 'Frosty' had 'spent so many of his 77 summers in the sun that he looks like a tall prune wearing a wig and half glasses'.[19]

It was rare for profiles of Hughes not to mention his use of language. Judges, opposing counsel and journalists sometimes needed a dictionary when Hughes launched words such as 'irrefragable' and 'minatory' into an argument (a journalist or a copy editor dealing with the Corby case reproduced the latter as 'military'). Hughes' approach to written opinions was slightly different.

> I have always been … very fussy about how I express myself when writing legal opinions. The aim being to be as brief as the nature of the case permits and clear, bearing in mind that opinions on legal subjects are to be read by clients who don't want long essays in which free rein is given to the expression of doubts … you're paid for your opinion and not for your doubts. It's incumbent upon counsel to reach an opinion on the particular question and express it clearly and concisely.

He made the further point that it required 'a great deal of polishing' to write concise and clear opinions. Hence, Hughes never used recording equipment, preferring to write everything in longhand and to 'correct it again and again'.[20] It is a very distinctive longhand, starting evenly across the top of the page before sliding to the right as he descended to the bottom.

Clarrie Harders observed that Hughes 'took great pride in his written work' and 'wrote very well'; his opinions were a pleasure to read, unlike those of some other Attorneys-General. Hughes never hesitated to put his slant and style on his opinions. After seeing Robert Hughes on television adopting a similar speaking and literary style, Harders decided it must be 'a family trait'.

Harders saw it as a great pity that Hughes never sat on the High Court; his judgments 'would have been a joy to read'.[21]

In 2008, Justin Gleeson SC, the present Commonwealth Solicitor-General, provided indirect support for McHugh's point about Hughes knowing what judges and juries 'would find most persuasive'. He drew attention to an approach where Hughes' words carefully shifted a court's attention away from something damaging to his client. Gleeson suggested that Hughes was an advocate who gave attention to Cicero's demand that any speech should begin with an *exordium* 'whose role was to evoke the good will of the listener' to its subsequent substance.[22] Gleeson cited the *Hospital Products case*,[23] where Hughes decided not to challenge findings of dishonesty made against his client, accepting privately that the client's behaviour was less than honourable. Rather, he opened by saying that the appeal to the High Court was about the choice of remedy. He conceded that the plaintiff was entitled to damages, but the trial judge and the Court of Appeal had granted equitable relief based on a fiduciary relationship between the plaintiff and the distributor. Hughes successfully argued that 'the Courts have been reluctant to inject fiduciary concepts into ordinary arm's length commercial dealings'.

Sir Anthony Mason observed that, unlike some exceptional advocates, Hughes 'was also a good lawyer'. For that reason, 'he was at home in any court, including the High Court where he argued constitutional questions with great ability'. Murray Gleeson also considered him 'an excellent lawyer', and made a similar point about his 'being equally at home in jury trials or before appellate courts'. Hughes had made his own contributions to precedent and statutory interpretations: among them in *Jones v Skelton*,[24] the *Concrete Pipes case*,[25] the *Hospital Products case*[26] and *Crimmins*.[27]

One obvious question, therefore, is why he did not go to the Bench. After all, even Frank McAlary, who clashed with Hughes in 11 Selborne, thought 'Old Tom could have been a judge if he wanted to be'.[28]

Hughes received a number of approaches, starting with McMahon's 'some sort of sop' for his sacking as Attorney-General. There was no possibility of accepting an invitation to join the NSW Supreme Court engineered by that Prime Minister.[29] Hughes' name would occasionally appear in the press when vacancies occurred in the High Court. In March 1985, he was asked if he would accept appointment as Chief Justice of the ACT Supreme Court. Gavan Griffith, the Commonwealth Solicitor-General, urged him to accept, and so did Lucy and Malcolm Turnbull. Hughes expressed initial interest but then decided it was not 'financially feasible', and his accountant told him the idea was 'out of the question'.[30] In any case, Hughes' brief interest in the ACT position was probably a temporary aberration. In addition to the compelling financial argument against any judicial appointment, Hughes also sensed that he was not, by temperament, suited to judicial activity. Dyson Heydon, who thought he would have been very good on the High Court or on any Court of Appeal, said Hughes would not have appreciated having to go at the pace of someone else. What Hughes called his lack of patience, Heydon described as having 'ants in his pants'.[31] No doubt correctly, Michael Kirby thought Hughes would never have been able to hide his impatience while sitting on the Bench.[32]

Terry Tobin stressed at the Notre Dame degree ceremony that there was more to Hughes than his 'genius as a trial lawyer'. There were also 'his qualities of restraint in the pursuit of victory and his faithfulness to the ethics of the profession'. Hughes liked to win, and could be grumpy in defeat, but sought always to play straight. Sir William Deane said that Hughes 'not only became the acknowledged leader of the Bar but was always a person who could be completely trusted'.[33] Murray Gleeson saw Hughes having 'a lot of credibility'; he agreed with Deane's point about trust and said Hughes 'was not going to pull wool over anyone's eyes'.[34] Tom himself ranked 'integrity' and 'honesty' above most if not all values, and these values were not restricted to advocacy. It will be recalled that in March 1971 Lieutenant General Tom Daly said he had 'a high regard' for Hughes' ability, and 'an even higher regard' for his integrity.

Hughes was concerned about more than adherence to codes of personal behaviour. He respected the processes of the law. Cases should not be decided outside of the evidence. Trials and appeals should be conducted according to the rules. Heydon believed that Hughes 'liked the integrity of the process'.[35] He did not appreciate judges who transgressed the rules or used their position to intimidate or show off. Hughes' diaries and letters are full of commentaries about judges who failed to meet his high standards. Two examples from 1985 will suffice; both men are now dead. Hughes referred to one judge being 'his usual pompous & difficult self. He <u>knew</u> that he would have to grant leave, but decided to put us through the hoops, taking 45 minutes to do so. If I had been a helpless junior, he would have granted leave in 10 minutes or less' (emphasis in the original). Hughes wrote of another judge that it was impossible to say anything laudatory about someone who 'was cordially disliked because he was ill-tempered, discourteous, suspicious and slow'.[36]

At the same time, Hughes was always quick off the mark with a congratulatory note when those he admired achieved elevation. He was forever writing to Michael Kirby who kept rising in eminence. Kirby, in turn, remembered how in the 1980s, when it was not acceptable for his partner, Johan van Vloten, to accompany him, Tom Hughes and Neville Wran made sure that at least Michael Kirby was included in social invitations.[37] Hughes' personal files are full of letters to and from barristers on their appointment to the Bench. Deane wrote to him in July 1982 thanking him for his letter of congratulations on Deane's appointment to the High Court: 'I know that I have your friendship … as you will always have mine.' He persisted in hoping that the two of them would one day serve on the same Bench.[38] Some 33 years later, and in retirement, Hughes continued to send messages of congratulation, for example, to Justice Geoffrey Nettle on his appointment to the High Court in February 2015. Not surprisingly, exchanges with new judges involved some mutual backslapping in the course of recollecting appearances together or in opposition as counsel. Yet, allowing for the unqualified warmth and generosity of letters written on such occasions, the striking feature of the replies is their consistent acknowledgement of Hughes' role as a teacher in the craft of advocacy.

Hughes had very definite ideas about what constituted the desired qualities of an advocate. Following the conferral of his honorary degree at Notre Dame University, he delivered the Michael O'Dea Oration, a lecture established to recognise those who held the highest ethical and professional values in the practice of the law. He proffered advice to those who were embarking on a career at the Bar or who were already in active practice. While not claiming to possess any of them in full measure, he listed what he saw as the important qualities of a good barrister: integrity, courage, competence, resilience and the ability to react to fast-moving situations in litigation. To them, he added a need for objectivity, tact and courtesy towards the judge and one's opponents. He highlighted a primary duty: 'complete candour and complete honesty.' It was better to bring a problem in an argument to the fore rather than try to hide it.

In autobiographical notes kept in his papers and in other public talks, Hughes expanded upon some of these themes. He especially liked Sir Owen Dixon's notion that advocacy 'is tact in action', which he interpreted to mean 'the intuitive perception of the right thing to do or say and adroitness in dealing with persons or circumstances'. On a very different and practical level, he argued that barristers should never over book and never dump clients at the last moment. 'If you have to bail out do it early, otherwise you will … deservedly make enemies.' A barrister should also understand that his life is 'a one man practice' [sic] and that 'the life of an advocate is essentially a lonely one'. You might work with juniors but, on your feet in court, 'it is entirely up to oneself'.[39]

Tense and edgy before speaking, Tom Hughes was nonetheless comfortable standing alone. He had arrived at the Bar holding many advantages, including inherited strong moral principles and a work ethic. The advocate McHugh described in 2013 bore traces of the barristers Hughes had observed in the 1950s. Along the way, however, Hughes developed his own method and style. He may well prove to be the last of the traditional barrister class but, on his own, he could draw a crowd, expose a witness, persuade a jury and ensure that judges paid attention.

A final judgment

The Hon Tom Bathurst, who had been one of the leading commercial silks in Australia, wrote to Hughes on 9 June 2011 in response to Hughes' letter congratulating him on his appointment as Chief Justice of New South Wales:

> Like many of my contemporaries I sought to model myself on you not only in relation to your outstanding forensic and legal abilities but also the dignity, honesty and integrity you brought to any matter in which you appeared. The profession has every reason to be grateful to you.[40]

Chapter Notes

Chapter 1

1 For Tom Hughes' direct male line, see the Family Tree on p xiii. For the Hughes family history recorded from 1760, see A Stevens, *Generations: The Hughes Family of Sydney 1840-2007*, Kudos Studio, Sydney, 2007.

2 Ibid, pp 15-18.

3 *Wagga Wagga Express*, 22 January 1916. See also George Buxton, 'Gormly, James (1836-1922)', *Australian Dictionary of Biography* (*ADB*), vol 4, Melbourne University Press, Melbourne, 1972. Gormly told Sir Thomas Hughes in December 1918 that he could remember everything since he was aged two: Hughes Family Papers, Mitchell Library (ML), MSS 1222, vol 4, pp 9-10.

4 The above paragraphs on immigration draw upon RB Madgwick, *Immigration into Eastern Australia 1788-1851*, Longman, Green and Co, London, 1937, chs 6-8; P O'Farrell, *The Irish in Australia*, reprinted edition, NSW University Press, Sydney, 1987, p 69ff; R Reid, 'From Ballyduff to Boorowa – Irish Assisted Immigration to New South Wales, 1830-1896', in R Reid and K Johnson (eds), *The Irish Australians: Selected Articles for Australian and Irish Family Historians*, Society of Australian Genealogists and Ulster Historical Foundation, Sydney, 1984; and J Waldersee, *Catholic Society in New South Wales 1788-1860*, Sydney University Press, Sydney, 1974, ch 6.

5 For a discussion on this point, see Stevens, *Generations*, p 17. Stevens noted that a Charles Hughes of Campbell Street, an infant of one week, died two days after Maria Hughes.

6 Ibid.

7 Ibid, pp 18-40; C Cunneen, 'Hughes, John (1825-1885)', *ADB*, Supplementary vol, Melbourne University Press, Melbourne, 2005.

8 E Digby (ed), *Australian Men of Mark: Illustrated and Authentic Portraits*, vol 1, Charles F Maxwell, Sydney, 1889, p 250.

9 Ibid.

10 *Freeman's Journal*, 8 December 1866.

11 *Empire*, 25 November 1871. See also his speech of 17 November reported in the *Freeman's Journal*, 25 November 1871. The *Journal* on 18 November said he should be elected if the ratepayers valued integrity and ability, and a willingness to discharge duties and to effect needed civic reform.

12 *SMH*, 12 March 1868; M Lyons, 'O'Sullivan, Richard (1840?-1880)', *ADB*, vol 5, Melbourne University Press, Melbourne, 1974.

13 Quoted in Stevens, *Generations*, pp 31-32.

14 Eventually, after the Elizabeth Bay property was redeveloped, the Kincoppal and Rose Bay convents of the Sacred Heart were amalgamated at Rose Bay in 1971.

15 Stevens, *Generations*, chs 4 and 10; P Spearritt, 'Hughes, John Francis (1857-1912) and Sir Thomas (1863-1930)', *ADB*, vol 9, Melbourne University Press, Melbourne, 1993.

16 For the reformers, see H Golder, *Sydney's Electoral History: A Short Electoral History of Sydney City Council, 1842-1992*, Sydney City Council, Sydney, 1995, pp 36-37.

17 *Catholic Press*, 9 September 1909.

18 *Catholic Press* and *Freeman's Journal*, 13 December 1917.

19 Quoted in M McKernan, *The Australian People and the Great War*, Nelson, Melbourne, 1980, p 40.

20 Edward Raine (his father was in the same class as Geoffrey) to Tom Hughes, 22 February 1984, Personal 1982, *Hughes Papers*; M Munro, *Shirley: The Story of a School in Sydney*, compiled for the Shirley Old Girls' Union, printed by GW Graham and Co Pty Ltd, 1967, pp 2-4, 14-17; L Trethewey and K Whitehead, 'Sowing the Seeds of a Pre-Service Model of Teacher Education in the Early Twentieth Century', *Australian Journal of Teacher Education*, vol 28, no 1, 2003, pp 30-39.

21 Hughes Family Papers, ML, MSS 1222, vol 4, p 33.

22 Ibid, vol 1, 679-81.

23 For Hughes' letters relating to the Vidal family see ibid, vol 2, p 179ff.

24 England Football Online, <http://www.englandfootballonline.com/TeamPlyrsBios/PlayersUV/BioVidalRWS.html>, accessed 6 January 2016. After attending Westminster School and Christ Church, Oxford, Robert took holy orders and became an outstanding parish priest. He dropped the name 'Vidal' in 1892.

25 Cricket Archive, <http://cricketarchive.com/Archive/Scorecards/216/216474.html>, accessed 6 January 2016. These matches consisted of four-ball overs; teams in the Marylebone matches used 12 players.

26 HA Morrah, *The Oxford Union 1823-1923*, Cassell, London, 1923, ch 14; C Hollis, *The Oxford Union*, Evan Brothers, London, 1965, ch 6.

27 Interview: Hughes, 11 July 2013.

28 See the Vidal entry in *Crockford's Clerical Dictionary*, 1918-19.

29 Long after her death, Margaret's youngest son, who did not think her 'religious by nature', wrote that 'the switch cannot have cost her too much sleep. She wanted her man': Robert Hughes, *Things I Didn't Know: A Memoir*, Vintage Books, Sydney, 2007, p 82. Robert's three siblings agreed that their mother's conversion was sincere and profound.

30 For commentary, including details of the gowns worn, see *Evening News*, 8 January 1923; *SMH*, 9 January 1923; *Freeman's Journal* and *Catholic Press*, 11 January 1923.

Chapter 2

1 Autobiographical Notes, Hughes Papers.

2 Interview: Hughes, 17 June 2013.

3 Interview: Hughes, 13 July 2013.

4 Interview: Constance Crisp, 4 January 2013.

5 Geoffrey Hughes to Sir Thomas and Lady Hughes, March to May 1928, GH Family Letters, Hughes Papers.

6 Interviews: Constance Crisp, 4 January 2013; Hughes, 31 January 2014.

7 Geoffrey Hughes to Sir Thomas and Lady Hughes, March to May 1928, GH Family Letters, Hughes Papers.

8 Interview: Constance Crisp, 4 January 2013.

9 Margaret Hughes to Geoffrey Hughes, no date, Hughes Family Papers, ML, MSS 1222, vol 3, pp 275-91.

10 *Goulburn Penny Post*, 22 February 1932; *National Advocate*, 26 February 1932.

11 Geoffrey Hughes to Sir Thomas and Lady Hughes, 7 August 1928, GH Family Letters, Hughes Papers.

12 Tom Hughes, Autobiography, Hughes Papers.

13 For the later development and refurbishment of 'Jonah's' as a restaurant and 'boutique hotel', see Not Quite Nigella, 'Jonah's', <http://www.notquitenigella.com/2011/09/16/jonahs-whale-beach>. The received wisdom is that Constance Vidal, 'an English widow' and 'a woman with a vision', bought the land for £740, 'foresaw the advancement of the motor vehicle', and opened a roadhouse.

14 R Hughes, *Things I Didn't Know: A Memoir*, Vintage Books, Sydney, 2007, see especially pp 95-98, 113-14 and 118.

15 Hughes, *Things I Didn't Know*, pp 130-31.

16 Interview: Constance Crisp, 4 January 2013; Interview: Tom Hughes, 13 July 2013.

17 Ibid.

18 For the above paragraph, see A Stevens, *Generations: The Hughes Family of Sydney 1840-2007*, Kudos Studio, Sydney, 2007, pp 443-45; I Mackersey, *Smithy – The Life of Sir Charles Kingsford Smith*, Little, Brown and Co, Great Britain, 1998, see especially p 223. The two crew members of the *Kookaburra* died of thirst before they could be found. 'Smithy' and Ulm were located in time and, though cleared of organising a 'stunt', the committee raised concerns about their preparations and handling of the flight.

19 *SMH*, 7 October 1932.

20 Geoffrey Hughes to Sir Thomas and Lady Hughes, March to May 1928, GH Family Letters, Hughes Papers. Labor retained South Sydney in 1928, a seat, with the exception of the 1925 poll, it had held comfortably since 1906. Geoffrey Hughes never again nominated for preselection,

sensibly rejecting an invitation from the United Australia Party (UAP), the successor to the Nationalists, to stand against Labor's unbeatable 'Eddie' Ward in East Sydney in 1940.

21 Geoffrey Hughes to Sir Thomas and Lady Hughes, 7 August 1928, GH Family Letters, Hughes Papers.

22 Hughes, Autobiography, Hughes Papers; Interview (John Farquharson, 2000): Hughes, NLA, ORAL, TRC 3952, pp 13-14; Interview, Hughes, 13 July 2013. The NLA interview with Hughes will be identified by the interviewer's name 'Farquharson'. The author conducted all the interviews referring simply to 'Hughes'.

23 *Bar News*, Winter 2009, p 24; Interview: Sir Anthony Mason, 24 February 2015; Mason to Hughes, 19 June 2009, Personal 2009-11, Hughes Papers. Mason, mistakenly, thought that Tom actually attended school at Kincoppal.

24 School Reports, Hughes Papers.

25 Interview (Farquharson): Hughes, p 13.

26 *Our Alma Mater*, 1939-40.

27 Interview (Farquharson): Hughes, p 40.

28 D'Arcy-Burke, described in an obituary as 'our own Dr Johnson' as a dinner table companion, was too frail physically for military service, did not fit into a secular university environment, worked briefly – and unhappily – under Dr Evatt in External Affairs and became a librarian. He died in 1997: *Our Alma Mater*, 1997. Ryan scored a series of Passes in the 1940 Leaving Certificate. He became a colourful Professor of Anthropology in Western Australia, describing himself for the Perth magazine *Starfish* in 2013 as 'Brilliant. Enchanting. A bit of a shit'. He died the following year.

29 Interview (Farquharson): Hughes, p 40.

30 Interview: Hughes, 9 December 2013.

31 Sir Anthony Mason later provided indirect support for the Rector's assessment. In his letter to Hughes of 19 June 2009 he wrote: 'I remember my uncle telling me that you were not the most popular but the most respected boy at Riverview.' Personal 2009-11, Hughes Papers.

32 Interview (Farquharson): Hughes, p 10.

33 Interview (Farquharson): Hughes, pp 10 and 15; John and Judy Mackinolty (eds), *A Century Down Town: Sydney University Law School's First Hundred Years*, Sydney University Law School, Sydney, 1990, p 73.

34 Geoffrey Hughes to Tom Hughes, 4 October 1945, Rhodes Scholarship, Hughes Papers.

Chapter 3

1 Interviews: Hughes, 17 June and 4 November 2013.

2 NAA: A9300, Hughes TEF.

3 For the Scheme and its operations, see J McCarthy, *A Last Call of Empire: Australian Airmen, Britain and the Empire Air Training Scheme*, Australian War Memorial, Canberra, 1988; P Dennis et al (eds), *The Oxford Companion to Australian Military History*, Oxford University Press, Melbourne, 1995, pp 226-27.

4 M Hogan, *Almost Like Home: Living in Bradfield Park*, Ku-ring-gai Historical Society, Sydney, 2012, pp 22-36.

5 RAAF, Unit History Sheets, Operations Record Book, 2 ITS, NAA: A9816/397/349-50. On 1 July there were 1230 trainees and, on 1 August, 1442.

6 For the above two reminiscences, see Hogan, *Almost Like Home*, p 30; McCarthy, *Last Call*, p 53.

7 Tom's contacts at Bradfield Park did not include the tall and striking-looking young man who would later repeatedly engage his attention. Edward Gough Whitlam, already married and more advanced in his law degree, joined 2 ITS one month after Tom.

8 Recollections, 2009, Hughes Papers.

9 Margaret Hughes to Lady Hughes, no date, Hughes Papers.

10 *Narrandera Argus*, 13 December 1940.

11 NAA: A9300, Hughes GF.

12 For the Narrandera letters, see Tom's Letters September to October 1942, Hughes Papers.

13 JD Balfe, *War Without Glory: Australians in the Air War with Japan 1941-45*, Macmillan, Melbourne, 1984, pp 242-43.

14 Wing Commander Ranger was one of eight senior pilots who, in the 'Moratai Mutiny' of April 1945, applied to resign their commissions in protest against the assignment of RAAF fighter squadrons to minor operations.
15 1941-50, Hughes Papers. Seventy trainee pilots in Tom's course at 2 ITS went to 10 EFTS at Temora.
16 *Narrandera Argus*, 3 November 1942.
17 Recollections, 2009, Hughes Papers.
18 Thomas McKay (1909-2004), educated at Shore and Sydney University, was admitted to the NSW Bar in 1934. A prize-winning amateur golfer, he enlisted in the RAAF in 1940, was commissioned, promoted to Squadron Leader (1942) and to Wing Commander (1944). McKay later served as a prosecutor in war crimes trials, and as a Liberal member of the NSW Legislative Council (1966-78).
19 The Arvo Anson, the 'Faithful Annie', a British twin-engine monoplane, was used as a trainer by the RAAF during the Second World War.
20 Squadron Leader Hendy, a veteran of the First AIF, who joined the Administrative and Special Duties Branch of the RAAF and served briefly under Geoffrey Hughes at Narrandera in 1940, was adjutant at 8 SFTS Bundaberg.
21 The above three paragraphs draw upon McKay's letters to Geoffrey Hughes, Hughes Family Papers, ML, MSS 1222, vol 3, pp 501-03, and TS McKay, 'Memoirs and Some Random Thoughts: An Autobiography', 1988, vol 1, ML, MSS 5165, pp 30-32.
22 Tom's letters from 8 SFTS are located in Bundaberg, Hughes Papers.
23 RAAF, No 8 Service Flying Training School, Personnel Occurrence Report, vol 3, 25 November 1942, NAA: A10605/863/2.
24 Ibid, vol 4, 5-7 April 1943, 863/3.
25 Interview: Hughes, 17 June 2013.
26 RAAF, Unit History Sheets, Operations Record Book, 1 Air Observers School, Cootamundra, NAA: A9186/380/60 and 64.
27 Hughes Family Papers, ML, MSS 1222, vol 3, pp 500 and 511.
28 The above paragraph draws upon Hughes' war diary and Letters from abroad 1943, Hughes Papers. For Russell, see the entry by PA Davidson, *ADB*, vol 18, Melbourne University Press, Melbourne, 2012.
29 For Tyers' service record, see NAA: B2455, Tyers Alexander MacKenzie.
30 Interview: Hughes, 12 July 2013.

Chapter 4

1 For Tom's letters from October to December 1943, see Letters from abroad 1943, Hughes Papers. This chapter also draws upon Tom's log book and his war diary, Hughes Papers.
2 For 10 Squadron see KC Baff, *'Maritime is Number Ten': a history of No 10 Squadron RAAF, the Sunderland era 1939-1945*, KC Baff, Adelaide, 1983. See also RAAF Historical Section, *Units of the Royal Australian Air Force: a concise history*, Australian Government Publishing Service, Canberra, 1995, pp 8-11; S Eather, *Flying Squadrons of the Australian Defence Force*, Aerospace Publications, ACT, 1995, pp 41-44; A Stephens, *The Royal Australian Air Force: a history*, Oxford University Press, Melbourne, 2006, pp 75-79.
3 KC Baff, *'Maritime is Number Ten'*, Annex J; M Lax, 'The RAAF in Coastal Command 1939-45', *Proceedings of the 1994 RAAF History Conference*, Canberra, October 1994, pp 74-75.
4 Tom's letters and other letters relating to his time at Mount Batten can be found in Letters from UK 1944 and Letters from UK 1945, Hughes Papers.
5 Mabbett later headed the automotive engineering company, Repco; Reeve, a very committed Christian, returned to the family dairy farm; and Robertson became a manager with the Bank of NSW.
6 For a brief account of the incident, see KC Baff, *'Maritime Number Ten'*, p 358.
7 Ibid, p 367.
8 Ibid, pp 370-74.
9 Tom was aware that Lord Astor and his wife, Nancy Astor MP, were leading members of the 'Cliveden set'. They had been accused of being actively pro-Hitler because, for a time in the 1930s, they supported an entente with Germany.

10 Squadron Leader Father John Harper, a Catholic Chaplain with the RAAF in the UK, told Tom's parents in June 1944 that their son looked 'remarkably well', was very happy in his job and was highly regarded in the Squadron: 'there is hardly need for me to tell you of his spiritual welfare – he is the same Tom and so I've said enough.'

11 Carleton Kemp Allen (known as 'CK') was born in 1887 in Melbourne, the son of a Congregational pastor, read classics at the University of Sydney, won a scholarship to Oxford, enlisted in the British Army, was awarded the Military Cross in 1918, became a prominent Oxford law 'don' and was appointed the second Warden of Rhodes House (1931-52).

12 He exaggerated slightly: those elected from the early 18th century were usually conservatives of one kind or another, except that Gladstone, after leaving the Tories, once retained the seat as a Liberal, and Liberal Unionists and independents occasionally won elections.

13 See also, KC Baff, *'Maritime is Number Ten'*, p 389.

14 Ibid, pp 404-06; A Storr, *RAAF WW2 Fatalities: 10 Squadron, RAAF*, Alan Storr Compilation, Canberra, 2006.

15 Interview: Hughes, 17 June 2013.

Chapter 5

1 McKay, 'Memoirs and Some Random Thoughts', vol 2, pp 689-70.

2 The above two paragraph draw mainly on an extended entry in Hughes' war diary for 9 June 1945, Hughes Papers.

3 Letters from UK, 1945, Hughes Papers.

4 When judging the seemingly anti-Semitic views of a 21-year-old Australian airman in the mid-1940s it is well to remember just how prevalent those views were in Australia at the time.

5 NAA: A9300, Hughes TEF.

6 Ironically, a different Wing Commander reported in September 1944 that Flight Lieutenant John Gorton, Hughes' great friend in later years, had shown 'superior ability in expressing himself': NAA: A9300, Gorton JG. As Prime Minister, Gorton acquired a reputation for mangling the English language; as Attorney-General and as a leading counsel, Hughes mastered it.

7 The conditions for election for the 1946 Rhodes scholarship differed in four important respects from the pre-War requirements: the allocation of two scholarships instead of one to each State; the restriction of eligibility to proof of 'war service'; the requirement of just one year of university education instead of the normal two years; and the removal of the marriage disqualification.

8 For the material used here relating to Tom's application, see Rhodes, Hughes Papers.

9 It appears that Homan became a shop owner in Southern Rhodesia and, like all the other candidates, was elected unopposed to the Legislative Council. He was defeated in 1911 and may have drowned in waters near Cape Town.

10 As Tom pointed out later in a letter to the Selection Committee, his father had mistakenly told him that the scholarship was for entrance to Oxford in October 1947; hence the reference to the possibility of completing his LLB before going to Oxford.

11 JB Peden to the acting secretary of the committee of selection for NSW Rhodes Scholarships, 7 November 1945, Hughes Papers.

12 Geoffrey Hughes to the acting secretary, 13 December 1945, Hughes Papers.

13 Interview (Farquharson): Hughes, pp 16-17.

14 Wing Commander Geoffrey Rossiter DFC, who briefly overlapped with Tom at 10 Squadron, was awarded one of the two scholarships available in Western Australia. Married and aged 29, Rossiter later became Warden of Burton Hall at the Australian National University.

15 Interview (Farquharson): Hughes, p 15.

Chapter 6

1 Interview: Hughes, 11 July 2013.

2 Ironically, around the same time, his father eschewed them. Vincent John Flynn may have been a Rhodes scholar but the Australian Club rejected his application for membership. Although Geoffrey Hughes maintained his subscription, he never entered the club again, suspecting that sectarianism was a factor in Flynn's rejection: Interview: Hughes, 9 December 2013.

3 Interview (Farquharson): Hughes, p 17.
4 Interview: Hughes, 11 July 2013.
5 Interview: Geoffrey Hughes, 11 September 2013.
6 R Therry, *Reminiscences of Thirty Years' Residence in New South Wales and Victoria*, Samson Low, Son and Coy, London, 1863, p 347.
7 NSW, *Law Almanac*, 1950.
8 *Australian Bar Gazette*, vol 1, no 3, 1964, p 13.
9 The above two paragraphs are based on: Interview: Mason, 24 February; Interview: Hughes, 13 March 2015; Interview (Farquharson): Hughes, p 20; Tom Hughes, Obituary: 'The Hon Antony Larkins QC', *Bar News*, Autumn, 1990; and Robert Hughes, *Things I Didn't Know*, pp 188-91.
10 Upon admission, a barrister was expected to serve a 12-month period as a pupil with a senior junior, to learn about turning theoretical knowledge to practical use and about techniques, the traditions of the Bar and everyday etiquette, as well as 'to profit by the experience of the senior': NSW Bar Association Rules, 1961.
11 The above two paragraphs are based on: Interview (Farquharson): Hughes, pp 25-26; Interview: Hughes 23 August 2013; Hughes, Address, 1987, pp 13-15 and 1949 + Letters, Hughes Papers.
12 For Robert and Aunt Mim, see especially, Robert Hughes, *Things I Didn't Know: A Memoir*, Vintage Books, Sydney, 2007, pp 118 and 125ff.
13 Tom's letters were kept in the 1949 + Letters file, Hughes Papers.
14 *Way v Commissioner for Stamp Duties* (1949) 79 CLR 477.
15 M McHugh, 'The Rise (and Fall?) of the Barrister Class', in JT Gleeson and RCA Higgins (eds), *Law, Language and the Practice of Persuasion*, Federation Press, Sydney, 2008, pp 185-86.
16 Hughes Fee Book, 1949-55, Hughes Papers. The estimate for average annual male earnings is based on Reserve Bank of Australia, Australian Economic Statistics, 1949/1950 to 1996/1997, Occasional Paper, Wages and Earnings, 4.17, no date.
17 Interview: Aleco Vrisakis, 13 October 2015.
18 TEF Hughes, Autobiography, Hughes Papers.
19 Interview (Farquharson): Hughes, p 29.
20 Ibid, pp 21-22.
21 Interview: Hughes, 11 July 2013.
22 *Mace v Murray* (1955) 92 CLR 370.
23 Politics (Arrival), Parkes, 1963, Hughes Papers, pp 5-6; Interview: Hughes, 13 March 2015.
24 For Hughes' account of his early appearances in the High Court, see 'High Court Recollections', *Australian Law Journal*, vol 77, 2003, pp 662-64.
25 Interview: Joanna Hughes, 3 May 2013; Interview: Hughes, 11 July 2013.
26 1951-60, Hughes Papers.
27 Interview: Hughes, 13 July 2013; R Hughes, *Things I Didn't Know*, p 144.
28 War Service, Hughes Papers.
29 Interview: John Whittle SC, 12 November 2014; Autobiography, Hughes Papers.
30 Interview: Constance Crisp, 4 January 2013.
31 G Hughes, *Starting Thredbo*, Walarah, NSW, 2008, p 36; Interview: Geoffrey Hughes, 11 September 2013; Interview: Tom Hughes, 4 March 2015. Geoffrey referred to 1958 as the year of the accident; the correct date is 1957.
32 R Hughes, *Things I Didn't Know*, p 154.
33 AP Reimer, *Inside Outside*, Collins, Angus & Robertson, Sydney, 1992, p 196. For Robert's account of his university years, see *Things I Didn't Know*, p 191ff.
34 Interview (Farquharson): Hughes, p 33.
35 Ibid, p 30.
36 *Jones v Skelton* (1961) 62 SR (NSW) 180.
37 *Jones v Skelton* [1963] 1 WLR 1362; (1963) 63 SR (NSW) 644.
38 For a recent citation, see *McAlpine v Bercow* [2013] EWHC 1342 (QB).
39 Interview (Farquharson): Hughes, p 33.
40 Interview: Hughes, 12 July 2013; Interview: Jim Merralls QC, 12 December 2013. Merralls, Dixon's associate at the time who was present on some of these occasions, became a long-term editor of the *Commonwealth Law Reports* and a leader of the Victorian Bar.
41 Tom Hughes to Margaret Hughes, 11 and 15 June 1972, Hughes Papers.
42 Letters on Taking Silk, Hughes Papers.

43 Asprey to Hughes, 20 December 1962; Street to Hughes, 3 January 1963; Letters on Taking Silk, 1962-63, Hughes Papers.

Chapter 7

1 *DT*, 22 October 1970.
2 City of Sydney Special Branch, Report of Committee on Functions of State Council, Liberal Party of Australia (LPA), ML, MSS 2385, Y4653/5.
3 Interview (Farquharson): Hughes, p 57.
4 Atwill later served as the Party's NSW State President and then Federal President.
5 Interview: Hughes, 15 April 2013.
6 The above two paragraphs are based on: Interview: Hughes, 15 April 2013.
7 Interview: Hughes, 15 April 2013; Interview: Howard, 13 February 2014.
8 For the Hughes statement and referees' reports, see LPA, ML, MSS 2385, Y4678/6.
9 The spelling, 'Labour' rather than 'Labor' remained in widespread use in the 1960s, including in Hansard.
10 Interview: Howard, 13 February 2014.
11 Politics (Arrival), pp 1-2, Hughes Papers; Interview: Howard, 13 February 2014.
12 LPA, ML, MSS 2385, Y4662/7.
13 L Haylen, *Chinese Journey: The Republic Revisited*, Angus and Robertson, Sydney, 1959; RE Northey, 'Haylen, Leslie Clement (1898-1977)', *ADB*, vol 14, Melbourne University Press, Melbourne, 1996.
14 Interview: Howard, 13 February 2014.
15 John Howard, 'Tribute: The Hon TEF Hughes AO QC', *Bar News*, Winter, 2009, p 26.
16 In 2009, Gleeson recalled being 'one of a group of young barristers … rounded up to distribute how-to-vote cards': *Bar News*, Winter 2009, p 28. Hughes firmly believes that another lawyer, 'Bill' Deane, a future High Court judge and Governor-General, also helped in his campaign. Sir William Deane emphatically denies any involvement. His friend, Murray Gleeson, has a clear recollection of both of them handing out how-to-vote cards for Hughes: Interview: Hughes, 15 April 2013; Interview: Deane, 20 November 2014; Interview: Gleeson, 27 January 2015.
17 *Weekly Flash*, 20 November 1963.
18 Politics (Arrival), p 4, Hughes Papers.
19 Interview: Howard, 13 February 2014.
20 *Weekly Flash*, 6 November 1963; Interview: Hughes, 15 April 2013; Howard, 'Tribute', p 26.
21 Interview: Howard, 13 February 2014.
22 The Campaign for Parkes, Hughes Papers.
23 The *Parkes Examiner* referred to Haylen as 'Left-Wing Les' 10 times in its four pages.
24 Politics (Arrival), pp 7-8, Hughes Papers.
25 *Bulletin*, 23 November 1963.
26 Carrick to Hughes, 12 November 1969, LPA, ML, MSS 2385, Y4706/9.
27 Interview: Hughes, 15 April 2013.
28 Whereas more than four-fifths of DLP preferences went to Government candidates in three of the NSW seats won back from Labor, just two-thirds went to Hughes in Parkes.
29 Interview: Howard 13 February 2014.
30 Interview: Lucy Turnbull, 30 September 2014.
31 *DT*, 2 December 1963.
32 *Sunday Mirror*, 8 December 1963.
33 WC Wentworth (Liberal, Mackellar), brilliant if erratic, was the Liberal Party's most persistent 'red-baiter'.
34 *Sunday Mirror*, 1 and 8 December and *SMH*, 2 December 1963.
35 *DT*, 2 December 1963.
36 *SMH*, 11 December 1963.
37 Haylen, *Twenty Years' Hard Labor*, Macmillan, Melbourne, 1969, p 173; Interview (Mel Pratt, 1976): Haylen, NLA, ORAL, TRC 121/84.
38 The Campaign for Parkes, Hughes Papers; Interview: Howard, 13 February 2014.

39 Interview: Howard, 13 February 2014.

Chapter 8

1 P Howson, *The Howson Diaries: The Life of Politics*, Viking Press, Melbourne, 1984, 12 December 1963 and 24 February 1964.
2 Interview: Hughes, 1 April 2014. English-born and educated, a former pilot with the Fleet Air Arm, Howson joined Foy & Gibson in Australia after the War. He started in the packing department of what was a former family department store chain and rose to become a staff manager and a member of the board. After three attempts, Howson won the Victorian seat of Fawkner in 1955.
3 Interview: Hughes 1 April 2014.
4 *Commonwealth Parliamentary Debates* (*CPD*), House of Representatives (H/R), vol 41, pp 188-91.
5 Ibid, pp 225 (Lindsay), 261 (Kent Hughes), 275 and 336 (Daly).
6 Ibid, pp 272-79; *Howson Diaries*, 4 March 1964; Interview: Hughes, 1 April 2014.
7 B Johns, 'The Unpredictable Liberal', *Bulletin*, 25 September 1965.
8 *CPD*, H/R, vol 42, pp 1475-76.
9 Ibid, vol 41, pp 720-22. In June, Hughes visited Formosa at the expense of the Nationalist Government.
10 For the above paragraph, see especially ibid, p 273 (Cairns); vol 44, pp 1670-71 (Uren), 1717 (Hayden), 1712-13 and 1720-21 (Hughes).
11 Ibid, pp 1794-97.
12 Interview: Hughes 7 March 2013.
13 C Cameron, *The Cameron Diaries*, Allen & Unwin, Sydney, 1990, pp 448-49.
14 *CPD*, H/R, vol 45, pp 832-46.
15 Australian Wool Board, *Report and Recommendations on Wool Marketing: Presented to the Australian Wool Industry Conference*, Canberra, July 1964.
16 Interview (Farquharson): Hughes, p 101. For Snedden's account of the fiat issue, see BM Snedden and MB Schedvin, *Billy Snedden: An Unlikely Liberal*, Macmillan, Melbourne, 1990, pp 59-60.
17 *CPD*, H/R, vol 47, pp 465-70.
18 For a version of Gunn's comments, see *Canberra Times* (*CT*), 9 September 1965.
19 *CPD*, H/R, vol 47, p 805.
20 For the speeches quoted above, see ibid, vol 47, pp 175-81, 465-70, 814-25 and 849-52.
21 'Australian Political Chronicle, September-December 1965', *Australian Journal of Politics and History*, vol 12, no 1, 1965, p 81.
22 Interview (Farquharson): Hughes, p 59.
23 Interview: Joanna Hughes, 3 May 2013; Interview: Howard, 13 February 2014.
24 Interview: Hughes, 1 April 2014.
25 LPA, ML, MSS 2385, Y4615/1.
26 For Hal Porter, see M Lord, *Hal Porter: Man of Many Parts*, Random House, Sydney, 1993 and P Pierce, 'Porter, Harold Edward (1911-1984)', *ADB*, vol 18, Melbourne University Press, Melbourne, 2012.
27 H Gordon, 'Hopman, Henrick Christian (1906-1985)', *ADB*, vol 17, Melbourne University Press, Melbourne, 2007.
28 *Launceston Examiner*, 4 December 1964.
29 *Porter v Mercury Newspaper Pty Ltd* [1964] Tas SR 235 at 275.
30 Interviews: Hughes, 17 July 2014 and 4 March 2015.
31 *Campsie News*, 19 October 1966; Election Campaign 1966, Hughes Papers.
32 The above paragraph draws on Howard to Members, 27 October and 16 November 1966, Election Campaign 1966, Hughes Papers; Interview: Howard, 13 February 2014.
33 Interview (Farquharson): Hughes, p 60.
34 Gavin Souter, *SMH*, 31 October 1966; *Weekly Flash*, 23 November 1966.
35 *SMH*, 16 November 1966.
36 Interview (Farquharson): Hughes, p 63.
37 Interview: Howard, 13 February 2014. For a subsequent court case involving an assault on Hughes, see *DT*, 9 December 1966.
38 Election Campaign 1966, Hughes Papers.

Chapter 9

1 I Hancock, 'The VIP Affair 1966-67: The Causes, Course and Consequences of a Ministerial and Public Service Cover-Up', special number, *Australasian Parliamentary Review*, vol 18, no 2, 2003, pp vi-xiii and 1-106.

2 *CPD*, H/R, vol 54, pp 147-50.

3 Interview: Hughes 1 April 2014; C Cunneen and JK McLaughlin, 'Evatt, Clive Raleigh (1900-1998)', *ADB*, vol 17, Melbourne University Press, Melbourne, 2007.

4 *Re Evatt; Ex p NSW Bar Association* (1967) 67 SR (NSW) 236; *Evatt v NSW Bar Association* (1968) 117 CLR 177; Interview: Hughes, 1 April 2014.

5 Interview: Hughes, 1 April 2014.

6 Hughes to Erwin, 22 March 1967, 1941-50, Hughes, Hughes Papers

7 Interview: Hughes, 1 April 2014; Interview (Farquharson): Hughes, p 65.

8 *CPD*, H/R, vol 58, pp 858-61.

9 Ibid, pp 653-54.

10 Ibid, vol 59, pp 1458-61.

11 Ibid, vol 60, pp 307-09.

12 Ibid, vol 61, pp 3132-33.

13 Interview: Hughes, 1 April 2014.

14 Carrick to Osborne, 26 July 1968, Osborne Papers, NLA, MS 3662/13/21.

15 Osborne to Carrick, 13 September 1968, ibid.

16 Berowra, Hughes Papers.

17 Berowra, Congratulations, Hughes Papers.

18 Under Party rules, all 20 outside members on the selection panel had to be delegates to State Council but, of them, any number could also be members of the State Executive.

19 Maddison to Osborne, 23 October 1968, Osborne Papers, NLA, MS 3662/13/21.

20 Lloyd to Carrick, 29 May 1969, LPA, ML, MSS 2385/Y4619/3.

21 Diary, 12 and 18 December 1968, Hughes Papers. This diary consisted of 10 pages of typed entries covering several days in each of December 1968 and February 1969, and is notable for recording McMahon, the Treasurer, 'full of his usual indiscretions', leaking Cabinet discussions to Hughes, a backbencher, and for Hughes' comment on Whitlam's 'besetting fault': 'he acts as if he is as clever as he thinks he is.'

22 Hughes to Family, 26 October 1968, Hughes Papers. Cramer, oblivious of any problems, wrote warmly about his own contribution and the honours bestowed on him: Sir John Cramer, *Pioneers, Politics and People: A Political Memoir*, Allen & Unwin, Sydney, 1989, pp 198-99. See also his speech of 27 February 1969 in *CPD*, H/R, vol 62, pp 245-48.

23 1941-50, Hughes, Hughes Papers.

24 For the delegation's comments on the Conference, see *CPD*, H/R, vol 62, pp 245-55.

25 Heather Henderson (ed), *Letters To My Daughter: Robert Menzies, Letters, 1955-1975*, Pier 9, Sydney, 2011, p 207.

26 For background and for the James and St John allegations and their immediate aftermath, see I Hancock, *John Gorton: He Did It His Way*, Hodder, Sydney 2002, pp 213-23. See also *CPD*, H/R, vol 62, p 694ff. For contemporary accounts see P Howson, *Life of Politics*, p 498ff; Alan Reid, *The Gorton Experiment*, Shakespeare Head Press, Sydney, 1971, p 220ff.

27 Originally, Hughes sat between St John and Killen who had exchanged insults in the lead up to the 1966 election. St John labelled Killen a 'racist' and a 'Fascist' for supporting continued white rule in southern Africa. Killen had denounced St John for having leftist connections and had sought his disendorsement. Given the seating arrangements, Killen considered that Tom Hughes provided a *cordon sanitaire*. Interview: Killen, 3 December 1999.

28 For some of the fanciful reports on the Mushroom Club, see *SMH*, 14 November 1969; Reid, *Gorton Experiment*, p 41; *Howson Diaries*, pp 543-44; Interview (Merran Samuel): John Jess, July 1983, NLA, ORAL, TRC, 4900/20/3: pp 4-6. The members of the club were Bill Arthur (NSW), 'Duke' Bonnett (Qld), Bridges-Maxwell (NSW), Fred Chaney Snr (WA), Chipp (Vic), Bruce Graham (NSW), Hughes (NSW), Don Jessop (SA), Killen (Qld), John McLeay (SA), Peacock (Vic), Tom Pearsall (Tas) and Tony Street (Vic). For insider views, see D Chipp and J Larkin, *Don Chipp: The Third Man*, Rigby, Adelaide, 1978, pp 89-91; J Killen, *Killen: Inside Australian Politics*, Mandarin, Melbourne, 1989, p 142; Interview: Chaney, 1 February 2000; Interview: Hughes, 15 April 2013.

29 For 'Edie' Parrish, see J Powell (ed), *Women of Hornsby Shire: Selected Lives*, Deerubbin Press in association with Hornsby Shire Council, Sydney, 2012, pp 59-61.
30 *Hornsby Advocate*, 5 February 1969; *Northern District Times*, 19 February 1969; *Sun-Herald*, 23 February 1969.
31 LPA, ML, MSS 2385/Y4619/3.
32 Personal, 1969, Hughes Papers.
33 *Hornsby Advocate*, 14 May 1969.
34 Carrick to President, Berowra FEC, 29 May 1969, LPA, ML, MSS 2385/Y4619/3.
35 *SMH*, 4 June 1969; *Hornsby Advocate*, 11 June 1969.
36 *Hornsby Advocate*, 30 July 1969,
37 Ibid.
38 *SMH* and *DT*, 11 August 1969.
39 *Australian*, *SMH* and *DT*, 11 August 1969.
40 G Robert Southern, *The Mysterious McLeod-Lindsay Case*, G Robert Southern, Wagstaff, 1970. For an account of the case that raised disturbing questions, see G Hawkins, *Beyond Reasonable Doubt*, ABC, Sydney, 1977, pp 105-30.
41 A McLeod-Lindsay, *An Ordinary Man*, Hale & Iremonger, Sydney, 1994, pp 112-13.
42 Southern, *McLeod-Lindsay Case*, p 31; Southern to Peter Brett, 12 June 1970, Brett Papers, NLA, MS 5603/51. Professor Brett, then of Monash University, who took an interest in the case from 1970, tried in vain to redirect Southern's counter-productive thinking and actions. Hughes, when Attorney-General, helped Brett obtain material from the inquiry.
43 *Report of the Inquiry held under Section 475 of the Crimes Act, 1900 into the Conviction of Alexander McLeod-Lindsay*, October 1969.
44 Ibid, pp 87-88.
45 Ibid, p 76.
46 Southern told Brett in July 1970 about several published works 'which soberly reveal the unscrupulous, pro-fascist, power-hungry political reality which hides behind the robes and draperies of Roman sanctity': Southern to Brett, 15 July 1970, Brett Papers, NLA, MS 5603/51.
47 McLeod-Lindsay, *An Ordinary Man*, p 261.
48 C Porter, *Walking on Water: A Life in the Law*, Random House, Sydney, 2003, ch 20.
49 Personal, 1969, Hughes Papers.
50 Geoffrey was conservative in many respects. When the Liberal State Council voted to support authorised medically-supervised abortions, he published an article with John Howard in the *Australian Liberal* entitled, 'Like a Taipan in a Baby Cot' (December 1968). They quoted medical authorities from around the world to demonstrate that a foetus was a human being, and other authorities such as 'History shows' and 'Studies indicate' to demonstrate the serious effects of abortions and the dangers of drawing artificial lines when defining human beings.
51 The Conservative British Prime Minister, Harold Macmillan, had said in 1957 'let us be frank about it – most of our people have never had it so good', which was later rendered as 'You've never had it so good' during the 1959 election in which the Tories increased their majority.
52 *Hornsby Advocate*, 22 October 1969.
53 Ibid, 15 October 1969.

Chapter 10

1 Ainsley Gotto (Gorton's Principal Private Secretary) to Gorton, 3 November 1969, Gorton Papers, NAA: M3787/1/48; Irwin to Gorton, 29 October and 10 November 1969, Gorton Papers, NAA: M3787/1/48.
2 'On becoming AG', no date, 1931-40, Hughes Papers.
3 Congratulations 'Attorney-General', Hughes Papers.
4 Carrick to Hughes, 12 November 1969, LPA, ML, MSS 2385, Y4706/9.
5 Interview (Farquharson): Hughes, pp 95-96.
6 'On becoming AG', no date, 1931-40, Hughes Papers; H Renfree to Attorney-General, 13 November 1969, Hughes Papers NLA, MS 4651/4/1.
7 Hughes said later that, because of the 'great number of things on my plate … ASIO was at the outer periphery of my responsibilities in practice'. ASIO's historian for 1963-75 concluded that 'such a hands-off approach to the management of ASIO's numerous sensitive concerns' left the

Director-General (Peter Barbour) 'with much responsibility and limited direction': J Blaxland, *The Protest Years: The Official History of ASIO 1973-1975*, vol II, Allen & Unwin, Sydney, 2015, p 58. Arguably, limited ministerial direction was both appropriate and desirable.

8 Hughes Papers, NLA, MS 4651/4/1. On at least one occasion, Hughes rejected the advice of his Department that wanted the Governor-General to grant remission for two outstanding fines each of $150 imposed for a failure to submit two tax returns. After writing 'Nonsense' and 'Balls' on the margins of the Department's submission, Hughes rejected the recommendation because the original – now deceased – miscreant 'was one of the most wicked con men ever known in recent years'. Hughes Papers, NLA, MS 4651/3/6/3.

9 'On becoming AG', no date, 1931-40, Hughes Papers.

10 Chairman PSB to Prime Minister 11 February 1970, Hughes Papers, NLA, MS 4651/3/1/2.

11 'On becoming AG', no date, 1931-40, Hughes Papers; Interview (Farquharson): Hughes, p 72.

12 Interview (Farquharson): Hughes, pp 69-70.

13 NAA: A11099, 1/106.

14 Ibid, 1/112.

15 For the above paragraph, see ibid; Kitto to Hughes, 13 August 1970, Hughes Papers, NLA, MS 4651/3/1/2; T Hughes, 'Sir Harry Gibbs: An Advocate's Perspective', *Proceedings of the Samuel Griffith Society*, vol 18, 2006, p 6. Stephen was appointed to the High Court in 1972.

16 *Age*, 4 December 1969.

17 *Australian*, 5 January 1970.

18 Robert Hughes, *Things I Didn't Know: A Memoir*, Vintage Books, Sydney, 2007, p 186.

19 NAA: A5619, C145.

20 For his speech on 27 May 1970, see Hughes Papers, NLA, MS 4651/4/4/13; *Age*, 2 and 24 September 1970.

21 Interview (Farquharson): Hughes, pp 123-24.

22 Hughes Papers, NLA, MS 4651/3/4/2; *Australian*, 21 April 1970.

23 Harris to Hughes, 24 March 1971, Hughes Papers, NLA, MS 4651/3/1/3.

24 *Daily Mirror*, 12 November, *Australian*, 13 November 1969.

25 NAA: A5919, C411, ff 19-22.

26 Interview (Farquharson); Hughes, p 102.

27 NAA, A5882, CO 600.

28 For a measured account of the Burchett story as it relates to this period, see P Edwards, *A Nation at War, Australian Politics, Society and Diplomacy during the Vietnam War 1965-1975*, Allen & Unwin in association with the Australian War Memorial, Sydney, 1997, pp 230-33.

29 Gotto to Gorton, 25 February 1970, Gorton Papers, NAA, M 3787/10/55/260-61.

30 Hughes to Gorton, 3 March 1970, ibid, 273-74.

31 Burchett could not be charged for activities relating to Vietnam because Australia had not made any formal declaration of war.

32 *CPD*, H/R, vol 66, p 194.

33 Hughes Papers, NLA, MS 4651/4/1.

Chapter 11

1 For the changing emphasis from attacking communist affiliations to highlighting violence in reaction to protest after 1965, see M Saunders, '"Law and Order" and the Anti-Vietnam War Movement: 1965-72', *Australian Journal of Politics and History*, vol 28, no 3, 1982, pp 367-79.

2 *Howson Diaries*, 22 April 1970; M Walsh, *AFR*, 24 April 1970.

3 *CPD*, H/R, vol 67, pp 1674-75.

4 Ibid, pp 1834-39 and 1861-67.

5 NAA: A5882, CO 600. In 1985, Williams became the first woman to head a Commonwealth Government department.

6 *Australian*, 2 October 1970.

7 *Australian*, *DT* and *SMH*, 31 July 1970.

8 Hughes Papers, NLA, MS 4651/3/1/2.

9 Interview: Michael Hughes, 28 October 2015.

10 Ibid.

11 For press coverage, see *DT* and *SMH*, 17-18 August 1970. ASIO, Special Branch (NSW) and the Commonwealth Police subsequently reported they had not received any warning of the demonstration.
12 Hughes Papers, NLA, MS 4651/3/1/2.
13 Ibid, p 3/6/3.
14 *CT*, 1 October 1970. Inside the theatre Jack Waterford, a prominent ANU student and later a Canberra journalist and newspaper editor, approached the platform carrying a Vietcong flag which he held up behind the speaker. Hughes eventually grabbed it, ripped the flag from its pole and placed it out of sight.
15 *Spectator*, 11 August 2012.
16 G Souter, 'Tom Hughes the Third', *West Australian*, 23 September 1970; Claudia Wright, 'Australia's Kennedys – with a difference', *Herald* (Melbourne), 29 September 1970.
17 *CPD*, H/R, vol 69, pp 139-41.
18 *DT*, 27 August 1970.
19 *CPD*, H/R, vol 69, p 499.
20 Sub 507, 31 August 1970, Dec 648, 2 September 1970, NAA: A5619, C513 and A5882, CO600.
21 NAA: A11099, 1/113.
22 Hughes Papers, NLA, MS 4561/3/3/8.
23 For an acute critique of the proposed Bill by Geoff Yeend of the Prime Minister's Department, see Notes on Cabinet Submission No 549, NAA: A5619, C513.
24 NAA: A11099, 1/114.
25 Hughes Papers, NLA, MS 4651/3/3/30.
26 *Age* and *SMH*, 10-11, December 1970.
27 *Age*, 1 and 12 December 1970.
28 'Advice', Hughes Papers, NLA, MS 4651/3/3/8.
29 Ibid, pp 22-45.
30 Interview (Farquharson): Hughes, p 77.
31 *Australian*, 29 January 1971.
32 Submission No 687, 17 February 1971; Cabinet Notebook, NAA: A11099/1/116.
33 NAA: CO 513; CO 600.
34 *CPD*, H/R, vol 71, pp 926-31. For a near-contemporary analysis of the legislation, see A Hiller, 'Law and Order under the Public Order Act 1971', *Australian Law Journal*, vol 47, May 1973, pp 251-62.
35 Howson referred in his diary to a 'rather dull party meeting' earlier in the morning of 16 March where Hughes outlined the proposed legislation.
36 E Smith, 'Protest Laws and Political Radicalism in 1970s Australia: The making of the Public Order Act 1971', <https://hatfulofhistory.wordpress.com/2012/10/18/protest-laws-and-political-radicalism-in-1970s-australia-the-making-of-the-public-order-act-1971>. For a current compilation of the *Public Order (Protection of Persons and Property) Act 1971* (Cth), see <https://www.comlaw.gov.au/Details/C2014C00245>.

Chapter 12

1 For Harders' analysis of the legislation, see CW Harders, 'Australia's Offshore Petroleum Legislation: A Survey of its Constitutional Background and its Federal Features', *Melbourne University Law Review*, vol 6, no 4, 1968, pp 414-28.
2 Gorton to DG Hutchinson, 4 July 1974, Gorton Papers, NLA, MS 7984/22.
3 Sub 92, 19 January 1970, NAA: A5619, C 17.
4 (1969) 122 CLR 177.
5 Sub 70, 7 January 1970, NAA: A5619, C 486. See copy 2 for Gorton's marginal comments.
6 NAA: A11099, 1/106.
7 Dec 74, 21 January 1970; NAA: A5882, CO537.
8 For a transcript, see Gorton Papers, NLA, MS 7984/22.
9 Interview (Farquharson): Hughes, p 93.
10 *CPD*, H/R, vol 67, pp 1897-1910.
11 Gorton Papers, NLA, MS 7984/22.
12 Memorandum, Off-Shore Minerals, no date, ibid.

13 Interim Report of the Senate Select Committee on Off-Shore Petroleum Resources, September 1970, p 126.
14 (1971) 124 CLR 468.
15 NAA: A432, 1970/5511, f 67.
16 JE Richardson, *Introduction to the Trade Practices Act*, Hicks Smith & Sons, Sydney, 1967, pp 11-14. For a summary of the Act, see ibid, pp 39-43.
17 *CPD*, H/R, vol 49, pp 3233-37 (Hughes); p 3269 (Whittorn).
18 Hughes Papers, NLA, MS 4651/4/3.
19 (1909) 8 CLR 330.
20 *Amalgamated Society of Engineers v Adelaide Steamship Co Ltd* (1920) 28 CLR 129.
21 *Victoria v Commonwealth* (1971) 122 CLR 353.
22 M Pelly, *Murray Gleeson: The Smiler*, Federation Press, Sydney, 2104, pp 52-54.
23 NAA: A432, 1970/5511, ff 40-23.
24 Interview: Gleeson, 27 January 2015.
25 Interview (Farquharson): Hughes, pp 73-74 and 83.
26 J Quick and RR Garran, *The Annotated Constitution of the Australian Commonwealth*, Angus and Robertson, Sydney, 1901.
27 In August 1970, Hughes had intervened by leave on behalf of the Commonwealth in a matrimonial dispute. He failed to persuade the Full Bench – Harry Gibbs was the lone dissentient – that the investiture of Commonwealth judicial power in the Supreme Court of New South Wales enabled a deputy registrar of that Court to make an order for interim costs in a matrimonial cause under the Commonwealth *Matrimonial Causes Act*. Barwick later made 'after his fashion, a jocularly disparaging but friendly remark about the strength of my argument'. Seventeen years later the High Court – Gibbs was then Chief Justice – unanimously overruled *Kotsis*. See *Kotsis v Kotsis* (1970) 122 CLR 69; Hughes, 'Sir Harry Gibbs', *Proceedings of the Samuel Griffith Society*, 2006, ch 2.
28 'Trade Practices Legislation', Concrete Pipes, Hughes Papers.
29 NAA: A432, 1970/5511, f 46.
30 Ibid, f 63.
31 [1907] AC 81.
32 *CT*, 19 December 1970.
33 Interview (Michael Coper and Fiona Wheeler): Tom Hughes, NLA, ORAL, TRC, 5947/75.
34 Fullagar suggested the Chief Justice might recuse himself from the hearing on the ground of his previous association with trade practices legislation. As Hughes put it, Barwick 'did not take kindly to the proposition which, however you dress it up, was a suggestion of apprehended bias': Interview (Coper and Wheeler): Hughes, p 120. Ellicott called Fullagar's action 'a stupid thing to do': Interview: Ellicott, 17 November 2014.
35 Transcript of Proceedings, High Court of Australia, 1-5 March 1971.
36 Interview (Coper and Wheeler): Hughes, p 65.
37 The above paragraph draws upon: Interview: Hughes, 11 July 2013; Interview: Ellicott, 24 November 2014; Interview: Gleeson, 27 January 2015.
38 Interview (John Farquharson): Harders, p 138. While Gleeson later said that 'Tom presented the case powerfully', he said it 'should be added that the then Chief Justice (also of a moderately centralist disposition) provided a following breeze': *Bar News*, Winter 2009, p 28.

Chapter 13

1 P Ayres, *Malcolm Fraser: A Biography*, William Heinemann Australia, Melbourne, 1987, p 183.
2 *CPD*, H/R, vol 71, pp 679-84.
3 For Hughes' version of these events, see Interview (Farquharson): Hughes, pp 84-88.
4 NAA: A11099, 1/111.
5 J Howard, *Lazarus Rising: A Personal and Political Biography*, HarperCollins, Sydney, 2010, p 46.
6 The above account draws upon hand-written notes in the Gorton Papers in the National Library that were taken during the meeting by an anonymous Gorton supporter. See also *Howson Diaries*, 10 March; N Brown, *On the Other Hand …: Sketches and Reflections from Political Life*, Poplar Press, Canberra, 1993, pp 59-60; Killen, *Inside Australian Politics*, p 173; Interview: Sir James Killen, 7

September 2001; Interview: Hughes, 16 July 2014. Neil Brown claims that Gorton did not 'vote' himself out; Gorton, and those sitting close by him, had the impression that he did.

7 Hughes to Prime Minister, 18 March 1971, Hughes Papers, NLA, MS 4651/3/2/1.

8 Interview: Howard, 13 February 2014; Interview: Ellicott, 16 November 2014.

9 Killen, *Inside Australian Politics*, pp 175-76; Interview (Farquharson): Hughes, p 110. When a CP backbencher greeted Mackay rising from the front bench to answer a question as 'His Oiliness' (Mackay had oil industry associations), many in the House grasped the double meaning.

10 NAA: A11099, 1/117.

11 Condolence Letters, Hughes Papers.

12 Interview (Farquharson): Harders, pp 137-39. In chronological order, Harders served under Hughes, Bowen, Greenwood, Whitlam, Murphy, Enderby, Greenwood (again), Ellicott and Durack.

13 The above two paragraphs draw upon: Interview: Hughes, 11 October 2013; Interview: Deane, 24 November 2014; written communication from Jenny Blackman, 23 October 2015.

14 Autobiography, Hughes Papers.

15 Interview: Anne Sloan, 16 October 2014; Interview: Hughes, 26 March 2015.

16 *CPD*, H/R, vol 73, pp 337 and 339 (Fraser), 560-62 (Hughes); vol 74, pp 1577-80, 1664-65.

17 For the above paragraph, see ibid, vol 73, pp 808 (Fraser), 1312, 1338-40 and 1400 (Hughes).

18 *Strickland v Rocla Concrete Pipes* (1971) 124 CLR 468.

19 (1909) 8 CLR 330.

20 Interview (Coper and Wheeler): Hughes, p 145.

21 *Concrete Pipes case* at 494; *CT*, 8 September 1971.

22 For the debate on 7 September 1971, see *CPD*, H/R, vol 73, pp 819-33.

23 Hughes was quoting George Dangerfield, *The Strange Death of Liberal England*, Constable, London, 1936, p 15.

24 *Advocate-Courier*, 13 October 1971.

25 Interview (Farquharson): Hughes, p 124.

26 Interview: Hughes, 23 August 2013. McMahon did write to 'My dear Tom' on 20 December 1971 appreciating his 'attitude' and expressing hope for frequent contact with 'both of you' in the future: 1941-50, Hughes, Hughes Papers.

27 *DT*, 23 November 1971.

28 *SMH*, 30 November 1971.

29 For Max Newton's perceptive appraisal of Hughes' position, see *Incentive*, 30 November 1971.

30 *CPD*, H/R, vol 76, pp 365-67.

31 Hughes to Prime Minister, 19 April 1972, Hughes Papers.

32 *CPD*, H/R, vol 78, pp 2711-12.

33 Ibid, pp 2785-88.

34 *CPD*, H/R, vol 81, p 3355ff.

35 Interview (Farquharson): Hughes, pp 115-16.

36 Ibid, pp 105-08.

37 Ibid, pp 103-04.

38 Ibid, pp 91-92.

39 Interview: Michael Mackellar, 25 July 2001. Later, apparently, Gorton's replacement 'was not to Fraser's liking': M Fraser and M Simons, *Malcolm Fraser: The Political Memoirs*, Miegunyah Press, Melbourne, 2010, p 225.

40 P Hasluck (edited and introduced by N Hasluck), *The Chance of Politics*, Text Publishing, Melbourne 1997, p 185.

41 Whitlam to Hughes, 28 December 1972, Hughes Papers.

Chapter 14

1 Interview: Hughes, 13 August 2013; Interview: Daley, 13 February 2015.

2 LG Glanfield, 'The Bar – in the Public Interest', in G Lindsay and C Webster (eds), *No Mere Mouthpiece: Servants of All, Yet of None*, LexisNexis Butterworths, Sydney, 2002, p 42.

3 JM Bennett, 'Some Reflections on *A History of the New South Wales Bar* (1969)' in Lindsay and Webster, *No Mere Mouthpiece*, p 67.

4 *Australian Bar Gazette*, vol 1, no 2, 1964, pp 10-11.
5 Ibid, pp 11-13 and no 3, 1964, pp 12-15.
6 NSW Bar Association Rules, 1961.
7 M Zander, *Lawyers and the Public Interest: A Study in Restrictive Practices*, Weidenfeld and Nicolson, London, 1968, p 157. See also DS Lees, *Economic Consequences of the Professions*, Institute of Economic Affairs, London, 1966, pp 2-4 and 35-45.
8 G Palmer, *Compensation for Incapacity: A Study of Law and Social Change in New Zealand and Australia*, Oxford University Press, Wellington, 1979; MA Robinson, *Accident Compensation in Australia: No-Fault Schemes*, Legal Books, Sydney, 1987, especially pp 17-21; H Luntz, 'Looking Back at Accident Compensations: An Australian Perspective', *Victoria University of Wellington Law Review*, vol 32, no 2, 2003, especially pp 280-90. See also *Report of the National Committee of Inquiry: Compensation and Rehabilitation in Australia*, AGPS, Canberra 1974, vol 1, pp 71-72 and 204-05.
9 Quoted in Luntz, 'Looking Back', p 280.
10 R Hunt, Answer to a Whitlam Question upon Notice, *CPD*, H/R, vol 103, p 509.
11 *Thirty-Seventh Annual Report of the NSW Bar Association*, pp 3-4.
12 Kirby to Hughes, 26 January and 8 June 1983, Personal 1982, Hughes Papers; 'Speeches by the Hon Michael Kirby', High Court of Australia.
13 Minutes of a Meeting of Council, 20 March 1975, Bar Association Papers.
14 *AFR*, 12 March and 8 April 1975.
15 Applications for Silk 1974, Hughes Papers.
16 *Strickland v Rocla Concrete Pipes Ltd* (1971) 124 CLR 468.
17 For the Bathurst Gaol riots and their aftermath, see E Whitton, *Can of Worms II*, Fairfax Library, Sydney, 2007, pp 327-38.
18 *National Times*, 30 September-5 October 1974.
19 *New South Wales Parliamentary Debates*, Third Series, vol 113, pp 1805-06. Maddison also referred to Staples' former membership of the Communist Party, his current membership of the Labor Party and his failed candidature for Labor preselection for the federal seat of Bennelong.
20 *Bulletin*, 25 June 1985. According to the minutes of the meeting, there were just 14 members present.
21 T Blackshield, 'Murphy, Lionel Keith' in T Blackshield, M Coper and G Williams (eds), *The Oxford Companion to the High Court of Australia*, Oxford University Press, Melbourne, 2001, p 485.
22 Interviews: Hughes, 23 August and 4 November 2013.
23 Dangerfield, *Strange Death of Liberal England*, p 15.
24 The words of the motion were taken from the one passed by the Victorian Bar in 1913 in protest at the appointment of Albert Piddington to the High Court. Billy Hughes, the Attorney-General, wanted to 'stack' the Court with judges favourable to the extension of Commonwealth power. Interview: Merralls, 12 December 2013. Piddington resigned within a month of his appointment, never having taken his seat.
25 The above paragraph draws upon: Interviews: Hughes, 23 August and 4 November 2013; Interview: Merralls, 12 December 2013; *Age* and *Australian*, 15 February 1975; T Blackshield, 'Judges and the Court System', in G Evans (ed), *Labor and the Constitution 1972-1975*, Heinemann, Richmond, 1977, pp 118-19.
26 *Thirty Seventh Annual Report of the NSW Bar Association*, p 4.
27 NSW Bar Association, *Submission to the Law Reform Commission of NSW on the Fixing and Maintenance of Ethical Standards*, no date, p 4.

Chapter 15

1 S Hall, 'A Class of His Own', *Australian Magazine*, 10-11 July 1993; A Clark, 'Tom Hughes: Life, Loves & the Law', *AFR Magazine*, June 2008.
2 Interview: Hughes, 13 October 2013.
3 1941-50, Hughes, Hughes Papers.
4 Autobiographical Notes, Hughes Papers.
5 Interview: Hughes, 23 August 2013.
6 Ibid.
7 K Fitzpatrick, *Name Dropping: An Incomplete Memoir*, HarperCollins, Sydney, 2004, p 333.

8 M McHugh, speech at the NSW Bar Association, 15 November 2013.
9 Interview: Deeta Colvin, 29 October; Interview: Tom Hughes Jnr, 16 December 2014; Interview: Michael Hughes, 28 October 2015. Colvin later ran her own specialist public relations company, married Rod McGeoch, the chief executive of the Sydney Olympic Games bid, became Director of Corporate Relations for PBL Marketing and, among other commitments, now serves on the board of UNICEF Australia.
10 Interview: Hughes, 12 August 2014; Lucy's letters, Hughes Papers. The author contacted Weigall in the course of researching this book. Unfortunately, she was not in a position to assist.
11 Interview (Veronica Keraitis): Edward St John QC, 29 September 1980, NLA, ORAL, TRC 830/71-4; Hughes to St John, 30 September 1975, 11th Floor Selborne Chambers, Hughes Papers.
12 The following account draws upon: 11th Floor Selborne Chambers, Hughes Papers; Interview: Hughes, 12 August 2014; Jenny Blackman, personal communication, 22 October 2015.
13 Conti took silk in 1977 and was a judge of the Federal Court (2000-07); Simon Sheller QC was a judge of the Court of Appeal (1991-2005); Vince Bruce took silk in 1982 and was a judge of the Supreme Court (1994-99).
14 Paul Daley, the floor clerk, did not detect the intrigue that others found palpable, and 'I miss nothing'. Interview: Daley, 13 February 2014.
15 The names were listed in alphabetical order: Blackman, Brown, Campbell, Cockburn, Collins, Cripps, Dunford, Herron, Hoeben, Hulme, Hunter, McAlary, Maconachie, Reddy, Renaud, Saywell, Simos, Sperling. The names 'Bruce' and 'Gray' were typed but there were no signatures.
16 Diary, 13 November 1979, Hughes Papers: see fn 3 of ch 17.
17 Interview: Hughes, 12 August 2014.
18 Interview: Anne Sloan, 16 October 2014.
19 *Herald* and *Sun* (Melbourne), 19-23 June 1973; PM Warrender, *Pamela: in her own right*, Hardie Grant Book, Melbourne, 2007, pp 218-19.
20 *CT* and *SMH*, 6-9 and 13-4 July 1973; *AFR*, 25 July 1973; Interview: Hughes, 10 June 2014.
21 Gorton to Hughes, 22 August 1973, Personal File: 1977-80.
22 T Reeves, *Mr Big: the true story of Lennie McPherson and his life of crime*, Allen & Unwin, Sydney, 2005, p 187. See also *Australian*, *DT* and *SMH*, 20 September 1973.
23 *Australian* and *SMH*, 5-8 and 13 June and 24 August 1974; *Mundey v Askin* [1982] 2 NSWLR 369; J Mundey, *Green Bans & Beyond*, Angus & Robertson, Sydney, 1981, p 129.
24 *Ratten v R* (1974) 131 CLR 510.
25 Brett Papers, NLA, MS 5603, Ratten, Folder 11.
26 G Hawkins, *Beyond Reasonable Doubt*, ABC, Sydney, 1977; T Molomby, *Ratten: The Web of Circumstance*, Outback Press, Melbourne, 1978; T Molomby, *Is There a Moderate on the Roof?: ABC Years*, William Heinemann Australia, Melbourne, 1991, pp 77-85.
27 *New South Wales v Commonwealth* (1975) 135 CLR 337. For an account of the Fraser Government's 'cooperative' approach to the effects of the High Court decision and of its consequences, see P Brazil, 'Offshore Constitutional Settlement 1980: A Case Study in Federalism', Occasional Paper, Public Law Discussion Group, ANU, 5 April 2001.
28 EG Whitlam, *The Whitlam Government 1972-1975*, Penguin Books, Melbourne, 1985, p 250.
29 *Victoria v Commonwealth* (1975) 136 CLR 170.
30 *Attorney-General (Cth) (Ex rel McKinlay) v Commonwealth* (1975) 135 CLR 1.
31 *CT*, 6 and 9 March 1976. Knight was the first elected ACT Senator in 1975 with 43 per cent of the primary vote and a quota of 1.307. Cavanough's 264 votes amounting to 0.008 of a quota were inconsequential. Garland returned to the ministry in 1977 and in 1981 went to the UK as High Commissioner for Australia.
32 *Newcastle Morning Herald and Miners' Advocate*, 25 February; *DT* and *Illawarra Mercury*, 26 February 1976.

Chapter 16

1 For a copy, see *CPD*, H/R, vol 108, p 1221.
2 D Markwell, 'Robinson, Eric Laidlaw (1929-1981)', *ADB*, vol 18, Melbourne University Publishing, Melbourne, 2012.

3 *Telegraph* (Brisbane), 29 December 1977; *Age*, 30 December 1977.
4 For a copy of the advice, see *CPD*, H/R, vol 108, pp 1308-12.
5 Ibid, pp 1218-23 and p 1306.
6 Interview: Hughes, 17 July 2014.
7 Royal Commission of Inquiry: Matters in Relation to Electoral Redistribution Queensland 1977, *Transcript of Proceedings*, pp 148-49.
8 Ibid, p 151.
9 Ibid, p 162.
10 Ibid, pp 230-34.
11 Ibid, pp 1829-31. Injured feelings did not alone explain Cameron's susceptibility to suspicions. He had an expectation of malpractice after witnessing at least one shonky rearrangement of Queensland electoral boundaries to save a State Liberal seat from a Labor takeover: Interview: Cameron, 5 July 2014.
12 For Rostedt, see in particular *Transcript of Proceedings*, pp 739-847.
13 For the above paragraph, see ibid, pp 747, 785 and 808.
14 Ibid, pp 900-02 and 3039-41.
15 Ibid, p 2224.
16 Ibid, p 3027.
17 *Report of the Royal Commission of Inquiry: Matters in Relation to Electoral Redistribution Queensland 1977*, AGPS, Canberra, 1978.
18 Ibid, p 158.
19 Ibid, p 243.
20 Interview: Hughes, 17 July 2014.
21 Sun (Sydney), 8 August 1978; *West Australian*, 9 August 1978.
22 Fraser and Simons, *Fraser*, pp 593 and 597.
23 Interview: Cameron, 5 July 2014.
24 *Transcript of Proceedings*, p 2090.
25 Interview: Hughes, 10 June 2014.

Chapter 17

1 ABC, *Australian Story: Malcolm Turnbull Interview – Transcript*, 3 August 2009, <http://www.abc.net.au/austory/content/2007/s2645849.htm>.
2 Interview: Lucy Turnbull, 30 September 2014.
3 Diary, 1979-80, Hughes Papers. This diary consists of three small notebooks and, unless otherwise stated, is the source of the quotations in the rest of this chapter.
4 For Clark's preparations and prescriptions for his biographer, see M McKenna, *An Eye for Eternity: The Life of Manning Clark*, Miegunyah Press, Melbourne, 2011, *passim*.
5 The *CT* reported the case, sometimes at length.
6 Interview (Juliette Brodsky): David Levine AO RFD QC, 4 May 2012, NSW Bar Association Oral History Project. While Levine's description fits perfectly with what happened in *Punch v Fairfax*, he said he was Hughes' junior in the unidentified case mentioned. In *Punch v Fairfax*, Levine appeared with Shand. This paragraph of the interview is no longer on the NSW Bar Association website.
7 Interview: Hughes, 17 April 2015.
8 Six weeks earlier (5 July 1979) he had written in another diary that he still loved her, wished they had not missed the boat six years ago – 'her decision' – and that he 'could get through to her … there should still be another trip. There is no other trip that I want'.
9 Lord Mountbatten was killed by an Irish Republican Army bomb blast on 27 August 1979 while sailing on his boat off County Sligo, north-west Ireland. After watching a Mountbatten retrospective on television, Hughes wrote 'What a great man!'.
10 Interview (Brodsky): Levine.
11 Tom Uren, *Straight Left*, Random House, Vintage edn, Sydney, 1995, p 316.
12 For distorted and self-serving reports of McGregor J's findings, see *CT* and *SMH*, 6 October 1979. Hughes did not refer to McGregor J's findings in his diary.
13 *John Fairfax and Sons Ltd v Punch* (1980) 47 FLR 458.

14 From the mid-1970s until early in the 1980s, Hughes represented the NSW Corporate Affairs Commission in charges brought against Alexander Barton and his son Thomas over their various business activities and attempts to avoid court appearances.
15 For Susan Smith, see T Stephens, 'A trailblazer in current affairs', *SMH*, 23 May 2006.
16 Hughes received $9300 in fees. For another account of the case, see *Royal Australian Navy News Pictorial*, 5 October 1979.
17 *Mukta Ben v Suva City Council* [1980] 1 WLR 767.

Chapter 18

1 Interviews: Lucy Turnbull, 30 September 2014 and Malcolm Turnbull, 20 January 2015.
2 ABC, *Australian Story: Transcript of Interview – Malcolm Turnbull*, 3 August 2009, <http//www.abc.net.au/austory/content/2007/s2645849.htm>.
3 See ibid, for the story of Malcolm Turnbull's unusual and sometimes fraught upbringing.
4 The eccentric and irrepressible Francis James, a one-time publisher of the *Anglican*, had opposed the Vietnam War, stood for Liberal Reform in 1966, and sent Tom a postcard from Moscow in 1969 threatening to embarrass him by supporting him in the 1969 election. Having remarked that Australia's 'real friends' were in Peking, James set out for China where he was incarcerated for four years as an alleged spy: Personal 1969, Hughes Papers.
5 The above two paragraphs draw substantially on London File 1976-79, Hughes Papers.
6 Personal File: 1977-80, Hughes Papers.
7 James Murray, *National Times*, 19-25 October 1980.
8 For this case, see Pelly, *Murray Gleeson: The Smiler*, ch 15.
9 Tony Staley, the Minister for Post and Telecommunications, appointed her for a five-year term. For her appointment and a photograph, see *National Times*, 3-9 August 1980. In 1985, Michael Duffy, Labor's Minister for Communications, reappointed her for a five-year term. Weigall resigned the following year.
10 *SMH* and *Northern Territory News*, 16 July 1980; *Messel v Davern* (unreported, NTSC, Gallop J, 20 May 1986), <http://www.supremecourt.nt.gov.au/archive/doc/sentencing_remarks/0/86/0/NS000410.htm>.
11 In 2001, when the author interviewed Fraser for his biography of Gorton, Fraser asked if Hewitt was still alive. On learning that he was, Fraser responded with one word: 'Pity.' Interview: Fraser, 31 August 2001.
12 Published by JR Walsh and GJ Munster, Sydney, 1980.
13 P Kelly and D Marr, *National Times*, 16-22 November 1979.
14 *CT*, 2 December 1980. For coverage of the case, see *AFR*, *Age*, *CT* and *SMH*, 12-13 November 1980.
15 For St John's version (he airbrushed his exchanges with Hughes out of the story) and his account of getting Davis back into practice after being disbarred for over 35 years, see Interview (Veronica Keraitis): St John, pp 77-79.
16 David McNicoll, *Bulletin*, 11 August 1981.
17 Billy married a member of the du Pont family in 1975, and died in New York in October 2011. His daughters spent some of their schooling in the United States, and Chrissie attended his funeral.
18 The above four paragraphs draw mainly upon: Interviews: Chrissie Hughes, 20 April 2014 and 17 April 2015; Interviews: Tom Hughes, 26 March and 17 April 2015; Wedding Folder; Hughes Papers.

Chapter 19

1 D Marr and W Bacon, *National Times*, 21-27 December 1984.
2 See M Gawenda's profile of Hughes, *Age*, 7 November 1984.
3 Ibid.
4 Diary, 1985, Hughes Papers.
5 *SMH*, 16 March 1985.

6 For the above paragraph, see M Farquhar, *Nine Words from the Grave: The Real Story as Revealed by Murray Farquhar*, Murray Farquhar, Sydney, 1986, pp 109-10 and 123.
7 *SMH*, 23 December 1983.
8 *CT*, 8 March 1985.
9 Diary, 6 March 1985, Hughes Papers.
10 Ibid, 8 March 1985.
11 Personal, 1986-87, Hughes Papers.
12 For Farquhar's criticisms of Muir, see *Nine Words*, pp 157-60.
13 Diary, 8 March 1985, Hughes Papers; Interview: Hughes, 28 January 2015; Interview, Neil, 6 February 2015.
14 Diary, 8 March 1985, Hughes Papers.
15 Ibid, 15 March 1985.
16 Transcript, Brief – Mr TEF Hughes QC, Senate Inquiry into Allegations Concerning a Judge, vol 1, Hughes Papers.
17 David Bennett and Annabelle Bennett, Submissions on the Inappropriateness of Interrogation of a Judge into whose Conduct an Inquiry is being Conducted, 4 July 1984, ibid.
18 Transcript of Evidence, Senate Select Committee on the Conduct of a Judge, 14 August 1984, ibid.
19 Interview: Hughes, 26 March 2015.
20 *AFR* and *CT*, 16 October 1984. Later, Stewart J found that the verbatim material 'has an acceptable degree of accuracy and probably fairly records that part of the conversation it purports to record' but cast serious doubt on the accuracy of transcriptions, including those claimed to have been made of verbatim material. *Report of the Royal Commission of Inquiry into Alleged Telephone Interceptions*, AGPS, Canberra, 1986, pp 1470-71.
21 *SMH*, 14 December 1984.
22 *SMH*, 6 March 2008.
23 Diary, 14 February 1985, Hughes Papers; Interview: Mason, 24 February 2015.
24 *SMH*, 19-20 July 1985.
25 Interview (Farquharson): Harders, p 139.
26 *R v Murphy* (1985) 158 CLR 596.
27 *CT*, 24 August 1985.
28 *SMH*, 4 September 1985.
29 *R v Murphy* (1985) 4 NSWLR 42.
30 *Australian*, 29 November 1985.
31 Interview (Farquharson): Harders, p 137.
32 In October 1982, Lindy Chamberlain was found guilty of the murder of her two-month-old child, Azaria, while on a camping holiday at Uluru in August 1980. She and her then husband, Michael, claimed that a dingo had killed their daughter. Tom Hughes was not directly involved but became an interested observer because of doubts about the conduct and outcome of the case.
33 Hughes to Ingrid Murphy, 31 October 1986, Personal 1986-87, Hughes Papers.

Chapter 20

1 The sum of $3250 amounted to $8800 in 2014 terms: RBA Inflation Calculator, <http://www.rba.gov.au/calculator/annualDecimal.html>.
2 For the much-admired McPhee, see the eulogy delivered by Justice Winneke, President of the Court of Appeal, and the article by J Hedigan QC, in *Victorian Bar News*, no 107, 1998. Winneke said McPhee was 'probably the finest exponent of the art of legal advocacy, in all its forms, of his generation'.
3 Theoretically, one avenue remains open via s 74 of the Australian Constitution, but such an appeal requires a certificate from the High Court. The Court has made clear it will not issue one.
4 The above paragraphs are based on newspaper reports; Diary, 14-21 June 1985, Hughes Papers: Interviews: Hughes, 13 October 2013 and 2 December 2014.
5 In 2014 terms, this figure amounted to $135,200: RBA Inflation Calculator, <http://www.rba.gov.au/calculator/annualDecimal.html>.

6 *Australian*, *DT*, *SMH*, 17-19 April 1984.
7 Peter Heerey to Hughes, 19 April 1984, Personal 1982, Hughes Papers. At that time, the *Age* was published at 250 Spencer Street, Melbourne.
8 *David Syme & Co Ltd v Lloyd* [1984] 3 NSWLR 346; *SMH*, 22 December 1984.
9 Interview: Carmen Champion, 15 April 2015. Champion was brought in to sort out the mess.
10 Alexander, called to the Bar of the Middle Temple in 1961, became a leader of the English Bar, Chairman of the Bar Council (1985-6) and appeared in a number of high profile cases before retiring in 1989 to take several company directorships and appointments as President of the Marylebone Cricket Club (MCC) and Chairman of the Royal Shakespeare Company. Elevated to the peerage as Baron Alexander of Weedon, he took the Conservative whip in the House of Lords. He died in 2003 at the age of 69.
11 Personal 1986-87, Hughes Papers. Although his playing days long preceded WSC and the Benson & Hedges World Cup, Lord Griffiths was awarded three Blues for cricket at Cambridge, played first class cricket for Glamorgan and was later President of the MCC.
12 *CT*, 23 March 1983.
13 *Austin v Mirror Newspapers Ltd* [1984] 2 NSWLR 383.
14 For the judgment favourable to Lloyd, see *Lloyd v David Syme & Co Ltd* [1986] AC 350.
15 Interview: Neil, 6 February 2015.
16 *Austin v Mirror Newspapers Ltd* (1985) 3 NSWLR 354.
17 Interview (Farquharson): Hughes, p 121.
18 Diary, 29 October 1985, Hughes Papers.
19 Personal, 1986-87, Hughes Papers.
20 Ibid.
21 *Seidler v John Fairfax & Sons Ltd* [1983] 2 NSWLR 390.
22 Hughes, 'Let Art be the Judge', Archibald Celebrity Talk, 8 June 1985, Hughes Papers.
23 *Harry Seidler & Associates Pty Ltd v John Fairfax & Sons Ltd* (1986) Aust Tort Reps 80-002.
24 Interview: Hughes, 4 March 2015.

Chapter 21

1 *Times on Sunday*, 6 December 1987. For a recent analysis of the boom and bust of the 1980s, see F Bongiorno, *The Eighties: The Decade that Transformed Australia*, Black Inc, Melbourne, 2015, especially chs 5 and 9.
2 *West Australian*, 12-16 June 1990; Interview: Stephen Archer, 24 November 2014.
3 *Australian* and *SMH*, 16 August 1990.
4 *SMH*, 27 November 1990.
5 *Australian*, 13 May 1991.
6 *Australian*, 29 June 1989; *SMH*, 6 March 1990 and *CT*, 21-22 May 1992.
7 MG Craig, Swearing in Speech, 2 March 2010, <http://www.lec.justice.nsw.gov.au/Documents/speech_02mar09_craigj_swearingin.pdf>.
8 *Sun-Herald*, 24 November 1991.
9 For a succinct summary of his prominent raids, see J McIlwraith, 'Holmes à Court, Michael Robert (1937-1990)', *ADB*, vol 17, Melbourne University Publishing, Melbourne, 2007.
10 Personal, 1986-87, Hughes Papers. For the OBL's case, see Outline of Case Delivered on Behalf of the Claimant, 4 May 1987, Hughes Papers. In May 1988, the Full Bench of the Victorian Supreme Court did not accept that the arbitrators' decision was 'erroneous in law'. In August, the High Court rejected the argument that the arbitration represented 'a substantial injustice' and dismissed an application for special leave to appeal. OBL lost the final round in London in October 1988.
11 Interview: Hughes, 23 August 2013.
12 The following account of the takeover and of the trial draws upon T Sykes, *Operation Dynasty: How Warwick took John Fairfax Ltd*, Greenhouse Publications, Melbourne, 1989, especially ch 16; VJ Carroll, *The Man Who Couldn't Wait*, Heinemann, Melbourne, 1990, especially ch 17; G Souter, *Heralds and Angels: The House of Fairfax 1841-1900*, Melbourne University Publishing, Melbourne, 1991, especially ch 9; R Tiffen, 'The Fall of the House of Fairfax', *Media Information*, no 68, 1993, pp 21-28.

13 Interview: Archer, 21 November 2014. Hughes also considered Connell 'highly intelligent, highly articulate': Interview (Farquharson): Hughes, p 168.
14 Souter, *Heralds and Angels*, p 298.
15 Hughes had worked with Bishop, the future senior minister in the Howard, Abbott and Turnbull Governments, in an earlier case in Perth and formed a very high opinion of her abilities. Interviews: Archer, 21 November 2014 and Hughes, 15 June 2015.
16 For details of the parties involved and of their legal representatives, see *SMH* and *AFR*, 14 October 1988.
17 Interview: Heydon, 15 December 2014.
18 Souter, *Heralds and Angels*, p 306.
19 Carroll, *Man Who Couldn't Wait*, p 354.
20 Sykes, *Operation Dynasty*, p 291.
21 Warwick Fairfax bailed out in 1991 and the Canadian-born Conrad Black bought the company in 1994.
22 Interview: Archer, 21 November 2014.
23 *Australian*, *CT* and *SMH*, 10 March 1989.
24 *Australian* and *West Australian*, 11 March 1989.
25 Personal, 1994-95, Hughes Papers.
26 Hughes to Ros Packer, 8 October 1990, Personal 1990, Hughes Papers.
27 For the exchange of letters in November and December 1991, see Consolidated Press Holdings: Fees, Hughes Papers. See also Interview (Farquharson): Hughes, pp 133-35.
28 For an account of the case after 10 years, see W Bacon, 'Lawyers, clients & their opponents', *Australian Society*, December 1991, pp 15-17.
29 *Carson v John Fairfax & Sons Ltd; Carson v Slee* (1994) 34 NSWLR 72.
30 *SMH*, 27 August 1992.
31 *Carson v John Fairfax & Sons Ltd* (1992) 178 CLR 44.
32 For a report of the second trial, see *Gazette of Law and Journalism*, no 23, 1994.
33 *Ettingshausen v Australian Consolidated Press Ltd* (1991) 23 NSWLR 443 at 444.
34 'Pom looks at penis', *Gazette of Law and Journalism*, no 31, May 1995, p 8. For a vivid account of Hughes' courtroom methods and demeanour, see S Hall, 'Master Class: The Law and Life of Tom Hughes', *Australian Magazine*, 10-11 July 1993.
35 For ET's later personal problems, see *Australian*, 26 March 2012; *Australian Women's Weekly*, 30 May 2012.
36 D Rolph, *Reputation, Celebrity and Defamation Law*, Ashgate, Aldershot and Burlington, England, 2008, p 151.
37 Hall, 'Master Class', *Australian Magazine*, 10-11 July 1993.
38 *Daily Telegraph Mirror*, 13 February 1993.
39 *SMH*, 13 February 1993.
40 According to local knowledge, Bannister was part of the land on which Saxe Bannister, the first Attorney-General of NSW (1824-26), briefly 'squatted': Interview: Hughes, 5 October 2015.
41 T Hughes, 'Sinking under a $1 billion pile', *Bulletin*, 19 February 1991.
42 For Hughes' comments on these matters, and for Robert Hughes' acute observations, see Personal, 1996-97, Hughes Papers.
43 *SMH*, 4 March 1994.
44 Interview: Hughes, 17 April 2015.
45 The above paragraphs draw on Father Emmet P Costello SJ, Hughes Papers; *Eureka Street*, 20 October; *Catholic Weekly*, 23 October; *SMH*, 25 October 2013; Interview: Hughes, 2 June 2015.
46 McCann to Hughes, 23 February 1993, Personal, 1994-95, Hughes Papers.
47 Hughes to Howard, 4 March 1996; Howard to Hughes, 3 April 1996, ibid.

Chapter 22

1 '150 Not Out', *Bar News*, Spring 1999.
2 *Bar Brief*, August 2001, p 3; personal communication, Philip Selth, 9 October 2015.
3 Autobiography, Speeches, Black Folder, Hughes Papers.

4 Interview: Hughes, 23 August 2013. He bought and eventually sold his Blackstone chambers for the same amount: $145,000: Interview: Lynette MacDonald, 29 October 2014.
5 Diary, 2009-10, Hughes Papers.
6 For the above paragraph, see *West Australian*, 18 and 20 March 1999.
7 A Ferguson, *Gina Rinehart*, Macmillan, Sydney, 2012, pp 196-97; D Marshall, *House of Hancock: The Rise and Rise of Gina Rinehart*, William Heinemann, Sydney, 2012, pp 213-24.
8 J Marsden, *I am what I am. My life and curious times*, Penguin, Melbourne, 2004, p 348.
9 Interview: Hughes, 15 June 2015.
10 Rivkin, former Senator Graham Richardson and former Packer executive, Trevor Kennedy, were investors in the company whose printing plant was mysteriously destroyed by fire in 1993.
11 Hughes to Lord Griffiths, 13 July 2001, Personal, 2000+, Hughes Papers.
12 *John Fairfax Publications Pty Ltd v Rivkin* (2003) 201 ALR 77. For a discussion of the findings, see D Rolph, 'Simple questions, difficult juries', *Commercial Law Quarterly*, vol 18, no 3, 2004, pp 9-20; D Rolph, *Reputation, Celebrity and Defamation Law*, pp 128-33; R Coleman, 'See You in Court', *Australian Author*, vol 44, no 1, 2012, pp 12-15.
13 Rivkin committed suicide on 1 May 2005. Convicted of Byrne's murder, Wood was gaoled in November 2008 but, in February 2012, the NSW Court of Criminal Appeal in a unanimous verdict acquitted him of murder and ordered his release.
14 *DT* and *SMH*, 27-28 February 2004.
15 B McWilliam, Hughes Papers.
16 The case was well covered by the *DT*, *SMH* and *Sunday Telegraph*, 30 May 2008.
17 McWilliam to Hughes, 5 December 2008, B McWilliam, Hughes Papers.
18 *R v Cook; ex p Twigg* (1980) 147 CLR 15.
19 For changes in the High Court, see S Gageler, 'Counsel, role of', *Oxford Companion to the High Court*, pp 167-68; G Brennan, 'Decision-making process', ibid, pp 197-98.
20 Interview: Kirby, 1 February 2015.
21 *Crimmins v Stevedoring Industry Finance Committee* (1999) 200 CLR 1 at 39.
22 *Ringrow Pty Ltd v BP Australia Pty Ltd* (2005) 224 CLR 656.
23 *Australian Competition and Consumer Commission v Channel Seven Brisbane Pty Ltd* (2009) 239 CLR 305.
24 Personal, 2009-11, Hughes Papers.
25 *Kable v Director of Public Prosecutions (NSW)* (1996) 189 CLR 51.
26 *International Finance Trust Co Ltd v NSW Crime Commission* (2009) 240 CLR 319; AA McCunn, 'The Resurgence of the *Kable* principle: *International Finance Trust Company*', *James Cook University Law Review*, vol 17, 2010, pp 110-31.
27 *Australian*, 4 December 2009; Interview: Hughes, 15 June 2015.
28 *R v LK and RK* (2010) 241 CLR 177. For an extended analysis of the case, see D Brakell, 'Conspiracy, a Jury, the Constitution and a Swiss Bank', *University of Western Sydney Law Review*, vol 14, 2010, pp 85-102.
29 Interview: Hughes, 2 December 2014. Contacts continued with the Waterhouse family; Tom and Chrissie had what Tom called 'a most agreeable dinner' with Gai and Robbie Waterhouse on 17 June 2009: Hughes to Waterhouse, 18 June 2009, Personal 2000+, Hughes Papers.
30 Hughes, 'Let Art be the Judge', Hughes Papers.
31 D Marr, *Barwick*, Allen & Unwin, Sydney, 1992.
32 G Barwick, *A Radical Tory: Garfield Barwick's Reflections and Recollections*, Federation Press, Sydney, 1995.
33 Notes, Hughes Papers.
34 For a revised version, see *Bar News*, Autumn 2014.
35 Diary, 22 April 1980, Hughes Papers.
36 Interview: Hughes, 17 April 2015.
37 ABC, *7.30 Report*, 22 February 2010, <http://www.abc.net.au/7.30/content/2010/s2827147.htm>. According to Fraser's book, 'Hughes missed the point'. Fraser had cited the Gazelle Peninsular, not as a cause of his resignation but 'only as evidence of a pattern of behaviour'. Apparently, Hughes also 'missed the point about proper process', though Fraser did not mention that he and Hughes persuaded Gorton to observe it: M Fraser and M Simons, *Fraser*, p 225.
38 Personal, 2000+, Hughes Papers.
39 *SMH*, 5 June 2002.
40 Hughes to Geoffrey Miller, 2 July 2009, Personal 2009-11, Hughes Papers.

41 The Hon DK Malcolm AC, *Eulogy: Sir Francis Theodore Page Burt AC KCMG QC LLM Hon LLD*, 8 September 2004, <http://www.supremecourt.wa.gov.au/_files/Eulogy-FrancisBurt.pdf>; Hughes to Janine Milton, 4 October and Milton to Hughes, 19 October 2004, Personal, 2000+, Hughes Papers.
42 Interview: Malcolm Turnbull, 20 January 2015.
43 Tom Hughes to Robert Hughes, 4 Oct. 2000, Robert Hughes, Hughes Papers. See also Tom's letter to Robert of 27 July 2010, ibid.
44 *CT*, 17 February 2004.
45 *Australian*, 19 March 2004.
46 Personal 2009-11, Hughes Papers.

Chapter 23

1 Tom Hughes to Phillip Boulton (President of the NSW Bar Association), 28 June 2012, Records of the NSW Bar Association.
2 Interview: John Whittle, 12 November 2014; Interview: Hughes, 5 October 2015.
3 Tom had briefly owned a property at Forbes to relocate sheep to protect them from ovine Johne's disease.
4 The above three paragraphs draw in part from an interview with Mark Boileau, 29 October 2015.
5 Speeches, Black Folder, Hughes Papers.
6 Constance to Tom, 9 December 1990, 1941-50, Hughes, Hughes Papers.
7 Private information.
8 Personal, 1982, Hughes Papers.
9 For examples, see Forsyth's letters to Hughes in 1987, Personal 1986-87, Hughes Papers.
10 Heydon and Hughes to McColl, 11 October 2000, Robert Hughes folder, Hughes Papers. Despite Archer's tribulations – the Bar Association refused to renew his practising certificate in 2001 and in 2009 successfully disbarred him – Hughes retains a very high regard for him as a barrister: Interviews: Hughes, 22 October 2014 and 15 June 2015.
11 Interview: Lynette MacDonald, 29 October 2014.
12 Interview: Heydon, 15 December 2015.
13 Diary, 28 July 1979, Hughes Papers.
14 Interview: Malcolm Turnbull, 19 January; Interview: Michael Hughes, 28 October 2015.
15 *SMH*, 25 May 1985; Hughes to Coleman 30 May and Coleman to Hughes 19 June 1985, Personal 1986-87, Hughes Papers.
16 Interview: Whittle, 12 November 2014.
17 Ibid.
18 Interview: Philip Selth, 23 August 2013; Interview: John Whittle SC, 12 November; Interview: Heydon, 15 December 2014.
19 *Australian*, 18 April 2001.
20 Interview (Farquharson): Hughes, p 41.
21 Interview (Farquharson): Harders, p 138.
22 J Gleeson, 'Rediscovering Rhetoric', in J Gleeson and R Higgins (eds), *Rediscovering Rhetoric: Law, Language and the Practice of Persuasion*, Federation Press, Sydney, 2008, pp 74-76.
23 *Hospital Products Ltd v United States Surgical Corporation* (1984) 156 CLR 41.
24 [1963] 1 WLR 1362; (1963) 63 SR (NSW) 644.
25 *Strickland v Rocla Concrete Pipes Ltd* (1971) 124 CLR 468.
26 *Hospital Products v United States Surgical Corporation* (1984) 156 CLR 41.
27 *Crimmins v Stevedoring Industry Finance Committee* (1999) 200 CLR 1.
28 Interview (John Farquharson): Frank McAlary, May 2001: NLA, ORAL, TRC 4742, p 101.
29 Interview (Farquharson): Hughes, p 119.
30 Diary, 21 March 1985, Hughes Papers.
31 Interview: Heydon, 2 December 2014.
32 Interview: Kirby, 15 February 2015.
33 Interview: Deane, 20 November 2014.
34 Interview: Gleeson, 27 January 2015.
35 Interview: Heydon, 15 December 2014.

36 Diary, 1985, Hughes Papers.
37 Interview: Kirby, 1 February 2015.
38 Personal, 1982, Hughes Papers.
39 Interview (Farquharson): Hughes, pp 177-78.
40 Bathurst to Hughes, 9 June 2011, Personal, 2009-11, Hughes Papers.

Select Bibliography

Official Records: National Archives of Australia
Cabinet documents, 1969-71
Cabinet notebooks, 1969-71
Individual service records, First and Second World Wars
Attorney-General's Department

Manuscripts

Liberal Party of Australia
    Federal Secretariat, National Library of Australia (NLA), Canberra
    New South Wales Division, Mitchell Library, Sydney
NSW Bar Association Papers
Personal Papers (held in the NLA)
    Brett, Peter
    Cramer, Sir John
    Gorton, Sir John
    Howson, Peter
    Hughes, TEF
    Osborne, FM
    Reid, Alan
    St John, Edward
Personal Papers held in the Mitchell Library
    Hughes Family Papers
Personal Papers held in the National Archives of Australia
    Sir John Gorton
Personal Papers held privately
    Hughes, TEF
Thomas Sidney McKay, Memoirs and Some Random Thoughts: an Autobiography

Newspapers and Periodicals

Age
Australian
Australian Bar Gazette
Australian Financial Review
Australian Journal of Politics and History
Australian Law Journal
Australian Society
Bar Gazette (NSW)
Bar News (NSW Bar Association)
Bulletin
Canberra Times
Catholic Press

Daily Mirror
Daily Telegraph
Freeman's Journal
Gazette of Law and Journalism
Hobart Mercury
Hornsby Advocate
Launceston Examiner
Media Information
National Times
Our Alma Mater
Justinian
Parkes Examiner
Sun-Herald
Sunday Mirror
Sunday Telegraph
Sydney Morning Herald
Victorian Bar News
Weekly Flash

Law Reports

Australian Law Reports
Commonwealth Law Reports
Federal Law Reports
NSW Law Reports
NSW State Reports
NSW Weekly Law Reports
Weekly Law Reports (UK)

Commission Reports

Report of the Inquiry held under Section 475 of the Crimes Act, 1900 into the Conviction of Alexander McLeod-Lindsay, October 1969.

Report of the Royal Commission of Inquiry: Matters in Relation to Electoral Redistribution Queensland 1977, August 1978

Transcripts

Transcripts of Proceedings, High Court of Australia

Transcript of Proceedings, Royal Commission of Inquiry: Matters in Relation to Electoral Redistribution Queensland 1977

Transcript, Senate Enquiry into Allegations Concerning a Judge, 1984

Books: Second World War

Baff, KC *'Maritime is Number Ten': A History of No 10 Squadron RAAF: The Sunderland Era*, KC Baff, South Australia, 1988.

Dennis, Peter, et al (eds), *The Oxford Companion to Australian Military History*, Oxford University Press, Melbourne, 1995.

Eather, Steve, *Flying Squadrons of the Australian Defence Force*, Aerospace Publications, ACT, 1995.
Hogan, Michael, *Almost Like Home: Living in Bradfield Park*, Ku-ring-gai Historical Society, Sydney, 2012.
Leach, Joe, *RAAF Flying Boats at War: The Way It Was*, Australian Military History Publications, Loftus, 1999.
McCarthy, John, *A Last Call of Empire: Australian Airmen, Britain and the Empire Air Training Scheme*, Australian War Memorial, Canberra, 1988.
McKernan, Michael, *The Australian People and the Great War*, Nelson, Melbourne, 1980.
Nelson, Hank, *Chased by the Sun: The Australians in Bomber Command in WWII*, Allen & Unwin, Sydney, 2006.
Stephens, Alan, *The Royal Australian Air Force: a history*, Oxford University Press, Melbourne, 2006.
Storr, Alan, *RAAF WW2 Fatalities: 10 Squadron, RAAF*, Alan Storr Compilation, Canberra, 2006.

Books: Political Memoirs and Diaries

Ayres, Philip, *Malcolm Fraser: A Biography*, William Heinemann Australia, Melbourne, 1987.
Brown, Neil, *On the Other Hand … : Sketches and Reflections from Political Life*, Poplar Press, Canberra, 1993.
Cameron, Clyde, *The Cameron Diaries*, Allen & Unwin, Sydney, 1990.
Chipp, Don and Larkin, John, *Don Chipp: The Third Man*, Rigby Limited, Adelaide, 1978.
Cramer, Sir John, *Pioneers, Politics and People: A Political Memoir*, Allen & Unwin, Sydney, 1989.
Fraser, Malcolm and Simons, Margaret, *Malcolm Fraser: The Political Memoirs*, Miegunyah Press, Melbourne, 2010.
Hasluck, Paul, *The Chance of Politics,* ed by Nicholas Hasluck, Text Publishing, Melbourne, 1997.
Haylen, Les, *Twenty Years' Hard Labor*, Macmillan, Melbourne, 1969.
Howard, John , *Lazarus Rising: A Personal and Political Biography*, HarperCollins, Sydney, 2010.
Howson, Peter, *The Life of Politics*, ed by Don Aitkin, Viking Press, Melbourne, 1984.
Killen, Sir James, *Killen: Inside Australian Politics*, Mandarin, Melbourne, 1989.
Larkin, John (ed), *Chipp*, Methuen Hayes, Sydney, 1987.
Snedden, Billy Mackie and Schedvin, M Bernie, *Billy Snedden: An Unlikely Liberal*, Macmillan, Melbourne, 1990.
Uren, Tom, *Straight Left*, Random House, Sydney, 1994.
Whitlam, Gough, *The Whitlam Government 1972-1975*, Penguin, Melbourne, 1985.

Books: Law and Lawyers

Ayres, Philip, *Owen Dixon*, Miegunyah Press, Melbourne, 2003.
Bennett, JM (ed), *A History of the New South Wales Bar*, Law Book Co., Sydney, 1969.
Freeman, Damien, *Roddy's Folly: RP Meagher QC: art lover and lawyer*, Connor Court, Ballan, 2012.
Gleeson, Justin T and Higgins, Ruth CA (eds), *Rediscovering Rhetoric: Law, Language and the Practice of Persuasion*, Federation Press, Sydney, 2008.
Hocking, Jenny, *Lionel Murphy: A Political Biography*, Cambridge University Press, Cambridge, 1997.
Lees, DS, *Economic Consequences of the Professions*, Institute of Economic Affairs, London, 1966.
Lindsay, Geoff and Webster, Carol (eds), *No Mere Mouthpiece: Servants of All, Yet of None*, New South Wales Bar Association Centenary Essays, LexisNexis Butterworths, Sydney, 2002.
Marr, David, *Barwick*, new edn, Allen & Unwin, Sydney, 1992.
Marsden, John, *I am what I am. My life and curious times*, Penguin, Camberwell, 2004.
Pelly, Michael, *Murray Gleeson: The Smiler*, Federation Press, Sydney, 2014.
Porter, Chester, *Walking on Water: A Life in the Law*, Random House, Sydney, 2003.
Rolph, David, *Reputation, Celebrity and Defamation Law*, Ashgate, Aldershot and Burlington, England, 2008.
Weisbrot, David, *Australian Lawyers*, Longmans Cheshire, Melbourne, 1989.
Zander, Michael, *Lawyers and the Public Interest: A Study in Restrictive Practices*, Weidenfeld and Nicolson, London, 1968.

Other Books

Blaxland, John, *The Protest Years: The Official History of ASIO 1973-1975*, vol II, Allen & Unwin, Sydney, 2015.

Bongiorno, Frank, *The Eighties: The Decade that Transformed Australia*, Black Inc., Melbourne, 2015.

Carroll, VJ, *The Man Who Couldn't Wait*, Heinemann, Melbourne, 1990.

Digby, Everard (ed), *Australian Men of Mark: Illustrated and Authentic Portraits*, vol 1, Charles F Maxwell, Sydney, 1889.

Edwards, Peter, *A Nation at War; Australian Politics, Society and Diplomacy during the Vietnam War 1965-1975*, Allen & Unwin in association with the Australian War Memorial, Sydney, 1997.

Evans, Gareth (ed), *Labor and the Constitution 1972-1975*, Heinemann, Melbourne, 1977.

Farquhar, Murray, *Nine Words from the Grave*, Murray Farquhar, Sydney, 1986.

Ferguson, Adele, *Gina Rinehart*, Macmillan, Sydney, 2012.

Fitzpatrick, Kate, *Name Dropping: An Incomplete Memoir*, HarperCollins, Sydney, 2004.

Freudenberg, Graham, *A Certain Grandeur: Gough Whitlam in Politics*, Macmillan, Melbourne, 1977.

Grattan, Michelle, *Australian Prime Ministers*, New Holland Publishers, Sydney, 2000.

Hancock, Ian, *John Gorton: He Did It His Way*, Hodder, Sydney, 2002.

Hawkins, Gordon, *Beyond Reasonable Doubt*, ABC, Sydney, 1977.

Henderson, Heather (ed), *Letters To My Daughter: Robert Menzies, letters, 1955-1975*, Pier 9, Sydney, 2011.

Horne, Donald, *Time of Hope: Australia 1966-72*, Angus & Robertson, Sydney, 1980.

Hughes, Colin A and Graham, BD, *A Handbook of Australian Government and Politics 1890-1964*, Australian National University Press, Canberra, 1968.

Hughes, Colin A, *A Handbook of Australian Government and Politics 1964-1974*, Australian National University Press, Canberra, 1977.

Hughes, Geoffrey, *Starting Thredbo*, Walarah, NSW, 2008.

Hughes, Robert, *Things I Didn't Know: A Memoir*, Vintage Books edn, Sydney, 2007.

McLeod-Lindsay, Alexander, *An Ordinary Man*, Hale & Iremonger, Sydney, 1994.

Madgwick, RB, *Immigration into Eastern Australia 1788-1851*, Longman, Green and Co., London, 1937.

Marshall, Debi, *House of Hancock: The Rise and Rise of Gina Rinehart*, William Heinemann, Sydney, 2012.

Molomby, Tom, *Ratten: The Web of Circumstance*, Outback Press, Melbourne, 1978.

Mundey, Jack, *Green Bans & Beyond*, Angus & Robertson, Sydney, 1981.

O' Farrell, Patrick, *The Irish in Australia*, reprinted edn, NSW University Press, Sydney, 1987.

Reid, Alan, *The Gorton Experiment*, Shakespeare Head Press, Sydney, 1971.

Reid, Richard and Johnson, Keith (eds), *The Irish Australians: Selected Articles for Australian and Irish Family Historians*, Society of Australian Genealogists and Ulster Historical Foundation, Sydney, 1984.

Richardson, JE, *Introduction to the Trade Practices Act*, Hicks Smith & Sons, Sydney, 1967.

Souter, Gavin, *Heralds and Angels: The House of Fairfax 1841-1900*, Melbourne University Publishing, Melbourne, 1991.

Southern, G Robert, *The Mysterious McLeod-Lindsay Case*, G Robert Southern, Melbourne, 1970.

Stevens, Anne, *Generations: The Hughes Family of Sydney 1840-2007*, Kudos Studio, Sydney, 2007.

Sykes, Trevor, *Operation Dynasty: How Warwick took John Fairfax Ltd*, Greenhouse Publications, Melbourne, 1989.

Waldersee, James, *Catholic Society in New South Wales 1788-1860*, Sydney University Press, Sydney, 1974.

Walsh, Maximillian, *Poor Little Rich Country: The Path to the Eighties*, Penguin, Melbourne, 1979.

Warrender, Pamela Myer, *Pamela: in her own right*, Hardie Grant Book, Melbourne, 2007.

Whitton, Evan, *Can of Worms II*, Fairfax Library, Broadway, 2007.

Reference works

Annual Reports of the NSW Bar Association

Australian Dictionary of Biography

Blackshield, Tony, Coper, Michael and Williams, George (eds), *The Oxford Companion to the High Court of Australia*, Oxford University Press, Melbourne, 2001.

NSW Law Almanac

Reserve Bank of Australia, Inflation Calculation

Index